# Readings in American Foreign Policy

# Readings in American Foreign Policy

## Historical and Contemporary Problems

**DAVID BERNELL**
*Oregon State University*

PEARSON
Longman

New York San Francisco Boston
London Toronto Sydney Tokyo Singapore Madrid
Mexico City Munich Paris Cape Town Hong Kong Montreal

Acquisitions Editor: Vikram Mukhija
Executive Marketing Manager: Ann Stypuloski
Production Manager: Donna DeBenedictis
Project Coordination, Text Design, and Electronic Page Makeup: GGS Book
    Services
Cover Design Manager: John Callahan
Cover Designer: Base Art Co.
Cover Photos: Upper and lower left: Corbis, Inc. Upper and lower right: Getty
    Images, Inc.
Senior Manufacturing Buyer: Roy L. Pickering Jr.
Printer and Binder and Cover Printer: R.R. Donnelley & Sons
    Company/Crawfordsville

**Library of Congress Cataloging-in-Publication Data**

Bernell, David.
  Readings in American foreign policy : historical and contemporary
problems/David Bernell. -- 1st. ed.
     p. cm.
  ISBN-13: 978-0-321-27622-3 (alk. paper)
  ISBN-10: 0-321-27622-1 (alk. paper)
  1. United States--Foreign relations.  I. Title.
  JZ1480.B47 2008
  327.73--dc22

                                                    2007043335

Please visit us at www.ablongman.com

ISBN-13: 978-0-321-27622-3
ISBN-10: 0-321-27622-1

1 2 3 4 5 6 7 8 9 10--DOC--10 09 08 07

# Contents

## PART III An Emerging Power at the Turn of the Century: Creating a Global American Foreign Policy   161

## PART IV The Cold War: The Foreign Policy of a Superpower   197

# PART V After the Cold War: A New World Order   311

# PART VI September 11 and Beyond: Contemporary American Foreign Policy   389

# P r e f a c e

Interest in American foreign policy is always significant, but has been more so since September 11 and the beginning of the war in Iraq. Scholars and students alike are engaging questions about why this country is so poorly regarded in many places around the world, how to successfully combat terrorism and the spread of weapons of mass destruction, why the American effort in Iraq is turning out so badly, what can be done about the huge U.S. trade deficit and its indebtedness to China, and how the United States can be such a rich and powerful country, but at the same time cannot seem to achieve some of its most important foreign policy goals.

*Readings in American Foreign Policy: Historical and Contemporary Problems* seeks to address these and other questions. The readings have been chosen with an eye toward examining the evolution of American foreign policy over the decades, highlighting the idea that there is both continuity and change in American actions overseas. American policy is continually evolving—policymakers are constantly responding to immediate crises and long-term developments, reacting to new opportunities and threats, and devising long-term strategies and ad-hoc responses. But at the same time, there are many constants in American foreign policy—the centrality of trade and economics, the recurrence of intervention in other countries, the promotion of democracy (even if only in rhetoric), the exercise of global leadership and influence, and the wariness with global rivals. All of these themes represent major elements in U.S. foreign policy.

There are, of course, a great many ways to understand and interpret American behavior in the world. The reaction of the United States to September 11 set in motion a set of policies in the Middle East and elsewhere that have been informed by neoconservatism. The United States has seen some successes and setbacks since this time. One of the significant problems has been that America's standing in the world has diminished; the country is more greatly feared, disliked, or held in low regard in many places around the world, both among governments and populations. Critics have suggested grounding American foreign policy more heavily along the lines of alternative perspectives, such as realism, or liberal internationalism, which would offer a way to correct America's relations with the world. The critics make good points and strong arguments, but these alternative views have their own limitations as well. They have been tried in the past, and each has its own record of successes and failures when put into practice. No single view of how to formulate and execute American foreign policy has all the answers, and no view can be easily dismissed. To the extent that readers of this book can better understand and evaluate these perspectives, as well as the policies that have emerged from them over the past several decades, this book can be judged a success.

## FEATURES

This reader is organized to include both a thematic and a chronological treatment of major problems in American foreign policy, offering an overview of the historical and contemporary issues and debates in U.S. foreign policy. The result is a book that consists of both primary source documents and essays from secondary sources to provide a reasonably thorough, but manageable overview of U.S. foreign policy—problems, policies, foundations, formation, critiques—from the beginning of the 20th century to the present. The two thematic sections look at theoretical foundations of U.S. foreign policy and actors in the policymaking process. The four historically oriented sections address, respectively, the early 20th century, the Cold War, the post–Cold War era up to September 11, and then after September 11. This combination of classic texts with more recent selections offers two important elements. The array of analyses and viewpoints provides students with tools for critical thinking. The historical approach provides background and context, allowing students to gain a better understanding of where American foreign policy has been, and therefore a more informed sense of where it may be going.

The authors of the readings represent a combination of scholars, public officials, think tanks, and other foreign policy analysts. Their works are excerpted to achieve the goal of communicating their arguments, interpretations, and policy prescriptions, while at the same time not being too long or burdensome for the reader. In order to offer additional explanation and context to the problems addressed in the selections, I have included introductions to each section, and an introduction to each reading. Even beyond the individual readings and the different sections, however, my goal is a book in which the whole is greater than the sum of the parts, so that it tells a story—written by multiple authors and from multiple perspectives—about the United States of America and its interactions with the rest of the world. My aim is to provide, if not definitive answers, then convincing analyses and interpretations of questions that students and scholars alike have regarding problems in U.S. foreign policy and their origins.

## SUPPLEMENTS

Longman is pleased to offer several resources to qualified adopters of this book and their students that will make teaching and learning from this book even more effective and enjoyable.

## For Instructors

**MyPoliSciKit Video Case Studies for International Relations and Comparative Politics (0-205-57436-X)**   Featuring video from major news sources and providing reporting and insight on recent world affairs, this DVD helps instructors integrate current events into their courses by letting them use the clips as lecture launchers or discussion starters.

## For Students

*Longman Atlas of World Issues* (0-321-22456-5)   Introduced and selected by Robert J. Art of Brandeis University and excerpted from the acclaimed Penguin Atlas Series, the *Longman Atlas of World Issues* is designed to help students understand the geography and major issues facing the world today, such as terrorism, debt, and HIV/AIDS. These thematic, full-color maps examine forces shaping politics today at a global level. Explanatory information accompanies each map to help students better grasp the concepts being shown and how they affect our world today. Available at no additional charge when packaged with this book.

*New Signet World Atlas* **(0-451-19732101)**   From Penguin Putnam, this pocket-sized yet detailed reference features 96 pages of full-color maps plus statistics, key data, and much more. Available at a discount when packaged with this book.

*Newsweek* **Discount Subscription (0-321-08895-6)**   *Newsweek* gets students reading, writing, and thinking about what's going on in the world around them. When a discount subscription card is packaged with this book, students will receive a 12-week subscription for only 59 cents an issue. To learn more about this and other discount subscriptions to newspapers and periodicals, please contact your Longman representative.

*Research and Writing in International Relations* **(0-321-27766-X)**   Written by Laura Roselle and Sharon Spray of Elon University, this brief and affordable guide provides the basic step-by-step process and essential resources that are needed to write political science papers that go beyond simple description and into more systematic and sophisticated inquiry. This text focuses on the key areas in which students need the most help: finding a topic, developing a question, reviewing literature, designing research, analyzing findings, and last, actually writing the paper. Available at a discount when packaged with this book.

*Careers in Political Science* **(0-321-113337-3)**   Offering insider advice and practical tips on how to make the most of a political science degree, this booklet by Joel Clark of George Mason University shows students the tremendous potential such a degree offers and guides them through: deciding whether political science is right for them; the different career options available; job requirements and skill sets; how to apply, interview, and compete for jobs after graduation; and much more. Available at a discount when packaged with this book.

## ACKNOWLEDGMENTS

I would like to thank those that helped me in completing this project. Eric Stano and Vik Mukhija of Longman have been great champions and talented editors. The external reviewers—Dave Benjamin, University of Connecticut; William Boettcher, North Carolina State University; Roger Durham, Aquinas College; Donald Hafner, Boston College; Peter Howard, American University; Richard Kilroy, Eastern Carolina University; Lawrence LeBlanc, Marquette University; David Lorenzo, Jamestown College; James Mitchell, California State University, Northridge; Ken Rodman, Colby College; Wayne Selcher, Elizabethtown College; and Jon Western, Mt. Holyoke College—made this a much better book; their time and attention to the task of reviewing the manuscript was impressive. Colleagues and students also provided assistance and advice along the way.

Most of all, I want to thank my family. My wife, Stephanie, and our boys, Eli and Miles, provide me with the inspiration to try and make a little more sense of this world. Perhaps we can make it a better place for them.

DAVID BERNELL

# Introduction

The United States currently finds itself, as it did after World War II and the Cold War, trying to craft a response to a set of global dangers and opportunities that have become central to its foreign policy. The terrorist attacks on September 11, 2001, as well as the vulnerabilities and potential threats they exposed, have prompted Americans and their political leadership to increasingly focus on combating terrorism and stopping the spread of weapons of mass destruction among states and non-state actors. The uncertainty regarding the chances of achieving these two goals by waging war in Iraq has not led to a reconsideration of these goals, only (thus far) the wisdom how effectively they have been pursued.

The intense focus on terrorism and weapons of mass destruction (WMD) is a recent development, and addressing these threats has become the central organizing principle of U.S. foreign policy. At the same time, this orientation is not entirely new, but part of an ongoing evolution of American foreign policy. It is instead a difference of degree, resulting from the continuation and intensification of the spread of disorder that has characterized international relations since the end of the Cold War. It is also the case that the American focus on terror, WMD proliferation, and other manifestations of disorder represent more than an attempt to prevent future attacks on American soil. It is a product of the United States' status as a globally dominant superpower, whose relative satisfaction with its political assets, its economic and military power, almost necessitates an intolerance for disorder, at least in certain parts of the globe.

As the world's only superpower, the United States has a big foreign policy agenda on the world stage. It involves a broad range of issues, numerous actors, and all parts of the world. Moreover, the United States maintains responsibilities not only for its own selfish interests, but also for a greater general interest around the globe. The second of these, ideally, should contribute to the first, but the two are by no means identical and may even work at cross-purposes. Sometimes the United States either seeks or is called upon to provide international public goods—institutional capacity, security, order, protection of human rights—that serve a larger, general interest, and that other counties cannot or will not provide (and that the United States may prefer not to provide). To be sure, a large part of the debate over U.S. foreign policy, both at home and abroad, revolves around the question of exactly how large a price the United States should pay to establish and preserve peace and order around the world. Of course, the flip side is also true. Often the United States acts on the global stage in ways that are believed by many at home and abroad to be contrary to world peace and order, against a greater general interest. This view has gained increasing acceptance around the world during the post–Cold War years, and especially since September 11, resulting in a situation where many governments that have strong ties to the United States, including some of its NATO allies, find themselves increasingly suspicious of U.S. power and global conduct, worried that the United States is willing to pursue its own parochial interests at the expense of global interests.

Views of United States policies, of course, run the spectrum, but that is indeed the key point: the foreign policy of the United States is so large and so influential, it cannot be easily ignored. On any given day, the attention and resources of U.S. foreign policymakers are devoted to problems involving not only terrorism and the proliferation of weapons of mass destruction, but also humanitarian intervention, democratization, trade and finance, development, globalization, the environment, energy, alliances, the U.N., and of course, the need for peace in the Middle East, to name but a few. These, along with a host of other issues, represent everything from immediate crises to long-term worries and threats that the United States must at some point address, either through action or a deliberate choice of inaction. Americans and other people around the globe may either extol or lament their fortune, but for better or worse, the United States often occupies a position as "the world's indispensable nation." When the United States acts, or refuses to act, the rest of the world is often affected.

In this book I have brought together a collection of readings that address the major issues and problems confronting the United States as it has engaged the world since becoming a global power. The goal is to provide an overview of the evolution of U.S. foreign policy—its challenges, its foundations, and how it is made. American foreign policy is characterized by both continuity and change. It has evolved and shifted to respond to changing global conditions, as well as economic and political developments at home. Industrialization across the United States, the decline of Britain, the power of the Soviet Union, the building of an atomic bomb, the collapse of communism, September 11—each of these represented points of change and departure. At the same time, however, there are consistent themes in American behavior, such as a belief in the spread of democratic ideals and practices, a desire to open up foreign markets to trade, and a degree of assertiveness that has led to numerous instances of expansion and intervention.

The larger focus of the book is on contemporary problems of the post–Cold War period, but it also includes several readings from the Cold War era and before. These earlier selections are included in order to explore the continuities and changes in U.S. foreign policy since the beginning of the 20th century. The end of the Cold War may have meant the end of an old order, but it did not necessarily mean an end to the goals of American foreign policy or the ways it is carried out. Many of the problems the United States deals with today are not unique to the past decade. Nor are America's contemporary challenges even unique to the past few years, despite a sense that September 11 "changed everything." The United States was combating terrorism, confronting Iraq, promoting democratization, responding to humanitarian disasters, dealing with globalization, and try-ing to manage political/religious conflict in the Middle East well before the World Trade Center was brought down. The most recent challenges con-fronting policymakers are not entirely new, despite dramatic changes that occurred in America and in the world since the watershed years of 1989 and 2001. The orientation and focus of U.S. foreign policy may be quite different than it was during the Cold War, or prior to September 11, but many of the goals of the United States remain the same, as do many of the problems.

Thus, in order to gain a more complete understanding of the United States' role as a superpower, and of contemporary issues and new direc-tions in the foreign policy of the United States, it is necessary to look not only at where the country finds itself currently, but also at what it has done in the world since it became a great power. To that end, this reader looks at U.S. foreign policy since the beginning of the 20th century, with a variety of articles and primary source documents that highlight American responses to its greatest challenges, opportunities and threats. It also includes a sec-tion that addresses different schools of thought explaining American for-eign policy, as well as a section dealing with the policymaking process and the actors who influence decision making.

The first part of the book looks at the theoretical and practical founda-tions of American behavior overseas, examining the ideas and traditions that have informed and explained American foreign policy over the past decades. The focus in this section is on contemporary and historical under-standings of U.S. policy, looking at isolationism, realism, and liberalism, the major schools of thought that have provided the grounding, explana-tion, and/or justification for U.S. policy. It also includes a look at the idea of American exceptionalism, as well as a critical look at the influence of eco-nomic and business interests on American policies. The first reading, by Cecil Crabb, addresses the country's first expression of isolationism, George Washington's Farewell Address, and discusses the history, mean-ing, and uses of isolationism in U.S. foreign policy. The readings then go on to consider other interpretive frameworks regarding the sources of U.S. for-eign policy, looking at the usefulness and appropriateness of realist and lib-eral approaches in U.S. policy. This includes a classic realist viewpoint by Hans Morgenthau, which, at more than 50 years old, continues to resonate as a clear *realpolitik* vision of the American national interest. This article is followed by a liberal interpretation of U.S. policy by John Ikenberry. Ikenberry looks toward institutions, norms, international law, economic interdependence, and a community of nations with shared values, all fostered and guided by American power, as the "glue" that both preserves peace and order in the world and promotes democracy and free markets. Next, Joshua Muravchik provides a neoconservative view of U.S. foreign policy. Neoconservatism, which currently holds sway in American policy, has some affinity with liberal internationalism. Like Ikenberry, Muravchik supports the liberal ideology that grounds American actions, but with different emphasis on what counts most in shaping global politics. Muravchik, contrasting the "new isolationism" of the 1990s with the Wilsonian tradition, suggests that American intervention and the use of force in the world's trouble spots—all grounded in America's democratic values—are the sources of American power and success, as well as the achievement of a peaceful, stable global order. Harold Hongju Koh follows, examining the idea of American exceptionalism as it has informed this country's engagement with the world. He offers a critique of how current policies and practices reflect this perspective, suggesting that while the view of an exceptional America has prompted the United States toward many successes, it also easily leads to applying a double standard when dealing with others. Lastly, the selection from Noam Chomsky offers a critical assessment of the goals and practices of U.S. foreign policy. A well-established critic of America's global actions, Chomsky looks at the American drive for dominance and the business interests that fuel its policies.

Part II addresses the process of making U.S. foreign policy. The readings in this section look at the people and institutions that make and influence U.S. actions overseas, as well as occurrences that highlight particular issues in the policymaking process. These selections underscore the politicized nature of the process, which rarely allows politics to "stop at the water's edge." They look first at the federal government, with Louis Fisher and James Lindsay examining the role of the presidency and the Congress, and the competition that often results over foreign policy influence between the two branches. Howard Wiarda then examines how different government agencies within the executive branch influence the formulation and implementation of U.S. foreign policy, looking specifically at the case of Mexico and how various agencies of the U.S. government may sometimes work at cross-purposes with one another. Government officials and agencies are by no means the only actors making U.S. foreign policy, and a few selections address these outside influences. Warren Strobel explores how the media influence foreign policy decisions. Tony Smith explains the role of ethnic groups in making policy and how a small vocal minority can prevail on certain issues. Finally, Richard Sobel explains how public opinion impacts decisions and outcomes in U.S. foreign policy, in spite of numerous presidential pronouncements to the contrary.

Part III marks a shift in the orientation of the book, moving from a thematic approach to a chronological approach. This section is devoted to looking at some of the historical antecedents of America's global engagement as a superpower. In spite of its isolationist orientation prior to the Cold War, the United States had long carried out an assertive, far-reaching foreign policy to serve the country's political and economic interests. The first three readings in the section are primary source documents, each reflecting an element of American regional or global activism. President Theodore Roosevelt's Corollary to the Monroe Doctrine, grounded in concerns of American power and influence in the region, and the subsequent strategic denial of such influence to European powers, discusses the justification for American intervention in Latin America and the Caribbean. Senator Albert Beveridge, in arguing the virtues of American empire based on the extension of American liberty and freedom, provides one of the strongest statements of American exceptionalism and demonstrates what the idea has meant in practice. The War Message of President Wilson provides a third example of U.S. activism and assertiveness prior to the Cold War, whereby the president sought to extend the reach of U.S. power in an effort to "make the world safe for democracy." The three primary source documents are followed by three analyses of U.S. behavior during this period. Robert Kagan considers America's current involvement in Iraq and suggests such action is not unusual for the United States. He looks back in U.S. history to highlight a consistent record of American intervention and assertiveness overseas. An excerpt from Walter LaFeber's *The New Empire* examines the economic and political developments of the late 19th century that prompted a global foreign policy. Finally, Walter Russell Mead examines the rise of the United States in the context of a changing world order, which was governed by the United States' economic and political relationship with a globally dominant Great Britain.

Part IV of the book addresses the Cold War and the emergence of the United States as a global superpower, looking at the many actions undertaken by the United States that made up the policy of containment. It first addresses the emergence of the United States as a superpower in the 1940s and the development of the anticommunist policy of containment. The classic article by George Kennan, "The Sources of Soviet Conduct," highlights the U.S. response to the Soviet challenge in the early years of the Cold War, as does Richard Crockett's more recent analysis of the Cuban Missile Crisis. Stephen Cohen examines the economic elements of American postwar actions, addressing how trade and economic policy served the policy of containment. The readings then turn to the war in Vietnam, détente, and U.S. reassertion, as the United States moved away from, and then back toward, a vigorous policy of confrontation with the Soviet Union. This period, from the late 1960s through the 1980s, when the war in Vietnam cast a shadow over so much of America's foreign relations, was marked by conflict over a number of issues such as the pursuit of arms control, détente, the use of force, competition for influence in the Third World, and U.S. support of "friendly" dictatorships, all of which took place in an economic context of oil shocks, debt crises, and the emergence of the United States as the world's largest debtor nation. These articles feature analyses by Richard Betts on Vietnam, focusing on the lessons learned from the war and how it changed U.S. actions in the world. In the aftermath of the war in Vietnam, the speech by President Carter provides an explanation and justification for the policy of détente and the pursuit of arms control, as well as a sense of new challenges for the United States. The difficulties of the 1970s—oil shortages, inflation, Third World revolution, and the weakening of détente—were seen by critics of Carter as evidence of U.S. decline, which prompted calls for the reassertion of American power around the globe. The well-known selections by Jeanne Kirkpatrick, "Dictatorships and Double Standards," and Ronald Reagan's address to the British Parliament capture the sense of this departure from détente. Reagan's speech also reflects the idea, later to be known at The Reagan Doctrine, that the United States should actively support democratic change by directly challenging socialist states around the world. Robert Gilpin provides an account of American economic policy at this time, looking at how the United States had lost its economic dominance and became a debtor nation. Part IV concludes by discussing the end of the Cold War, with John Lewis Gaddis' analysis of the Cold War as a "Long Peace," and an examination by Raymond Garthoff of why the Soviet Union and the Communist bloc collapsed.

Part V looks at the period between the end of the Cold War and September 11, 2001. After the Cold War American foreign policy often seemed to be characterized as adrift, without a grand strategy such as containment to guide it. In spite of (the first) President Bush's proclamation of a "new world order," what seemed to emerge instead was greater disorder—in the Balkans, in Somalia, in the former Soviet republics, in Iraq and Kuwait—with no overall plan to address it. Initial uncertainty about what the United States should do after it had achieved and exceeded its longstanding goals with respect to the Soviet Union are illustrated in the articles by Charles Krauthammer and Ronald Steel. Krauthammer suggested that the United States was in the midst of "The Unipolar Moment" and should take advantage of its position. Steel, on the other hand, looked at the ambiguities that accompanied the end of the Cold War. The Clinton Administration eventually decided on a strategy of "democratic enlargement," the simultaneous pursuit of expanding democratic government and free market economies. The excerpt from the National Security Strategy of

1996 and the article by Douglas Brinkley explain and critique this framework, commenting on the goal and wisdom of emphasizing liberal values as a strategic interest, and bringing concerns regarding economic globalization into the realm of high politics. In spite of this approach to global politics, multiple crises continually demanded American attention throughout the 1990s. The proliferation of weapons of mass destruction, terrorism, ethnic conflict, humanitarian disasters, and conflict in the Middle East all rose in prominence in U.S. foreign policy, often because of the diminution of global order that had previously been imposed by the Cold War. Several selections, by Graham Allison and Owen Cote, James Dobbins, and the Sharm El-Sheik Fact Finding Committee, address the problems and opportunities that each of these issues represented to the United States. As the decade of the 1990s neared an end, America's foreign policy was very much oriented toward economic concerns, and U.S. economic strength had resulted in a global economic order increasingly dominated by the United States. In this context, President Clinton gave a speech offering an assessment of his economic policies and the increasing trend toward globalization. At the same time, American economic power was complemented by a concurrent increase in military capabilities and what was seen as an increasing tendency to act unilaterally. The country had eclipsed its rivals to such an extent it was dubbed not merely a superpower, but a "hyperpower." This supremacy at the close of the century prompted several analyses of America's purposes, strategies and tactics. One of the most notable was by Samuel Huntington, who characterized the United States as "The Lonely Superpower."

Part VI, the final section of the book, looks at new developments in U.S. foreign policy after September 11, 2001, examining the contemporary international environment and the policy choices made by the George W. Bush Administration. The two largest issues, the war on terrorism and the war in Iraq, have dominated the time and attention of U.S. policymakers, as well as the lion's share of commentary and analysis of U.S. foreign policy. The selection by President Bush characterizes the nature of America's initial response to the attacks of September 11. The excerpt from the National Security Strategy of 2002 demonstrates how this early reaction evolved to include "preemption" as an important element in U.S. policymaking. Preemption provided an explanation and justification for war with Iraq, whose merits are discussed in a selection by Robert Lieber, with an opposing view by John Mearsheimer and Stephen Walt. The war on terror and the war in Iraq have prompted a significant debate over U.S. foreign policy, with one of the central issues involving American unilateralism and the extent to which the United States can and will seek to impose its version of order around the world. This is addressed in the article by James Chace, who provides a critique of the wisdom of this approach to implementing policy. The actual conduct of the war in Iraq is addressed by the Iraq Study Group led by James Baker and Lee Hamilton, which provides an assessment of what has gone wrong in the war and how such problems should be addressed. While the focus of U.S. foreign policy in recent years has been on military and strategic concerns involving terrorism and the war in Iraq, a number of other problems have required attention as well, such as weapons of mass destruction, American economic policies, and global climate change. The article by Patrick Long and Larry Johnson considers the problem of nuclear weapons proliferation, looking specifically at the case of Iran and how there seem to be no easy answers for combating or managing proliferation. In "Riding for a Fall," Peter Peterson examines American economic policies that have led to massive budget and trade deficits, and he considers their potential impact on American power, the U.S. economy, and global politics. Lee Lane and Samuel Thernstrom look at global climate change, the role the United States has played in addressing this looming problem, and how its actions should be modified. The next three articles look at regional issues. Wang Jisi, the Council on Foreign Relations, and Peter Hakim take stock of the state of affairs surrounding America's relations with key countries and regions in the world. They look, respectively, at the American relationship with China, developments within Russia and the possible U.S. response, and the deteriorating state of inter-American affairs. Finally, the last selection in the book by Thomas P. M. Barnett looks at the "big picture" issue of American grand strategy. He offers an assessment of America's global role since World War II, and provides a vision of the goals and objectives the United States should pursue to build not only a strong, successful United States, but a peaceful, prosperous world.

# PART 1

# Foundations of
# American Foreign Policy

A book examining U.S. foreign policy should rightly begin with a look at the theoretical foundations that have both explained and informed American actions over the decades. It is not enough to study the major problems and issues in American foreign policy. A close look at the interpretations and understandings of policy is also essential in order to better understand and make sense of actual policies and decisions, and there are a number of perspectives that have competed for the attention of policymakers and analysts. Part I, therefore, is designed to offer the reader a look at a variety of competing perspectives, including isolationism, realism, liberal internationalism, and neoconservatism, as well as views that see U.S. actions as a function of American exceptionalism or an expansionist drive to dominate global politics and economics.

These perspectives represent not only distinct frameworks for looking at American foreign policy, they have also emerged as responses to America's changing role in the world, and responses to each other. Just as the American role in the world has evolved over time, so too have the theoretical perspectives explaining that American role. The isolationist view emerged in a new nation looking to preserve its independence and maintain freedom of action to expand across North America, and to do this in a world dominated by European powers. When that view seemed to no longer fully meet the needs and goals of a country that had grown rich and powerful, there emerged a growing realist school of international relations, whose prominence arose in the United States in response to World War II, the beginning of the Cold War, and America's leadership role in the international system. The liberal internationalist view and what has come to be called the *neoconservative view* are, in many ways, close relatives, both

1

grounded in the idea that the spread of American democratic values and practices, including market capitalism, are worthy goals to pursue. However, these two perspectives part company on many points, most importantly regarding the appropriateness of the use of force to achieve greater democratization. Elements of liberal internationalism and neoconservatism played a prominent role during the Cold War in informing American policymakers, and these often coexisted along with realism to create a complete, if not always coherent, set of Cold War policies. After the Cold War, these two perspectives gained added strength, as the United States emerged as the world's sole superpower, and the question to be answered was what the country should do with its advantageous position in the world.

The theoretical perspectives included in this part talk to each other, to some extent, and they can be read with an eye to seeing how they do this. The section begins with Crabb's examination of isolationism and its important role in American foreign policy up until World War II. Morgenthau, advocating a policy informed by realism, is sharply criticizing the liberal and isolationist views, pointing out how adherence to them has resulted in misunderstanding global politics. In particular, he points out how a realist approach would likely have made World War II avoidable or less costly. Muravchik, by contrast, advocates neoconservatism after the end of the Cold War and argues that isolationism and realism have resulted in similar outlooks and similar responses to threats that have been harmful to the United States and the world. Ikenberry suggests that one of the overlooked secrets of America's global power and success has been its liberal orientation, and the building of a safe, orderly international system during the Cold War that benefited, and continues to benefit, participants in an American-led system. Alongside these articles, Chomsky and Koh offer reminders that there are alternative ways to read American behavior, and that these do not always illustrate the American project in a favorable light.

# 1

# The Isolationist Heritage
## CECIL V. CRABB

The beginning of this book looks to the beginning of the American republic to examine the foundations of U.S. foreign policy. The first expression of American foreign policy doctrine was that of isolationism. In his farewell address, George Washington declared that it would be unwise for the United States to allow itself to become implicated in the continual political conflicts of the European powers. Thomas Jefferson, in a similar vein, warned of becoming involved in entangling alliances. While these warnings at the time reflected the concerns of the new nation regarding the French Revolution and the Napoleonic wars, and the threats these posed to American security, the general principles continued to inform and shape American policy in the world for more than a century and a half.

Cecil Crabb provides an overview of this foreign policy tradition, explaining that isolationism was not about cutting America off from the rest of the world. It did not mean dissolving political and diplomatic ties, and it most certainly did not apply to commercial relations. Isolationism meant engagement in all these areas, most especially with respect to commerce and trade. American engagement, however, reflecting an isolationist stance, would take place on terms that allowed the United States freedom of action without obligating the country to others. Neither Washington nor Jefferson ruled out all alliances, only those that would ensnare the United States in conflicts where it had no direct interest.

Until World War II, isolationism was seen by Americans as being essential to their national security. It kept the United States out of European conflict and allowed the country to expand across North America, developing its own economic, political, and military strength. It is argued, however, that the United States was merely lucky in being allowed the luxury to choose isolationism. Europe avoided a major war for 100 years and therefore never dragged the United States into conflict. Although the Spanish-American War and involvement in World War I represented breaks with isolationist thinking, these were only temporary instances. Isolationism was only discarded after World War II, when the United States took the lead in global affairs, deliberately creating "entangling alliances" and

From *Policymakers and Critics: Conflicting Theories of American Foreign Policy*, 2nd ed. by Cecil V. Crabb, Jr. Copyright © 1986. Reproduced with permission of Greenwood Publishing Group, Inc., Westport, CT.

involving itself in all parts of the world, which by that time was seen as essential to the protection of American security and safety.

This break with the past was by no means complete, as Crabb points out. In spite of the fact that isolationism no longer dominates American foreign policy thinking, and that to call someone an isolationist is considered derogatory, elements of it have continued to surface in American politics, affecting U.S. actions in the world long after the end of the Second World War.

---

On June 12, 1783, the Congress of the United States resolved that "the true interests of these states [i.e., the United States] require that they should be as little as possible entangled in the politics and controversies of European nations."[1]

Thirteen years later, in one of the most celebrated state papers in the nation's history, President George Washington's Farewell Address, Americans were solemnly warned against "permanent antipathies against particular nations and passionate attachments for others"; instead, the new Republic should cultivate "just and amicable feelings toward all" nations. Then, in what came to be referred to widely in later years as "Washington's rule," the President declared:

> The great rule of conduct for us in regard to foreign nations is, in extending our commercial relations to have with them [the nations of Europe] as little political connection as possible. . . . Europe has a set of primary interests which to us have none or a very remote relation. Hence she must be engaged in frequent controversies, the causes of which are essentially foreign to our corners. Hence, therefore, it must be unwise in us to implicate ourselves by artificial ties in the ordinary vicissitudes of her politics or the ordinary combinations and collisions of her friendships or enmities. . . . It is our true policy to steer clear of permanent alliances with any portion of the foreign world. . . . Taking care always to keep ourselves by suitable establishments on a respectable posture, we may safely trust to temporary alliances for extraordinary emergencies.

Referring to the existence of warfare in Europe, President Washington reaffirmed America's "neutral position" toward the conflict. A neutral stance would "gain time to our country to settle and mature its yet recent institutions, and to progress without interruption to that degree of strength and consistency which is necessary to give it . . . the command of its own fortunes."

Later Presidents and statesmen amplified the meaning of "Washington's rule," applying it to concrete issues that arose in American foreign relations and adapting it to new conditions confronting the United States abroad. Despite a popular tendency to attribute the phrase to Washington, for example, it was President Thomas Jefferson who in 1801 admonished Americans to shun "entangling alliances" with other nations.[2] In a message to Congress on December 2, 1823, President James Monroe reaffirmed and amplified these principles, applying them specifically to the twofold threat of intervention by the Holy Alliance in the Western Hemisphere and Czarist Russia's territorial ambitions in the Pacific Northwest. In what came to be known in the years thereafter as the "Monroe Doctrine," Monroe stated that "the American continents, by the free and independent condition which they have assumed and maintain, are henceforth not to be considered as subjects for future colonization by any European powers." At the same time Monroe pledged, "In the wars of the European powers in matters relating to themselves we have never taken any part, nor does it comport with our policy to do so." He observed that "the political system of the allied [i.e., European] powers is essentially different . . . from that of America." Accordingly, the United States would "consider any attempt on their part to extend their system to any portion of this hemisphere as dangerous to our peace and safety." Yet with Europe's "existing colonies" in the New World, Monroe added, "we have not interfered and shall not interfere."

For more than a century and a half—from the time it declared its independence in 1776 until the outbreak of World War II—the United States was devoted to an "isolationist" position in world affairs.[3] As we shall see, isolationism is not an easy or simple concept to define. Throughout the course of American history, the doctrine acquired numerous implications and tenets, some of which were not always mutually consistent or compatible. From the time of Washington's Farewell Address onward, isolationism was in reality a *cluster of attitudes and assumptions* about America's proper relationship with the outside world. Isolationism had several components from the beginning, and every age tended to modify its content as the concept was applied to specific conditions prevailing at home and abroad.

We shall examine the main components or facets of isolationism at a later stage. Meanwhile, two points about the doctrine require emphasis at the outset. The first is that, for a hundred and fifty years or so after the United States became an independent nation, a foreign policy of isolationism was viewed by most citizens as an *indispensable condition* for their national security, the continued success of their democratic experiment, their political stability, their economic prosperity—in brief, for all the benefits conferred by successful pursuit of the "American way of life." However much they often disagreed upon domestic issues, most Americans subscribed to the view that the "timeless principles" enunciated by Presidents Washington, Jefferson, and Monroe must be adhered to diligently in foreign relations. Continued devotion to them would enable the society to realize the promises implicit in the American society's unique way of life.

Conversely, departure from them risked a host of evils: foreign intervention in the political and economic affairs of the nation; the growth of "militarism" and escalating armaments expenditures; the loss of freedoms guaranteed by the Bill of Rights and other liberties; the emergence of presidential "dictatorship" and the consequent "decline" of Congress; a steadily mounting national debt; internal divisiveness and acute political factionalism; economic retrogression, precipitated by the loss of foreign markets—to mention but a few of the dangers that proponents of an isolationist position sought to avoid. As time passed, prominent American historians discerned a *direct causal relationship* between stability and progress at home, and steadfast adherence to a policy of isolationism abroad. Thus one of the nation's most eminent historians in the pre-World War II period, Charles A. Beard, was convinced that an isolationist policy had ". . . enabled the American people to go ahead under the principles of 1776, conquering a continent and building a civilization which, with all its faults, has precious merits for us and is, at all events, our own." Under the shelter provided by this doctrine, Beard was convinced, ". . . human beings were set free to see what they could do on this continent, when emancipated from the privilege-encrusted institutions of Europe and from entanglement in the endless revolutions and wars of that continent.[4]

Some fifty years earlier, the perceptive British observer Lord Bryce had said much the same thing about the United States: "America lives in a world of her own. . . . Safe from attack, safe even from menace, she hears from afar the warring cries of European races and faiths. . . . But for the present at least—it may not always be so—she sails upon a summer sea.[5]

Such viewpoints are not cited to prove that a foreign policy of isolationism was in fact directly responsible for the promise and progress that Americans identified with their way of life. But what people believe to be true is sometimes even more crucial in accounting for their behavior than what is objectively true. Correctly or not, down to World War II millions of Americans were prone to view an isolationist position in foreign affairs abroad as part of the unchallenged "wisdom" of the Founding Fathers; the soundness of their advice appeared to have been reinforced by a century and a half of secure existence as a free nation.

A second point requires emphasis at the outset of our study of the isolationist approach to American foreign relations. Pervasive and deeply rooted as it was down to World War II, today isolationism *per se* no longer commands the allegiance of the American society. Following the most destructive global conflict in the history of the world, the American people and their leaders overwhelmingly rejected an isolationist stance for the United States in the postwar period.[6] One of the most vocal and influential spokesmen for pre-World War II isolationism, Senator Robert A. Taft (Republican of Ohio), said in 1950: "I don't know what they mean by isolationism, nobody is an isolationist today."[7] Even before the end of World War II, another prominent spokesman for the isolationist viewpoint, Senator Arthur H. Vandenberg (Republican of Michigan) delivered a widely circulated "confession" on the floor of the Senate, in which he formally renounced his isolationist principles and called for a "hard-and-fast treaty" between the United States and the principal wartime Allies to assure peace and security in the postwar period.[8] After Senator Vandenberg's dramatic conversion to an internationalist point of view, he emerged as a leading architect of a bipartisan approach to foreign relations, based on collaboration between the Democratic and Republican parties in behalf of common foreign policy principles and programs.[9] In Vandenberg's new role as advocate of a bipartisan approach to external problems, one of his outstanding contributions to a unified foreign policy was "to keep in line the obstructionists and diehard isolationists in his own party."[10]

The transformation witnessed in the viewpoints of figures like Senators Taft and Vandenberg about foreign affairs may be taken as representative of the fundamental shift in American opinion toward the outside world as a result of World War II. A substantial majority of Americans now accepted the fact that after World War II isolationism no longer served as a viable foreign policy posture for the most influential nation on the world scene. Indeed, by the end of World War II the concept of isolationism not only had few overt adherents; the very term had rapidly fallen into disrepute and had become something of an epithet, signifying myopia toward the course of world events and an unwillingness to accept the most elementary realities about America's involvement in them. Thus one of the most tireless champions of the doctrine prior to World War II, Senator Gerald P. Nye (Republican of North Dakota), said in 1944 that isolationism had become identified with "everything that was bad, terrible, un-American, and indecent."[11] In the postwar period, very few Americans have been willing to identify themselves openly as "isolationists," out of fear perhaps that whatever they said about America's proper course in foreign relations would be discredited by virtue of that admission.

Admittedly, therefore, it is difficult for the contemporary student of American foreign policy to evaluate the traditional isolationist point of view sympathetically and with due regard for its more positive and beneficial features. Isolationism often seems as relevant for the successful conduct of foreign policy in the modern period as mercantilism for the operation of the economic system or an understanding of pre-Copernican astronomy for insight into the problems of the space age. Yet it is an assumption of this chapter that—while very few Americans subscribe to an avowedly isolationist position—the nation's more or less consistent adherence to an isolationist stance for over a century and a half *profoundly affected the American approach to foreign relations after World War II, as well as before it.*

The doctrine of isolationism may no longer be in vogue—and likely will never be again. But many of the assumptions, preconceptions, popular images, attitudes, sentiments, and the like associated with the isolationist mentality for more than one hundred and fifty years remain deeply embedded in the American ethos and continue to affect the thinking of the American people and their leaders about events outside their own borders. As we shall see, since 1945 there has often been a remarkable continuity between the reaction displayed by Americans toward developments overseas and the assessment of Americans in the mid-nineteenth century or during the 1930s.

Despite America's formal renunciation of isolationism, many citizens in the postwar period continue to exhibit behavior tendencies and attitudes toward foreign affairs remarkably akin to those identified with the traditional isolationist mentality. At this stage, let us take note merely of two recent examples. By the 1970s, a substantial number of citizens had become convinced that perhaps America's most useful contribution to global peace and security would be to "set its own house in order," thereby providing a worthy example (contemporary political scientists tended to call it an attractive "model") that other societies would be motivated to follow. As we shall see, this conviction—the idea that the solution of major *domestic* problems had first claim upon the energies and resources of the American society—was also a fundamental tenet of classical isolationist outlook.[12]

Toward a different problem in the contemporary period—American military intervention in Southeast Asia or other regions—a significant number of Americans have become persuaded that the intervention of the United States in political or ideological controversies far from its own shores was indefensible for a number of reasons. One of them was the conviction that America's involvement in such crises will in the end "make no difference" in their outcome. Critics of the nation's prolonged involvement in the Vietnam conflict, for example, frequently contended that it did not lie within the power of the United States to determine the result of political contests in settings like Southeast Asia. Other critics applied the same reasoning to crises in the Middle East, Black Africa, and Latin America. This same conviction underlay the thinking of early isolationists with regard to American involvement in Europe's political rivalries. It was particularly prominent during the 1930s in the opposition of isolationists to American policies designed to limit Axis expansionism in Europe or to curb Japanese aggression in the Far East. These two instances are cited to illustrate a more general phenomenon: While "isolationism" is no longer a doctrine commanding the overtly enthusiastic support of the American people, an understanding of the traditional isolationist mentality yields many insights applicable to the American approach to foreign relations in the modern period.

# THE MANY FACETS OF "ISOLATIONISM"

A remarkable quality of the concept of isolationism—and a characteristic that was crucial in enabling it to serve as the basis for the nation's foreign policy over a century and a half—was the richness and adaptability of the doctrine. During no era of American history did isolationism comprise a coherent, internally consistent body of foreign policy principles. Instead, the exact content of isolationism tended to vary from era to era; even within any given historical period, no two proponents of the doctrine were likely to define it identically. The isolationism of the late eighteenth century Jeffersonian was likely to differ in several important respects from the isolationism espoused by the "agrarian radicals" a century later, and the foreign policy viewpoint of this latter group in turn could be contrasted with the isolationism of the America First Committee and other groups that attacked the Roosevelt Administration's foreign policies during the 1930s. From the time of Washington's Farewell Address onward, there has always been a tendency for isolationism to be defined by reference to concrete policy issues confronting the United States in its foreign and domestic affairs.

Moreover, as Rieselbach has emphasized, isolationist thought could and did exist *on several levels*. The concept might emphasize America's *geographic separation* from other continents, particularly Europe. It might stress mainly America's *spiritual and philosophical separation* from Europe, underscoring the contrast between the progressive "American way of life" versus Europe's stagnant social and economic systems. It might call attention primarily to *fundamental political and ideological distinctions* between the democracy of the New World and the authoritarian or despotic political systems and ideologies of the Old World. By the twentieth century, isolationism might also have reference to America's relative *economic self-sufficiency* and its ability to prosper, if need be, without access to the markets of the world. After 1900 isolationism might denote the nation's *relative military security and invincibility in the Western Hemisphere*. Many of the isolationists of the 1930s, for example, were convinced that an Axis victory in Europe, or even worldwide, posed no serious military consequences for the security of the United States. Isolationism could also convey the American people's inherent *apathy and antipathy toward foreign affairs generally vis-à-vis domestic affairs*. The former was a realm abounding in problems, frustrations, unwanted burdens, and dangers for the American Republic, whereas the latter was a sphere in which the promises and benefits implicit in the "American way of life" could be, and were being, rapidly realized. The "isolationism" expressed by a particular individual or school of thought might embody an almost infinite combination of these and other elements; or it might give almost exclusive attention to one of the above dimensions of the idea, while largely ignoring other dimensions.

Within these general limitations, let us take note of several specific facets or connotations of the term "isolationism," recognizing at all times that the concept never comprised a universally accepted or internally consistent set of foreign policy guidelines. Throughout the course of American history, perhaps the most widely accepted definition for isolationism—the idea viewed by many authorities as its "core" or most intrinsic meaning—was the idea of *diplomatic and military nonentanglement*, as illustrated by President Jefferson's admonition in 1801 against "entangling alliances."[13] The variant phrase—"no entangling alliances"—in time became the watchword of isolationism and a keynote of the American national credo. After 1800 nearly every American president was compelled to reassure the nation that his policies were designed to avoid "entangling alliances" with other countries, in conformity with principles enunciated by the Founding Fathers.

It must be emphasized that Jefferson was merely giving authoritative and forceful expression to a principle that had already found wide acceptance among the American people and their leaders.[14] Adherence to the principle of "no entangling alliances" was designed to safeguard the new Republic against a specific danger: involvement in the upheavals that gripped Europe during the period of the French Revolution and the Napoleonic era. French assistance during the American Revolution had been of inestimable importance—some historians have regarded it in fact as absolutely essential—for an American victory and the achievement of independence from England. On February 6, 1778, the United States and France signed a treaty of alliance; according to its terms, the United States was obligated to assist France "forever" in retaining possession of its New World colonies, like the French West Indies.[15] Even before the pact was signed, and even more so while it was in force, French officials had repeatedly intervened in the internal affairs of the United States (vigorous French efforts designed to prevent ratification of the Jay Treaty, signed with England on November 19, 1794, was a case in point). As new conflicts erupted among the European powers at the end of the eighteenth century, there was the real danger that the United States might find itself involved in another war with England to fulfill its obligations under the alliance with France. As had occurred many times in the past, the risk existed that Americans would find themselves "entangled" once more in a European struggle, in which their interests were secondary to those of the more powerful belligerents and in which their capacity to affect the outcome was minimal. This was the specific danger against which Jefferson's admonition against "entangling alliances" was directed.

As was not unusual with later principles of American foreign policy (such as those associated with the Monroe Doctrine in 1823), the injunction against "entangling alliances" in time came to be universalized and sanctified into a kind of law. The tendency was to interpret and apply it far more rigidly and indiscriminately than its early advocates had intended. The principle was enunciated, we need to be reminded, *in response to a particular set of circumstances*, which appeared to threaten the security and well-being of the young and vulnerable American democracy. The threat arose from the machinations of *European powers*. As with nearly all other tenets of isolationism, it was at prevention of American involvement in *European conflicts* that the maxim was aimed. Note should also be taken of the fact that the specific danger identified was "entangling" *alliances*. Neither Washington nor Jefferson, nor any other early statesman had urged the United States to avoid involvement in foreign (and certainly not in foreign economic and commercial) affairs; the injunction of Washington and Jefferson contained no suggestion that America could be indifferent to events outside its own borders, take its precarious security for granted, or pretend that its destiny was otherwise unaffected by the behavior of other countries.

A closely related connotation of "isolationism" from the infancy of the Republic to the period of World War II was preservation of *national sovereignty and independence in decision-making*. Why should the United States avoid "entangling alliances" with more powerful European states? It should do so primarily because, as a weak and vulnerable country, its independence might be jeopardized by close diplomatic and military association with more powerful nations. For example, Secretary of State Timothy Pickering believed that the government of France had aided the colonial cause during the American Revolution chiefly to promote its own interests—a leading French objective being *to keep the United States dependent upon France for an indefinite period thereafter*.[16]

President Monroe's famous message to Congress (December 2, 1823), laying the foundation for what came to be called the Monroe Doctrine, was directed against two (real or imaginary) dangers: a threatened intervention by the Holy Alliance in Latin America and expansionism by Czarist Russia in the Pacific Northwest. Although the principles enunciated by President Monroe became well known in the years to follow, it was sometimes overlooked that his paramount concern was *the security and independence of the United States*.[17] Invited to join with Great Britain in asserting the concepts contained in his doctrine, President Monroe refused. A joint declaration with the vastly more powerful England, Secretary of State John Quincy Adams wrote, would have reduced the United States to "a cock-boat in the wake of the British man-of-war."[18]

Another facet of the doctrine of isolationism was *unilateralism*: during the twenty years that followed World War I, this was perhaps the doctrine's dominant connotation. According to Paul Seabury, the term signified America's "preference for autonomous action in world politics and a disinclination to be bound by alliances or by any supranational agreements committing the nation in advance to policies which might involve the use of force or war."[19] In 1924, Secretary of State Charles Evans Hughes declared that, although the United States was willing to participate in certain forms of international collaboration (like arms reduction), it "would not tolerate the submission of such questions which pertain to our own policy to the determination of any group of Powers. . . . We should not be willing to enter any organization through which a group of Powers would be in a position to intervene to attempt to determine our policies for us."[20] Called the "perfect isolationist," Senator William E. Borah once declared: "What I have opposed from the beginning is any commitment of this nation to a given line of procedure in a future exigency, the facts as to which could not be known before the event."[21]

As war clouds gathered in Europe (and more specifically after Italy invaded Ethiopia in 1935), the Roosevelt Administration tried to take limited steps to prevent further aggression. In this process, one commentator has written, Secretary of State Cordell Hull "was careful to avoid any appearance of being led by the League [of Nations]."[22] Irrespective of what America's particular response to Axis expansionism might be—and there was a considerable range of opinion, even among isolationists, on this issue—the United States was required to act unilaterally. It was precluded by the isolationist heritage from using its military, economic, and frequently even its moral influence abroad in concert with other nations.

Still another component or fact of the isolationist credo was its insistence upon *America's nonparticipation in foreign wars*. In the Monroe Doctrine, President Monroe had declared:

> In the wars of the European powers in matters relating to themselves we have never taken any part, nor does it comport with our policy to do so. It is only when our rights are invaded or seriously menaced that we resent injuries or make preparation for our defense.

As with other aspects of the isolationist mentality, America's desire to escape involvement in foreign wars was no abstract principle formulated by the fathers of the Republic. To the contrary, it was a determination which had evolved out of the American society's experience during the colonial period and the early years under the Constitution. The diplomatic historian, Thomas A. Bailey, has noted that between 1689 and 1815 England and France fought each other seven times, engaging in conflict for 60 out of 126 years. Americans had been involved in every one of these major and minor wars, irrespective of their own wishes in the matter.[23] The benefits accruing to Americans from avoidance in Europe's wars had been one of the main advantages of "separation" from England, as advocated by Thomas Paine in *Common Sense* and by other pre-Revolutionary leaders.[24]

Something of the dominant American attitude on this point is conveyed by President Woodrow Wilson's mental anguish during World War I, after he had prepared his "war message" (presented to Congress on February 26, 1917). According to one historian, Wilson feared that America's entry into the First World War would "overturn the world we had known."

Down to World War II, the connection between staunch adherence to a policy of isolationism and nonparticipation in war was twofold. First, *if* the American society could successfully avoid becoming embroiled in foreign conflicts, it could escape such evils as infringement upon its independent decision-making by more powerful states, a tendency toward militarism at home, the possible loss of such liberties as those incorporated in the Bill of Rights, higher taxes, and distraction from more important and promising domestic pursuits. Second, the evident success of their isolationist stance, in enabling the United States to avoid involvement in major foreign conflicts for more than a century after the War of 1812, tended to confirm Americans in the wisdom of their behavior toward other countries. (As Sheldon Appleton has pointed out, Americans tended to overlook the fact that for some one hundred years after the defeat of Napoleon in 1815, in fact there was no general European war!)[25]

Yet, fundamental as it was to the concept of isolationism, we should not imagine that the principle of avoiding war was unqualified or free of ambiguities and limitations. The Monroe Doctrine's provisions, for example, were more heavily qualified than most Americans realized. President Monroe had pledged the United States to abstain from participation in Europe's wars; as with certain other dimensions of the isolationist viewpoint, the restrictions envisioned upon American diplomatic behavior were directed primarily at "entanglement" *in Europe's rivalries and conflicts.* But President Monroe had gone even further: He affirmed that the United States would not participate in "the wars of the European powers *in matters relating to themselves* [Italics added]." Moreover, he had emphatically warned the European Powers that "when our rights are invaded or seriously menaced" America would "make preparation for our defense." Despite the mythology that came to surround it, the Monroe Doctrine, in other words, *contained no blanket prohibition against American participation in foreign wars.* The United States proposed to be a nonbelligerent—or adopt a position of "neutrality"—(1) toward wars involving the major powers of Continental Europe, (2) with regard to disputes that were of concern to these states, (3) so long as America's own security was not jeopardized. This is quite literally what President Monroe announced to the world. As time passed, the American people (not excluding sometimes their leaders) lost sight of the qualifications surrounding the nonbelligerency principle. Thus, President Franklin D. Roosevelt informed the Australian Prime Minister, Joseph A. Lyons, in 1935 that the United States would never again be drawn into a European war *for any reason.*[26]

Although the nonbelligerency concept became associated with the isolationist credo, we must not imagine that isolationism was synonymous with pacificism or total indifference toward the problem of national defense and security. As with other specific connotations of the isolationist doctrine, the meaning and relative importance of the nonbelligerency idea tended to vary, depending upon circumstances at home and abroad. Those Americans who opposed interventionism in Europe's conflicts during the 1930s, for example, were convinced that isolationism *was* a viable diplomatic strategy, which would enable the United States to defend its interests and security successfully. For many isolationists, a salient feature of their approach to foreign policy, for example, was the premise that *within the Western Hemisphere, the power of the United States was supreme, and it must continue to be supreme.* As long as this was the case, American security was not endangered by the Axis Powers.[27] Robert E. Sherwood has emphasized that most pre-World War II isolationists were in no sense pacifists. Their attitude toward Japan and Soviet Russia, for example, was sometime very belligerent! More generally, they favored reliance upon armed force to achieve national policy goals under two conditions: All battles must be waged on America's so-called home ground in the Western Hemisphere, and the United States must fight its military engagements *alone*, without allies, thereby presumably avoiding the "mistakes" of World War I.[28]

Isolationists of an earlier era had sometimes taken a different view of the proper use of military force for the achievement of American foreign policy objectives. Thus, in the period from the end of the nineteenth century to World War I, one school of thought, typified by Senator Henry Cabot Lodge (Republican of Massachusetts), advocated a "large" American policy, involving expansionism and territorial annexations. Lodge entered political life at a time when the advantages accruing from America's geographic isolation were being undermined by modern means of communication and transportation. In this period America was "coming of age," emerging as one of the most powerful nations on the globe. A disciple of Admiral Alfred Mahan, America's foremost advocate of seapower and of control over sea lanes and bases upon which its effective exercise depended,[29] Lodge called for an energetic and expansionist foreign policy for the United States, entailing a rapid buildup in naval strength, particularly in the Pacific region. Thus, Lodge favored America's annexation of Hawaii on strategic-military grounds: Possession of these islands gave the United States mastery of the Pacific sea lanes, and the United States had to deny ownership of them to any foreign power.[30] Similarly, on the eve of World War I, Senator William E. Borah urged the Republican party to "make our position strong for America first, for the protection of American rights here and abroad." Responding to President Wilson's assertion (May 10, 1915) that "there is such a thing as a man [or nation] being too proud to fight," Borah stated: "A nation which declares itself too proud to fight will soon be regarded by the nations of the earth as too cowardly to live." In Borah's view, "weakness is a source of war." Borah was the author of the phrase (from which the "America First" movement, one of the most influential organizations during the 1930s, took its name): "America first, let it cost what it may."[31]

In connection with a controversy with Great Britain, on January 21, 1821, Secretary of State John Quincy Adams had informed London: "Keep what is yours, but leave the rest of the [American] Continent to us."[32] This highlights another component of isolationist thought: the idea of *continentalism*. After independence, one of the goals served by an isolationist stance was "filling out" America's boundaries westward and extending the hegemony of the United States up to its "natural frontiers" on the Pacific Ocean, the Canadian border, and the Gulf of Mexico. (Some Americans of course believed that eventually Canada, and perhaps Cuba, were destined to form part of the American Union.) This aspiration was unquestionably implicit in the "non-colonization" principle of the Monroe Doctrine and reiterated many times after 1823. As expressed in President James K. Polk's celebrated "corollary" to the Monroe Doctrine (December 2, 1845), the United States was dedicated to the "settled policy that no future European colony or dominion shall with our consent be planted or established on any part of the North American continent." Polk continued that the United States was committed to

> . . . the principle that the people of this continent alone have the right to decide their own destiny. Should any portion of them, constituting an independent state, propose to unite themselves with our Confederacy, this will be a question for them and us to determine without any foreign interposition.[33]

A generation earlier, Congress had forcefully asserted another concept—the "no-transfer" principle—in connection with Spanish possessions in Florida. On January 15, 1811, a congressional resolution announced that the United States could not, "without serious inquietude, see any part of the said territory [East and West Florida] pass into the hands of any foreign Power." Proponents of the no-transfer injunction were unquestionably aware that ultimately the United States might wish to annex Florida and other European colonial possessions in North America.[34] When the Monroe Doctrine and the no-transfer principle were invoked against outside powers, therefore, this was done in some degree on the premise that it was the destiny of the United States to incorporate foreign territorial possessions on the North American continent.

To the American mind, such expansionist impulses had little in common with the hegemonial tendencies of nations in the Old World. Pursuit of "continentalism" not only would benefit the United States but ultimately would uplift human society at large, not excluding the conduct of international affairs. This mentality perhaps reached its culmination in the approach of Wilsonian idealists to foreign policy questions. Compelled by events to abandon America's preferred position of neutrality toward the belligerents in World War I, President Wilson was determined that, as a result of America's entry into the war, the basic pattern of international relations would thereafter be fundamentally changed. For Wilsonians, this conflict became "the war to end wars" and to "make the world safe for democracy." As Walter Lippmann expressed the idea, "The Wilsonian doctrine was the adaptation of the American tradition to an unexpected necessity—that of returning to Europe, of fighting on the soil of Europe, and of reuniting politically with the European nations." In order to achieve these Wilsonian ends, "the principles of democracy would have to be made universal throughout the world. The Wilsonian ideology is American fundamentalism made into universal doctrine."[35]

## Notes

1. Quoted in Richard W. Leopold, *The Growth of American Foreign Policy: A History* (New York: Alfred A. Knopf, 1962), p. 18.
2. See Jefferson's First Inaugural Address (March 4, 1801), in House of Representatives, *Miscellaneous Documents*. 53d Congress, 2d Session, 1893–94 (Washington: Government Printing Office, 1895), pp. 321–24.
3. When the United States "abandoned" isolationism is a debatable question, which elicits diverse answers from commentators. Some believe that President Franklin D. Roosevelt's "Quarantine Speech" of October 5, 1937, in which he likened Axis aggression to a disease and called on the nations of the world to quarantine it, marked the end of America's isolationist posture. See William L. Langer and S. Everett Gleason, *The Challenge to Isolation: 1937–1940* (New York: Harper and Row, 1952), p. 11.
4. Quoted from Charles A. Beard, *Giddy Minds and Foreign Quarrels* (New York: Macmillan, 1939), reprinted in Robert A. Goldwin, ed., *Readings in American Foreign Policy*, 2d ed. (New York: Oxford University Press, 1971), pp. 131–33.
5. Quoted in Norman A. Graebner, "Isolationism," *International Encyclopedia of the Social Sciences* (New York: Crowell Collier and Macmillan, 1968), Vol. 8, p. 218.
6. After analyzing the results of public opinion polls in the early postwar period, one commentator concluded that no more than 10 per cent of the American people could accurately be described as "isolationists." See Alfred O. Hero, *Americans in World Affairs* (Boston: World Peace Foundation, 1959), pp. 10–11.
7. Quoted in Graebner, "Isolationism," p. 219.
8. See Arthur H. Vandenberg, Jr., ed., *The Private Papers of Senator Vandenberg* (Boston: Houghton Mifflin, 1952), pp. 131, 139.
9. For a detailed discussion of Senator Vandenberg's role, see Cecil V. Crabb, Jr., *Bipartisan Foreign Policy: Myth or Reality?* (New York: Harper and Row, 1957), esp. pp. 44–116.

10. Vandenberg, *The Private Papers of Senator Vandenberg*, p. 139.
11. Quoted in Wayne S. Cole, *Senator Gerald P. Nye and American Foreign Relations* (Minneapolis: University of Minnesota Press, 1962), p. 216.
12. The idea that America's most beneficial contribution to global peace and security was to solve its own internal problems and conduct itself in an exemplary manner is one of the most consistent themes associated with traditional isolationist thought. President Millard Fillmore in 1851 said that America's "true mission" was "to teach by example and show by our success . . . the advantages of free institutions." Quoted in Leopold, *The Growth of American Foreign Policy*, p. 26, and in Arthur A. Ekirch, Jr., *Ideas, Ideals and American Diplomacy* (New York: Appleton-Century-Crofts, 1966), pp. 36–37. Many years later, Secretary of State Cordell Hull declared in a speech in 1937 that America's most effective contribution to world peace was "to have this country respected throughout the world for integrity, justice, good will, strength, and unswerving loyalty to principles." Quoted in Julius W. Pratt, "Cordell Hull," in Samuel F. Bemis, ed., *The American Secretaries of State and Their Diplomacy* (New York: Cooper Square Publishers, 1964), 1:288.
13. Although Jefferson did not use the term "isolationism," in time the phrase "no entangling alliances" became synonymous with it. See Samuel F. Bemis, *A Diplomatic History of the United States*, 2d ed. (New York: Henry Holt, 1942), pp. 202–3, and Leopold, *The Growth of American Foreign Policy*, pp. 22–23.
14. As we have already observed, the warning had been foreshadowed in Washington's Farewell Address (1796). See Appendix 1.
15. Despite the fact that supposedly its terms were to last *in perpetuo*, on July 7, 1798, Congress declared the French alliance void on the grounds that the French government had violated its terms. Thomas A. Bailey, *A Diplomatic History of the American People*, 8th ed. (New York: Appleton-Century-Crofts, 1969), p. 95.
16. Henry J. Ford, "Timothy Pickering," in Bemis, ed., *The American Secretaries of State*, pp. 205–6. Pickering served as Secretary of State during the period 1795–1800.
17. Frank Donovan, *Mr. Monroe's Message: The Story of the Monroe Doctrine* (New York: Dodd, Mead, 1963), p. 9.
18. Quoted in Bailey, *A Diplomatic History of the American People*, p. 182, citing C. F. Adams, *Memoirs*, 6:179 (November 7, 1823).
19. Paul Seabury, *Power, Freedom, and Diplomacy: The Foreign Policy of the United States of American* (New York: Random House, 1963), p. 38.
20. Quoted in Charles C. Hyde, "Charles Evans Hughes," in Bemis, ed., *The American Secretaries of State*, p. 356.
21. John C. Vinson, *William E. Borah and the Outlawry of War* (Athens: University of Georgia Press, 1957), p. 1.
22. Quoted in Pratt, "Cordell Hull," 1:199.
23. See the views of Thomas A. Bailey, as cited in Sheldon Appleton, *United States Foreign Policy: An Introduction with Cases* (Boston: Little, Brown, 1968), p. 39.
24. Bemis, *A Diplomatic History of the United States*, p. 12.
25. Appleton, *United States Foreign Policy*, p. 56.
26. For Roosevelt's views, see Robert H. Ferrell, *American Diplomacy: A History* (New York: Norton, 1959), p. 367.

27. See Burton K. Wheeler, *Yankee from the West* (Garden City, N. Y.: Doubleday, 1962), p. 22, and Pratt, "Cordell Hull," 1:251.
28. See Robert E. Sherwood, *Roosevelt and Hopkins* (New York: Bantam Books, 1950), 1:161.
29. Admiral Alfred Mahan (1840–1914) exercised a profound influence upon American military strategy for perhaps a half-century or more after 1900. He was a prolific author and well-known lecturer; his most famous book was *The Influence of Seapower Upon History* (1918). For a succinct discussion of Mahan's views, see Margaret T. Sprout, "Mahan: Evangelist of Sea Power," in Edward M. Earle, ed., *Makers of Modern Strategy* (New York: Atheneum, 1966), pp. 415–46.
30. John A. Garraty, *Henry Cabot Lodge: A Biography* (New York: Alfred A. Knopf, 1953), pp. 150–55.
31. Marian C. McKenna, *Borah* (Ann Arbor: University of Michigan Press, 1961), pp. 138–43.
32. See Adams's views as quoted in Leopold, *The Growth of American Foreign Policy*, p. 42.
33. Julius W. Pratt, *A History of United States Foreign Policy* (Englewood Cliffs, N.J.: Prentice-Hall, 1955), pp. 243–44.
34. See *ibid.*, pp. 129, 165.
35. See Walter Lippmann, *Isolation and Alliances: An American Speaks to the British* (Boston: Little, Brown, 1952), pp. 21–22.

## 2  The Mainsprings of American Foreign Policy

### HANS J. MORGENTHAU

Hans Morgenthau is perhaps the best known proponent of realism in international politics. One of its earliest theorists and advocates, Morgenthau wrote *Politics Among Nations* in 1948 (revised several times over the subsequent years), which explained the principles of realism. This theory suggests that the foreign policies of states are, and ought to be, based upon a narrow assessment of national interests, whereby states' primary concerns are with the protection of their security, the acquisition of power, and the global balance of power, not the fulfillment of their ideals. In other words, states act and should act in terms of power politics to protect their material interests, not their ideological goals. According to realism, state

Hans Morgenthau, from *In Defense of the National Interest: A Critical Examination of American Foreign Policy.* Copyright 1951. Reprinted by permission of Matthew Morgenthau.

action grounded in idealism (utopianism as Morgenthau calls it), morality, law, values, ethics, and/or the promotion of democracy is both wrongheaded and potentially dangerous. The laws that govern domestic society and relations among individuals are fundamentally different from those that govern relations among nations. Morgenthau believes that policymakers and statesmen had ignored these realities in the first half of the 20th century, leading to two world wars in a generation.

In "The Mainsprings of American Foreign Policy," Morgenthau applies his theoretical framework to American engagement in foreign relations. He argues that the pinnacle of American realist thinking came in the first decade of the country's existence, when George Washington spoke the language of realism—interest defined as power and security—and acted according to its principles. Since this time, according to Morgenthau, American political thought has been divorced from the country's political action. American political leaders have thought in ideological terms and moral imperatives, grounding U.S. foreign policy in ideas about a distinctly American system whose democratic practices were unique and whose adversaries had to be vanquished. The results, says Morgenthau, have been detrimental to U.S. and global security.

Realism has been an important element of U.S. foreign policy, and has influenced American policymakers for generations. It played a particularly strong role during the Cold War, informing American policy toward the Soviet Union. President Nixon and Secretary of State Henry Kissinger were its most faithful practitioners in the United States, but its importance has not eclipsed with time, and it continues to be a prominent part of American foreign policy thinking. Quite often, American foreign policy reflects a combination of realist considerations and other perspectives.

---

It is often said that the foreign policy of the United States needs to mature and that the American people and their government must grow up if they want to emerge victorious from the trials of our age. It would be truer to say that this generation of Americans must shed the illusions of its fathers and grandfathers and relearn the great principles of statecraft which guided the republic in the first decade and—in moralistic disguise—in the first century of its existence. The United States offers the singular spectacle of a commonwealth whose political wisdom has not grown slowly through the accumulation and articulation of experiences. On the contrary, the full flowering of its political wisdom was coeval with its birth as an independent nation; indeed, it owed its existence and survival as an independent nation to those extraordinary qualities of political insight, historical perspective, and common sense which the first generation of Americans applied to the affairs of state.

This classic age of American statecraft came to an end with the disappearance of that generation of American statesmen. Cut off from its vital sources, the rich and varied landscape in which they had planted all that is worth while in the tradition of Western political thought was allowed to go to waste. That age and its wisdom became a faint and baffling remembrance, a symbol to be worshipped rather than a source of inspiration and a guide for action. Until very recently the American people have appeared content to live in a political desert whose intellectual barrenness and aridity was relieved only by some sparse and neglected oases of insight and wisdom. What passed for foreign policy was either improvisation or—especially in our century—the invocation of some abstract moral principle in whose image the world was to be made over. Improvisation was largely successful, for in the past the margin of American and allied power has generally exceeded the degree to which American improvidence has failed the demands of the hour. The invocation of abstract moral principles was in part hardly more than an innocuous pastime; embracing everything, it came to grips with nothing. In part, however, it was a magnificent instrument for marshaling public opinion in support of war and warlike policies—and for losing the peace. The intoxication with moral abstractions, which as a mass phenomenon started with the Spanish-American War and which in our time has become the prevailing substitute for political thought, is indeed one of the great sources of weakness and failure in American foreign policy. Much will have to be said about this later.

Still it is worthy of note that underneath this political dilettantism, which is nourished by improvidence and a sense of moral mission, there lives an almost instinctive awareness of the perennial interests of the United States. This has been especially true with regard to Europe and the Western Hemisphere, for in these regions the national interest of the United States has always been obvious and clearly defined.

## 1. THE NATIONAL INTEREST OF THE UNITED STATES

In the Western Hemisphere we have always endeavored to preserve the unique position of the United States as a predominant power without rival. We have not been slow in recognizing that our predominance was not likely to be effectively threatened by any one American nation or combination of nations acting without support from outside the hemisphere. This peculiar situation has made it imperative for the United States to isolate the Western Hemisphere from the political and military policies of non-American nations. The interference of non-American nations in the affairs of the Western Hemisphere, especially through the acquisition of territory, was the only way in which the predominance of the United States could have been challenged from within the hemisphere itself. The Monroe Doctrine and the policies implementing it express that permanent national interest of the United States in the Western Hemisphere.

Since a threat to our national interest in the Western Hemisphere can only come from outside it—historically, from Europe—we have always striven to prevent the development of conditions in Europe which would be conductive to a European nation's interfering in the affairs of the Western Hemisphere or contemplating a direct attack upon the United States. These conditions would be most likely to arise if a European nation, its predominance unchallenged within Europe, could look across the sea for conquest without fear of being menaced at the center of its power; that is, in Europe itself.

It is for this reason that the United States has consistently—the War of 1812 is the sole major exception—pursued policies aiming at the maintenance of the balance of power in Europe. It has opposed whatever European nation—be it Great Britain, France, Germany, or Russia—was likely to gain that ascendancy over its European competitors which would have jeopardized the hemispheric predominance and eventually the very independence of the United States. Conversely, it has supported whatever European nation appeared capable of restoring the balance of power by offering successful resistance to the would-be conqueror. While it is hard to imagine a greater contrast in ways of thinking about matters political than that between Alexander Hamilton and Woodrow Wilson, in this concern for the maintenance of the balance of power in Europe—for whatever different reasons—they are one. It is with this concern that the United States has intervened in both World Wars on the side of the initially weaker coalition, and has pursued European policies so largely paralleling those of Great Britain; for from Henry VIII to this day Great Britain has had a single objective in Europe: the maintenance of the balance of power.

## 2. THE AMERICAN EXPERIENCE IN FOREIGN AFFAIRS

Wherever American foreign policy has operated, political thought has been divorced from political action. Even where our long-range policies reflect faithfully, as they do in the Americas and in Europe, the true interests of the United States, we think about them in terms that have at best but a tenuous connection with the actual character of the policies pursued. We have acted on the international scene, as all nations must, in power-political terms; but we have tended to conceive of our actions in non-political, moralistic terms.

## 3.  THE THREE PERIODS OF AMERICAN FOREIGN POLICY

### The Realistic Period

The illusion that a nation can escape, if it wants to, from power politics into a realm where action is guided by moral principles rather than by considerations of power is deeply rooted in the American mind. Yet it took more than a century for that illusion to crowd out the older notion that international politics is an unending struggle for power in which the interests of individual nations must necessarily be defined in terms of power. Out of the struggle between these two opposing conceptions, three types of American foreign policy have emerged: the realistic—thinking and acting in terms of power—represented by Alexander Hamilton; the ideological—thinking in terms of moral principles but acting in terms of power—represented by Thomas Jefferson and John Quincy Adams; and the moralistic—thinking and acting in terms of moral principles—represented by Woodrow Wilson. To these three types, three periods of American foreign policy roughly correspond, the first covering the first decade of the history of the United States as an independent nation, the second covering the nineteenth century to the Spanish-American War, and the third covering the half century after that war. This division of the history of American foreign policy—as will become obvious in our discussion—refers only to prevailing tendencies, without precluding the operation side by side of different tendencies in the same period.

It illustrates both the depth of the moralistic illusion and the original strength of the opposition to it that the issue between these two opposing conceptions of foreign policy was joined at the very beginning of the history of the United States, was decided in favor of the realistic position, and was formulated with unsurpassed simplicity and penetration by Alexander Hamilton. The memorable occasion was Washington's proclamation of neutrality in the War of the First Coalition against revolutionary France.

In 1792, the War of the First Coalition had ranged Austria, Prussia, Sardinia, Great Britain, and the United Netherlands against revolutionary France, which was tied to the United States by a treaty of alliance. On April 22, 1793, Washington issued a proclamation of neutrality, and it was in defense of that proclamation that Hamilton wrote the "Pacificus" and "Americanus" articles. Among the arguments directed against the proclamation were three derived from moral principles. Faithfulness to treaty obligations, gratitude toward a country that had lent its assistance to the colonies in their struggle for independence, and the affinity of republican institutions, were cited to prove that the United States must side with

France. Against these moral principles, Hamilton invoked the national interest of the United States:

> There would be no proportion between the mischiefs and perils to which the United States would expose themselves, by embarking in the war, and the benefit which the nature of their stipulation aims at securing to France, or that which it would be in their power actually to render her by becoming a party.
>
> This disproportion would be a valid reason for not executing the guaranty. All contracts are to receive a reasonable construction. Self-preservation is the first duty of a nation; and though in the performance of stipulations relating to war, good faith requires that its ordinary hazards should be fairly met, because they are directly contemplated by such stipulations, yet it does not require that extraordinary and extreme hazards should be run. . . .
>
> Whence it follows that an individual may, on numerous occasions, meritoriously indulge the emotions of generosity and benevolence, not only without an eye to, but even at the expense of, his own interest. But a government can rarely, if at all, be justifiable in pursuing a similar course; and, if it does so, ought to confine itself within much stricter bounds. . . .

Must a nation subordinate its security, its happiness, nay, its very existence to the respect for treaty obligations, to the sentiment of gratitude, to sympathy with a kindred political system? This was the question Hamilton proposed to answer, and his answer was an unequivocal "no." To the issues raised by the opposition to Washington's proclamation of neutrality Hamilton unswervingly applied one standard: the national interest of the United States. He put the legalistic and moralistic arguments of the opposition, represented by Madison under the pseudonym "Helvidius," into the context of the concrete power situation in which the United States found itself on the international scene, and asked: If the United States were to join France against virtually all of Europe, what risks would the United States run, what advantages could it expect, what good could it do to its ally?

## The Ideological Period

Considerations such as these, recognized for what they were, guided American foreign policy for but a short period; that is, as long as the Federalists were in power. *The Federalist* and Washington's Farewell Address are their classic expression. Yet we have seen that these considerations, not recognized for what they were or even rejected, have determined the great objectives of American foreign policy to this day. During the century following their brief flowering, their influence has persisted, under the cover of those moral principles with which from Jefferson onward American statesmen have liked to justify their moves on the international scene. Thus this second period witnessed a discrepancy between political thought and political action, yet a coincidence in the intended results of both. What was said of Gladstone could also have been said of Jefferson, John Quincy Adams, Grover Cleveland, Theodore Roosevelt, the war policies of Wilson and of Franklin D. Roosevelt: what the moral law demanded was by a felicitous coincidence always identical with what the national interest seemed to require. Political thought and political action moved on different planes, which, however, inclined to merge in the end.

John Quincy Adams is the classic example of the political moralist in thought and word, who cannot help being a political realist in action. Yet even in Jefferson, whose dedication to abstract morality was much stronger and whose realist touch in foreign affairs was much less sure, the moral pretense yielded often, especially in private utterance, to the impact of the national interest upon native good sense.

Thus during the concluding decade of the Napoleonic Wars Jefferson's thought on international affairs was a reflection of the ever changing distribution of power in the world rather than of immutable moral principles. In 1806, he favored "an English ascendancy on the ocean" as being "safer for us than that of France." In 1807, he was by the logic of events forced to admit:

> I never expected to be under the necessity of wishing success to Buonaparte. But the English being equally tyrannical at sea as he is on land, & that tyranny bearing on us in every point of either honor or interest, I say "down with England" and as for what Buonaparte is then to do to us, let us trust to the chapter of accidents, I cannot, with the Anglomen, prefer a certain present evil to a future hypothetical one.

However, in 1812, when Napoleon was at the pinnacle of his power. Jefferson hoped for the restoration of the balance. Speaking of England, he said:

> It is for the general interest that she should be a sensible and independent weight in the scale of nations, and be able to contribute, when a favorable moment presents itself, to reduce under the same order, her great rival in flagitiousness. We especially ought to pray that the powers of Europe may be so poised and counterpoised among themselves, that their own security may require the presence of all their forces at home, leaving the other quarters of the globe in undistrubed tranquility.

In 1814, again compelled by the logic of events, he came clearly out against Napoleon and in favor of a balance of power which would leave the power of Napoleon and of England limited, but intact.

> Surely none of us wish to see Bonaparte conquer Russia, and lay thus at his feet the whole continent of Europe. This done, England would be but a breakfast; and, although I am free from the visionary fears which

the votaries of England have effected to entertain, because I believe he cannot effect the conquest of Europe; yet put all Europe into his hands, and he might spare such a force to be sent in British ships, as I would as leave not have to encounter, when I see how much trouble a handful of British soldiers in Canada has given us. No. It cannot be to our interest that all Europe should be reduced to a single monarchy.

It was only when, after 1815, the danger to the balance of power seemed to have passed that Jefferson allowed himself again to indulge in the cultivation of moral principles divorced from political exigencies.

From this tendency, to which Jefferson only too readily yielded, John Quincy Adams was well-nigh immune. We are here in the presence of a statesman who had been reared in the realist tradition of the first period of American foreign policy, who had done the better part of his work of statecraft in an atmosphere saturated with Jeffersonian principles, and who had achieved the merger of these two elements of his experience into a harmonious whole. Between John Quincy Adams's moral principles and the traditional interest of the United States there was hardly ever a conflict. The moral principles were nothing but the political interests formulated in moral terms, and vice versa. They fit the interests as a glove fits the hand. Adams's great contributions to the tradition of American foreign policy—freedom of the seas, the Monroe Doctrine, and Manifest Destiny—are witness to this achievement.

In the hands of Adams, the legal and moral principle of the freedom of the seas was a weapon, as it had been two centuries earlier when Grotius wielded it on behalf of the Low Countries, through which an inferior naval power endeavored to safeguard its independence against Great Britain, the mistress of the seas. The Monroe Doctrine's moral postulates of anti-imperialism and mutual nonintervention were the negative conditions for the safety and enduring greatness of the United States. Their fulfillment secured the isolation of the United States from the power struggles of Europe and, through it, the continuing predominance of the United States in the Western Hemisphere. Manifest Destiny was the moral justification as well as the moral incentive for the westward expansion of the United States. The peculiar American way—foreordained by the objective conditions of American existence—of founding an empire, the "American Empire," as one of the contemporary opponents of Adams's policies put it.

## The Utopian Period

Jefferson and John Quincy Adams stand at the beginning of the second period of American thought on foreign policy, both its most eminent representatives and the heirs of a realist tradition that continued to mold political action, while it had largely ceased to influence political thought. At the beginning of the third period, McKinley leads the United States as a great world power beyond the confines of the Western Hemisphere, ignorant of the bearing of this step upon the national interest, and guided by moral principles completely divorced from the national interest. When at the end of the Spanish-American War the status of the Philippines had to be determined, McKinley expected and found no guidance in the traditional national interests of the United States. According to his own testimony, he knelt beside his bed in prayer, and in the wee hours of the morning he heard the voice of God telling him—as was to be expected—to annex the Philippines.

This period initiated by McKinley, in which moral principles no longer justify the enduring national interest as in the second, but replace it as a guide for action, finds its fulfillment in the political thought of Woodrow Wilson. Wilson's thought not only disregards the national interest, but is explicitly opposed to it on moral grounds. "It is a very perilous thing," he said in his address at Mobile on October 27, 1913,

> to determine the foreign policy of a nation in the terms of material interest. It not only is unfair to those with whom you are dealing, but it is degrading as regards your own actions. . . . We dare not turn from the principle that morality and not expediency is the thing that must guide us, and that we will never condone iniquity because it is most convenient to do so.

Yet in his political actions, especially under the pressure of the First World War, Wilson could not discount completely the national interest of the United States, any more than could Jefferson before him. Wilson's case, however, was different from Jefferson's in two respects. For one thing, Wilson was never able, even when the national interest of the United States was directly menaced, to conceive of the danger in other than moral terms. It was only the objective force of the national interest, which no rational man could escape, that imposed the source of America's mortal danger upon him as the object of his moral indignation. Thus Wilson in 1917 led the United States into war against Germany for the same reasons, only half-known to himself, for which Jefferson had wished and worked alternately for the victory of England and France. Germany threatened the balance of power in Europe, and it was in order to remove that threat—and not to make the world safe for democracy—that the United States put its weight into the Allies' scale. Wilson pursued the right policy, but he pursued it for the wrong reasons.

## 4.  WILSONIANISM, ISOLATIONISM, INTERNATIONALISM—THREE FORMS OF UTOPIANISM

Whereas before Paris and Versailles these moral principles rang true with the promise of a new and better world, afterwards they must have sounded rather hollow and platitudinous to many. Yet what is significant for the course American foreign policy was to take in the interwar years is not so much that the American people rejected Wilsonianism, but that they rejected it by ratifying the denial of the American tradition of foreign policy which was implicit in the political thought of Wilson. We are here indeed dealing with a tragedy not of one man, but of a political doctrine and, as far as the United States is concerned, of a political tradition. The isolationism of the interwar period could delude itself into believing that it was but the restorer of the early realistic tradition of American foreign policy. Did it not, like that tradition, proclaim the self-sufficiency of the United States within the Western Hemisphere? Did it not, like that tradition, refuse to become involved in the rivalries of European nations? The isolationists of the twenties and thirties did not see—and this was the very essence of the policies of the Founding Fathers—that both the isolated and the preponderant position of the United States in the Western Hemisphere was not a fact of nature, and that the freedom from entanglements in European conflicts was not the result of mere abstention on the part of the United States. Both benefits were the result of political conditions outside the Western Hemisphere and of policies carefully contrived and purposefully executed in their support. For the realists of the first period, isolation was an objective of policy, and had to be striven for to be attained. For the isolationists of the interwar period, isolation was a natural state, and only needed to be left undisturbed in order to continue forever. Conceived in such terms, it was the very negation of foreign policy.

Isolationism, then, is in its way as oblivious to political reality as is Wilsonianism—the internationalist challenge, to which it thought to have found the American answer. In consequence, they are both strangers not only to the first, realistic phase of American foreign policy, but to its whole tradition. Both refused to face political reality either in realistic or ideological terms. They refused to face it at all. Thus isolationism and Wilsonianism have more in common than their historic enmity would lead one to suspect. In a profound sense they are brothers under the skin. Both are one in maintaining that the United States has no interest in any particular political and military configuration outside the Western Hemisphere. While isolationism stops here, Wilsonianism asserts that the American national interest is not somewhere in particular, but everywhere, being identical with the interests of mankind itself. Both refuse to concern themselves with the concrete issues upon which the national interest must be asserted. Isolationism stops short of them, Wilsonianism soars beyond them. Both have but a negative relation to the national interest of the United States outside the Western Hemisphere. They are unaware of its very existence. This being so, both substitute abstract moral principles for the guidance of the national interest, derived from the actual conditions of American existence. Wilsonianism applies the illusory expectations of liberal reform to the whole world, isolationism empties of all concrete political content the realistic political principle of isolation and transforms it into the unattainable parochial ideal of automatic separation.

In view of this inner affinity between isolationism and Wilsonianism, it is not surprising that the great debate of the twenties and thirties between internationalism and isolationism was carried on primarily in moral terms. Was there a moral obligation for the United States to make its contribution to world peace by joining the League of Nations and the World Court? Was it morally incumbent upon the United States, as a democracy, to oppose Fascism in Europe and to uphold international law in Asia? Such were the questions raised in that debate, and the answers depended upon the moral position taken. The question central to the national interest of the United States, that of the balance of power in Europe and Asia, was hardly ever faced squarely, and when it was faced it was dismissed on moral grounds. Mr. Cordell Hull, Secretary of State of the United States from 1933 to 1944, and one of the most respected spokesmen of internationalism, summarizes in his *Memoirs* his attitude toward this central problem of American foreign policy:

> I was not, and am not, a believer in the idea of balance of power or spheres of influence as a means of keeping the peace. During the First World War I had made an intensive study of the system of spheres of influence and balance of power, and I was grounded to the taproots in their iniquitous consequences. The conclusions I then formed in total opposition to this system stayed with me.

When internationalism triumphed in the late thirties, it did so in the moral terms of Wilsonianism. That in this instance the moral postulates inspiring the administration of Franklin D. Roosevelt happened to coincide with the exigencies of the American national interest was again, as in the case of Jefferson and of the Wilson of 1917, due to the impact of a national emergency upon innate common sense, and to the strength of a national tradition that holds in its spell the actions of even those who deny its validity in words. However, as soon as the minds of the American leaders, freed from these inescapable pressures of a primarily military nature, turned toward the political problems of the Second World War and its aftermath, they thought and acted again as Wilson had acted under similar circumstances. That is to say, they thought and acted in moral terms, divorced from the political conditions of America's existence.

The practical results of this philosophy of international affairs, as applied to the political problems of the war and postwar period, were therefore bound to be quite similar to those which had made the Allied victory in the First World War politically meaningless. Conceived as it was as a "crusade"—to borrow from the title of General Eisenhower's book—against the evil incarnate in the Axis powers, the purpose of the Second World War could only be the destruction of that evil, brought about through the instrumentality of "unconditional surrender." Since the threat to the Western world emanating from the Axis was conceived primarily in moral terms, it was easy to imagine that all conceivable danger was concentrated in that historic constellation of hostile powers and that with its destruction political evil itself would disappear from the world. Beyond "unconditional surrender" there was to be, then, a brave new world after the model of Wilson's, which would liquidate the heritage of the defeated nations—evil and not "peace-loving"—and establish an order of things where war, aggressiveness, and the struggle for power itself would be no more.

With this philosophy dominant in the West—Mr. Churchill provides almost the sole, however ineffective, exception—the strategy of the war and of the peace to follow could not help being oblivious to those considerations of the national interest which the great statesmen of the West, from Hamilton through Castlereagh, Canning, and John Quincy Adams, to Disraeli and Salisbury, had brought to bear upon the international problems of their day. War was no longer regarded as a means to a political end. The only end the war was to serve was total victory, which is another way of saying that the war became an end in itself. Hence, it became irrelevant how the war was won politically, as long as it was won speedily, cheaply, and totally. The thought that the war might be waged in view of a new balance of power to be established after the war, occurred in the West only to Winston Churchill—and, of course, it occurred to Joseph Stalin. The national interest of the Western nations was, then, satisfied in so far as it required the destruction of the threat to the balance of power emanating from Germany and Japan; for to that extent the moral purposes of the war happened to coincide with the national interest. However, the national interest of the Western nations was jeopardized in so far as their security required the creation of a new viable balance of power after the war.

How could statesmen who boasted that they were not "believers in the idea of balance of power"—like a scientist not believing in the law of gravity—and who were out "to kill power politics," understand the very idea of the national interest which demanded, above all, protection from the power of others? Thus it was with deep and sincere moral indignation that the Western world, expecting a utopia without power politics, found itself confronted with a new and more formidable threat to its security as soon as the old one had been subdued. There was good reason for moral indignation, however misdirected it was. That a new balance of power will rise out of the ruins of an old balance and that nations with political sense will avail themselves of the opportunity to improve their position within it, is a law of politics for whose validity nobody is to blame. Yet they are indeed blameworthy who in their moralistic disdain for the laws of politics endanger the interests of the nations in their care.

## 5.  THE MORAL DIGNITY OF THE NATIONAL INTEREST

The fundamental error that has thwarted American foreign policy in thought and action is the antithesis of national interest and moral principles. The equation of political moralizing with morality and of political realism with immorality is itself untenable. The choice is not between moral principles and the national interest, devoid of moral dignity, but between one set of moral principles divorced from political reality, and another set of moral principles derived from political reality.

The extreme instance of political failure on the international plane is national suicide. It may well be said that a foreign policy guided by universal moral principles, by definition relegating the national interest to the background, is under contemporary conditions of foreign policy and warfare a policy of national suicide, actual or potential. Within a national society the individual can at times afford, and may even be required, to subordinate his interests and even to sacrifice his very existence to a supra-individual moral principle—for in national societies such principles exist, capable of providing concrete standards for individual action. What is more important still, national societies take it upon themselves within certain limits to protect and promote the interests of the individual and, in particular, to guard his existence against violent attack. National societies of this kind can exist and fulfill their functions only if their individual members are willing to subordinate their individual interests in a certain measure to the common good of society. Altruism and self-sacrifice are in that measure morally required.

The mutual relations of national societies are fundamentally different. These relations are not controlled by universal moral principles concrete enough to guide the political actions of individual nations. What again is more important, no agency is able to promote and protect the interests of individual nations and to guard their existence—and that is emphatically true of the great powers—but the individual nations themselves. To ask, then, a nation to embark upon altruistic policies oblivious of the national interest, is really to ask something immoral. For such disregard of the individual interest, on the part of nations as of individuals, can be morally justified only by the existence of social institutions, the embodiment of concrete moral principles, which are able to do what otherwise the individual would have to do. In the absence of such institutions it would be both foolish and morally wrong to ask a nation to forego its national interests not for the good of a society with a superior moral claim but for a chimera. Morally speaking, national egotism is not the same as individual egotism because the functions of the international society are not identical with those of a national society.

# 3

# America's Liberal Grand Strategy: Democracy and National Security in the Post–War Era

## G. JOHN IKENBERRY

One of the major goals of U.S. foreign policy has been the promotion of democracy abroad. This idea has included not only a drive for encouraging or creating democratic political practices, but also a desire to expand market capitalism. Indeed, nations that possess both free political institutions and capitalist economies are often referred to as 'market democracies'. These two elements are considered to go hand-in-hand according to the liberal internationalist (or simply 'liberal') perspective of international relations, which suggests that free political institutions and free markets support one another, and that they help to foster global order, peace, and prosperity.

Liberalism is often termed *idealism*, which evokes notions of the Wilsonian vision of a global order characterized by respect for international law, collective security, and morality. Considering the failure of this vision to be realized, idealism has been repeatedly dismissed as 'unrealistic'. However, as John Ikenberry argues, the United States has actually successfully pursued a liberal grand strategy in the world since World War II, creating a liberal international order in both political and economic realms. While this grand strategy may have often seemed hidden behind the priorities of the Cold War, it has been a significant part of American foreign policy, and it has continued well beyond the Cold War. This liberal, American-centered order is not based primarily on idealistic moralism or legalistic understandings of global politics. Rather, it consists of institutions, rules, norms, and practices involving political and economic interactions among states. It professes a strong preference for democracy and understands that democracies tend to have friendly relations and common interests due to shared values and common practices. Moreover, as Ikenberry points out, they do not engage in war with one another. The liberal world order Ikenberry describes also reflects an understanding that states that participate in the IMF, the WTO, the U.N., and other organizations do so because the rules and practices they prescribe generally provide benefits for compliance, while creating costs for noncompliance. This system, which has served to entice countries around the world to join the institutions that the

G. John Ikenberry, from "America's Liberal Grand Strategy: Democracy and National Security in the Post-War Era" in *American Democracy Promotion: Impulses, Strategies and Impacts*, edited by Cox, Ikenberry, and Inoguchi. © 2000. By permission of Oxford University Press.

United States created, offers predictability and stability that result from adherence to certain practices and norms in the international system. This, in turn, contributes greatly to global peace, order, and prosperity, and allows the United States to lead without the continual need to resort to coercion.

# INTRODUCTION

It is thought by many that America's preoccupation with the promotion of democracy around the world is essentially an 'idealist' impulse rooted in the moralism and exceptionalism of the American political tradition. To the extent that this American preoccupation with democracy spills over into actual foreign policy, it is seen as the triumph of American ideas and ideology—often at the expense of the more sober pursuit of American national interests. At best, the American democratic impulse is a minor distraction, rhetorical window dressing fashioned to make foreign policy commitments more acceptable to the American public. At worst, it is a dangerous and overweening moralistic zeal, built around profound misconceptions about how international politics really operates, and fuelling periodic 'crusades' to remake the world—and, as Woodrow Wilson discovered after 1919, this democratic impulse can get the country in serious trouble.

This common view is wrong. The American promotion of democracy abroad in the broadest sense, particularly as it has been pursued after World War II, reflects a pragmatic, evolving, and sophisticated understanding of how to create a stable international political order and a congenial security environment: what might be called an American liberal grand strategy.[1] This orientation sees the character of the domestic regimes of other states as hugely important for the attainment of American security and material interests. Put simply, the United States is better able to pursue its interests, reduce security threats in its environment, and foster a stable political order when other states—particularly the major great powers—are democracies rather than non-democracies. This view is not an idealist preoccupation but a distinctively American national security orientation that helps explain the American encouragement of democracy abroad as well as the wider imprint that the United States has left on the post-war world.

The argument of this chapter is three-fold. First, the American preoccupation with democracy promotion is part of a larger liberal view about the sources of a stable, legitimate, secure, and remunerative international order. This liberal orientation may be intellectually right or wrong, historically successful or unsuccessful, and in a given American foreign policy episode it may be a dominant or recessive characteristic. But it is a relatively coherent orientation rooted in the American political experience and an understanding of history, economics, and the sources of political stability. This American liberal grand strategy can be contrasted with more traditional grand strategies that grow out of the realist tradition and the foreign policy practices of balance of power, *Realpolitik*, and containment.

Second, this distinctively American liberal grand strategy is built around a wide-ranging set of claims and assumptions about how democratic politics, economic interdependence, international institutions, and political identity contribute independently and together to encourage stable and mutually acceptable political order. The richness and persistence of this American orientation is due in part to its manifold character; it is not just a single theoretical claim—for example, power transitions cause wars, democracies do not fight each other, stable order is built on a balance of power—but is a composite view built on a wide range of related claims about democracy, interests, learning, institutions, and economic change. Its richness and persistence is also due to the fact that various aspects of the liberal grand strategy are argued by different groups in the foreign policy community—this is what makes it a composite but also so stable. Some stressed democracy promotion, some stressed free trade and economic liberalization, and others stressed the construction of ambitious new international and regional economic and security institutions. But these separate emphases and agendas complemented each other—and together they came to constitute a liberal grand strategy.

Third, the dominance and appeal of this liberal grand strategy have survived the end of the cold war, even as most observers of American foreign policy do not fully recognize its character or accomplishments. It is an orientation that unites factions of the left and the right in American politics. Conservatives point to Ronald Reagan as the great cold war champion of the free world, democracy, and self-determination—ironically, Reagan is the great Wilsonian of our age. Liberals emphasize the role of human rights, multilateral institutions, and the progressive political effects of economic interdependence. For all the talk about drift and confusion in contemporary American foreign policy, the United States is seized by a robust and distinctive grand strategy.

## THE LIBERAL POST-WAR SETTLEMENT

It is useful to observe that American foreign policy after 1945 produced two post-war settlements. One was a reaction to deteriorating relations with the Soviet Union, and it culminated in the 'containment order'. It was a settlement based on the balance of power, nuclear deterrence, and political and ideological competition. The other settlement was a reaction to the economic rivalry and political turmoil of the 1930s and the resulting world war, and it culminated in a wide range of new institutions and relations among the Western industrial democracies—call it the 'liberal democratic order'. This settlement was built around economic openness, political reciprocity, and institutionalized management of an American-led liberal political order.[2]

The two settlements had distinct political visions and intellectual rationales, and at key moments the American president gave voice to each. On 12 March 1947, President Truman gave his celebrated speech before Congress announcing aid to Greece and Turkey, wrapping it in a new American commitment to support the cause of freedom around the world. The Truman Doctrine speech was a founding moment of the 'containment order'—rallying the American people to a new great struggle, this one against the perils of world domination by Soviet communism. A 'fateful hour' had arrived, Truman told the American people. The people of the world 'must choose between two alternative ways of life'. If the United States failed in its leadership, Truman declared, 'we may endanger the peace of the world'.[3]

It is forgotten, however, that six days before this historic declaration, Truman gave an equally sweeping speech at Baylor University. On this occasion, Truman spoke of the lessons the world must learn from the disasters of the 1930s. 'As each battle of the economic war of the thirties was fought, the inevitable tragic result became more and more apparent. From the tariff policy of Hawley and Smoot, the world went on to Ottawa and the system of imperial preferences, from Ottawa to the kind of elaborate and detailed restrictions adopted by Nazi Germany'. Truman reaffirmed American commitment to 'economic peace', which would involve tariff reductions and rules and institutions of trade and investment. In the settlement of economic differences, 'the interests of all will be considered, and a fair and just solution will be found'. Conflicts would be captured and domesticated in an iron cage of multilateral rules, standards, safeguards, and dispute resolution procedures. According to Truman, 'this is the way of a civilized community'.[4]

The 'containment order' is well known in the popular imagination. It is celebrated in our historical accounts of the early years after World War II, when intrepid American officials struggled to make sense of Soviet military power and geopolitical intentions. In these early years, a few 'wise men' fashioned a coherent and reasoned response to the global challenge of Soviet communism.[5] The doctrine of containment that emerged was the core concept that gave clarity and purpose to several decades of American foreign policy.[6] In the decades that followed, sprawling bureaucratic and military organizations were built on the containment orientation. The bipolar division of the world, nuclear weapons of growing size and sophistication, the ongoing clash of two expansive ideologies—all these circumstances gave life to and reinforced the centrality of the 'containment order'.

By comparison, the ideas and policies of the liberal democratic order were more diffuse and wide-ranging. It was less obvious that the liberal democratic agenda was a 'grand strategy' designed to advance American security interests. As a result, during the cold war it was inevitable that this agenda would be seen as secondary—a preoccupation of economists and American business. The policies and institutions that supported free trade and economic openness among the advanced industrial societies were quintessentially the stuff of 'low politics'. But this is an historical misconception. The liberal democratic agenda was built on a robust and sophisticated set of ideas about American security interests, the causes of war and depression, and the proper and desirable foundations of post-war political order. Indeed, although the 'containment order' overshadowed it, the ideas behind post-war liberal democratic order were more deeply rooted in the American experience and a thorough-going understanding of history, economics, and the sources of political order.

The most basic conviction behind the post-war liberal agenda was that the closed autarkic regions that had contributed to world depression and split the world into competing blocs before the war must be broken up and replaced by an open and non-discriminatory world economic system. Peace and security were impossible in a world of closed and exclusive economic regions. The challengers to liberal multilateralism occupied almost every corner of the advanced industrial world. Germany and Japan, of course, were the most overt and hostile challengers. Each had pursued a dangerous pathway into the modern industrial age that combined authoritarian capitalism with military dictatorship and coercive regional autarky. But the British Commonwealth and its imperial preference system was also a challenge to liberal multilateral order.[7] The hastily drafted Atlantic Charter was an American effort to insure that Britain signed on to its liberal democratic war aims.[8] The joint statement of principles affirmed free trade, equal access for countries to the raw materials of the world, and international collaboration in the economic field so as to advance labour standards, employment security, and social welfare. Roosevelt and Churchill were intent on telling the world that they had learned the lessons of the inter-war years—and those lessons were fundamentally about the proper organization of the Western world economy. It was not just American's enemies, but also its friends, that had to be reformed and integrated.

It was in this context that the post-1945 settlement within the advanced industrial world can be seen. It was a scattering of institutions and arrangements, reflecting the lessons of the 1930s and the new imperatives that emerged from a collapsed war-ravaged world and a newly powerful America. The cold war did overpower the thinking of American officials sooner or later, but the principles and practices of Western order came earlier and survived longer. They were principles and practices that emerged as officials grappled with real post-war problems—the liberal post-war agenda emerged as officials sought to stabilize, manage, integrate, organize, regulate, reciprocate, control, and achieve agreement. The specific ideas and operational visions can be identified more precisely and linked to the post-war transformation.

## AMERICAN LIBERAL VISIONS AND STRATEGIES

America's liberal grand strategy is an amalgam of related but distinct claims about the sources of political order—and each has been pushed into the post-war foreign policy process by different groups and parts of the foreign policy establishment. Post-war presidents have stressed different aspects of this agenda, even though the various strategies complement and reinforce each other. Five strategies can be identified, each with its own theory and claims about international relations and each with its own distinctive impact on American foreign policy. In each instance these are liberal ideas that emerge from the American experience and its conceptions of the sources of desirable political order.

### Democracy and Peace

Ideas about democratic peace, traced to Kant and developed recently by many analysts, hold that liberal constitutional democracies—or what Kant called 'republics'—tend to have peaceful relations with one another, because of both their internal structures and shared norms.[9] Some argue that the structures of democratic government limit and constrain the types of conflicts over which democratic leaders can mobilize society. Others stress the norms of peaceful resolution of conflict and the ways in which reciprocal democratic legitimacy places limits on the use of violence, while others emphasize the effect of democratic institutions on information and signaling in strategic interaction. Behind these institutional dynamics, others focus on the way in which democracies are built on shared social purposes and an underlying congruence of interests that limit the rise of conflicts worthy of war.[10]

American officials at various junctures have acted on this basic liberal view. Wilson, of course, placed the role of democracy at the centre of his optimism about the durability of a post-war peace. It was also his conception of the sources of war that led to his distinction between the German people and the German government: the former the legitimate source of authority and interest and the latter a dangerous militarist autocracy. The United States did not have a quarrel with the German people, but with their military dictators who had brought war to Europe. 'A steadfast concert of peace can never be maintained except by a partnership of democratic nations. No autocratic government could be trusted to keep faith within it or observe its convenants.'[11]

Wilson's claim was just the most emphatic version of a long tradition in American diplomacy arguing that the United States would be able to trust and get along better with democracies than non-democracies. The American decision to use its post-war occupation of Japan and Germany to attempt ambitious and unprecedented reforms of their states and societies was driven in large part by this belief in the security implications that would flow if Germany and Japan developed more democratic polities.[12] This impulse, of course, was not absolute, and cold war imperatives moderated the extent of actual democratic reform, particularly in Japan. But the argument that the world wars were caused fundamentally by the rise of illiberal, autocratic states and that American post-war security was dependent on the successful transition of these states to democracy was widespread and at the heart of American foreign policy. It was echoed recently by an American official who summarized the view:

> Our answer to the sceptics, the critics, and the self-styled realists is straightforward: look at history, and look at the world around us. Democracy contributes to safety and prosperity, both in national life and in international life—it's that simple. The ability of a people to hold their leaders accountable at the ballot box is good not just for a citizenry so enfranchised—it is also good for that country's neighbours, and therefore for the community of states.[13]

Beyond the democratic peace thesis, other arguments abound that link democracy and the rule of law to international agreement and the stable functioning of international institutions. One argument is that democracies are able to develop relations based on the rule of law rather than political expediency, and this facilitates stable and mutually beneficial dealings.[14] Another argument is that democracies are better able to cooperate in alliance organizations and establish binding institutional relations. The open and permeable character of democracies allows potential institutional partners to overcome uncertainties about domination or abandonment. This is true for three reasons. Democracies are more transparent than non-democracies, and this allows states to observe the domestic system of the other states, and therefore to have more confidence in promises and commitments. Democracies are also more open and accessible to the direct representations of other states, allowing potential partners to not just make agreements, but also to create a political process that allows them to actually influence policy in the other democracies. Finally, the multiple power centres of democracies make abrupt and untoward state actions more difficult—sharp change in policy requires more actors and institutions to sign up to it than in non-democracies.[15]

Overall, the liberal claim is that democracies are more capable of developing peaceful, continuous, rule-based, institutionalized, and legitimate relations among each other than is possible with or between non-democracies. This thesis was put forward by former National Security Council Director Anthony Lake in 1995 in explaining American foreign policy after World War II:

> We led the struggle for democracy because the larger the pool of democracies, the greater our own security and prosperity. Democracies, we know, are less likely to make war on us or on other nations. They tend not to abuse the rights of their people. They make for more reliable trading partners. And each new democracy is a potential ally in the struggle against the challenges of our time—containing ethnic and religious conflict; reducing the nuclear threat; combating terrorism and organized crime; overcoming environmental degradation.[16]

## Free Trade, Economic Openness, and Democracy

Another liberal argument that found its way into American post-war policy stresses the importance of trade and economic openness in creating and reinforcing democracy. The claim is that open markets have a salutary impact on the political character of the regimes of other countries, dissolving autocratic and authoritarian structures and encouraging more pluralistic and accountable regimes. Because trade and economic openness have liberalizing political impacts, international order that is organized around free markets promotes and reinforces the types of states that are most inclined to pursue free markets. It is a self-reinforcing order.

Several different lines of argument are advanced. The most general argument is that trade has a positive impact on economic growth and this in turn encourages democratic institutions, and this in turn creates more stable and peaceful international relations. The logic is straightforward: FREE TRADE→PROSPERITY→DEMOCRACY→PEACE. The two claims that are introduced in this area are that trade promotes economic growth and that economic growth encourages democracy. The first of these arguments is an almost undisputed truth, at least among economists and theorists of economic growth. Economists understand why trade stimulates growth faster than with closed economies—factors of production are employed more efficiently, allowing the development and spread of technology and stimulating productivity gains. Opponents of free trade rarely dispute the growth effects of trade, but rather focus on its potentially adverse distributive, social, or national security implications.[17]

The argument that economic growth encourages democracies is more complicated and debated. But as two scholars recently summarize one version of the argument, 'it is only under conditions of prosperity and capitalism that elites can accept defeat peacefully at the polls, secure in the knowledge that they will have fair opportunities to regain political power, and opportunities for economic benefit when they are out of power'.[18] Moreover, there is strong empirical evidence to support the claim. Not all democracies are high-income and prosperous, but there is a strong correlation.[19]

The classic statement of the theory was advanced by Lipset in the 1950s, who attempted to explain why economic development had a positive effect on the likelihood of a country establishing and maintaining democracy. Two intervening factors were most important. First, economic development tends to produce increases in education, which in turn promotes a political culture and political attitudes that are conducive to democracy; and second, economic development tends to produce a social structure dominated by a rising middle class, which moderates class struggle and the appeal of anti-democratic parties and ideologies and increases the size of the population that supports democratic parties.[20] In this view, a rising middle class is the key to the rise and maintenance of democratic institutions, and this class increases in size and importance with economic growth and capitalist development.[21]

Subsequent debate on this argument has stressed complicating factors, particularly the role of income inequality, which some argue tends to counteract the positive influence of economic development on democracy. There also seem to be non-linear and threshold effects on the relationship: economic growth is most important at the lower and medium levels of development, and after some threshold the level of democracy tends to hold regardless of further economic development.[22]

This claim about the positive impact of trade on economic development and economic development on politics has had a long and well-established hold on official American foreign policy thinking. The American embrace of free trade and open markets gained its most secure foothold at the turn of the twentieth century with the articulation of the Open Door policy, driven most forcefully by American efforts to gain market access in Asia. Later, during the progressive era, arguments in favour of free trade moved beyond the simple struggle for markets or the restatement of Ricardo's classic claims. It was Wilson who claimed that free trade would have the added benefit of checking or undercutting domestic monopoly. Protectionism encouraged collusion and reinforced the dominance of big business, and this in turn distorted democratic politics.[23] This progressive era view was seen to hold outside the United States as well—free trade was a necessary condition for the spread of democracy abroad.

This liberal view makes an intensely materialist assumption: that economics shapes politics. Free trade and open markets strengthen society and create zones of autonomy that limit the reach of the state, empowering individuals and altering what they want and expect out of politics. This view lies at the core of American foreign policy efforts at 'engagement'—whether it is directed at South Africa, the Soviet Union, or China. Often unappreciated by the antidemocratic elites whose countries are engaged, trade and market openings are the sharp end of a liberalizing wedge that ultimately promotes economic development and democracy.

## Free Trade, Economic Interdependence, and Peace

A related argument is that free trade and open markets promote not just economic advancement and democracy, but also encourage more intense and interdependent relations between states, which in turn foster mutual dependence and new vested interests that favour greater restraint and stability in international relations. This claim takes several forms. Some argue that trade makes states more prosperous, and therefore they are less likely to have grievances that lead to war. 'Prosperous neighbours are the best neighbours', remarked Roosevelt era Treasury official Harry Dexter White.[24] Others argue that trade breaks down the sources of antagonism and war.

These claims were advanced by American officials involved in the creation of an open trading system after World War II. The most forceful advocates of this position came from the Department of State and its Secretary, Cordell Hull. Throughout the Roosevelt presidency, Hull and other State Department officials consistently held the conviction that an open international trading system was central to American economic and security interests and was also fundamental to the maintenance of peace. Hull believed that bilateralism and the economic blocs of the 1930s, practised by Germany and Japan but also Britain, were the root cause of the instability of the period and the onset of war.[25] Charged with responsibility for commercial policy, the State Department championed tariff reduction agreements, most prominently in the 1934 Reciprocal Trade Agreement Act and the 1938 US–British trade agreement. Trade officials at the State Department saw liberal trade as a core American interest that reached black to the Open Door policy of the 1890s.[26] In the early years of World War II, this liberal economic vision dominated initial American thinking about the future world order and became the initial opening position as the United States engaged Britain over the post-war settlement. Emerging from the war with the largest and most competitive economic order would serve American interests. An open system was also seen as an essential element of a stable world political order; it would discourage ruinous economic competition and protectionism that was a source of depression and war. But just as importantly, this vision of openness—a sort of 'economic one-worldism'—would lead to an international order in which American 'hands on' management would be modest. The system, would, in effect, govern itself.[27]

The connection between trade and the source of order is made at several levels. There is an expectation that trade will create new forms of mutual dependence through the progressive evolution of specialization and functional differentiation of national economies. This process in turn creates a blurring of national economic borders and interests, which in turn debilitates the capacity of the state to determine and act upon narrow nationalist economic interests. The state's interests are broadened to include a stake in the stability and functioning of the larger international order. At the level of the state, the expansion of trade and investment creates new vested interests in economic openness and the political organization of international politics that is congenial with openness. For example, there is evidence that when firms invest overseas they not only develop an interest in international conditions that foster and protect those operations, but they also become a new voice back home in advocating the opening of the domestic market.[28]

More generally, when American foreign policy has sought to bring countries into the open trade order, they have had expectations that these involvements would have 'socializing' effects on these countries that would be conducive to the maintenance of order. Nowhere was this more explicit than in the Clinton administration's approach toward China. The administration argued that a 'China as a power that is stable, open, and non-aggressive, that embraces free markets, political pluralism, and the rule of law, that works with us to build a secure international order—that kind of China, rather than a China turned inward and confrontational, is deeply in the interests of the American people'. To move China in this direction, the administration embraced the dynamic vision of liberalism: that integration into the international economic order would promote reform at home, encourage the development of the rule of law, and socialize China into the prevailing order. This liberal vision was put directly by Clinton:

> China's economic growth has made it more and more dependent on the outside world for investment, markets, and energy. Last year it was the second recipient of foreign direct investment in the world. These linkages bring with them powerful forces for change. Computers and the Internet, fax machines and photo-copiers, modems and satellites all increase the exposure to people, ideas, and the world beyond China's borders. The effect is only just beginning to be felt.[29]

This is essentially the same argument made by Wilson, Roosevelt, Truman, and other American presidents. It now takes a more sweeping and vivid form because of recent developments: the dramatic collapse of the Soviet Union, the rapid rise of new technologies, and the continuing work of the relentless integrating forces of trade and investment. Free markets tend to force open societies, liberalize politics, and integrate and socialize countries.

## Institutions and the Containment of Conflict

Another enduring and strongly held liberal view that is deeply entrenched in American foreign policy thinking is that institutions matter. The claim is that when states create and operate within international institutions, the scope and severity of their conflicts are reduced. The reasons involve a series of arguments about the relationship between states, interests, and the logic of dispute resolution. But fundamentally, when states agree to operate within international institutions (within a particular realm), they are in effect creating a political process that shapes, constrains, and channels state actions in desirable ways. Interstate institutions establish a political process that helps to contain conflict by creating mechanisms that can move the dispute toward some sort of mutually acceptable resolution.

At the heart of the American political tradition is the view that institutions can serve to overcome and integrate diverse and competing interests—state, section, ethnicity, class, and religion. American constitutionalism is infused with the belief that state power can be restrained and rights and protections of individuals insured through the many institutional devices and procedures that they specify. Separation of power, checks and balances, and other devices of the balanced constitution were advanced as ways to ensure limits on power. Theories of institutional balance, separation, oversight, and judicial review have an intellectual lineage that traces from Aristotle to Locke and Montesquieu. By specializing functional roles and dispersing political authority, the concentration of power and the possibility of tyranny is prevented.[30] In this way, institutional design can help define and ensure the durability of desirable political order.

It is this deeply held view that has made American officials so inclined to build and operate international institutions. Indeed, the historical record is striking. When the United States has had an opportunity to organize international relations—such as after the two world wars—it has been unusually eager to establish regimes and multilateral institutions.[31] After 1919 it was the League of Nations, and after 1945 it was a flood of institutions with different purposes, functions, and scope. The American architects of postwar order are justly famous for their efforts to institutionalize just about everything: security, monetary relations, trade, development assistance, peacekeeping, and dispute resolution.[32] When one compares and contrasts *Pax Britannica and Pax Americana*, one of the first things to note is that the American era was much more institutionalized.[33]

Of course, American interest in institutionalizing international relations is driven by a variety of factors. It mattered that the United States was in an unprecedented power position after the war. The sheer asymmetry of power relations between the United States and its potential post-war partners made institutions an attractive way to reassure Europe and Japan that it would neither dominate nor abandon them, and a functioning political process made possible by the wide array of institutions was useful in legitimizing America's post-war hegemony.[34] Likewise, the industrial great powers at mid-twentieth century passage were much more complex and interdependent than in the early nineteenth century—so there was just a lot more stuff to organize than before. The political calculus and social purpose of states had evolved, and this was reflected in the functional imperatives of the 1940s.[35]

But there are specific expectations that Americans had about how states operating within international institutions would dampen conflict and mitigate anarchy. Two types of general institutional 'effects' are most important: institutions constrain and socialize. Institutions constrain in that the rules and roles that institutions set out for states serve to create incentives and costs that channel states in particular directions. Violating the rules may create costs by provoking responses by others—such as sanctions and retaliation—or constraints may be manifest by creating 'sunk costs' that make it relatively more expensive to start from scratch and create a new institution. International institutions are not unlike domestic institutions; they create a 'political landscape' that provides advantages, constraints, obstacles, and opportunities for actors who inhabit them.[36] Properly engineered, they can bias state actions toward the desired rules and roles.

International institutions can also socialize states, which happens when they influence the way in which states think about their interests. In becoming socialized to accept certain ways of thinking, as Martha Finnemore argues, states 'internalize the roles and rules as scripts to which they conform, not out of conscious choice, but because they understand these behaviours to be appropriate'.[37] The underlying view is that the interests and preferences of states are not completely fixed, and that institutions could play a role in cultivating certain types of foreign and domestic policy orientations. States might initially agree to operate in an international institution because of the manipulation of incentives by the hegemon, but after a while through a complex process of socialization the rules and values of the institution would be embraced by the state as right and proper.[38]

American officials hoped that the post-war institutions would 'rub off' on the other states that agreed to join. In creating the United Nations, officials worked under the assumption that the establishment of mechanisms for dispute resolution would channel conflicts in non-violent directions.[39] In creating the GATT, officials also anticipated the economic conflicts that could be trapped and diffused in framework of rules, standards, and dispute resolution procedures. In establishing the Marshall Plan for aiding post-war Europe, American officials insisted that the Europeans create a joint institution that would force them to work together in allocating funds, and the hope was that a habit of cooperation would emerge.[40]

Both these ways in which institutions matter echo the American political tradition. The notion of institutional constraints is implicit in republican political theory, where the constitution, separation of powers, and the institutional layers and limits on authority create power distribution and checking mechanisms that inhibit the aggrandizement of power. The view that institutions can socialize is also an extension of the classical liberal view that the political system is not simply a mechanical process where preferences are aggregated, but it is a system where persuasion and justification matter as well.

## Community and Identity

A final liberal claim is that a common identity among states facilitates the establishment of a peaceful and durable order. Values and a sense of community matter as sources of order—not just power and interests. Again, there are several layers of argument. One is that states with similar political values and social purposes will be more likely to understand each other, which facilitates cooperation. Another is that if the common values are liberal and democratic, substantive norms exist that specify expectations about how conflicts are to be resolved.

American foreign policy thinkers have been attracted to this liberal view, but the specific way they have sought to identify and develop common identity and community has varied. Wilson talked about a 'community of power' and associated common identity with democracy. This followed directly from his view that the world stood on the brink of a great democratic revolution, and so to build order around a universal democratic community was obvious. The problem was that the world did not culminate in democratic revolution after 1919; Russia, of course, moved in a different direction, but continental Europe also failed to develop democratic societies in the way Wilson expected. As a result, the universalism of the League of Nations was built on unfulfilled expectations.

This failure was a central lesson of the generation of American leaders who followed Wilson. The lesson was not that democracy was unrelated to American security and a durable post-war order, but that universalism was a bridge too far. Democracy was not as easily spread or deeply rooted as Wilson had assumed. Building order around like-mind democracies was still a desired goal of Roosevelt and Truman, but the realm of world politics that would be within this order and the way the order would be institutionalized differed after World War II.[41] The democratic community would exist primarily within the Atlantic world, and its institutional foundations would be more complex and layered.

This view was articulated by a variety of officials and activists in the 1940s who were primarily concerned with creating political order among the democracies of the North Atlantic region. The vision was of a community or union between the United States, Britain, and the wider Atlantic world. Ideas of an Atlantic union can be traced to the turn of the twentieth century and a few British and American statesmen and thinkers, such as John Hay, British Ambassador to Washington Lord Bryce, American Ambassador to London Walter Hines Page, Admiral Alfred T. Mahan, and Henry Adams. These writers and political figures all grasped the unusual character and significance of Anglo-American comity, and they embraced a vision of closer transatlantic ties.[42] These ideas were articulated and rearticulated over the following decades. During World War II, Walter Lippmann gave voice to this view, that the 'Atlantic Ocean is not the frontier between Europe and the Americas. It is the inland sea of a community of nations allied with one another by geography, history, and vital necessity'.[43]

Various experiences and interests fed into the Atlantic idea. One was strategic and articulated during and after the two world wars. Suspicious of Woodrow Wilson's League of Nations proposal, French Premier Georges Clemenceau proposed in 1919 an alliance between France, Britain, and the United States—an alliance only among what he called 'constitutional countries'.[44] The failure of the League of Nations reaffirmed in the minds of many Americans and Europeans the virtues of a less universal security community that encompassed the North Atlantic area.

Others focused on the protection of the shared democratic values that united the Atlantic world. These ideas were most famously expressed in Clarence Streit's 1939 book, *Union Now: The Proposal for Inter-democracy Federal Union*.[45] Concerned with the rise of fascism and militarism and the fragility of the Western democracies in the wake of a failed League of Nations, Streit proposed a federal union of the North Atlantic democracies.[46] In the years that followed, a fledgling Atlantic Union movement came to life. An Atlantic Union Committee was organized after the war and prominent Americans called for the creation of various sorts of Atlantic organizations and structures. American and European officials were willing to endorse principles of Atlantic community and unity—most explicitly in the 1941 Atlantic Charter—but they were less interested in supranational organization.

In more recent years, American officials have returned to this theme. In the aftermath of the cold war, the Bush administration was quick to remind its allies that they were more than a defensive alliance against communism— that the alliance was equally a positive embodiment of the values and community that they shared. In major speeches both President Bush and Secretary of State Baker talked about the Euro-Atlantic Community and the 'zone of democratic peace'. It had been relatively easy during the cold war to talk about the unity of the 'free world'. After 1991, this became more difficult and the older notions of democratic community were rediscovered. The Clinton administration also came to evoke similar sentiments about democratic community in making the case for NATO expansion.

There is an inherent ambiguity in specifying the precise character of democratic community, and this is reflected in foreign policy thinking. Some draw the borders of shared community rather narrowly. Samuel Huntington's famous argument about civilization, for example has a rather limited notion of the West and shared community. It exists primarily in the Atlantic world. Others have more expansive notions. James Huntley has developed an elaborate set of criteria for determining the 'like-mindedness' of states, which in turn explains why 'some countries and their governments are more ready than others to engage in sophisticated forms of international cooperation'. These include a stable, experienced, and advanced democratic regime, advanced and knowledge-based modern economies and societies, and a substantial body of diplomats, civil servants, political leaders, and other elites who are oriented toward international cooperation.[47] In this view, democratic community is not absolute, but runs along a gradient, concentrated in a core of states and moving outward to less similar states.

## CONCLUSION

For those who thought cooperation among the advanced industrial democracies was primarily driven by cold war threats, the last few years must appear puzzling. Relations among the major Western countries have not deteriorated or broken down. What the cold war focus misses is an appreciation of the other and less heralded post-war American project: building a liberal democratic order within the West. The ideas, practices, lessons, and designs that American officials brought to bear on the problem of rebuilding order among the Western states was, taken together, a distinctively American grand strategy.

The robustness of the ideas behind Western liberal democratic order was partly a result of the manifold lessons and experiences that stimulated these ideas. It is sometimes argued that what differentiated the successful settlement after 1945 from the 'unsuccessful' settlement after 1919 is that it was based on more 'realist' understandings of power and order. Roosevelt, for example, was sensitive to considerations of power, and his notion of the 'Four Policemen' was a self-conscious effort to build a post-war settlement around a great-power collective security organization. But the actual post-war settlement reflected a more mixed set of lessons and calculations. 'Realist' lessons from the League of Nations debacle of the 1920s were combined with 'liberal' lessons from the regional imperialism and mercan-tilist conflict of the 1930s. The United States did show more willingness to use its military victory and occupation policy after 1945 to implement its post-war aims in Germany and Japan, but those aims were manifestly liberal in character.

It is commonly argued today that post-cold war American foreign policy has lost its way. The loss of containment as an organizing concept and grand strategy has left some bewildered. But if the other elements of American post-war grand strategy sketched in this paper are recognized, this perspective is less compelling. The United States has a deeper and more sophisticated set of policies and practices than a narrow focus on American cold was diplomacy would reveal. So to analysts who equate grand strategy with 'containment' and 'managing the balance of power', the liberal strategies of the United States will not be recognized, and these analysts will acknowledge the arrival of a new American grand strategy only when a new threat emerges that helps stimulate and organize balanc-ing policies. But this is an intellectually and historically impoverished view, and it misses huge foreign policy opportunities in the meanwhile.

What is striking, in fact, and perhaps ironic, about American foreign policy after the cold war is how deeply bipartisan liberal internationalism is in foreign policy circles. Reagan and Bush pursued policies that reflected a strong commitment to the expansion of democracy, markets, and the rule of law. The Reagan administration's involvement in El Salvador, the Philippines, Chile, and elsewhere all reflected this orientation. Its shift from the Nixon-Kissinger 'permanent coexistence' approach to the Soviet Union toward a more active pursuit of a human rights and democracy promotion agenda also revealed this orientation. Following in line with a view articu-lated by Wilson, Roosevelt, Truman and others, the Reagan administration articulated the democratic peace argument—that the regime type of other states matters, and if they are democracies they will be less threatening to the United States. Jeanne Kirkpatrick and other Kissinger-type realists were brought into the administration, but their view that democracy promotion was a counterproductive luxury did not dominate.

Today, a foreign policy agenda organized around business international-ism, multilateral economic and security organizations, and democratic community building is embraced by elites in both parties. It is a coalition not unlike the one that formed in the 1940s. Some elites embrace democracy, the rule of law, and human rights as an end in itself; others see its promo-tion as a way to expand and safeguard business and markets; and others see indirect payoffs for national security and alliance management. The Clinton administration's doctrine of 'enlargement' and its policy of engage-ment toward China were mere reflections of this long-standing liberal American orientation.[48] Many of the speeches that Clinton administration officials made on enlargement and engagement could just as easily have been generated by Reagan and Bush speech writers. There were differences of details, but the two major parties did not articulate two radically—or even moderately—different worldviews.

Part of the reason for the stability of this general liberal strategic orientation is that the overall organizational character of the American system encourages it. International business is a coalition partner. Engagement of China, for example, was really the only option, given the huge stakes that American multinationals have in the Chinese and Asian markets. The United States also has a huge domestic constituency for democracy promotion and numerous non-government organizations keep the issue on the agenda. The groups and associations that have sought to build a more formal Atlantic community are also at work articulating notions of wider democratic community. Transnational groups that support the United Nations, the IMF and World Bank, and other major multilateral organizations also feed into the American foreign policy process. In other words, American foreign policy is only part of what generates and sustains the American liberal orientation. Democracies—particularly big and rich ones like the United States—seem to have an inherent sociability. Democracies are biased, structurally speaking, in favour of engagement, enlargement, interdependence, and institutionalization, and they are biased against containment, separation, balance, and exclusion. The United States is doomed to pursue a liberal grand strategy.

## Notes

1. The most sophisticated and systematic survey of American democracy promotion in this century is Tony Smith, *America's Mission: The United States and the Worldwide Struggle for Democracy in the Twentieth Century* (Princeton: Princeton University Press, 1994).
2. This section draws on G. John Ikenberry, 'The Myth of Post-Cold War Chaos', *Foreign Affairs*, 75/3 (1996), pp. 79–91.
3. H. Truman, 'Address to Joint Session of Congress on Aid to Greece and Turkey', 12 March 1946. For historical accounts of this foreign policy turning point, see Dean G. Acheson, *Present at the Creation: My Years at the State Department* (New York: Norton, 1969); Howard Jones, *'A New Kind of War': America's Global Strategy and the Truman Doctrine in Greece* (New York: Oxford University Press, 1989). On whether the Truman Doctrine was a cold war watershed, see John Lewis Gaddis, 'Was the Truman Doctrine a Real Turning Point?', *Foreign Affairs*, 52 (1974), pp. 386–92.
4. H. Truman, 'Address on Foreign Economic Policy' (Baylor University: 6 March 1947).
5. For a popular account of the 'founding fathers' of the containment order, see Walter Issacson and Evan Thomas, *The Wise Men: Six Friends and the World They Made* (New York: Simon and Schuster, 1986).

6. The seminal role of George Kennan as architect of containment policy is stressed in John Lewis Gaddis, *Strategies of Containment* (New York: Oxford University Press, 1984). More recently, Melvyn Leffler has argued that many American officials and experts from across the foreign and defence establishment independently began to embrace containment thinking. See *A Preponderance of Power* (Stanford: Stanford University Press, 1992). On Kennan's changing views of containment, see Kennan, *American Diplomacy, 1925–50* (Chicago: University of Chicago Press, 1951); Memoirs, 1925–50 (Boston: Little, Brown and Co, 1967); and the interview with Kennan in 'X-Plus 25', *Foreign Policy*, 7 (1872), p. 353.

7. For arguments that the great mid-century struggle was between an open capitalist order and various regional autarkic challengers, see Bruce Cumings, 'Trilaterilism and the New World Order', *World Policy Journal*, 8/2 (1991), pp. 195–226; and Charles Maier, 'The Two Postwar Eras and the Conditions for Stability in Twentieth-Century Western Europe', in Charles Maier, *In Search of Stability: Explorations in Historical Political Economy*, part 1 (New York: Cambridge University Press, 1987), pp. 153–84. A similar sweeping historical argument, described as a struggle between 'liberal' and 'collectivist' alternatives, is made in Robert Skidelsky, *The World After Communism* (London: Macmillan, 1995).

8. Churchill insisted that the charter did not mandate the dismantlement of the British empire and its system of trade preferences, and only the last-minute sidestepping of this controversial issue ensured agreement. See Lloyd C. Gardner, 'The Atlantic Charter: Idea and Reality, 1942–1945', in Douglas Brinkley and David R. Facey-Crowther (eds), *The Atlantic Charter* (London: Macmillan, 1994), pp. 45–81.

9. See Michael Doyle, 'Kant, Liberal Legacies, and Foreign Affairs', *Philosophy and Public Affairs*, 12 (1983), pp. 205–35, 32–53; Michael Doyle, 'Liberalism and World Politics', *American Political Science Review*, 80/4 (1986), pp. 1151–69; Bruce Russett, *Grasping the Democratic Peace: Principles for a Post-Cold War World* (Princeton: Princeton University Press, 1993); James Lee Ray, *Democracy and International Conflict: An Evaluation of the Democratic Peace Proposition* (Columbia: University of South Carolina Press, 1995); and William J. Dixon, 'Democracy and the Peaceful Settlement of International Conflict', *American Political Science Review*, 88/1 (1994), pp. 14–32.

10. Many of these arguments are brought together in Michael E. Brown, Sean Lynn-Jones, and Steven Miller (eds), *Debating the Democratic Peace* (Cambridge, MA: MIT Press, 1996).

11. Address to a Joint Session of Congress, 2 April 1917; in Arthur S. Link (ed.), *The Public Papers of Woodrow Wilson*, 41 (Princeton: Princeton University Press, 1983), pp. 519–27.

12. See Smith, *America's Mission*, Ch. 6.

13. 'Democracy and the International Interest', remarks by Deputy Secretary of State Strobe Talbott to the Denver Summit of the Eight Initiative on Democracy and Human Rights, 11 October 1997, p. 2. See also Strobe Talbott, 'Democracy and the National Interest', *Foreign Affairs*, 75/6 (1996), pp. 47–63.

14. See Anne-Marie Burley, 'Toward the Age of Liberal Nations', *Harvard International Law Journal*, 33/2 (1992), pp. 393–405; and 'Law Among Liberal

States: Liberal Internationalism and the Act of State Doctrine', *Columbia Law Review*, 92/8 (1992), pp. 1907–96.

15. These arguments are developed in G. John Ikenberry, 'Liberal Hegemony: The Logic and Future of America's Postwar Order' (unpublished paper, 1997). See also Daniel Deudney and G. John Ikenberry, 'Liberal Competence: The Performance of Democracies in Great Power Balancing' (unpublished paper, 1994). For a good summary of this literature, see Kurt Taylor Gaubatz, 'Democratic States and Commitment in International Relations', *International Organization*, 50/1 (1997), pp. 109–39.

16. Anthony Lake, 'Remarks on the Occasion of the 10th Anniversary of the Center for Democracy' (Washington, DC: 26 September 1995).

17. See Douglas A. Irwin, *Against the Tide: An Intellectual History of Free Trade* (Princeton: Princeton University Press, 1996).

18. Thomas J. Volgy and John E. Schwarz, 'Free Trade, Economic Inequality and the Stability of Democracies in the Democratic Core of Peace', *European Journal of International Relations*, 3/2 (1997), p. 240.

19. See John B. Longregan and Keith Poole, 'Does High Income Promote Democracy?', *World Politics*, 49 (1996), pp. 1–30.

20. Seymour Martin Lipset, 'Some Social Requisites of Democracy: Economic Development and Political Legitimacy', *American Political Science Review*, 53 (1959), pp. 69–105.

21. The literature is summarized by Dietrich Rueschemeyer, Evelyne Huber Stephens, and John D. Stephens, *Capitalist Development and Democracy* (Chicago: University of Chicago Press, 1992). These authors modify the Lispet model, stressing the specific role of the urban working class.

22. See Edward N. Muller, 'Economic Determinants of Democracy', *American Sociological Review*, 60 (1995), pp. 966–82.

23. See Arthur S. Link, *Woodrow Wilson and the Progressive Era, 1910–1917* (New York: Harper and Row, 1954).

24. Alfred E. Eckes, Jr., *A Search for Solvency: Bretton Woods and the International Monetary System, 1944–71* (Austin: University of Texas Press, 1971), p. 52. This was a reflection of the Cobdenite philosophy that trade protection and tariffs were linked to political conflict and, ultimately, war.

25. As Secretary Hull argued, 'unhampered trade dovetailed with peace; high tariffs, trade barriers, and unfair economic competition, with war'. Cordell Hull, *The Memoirs of Cordell Hull*, Vol. 1 (New York: Macmillan, 1948), p. 81.

26. Herbert Feis, the State Department's economic adviser, noted the continuity of the department's position when he argued during the war that 'the extension of the Open Door remains a sound American aim'. See Herbert Feis, 'Economics and Peace', *Foreign Policy Reports*, 30 (April 1944), pp. 14–19. On the State Department's commitment to a post-war open trading system, see Lloyd Gardner, *Economic Aspects of New Deal Diplomacy* (Madison: University of Wisconsin Press, 1964); Richard Gardner, *Sterling-Dollar Diplomacy: The Origins and the Prospects of Our International Economic Order* (New York: McGraw Hill, 1969); and Alfred E. Eckes, Jr., *Opening America's market: U.S. Foreign Policy Since 1776* (Chapel Hill: The University of North Carolina Press, 1995), Ch. 5.

27. This argument is made in G. John Ikenberry, 'Rethinking the Origins of American Hegemony', *Political Science Quarterly*, 104 (1989), pp. 375–400.

28. Helen Milner and David B. Joffie, 'Between Free Trade and Protectionism: Strategic Trade Policy and a Theory of Corporate Trade Demands', *International Organization*, 42/2 1989), pp. 239–72; and Hidetaka Yoshimatsu, 'Economic Interdependence and the Making of Trade Policy: Industrial Demand for an Open Market in Japan', *The Pacific Review*, 11/1 (1998), pp. 28–50.

29. White House Press Release, 'Remarks by the President in Address on China and the National Interest' (24 October 1997).

30. See M. Richter, *The Political Theory of Montesquieu* (Cambridge: Cambridge University Press, 1977).

31. Of course, the United States has also been assiduous is ensuring that there are limits and escape clauses in the binding effects of institutions.

32. On the post-war surge in institution building, see Craig Murphy, *International Organization and Industrial Change* (New York: Oxford University Press, 1994).

33. For comparisons of American and British hegemony, see Robert Gilpin, *U.S. Power and the Multinational Corporation: The Political Economy of Foreign Direct Investment* (New York: Basic Books, 1975); and David Lake, 'British and American Hegemony Compared: Lessons for the Current Era of Decline', in Michael Fry (ed.), *History, the White House, and the Kremlin: Statesmen As Historians* (New York: Columbia University Press, 1991), pp. 106–22.

34. These arguments are made in G. John Ikenberry, *After Victory: Institutions, Strategic Restraint, and the Rebuilding of Order After Major Wars* (Princeton: Princeton University Press, 2000).

35. See John G. Ruggie, *Winning the Peace: America and World Order in the New Era* (New York: Columbia University Press, 1996).

36. For an overview of this perspective on institutions, see James G. March and Johan Olsen, 'The New Institutionalism: Organizational Factors in Political Life', *American Political Science Review*, 78 (1984), pp. 734–49.

37. Martha Finnemore, *National Interests in International Society* (Ithaca: Cornell University Press, 1996), p. 29.

38. See G. John Ikenberry and Charles Kupchan, 'Socialization and Hegemonic Power', *International Organization*, 43/3 (1990), pp. 283–315.

39. See Ruth B. Russell, *A History of The United Nations Charter: The Role of the United States, 1940–1945* (Washington, DC: The Brookings Institution, 1958).

40. See Ernst H. Van Der Beugel, *From Marshall Plan to Atlantic Partnership* (Amsterdam: Elsevier Publishing Co., 1966).

41. On the lessons drawn by order builders in 1945 from the failures of 1919, see David Fromkin, *In the Time of the Americans: The Generation that Changed America's Role in the World* (New York: Alfred Knopf, 1995).

42. See James Robert Huntley, *Uniting the Democracies: Institutions of the Emerging Atlantic-Pacific System* (New York: New York University Press, 1980), p. 4.

43. Walter Lippmann, *U.S. Foreign Policy: Shield of the Republic* (Boston: Little, Brown, 1943), p. 83.

44. The French proposal was to transform the League of Nations into a North Atlantic treaty organization—a union complete with an international army and a general staff. See Thomas J. Knock, *To End All Wars: Woodrow Wilson*

*and the Quest for a New World Order* (New York: Oxford University Press, 1992), pp. 221–22.

45.  Clarence Streit, *Union Now: The Proposal for Inter-democracy Federal Union* (New York: Harper and Brothers, 1939).

46.  It would be a 'union of these few peoples in a great federal republic built on and for the thing they share most, their common democratic principle of government for the sake of individual freedom'. Streit, *Union Now*, p. 4.

47.  James Robert Huntley, *Pax Democratica: A Strategy for the Twenty-first Century* (London: Macmillan, 1998), Appendix A.

48.  See Douglas Brinkley, 'Democratic Enlargement: The Clinton Doctrine', *Foreign Policy*, 106 (1997), pp. 111–27.

# 4  The New Great Debate—Washington Versus Wilson

## JOSHUA MURAVCHIK

The current leadership of the United States has grounded its foreign policy thinking and actions in a view that is known as "neoconservatism." Neoconservatism shares some affinities with liberalism—as Joshua Muravchik argues, it has its roots in Wilsonian practices that sought to "make the world safe for democracy,"— but it is fundamentally different from liberalism and is considered an entirely different perspective on U.S. foreign policy. Neoconservatism joins the idea of promoting democracy and American political values with American power, often military power, in order to proactively shape the global environment and at best, to establish democracies in foreign lands where they do not exist. Neoconservatism tends to consider the strength of international law and institutions to be quite limited, and thus looks to American might and action to produce favorable outcomes in foreign relations. An example of this thinking put into practice is the war in Iraq.

Muravchik juxtaposes the neoconservative view (which he refers to as Wilsonian, even though it does not embody the entirety of Wilsonian views on international law, institutions, and morality) to the realist and isolationist views (which he combines and calls "Washingtonian"), arguing that the United States has a choice to make about how to engage the world. The issue that ultimately separates these two perspectives, according to Muravchik, involves when the United States must take strong action to maintain or restore peace and security. Neoconservatives set a much lower threshold for American intervention abroad, preferring to act at an early point along a chain of contingency in order to keep small problems from turning into big problems.

The war in Iraq has demonstrated some of the problems that can accompany a neoconservative perspective. Democracy may not always be easily imposed by outside forces, and an assertive policy of democracy promotion can prompt a strong reaction by both foes and longstanding friends. As Woodrow Wilson learned upon intervening in Mexico, the Dominican Republic and Haiti, the United States has not often been able to achieve the goal, as Wilson put it, of "teaching [others] to elect good men."

---

Although those who today are summoning America home from its international engagements may not be much different from, or much wiser than, those who did the same seventy years ago, I have no wish to engage them in semantic argument. Rather than call them isolationists, we might call them Washingtonians (in a reference to our first president's views on foreign entanglements), surely not a prejudicial label. And we might say that the main debate over U.S. foreign policy is between the Washingtonian and the Wilsonian outlooks.

## WASHINGTONIANS AND WILSONIANS

Throughout the cold war, or at least since Vietnam, the main divide on foreign policy pitted "doves" against "hawks." Both sides understood that the question was how to protect ourselves against the power of Soviet communism or the danger of war with the Soviet Union. Hawks believed that the answer lay in strength and toughness, while doves believed it lay in understanding and accommodation. Although labels necessarily simplify and group people together and override nuances, most national politicians and commentators fell in one camp or the other, and on this basis it was fairly easy to foretell accurately what position each would take as the theater shifted from East Asia to Central America to southern Africa to the Middle East and so on.

The great debate between hawks and doves ended with the cold war. In its place has emerged the debate between Washingtonians and Wilsonians. These embody the two contrasting answers to what—in the absence of a more specific threat like the Soviet—the generic basic question for foreign policy is, How do we keep ourselves secure?

By "Washingtonian," I mean to invoke the famous Farewell Address. To President Washington, the world outside—the operative part of which was

Europe—was replete with conflict. The key to our safety was to avoid getting drawn into other people's quarrels. "Why . . . entangle our peace and prosperity in the toils of European ambition, Rivalship, Interest, Humour or Caprice?" he asked. To gird ourselves against such entanglement we needed to guard against sentimentality, that is, against "excessive partiality for one foreign nation and excessive dislike of another." In sum, look out for ourselves and avoid trouble.

The Wilsonian approach shares the premise that the world is full of conflicts. But President Wilson learned from the bitter experience of World War I how difficult it is to keep America aloof from foreign broils. His solution was that America try to shape and guard the peace, keeping itself safe by making the world a safer place. This approach sets a much lower threshold for American involvement abroad, on the theory that early intervention on a small scale may forestall a much heavier commitment later on. The Washingtonian's characteristic question about any foreign quarrel is, Does it threaten us? The Wilsonian's is, Might it come to threaten us?

Wilson is probably the most controversial major figure in the history of American diplomacy, and by using his name I risk inviting a host of tangential arguments. But the specific provisions of the Versailles Treaty are no more intrinsic to the Wilsonian outlook than any particular interpretation of the 1778 treaty with France is to the Washingtonian. Political scientist Arnold Wolfers divided the goals of states between "possession goals" and "milieu goals." The former designates tangible goods or benefits; the latter, "the shape of the environment in which the nation operates."[1] The essence of the difference between Washingtonians and Wilsonians is how much attention to give to milieu goals.

To put it another way, the question is how far from home America should begin trying to defend itself. I refer not primarily to geographic distance but to distance along the chain of contingency. Extreme Washingtonians—true isolationists—believe that American defense begins when an enemy army approaches our shores. Less extreme Washingtonians—otherwise known as "realists"—would defend key allies or pieces of geography that in hostile hands might soon translate into the approach of an enemy army. But they insist on a rather close connection. Wilsonians are willing to travel much further along the chain of contingency to confront problems whose effect on us might be indirect or several steps removed. They are more concerned about the internal evolution of states, believing that it often affects external behavior. They put more stock in the psychological effects that events in one situation may have on another, therefore caring more about the force of example and the strength of international laws and norms. They also tend to attach more importance to the power of "hearts and minds" relative to that of guns and dollars.

## INTEREST AND MORALITY

The difference between the two camps has less to do with the conflict between interest and morality than is often supposed. On some issues Wilsonians might give priority to a moral principle or humanitarian concern, while Washingtonians would put first an American material interest. On the question of trade with China, for example, Washingtonians might emphasize America's commercial stakes, while Wilsonians emphasize human rights. But where American security is at issue, no thoughtful Wilsonian would put other values first. On the contrary, Wilsonians argue that self-defense is completely harmonious with sound morality. They tend toward Jefferson's view that "with nations as with individuals our interests soundly calculated will ever be inseparable from our moral duties."[2]

Will Wilsonians, however, more often hazard military action where no U.S. interests are at stake? Sometimes yes. They will be more open than Washingtonians to humanitarian interventions, but the occasions for such are rare and extreme. Indeed, the cases most often discussed as ripe for humanitarian intervention are hypothetical—against Pol Pot's mass slaughter or Hitler's genocide. One contemporary tragedy where a strong case could have been made for humanitarian intervention was Rwanda, but oddly no one made the case since America had only recently been burned in Somalia, where a low-risk humanitarian mission, launched by a very non-Wilsonian president, had been spoiled by "mission creep."

On the other side, Washingtonians, in the main, would deny that their approach ignores moral reasoning. David C. Hendrickson, for example, summoning Americans to the foreign policy of the Founding Fathers, calls it a "tradition of thought and web of principle."[3]

In this century, America has tried both the Wilsonian and the Washingtonian approaches with instructive effect. After World War I, Wilson unveiled his visionary scheme, but in the end he failed to bring his countrymen behind him. The nation turned instead down the Washingtonian path. We refused to join the League of Nations, we erected trade barriers, and we focused our attention on domestic affairs. The themes behind that decision were very like what we hear today. "It is not that which is happening in Russia ... that is bringing doubt and worry to our own people," said the famous Progressive, Senator William Borah. "It is the conditions here in our own land. ... Capitalism must turn its eyes inwardly ... and solve its own internal problems."[4] The other leading opponent of ratifying the Versailles Treaty, Senator Henry Cabot Lodge, said, "The United States can best serve the world, first, by preserving its own strength and the fabric of its civilization."[5]

Then, the Washingtonian path led directly to the worst catastrophe in history: World War II. Of course, there were many causes of the war, starting with Hitler's evil genius and including much folly—on the part of

German politicians, British statesmen, French strategists, and the Soviet dictator. Still, had America shouldered the burdens of international engagement and enforced the terms of the Versailles Treaty, the war might never have happened.

After World War II, the pull of Washingtonianism made itself felt again. Even as Stalin spread his empire over Eastern Europe, thereby launching the cold war, America demobilized at breakneck speed, reducing its forces from 12 million to 1 million within a year. But by 1947 Americans had wakened to the Soviet threat, and we came roaring back. We embarked on the most Wilsonian of policies. Never has a country undertaken such an internationalist policy, with the possible exception of the great empire builders, and even they may not compare. We established scores of military bases around the world. We forged a dense web of entangling alliances. We remade Germany and Japan if not quite in our image then according to our lights. We carried out the Marshall Plan, on which we spent, together with other foreign aid, some 2 percent of our gross national product for six years. We fostered the United Nations and the Bretton Woods international economic regime. Above all, we adopted the strategy of containment, audaciously taking the whole globe as our chessboard, determined, as George Kennan put it in his famous "X" article, to resist Soviet expansion through "the adroit and vigilant application of counter-force at a series of constantly shifting geographical and political points, corresponding to the shifts and maneuvers of Soviet policy."[6]

The results of this radically internationalist policy were sublime. We faced the most fearsome foe the world has ever known, and we triumphed without having to fight a general war. Some "realists" may object that the post-World War II policies that issued in victory in the cold war ought not to be credited to Wilsonianism. The Carnegie Endowment explicitly contrasts Wilson's "too idealistically conceived" policies with those "after World War II [when] wise leaders tempered idealism with realism."[7] Wilson's notions about things like collective security and disarmament *were* woolly-headed, and America's postwar policies were more tough-minded, but they were not "realist" policies in the formal sense of that term.[8] They were, in the largest sense, distinctly Wilsonian. At a time when America enjoyed a nuclear monopoly, it might have sought security in military technology and separated its security from that of every other country. Instead, it took the view that its security was invested in almost everyone else's. The goal was to defend America. The strategy was to defend as far along the chain of contingency as we could get.

Moreover, not only was our postwar strategy Wilsonian, but it reached its successful climax under our most Wilsonian president since Wilson—Ronald Reagan. To speak of Reagan in this way may confuse some who, quite rightly, think of Wilson as a premier liberal and Reagan as an arch conservative or who recall Wilson's faith in international organizations and Reagan's apparent low regard for the United Nations. But "liberal" and "conservative" have little to do with it. And Wilson's attachment to international organization was but one part of his legacy—I would say the hollowest. In other respects, Reagan's policies were quintessentially Wilsonian.

One hallmark of Wilson's view was the belief in a nexus of America's security and that of many others. Reagan acted from the premise that American security was bound up with events in places far from home and in countries of little intrinsic weight: Nicaragua, El Salvador, Angola, Afghanistan, and even Grenada. Wilson also put great store by the power of ideas and moral values in international politics, and so did Reagan, even to the point of including ideological thrusts in his speeches that were regarded as great diplomatic blunders, such as calling the Soviet Union an "evil empire." Wilson championed the spread of democracy, seeing it as a key to solving many of the world's problems. Likewise, Reagan launched the National Endowment for Democracy and succored a global trend of democratization. Above all, Reagan, like Wilson, viewed American leadership as the linchpin of world order.

Because historical events and circumstances do not repeat themselves, the success or failure of a policy in the past is no sure guide to the future. Still, the very dramatic contrast between the catastrophe that resulted from the Washingtonian approach after the first world war and the spectacular success of the Wilsonian approach after the second constitute a prima facie case for staying on the Wilsonian path as we search for a post-cold war policy.

What makes that quest so difficult is that no single palpable threat appears on our horizon as Soviet imperialism did in the aftermath of World War II. In that sense, our situation more resembles what we faced after World War I. In 1919, neither fascism nor Nazism had yet been invented, and while Bolshevism had seized Russia, few believed it could endure, much less bid for world supremacy. No one foresaw that we would spend the next seventy years fighting for our lives against these totalitarian movements. That we can identify no single such menace now does not mean that none will emerge: that failure may only show the limits of our imaginations. Moreover, whether such a menace will materialize is not written in the stars or predetermined. Our own engagement or abdication will help decide it.

Hitler and Stalin did not have to happen. They were partly of our making. It is widely appreciated that our isolationism stoked the Nazi juggernaut. Less widely appreciated is that we might have nipped Bolshevism in the bud and thus forestalled the spawning of all this century's totalitarian regimes, for it was the model the others copied. In Lloyd George's war cabinet in 1918, Winston Churchill urged that the Allies impose, either by diplomacy or by force if need be, a free, supervised election on Russia, which he was confident would lead to the defeat of the Bolsheviks.[9] But he was turned down. He recorded his thoughts in a memorandum that makes interesting reading today:

> Most people wish to get free from Russia and to leave her to work out her own salvation or stew in her own juice. . . . Nobody wants to intervene in Russian affairs. Russia is a very large country, a very old country, a very disagreeable country inhabited by immense numbers of ignorant people largely possessed of lethal weapons and in a state of extreme disorder. Also Russia is a long way off. We on the other hand have just finished an important and expensive war against the Germans. . . . We wish now to bring home our soldiers, reduce our taxes and enjoy our victory. . . . We may abandon Russia: but Russia will not abandon us. We shall retire and she will follow.[10]

## FUTURE THREATS

Where today may lurk the embryo of future monsters to torment us or our children, as Russian Bolshevism tormented our parents and ourselves? Perhaps again in Russia, although probably not in the form of resurgent communism but of ultranationalism or fascism or, more likely still, some completely original ideological mutation. These forces emerged in the parliamentary elections of 1993 in part as the result of Western inaction. As Jeffrey Sachs, former economic adviser to President Yeltsin, put it, "For two years, reformers in Moscow struggled for power while Western governments promised them large-scale aid. The reformers could not win without our help, but help never arrived."[11]

Or it may lurk in China, which has won almost as much Western admiration for its rapid creation of capitalism as it won a few decades ago for its rapid creation of communism. Although it may now prefer the economic theories of Friedman to those of Marx, the Communist Party still rules China, and it remains ruthless and ambitious. Nicholas Kristof, former Beijing bureau chief for the *New York Times*, observed: "China . . . has nuclear weapons, border disputes with most of its neighbors, and a rapidly improving army that may—within a decade or so—be able to resolve old quarrels in its own favor. . . . While most countries have been cutting military budgets . . . China has been using its economic boom to finance a far-reaching buildup. It seeks the influence of a great power."[12] With its vast population, if China's economy continues to grow like those of the other Asian "tigers," it could come to rival America's. If this growth is not accompanied by political transformation, then China could become a big threat to world peace. Americans of the Washingtonian school regard the issue of human rights in China as mere sentimentalism that must not be allowed to disrupt our access to "the world's biggest market" or to complicate our diplomacy. But the fate of human rights there—which means the nature of the regime—may well determine our ability to live with China in the next century.

Or our future bane may lurk in Tehran, which has succeeded in spreading the virus of Islamic fanaticism to the Sudan, Algeria, Egypt, Lebanon, and Palestine and even into Turkey. Muslims make up nearly one-fifth of the world's population, and if radical Islam becomes dominant among them, it will cause unimaginable turmoil. Yet Western governments have consistently endeavored to get along with Tehran rather than combat the virus.

Serious threats may also arise in places now hard to foresee or through a synergy of troubles in disparate places. The events that led from 1919 to 1939, from peace to war, were to some extent disconnected, but they fed on each other. Democratic regimes succumbed in Italy, then in Central and Eastern Europe; the Japanese occupied Manchuria; Hitler rose to power; Italy invaded Abyssinia (now, Ethiopia), and the West responded with feckless economic sanctions; Germany rearmed in violation of the Versailles Treaty, and the West responded with appeasement; civil war broke out in Spain. A terrible momentum built. Although today's circumstances look far less ominous, it is not hard to picture dangerous events once again reinforcing each other. North Korea begins to assemble a nuclear arsenal; Islamic fanaticism takes hold of a growing portion of the Muslim world; a breakdown of law enforcement in Russia allows more weapons of mass destruction into international circulation; from one source or the other, "rogue" regimes in Iran, Iraq, and Libya get their hands on nuclear weapons, and so do some of the terrorist groups they sponsor; Serbian nationalism metastasizes in ethnic cleansing bordering on genocide against Bosnian Muslims, giving Muslims everywhere a festering grievance at their treatment in Europe and weakening the norms of international law. Do any of these events seem unlikely? Together they make an explosive mixture.

We can deal with such an explosion when it comes, or we can do our best to prevent it by dealing with its contributory elements as they arise. That is the essential choice we face. Washingtonians would have us keep our heads down until threats loom on our doorsteps or in our front yards. Does this caricature their position? Consider this editorial from the *New York Times*: "For America to remain truly strong now, Congress has to distinguish clear and present dangers from overblown and distant threats."[13] To wait until dangers become clear and present, however, is to wait until very late in the game.

The point was underscored by a comment Colin Powell made while serving as chairman of the Joint Chiefs of Staff: "I've been chairman for 18 months . . . and I've had . . . six opportunities to use the armed forces of the United States and no one had predicted [any] of them 18 months and one day ago."[14] In an unintentional illustration of that point, in 1992 Foreign Relations Committee Chairman Lee Hamilton observed about the Gulf War that "few threats to the peace will be so clear-cut ... as a direct military threat to the world's supply of oil."[15] What Hamilton apparently forgot was that he had opposed the Gulf War. Threats are usually much more clear-cut in retrospect than in prospect.

## PREVENTING WAR, DEFENDING PEACE

The Wilsonian alternative is not to wait for "clear and present dangers" but to make every effort to defend the peace. Sometimes such a defense will entail political exertions to influence developments between or within other nations. Sometimes it will entail military action to deter aggression or to stop its development. Many of the Americans who drive around with bumper stickers urging fellow motorists to "work for peace" have in mind methods, like unilateral disarmament, that would bring results opposite to those intended. But the spirit is right. Peace is hard to come by and hard to keep. And we must labor for it, although better by arming than by disarming.

Washingtonians may respond by saying that preventing wars is hopeless, so our goal must be to stay out of them. But we have a poor record of staying out of wars. We determined to stay out of World War I and trumpeted our neutrality, only to be drawn in. We attempted neutrality of a sort again in World War II, but we were not neutral enough to satisfy Tojo and Hitler, so they made war on us. In 1950, we implied that we would not go to war on behalf of South Korea, but when it was attacked, we concluded we had to defend it. Korea and World War II might both have been averted had America acted robustly early to deter the aggressor. And the same is true, mutatis mutandis, for World War I, had Britain—which was then the leading power—so acted. (Even Vietnam was a war we tried unsuccessfully to stay out of by denying French entreaties for help in 1954, although in that case it is much harder to say what we should have done.)

Americans sometimes overlook the fragility of peace because we have suffered less from war than have most other peoples. And this good fortune can lead us to react too slowly. Columnist Robert J. Samuelson has made the point that we think too contentedly about the outcome of World War II, "the good war," from which we emerged victorious. We sometimes forget the terrible cost of having entered it so late and so unprepared. Had we fought sooner, we might have prevented the Holocaust and Soviet conquest of Eastern Europe. Indeed, Samuelson speculates, following historian William O'Neill, that had Japan not attacked us, America might not have entered the war. As a result, Hitler would likely have made all Europe his own, or he and Stalin would eventually have divided it.[16]

The urgency of working to preserve peace is magnified by the proliferation, or its prospect, of nuclear weapons. Iraq, we discovered, was very close to acquiring a nuclear bomb. North Korea, it seems, already has one or two. Neither is an advanced country. We are thus clearly poised on the brink of a substantial increase in the number of nuclear-armed states. Of course, it would be suicidal for any of these new members of the nuclear club to attack the United States, but that is hardly our only concern. Nuclear weapons in the hands of a Saddam Hussein or the heirs to Kim Il Sung could pose a very real danger to the states near to them and could also be used to deter American intervention against a local aggression. How would the Persian Gulf crisis have unfolded had Saddam already completed his bomb? Would Egypt, Saudi Arabia, and Syria have given us their cooperation in the face of such a peril? Could we ourselves have been deterred by a threat to respond to the bombing of Baghdad by a nuclear strike on an American city?[17]

We can attempt to counteract proliferation through diplomacy, intelligence, controls on the transfer of technology, and economic sanctions and even through preemptive military strikes, as Israel carried out against Iraq in 1981 and we may at some point execute against North Korea. But Edward Luck, president of the United Nations Association, argues convincingly that the prospects for success against proliferation are tied to the general level of peacefulness in the world: "Ultimately... it will be necessary to create conditions that reduce the demand for advanced weapons of mass destruction. That effort will entail more decisive and consistent efforts by the international community to enforce a geographically inclusive concept of collective security. A laissez-faire American approach to regional conflicts would have the opposite effect."[18]

Realists will scoff at the idea of "a geographically inclusive concept of collective security," and perhaps they are right. But their mantra that the future will mostly resemble the past takes on a macabre aspect in light of nuclear proliferation. Should we simply resign ourselves to a conviction that nuclear war will become part of our environment? Even if Luck is naive in his aspiration for collective security, the point stands that local or regional conflicts will spur nuclear proliferation, a fact that gives America a stake in their resolution.

Realists are right that the world is not transformed easily or painlessly, but it does change. Adherents of the Washingtonian approach invoke the wisdom of the Founding Fathers. But with the advent of nuclear weapons, and missiles that can carry them across continents in minutes, how different the world is today from that with which Washington had to cope. At its founding, America was a nation of 2 million, one of the smallest and weakest states on earth. Its main goal was to avoid being crushed by any of the great powers. The policies appropriate to that goal hold little relevance for our current circumstance.

## AMERICAN POWER

America is no longer small, nor is it just one power among others. Its power has largely shaped the world we know, and its decisive weight is the ballast that provides what stability the world of nations enjoys. Imagine for a moment the world of today without the United States or in which the United States withdrew into a policy of "fortress America." We can predict that Japan would rearm, and probably "go nuclear," as would Germany. Russia, where everything else is going wrong, would be irresistibly tempted to compensate by exerting its chief asset, its supreme military power. Moderate Arab regimes would fall before the onslaught of Islamic radicalism, compelling Israel to put its nuclear arsenal on a hair trigger. Competition and mutual distrust between China and Japan and between Russia and Germany would mount. Would World War III be very far from hand?

What makes this scenario unlikely is the presence of America, which gives some measure of security all around. The basis for world peace is that there is one preeminent power, and it is peaceful and nonaggrandizing. This condition is unprecedented. At other moments in history, when a single state has been supreme, it has always been imperial. America's unique role provides a basis for hope that relative peace can be preserved for a long time.

America was victorious in World War I and World War II, after each of which it largely shaped the peace. Then it was victorious once again in the cold war. The spread of democracy, the end of colonialism, the international economic system born at Bretton Woods, and the creation of the United Nations are all large, deliberate policy achievements of America's. In seeking wise approaches to the post-cold war world, we ought to begin by asking not how we can "change our ways" (as the Carnegie Commission recommended) but how we can continue our success. What can we learn from this great record, especially from its crowning glory, our bloodless victory in the cold war?

## THE SUCCESS OF IDEALISM

For one thing, this success constitutes a loud rebuke to the "realist" school of thought. For America's foreign policy tradition is laced with idealism, especially in the twentieth century as the nation has struggled to emerge from isolation. Indeed, the most telling criticism of that tradition is that its idealism has often shaded into naivete. The United States invested great political capital in creating the League of Nations and the United Nations. It has repeatedly sought to solve international problems through legal mechanisms that often lacked means of enforcement, such as the 1928 Kellogg-Briand Pact that "outlawed" war. It has championed principles of self-determination, human rights, democracy, nonrecognition of acquisition of territory by force, one-man-one-vote, and the like that have caused no end of irritation to the diplomats of older, more sophisticated nations and to Washingtonian thinkers like George Kennan, who decried America's "legalistic-moralistic approach to international problems,"[19] and Hans Morgenthau, who believed American foreign policy had gone relentlessly downhill since the late 1700s.[20]

In contrast, France, Britain, other European states, and Japan have been guided much more by "realist" sensibilities. This may be said even for Russia, despite the heavy overlay of ideology during the decades of communism. It was Stalin who spoke that famous realist apothegm, "How many divisions has the Pope?" And yet all of these are no more than secondary powers today, having fallen from times of greater glory, while America, the naive, reigns supreme. Could it be that, as President Lincoln said, "right makes might"?

To some extent surely it does, or at least the conviction of right makes might, because it enhances a state's ability to rally its citizens and to summon the best efforts of its leaders, officials, and soldiers. In a painstaking study of sixteen international crises spanning the period 1895 to 1973 that was designed to test various theories of international relations, Glenn H. Snyder and Paul Diesing happened on an unanticipated finding. "Perceptions of legitimacy are potent in determining bargaining power and outcomes," they wrote. "That is, the party that believes it is in the right and communicates this belief to an opponent who has some doubts about the legitimacy of its own position, nearly always wins."[21] Snyder and Diesing were using the tools of social science to rediscover what Napoleon had tried to explain nearly two centuries earlier, when he said that in warfare, moral factors are three times more important than material ones.

Right may also make might by encouraging more accommodating behavior from other states who know that they have little to fear or distrust from a righteous state. One of the sources of American influence is that many other states trust America to be an honest mediator of their quarrels, and they often welcome the presence of American forces, not fearing that they will act as subjugators. Whatever the cause, the fact that America, the idealistic, has been so successful hardly suggests that it should now follow in the more "realistic" footsteps of the has-been powers.

What we should conclude from the end of the cold war is not that the time has come to lay down our burdens. Rather it is that America can be wondrously effective pursuing a "Wilsonian," or an intensely activist, engaged foreign policy—playing the role of world leader. Unfortunately, upholding the peace is not something that can be done just one time: it is a perpetual task. Fortunately, America has proved that it is very good at this task. The question is, Does it have the will and courage to keep doing it?

## Notes

1. Arnold Wolfers, *Discord and Collaboration* (Baltimore: Johns Hopkins University Press, 1962), p. 73.
2. Thomas Jefferson, *Second Inaugural Address*, March 4, 1805. U.S. Congress, House of Representatives, Committee on House Administration, *Inaugural Addresses of the Presidents of the United States from George Washington to Harry S. Truman*, 82d Cong., 2d sess., House doc. no. 540, 1952, p. 15.
3. David C. Hendrickson, "The Renovation of Foreign Policy," *Foreign Affairs*, vol. 71, no. 2 (Spring 1992), p. 63.
4. William E. Borah, *Bedrock: Views on Basic National Problems* (Washington, D.C.: National Home Library Foundation, 1936), pp. 52–53.
5. Henry Cabot Lodge, "Foreign Relations of the United States, 1921–1924," *Foreign Affairs*, vol. 2, no. 4 (June 15, 1924), p. 538.
6. "X" [George Kennan], "The Sources of Soviet Conduct," *Foreign Affairs*, vol. 25 (July 1947), p. 576.
7. Carnegie Endowment for International Peace National Commission on America and the New World, *Changing Our Ways* (Washington, D.C.: Carnegie Endowment for International Peace, 1992), p. 1.
8. Realism is a school of thought about international relations whose leading figures are Hans Morgenthau, George Kennan, Walter Lippmann, Reinhold Niebuhr, E. H. Carr, and Henry Kissinger. Its core idea is that international relations consist of the interplay of states driven by innate interests that are usually determined by geography and that any policy that deviates from this, or appears to, is either illusory or misconceived. For a fuller explication and critique, see my *Exporting Democracy: Fulfilling America's Destiny* (Washington, D.C.: AEI Press, 1991), chap. 3.
9. Martin Gilbert, *Winston S. Churchill*, vol. 4, *The Stricken World, 1916–1922* (Boston: Houghton Mifflin, 1975), p. 229.
10. Quoted in ibid., p. 228.
11. Jeffrey Sachs, "The Reformers' Tragedy," *New York Times*, January 23, 1994.
12. Nicholas D. Kristof, "The Rise of China," *Foreign Affairs*, vol. 72, no. 5 (November–December 1993), pp. 59, 65.
13. "War Games, Money Games," *New York Times*, February 19, 1992.
14. Quoted in Jim Wolfe, "Iraqi Army's Ruin Makes Drawdown Safer: Powell," *Navy Times*, April 15, 1991, p. 24.
15. Lee H. Hamilton, "A Democrat Looks at Foreign Policy," *Foreign Affairs*, vol. 71, no. 3 (Summer 1992), p. 39.
16. Robert J. Samuelson, "War and Remembrance," *Washington Post*, January 12, 1994.
17. Saddam does not yet have the means to deliver a nuclear weapon, except perhaps by terrorist infiltration, but the technology of missiles is proliferating even faster than that of bombs, so the possibility that he, or others like him, could within a few years possess both the weapon and the means of delivery is not far-fetched.
18. Edward C. Luck, "Making Peace," *Foreign Policy*, no. 89 (Winter 1992–1993), p. 140.
19. George F. Kennan, *American Diplomacy, 1900–1950* (New York: Mentor Books, 1952), p. 82.

20. Hans J. Morgenthau, *In Defense of the National Interest* (New York: Knopf, 1951), p. 3.
21. Glenn H. Snyder and Paul Diesing, *Conflict among Nations* (Princeton: Princeton University Press, 1977), p. 498.

# 5    America's Jekyll-and-Hyde Exceptionalism

## *Harold Hongju Koh*

The idea of American exceptionalism has played an important part in American foreign policy. It does not constitute a coherent perspective on American foreign policy, or offer a collection of prescriptive policies or guidelines for American action abroad, in the way that the other schools of thought reviewed here do. Rather, it offers an understanding of the United States as qualitatively different from other developed countries—one that is defined by its commitment to liberty and individualism, its origins, its political institutions, and other unique attributes that make it unlike any other country in the world. Exceptionalism has been invoked to inform, explain, and justify America's independence from Britain, its settlement of a continent, its acquisition of empire, and its leadership of the West against the Soviet Union, among other actions. It has also been invoked to suggest a degree of American superiority in its dealings with others, and that America's good fortunes have been the result of such superiority.

Exceptionalism has played an important role in informing American foreign policy from the earliest days of the republic, though at times only implicitly and subtly. Isolationism has certainly embodied the idea, bolstering a view of the world and a set of policies that helped to set the United States apart from other countries, especially the European powers. Liberalism as well (especially Woodrow Wilson's version of it), encompassing the idea that liberal democracy is a form of government preferable to all others and that all peoples around the world have a right to it, has displayed some

Harold Hongju Koh, from "On American Exceptionalism." Used with permission from the *Stanford Law Review*, 55.5, May 2003. © 2003 by the Board of Trustees of the Leland Stanford Junior University. Permission conveyed through Copyright Clearance Center, Inc.

affinity for the notion of an exceptional America. And neoconservatism most certainly includes the idea, arguing that American power, informed by its values, has benefited the world and should continue to do so.

Harold Hongju Koh provides an examination of exceptionalism and offers an interpretation of how to view its place in U.S. foreign policy. He distinguishes among five different types of American exceptionalism, highlighting the different ways the United States is different from other countries, while analyzing the benefits and drawbacks of each. From this discussion he turns to American foreign policy after September 11, looking at each of these types of differences and how they are applicable in the current setting. While Koh identifies many positive and benign aspects of American exceptionalism, he argues that in recent years the United States has all too frequently exemplified the more negative aspects of exceptionalism, applying double standards in its dealings with other countries.

---

Since September 11, "American exceptionalism" has emerged as a dominant leitmotif in the daily headlines. But the very phrase raises three questions: First, precisely what we do mean by American exceptionalism? Second, how do we distinguish among the negative and overlooked positive faces of what I call "America's Jekyll-and-Hyde exceptionalism"? And third, how should we, as Americans, respond to the most negative aspects of American exceptionalism after September 11?

During the last fifteen years, I have had a special opportunity to look at American exceptionalism from both sides now: not just from the perspective of the academy and the human rights world, but from two distinct vantage points *within* the human rights arena: from one angle, as a human rights scholar and nongovernmental advocate; from another, as a U.S. government official.[1] From these twin perspectives, I now see, the term "American exceptionalism" has been used far too loosely and without meaningful nuance. When we talk about American exceptionalism, what, precisely, do we mean?

## THE FACES OF AMERICAN EXCEPTIONALISM

Over the centuries, the very concept of "American exceptionalism" has sparked fierce debate in both the academic and political realms. The term, usually attributed to Alexis de Tocqueville, has historically referred to the perception that the United States differs qualitatively from other developed nations, because of its unique origins, national Credo, historical evolution, and distinctive political and religious institutions.[2] The phrase sometimes also connotes the idea that America's canonical commitments to liberty, equality, individualism, populism, and laissez-faire exempt it from the historical forces that have led to the corruption of other societies. In American political life, the concept flows through the rhetoric of nearly every American president, from Washington's Farewell Address, to Lincoln's Gettysburg Address, to Reagan's image of a "shining city on the hill," to nearly every post-September 11 speech of George W. Bush.

In the academic realm, the phrase has been variously used to explain America's distinctive cultural traditions, the evolution of the American labor movement, America's differences from Europe, America's peculiar approach to social welfare policy, and America's "frontier anxiety."[3] In foreign policy, the notion of American exceptionalism generally "holds that Americans deprecate power politics and old-fashioned diplomacy, mistrust powerful standing armies and entangling peacetime commitments, make moralistic judgments about other people's domestic systems, and believe that liberal values transfer readily to foreign affairs."[4]

Michael Ignatieff has approached the matter more systematically. He catalogs various kinds of American exceptionalism, in the process distinguishing at least three different faces of American engagement with the world.[5] The first face Ignatieff calls "American exemptionalism"—ways in which the United States actually *exempts itself* from certain international law rules and agreements, even ones that it may have played a critical role in framing, through such techniques as noncompliance; nonratification;[6] ratification with reservations, understandings, and declarations; the non-self-executing treaty doctrine; or the latest U.S. gambit, unsigning the Rome Statute of the International Criminal Court (ICC).[7] Second, he notes America's *legal self-sufficiency*, typified by Justice Scalia's statement in *Stanford v. Kentucky* that the practices of foreign countries are irrelevant to U.S. constitutional interpretation, because, in the construing of open-ended provisions of the Bill of Rights, "it is *American* conceptions of decency that are dispositive."[8] Third, he points to *double standards*, whereby the United States judges itself by different standards from those it uses to judge other states, and judges its friends and its enemies by different standards.

This helpful trichotomy nevertheless lumps together certain forms of exceptionalism and misses others. I prefer to distinguish among four somewhat different faces of American exceptionalism, which I call, in order of ascending opprobrium: distinctive rights, different labels, the "flying buttress" mentality, and double standards. In my view, it is the fourth face—double standards—that presents the most dangerous and destructive form of American exceptionalism.

America undoubtedly has a *distinctive rights culture*, growing out of its peculiar social, political, and economic history. Because of that history, some human rights, such as the norm of nondiscrimination based on race or First Amendment protections for speech and religion, have received far greater emphasis and judicial protection in America than in Europe or Asia. So, for example, the U.S. First Amendment is far more protective than other countries' laws of hate speech,[9] libel,[10] commercial speech,[11] and publication of national security information.[12] But is this distinctive rights culture, rooted in our American tradition, really inconsistent with universal human rights values? On examination, I do not find this distinctiveness too deeply unsettling to world order. The judicial doctrine of "margin of appreciation," familiar in European Union law, permits sufficient national variance in protection of the same rights as to promote some tolerance of this kind of rights distinctiveness.[13] Admittedly, in a globalizing world, our exceptional free speech tradition can cause problems abroad, as may, for example, occur when hate speech is disseminated over the Internet. In my view, however, our Supreme Court can moderate these conflicts by applying more consistently the transnationalist approach to judicial interpretation discussed below.

Similarly, America's tendency to use *different labels* to describe synonymous concepts turns out to be more of an annoyance than a philosophical attack upon the rest of the world. When I appeared before the Committee Against Torture in Geneva to defend the first American report on U.S. compliance with the Torture Convention, I was asked a reasonable question: why the United States does not "maintain a single, comprehensive collation of statistics regarding incidents of torture and cruel, inhuman or degrading treatment or punishment," a universally understood concept.[14] My answer, in effect, was that the myriad bureaucracies of the federal government, the fifty states, and the territories *did* gather statistics regarding torture and cruel, inhuman, or degrading treatment, but we called that practice by different labels, including "cruel and unusual punishment," "police brutality," "section 1983 actions," applications of the exclusionary rule, violations of civil rights under color of state law, and the like. Refusing to accept the internationally accepted human rights standard as the American legal term thus reflects a quirky, nonintegrationist feature of our cultural distinctiveness (akin to our continuing use of feet and inches, rather than the metric system). But different labels don't necessarily mean different rules. Except for some troubling post-September 11 backsliding, which the Bush administration has now renounced, the United States generally accepts the prohibition against torture, even if it calls that prohibition by a different name.[15]

Third, I believe that lumping all of America's exclusionary treaty practices—e.g., nonratification, ratification with reservations, and the non-self-executing treaty doctrine—under the general heading of "American exemptionalism" misses an important point: that not all the ways in which the United States exempts itself from global treaty obligations are equally problematic. For example, although the United States has a notoriously embarrassing record for the late ratification, nonratification, or "Swiss cheese ratification"[16] of various human rights treaties, the relevant question is not nonratification but *noncompliance* with the underlying norms, a problem from which the rest of the world tends to suffer more than does the United States.[17] Many countries adopt a strategy of ratification without compliance; in contrast, the United States has adopted the perverse practice of human rights *compliance without ratification*. So, for example, during the thirty-seven years after the United States signed, but before it ratified, the Genocide Convention,[18] no one plausibly claimed that U.S. officials were committing genocide. This was simply another glaring example of American compliance without ratification.

This third face of American exceptionalism Louis Henkin long ago dubbed "America's *flying buttress* mentality." Why is it, he asked, that in the cathedral of international human rights, the United States is so often seen as a flying buttress, rather than a pillar, willing to stand outside the structure supporting it, but unwilling to subject itself to the critical examination and rules of that structure? The short answer is that compliance without ratification gives a false sense of freedom. By supporting and following the rules of the international realm most of the time, but always out of a sense of political prudence rather than legal obligation, the United States enjoys the appearance of compliance, while maintaining the illusion of unfettered sovereignty.[19]

Like "distinctive rights" and "different labels," the flying buttress mentality is ultimately more America's problem than the world's. For example, it is a huge embarrassment that only two nations in the world—the United States and Somalia, which until recently did not have an organized government—have not ratified the Convention on the Rights of the Child. Nevertheless, this ultimately is more America's loss than that of the world. Why? Because the United States rarely gets enough credit for the large-scale moral and financial support that it actually gives to children's rights around the world, in no small part because of its promiscuous failure to ratify a convention with which it actually complies in most respects.[20] But once one weighs in the currently unfavorable alignment of proratification votes in the

Republican-controlled Senate, and considers the amount of political capital that U.S. activists would expend to obtain the sixty-seven votes needed for ratification any time soon, one soon concludes that children's rights advocates are probably better off directing their limited energies not toward ratification, but rather toward real strategies to reduce the exploitation of child labor on the ground or to expand the prohibitions in the child-soldiers protocol.

This brings me to the fourth and most problematic face of American exceptionalism: when the United States actually uses its exceptional power and wealth to promote a *double standard*. The most problematic exceptionalism is not distinctive American rights culture, a taste for different labels, or a flying buttress mentality, but rather instances when the United States proposes that a different rule should apply to itself and its allies from the one that should apply to the rest of the world. Recent well-known examples include such diverse issues as the International Criminal Court,[21] the Kyoto Protocol on Climate Change,[22] executing juvenile offenders or persons with mental disabilities,[23] declining to implement orders of the International Court of Justice with regard to the death penalty,[24] or claiming a Second Amendment exclusion from a proposed global ban on the illicit transfer of small arms and light weapons.[25] In the post-9/11 environment, further examples have proliferated: particularly, America's attitudes toward the global justice system, and holding Taliban detainees on Guantanamo without Geneva Convention hearings, about which I will say more later.

For now, we should recognize at least four problems with double standards. The first is that when the United States promotes double standards, it invariably ends up not on the higher rung, but on the lower rung with horrid bedfellows—for example, with such countries as Iran, Nigeria, and Saudi Arabia, the only other countries that have not in practice either abolished or declared a moratorium upon the imposition of the death penalty on juvenile offenders.[26] This appearance of hypocrisy undercuts America's ability to pursue an affirmative human rights agenda. Worse yet, by espousing the double standard, the United States often finds itself co-opted into either condoning or defending other countries' human rights abuses, even when it previously criticized them (as has happened, for example, with the U.S. critique of military tribunals in Peru, Russia's war on Chechen "terrorists," or China's crackdown on Uighur Muslims).[27]

Third, the perception that the United States applies one standard to the world and another to itself sharply weakens America's claim to lead globally through moral authority. This diminishes U.S. power to persuade through principle, a critical element of American "soft power." Fourth, and perhaps most important, by opposing the global rules with the aim of modifying them to suit America's purposes, the United States can end up undermining the legitimacy of the rules themselves. The irony, of course, is that, by doing so, the United States disempowers itself from invoking those rules, at precisely the moment when it needs those rules to serve its own national purposes.

## AMERICA'S OVERLOOKED EXCEPTIONALISM

Having focused until now on the four negative faces of American exceptionalism, I must address a fifth, much-overlooked dimension in which the United States is genuinely exceptional in international affairs. Looking only at the half-empty part of the glass, I would argue, obscures the most important respect in which the United States has been genuinely exceptional, with regard to international affairs, international law, and promotion of human rights: namely, in its *exceptional global leadership* and activism. To this day, the United States remains the only superpower capable, and at times willing, to commit real resources and make real sacrifices to build, sustain, and drive an international system committed to international law, democracy, and the promotion of human rights. Experience teaches that when the United States leads on human rights, from Nuremberg to Kosovo, other countries follow. When the United States does not lead, often nothing happens, or worse yet, as in Rwanda and Bosnia, disasters occur because the United States does not get involved.[28]

Let me illustrate with two anecdotes from my own experience. The first comes from my time as assistant secretary of state. A young British diplomat I knew came from the British Foreign and Commonwealth Office to work "on detail" at the State Department's Bureau of European Affairs. As he was returning to the British Embassy, I asked him, "So what was the major difference between your two jobs?" His immediate answer: "When something happens in the world, the Americans ask, 'What should we do?' The British ask, 'What will the Americans do?'"

This explains in part the Bush administration's cynicism about the French. Can you remember the last major human rights campaign led by the French? If you cannot remember, it is because in fact they have led very few, even while notoriously fraternizing with abusive regimes in such countries as China, Iraq, and Burma.

My second, bittersweet anecdote comes from my childhood. My late father, Dr. Kwang Lim Koh, served as minister to the United States for the first democratically elected government in South Korea. In 1961, a military coup overthrew the democratic government of Prime Minister Chang Myon, who was placed under house arrest amid rumors that he would shortly be executed. To plead for Change's life, my parents brought Chang's teenage son to see Walt W. Rostow, then the deputy national security adviser to the president. Rostow turned to the boy and said simply, "We know where your father is. Let me assure you, he will not be harmed." Rostow's words stunned my father, who simply could not believe that any country could have such global power, reach, and interest. The story so impressed my father that he repeated it on countless occasions as I grew up, as proof of the exceptional goodness of American power.

But after I entered the State Department, I came to realize that what I had understood to be exceptional behavior is in fact America's diplomatic rule: every day in virtually every embassy and consulate around the world, American diplomats make similar interventions for and inquiries about political prisoners, opposition politicians, and labor leaders, even in countries that most Americans could not locate on any map. Without question, no other country takes a comparable interest or has comparable influence worldwide. Both America's global interest and its global influence are genuinely exceptional.

Ironically, as I grew older, I came to realize that this canonical story was inherently double-edged. On the one hand, it showed that America both has and exercises exceptional power, every day and in every country on the planet. But the real problem in the Korean case was not that the United States did too much, but that it probably did too little.[29] The United States was ready to intervene to save Prime Minister Chang's life, but not to take the additional steps necessary to restore democracy in South Korea. Instead of doing more to effectuate its human rights commitment, for several decades during the Cold War, the United States instead supported a military government committed to authoritarian rule and economic growth.

## ENTRENCHING EXCEPTIONALISM

The second Gulf War with Iraq in March 2003 brought with it the inescapable sense that the phenomenon of American exceptionalism and the debate over it had reached a new watershed.[30] Under the Bush administration, an exceptionalist strategy seems to have become America's dominant response to the horrendous terrorist attacks of September 11.

Looking back, we can now see that September 11 created a cleft in the age of globalization that began with the fall of the Berlin Wall. In hindsight, the immediate post-Cold War era now looms as a time of "global optimism," when too many commentators were exuberantly optimistic about the constructive possibilities posed by the globalization of transport, commerce, finance, and communications. But then we learned that the same coin has a dark side: that terrorists can exploit that same interconnected-ness to turn airplanes into missiles, to use the global financial system to move money across borders, to turn ordinary mail into a delivery system for biological weapons, and to plant viruses in email as a tool for cyberter-rorism. Since September 11, we have almost literally left the light and entered the shadows of a new age of global pessimism, in which we have realized with alarm that all of the interdependent dimensions of the age of globalization could be equally turned against us.

The Bush administration's response to this startling challenge has been not interstitial but architectural. The emerging Bush Doctrine now has five identifiable elements:

- First, *Achilles and his heel.* September 11 brought upon the United States, like Achilles, a schizophrenic sense of its exceptional power coupled with its exceptional vulnerability. Never has a superpower seemed so powerful and vulnerable at the same time. Given that we have already suffered some three thousand civilian casualties in the war against terrorism, the question fun-damentally posed by the Bush Doctrine is how to use our superpower resources to protect our vulnerability.

- The answer given has been *Homeland Security,* in both the defen-sive and preemptive senses of that term. In the name of preserv-ing American power and forestalling future attack, the United States government has instituted sweeping strategies of domes-tic security, law enforcement, immigration control, security detention, governmental secrecy, and information awareness at home,[31] even while asserting a novel right under international law to forced disarmament of any country that poses a gather-ing threat, through strategies of preemptive self-defense if necessary.[32]

- Third, the administration has justified this claimed sovereign right under international law by a shift in emphasis in human rights. In 1941, when Franklin Delano Roosevelt summoned the Allies to arms against an earlier "Axis of Evil," he did not sim-ply call America to war. Instead, he painted a positive vision of the world we were trying to make: a postwar world of four fundamental freedoms: freedom of speech, freedom of religion, freedom from want, freedom from fear.[33] Since 1941, U.S. human rights policy in both Democratic and Republican administrations has followed the broad contours of the "Four Freedoms" speech. This framework foreshadowed a postwar human rights construct—eventually embedded in Eleanor Roosevelt's Universal Declaration of Human Rights[34] and subsequent international covenants—that would emphasize comprehensive protection of civil and political rights (freedom of speech and religion), economic, social, and cultural rights (freedom from want), and freedom from gross violations and persecution (e.g., the Refugee Convention, the Genocide Convention, and the Torture Convention). But after September 11, administration officials have reprioritized *"freedom from fear"* as the number one freedom the American people need to preserve. Instead of declaring a state of emergency, however, or announcing broad-scale changes in the rules by which the United States had previously accepted and internalized international human rights standards, the administration has opted instead for a two-pronged strategy of creating *extralegal zones*, most prominently the U.S. naval base at Guantanamo Bay, Cuba, where scores of security detainees are held without legal recourse, and *extralegal persons*—particularly those detainees labeled "enemy combatants," who, even if American citizens on American soil, are effectively accorded no recognized legal avenue to assert either substantive or procedural rights.

- Fourth, beginning with Afghanistan and now continuing with Iraq, the administration has asserted a new strategy toward democracy promotion. From Ronald Reagan's famous 1982 Westminster speech until September 11, successive administrations had supported the promotion of democracy as a fundamental goal of U.S. foreign policy.[35] President Reagan's address to the Houses of Parliament called for a broad public-private effort "to foster the infrastructure of democracy—the system of a free press, unions, political parties, universities—which allows a people to choose their own way, their own culture, to reconcile their own differences through peaceful means."[36] During the Bush-Clinton years, the democracy-promotion strategy developed into a broader aspiration, captured by President George H.W. Bush's January 29, 1991, State of the Union message, for "a new world order—where diverse nations are drawn together in common cause, to achieve the universal aspirations of mankind: peace and security, freedom and the rule of law."[37] But the consistent theme during these years was "democracy promotion from the bottom up," not imposed from the top down. Since the U.S. invasion of Afghanistan, democracy-promotion efforts have shifted toward *militarily imposed democracy*, characterized by U.S.-led military attack, prolonged occupation, restored opposition leaders, and the creation of resource-needy postconflict protectorates.[38] At this writing, a new, four-pronged strategy seems to be emerging: "hard," militarily imposed democracy promotion in Iraq and Afghanistan; "soft," diplomatic democracy promotion in Palestine; optimistic predictions of "domino democratization" elsewhere in the Middle East; and reduced democracy-promotion efforts elsewhere. But if extended globally, as was done during the Cold War, such a U.S. strategy of making "the world safe through imposed democracy" could soon transform into an unsustainable strategy requiring near-unilateral military inter- ventionism, extended support for client governments, and imperial overstretch.[39]

- Fifth and finally, as Strobe Talbott has observed, to implement the various elements of this emerging doctrine, the Bush administration has opted for *"strategic unilateralism and tactical multilateralism."* By its nature, such a strategy resists enforced obedience to international treaties and institutions as danger- ously constraining on U.S. national sovereignty.[40] But as with the "flying buttress" mentality described above, to win the illu- sion of unfettered sovereignty, the United States surrenders its reputation for being law-abiding. This loss of rectitude dimin- ishes America's moral authority and reduces the soft power American needs to mobilize multilateral responses in a post- September 11 world.

If these are the elements of the emerging Bush Doctrine, why is it so trou- bling? *Because such a doctrine makes double standards—the most virulent strain of American exceptionalism—not just the exception but the rule.* Each element of the emerging Bush Doctrine places the United States in the position of pro- moting genuine double standards, one for itself and another for the rest of the world. The exclusive focus on American vulnerability ignores the far greater vulnerability of such countries as, for example, Israel and Turkey (which, being a neighbor of Iraq, surely had more to fear from Saddam Hussein than did the United States, yet still denied American soldiers the right to stage ground operations from Turkish bases). Even while asserting its own right of preemptive self-defense, the United States has properly hesitated to recognize any other country's claim to engage in forced disar- mament or preemptive self-defense in the name of homeland security.[41] The technique of creating extralegal "rights-free" zones and individuals under U.S. jurisdiction necessarily erects a double standard *within* American jurisprudence, by separating those places and people to whom

America must accord rights from those it may treat effectively as human beings without human rights.

Similarly, the oxymoronic concept of "imposed democracy" authorizes top-down regime change in the name of democracy. Yet the United States has always argued that genuine democracy must flow from the will of the people, not from military occupation.[42] Finally, a policy of strategic unilateralism seems unsustainable in an interdependent world. Because the United States is party to a global network of closely interconnected treaties enmeshed in multiple frameworks of international institutions, unilateral administration decisions to break or bend one treaty commitment usually trigger vicious cycles of treaty violation. In an interdependent world, the United States simply cannot afford to ignore its treaty obligations while at the same time expecting its treaty partners to help it solve the myriad global problems that extend far beyond any one nation's control: the global AIDS and SARS crises, climate change, international debt, drug smuggling, trade imbalances, currency coordination, and trafficking in human beings, to name just a few. Strategic unilateralism undermines American soft power at the exact moment when the United States is trying to use that soft power to mobilize those same partners to help it solve problems it simply cannot solve alone: most obviously, the war against global terrorism, but also the postwar reconstruction of Iraq, the Middle East crisis, and the renewed nuclear militarization of North Korea.

If the emerging Bush Doctrine takes hold, the United States may well emerge from the post-9/11 era still powerful, but deeply committed to double standards as a means of preserving U.S. hegemony. Promoting standards that apply to others but not to us represents the very antithesis of America's claim, since the end of World War II, to apply *universal* legal and human rights standards. The real danger of the Bush Doctrine is thus that it will turn the United States, which since 1945 has been the major architect and buttress of the global system of international law and human rights, into its major outlier, weakening that system and reducing its capacity to promote universal values and protect American interests.

## Notes

1. While in government, I served in the Reagan administration as a Justice Department lawyer and in the Clinton administration as assistant secretary of state for democracy, human rights, and labor. In those positions, I acted, in effect, as America's plaintiff's lawyer in cases where the United States holds a

human rights grievance, as well as its defense lawyer when the United States has been charged with human rights abuse. Both before and after my government service, I spent considerable time suing the U.S. government, with regard to its refugee policy, foreign affairs decision making, use of force abroad, and human rights practices. *See, e.g.*, Harold Hongju Koh, *America's Offshore Refugee Camps*, 29 U. Rich. L. Rev. 139 (1994) (Allen Chair issure) (reviewing litigation).

2. *See generally Is America Different? A New Look at American Exceptionalism* (Byron E. Shafer ed., 1991); John W. Kingdon, *America the Unusual* (1999); Seymour M. Lipset, *American Exceptionalism: A Double-Edged Sword* (1996); 2 Alexis de Tocqueville, *Democracy in America* 36–37 (Phillips Bradley ed., Henry Reeve trans., A. A. Knopf 1948) (1835).

3. *See, e.g.*, Deborah L. Madsen, *American Exceptionalism* (1998) (cultural traditions); Jonathan A. Glickstein, *American Exceptionalism, American Anxiety: Wages, Competition, and Degraded Labor in the Antebellum United States* (2002); *but see* Sean Wilentz, *Against Exceptionalism: Class Consciousness and the American Labor Movement, 1790–1820*, 26 Int'l Lab. & Working Class Hist. 1 (1984) (labor movement); Robert Kagan, *Of Paradise and Power: America vs. Europe in the New World Order* (2003) (America's differences from Europe); Seymour M. Lipset & Gary Marks, *It Didn't Happen Here: Why Socialism Failed in the United States* (2001) (failure of socialism in America); Jacob S. Hacker, *The Divided Welfare State: The Battle over Public and Private Social Benefits in the United States* 5–28 (2002) (America's approach to social welfare policy); David M. Wrobel, *The End of American Exceptionalism: Frontier Anxiety from the Old West to the New Deal* (1996); Frederick Jackson Turner, *The Significance of the Frontier in American History*, in *Does the Frontier Experience Make America Exceptional?* 18 (Richard W. Etulain ed., 1999) (America's frontier anxiety).

4. Joseph Lepgold & Timothy McKeown, *Is American Foreign Policy Exceptional? An Empirical Analysis*, 110 Pol. Sci. Q. 369, 369 (1995).

5. Michael Ignatieff, *American Exceptionalism and Human Rights*, chapter 1.

6. Ignatieff treats noncompliance and nonratification as separate categories of American exceptionalism, but for present purposes, I also group these phenomena under the "exemptionalism" heading. *See* Ignatieff, *supra* note 5.

7. *See* Edward T. Swaine, *Unsigning*, 55 Stan. L. Rev. 2061 (2003).

8. 492 U.S. 361, 369 n.1 (1989) (emphasis in original).

9. *Brandenburg v. Ohio*, 395 U.S. 444, 447 (1969).

10. *New York Times v. Sullivan*, 376 U.S. 254, 269 (1964).

11. *Landmark Communications, Inc. v. Virginia*, 435 U.S. 829 (1978).

12. *N.Y. Times Co. v. United States*, 403 U.S. 713 (1971).

13. *See generally* Louis Henkin, Gerald L. Neuman, Diane F. Orentlicher & David W. Leebron, *Human Rights* 564 (1999).

14. *See* Harold Hongju Koh, U.S. Assistant Secretary of State, Democracy, Human Rights & Labor, & William R. Yeomans, Chief of Staff, Civil Rights Division, U.S. Dep't of Justice, *Reply to Questions from the U.N. Committee Against Torture* 3 (May 11, 2000) (on file with author).

15. The most prominent of these, of course, is the outrageous treatment of Iraqi prisoners at Abu Ghraib prison, but in the wake of that disaster, President Bush has reiterated the categorical U.S. position against torture as an instrument of state policy. See *President's Statement on the U.N. International Day in Support of Victims of Torture,* June 26, 2004, *available at* http://www.whitehouse.gov/news/releases/2004/06/20040626-19.html ("the United States reaffirms its commitment to the worldwide elimination of torture. . . . Freedom from torture is an inalienable human right, and we are committed to building a world where human rights are respected and protected by the rule of law. To help fulfill this commitment, the United States has joined 135 other nations in ratifying the Convention Against Torture and Other Cruel, Inhuman or Degrading Treatment or Punishment. America stands against and will not tolerate torture. We will investigate and prosecute all acts of torture and undertake to prevent other cruel and unusual punishment in all territory under our jurisdiction. American personnel are required to comply with all U.S. laws, including the United States Constitution, Federal statutes, including statutes prohibiting torture, and our treaty obligations with respect to the treatment of all detainees").

16. By "Swiss cheese ratification," I mean U.S. ratification of multilateral treaties with so many reservations, understandings, and declarations that these conditions substantially limit the U.S. acceptance of these treaties.

17. Oona A. Hathaway, *Do Human Rights Treaties Make a Difference?*, 111 Yale L.J. 1935, 1977, 1980 (2002).

18. Convention on the Prevention and Punishment of the Crime of Genocide, Dec. 9, 1948, 78 U.N.T.S. 277 (approved by Senate on Feb. 19, 1986).

19. It is a bit like the driver who regularly breaks the speed limit but rarely gets a ticket, because he uses radar detectors, cruise control, CB radios, and similar tricks to stay just this side of the law. He complies but does not obey, because to obey visibly would mean surrendering his freedom and admitting to constraints, while appearing "free" better serves his self-image than the more sedate label of being law-abiding. *See* Harold Hongju Koh, *The 1998 Frankel Lecture: Bringing International Law Home,* 35 Hous. L. Rev. 623, 626–32 (1998) (describing difference between compliance and obedience).

20. The glaring exception, of course, is article 37(a) of the Children's Rights Convention, which says that "capital punishment . . . shall [not] be imposed for offences committed by persons below eighteen years of age." Convention on the Rights of the Child, G.A. Res. 44/25, annex, U.N. GAOR, 44th Sess., Supp. No. 49, art. 37(a), U.N. Doc. A/44/49 (1989) (entered into force Sept. 2, 1990). See *Roper v. Simmons,* 125 S. Ct. 1183 (2005) (holding, by a five-to-four vote, that the Eighth Amendment prohibits execution of juvenile offenders who committed their offenses while under the age of eighteen).

21. Although the United States initially refused to accede to the Rome Statute of the International Criminal Court, President Clinton signed the treaty on December 31, 2000, without submitting it to the Senate. *See Clinton's Words: "The Right Action,"* N.Y. Times, Jan. 1, 2001, at A6. In May 2002, however, the

Bush administration purported to unsign the treaty and notified the United Nations that it did not intend to become a party to the Rome Statute. *See* Letter from John R. Bolton, Under Secretary of State for Arms Control and International Security, to Kofi Annan, U.N. Secretary General (May 6, 2002), *available at* http://www.state.gov/r/pa/prs/ps/2002/9968.htm.

22. *See Kyoto Protocol to the Framework Convention on Climate Change*, U.N. FCCC, 3d Sess., U.N. Doc. FCCC/CP/1997/7/Add.2 (1997), *reprinted in* 37 I.L.M. 22 (1998).

23. *See Atkins v. Virginia*, 536 U.S. 304 (2002) (persons with mental retardation); *In re Stanford*, 123 S. Ct. 472 (2002) (Stevens, J., dissenting) (juvenile offenders). At the time that the Supreme Court voted to ban the execution of persons with mental retardation, the United States was the only nation in the world engaging in this practice, and the United States had criticized other nations for harsh treatment of those with retardation. *See generally* Harold Hongju Koh, *Paying "Decent Respect" to World Opinion on the Death Penalty*, 35 U.C. Davis L. Rev. 1085 (2002) (arguing for internalization of international standards regarding the execution of persons with mental disabilities). Until 2005, of all the established democracies in the world, only the United States was known to execute individuals who were younger than eighteen when the crime was committed, and three states—Texas, Virginia and Oklahoma—account for 81 percent of the 22 executions of children since 1972. Curiously, in 1979, representatives of the U.S. State Department had represented to Congress that juvenile execution was no longer a practice engaged in by the United States. See Harold Hongju Koh, *International Law as Part of Our Law*, 98 Am. J. Int'l L. 43, 51 (2004). In *Roper v. Simmons*, 125 S. Ct. 1183 (2005), The Supreme Court finally declared that practice unconstitutional.

24. In the LaGrand Case (*F.R.G. v. U.S.*), 2001 I.C.J. 104 (June 27), Germany sued the United States in the World Court for threatening to execute two German nationals without according them rights pursuant to the Vienna Convention on Consular Relations. Although the ICJ issued provisional measures enjoining the execution of Karl LaGrand, American officials ignored the orders, the United States Supreme Court declined to intervene, and LaGrand was executed. The World Court finally found that the United States had violated the Vienna Convention, but, subsequently, American courts have treated the ICJ's ruling as having no legal effect within the United States. *See generally Symposium, Reflections on the ICJ's LaGrand Decision: Foreword*, 27 Yale J. Int'l L. 423, 424 (2002); Harold Hongju Koh, *Paying Decent Respect to International Tribunal Rulings*, 2002 Proc. Am. Soc'y of Int'l L. 45 (discussing post-LaGrand U.S. cases).

Recently, in *Avena v. Other Mexican Nationals (Mexico v. United States)*, March 31, 2004, *available at* http://www.icj-cij.org/icjwww/idocket/imus/imusframe.htm, the International Court of Justice ruled that the United States had breached its obligations to Mexico and to fifty-one Mexican nationals by the failure of state officials to inform the detained foreign nationals of their right to contact consular officials for assistance under the Vienna Convention before sentencing them to death. The ICJ directed the United States to review and reconsider the convictions and sentences of the Mexican nationals in light of the treaty violation. In March 2005, President Bush finally ordered the Texas state courts, as a matter of comity, to grant the review and reconsideration required by the ICJ's judgment.

25. *See* John R. Bolton, *Statement to the Plenary Session of the U.N. Conference on the Illicit Trade in Small Arms and Light Weapons in all Its Aspects* (July 9, 2001), *available at* http://www.un.int/usa/01_104.htm ("The United States will not join consensus on a final document that contains measures abrogating the Constitutional right to bear arms"). For a critique of this argument, see Harold Hongju Koh, *A World Drowning in Guns*, 71 Fordham L. Rev. 2333 (2003).

26. According to Amnesty International, the United States has executed 70 percent of the juvenile offenders executed worldwide since 1998, and, in 2002, the state of Texas (with three executions) was the only known jurisdiction in the world to execute a juvenile offender. *See* Amnesty Int'l, *Indecent and Internationally Illegal: The Death Penalty against Child Offenders* (abridged ed. 2002), *available at* http://www.amnestyusa.org/abolish/reports/amr51_144_2002.pdf.

27. *See, e.g.*, Tom Malinowski, *Overlooking Chechen Terror*, Wash. Post, Mar. 1, 2003, at A19 (noting that the United States has added three Chechen organizations to the State Department list of terrorist groups, apparently to avoid Moscow's veto of the Iraq resolution before the UN Security Council).

28. For compelling discussions of how the United States failed to intervene in time in Bosnia and Rwanda, *see* Richard C. Holbrooke, *To End a War* (1998); Samantha Power, *A Problem from Hell: America and the Age of Genocide* (2002).

29. For historical accounts of this period in South Korean political life, see Sungjoo Han, *The Failure of Democracy in South Korea* (1974); Gregory Henderson, *Korea: The Politics of the Vortex* 177–91 (1968).

30. *See, e.g.*, Fareed Zakaria, *The Arrogant Empire*, Newsweek, Mar. 24, 2003, at 18.

31. *See generally* Lawyers Comm. for Human Rights, *Imbalance of Powers: How Changes to U.S. Law and Security since 9/11 Erode Human Rights and Civil Liberties* (2003), *available at* http://www.lchr.org/us_law/loss/imbalance/powers.pdf; Lawyers Committee for Human Rights, *A Year of Loss: Reexamining Civil Liberties since September 11* (2002), *available at* http://www.lchr.org/pubs/descriptions/loss_report.pdf.

32. *See* President of the United States, *The National Security Strategy of the United States of America* 34 (2002), *available at* http://www.whitehouse.gov/nsc/nss.pdf; Bill Keller, *The I-Can't-Believe-I'm-a-Hawk Club*, N.Y. Times, Feb. 8, 2003, at A17 (noting claim of right of forced disarmament).

33. Franklin Delano Roosevelt, *Eighth Annual Message to Congress* (Jan. 6, 1941), in 3 *The State of the Union Messages of the Presidents, 1790–1966*, at 2855 (Fred L. Israel ed., 1966).

34. *See generally* Mary Ann Glendon, *A World Made New: Eleanor Roosevelt and the Universal Declaration of Human Rights* (2001).

35. For history, see Thomas Carothers, *Aiding Democracy Abroad: The Learning Curve* 30–32 (1999); Tony Smith, *America's Mission: The United States and the Worldwide Struggle for Democracy in the Twentieth Century* (1994); Harold Hongju Koh, *A United States Human Rights Policy for the 21st Century*, 46 St. Louis U. L.J. 293 (2002).

36. President Ronald Reagan, *Promoting Democracy and Peace* (June 8, 1982), *available at* http://www.iri.org/reaganspeech.asp. At that time, Congress

approved the National Endowment for Democracy—a government-financed, private nonprofit fund that has continued to this day to make significant grants to business and labor—and effectively gave birth to the two political party institutes that now give support for the development of political parties and electoral processes overseas—the National Democratic Institute, of which former Secretary of State Madeleine Albright is now the chair, and the International Republican Institute, of which Senator John McCain is now the chair.

37. In his successful campaign for president, Bill Clinton criticized George H. W. Bush by arguing that "[o]ur nation has a higher purpose than to coddle dictators and stand aside from the global movement toward democracies. . . . President Bush seems too often to prefer a foreign policy that embraces stability at the expense of freedom." Harold Hongju Koh, *The "Haiti Paradigm" in United States Human Rights Policy*, 103 Yale L.J. 2391, 2427 n.206 (quoting Governor Bill Clinton, Remarks to the University of Wisconsin Institute of World Affairs (Oct. 1, 1992)).

38. *See* Chibli Mallat, *Focus on Human Rights Offers Hope of Reconciliation*, Times (London), Mar. 29, 2003, at A13. "Welcome to the post-modern war. Even before it started, this war appeared surreal, not least for the idea that the United States and Britain were 'liberating Iraq' while refusing to involve any Iraqi in the process of change. ... Even [hawkish Iraqis] are uneasy about American plans to rule Iraq 'directly,' echoing a universal rejection in the Arab world of American or British occupation." *Id.*

39. Even the successful impositions of top-down democracy in Germany and Japan were accomplished after a single conflict, not pursuant to the laborious and expensive "seriatim strategy" that Afghanistan and Iraq may now portend.

40. Talbott argues that, by contrast, the Clinton administration, in which he served as deputy secretary of state, pursued a foreign policy based on strategic multilateralism and tactical unilateralism.

41. *See* Mary-Ellen O'Connell, *The Myth of Preemptive Self-Defense* 3 (2002) (stating "the United States as a government has consistently supported the prohibition on such preemptive use of force"), *at* http://www.asil.org/taskforce/oconnell .pdf. Indeed, had such a doctrine existed at the time of the Cuban Missile Crisis, one wonders whether Castro would have invoked it to engage in preemptive self-defense against the United States.

42. *See* U.S.-Sponsored Resolutions on the "Right to Democracy," C.H.R. Res. 1999/57, U.N. CHR, 55th Sess., U.N. Doc. E/CN.4/RES/1999/57 (1999) (51–0, with two abstentions); C.H.R. Res. 2000/62, U.N. CHR, 56th Sess., U.N. Doc. E/CN.4/RES/2000/62 (2000) (30–17, with six abstentions). In so arguing, the United States explicitly invoked legal scholarship asserting the existence of a right to democratic governance under international law. *See, e.g., Democratic Governance and International Law* (Gregory H. Fox & Brad R. Roth eds., 2000); Gregory H. Fox, *The Right to Political Participation in International Law*, 17 Yale J. Int'l L. 539 (1992); Thomas M. Franck, *The Emerging Right to Democratic Governance*, 86 Am. J. Int'l L. 46 (1992); Henry J. Steiner, *Political Participation as a Human Right*, 1 Harv. Hum. Rts. Y.B. 77 (1988).

# 6

# Dilemmas of Dominance

## NOAM CHOMSKY

In addition to the prevailing schools of thought regarding the underpinnings of U.S. foreign policy, there is also an interpretation—a critique—that views American actions as imperialist, driven by the desire to advance American economic interests and achieve or maintain global dominance. This analytical perspective is highly critical of American policy, suggesting that U.S. business interests dominate the formulation of policy, and that American policy largely serves such interests.

Noam Chomsky has been one of the better known proponents of this view in the United States, providing over the course of many years a robust critique of American foreign policy. From the Cold War years to the present day, Chomsky has consistently questioned American behavior overseas and its stated justifications. Rather than accept official explanations or conventional theoretical approaches, he has posited that a more convincing explanation of American policy is one that sees the results of American actions—the accumulation of vast economic and political power—as the actual aims of U.S. foreign policy. In this selection, Chomsky looks at the sweep of U.S. policy after World War II, stating that in the postwar era, "the new global order was to be subordinated to the needs of the U.S. economy and subject to U.S. political control." He suggests that the United States has been very successful in achieving its objectives since this time, but also argues that American dominance is increasingly threatened in the present day, especially by the resurgence of Asia as a center of wealth and power.

This analytical perspective of U.S. foreign policy remains a minority view in the United States, (though it has greater acceptance overseas, especially in recent years). At the same time, however, it continues to offer a thoughtful, vigorous, and sometimes convincing critique of American actions around the globe. It is for this reason that Chomsky and others making a similar assessment remain an important part of the ongoing dialogue regarding American foreign policy.

Enthusiasm about the New Europe of the former Soviet empire is not solely based on the fact that its leadership is willing to "salute and shout, 'Yes sir.'" More fundamental reasons were articulated as the European Union considered extension of membership to these countries. The US strongly supported this move. The countries of the East are "Europe's real modernizers," political commentator David Ignatius explained. "They can blow apart the bureaucratism and welfare-state culture that still hobble much of Europe" and "let free markets function the way they should"[1]—as in the US, where the economy relies heavily on the state sector, and the current incumbents broke postwar records in protectionism during their first tenure in office.

Since "the freedom-loving, technology-adapting people of the East are paid a small fraction of what workers in the West earn," Ignatius continues, they can drive all of Europe toward "the realities of modern capitalism": the American model, apparently ideal by definition. The model has per capita growth rates approximately equal to Europe's and unemployment at about the same level, along with the highest rates of inequality and poverty, the highest workloads, and some of the weakest benefits and support systems in the advanced industrial world. The median male wage in 2000 was still below the 1979 level after the late-nineties boomlet, though productivity was 45 percent higher, one sign of the sharp shift toward benefits for capital that is being accelerated more radically under Bush II.

The potential contribution of Eastern Europe to undermining quality of life for the majority in the West was recognized immediately after the fall of the Berlin Wall. The business press was exultant about the "green shoots in Communism's ruins," where "rising unemployment and pauperization of large sections of the industrial working class" meant that people were willing "to work longer hours than their pampered colleagues" in the West, at 40 percent of the wages and with few benefits. Further "green shoots" include enough repression to keep working people in line and attractive state subsidies for Western investors. These market reforms would enable Europe to "hammer away at high wages and corporate taxes, short working hours, labor immobility, and luxurious social programs." Europe would be able to follow the American pattern, where the decline of real wages in the Reagan years to the lowest level among the advanced industrial societies (apart from Britain) was "a welcome development of transcendent importance." With Communism's ruins playing something like the role of Mexico, the advantages can now be brought to Western Europe as well, driving it toward the US-British model.[2]

Communism's ruins have many advantages over the regions that have been under unbroken Western domination for centuries. Those on the eastern side of the 500-year-old fault line dividing East and West (not quite that of the Cold War, but similar) enjoyed much higher standards of health and education after the East exited from its status as the West's original "third world," and they even have the right skin color. With the return of something like traditional relationships, the East can now provide other benefits, including a huge flood of easily exploited labor. The Ukraine is now reported to be replacing Southern Europe as the source of cheap labor in the West, depriving the collapsing Ukrainian economy of its most productive workers. Like their counterparts from Central America, Ukrainian emigrants send back enormous remittances, thus helping to keep what remains of the society alive. Working and living conditions are so awful that death rates are high, and perhaps 100,000 Ukrainian women are held in sexual slavery. Not an unfamiliar story.[3]

It is clear enough why the "de facto world government" described in the business press should welcome Eastern Europe's "market reforms," but for US elites they have a further significance. Like independent social and economic development in the third world, Western Europe's social-market system could be a "virus that might infect others," hence a form of "successful defiance" that must be dispatched to oblivion. The European welfare state systems could have a dangerous impact on American public opinion, as revealed by the continued popularity in the US of a universal tax-based health care system, despite constant denigration in the media and the exclusion of the option from the electoral agenda on grounds that it is "politically impossible" no matter what the public may think about it.

The "realities of modern capitalism" illustrated in the regions long subject to Western control have been brought to much of Eastern Europe as its economies have been "Latin-Americanized." The reasons are debated, but the essential facts of the social and economic collapse are not.

The principles remain in force despite changing circumstances. Quite apart from their potential contributions to undermining the social-market systems of Western Europe, Eastern European countries are expected to be a "Trojan horse" for US interests, undermining any drift toward an independent role in the world.

By 1973, US global dominance had declined from its post–World War II peak. One measure is US control of the world's wealth, which is estimated to have shrunk from roughly 50 percent to half of that as the world economy moved to a "tripolar" order, with three major power centers: North America, Europe, and Japan-based Asia. These structures have since been modified further, particularly with the rise of the East Asian "tigers" and the entry of China into the global system as a major player. The basic concerns about the prospect of an independent Europe extend to Asia as well, in new ways.

Long before World War II, the US was by far the greatest economic power in the world but not a leading actor in global management. The war changed that. Rival powers were either devastated or severely weakened, while the US gained enormously. Industrial production almost quadrupled under the semi-command economy. By 1945 the US had not only over-whelming economic dominance but also a position of incomparable security: it controlled the hemisphere, the surrounding oceans, and most of the territory bordering them. US planners moved quickly to organize the global system, following plans that had already been developed to satisfy the "requirement[s] of the United States in a world in which it proposed to hold unquestioned power" while limiting the sovereignty of those who might pose a challenge.[4]

The new global order was to be subordinated to the needs of the US economy and subject to US political control as much as possible. Imperial controls, especially the British, were to be dismantled while Washington extended its own regional systems in Latin America and the Pacific on the principle, explained by Abe Fortas, that "what was good for us was good for the world." This altruistic concern was not appreciated by the British Foreign Office. Officials recognized that Washington, guided by "the eco-nomic imperialism of American business interests, [is] attempting to elbow us out," but could do little about it. The minister of state at the Foreign Office commented to his cabinet colleagues that Americans believe "that the United States stands for something in the world—something of which the world has need, something which the world is going to like, something, in the final analysis, which the world is going to take, whether it likes it or not."[5] He was articulating the real-world version of Wilsonian idealism, the version that conforms to the historical record.

US planning at the time was sophisticated and thorough. The highest priority was to reconstruct the industrial world along lines that would sat-isfy the requirements of the business interests that dominate policy forma-tion: in particular, to absorb US manufacturing surpluses, overcome the "dollar gap," and offer opportunities for investment. The outcomes were appreciated by the domestic beneficiaries. Reagan's Commerce Department observed that the Marshall Plan "set the stage for large amounts of private U.S. direct investment in Europe," laying the groundwork for multina-tional corporations (MNCs). *Business Week* described MNCs in 1975 as "the economic expression" of the "political framework" established by postwar policymakers in which "American business prospered and expanded on overseas orders ... fueled initially by the dollars of the Marshall Plan" and protected from "negative developments" by "the umbrella of American power."[6]

Other parts of the world were assigned their "functions" by State Department planners. Thus Southeast Asia was to provide resources and raw materials to the former imperial masters, crucially Britain but also Japan, which was to be granted "some sort of empire toward the south," in the phrase of George Kennan, head of the State Department's Policy Planning Staff.[7] Some areas were of little interest to the planners, notably Africa, which Kennan advised should be handed over to Europeans to "exploit" for their reconstruction. A different postwar Europe-Africa relationship comes to mind in the light of history but does not seem to have been considered.

The Middle East, in contrast, was to be taken over by the United States. In 1945, State Department officials described Saudi Arabian energy resources as "a stupendous source of strategic power, and one of the greatest material prizes in world history"; the Gulf region generally was considered "probably the richest economic prize in the field of foreign investment." Eisenhower later described it as the "most strategically important area of the world." Britain agreed. Its planners described the resources of the region in 1947 as "a vital prize for any power interested in world influence or domination."[8] France was expelled from the Middle East by legalistic maneuvers, and Britain declined over time to junior partner.

Kennan, who was farsighted, recognized that by controlling Japan's supplies of energy, primarily in the Middle East at the time, the US would achieve some "veto power" over Japan's potential military and industrial policy, though Japanese prospects were generally disparaged at the time. The issue has been the source of continued conflict since, with regard to Europe as well, as both Europe and Japan have sought a degree of energy independence.

Meanwhile Asia was changing. A prestigious task force, reporting in 2003, described Northeast Asia as "the epicenter of international commerce and technological innovation. . . . the fastest-growing economic region in the world for much of the past two decades," by now accounting "for nearly 30 percent of global GDP, far ahead of the United States," and also holding about half of global foreign exchange reserves. These economies also "account for nearly half of global inbound foreign direct investment" and are becoming an increasing source of outbound FDI, flowing within East Asia and to Europe and North America, which now trade more with Northeast Asia than with each other.[9]

The region is, furthermore, an integrated one. Eastern Russia is rich in natural resources, for which the industrial centers of Northeast Asia are the natural market. Integration would be enhanced by economic unification of the two Koreas with gas pipelines passing through North Korea and extension of the trans-Siberian railroad on the same course.

In 1998 the National Bureau of Asian Research warned that "pipelines that promote greater regional integration in Northeast Asia might exclude U.S. involvement except in a marginal way" and could accelerate a process of evolution "into regional blocs."[10] These pipelines "could enhance regional stability and provide a cheap alternative to oil imported from the Middle East," Selig Harrison adds, but "the United States seems uneasily wary of pipeline networks in Northeast Asia." The US is aware that the countries of the region "want to reduce what they find to be an increasingly uncomfortable reliance on the US"; or from another point of view, the "veto power" the US exercises by virtue of its control of Middle East oil and the sea-lanes for tanker traffic. The threat of potential independence may prove an impediment to diplomatic settlement. For partially related reasons, China is regarded as a prime potential enemy by Washington hawks, and much military planning is geared to that contingency. Recent efforts to strengthen India-US strategic relations are partly motivated by the same concerns, along with Washington's concerns about its control over the world's largest energy reserves in the Middle East.

In the early postwar years, US planners sought to fashion East and Southeast Asia into a Japan-centered system within the "overall framework of order" maintained by the US. The basic framework was outlined in the San Francisco Peace Treaty (SFPT) of 1951, which formally ended the war in Asia.[11] Apart from the three French colonies in Indochina, the only Asian countries that accepted the SFPT were Pakistan and Ceylon, both recently freed from British rule and remote from the Asian war. India refused to attend the San Francisco conference because of the terms of the treaty, among them the US insistence on retaining Okinawa as a military base, as it still does, over strong protests from Okinawans, whose voices barely register in the US.

Truman was outraged by India's disobedience. His reaction, no less elegant than the current reaction to the disobedience of Old Europe and Turkey, was that India must have "consulted Uncle Joe and Mousie Dung of China." The white man got a name, not just a vulgar epithet. Partly that may be ordinary racism, or perhaps it is because Truman genuinely liked and admired "Old Joe," who reminded him of the Missouri boss who had launched his political career. In the late 1940s, Truman found Old Joe to be a "decent fellow," though "a prisoner of the Politburo" who "can't do what he wants to." Mousie Dung, however, was a yellow devil.

These distinctions extended wartime propaganda. Nazis were evil but merited a certain respect: in the stereotype, at least, they were blond, blue-eyed, orderly, far more appealing than the Frogs, whom Truman particularly disliked, not to speak of the Wops. And they were a wholly different species from the Japs, who were vermin to be crushed, at least once they became enemies; before that, the US was ambivalent about Japanese depredations in Asia, as long as US business interests were protected.

The primary victims of Japanese fascism and its predecessors—China and the Japanese colonies of Korea and Formosa (Taiwan)—did not attend the San Francisco Peace Conference and were accorded no serious concern. Koreans and Chinese received no reparations from Japan; nor did the Philippines, which also did not attend the conference. Secretary of State Dulles condemned Filipinos for the "emotional prejudices" that kept them from grasping why they would have no relief for the torture they had endured. Initially, Japan was to pay reparations, but only to the US and other colonial powers, despite the fact that the war was a Japanese war of aggression in Asia through the 1930s and only became a US-led Western war with Japan after Pearl Harbor. Japan was also to reimburse the US for the costs of the occupation. For its Asian victims, Japan was to pay "compensation" in the form of export of Japanese manufacturing products using Southeast Asian resources, a central part of the arrangements that, in effect, reconstructed something like the "New Order in Asia" that Japan had attempted to construct by conquest, but was now gaining under US domination, so that it was unproblematic.

The tripolar order that was taking shape form the early 1970s has since become more firm, and with it, the concern of US planners that not only Europe but also Asia might seek a more independent course. From a longer historical perspective, that would not be too surprising. In the eighteenth century, China and India were major commercial and industrial centers. East Asia was far ahead of Europe in public health and probably sophistication of market systems. Life expectancy in Japan may have been higher than in Europe. England was trying to catch up in textiles and other manufactures, borrowing from India in ways that are now called piracy and are banned in the international trade agreements imposed by the rich states under a cynical pretense of "free trade"; the US relied heavily on the same mechanisms, as have other states that have developed. As late as the mid-nineteenth century, British observers claimed that Indian iron was as good as or better than British iron, and much cheaper. Colonization and forced liberalization converted India to a British dependency. It only resumed its growth and ended murderous famines after independence. China was not subjugated until the second British opium war 150 years ago, and also only resumed development after independence. Japan was the only part of Asia to resist colonization successfully, and the only one to develop, along with its colonies. It is not, then, a great surprise that Asia is returning to a position of considerable wealth and power after regaining sovereignty.

These long-term historical processes, however, extend the problems of sustaining the "overall framework of order" in which others must respect their proper place. The problems are not restricted to "successful defiance" in the third world, a major theme of the Cold War years, but reach the industrial heartlands themselves. Violence is a powerful instrument of control, as history demonstrates. But the dilemmas of dominance are not slight.

# Notes

1. David Ignatius, *International Herald Tribune*, 14–15 December 2002, from *Washington Post*.
2. For *Financial Times, Business Week, Wall Street Journal* and other sources, see my *World Orders Old and New*, chapter 2.
3. Arie Farnam, *Christian Science Monitor*, 10 June 2003.
4. See Henry Kissinger, *American Foreign Policy* (expanded edition, Norton, 1974), p. 15.
5. Christopher Thorne, *The Issue of War* (Oxford, 1985), pp. 225, 211. For sources and general context, see my *Deterring Democracy*.
6. Howard Wachtel, *The Money Mandarins* (M. E. Sharpe, 1990), pp. 44ff. *Business Week*, 7 April 1975.
7. Melvyn Leffler, *Preponderance of Power*, p. 339.
8. Britain, see Mark Curtis, *Web of Deceit*, pp. 15–16. For the others, see Aaron David Miller, *Search for Security* (North Carolina, 1980); Irvine Anderson, *Aramco, the United States and Saudi Arabia* (Princeton, 1981); and Michael Stoff, *Oil, War, and American Security* (Yale, 1980). Eisenhower cited in Steven Spiegel, *The Other Arab-Israeli Conflict* (Chicago, 1985, p. 51.
9. Task Force on US-Korea Policy (Center for International Policy, Washington, and Center for East Asian Studies, Chicago), "The Nuclear Crisis on the Korean Peninsula: Avoiding the Road to Perdition"; abridged version, *Current History*, April 2003.
10. Cited by Selig Harrison, *World Policy Journal*, winter 2002–03.
11. What follows concerning the San Francisco Peace Treaty is drawn from John Price, Working Paper No. 78, Japan Policy Research Institute, June 2001.

# PART 11

# Making Foreign Policy: Individuals, Institutions, Politics

The theoretical foundations of U.S. foreign policy addressed in Part I offer a way to explain the actions taken by the United States around the world. They offer, however, only a partial explanation. There are additional elements to consider, namely, the individuals and institutions that formulate and implement policy, as well as the politics of how different participants in the process interact with one another. Examining the question of who influences, develops, and carries out foreign policy is of great importance in understanding how and why the United States behaves as it does in the international system. Part II examines these aspects of American foreign policy, offering selections that address the role of the executive branch and Congress, as well as the roles of the press, interest groups, and the public in influencing policy.

The roles and functions of different actors in the policymaking process have changed somewhat over time; their roles have evolved. People may have long ago described Washington, DC, as a rather sleepy town, but the growth of American power, global interests, and responsibilities has produced a big government with significant powers. One of the impacts of this change has been a more powerful presidency. Louis Fisher argues that one of the biggest changes since the end of World War II has been the growing power of the president in foreign policy, especially with regard to committing the nation to war. While Fisher suggests that Congress has essentially abdicated its responsibility, James Lindsay offers an additional consideration. He argues that the presidency is indeed strong in foreign affairs, but not consistently. It depends upon the political dynamic between Congress and the president. The president usually gets his way in time of danger (or perceived danger), but in times of peace, where threats do not seem to loom over the country, Congress tends to more actively assert its power and pre-rogatives, challenging the president on a variety of fronts. Howard Wiarda, in looking at bureaucratic politics, takes a different tack. While the president and Congress formulate policy, bureaucratic agencies actually implement it. The ever-growing size of the executive branch, as well as the great myriad of interests sought by different agencies, has produced a situation in which the U.S. government is often at odds with itself, resulting in problems of how to effectively carry out American policy.

Outside of government institutions, there are significant influences on the policymaking process. Interest groups lobby for their preferred policies, the public at times weighs in on important matters, the press continually communicates the policy process while also framing an understanding of it, and others— from think tanks to foreign governments—all try to impact the politics and the policy of foreign relations. The selections here address some of these multiple influences, while also considering their impacts over time. The role of the press has certainly changed and expanded, and it continues to do so. Warren Strobel, in looking at 24-hour cable news, finds that this is true, but he is careful to note that not everything has changed. The press should not be credited with too much power, in spite of its seeming omnipresence. The influence of ethnic groups, by contrast, seems to wax and wane. Moreover, according to Tony Smith, through different stages in their history, ethnic lobbies have significantly impacted American policy, sometimes to the detriment of broader national interests. And, of course, since the war in Vietnam, the public has become increasingly skeptical of the use of force, limiting the government's power to intervene in faraway lands—a skepticism that is quite evident with regard to the current war in Iraq.

# 7 Presidential Wars
## LOUIS FISHER

There are a number of actors who participate in the formulation and implementation of U.S. foreign policy, and their respective roles are considered in this section on the policymaking process. Chief among these participants is the president. Although the Constitution of the United States specifies very few foreign policy responsibilities for the president—serve as commander-in-chief, make treaties, appoint ambassadors—in practice his role is larger than anyone else's. The president makes the major decisions on foreign policy strategy, decides what issues will be most important, and exercises day-to-day responsibilities for managing the formulation and implementation of American policies.

The president also acts as the primary decision maker when it comes to using American armed forces around the world. The president is commander-in-chief, but it is Congress that has the power to declare war. This division of responsibilities often creates conflict between the two branches of government, as presidents sometimes commit American troops to engage in hostilities around the globe without congressional approval. Louis Fisher argues that this tendency in American politics has been on the increase since the beginning of the Cold War, and it continues to the present. He states that "presidents over the past half century have felt increasingly comfortable in acting unilaterally when using military force against other countries." In Korea, twice in Iraq, in Bosnia, Kosovo, and Haiti, U.S. presidents have circumvented Congress in a variety of ways. Fisher argues that the exercise of strong presidential powers in making war is a violation of the Constitution that is inconsistent with the framers' intentions. But he also suggests that the problem is not only one of presidents stretching their powers to be more and more expansive. Congress also bears responsibility for this state of affairs. It has essentially abdicated its roles and its responsibilities for foreign affairs, effectively conceding them to the president. Until Congress reasserts itself to redress the imbalance, unilateral presidential action in war-making will continue to be the norm in the United States.

Louis Fisher, from "Presidential Wars" in Wittkopf and McCormick eds., *The Domestic Sources of American Foreign Policy*, 4th ed., Rowman & Littlefield Publishers, 2004. Reprinted by permission of Rowman & Littlefield Publishing Group.

From 1789 to 1950, all major military initiatives by the United States were decided by Congress, either by a formal declaration of war or by a statute authorizing the president to use military force. There were some notable exceptions, such as the actions by President James Polk that led to hostilities between the United States and Mexico. Presidents also used military force for various "life and property" actions, but they were typically limited, short-term engagements. By and large, the first century and a half followed the framers' expectations that matters of war and peace would be vested in the government's representative branch—Congress.

The record since 1950 has been dramatically different. Presidents over the past half century have felt increasingly comfortable in acting unilaterally when using military force against other countries. Instead of coming to Congress for authority, they justify military actions either on the commander in chief clause in the Constitution or on decisions reached by the UN Security Council and NATO. Even with these departures, however, only two major U.S. wars have been entered into without a congressional declaration or authorization of war—Korea in 1950 and Yugoslavia in 1999.

## CONSTITUTIONAL PRINCIPLES

When the American Constitution was drafted in 1787, the framers were aware that existing models of government placed the war power and foreign affairs solely in the hands of the king. Thus, matters of treaties, appointment of ambassadors, the raising and regulation of fleets and armies, and the initiation of military actions against other countries had been vested in the king. Accordingly, John Locke and William Blackstone, whose writings deeply influenced the framers, assigned war powers and foreign affairs exclusively to the executive branch.

This monarchical model was expressly rejected at the Philadelphia convention. As revealed in the historical records of the Constitutional Convention,[1] Charles Pinckney said he was for "a vigorous Executive but was afraid the Executive powers of [the existing] Congress might extend to peace & war &c which would render the Executive a Monarchy, of the worst kind, to wit an elective one." Although John Rutledge wanted the executive power placed in a single person, "he was not for giving him the power of war and peace." James Wilson supported a single executive but "did not consider the Prerogative of the British Monarch as a proper guide in defining the Executive powers. Some of these prerogatives were of a Legislative nature. Among others that of war & peace &c." Edmund Randolph worried about executive power, calling it "the foetus of monarchy."

The framers recognized that the president would need unilateral power in one area: defensive actions to repel sudden attacks when Congress was not in session to legislate. The early draft of the Constitution empowered Congress to "make war." Charles Pinckney objected that legislative proceedings "were too slow" for the safety of the country in an emergency, since he expected Congress to meet but once a year. James Madison and Elbridge Gerry moved to insert "declare" for "make," leaving to the president "the power to repel sudden attacks."

In making the president the commander in chief, Congress retained for Congress the important check over spending. Madison set forth this tenet: "Those who are to *conduct a war* cannot in the nature of things, be proper or safe judges, whether *a war ought* to be *commenced, continued*, or *concluded*. They are barred from the latter functions by a great principle in free government, analogous to that which separates the sword from the purse, or the power of executing from the power of enacting laws." At the Philadelphia convention, George Mason counseled that the "purse & the sword ought never to get into the same hands (whether Legislative or Executive)."

Throughout the next century and a half, major military actions were either declared by Congress (the War of 1812, the Mexican War of 1846, the Spanish-American War of 1898, World War I, and World War II) or authorized by Congress (the Quasi-War against France from 1798 to 1800 and the Barbary Wars during the administrations of Thomas Jefferson and James Madison). In either case, presidents came to Congress for authority to take part in offensive actions.

The record since 1950 has been fundamentally different. In that year President Harry Truman sent American troops to Korea, without ever coming to Congress for authority. He based his actions in part on resolutions adopted by the UN Security Council, but nothing in the history of the UN Charter implies that Congress ever contemplated placing in the hands of the president the unilateral power to wage war. Truman's initiative became a model for President George H. W. Bush in going to war against Iraq in 1991 and President Bill Clinton in threatening to invade Haiti in 1994. In addition, Clinton cited NATO as authority for air strikes in Bosnia and sending ground troops to that region. In 1999, he relied on NATO to wage war against Yugoslavia. But the legislative histories of the UN and NATO show no intent on the part of Congress to sanction independent presidential war power.

## THE UNITED NATIONS AND NATO

In 1945, during Senate debate on the UN Charter, President Truman sent a cable from Potsdam stating that all agreements involving U.S. troop commitments to the United Nations would first have to be approved by both houses of Congress. He pledged without equivocation: "When any such agreement or agreements are negotiated it will be my purpose to ask the Congress for appropriate legislation to approve them."[2] By "agreements" he meant the procedures that would permit UN military force in dealing with threats to peace, breaches of the peace, and acts of aggression. All UN members would make available to the Security Council, "on its call and in accordance with a special agreement or agreements," armed forces and other assistance for the purpose of maintaining international peace and security.

The UN Charter provided that these agreements, concluded between the Security Council and member states, "shall be subject to ratification by the signatory states in accordance with their respective constitutional processes." Each nation would have to adopt its own procedures for meeting their international obligations.

After the Senate approved the UN Charter, Congress had to decide the meaning of "constitutional processes." What procedure was necessary, under the U.S. Constitution, to bring into effect the special agreements needed to contribute American troops to UN military actions? That issue was decided by the UN Participation Act of 1945, which stated without the slightest ambiguity that the agreements "shall be subject to the approval of the Congress by appropriate Act or joint resolution." The agreements between the United States and the Security Council would not result from unilateral executive action, nor would they be brought into force only by the Senate acting through the treaty process. Action by both houses of Congress would be required.

At every step in the legislative history of the UN Participation Act— hearings, committee reports, and floor debate—these elementary points were underscored and reinforced. Executive officials repeatedly assured members of Congress that the president could not commit troops to UN military actions unless Congress first approved.

During this time the Senate also approved the NATO treaty of 1949, which provides that an armed attack against one or more of the parties in Europe or North America "shall be considered an attack against them all." In the event of an attack, member states could exercise the right of individual or collective self-defense recognized by Article 51 of the UN Charter and assist the country or countries attacked by taking "such action as it deems necessary, including the use of armed force." However, Article 11 of the treaty states that it shall be ratified "and its provisions carried out by the Parties in accordance with their respective constitutional processes." The Southeast Asia Treaty (SEATO) of 1954 also stated that the treaty "shall be ratified and its provisions carried out by the Parties in accordance with their respective constitutional processes."

Do these treaties grant the president unilateral power to use military force against other nations? First, it is well recognized that the concept in mutual security treaties of an attack on one nation being an attack on all does not require from any nation an immediate response. Each country maintains the sovereign right to decide such matters by itself. As noted in the Rio Treaty of 1947, "no State shall be required to use armed force without its consent." In the U.S. system, who decides to use armed force?

During hearings in 1949 on NATO, Secretary of State Dean Acheson told the Senate Foreign Relations Committee that it "does not mean that the United States would automatically be at war if one of the other signatory nations were the victim of an armed attack. Under our Constitution, the Congress alone has the power to declare war." Of course he was merely saying what is expressly provided for in the Constitution. However, nothing in the legislative history of NATO gives the president any type of unilateral authority in the event of an attack. That the president lacks unilateral powers under the UN Charter or NATO should be obvious from the fact that both are international treaties entered into by way of a presidential proposal and Senate advice and consent. The president and the Senate cannot use the treaty process to strip the House of Representatives of its prerogatives over the use of military force.

In the words of one scholar, the provisions in the NATO treaty that it be carried out according to constitutional processes was "intended to ensure that the Executive Branch of the Government should come back to the Congress when decisions were required in which the Congress has a constitutional responsibility." The NATO treaty "does not transfer to the President the Congressional power to make war."[3] Those predictions would be eroded by practices during the Clinton administration.

## TRUMAN IN KOREA

With these treaty and statutory safeguards supposedly in place to protect legislative prerogatives, President Truman nonetheless sent U.S. troops to Korea in 1950 without ever seeking or obtaining congressional authority. How could this happen? How could so many explicit executive assurances to Congress be ignored and circumvented?

On June 26, Truman announced that the UN Security Council had ordered North Korea to withdraw its invading forces to positions north of the thirty-eighth parallel and that "in accordance with the resolution of the Security Council, the United States will vigorously support the effort of the Council to terminate this serious breach of the peace." The next day he ordered U.S. air and sea forces to provide military support to South Korea. It was not until the evening of June 27 that the Security Council actually called for military action. In his memoirs, *Present at the Creation*, Dean Acheson admitted that "some American action, said to be in support of the resolution of June 27, was in fact ordered, and possibly taken, prior to the resolution."

Truman violated the statutory language and legislative history of the UN Participation Act, including his own assurance from Potsdam that he would first obtain the approval of Congress before sending U.S. forces to a UN action. How was this possible? He simply ignored the special agreements that were supposed to be the guarantee of congressional control. Indeed, no state has ever entered into a special agreement with the Security Council—and none is ever likely to do so.

Truman exploited the UN machinery in part because of a fluke: the Soviet Union had absented itself from the Security Council during two crucial votes taken during the early days of the crisis. It is difficult to argue that the president's constitutional powers vary with the presence or absence of Soviet (or other) delegates to the Security Council. As Robert Bork noted in 1971, "the approval of the United Nations was obtained only because the Soviet Union happened to be boycotting the Security Council at the time, and the president's Constitutional powers can hardly be said to ebb and flow with the veto of the Soviet Union in the Security Council."[4]

Truman tried to justify his actions in Korea by calling it a UN "police action" rather than an American war. That argument was suspect from the start and deteriorated as U.S. casualties mounted. The UN exercised no real authority over the conduct of the war. Other than token support from a few nations, it remained an American war—measured by troops, money, casualties, and deaths—from start to finish. The euphemism "police action" was never persuasive. As a federal court concluded in 1953, "We doubt very much if there is any question in the minds of the majority of the people of this country that the conflict now raging in Korea can be anything but war."[5]

## BUSH IN IRAQ (1990–1991)

Truman's initiative in Korea became a precedent for actions taken in 1990 by President George H. W. Bush. In response to Iraq's invasion of Kuwait on August 2, Bush sent several hundred thousand troops to Saudi Arabia for defensive purposes. Over the next few months, the size of the American force climbed to 500,000, giving Bush the capability for mounting an offensive strike.

Instead of seeking authority from Congress, Bush created a multinational alliance and encouraged the UN Security Council to authorize the use of military force. The strategic calculations have been recorded by James A. Baker III, who served as secretary of state in the Bush administration. In his book *The Politics of Diplomacy*, Baker says he realized that military initiatives by Presidents Reagan in Grenada and Bush in Panama had reinforced in the international community the impression that American foreign policy followed a "cowboy mentality." In response to those concerns, Bush wanted to assemble an international political coalition. Baker notes: "From the very beginning, the president recognized the importance of having the express approval of the international community if at all possible." It is noteworthy that Bush would seek the express approval of other nations but not the express approval of Congress.

On November 20, Bush said he wanted to delay asking Congress for authorization until after the Security Council considered a proposed resolution supporting the use of force against Iraq. About a week later, on November 29, the Security Council authorized member states to use "all necessary means" to force Iraqi troops out of Kuwait. "All necessary means" is code language for military action. To avoid war, Iraq had to withdraw from Kuwait by January 15, 1991. Although the Security Council "authorized" each member state to act militarily against Iraq, the resolution did not compel nor obligate them to participate. Instead, member states were free to use (or refuse) force pursuant to their own constitutional systems and judgments about national interests.

What procedure would the United States follow in deciding to use force? When Secretary of Defense Dick Cheney appeared before the Senate Armed Services Committee on December 3, 1990, he said that President Bush did not require "any additional authorization from the Congress" before attacking Iraq. Through such language he implied that authorization from the UN was sufficient. The UN action, he said, made congressional action not only unnecessary but counterproductive:

> As a general proposition, I can think that the notion of a declaration of war to some extent flies in the face of what we are trying to accomplish here. And what we are trying to accomplish is to marshal an international force, some 26, 27 nations having committed forces to the enterprise, working under the auspices of the United Nations Security Council.

In other words, once presidents assembled an international force and obtained support through a Security Council resolution, Congress had no role except perhaps to pass a resolution indicating its support. According to this position, whether Congress acted or not had no bearing on the president's freedom to move ahead with the multinational force.

The Justice Department argued in court that President Bush could order offensive actions against Iraq without seeking advance authority from Congress. On December 13, 1990, in *Dellums v. Bush*, the court expressly and forcefully rejected the sweeping interpretation of presidential war power advanced by the Justice Department. If the president had the sole power to determine that any offensive military operation, "no matter how vast, does not constitute war-making but only an offensive military attack, the congressional power to declare war will be at the mercy of a semantic decision by the Executive." But, having dismissed the Justice

Department's interpretation, the court then held that the case was not ripe for adjudication.

On January 8, 1991, President Bush asked Congress to pass legislation supporting the UN position. Clearly he was asking for "support," not authority. The next day reporters asked whether he needed authority from Congress. His reply: "I don't think I need it. . . . I feel that I have the authority to fully implement the United Nations resolutions." The legal crisis was avoided on January 12 when Congress authorized offensive actions against Iraq. In signing the bill, Bush indicated that he could have acted without legislation: "As I made clear to congressional leaders at the outset, my request for congressional support did not, and my signing this resolution does not, constitute any change in the longstanding positions of the executive branch on either the president's constitutional authority to use the Armed Forces to defend vital U.S. interests or the constitutionality of the War Powers Resolution." Despite his comments, the bill expressly authorized the action against Iraq. A signed statement does not alter the contents of a public law.

In one of his last addresses as president, Bush used a speech at West Point to explain his theory of presidential war power. Referring to President Washington's warning of the dangers of "entangling alliances," and saying that Washington was correct at that point in history, Bush noted that what was "entangling" in Washington's day "is now essential." Congress had a constitutional role in these involvements, but apparently more to offer support rather than to grant authority. Presidential leadership "involves working with the Congress and the American people to provide the essential domestic underpinning if U.S. military commitments are to be sustainable." "Authority" seems to come only from international organizations. In both Iraq and Somalia, Bush said, U.S. forces were "acting under the full authority of the United Nations."

## INTERVENTION IN BOSNIA

In concert with the United Nations and NATO, the Bush and Clinton administrations participated in humanitarian airlifts in Sarajevo and helped enforce a "no-fly zone" (a ban on unauthorized flights over Bosnia-Herzegovina). In 1993 Clinton indicated that he would have to seek support and authorization from Congress before ordering air strikes. On May 7 he stated: "If I decide to ask the American people and the United States Congress to support an approach that would include the use of air power, I would have a very specific, clearly defined strategy." He anticipated asking "for the authority to use air power from the Congress and the American people."

Later in the year he began to object to legislative efforts to restrict his military options. Instead of seeking authority from Congress, Clinton now said he would seek from Congress advice and support. He was "funda-mentally opposed" to any statutory provisions that "improperly limit my ability to perform my constitutional duties as Commander-in-Chief." He would operate through NATO, even though NATO had never used mili-tary force during its almost half-century of existence.

In 1994, Clinton announced that decisions to use air power would be taken in response to UN Security Council resolutions, operating through NATO's military command. There was no more talk about seeking author-ity from Congress. Curiously, by operating through NATO, Clinton would seek the agreement of England, France, Italy, and other NATO allies, but not Congress. NATO air strikes began in February 1994 and were followed by additional strikes throughout the year and into the next. The authoriz-ing body was a multinational organization, not Congress.

The next escalation of U.S. military action was Clinton's decision to introduce ground troops into Bosnia. When reporters asked him on October 19, 1995, if he would send the troops even if Congress did not approve, he replied: "I am not going to lay down any of my constitutional prerogatives here today." On the basis of what he considered sufficient authority under Article II of the Constitution and under NATO, he ordered the deployment of twenty thousand American ground troops to Bosnia without obtaining authority or support from Congress. In an address on November 27, 1995, he said that deployment of U.S. ground troops to Bosnia was "the right thing to do," paralleling his justification for invading Haiti. It was the right thing, even if not the legal thing.

On December 21, Clinton expected that the military mission to Bosnia "can be accomplished in about a year." A year later, on December 17, 1996, he extended the troop deployment for another eighteen months. At the end of 1997 he announced that the deployment for another eighteen months. At the end of 1997 he announced that the deployment would have to be extended again, but this time without attempting to fix a deadline. In 2003, U.S. troops were still in Bosnia.

## THE WAR IN YUGOSLAVIA

In October 1998, the Clinton administration was again threatening the Serbs with air strikes, this time because of Serb attacks on the ethnic Albania majority in Kosovo. At a news conference on October 8, Clinton stated: "Yesterday I decided that the United States would vote to give NATO the authority to carry out military strikes against Serbia if President Milosevic continues to defy the international community." An interesting sentence—"*I* decided that the United States . . ." Whatever Clinton decided would be America's policy.

Clinton's chief foreign policy advisers went to Capitol Hill to consult with lawmakers, but not to obtain their approval. Although Congress was to be given no formal role in the use of force against Serbs, legislatures in other NATO countries took votes to authorize military action in Yugoslavia. The Italian Parliament had to vote approval for the NATO strikes, and the German Supreme Court ruled that the Bundestag, which had been dissolved with the election that ousted Chancellor Kohl, had to be recalled to approve deployment of German aircraft and troops to Kosovo.

With air strikes imminent in March 1999, the Senate voted fifty-eight to forty-one in support of military air operations and missile strikes against Serbia. On April 28, after the first month of bombing, the House took a series of votes on war in Yugoslavia. A vote to authorize the air operations and missiles strikes lost on a tie vote, 213 to 213. Several resolutions were offered in the Senate, to either authorize or restrict the war, but they were tabled. The Senate chose procedural remedies rather than voting on the merits.

During the bombing of Serbia and Kosovo, Representative Tom Campbell (R-Cal.) went to court with twenty-five other House colleagues to seek a declaration that President Clinton had violated the Constitution and the War Powers Resolution by conducting the air offensive without congressional authorization. A district judge held that Campbell did not have standing to raise his claims. Although each House had taken a number of votes, Congress had never as an entire institution ordered Clinton to cease military operations. In that sense, there was no "constitutional impasse" or "actual confrontation" for the court to resolve.[6]

## THE IRAQ RESOLUTION IN 2002

When the Bush administration first began talking about war against Iraq in 2002, the White House cautioned that President George W. Bush was carefully studying a number of options. On August 21, stating that "we will look at all options," he said the country was too preoccupied with military action against Iraq. Yet five days later Vice President Dick Cheney delivered a forceful speech that implied that only one option existed: going to war. He warned that Saddam Hussein would "fairly soon" have nuclear weapons and that it would be useless to seek a Security Council resolution requiring Iraq to submit to weapons inspectors. Newspaper editorials concluded that Cheney's speech left little room for measures short of destroying Hussein's regime through preemptive military action. What happened to the options carefully being weighed by Bush?

The meaning of "regime change" shifted with time. On April 4, 2002, Bush said that he had made up his mind "that Saddam needs to go. . . . The policy of my Government is that he goes." Yet when Bush addressed the United Nations on September 12, he laid down five conditions (including inspections) that could lead to a peaceful settlement. If Hussein complied with those demands, he could stay in power.

What had happened to the policy of regime change?

After the September 12 speech, Iraq agreed four days later to unconditional inspections. At that point, the administration began to belittle the importance of inspections. If they were of little use, why have Bush go to the UN and place that demand on Iraq and the Security Council?

Initially, the White House concluded that Bush did not need authority from Congress. However, for one reason or another, Bush decided in early September to seek authorization from Congress. There was pressure on lawmakers to complete action on the authorizing resolution before they adjourned for the elections, inviting partisan exploitation of the war issue. Several Republican nominees in congressional contests made a political weapon out of Iraq, comparing their "strong stand" on Iraq to "weak" positions by Democratic campaigners.

There was little doubt that Bush would gain House support. The question was whether the vote would divide along party lines. The partisan issue blurred when House Minority Leader Dick Gephardt (D-Mo.) broke ranks with many in his party and announced support for a slightly redrafted resolution. He said: "We had to go through this, putting politics aside, so we have a chance to get a consensus that will lead the country in the right direction." Of course, politics could not be put aside. The vote on the resolution was inescapably and legitimately a political decision. Lawmakers would be voting on whether to commit as much as $100 billion or $200 billion to the war, stretching over a period of years. Their actions would stabilize or destabilize the Middle East, strengthen or weaken the war against terrorism, enhance or debase the nation's prestige.

Why were Democrats so worried about being labeled "antiwar"? There was no evidence that the public, in any broad sense, supported war against Iraq. A *New York Times* poll published on October 7 indicated that 69 percent of Americans believed that Bush should be paying more attention to the economy. On the question "Should the U.S. take military action against Iraq fairly soon or wait and give the U.N. more time to get weapons inspectors into Iraq?," 63 percent wanted to wait. A *Washington Post* story on October 8 noted that the public's enthusiasm for war against Iraq "is tepid and declining."

On October 10, the House passed the Iraq resolution, 296-133. That evening, the Senate voted seventy-seven to twenty-three for the resolution. It would have been better for Congress as an institution, and for the country as a whole, to have Bush request the Security Council to authorize inspections in Iraq, and then to come to Congress after the elections (as was done in 1990–1991). Congress would have been in the position at that point to make an informed choice. It chose, instead, to vote under partisan pressures, with inadequate information, and thereby abdicated its constitutional duties to the president. In passing the resolution, lawmakers decided only that President Bush should decide. After the Security Council voted on November 8 that Iraq must allow inspectors into the country, the judgment on whether war would be necessary was in the hands of Bush, not Congress.

## A FAILURE OF CHECKS AND BALANCES

The framers of the Constitution assumed that each branch of the government would protect its own prerogatives. Efforts by one branch to encroach upon another would be beaten back. As Madison explained in *Federalist* No. 51: "the great security against a gradual concentration of the several powers in the same department, consists in giving to those who administer each department the necessary constitutional means and personal motives to resist encroachments of the others. . . . Ambition must be made to counter ambition." To some extent, this theory has worked well. The president and the judiciary invoke a multitude of powers to protect their institutions.

Congress, on the other hand, not only fails to fight back but even volunteers in surrendering fundamental legislative powers, including the war power and the power of the purse. Members of Congress seem uncertain about the scope of their constitutional powers. Some claim that Congress can limit funds for presidential actions that were taken in the past but never for future actions. There is no constitutional support for that position. The decision to use military force against other nations is reserved to Congress, other than for defensive actions. Members may restrict a president's actions prospectively as well as retrospectively.

Some legislators suggest that a cutoff of funds would leave American soldiers stranded and without ammunition. During debate in 1995 on prohibiting funds from being used for the deployment of ground forces to Bosnia and Herzegovina, Congressman Porter Goss said: "I cannot support a complete withdrawal of funds and support for the United States troops who are already on the ground in the former Yugoslavia. These men and women are wearing the uniform of the U.S. military and obeying orders, and we cannot leave them stranded in hostile territory." Congressman George Gekas added: "I cannot vote under any circumstances to abandon our troops. Not to fund them? Unheard of. I cannot support that. Not to supply them with foods, material, ammunition, all the weapons that they require to do their mission?"[7] Cutting off funds would not have that effect. A funding prohibition would force the withdrawal of whatever troops were in place and prevent the deployment of any other troops to that region.

Theories of presidential war power that would have been shocking fifty years ago are now offered as though they were obvious and free of controversy. Instead of the two branches working in concert to create a program that has broad public support and understanding, with some hope of continuity, presidents take unilateral steps to engage the country in military operations abroad. They typically justify their actions not only on broad interpretations of the Constitution but cite "authority" granted by multinational institutions in which the United States is but one of many state actors. This pattern does not merely weaken Congress and the power of the purse. It undermines public control, the system of checks and balances, and constitutional government.

## Notes

1. See Max Farrand, ed., *The Records of the Federal Convention of 1787* (New Haven, Conn.: Yale University Press, 1937), especially vol. 1, 64–66, and vol. 2, 318–19.
2. 91 *Cong. Rec.* 8185 (1945).
3. Richard H. Heindel et al., "The North Atlantic Treaty in the United States Senate," *American Journal of International Law* 43: 649, 650 (1949).
4. Robert H. Bork, "Comments on the Articles on the Legality of the United States Action in Cambodia," *American Journal of International Law* 65: 81 (1971).
5. *Weissman v. Metropolitan Life Ins. Co.*, 112 F. Supp. 420, 425 (S.D. Cal. 1953).
6. *Campbell v. Clinton*, 52 F.Supp.2d 34 (D.D.C. 1999), aff'd, *Campbell v. Clinton*, 203 F.3d 19 (D.C. 2000).
7. 141 *Cong. Rec.* H14820, H14822 (daily ed. December 13, 1995).

# 8   Deference and Defiance: The Shifting Rhythms of Executive-Legislative Relations in Foreign Policy

## JAMES M. LINDSAY

Congress is an important contributor in the development of U.S. foreign policy, with the Constitution specifying several roles the Congress is to carry out—declare war, approve treaties and ambassadors, and establish an army and navy, among others. In spite of constitutional language, however, Congress and the president continually jockey over the exercise of power in making foreign policy, and the relationship is constantly shifting. James Lindsay points out that

James Lindsay, from "Deference and Defiance: The Shifting Rhythms of Executive-Legislative Relations in Foreign Policy," *Presidential Studies Quarterly*, 33, No. 3, Sept. 2005. Reprinted by permission of Blackwell Publishing Ltd.

there is an ebb and flow in congressional assertiveness in foreign policy. There are times, such as after the Vietnam War and after the Cold War, when Congress was quite assertive in making foreign policy and limiting the freedom of action of the president. In other instances Congress is, by contrast, quite deferential to the president, willing to give him a great deal of freedom in making and carrying out policy.

Lindsay argues that these "shifting rhythms" are due to the political circumstances of a given administration or period in American history. He suggests that the degree to which Congress exercises its constitutional authorities is determined primarily by two questions. The first of these involves whether the country is threatened or secure. Times of international crisis and danger to American security produce very different congressional actions than do times of relative peace and security. Secondly, the question of whether or not the president's policies are succeeding or failing results in different responses from Congress. To put it simply, Lindsay states, "Times of peace and presidential missteps favor Congressional defiance. Times of war and presidential success favor Congressional deference." This is a pattern that has been repeated throughout American history, and as Lindsay argues it has been especially in evidence since the attacks on September 11.

---

The presidencies of Bill Clinton and George W. Bush contrast in many ways, perhaps no more so than in their divergent experiences in dealing with Congress on foreign policy. Clinton confronted a Congress that frequently sought to defy his initiatives and at times seemed to take glee in doing so. His list of defeats on Capitol Hill is long. Congress forced him to withdraw U.S. troops from Somalia in 1994. It slashed his foreign aid requests. It refused to grant him fast-track trade negotiating authority. It forced him to accept national missile defense and regime change in Iraq as goals of U.S. foreign policy even though he and many of his advisers doubted the wisdom and practicality of both. It blocked his efforts to pay U.S. back dues to the United Nations. The Senate rejected the Comprehensive Test Ban Treaty. Even when Congress backed Clinton on foreign policy, as with the dispatch of U.S. peacekeepers to Bosnia and the Senate's approval of the Chemical Weapons Convention and NATO enlargement, the victories seemed to require inordinate administration effort.

Bush's experience has been far different. Congress was eager to defer to his leadership on many foreign policy issues. It overwhelmingly authorized him to wage not one but two wars. It acceded to his decisions to leave the 1972 Anti-Ballistic Missile (ABM) Treaty and move to develop an expansive new national missile defense. It gave him most everything he requested for defense and foreign affairs spending. It embraced his request to begin the largest reorganization of the federal government in more than a century. It gave him the trade-promotion (formerly fast-track) authority it had denied Clinton. Perhaps most significant, he had all Republicans and many Democrats rushing to tell voters that they supported his national security policies.

September 11 explains Congress's shift from defiance of Clinton to deference to Bush. The attacks on the World Trade Center and the Pentagon altered the American political landscape in the United States. Members of Congress who previously took pride in standing up to the White House suddenly saw the better part of good policy and good politics lying in a willingness to rally around the president.

The change that September 11 caused in executive-legislative relations was extreme but not unprecedented. The pendulum of power on foreign policy has shifted back and forth between Congress and the president many times over the course of American history. The reason for this ebb and flow does not lie in the Constitution. Its formal allocation of foreign policy powers, which gives important authorities to both Congress and the president, has not changed since it was drafted. Rather, the answer lies in politics. How aggressively Congress exercises its foreign policy powers turns on the critical questions of whether the country sees itself as threatened or secure and whether the president's policies are succeeding or failing. Simply put, times of peace and presidential missteps favor congressional defiance. Times of war and presidential success favor congressional deference.

## THE CONSTITUTION AND FOREIGN POLICY

Ask most Americans who makes foreign policy in the United States and their immediate answer is: the president. To a point they are right. Still, even a cursory reading of the Constitution makes clear that Congress possesses extensive foreign policy powers. Article 1, Section 8 assigns Congress the power to "provide for the common Defence," "To regulate Commerce with foreign Nations," "To define and punish Piracies and Felonies committed on the high Seas," "To declare War," "To raise and support Armies," "To provide and maintain a Navy," and "To make Rules for the Government and Regulation of the land and naval Forces." Article 2, Section 2 specifies that the Senate must give its advice and consent to all treaties and ambassadorial appointments. Congress's more general powers to appropriate all government funds and to confirm Cabinet officials provide additional means to influence foreign policy.

The lesson here is that when it comes to foreign affairs, Congress and the president *both* can claim ample constitutional authority. The two branches are, in Richard Neustadt's (1990, 29) oft-repeated formulation, "separated institutions *sharing* power." The question of which branch should prevail as a matter of principle when their powers conflict has been disputed ever since Alexander Hamilton and James Madison squared off two centuries ago in their famed Pacificus-Helvidius debate. Hamilton argued that the president was free to exercise his powers as he saw fit even if those actions might "affect the exercise of the power of the legislature. . . . The legislature is still free to perform its duties, according to its own sense of them; though the executive, in the exercise of its constitutional powers, may establish an antecedent state of things, which ought to weigh in the legislative decision" (Smith 1989, 52). Madison denied that there could be such a thing as concurrent authority and insisted that the president could not exercise his authority in ways that would "abridge or affect" the enumerated powers of the legislature (Smith 1989, 56).

At the start of the twenty-first century, Hamilton's and Madison's intellectual descendants continue to spar, and they will undoubtedly continue to do so for years to come. Their battles often unleash the same passion they did two hundred years ago. Yet, these battles are also largely academic, interesting intellectual exercises but seldom applicable to real world policy debates. The fact that the Constitution grants Congress extensive foreign policy powers means that most executive-legislative disputes do not raise constitutional issues. They instead raise political issues and involve the exercise of political power. That is the insight behind Edward Corwin's oft-repeated observation that the Constitution is "an invitation to struggle for the privilege of directing American foreign policy" (Corwin 1957, 171).

To say that Congress can put its mark on foreign policy, however, is not the same as saying that it will try to do so. To understand why congressional activism on foreign policy varies over time, it is necessary to leave the realm of law and enter the realm of politics.

## POLITICS AND FOREIGN POLICY

The first explanation for Congress's fluctuating say in foreign policy lies in an observation that Alexis de Tocqueville made more than 150 years ago. Surprised to find that the pre-Civil War Congress played a major role in foreign policy, he speculated that congressional activism stemmed from the country's isolation from external threat. "If the Union's existence were constantly menaced, and if its great interests were continually interwoven with those of other powerful nations, one would see the prestige of the executive growing, because of what was expected from it and of what it did" (de Tocqueville 1969, 126).

Why might threat perceptions affect how Congress behaves? When Americans believe they face few external threats—or think that international engagement could itself produce a threat—they see less merit in deferring to the White House on foreign policy and more merit to congressional activism. Debate and disagreement are not likely to pose significant costs; after all, the country is secure. When Americans believe the country faces an external threat, however, they quickly convert to the belief that the country needs strong presidential leadership. Congressional dissent that was previously acceptable suddenly looks to be unhelpful meddling at best and unpatriotic at worst. Members of Congress are no different than their constituents. They feel the same shifting sentiments toward the wisdom of deferring to the president. They are also profoundly aware that being on the wrong side of that shift could hurt them come the next election.

Throughout American history, power over foreign policy has flowed back and forth between the two ends of Pennsylvania Avenue according to this basic dynamic. In the second half of the nineteenth century, the United States was as secure from foreign attack as at any time in American history. This was also a time when Congress so dominated foreign policy that it has been called the era of "congressional government," "congressional supremacy," and "government-by-Congress." When the United States entered World War I, the pendulum of power swung to the White House. Woodrow Wilson experienced few congressional challenges during his war presidency. But once the war ended, Congress—and the Senate in particular—reasserted itself. Congressional activism persisted into the 1930s and even intensified. Convinced that America would be safe only as long as it kept out of Europe's political affairs, Congress's isolationist majority bitterly resisted any step President Franklin Roosevelt might take that could involve the United States in the war brewing across the Atlantic.

Japan's bombing of Pearl Harbor punctured the isolationists' arguments and greatly expanded FDR's freedom to conduct foreign policy. He made virtually all of his major wartime decisions without reference to or input from Capitol Hill. When World War II ended, Congress began to reassert itself. Senior members of the House Foreign Affairs and Senate Foreign Relations Committees helped draft the United Nations Charter, the peace treaties for the Axis satellite states, and mutual security pacts such as the NATO Treaty.

But growing concerns about the Soviet Union slowed the shift of power away from the White House. As Americans became convinced in the late 1940s that hostile communist states threatened the United States and the rest of the free world, they increasingly came to agree on two basic ideas: the United States needed to resist communist expansion, and achieving this goal demanded strong presidential leadership. Most members of Congress shared these two basic beliefs (and helped promote them); those who disagreed risked punishment at the polls. The process became self-reinforcing. As more lawmakers stepped to the sidelines on defense and foreign policy over the course of the 1950s, others saw it as increasingly futile, not to mention dangerous politically, to continue to speak out. By 1960, the "imperial presidency," the flip side of a deferential Congress, was in full bloom (Schlesinger 1973). As one senator complained in 1965, members of Congress were responding to even the most far-reaching presidential decisions on foreign affairs by "stumbling over each other to see who can say 'yea' the quickest and loudest" (Sundquist 1981, 125).

The era of congressional deference to the imperial presidency came to a crashing halt with the souring of public opinion on the Vietnam War. Many Americans became convinced that communist revolutions in the third world posed no direct threat to core U.S. security interests, just as détente persuaded many that Leonid Brezhnev's Soviet Union posed less of a threat to core U.S. security interests. With the public more willing to question administration policies, so too were members of Congress. Many more had substantive disagreements with the White House over what constituted America's vital interests and how best to protect and advance them. Moreover, lawmakers had less to fear politically by the early 1970s in challenging the White House than they had only a few years earlier. Indeed, many calculated that challenging the president's foreign policies could actually help them at the ballot box by enabling them to stake out positions that their constituents favored. The result was a predictable surge in congressional activism.

Members of Congress did not always succeed in putting their stamp on foreign policy in the 1970s and 1980s. Knee-jerk support of the president was gone, but elements of congressional deference persisted among senior lawmakers (who had come of age during the era of congressional deference) and moderates (who worried that defeating the president could harm the country's credibility). Presidents from Richard Nixon through the elder George Bush often prevailed on major issues because they could persuade these groups to join them with a simple argument: the administration's policy might have shortcomings, but rejecting the president's request would damage his standing abroad, perhaps embolden Moscow to act more aggressively, and ultimately harm American interests. Yet the mere fact that post-Vietnam presidents had to make this argument showed how much had changed from the days of the imperial presidency. Presidents Ford, Carter, and Reagan did not get the acquiescence from Capitol Hill that Presidents Eisenhower and Kennedy did.

Although perception of the external threat facing the country provides the primary impetus to the shifting pendulum of power along Pennsylvania Avenue, it is not the only one. A second, and interrelated, factor is how well the president's foreign policy initiatives work. Presidents like Ronald Reagan who spend their political capital wisely and can show successes for their efforts can take power back from a Congress accustomed to flexing its muscles. In contrast, presidents who commit major foreign policy blunders, as Reagan did with Iran-Contra and Clinton did in

Somalia, invite congressional challenges to their power. In that respect, John F. Kennedy's (1962, 316–17) observation that "victory has 100 fathers and defeat is an orphan" is an iron law of the politics of foreign policy. In the extreme case where presidential decisions turn into historic debacles, as happened first with Lyndon Johnson and then with Richard Nixon in Vietnam, the result can be to change the very way Americans think about threats to their security and prosperity.

## DEFIANCE REBORN

The end of the Cold War accelerated and exacerbated the trend toward greater congressional defiance that Vietnam had triggered. With the Soviet Union relegated to the ash heap of history, most Americans looked abroad and saw no threat of similar magnitude on the horizon. When asked to name the most important problem facing the United States, polls in the 1990s rarely found that more than 5 percent of Americans named a foreign policy issue. That was a steep drop from the upward of 50 percent who named a foreign policy issue during the height of the Cold War. Moreover, many Americans had trouble identifying *any* foreign policy issue that worried them. One 1998 poll asked people to name "two or three of the biggest foreign-policy problems facing the United States today." The most common response by far, at 21 percent, was "don't know" (Reilly 1999, 111).

These public attitudes meant that members of Congress who challenged the White House on foreign policy ran almost no electoral risks. With the public not caring enough to punish them for any excesses, lawmakers went busily about challenging Bill Clinton's foreign policy. In April 1999, for instance, during the Kosovo war, the House refused to vote to support the bombing. Not to be outdone, the Senate six months later voted down the test ban treaty even though President Clinton and 62 senators had asked that it be withdrawn from consideration. These episodes were major departures from past practice. When members of Congress had squared off against the White House in the latter half of the Cold War on issues such as Vietnam, the MX missile, and aid to the Nicaraguan contras, they had vocal public support. On Kosovo and the test ban, however, few Americans were urging Congress to challenge Clinton. To the extent that they had opinions— and many did not—most Americans sided with the president.

Just as important, the once powerful argument that members of Congress should defer to the White House on key issues lest they harm broader American interests fell on deaf ears. In 1997 the Clinton administration sought to convince Congress to give it "fast-track" negotiating authority for international trade agreements. (With fast-track authority, Congress agrees to approve or reject any trade agreement the president negotiates without amendment. This simplifies trade negotiations because other countries do not have to worry that Congress will rewrite any trade deal.) When it became clear that he lacked the votes needed to prevail, President Clinton escalated the stakes by arguing that fast track was needed because "more than ever, our economic security is also the foundation of our national strategy" (Broder 1997, A1). The decision to recast a trade issue as a national security issue—a tried and true Cold War strategy—changed few minds, however. Recognizing defeat, Clinton asked congressional leaders to withdraw the bill from consideration, marking the first time in decades that a president had failed to persuade Congress to support a major trade initiative.

Besides encouraging members of Congress to flex their foreign policy muscles, the public's diminished interest in foreign affairs after the collapse of the Soviet Union also encouraged them to cater to groups with narrow but intense preferences on foreign policy. It did so for two reasons. First, with most people focused on domestic concerns, interest groups constituted a major source of political profit or loss for politicians who did focus on foreign policy issues. Groups that had something to gain by influencing government policy became squeaky wheels, and they got the grease. Second, with the broad public looking elsewhere, the cost to members of Congress of tending to narrow interests dropped. Voters could not punish behavior they did not see.

The result of both these trends was that foreign policy in the 1990s increasingly became—to paraphrase the famed German military strategist Clausewitz—the continuation of domestic politics by other means. Lawmakers were more interested in how ethnic, business, and single-issue groups might help them win reelection and less whether the programs they championed added up to a coherent foreign policy. As former Rep. Lee H. Hamilton (D-Indiana) put it: "Too many people place constituent interests above national interests. They don't see much difference between lobbying for highway funds and slanting foreign policy toward a particular interest group" (Mufson 2000, A1). U.S. Ambassador Chas W. Freeman, Jr., put the same point somewhat differently, arguing that the 1990s represented "the franchising of foreign policy" to interest groups (Mufson 2000, A1).

A case in point was the House of Representatives' effort in 2000 to pass a non-binding resolution labeling the massacres of Armenians that occurred in the Ottoman Empire from 1915 to 1923 as "genocide." Rep. James Rogan (R-California) sponsored the resolution. He made no claim to be a foreign policy expert—none of his committee assignments dealt with foreign policy and he had traveled outside the United States only once in his life—but he was caught in a tight reelection race. And his congressional district happened to have the highest concentration of Armenian-Americans of any district in the United States. The resolution offered an easy way to build goodwill with constituents by promoting a cause they held dear. The Armenian Assembly of America, which routinely grades how members of Congress vote on issues affecting Armenia, had long lobbied for the resolution.

In another time, Rogan's resolution would have languished in commit-tee. Party leaders would have allowed him to introduce the bill—enabling him to gain political credit with his constituents for "fighting the good fight"—but kept the bill from advancing—thereby protecting the country's broader interests. But in 2000, House Republican leaders, eager to maintain their slim majority in the face of potential Democratic inroads in the upcoming elections, embraced the bill. Speaker of the House Dennis Hastert (R-Illinois) promised Rogan that he would bring the resolution to a vote on the House floor. He personally placed the measure on the House legislative calendar. The House International Relations Committee subse-quently approved it by a large margin.

As Rogan, Hastert, and other House members pushed the genocide resolution forward, they gave little thought to the consequences their sym-bolic gesture would have on broader U.S. interests. The result was escalat-ing tensions with Turkey, a major American ally that among other things let U.S. and British fighter planes use Incirlik Air Base to patrol the skies over northern Iraq. Turkey's president expressed "grave reservations" about the resolution, repeating his country's long-standing insistence that there had been no genocide (Mufson 2000, A1). Suddenly U.S. defense companies faced the possibility that they might lose sales to Turkey, and the Pentagon the possibility that it would lose the right to fly out of Incirlik. After a bar-rage of phone calls from Bill Clinton, other administration officials, and senior military officers warning that the resolution would significantly harm U.S. foreign policy, Hastert agreed to put off a vote on Rogan's bill.

## THE DEFERENTIAL CONGRESS RETURNS

Congress's defiance of Bill Clinton in the first post-Cold War decade rested on the public's belief that what happened outside America's borders mat-tered little for their lives. September 11 punctured that illusion and ended America's decade-long "holiday from history" (Krauthammer 2001, 156). Foreign policy suddenly became a top priority with the public. Not surpris-ingly, the pendulum of power swung sharply back toward the White House.

### Early Actions

The shift in political power from Capitol Hill to the White House was evi-dent immediately. On September 14, 2001, after little debate about the con-sequences of what they were about to do, all but one member of Congress voted to give the president authority to retaliate against those responsible. The resolution was stunning in the breadth of authority it granted. It stated that the president could "use all necessary and appropriate force against those nations, organizations, or persons he determines planned, authorized, committed, or aided the terrorist attacks that occurred on September 11, 2001, or harbored such organizations or persons." In short, Congress effectively declared war and left it up to President Bush to decide who the enemy was.

The new congressional deference manifested itself quickly on other issues as well. In 1997, the Clinton administration had struck a deal with Senators Jesse Helms (R-North Carolina) and Joseph Biden (D-Delaware), the chair and ranking member of the Senate Foreign Relations Committee, respectively, to pay most (but not all) of the back dues the United States owed to the United Nations. Efforts to appropriate all the funds needed to carry out the so-called Helms-Biden law, however, bogged down in the House. Many House Republicans were deeply skeptical of the value of the United Nations, and some representatives used the bill in an attempt to force changes in the Clinton administration's policy on the International Criminal Court and assistance to family planning organizations.

The Bush administration had taken up the cause of Helms-Biden when it assumed office. As of early September 2001, however, it had little to show for its efforts. Once the attacks on the World Trade Center and the Pentagon occurred and it became essential to build a multinational coalition to prosecute the war on terrorism, the White House found Congress much more receptive to its arguments. House leaders quickly agreed to work for passage of a stand-alone bill providing the necessary funding. They placed it on the suspension calendar, which limited debate but also required a two-thirds majority vote to pass. The bill, which the Senate had passed in February 2001, cleared on a voice vote (Pomper 2001b, 2276).

The Bush White House also tackled another previously hot issue—sanctions on Pakistan. Islamabad had triggered one set of sanctions with its May 1998 nuclear tests. U.S. law required the imposition of another set of sanctions in response to Gen. Pervez Musharraf's overthrow of Pakistan's democratically elected government in October 1999. The Clinton administration recognized that these sanctions did not necessarily serve U.S. interests. However, persuading Congress to accept that judgment was another matter entirely. In the 1990s, congressional sentiment had tilted sharply in favor of Pakistan's rival India. More than a hundred lawmakers belonged to the Congressional Indian Caucus, and the Clinton administration decided not to expend its limited foreign policy capital invoking a provision in the law that allowed the president to waive the sanctions imposed in response to the nuclear tests. Immediately after the September 11 attacks, however, President Bush exercised that waiver as part of his effort to ensure Pakistani support for the war on terrorism and military action against Afghanistan. In mid-October, Congress passed legislation authorizing him to waive the other sanctions that had been placed on Islamabad (Pomper 2001a, 2487).

One issue that saw congressional Democrats reverse themselves was national missile defense. Throughout the spring and summer of 2001 they had regularly criticized the administration for suggesting that it was preparing to withdraw the United States from the ABM Treaty. They argued that destroying what they called the "cornerstone of international stability" so that the Pentagon could test unproven defensive technologies was reckless at best. Many Democrats also concluded that opposing the Bush administration's missile defense plans would be politically reward-ing. They believed that their decision to oppose Ronald Reagan's Strategic Defense Initiative in the 1980s had been politically profitable, and they hoped to reprise that success.

Democrats had one strong card to play in this debate—their control of the Senate. Sen. Carl Levin (D-Michigan) used his prerogative as chair of the Senate Armed Services Committee to insert a provision in the fiscal year 2002 defense authorization bill that would have cut $1.3 billion of the $8.3 billion the administration had requested for missile defense and pro-hibited the Defense Department from conducting any antimissile test that violated the ABM Treaty. The committee sustained his "chairman's mark" on a straight-line party vote. A "fierce Senate showdown" looked to be in the offing (Towell 2001, 2079). In the wake of September 11, however, Senate Democrats stripped the authorization bill of the testing provision and restored nearly all the funding the White House had requested. (A small amount was shifted to counter-terrorism accounts.) In December 2001, President Bush announced U.S. withdrawal from the ABM Treaty. The decision passed without much comment on Capitol Hill.

Just weeks before the ABM withdrawal announcement, the White House issued the Military Order of November 13 (Bush 2001). It declared that the foreign citizens the United States detained while waging its war on terror-ism could be tried before military commissions. The order offended many civil libertarians and prompted more than 300 law professors to sign a let-ter calling the commissions "legally deficient, unnecessary, and unwise" (Seelye 2001, B7). The order presumably implicated Congress's constitu-tional authority to "define and punish ... offenses against the law of nations" and its power to make all other laws "necessary and proper" for executing the federal government enumerated power (Tribe 2001). Still, Congress neither rejected the president's decision nor acted to reinforce its legal basis. Even lawmakers who strongly endorsed the idea, such as for-mer vice presidential candidate Sen. Joseph Lieberman (D-Connecticut), saw no need for congressional action. Those lawmakers who doubted the wisdom of the military commission idea, or who worried that it might have consequences for the civil liberties of American citizens, were either few in number or remarkably quiet. Little changed when the Justice Department turned Jose Padilla, a suspected American-born member of al Qaeda, over to the Defense Department to be held as an enemy combatant.[1] Few members wanted to be seen sympathizing with an alleged terrorist and criticizing a very popular president.

## From Tora Bora to Baghdad

President Bush's dominance of foreign affairs continued into 2002. In February 2002, he proposed increasing the defense budget by $48 billion. It was the largest requested increase in real dollars in defense spending since the early years of the Reagan buildup—and a sum roughly equal to China's total defense budget. The request elicited few complaints from Congress, even though the bulk of the spending increase was targeted at funding defense programs that had been on the drawing boards for years rather than to meet new needs created by the war on terrorism. Congress did make technical adjustments that cut slightly more than $1 billion in funding. It also stripped out a provision to create a $10 billion contingency fund that the Pentagon could have used as it saw fit; even deferential lawmakers were reluctant to give the Defense Department that much walking around money. Nonetheless, they signaled that they would be receptive to any specific funding requests that the Pentagon might submit. The eventual FY 2003 appropriation increased defense spending by nearly $37 billion, or a sum equal to Great Britain's entire military budget.

In his January 29, 2002 State of the Union Speech, Bush (2002b) had named Iraq, Iran, and North Korea as members of an "axis of evil, arming to threaten the peace of the world." He went on to declare that "time is not on our side. I will not wait on events, while dangers gather." He and his aides subsequently ruled out using military force to deal with the threats from Iran and North Korea. They gave no such reassurances about U.S. dealings with Iraq. Concerns that Bush (2002a) was planning to attack Iraq grew after he declared in his June 1, 2002 commencement address at West Point that Americans must "be ready for preemptive action" and his senior aides talked openly of the need for regime change in Iraq.

The administration's threats to overthrow Saddam Hussein prompted calls for members of Congress to speak to the possibility of war. The Senate Foreign Relations Committee held its first hearings on the topic at the end of July. Over the next several weeks, lawmakers from both parties began arguing that the administration could not take the country to war without congressional approval. The White House's initial response was that the 1991 Gulf War resolution, the September 11 resolution, and the president's inherent powers as commander in chief made that step unnecessary. But then in early September, the White House relented and sent to Capitol Hill a draft use-of-force resolution that would have given the president nearly unbounded power. The decision to call for a congressional vote was easy to make. Administration officials recognized that Congress was virtually certain to grant its request. If Democrats decided to vote against a use-of-force resolution, Republicans could use that against them in the midterm elections.

The administration's calculations proved correct. Democratic attempts to postpone the vote until after the elections failed. Senate Majority Leader Daschle's fallback position was to substitute a restrictive resolution for the open-ended one the White House had proposed. That strategy collapsed, however, when House Minority Leader Gephardt broke ranks. He met privately with the president and agreed to support a slightly modified version of the White House proposal. Other lawmakers quickly abandoned their efforts to craft alternative resolutions. In early October, both the House and Senate voted overwhelmingly to authorize the president to go to war.

The resolution that Congress passed differed in a few ways from the one the White House initially proposed. The final resolution dropped the most egregious provision in the original, which would have authorized the president "to use all means that he determines to be appropriate" to "restore international peace and security in the region." The final resolution also contained greatly expanded language detailing the horrors of Saddam Hussein's rule, and it imposed reporting requirements on the White House. Nonetheless, the thrust of the operative paragraph remained the same: the president could take the country to war as he saw fit. In that respect, the October 2002 Iraq War resolution is unique in American history. Congress authorized the president to wage a war that he himself had not yet decided (at least publicly) to fight.[2]

When asked why Democrats had not done more to oppose a resolution so many of them thought unwise, Senate Majority Leader Daschle wearily replied: "The bottom line is . . . we want to move on" (Rich 2002, A21). Congress's eagerness to delegate its war power to the president drew the ire of Sen. Robert Byrd (D-West Virginia), a veteran of five decades of service on Capitol Hill. "How have we gotten to this low point in the history of Congress? Are we too feeble to resist the demand of a president who is determined to bend the collective will of Congress to his will?" (Byrd 2002, A39).

## CONCLUSION

Congress's shifting deference to and defiance of presidential leadership in foreign affairs reflects a political dynamic that stretches back to the beginnings of the American republic. Lawmakers are willing to assert their constitutional prerogatives when they believe the United States has little to worry about abroad or the president's proposed course of action threatens to imperil American security. Conversely, when threats are clear and presidential decisions have produced success rather than failure, both politics and a sense of good policy encourage members of Congress to rally round the flag.

It is impossible to say how long the current era of congressional defer-ence will last. Unlike domestic policy, where critics have strong political incentives to criticize the White House, the political winds at the start of July 2003 blew in the opposite direction. A sustained period of peace could change those calculations, but that hardly seemed to be in the offing. The country was occupying Iraq, al Qaeda's most senior leaders remained on the loose, and confrontation over Iran's and North Korea's nuclear pro-gram threatened to escalate.

The greater threat to the imperial presidency seemed to come then from the opposite direction—the threat of executive overreaching. In deciding to wage war on Iraq, President Bush took a strategic gamble of potentially his-toric proportions. He vowed not just to unseat a ruthless dictator and destroy his weapons of mass destruction but also to bring democracy to the Iraqi people and to the Middle East. Should the military occupation of Iraq begin to look like the U.S. peacekeeping mission in Lebanon in 1983, the political winds could quickly reverse. In that event, President Bush would discover what President Johnson learned more than three decades ago— the fact that members of Congress defer to the White House when his for-eign policy takes off does not mean they will be deferential when it crashes.

## Notes

1. The military commission order explicitly applies only to foreign citizens. Padilla's ultimate legal fate was undetermined as of July 2003.
2. The founders rejected the notion that Congress could, or should, give such con-tingent authority to the president (Schlesinger 1973, 26–29).

---

## 9  Beyond the Pale: The Bureaucratic Politics of United States Policy in Mexico

### HOWARD WIARDA

The president, and to a lesser extent the Congress, determine the direc-tion of U.S. foreign policy, but it is the executive agencies that carry it out, making a wide range of decisions about how policies will actually be implemented. What's more, most problems and decisions do not rise to a presidential or Congressional level and therefore escape

Howard Wiarda, from "Beyond the Pale: The Bureaucratic Politics of United States Policy in Mexico," World Affairs, 162, No. 4, Spring 2000. Reprinted by permission of the author.

attention from elected officials. This has important implications for the conduct of American foreign policy. The United States has interests around the world, and a wide variety of executive agencies work to advance those interests, far more than those that are usually associated with foreign policy—State, Defense, NSC, and CIA. In addition, trade, drug enforcement, agriculture, finance, and environmental concerns all are a part of U.S. foreign policy. However, as Howard Wiarda argues, the goals of different agencies may sometimes work at cross purposes, reflecting not only different policy preferences, but also agency attitudes and points of view. At worst, agencies sometimes do not communicate with one another, either inadvertently or by design, and they battle quite strenuously to have their preferred policies prevail. The result can be bureaucratic rivalries and confused American policy.

Wiarda examines the case of Mexico as one of the worst examples of bureaucratic politics—he suggests that the United States does not have a foreign policy toward Mexico, but 67 of them, one for every agency operating there—but it is by no means an isolated case. Such bureaucratic divisions are quite common, and are reflected in American policies throughout the world. This has even been evident with respect to current American policy in Iraq, with the Departments of State and Defense often rivaling one another for supremacy in making policy.

---

In the last two decades, Mexico has emerged as one of the most important countries in the world from the point of view of U.S. foreign policy. Its potential for instability, either economic or political or both, has vaulted Mexico to a position of importance in U.S. foreign policy comparable to that of Japan, Germany, or Russia. It is not that Mexico represents a threat to the United States in any classic strategic or military sense. Mexico is not about to invade the United States militarily, nor are there Mexican missiles armed with nuclear, chemical, or biological weapons aimed at the United States. Instead, Mexico is important to us because of its ability to affect us domestically in many ways. Even the slightest hint of actual or potential economic or political instability in Mexico sends tens of thousands of Mexicans fleeing toward or across the U.S. border. And that has immense consequences for U.S. school systems, housing, employment, social programs, law enforcement, and other domestic programs—mainly in the Southwest, but now increasingly in other areas as well. It also triggers a domestic political backlash, resulting in pressures for increased border patrols, immigration restrictions, and insistence on English as the official U.S. language. These measures in turn trigger their own backlash in Mexico, which exacerbates the problem and increases the pressures on Mexican stability.[1]

Therefore, the best way to think about Mexico in an international relations sense is not through the lens of hardheaded, classic realism—Mexico is not a military threat—but through the newer prism of what Joseph Nye and Robert Keohane called "complex interdependence."[2] Mexico is interdependent with the United States on a host of issues: oil and natural gas, tourism, trade, NAFTA, water rights, pollution and the environment, immigration and labor supplies, banking and investment, manufactured products, and now drugs, crime, gangs, and violence. There is perhaps no other country in the world, besides Canada, with which the United States is more interdependent on such a wide range of issues. Note that most of these issues are not what we might call "hard" strategic threats, but rather what Nye and Keohane call "soft" interdependency issues. Note also that most of these are not what we think of as classic international relations issues over power and dominance (although that is also involved); rather, they are issues that are both international and domestic—what we now call "intermestic." Moreover, all of them are hot, post-cold war, front-burner issues.

That means that a host of U.S. agencies—primarily domestic affairs agencies—have jurisdiction over and are interested and involved in U.S. policy toward Mexico. Few of these traditionally domestic agencies—EPA, FBI, DEA, and so forth—have a long history of involvement in foreign affairs or in Mexico; they frequently lack the language skills, international affairs experience, or foreign policy background to carry out their assigned roles successfully. Perhaps of even greater importance, they add to the "bureaucratic politics"—the jostling and even rivalries among agencies—that has long characterized and often frustrated the successful carrying out of U.S. policy. We do not have a single U.S. foreign policy in Mexico; instead we have approximately sixty-seven policies—one or several policies for each of the U.S. agencies operating there. It is the thesis of this article that the bureaucratic politics of U.S.–Mexican relations has now become so complex, so multilayered, so conflicting, that it hamstrings, frustrates, and often paralyzes policy and makes it virtually impossible for the United States to carry out a successful foreign policy there.

## BUREAUCRATIC POLITICS

In a justly famous book written some years ago about the Cuban Missile Crisis, Harvard scholar Graham Allison described the "rational actor model" of American foreign policymaking.[3] This model suggests that a series of options, with the pros and cons carefully weighed, are presented to the president or foreign policy decisionmaker, who makes the decision based on a "rational" calculation of which option best serves U.S. interests. Allison pointed out that American foreign policymaking did not always conform to the rational actor model, though that was how most Americans conceived of foreign policymaking—when and if they thought about it at all.

But Allison argued that at least two other "models" were also present in foreign policy decisionmaking: an organizational model and a bureaucratic model. The organizational model indicates that foreign policy agencies have habits, guidelines, cultures, and standard operating procedures of their own quite independent of presidential decision making; in the case of the Cuban Missile Crisis, the Navy went ahead with its own way of blockading Soviet ships regardless of President Kennedy's detailed instructions, even though the "Navy way" had the potential to trigger World War III. The bureaucratic model (the main focus of our analysis here) suggests that agencies such as the State Department, the Department of Defense, the Central Intelligence Agency, and others have independent bureaucratic interests (budgets, power, prestige, access to the White House) that they seek to enhance and protect, which are also quite independent of "rational" foreign policy decisionmaking. In interviews conducted during the 1980s, for example, at the height of the cold war, State Department officials frequently lamented that dealing with the Soviets was easy compared with their discussions with a certain rival agency in a five-sided building in "foreign territory" across the Potomac.[4]

Now let us apply the bureaucratic politics model to Mexico. In the following I present my conclusions in the form of an executive summary; I will offer much of the data and analysis on which they are based later in the article.

- There are more U.S. government agencies assigned to the American embassy in Mexico than to any other country in the world: thirty by my count. There are over 1,200 official, civilian, U.S. government personnel in Mexico, again the largest number in the world. These numbers do not include the significant number of CIA, DOD, and Defense Intelligence Agency personnel in Mexico.
- The bureaucratic politics of foreign policymaking used to be confined to three main, sometimes rival agencies: State, DOD, and CIA. Now it includes many more. There are no less than forty-three agencies involved in the drug war alone, and almost all of these are in one way or another involved in activities in Mexico.
- Not only is there often rivalry and bureaucratic politics between cabinet departments, but there are other rivalries within departments—for instance, between the Army and Navy within Defense, between Customs and INS within Treasury, between FBI and DEA within Justice. To say these agencies are not always on the same wavelength would be an understatement.
- Clearly, some agencies do not trust others with information and do not inform them of major policy initiatives. The most striking

case, analyzed in detail below, involved the Justice Department's sting operation in Mexico, Operation Casablanca, which nabbed members of Mexico's banking community on charges of laundering drug money. Justice carried out this operation without informing the White House drug czar's office or the State Department—because they feared that State and the drug czar might object and scuttle the operation. From this episode it became clear that the United States has two drug policies in Mexico: one run by Justice and DEA and one run by State and the White House. Neither the right hand nor the left knows fully what the other is doing. Actually, our research shows we have not just two but multiple, often unconnected, sometimes rival drug policies toward Mexico.

Virtually every U.S. government agency operating in Mexico is pursuing its own policy there—usually several policies at once, which are often secret, contradictory, and conducted with varying levels of coordination with the ambassador. Although this means that each agency has a piece of the action and a vested interest in its own programs, the agencies lose overall coordination, harmony, and focus on the larger goals. The lack of coordination, including the downright secrecy in which some programs are shrouded—as evidenced by the infamous Justice Department sting operation—have damaged both U.S. interests and U.S.–Mexican relations. The United States does not have one single, well-thought-out policy that it arrived at through the rational actor model. Rather, it has scores of policies toward Mexico. Ultimately, having so many policies means having no policy at all, and that is both dysfunctional and self-defeating.

## DRUG POLICY

There are, at last count, no less than forty-three U.S. government agencies involved in counternarcotics. Because of its proximity, and because Mexico is a (maybe the) primary producer and transshipment point for drugs entering the United States, Mexico has become the primary focus for virtually every one of these agencies.

Heroic efforts have been made, particularly by the Office of the Drug Czar, to coordinate these agencies and present a single, clear, coherent policy and strategy. The creation of the drug czar's office during the Reagan administration was itself an admission that the then-existing drug policy needed better coordination. Then, as now, State, Defense, DEA, Customs, Coast Guard, and others were all independently carrying out their own counternarcotics policies, meanwhile entangling in bureaucratic rivalries, jealousies, turf battles, and fights over budgets and responsibilities. The drug czar's office was therefore located in the White House to give it added clout, and the drug czar was supposed to be a cabinet member. The elevated status would enable him to meet and negotiate with other cabinet secretaries as an equal, knock heads if necessary, and arrive at a coordinated policy. The key question has always been whether the drug czar would be a member of the cabinet or not, and administrations have changed direction several times on this issue. The present drug czar, Barry McCaffrey, is not a member of the cabinet. Therefore, there are severe limits on his ability to coordinate drug policy among the several departments. The law enforcement agencies see State as "soft" on drugs and have even threatened to bring obstruction of justice charges against U.S. officials who refuse to go along with some schemes.

A variety of coordinating groups, interagency task forces, undersecretaries, assistant secretaries, and subprincipals' groups operate below the drug czar. Quite a number of these serve useful functions, particularly by sharing information. But below the top cabinet level, almost no decision can be made—unless the principals also concur, which happens irregularly. Many of the meetings of these groups are not necessarily full information-sharing meetings; rather, one agency hosts a briefing that may or may not provide full information. The other agencies may listen and take notes, but they will not necessarily share their own full information or report fully on the policy initiatives of their agencies. Frequently the representatives at these meetings are not fully informed about the policies of their own agencies. Nor can lower-level officials be expected to reach agreement, let alone have the authority to coordinate policy, since their principals may not be in agreement, fully informed on new initiatives, or yet "on board." Hence at all levels, but particularly at the very top, there is neither full coordination of U.S. drug policy nor the incentives or authority to achieve it.[5]

The basic split in policy is between those agencies that have primarily law enforcement backgrounds, orientations, and responsibilities (Justice, Treasury, DEA, FBI, Customs) and those that are primarily political and diplomatic (CIA, State, White House, including the Office of the Drug Czar). My earlier research[6] revealed that these law enforcement agencies (Justice, DEA, and FBI) are mainly staffed at policy levels—not surprisingly—by lawyers. All of these agencies are relatively new to the foreign affairs arena; they tend to have few personnel who speak foreign languages or are trained in foreign cultures, to be dominated by ethnocentrism, and often to have a tunnel vision concerning policy. That is, as law enforcement agencies, legitimately and quite properly charged with the responsibility of implementing and enforcing the law (U.S. law—and there is one of the nubs of the problem), their job is to carry out U.S. counternarcotics policy. If carrying out this responsibility means harassing, arresting, or ousting military officers, cabinet members, or even the president of another country (as in the case of Colombia's Ernesto Samper), then so be it. If it means kidnapping Mexicans from their own nation and bringing them to the United States for trial, then so be it. If it means violating Mexican law by carrying guns while operating in Mexican national territory, then that must be done too. If it means conducting a sting operation among bankers in Mexico (also illegal under Mexican law) and luring them to the United States for arrest, then that too must be approved. There is obviously a pattern here: these are law enforcement agencies whose single-track vision and legitimate responsibilities oblige them to enforce the law—even if that implies enormous costs in terms of overall U.S.–Mexican relations and even if that is often self-defeating on its own law enforcement terms.

The second set of agencies mentioned above has a different set of priorities and responsibilities. State, CIA (at least its analytic arm), and the White House—including, although the orientation is not 100 percent, the drug czar's office—tend to emphasize the larger picture of U.S.–Mexican relations. They tend to see the law enforcement types as cowboys who may well damage U.S.–Mexican relations by their one-track policies and overzealous implementation of them. They do not believe that arresting high-level Mexican officials or drumming high-ranking military officers out of the armed forces is the correct policy. Kidnapping Mexican officials from their own territory, riding roughshod over Mexican laws, and de facto taking over some Mexican government functions is not, they believe, in the long-term best interests of either Mexico or the United States.

Although they don't say this publicly, quite a number of these officials are opposed to much of the U.S. counternarcotics strategy, since they believe that drug sales are a crucial element in the Mexican national economy and that successfully removing that component might well destabilize Mexico. Many are not convinced that a "war on drugs" is the right course to pursue or that the drug problem can be solved by focusing on the supply or production side. These agencies, in other words, are concerned with the big picture of U.S.–Mexican relations, which takes place on multiple, complex, interdependent levels and which may well be harmed by a too zealous, unilateral, single-agency enforcement of the U.S. drug policy. In response, the law enforcement agencies see State as "soft" on drugs and have even threatened to bring obstruction of justice charges against U.S. officials who refuse to go along with some of Justice's more harebrained schemes. When one agency of the U.S. government threatens the officials of another (including a U.S. ambassador, although in another country besides Mexico) with prosecution for obstruction of justice for failing to carry out what the first agency wants to do, that is more than bureaucratic politics run amok; that is complete chaos and dysfunction. In other words, we have no single counternarcotics policy towards Mexico, but two (and many more) conflicting policies, run by conflicting agencies, whose constant feuding and competition threaten to destroy U.S.–Mexican relations.

The case that best illustrates these destructive bureaucratic conflicts is the sting operation known as "Casablanca," carried out by the Justice and Treasury Departments against a number of Mexican bank officials in an effort to catch them on a money laundering charge. Over a three-year period, U.S. undercover agents apparently lured bankers working mainly with Mexico's Juarez narcotraffickers to launder drug money, using such techniques as wire transfers and bankers' drafts. For their service, the bankers received 2 to 3 percent of the transactions. The culmination of the sting came when American officials lured the bankers to the United States with the promise of a free holiday in San Diego and Las Vegas, and then arrested them.[7]

Mexico was often viewed by U.S. policymakers as a difficult, prickly, non-cooperative country on such issues as Mexico's failure to break relations with communist Cuba or to adhere to the U.S. blockade. This case is particularly interesting for a number of reasons. First, Mexican law does not allow sting operations, so U.S. officials were using U.S. laws to indict Mexican bank officials operating in Mexican national territory. Second, for the reason just cited as well as Mexican nationalism—specifically the sense that Mexican officials were cowed by the United States—the sting elicited a howl of protest in Mexico, which not only formally objected but threatened to prosecute the U.S. officials who ran the antidrug sting. Third, although we are supposed to be cooperating with Mexico at all levels in the drug war, the sting was carried out without informing Mexican high government authorities or gaining their legal approval for the U.S. actions—apparently because of American impatience with the failure of Mexican prosecutors to make any real progress against drug corruption and for fear that Mexican officials would inform the bankers and drug lords about the sting. Fourth, and most important for our discussion of bureaucratic politics, the Justice-Treasury sting was carried out without informing either the Department of State or the Office of the Drug Czar, or informing them at such low levels and in such a purposely obscurant way that no one would recognize the larger policy implications of the sting. The reason for not fully informing the latter two agencies was Justice's and Treasury's fears that State and the drug czar, with their "softer" attitudes on drugs and focus on "the big picture," would object, leak the information, or scuttle the operation by appealing to President Clinton. Needless to say, State and the drug czar's office were very angry over being left out of the loop on Casablanca.

In an editorial, the New York Times denounced the sting as both unlawful and undiplomatic.[8] It said that Washington's failure to obtain Mexico's approval for an undercover operation carried out on Mexican soil was inexcusable and had turned a law enforcement coup into a diplomatic fiasco. President Clinton was obliged to express "regrets" to Mexican President Ernesto Zedillo after a wave of denunciation and threats from Mexico. But elsewhere in the United States, denunciations were rather muted, reflecting

American impatience with apparent Mexican foot-dragging on the issue and the tendency (or preference) of Americans to blame Mexico for our own drug problems. The public undoubtedly supported the sting, and DEA was quick to claim credit for the operation regardless of State's views.

A far more informed and biting criticism came from CSIS's Mexico Project director Delal Baer,[9] who at the time of the sting was living and conducting in-depth research in Mexico. She was thus able to assess the impact of the sting as well as of overall U.S. drug policy in Mexico at a level far deeper than U.S. editorialists. Baer criticized a policy in which law enforcement agencies (Customs at Treasury and DEA at Justice) are in the pilot's seat and allowed to operate autonomously from other U.S. agencies and from overall U.S. policy. She argued that the law enforcement agencies of the U.S. government, untrained in foreign policy, have little understanding of the larger consequences of their tactics. Not only was the sting a diplomatic embarrassment for the United States, but its consequences reverberated negatively through the whole Mexican political system and the entire U.S.–Mexico bilateral relationship, of which Customs and DEA are often blissfully unaware. For example, the timing of the sting threw a monkey wrench into delicate negotiations President Zedillo was conducting with the Mexican Congress over financial reforms—reforms which are in the U.S. interest to see enacted. The sting also panicked investors—whom U.S. policy has an interest in encouraging—who interpreted the operation as indicating the U.S. government lacked confidence in Mexican institutions. The sting and the intense Mexican reaction to it also led to several calls in Mexico for the resignation of their central bank governor and attorney general—officials whom the U.S. has tried discreetly to support.[10]

Baer goes on to say that while it may not be the responsibility of U.S. law enforcement officials to monitor the political and economic fallout of their unilateral actions with Mexico, it is the responsibility of senior officials to coordinate policy among the various agencies involved. They should ensure that such operations are conducted with at least some respect for signed agreements and rules of bilateral cooperation between the two countries, as well as with a sense of the impact of such policies in Mexico and their effect on overall U.S.–Mexican relations. Apparently that was not done in this case—and indeed this case is part of a pattern in overall US.–Mexican relations. The stage is thus set for a new and recurring confrontation between the United States and Mexico. For instance, Justice and Treasury can be expected to pressure hard for decertifying Mexico as a country cooperating in the drug war, while State and, one hopes, the White House will be scrambling to present the larger picture of U.S.–Mexico interrelations to prevent Congress from making that blunder. Baer concludes sarcastically: What a "victory" for Janet Reno, Customs, and DEA! They have proven that if the United States dangles $30 million in front of low-level Mexican bank branch managers, we can corrupt them in the same way drug traffickers already have. For this dubious revelation we have put the entire framework of U.S.–Mexican relations at risk.

Unfortunately, this case is not atypical of a wide range of U.S. policies—on drugs and a host of other issues—in Mexico that emerge as the result of the bureaucratic politics of American policymaking. Reviewing only my own files on Mexico from the last few month reveals such headlines as "The U.S. at Odds With Itself on Mexico," "Drug War Leader Is Frustrated: Kramek Says Politics Hamper Coast Guard,"[11] and "2000 Miles of Disarray in Drug War: U.S.–Mexico Border Effort a Shambles."[12] Meanwhile, through the Southwest Border Initiative, the Justice Department continues to operate in Mexico with the same coalition of law enforcement agencies (Customs, DEA, FBI, the Criminal Division of Justice, the U.S. Attorneys' Offices, the High-Intensity Drug Trafficking Area Program, and state and local counterparts) that brought us Casablanca.[13] Note that once again neither State, CIA, the drug czar, or the NSC is represented. Finally, we have the devastating reports of the General Accounting Office—about as objective a voice as we are going to get on this issue—whose consistent conclusion through a series of reports has been: (a) "Mexico continues to be the principal transit country for cocaine entering the United States"; (b) "despite U.S. and Mexican counternarcotics efforts, the flow of illegal drugs into the United States has not significantly diminished"; and (c) the effectiveness and usefulness of new laws, new counternarcotics agencies, and new initiatives is limited "due to inadequate planning and coordination *among U.S. agencies*" [emphasis added].[14]

## CONCLUSION

The United States cannot continue to run its foreign policy on this basis. With the end of the cold war, it is domestic politics and bureaucratic rivalries that almost exclusively drive U.S. foreign policy, rather than a hard-headed but enlightened calculation of the national interest and a sense of how to manage a host of complex, interdependent issues with a large, important neighbor like Mexico. Congress and the White House play politics with foreign policymaking, doling out whole programs to different agencies on political and bureaucratic grounds. Then each agency conducts its own foreign policy with little or no attachment to a central core of principles and interests. And there is precious little coordination between, among, or even within the distinct agencies involved. Both the politicians and the agencies involved seek to curry favor with particular constituencies and pursue their own organizational and bureaucratic self-interests. Operation Casablanca and the JMET programs are the two most blatant examples, but there are many others.[15]

The bureaucratic politics of U.S.–Mexican policymaking has now snow-balled way beyond Allison's original formulation to encompass dozens of offices, departments, and agencies carrying out hundreds if not thousands of programs. The White House, the president, and the National Security Council are supposed to coordinate all these distinct programs, but that is being done ineffectively or so superficially that each agency continues to follow its own route. The bureaucratic politics of American policymaking encompasses not only agencies in Washington but also the myriad offices in the Mexico City embassy, which has more U.S. agencies represented than any other U.S. embassy in the world. What in the embassy is supposed to be a coordinated "family" of operations has become dysfunctional. It is said that "we have no one policy toward Mexico but sixty-seven policies."

The incredible pluralism, verging on chaos, has by now begun to affect the substance of American policy toward Mexico. There are two things that exercise the Mexicans: one is the specific contents of individual U.S. policies—not our main subject here; the other is the sheer confusion in U.S. policy, the lack of clear direction, the fact that the United States speaks with many voices on foreign policy, not one. Other nations in this and other times have lamented these characteristics of American foreign policy, but now, and specifically in the Mexico case, the situation is far worse and going beyond the pale. The sheer proliferation (the world's largest) of agencies and pro-grams, the fact that the left hand of U.S. policymaking seldom knows fully what the right hand (actually, fifty or sixty other "hands") is doing, and increasingly the political and bureaucratic "games" that one part of the American government tries to play on others (as in Casablanca) are now becoming exceedingly destructive and self-defeating. Not only is there rising anger and indignation in Mexico[16]—hardly conducive to gaining Mexican cooperation on a host of issues—but policy effectiveness is also breaking down. This is more than Allison's famous model run amok; it is Allis 'n Wonderland.

## Notes

1. The contrasting U.S. and Mexican views are propounded in Robert A. Pastor and Jorge G. Casta—eds, *Limits to Friendship: The United States and Mexico* (New York: Knopf, 1988).
2. Robert O. Keohane and Joseph S. Nye, Jr., eds., *Transnational Relations and World Politics* (Cambridge, M.A.: Harvard University Press, 1970).
3. Graham T. Allison, *Essence of Decision: Explaining the Cuban Missile Crisis* (Boston: Little Brown, 1971).
4. Howard J. Wiarda, *Foreign Policy Without Illusion: How Foreign Policy Works and Fails to Work in the United States* (New York: Scott Foresman/Little Brown, 1990).
5. Based on interviews I conducted at the National Security Council, the Office of the Drug Czar, and the Department of State.

6.  Reported in *Foreign Policy Without Illusion* and *American Foreign Policy*.
7.  The case received intensive coverage in the *New York Times* and *Washington Post* during May 1998.
8.  As reprinted in the *International Herald Tribune*, 13–14 June 1998, 6.
9.  See her op-ed in *Washington Post*, 1 June 1998, p. A17.
10. This article focuses on the Byzantine character of American bureaucratic politics in dealing with Mexico; at least as complicated is Mexican bureaucratic politics— the interrelations and machinations of the party, the government, the Central Bank, the president, the attorney general's office, the interior ministry, the press, the opposition parties, state governments, the armed forces, the police, special forces, and so on. If these two bureaucratic politics models could ever be brought together, then we would truly understand Mexico as well as U.S. policymaking and the complex interrelation between the two. Such an effort could be the subject of a doctoral dissertation; it is beyond the scope of this article.
11. *Washington Post*, 2 June 1998, A11.
12. *Washington Post*, 9 May 1998, A1.
13. James S. Milford, Acting Deputy Administrator of the Drug Enforcement Administration, "Antinarcotics Cooperation with the Government of Mexico," DEA Congressional Testimony before the Senate Drug Caucus, 29 October 1997.
14. General Accounting Office, *Drug Control: Status of Counternarcotics Efforts in Mexico* (Washington, D.C.: GAO, 18 March 1998).
15. For additional cases and analysis see Wiarda, *American Foreign Policy*.
16. *Washington Post*, 29 July 1998, A17.

# 10 The CNN Effect: Myth or Reality

## Warren P. Strobel

The influences that go into making American foreign policy are not restricted to governmental institutions and actors. Outside of government offices, other actors—interest groups, the press, ethnic lobbies, the general public—can play a significant role in determining the direction of policy. The press in particular, and especially cable television news, is often seen as having great influence on U.S. foreign policy. This seemed to be especially true after the end of the Cold War, which coincided not only with a number of ethnic wars and humanitarian disasters, but also the rise of CNN and other 24-hour-a-day

Warren Strobel, "The CNN Effect," *American Journalism Review*, May 1996. By permission of American Journalism Review.

news stations, which could instantly transmit a continuous and endless stream of up-to-the-minute information.

Warren Strobel discusses how this phenomenon seems to have had the effect of eliminating the news cycle, in which politicians and the public previously had time to digest and respond to new developments. Instead, the process is now much faster. Information is everywhere, coming from multiple sources. Television images incite the public, which demands instant responses from government officials, who in turn continually reshape foreign policy. Strobel called this "The CNN Effect," the extent to which television and the media increasingly determine policy. His analysis became almost an instant classic when it was published.

The CNN Effect has been credited with contributing to American intervention in Somalia and the Balkans, and with placing significant pressures on government leaders to act when they might not otherwise be inclined to do so. Strobel, however, seeks to contradict the idea of strong media influence over policy, analyzing several facets of the CNN Effect that are accepted as conventional wisdom and finding them to be "myths."

---

It's May 31, 1995, there's another flare-up in the long-running Bosnia crisis and the Defense Department spokesman, Kenneth Bacon, is sitting in his office on the Pentagon's policy making E Ring. A clock is ticking over his head. On the wall right outside the door to Bacon's inner office is a television. Aide Brian Cullen glances at it from time to time.

On the bottom of the screen is the familiar CNN logo. Above it is the equally familiar figure of Peter Arnett in flak jacket and helmet, reporting breathlessly from Bosnia, analyzing the latest NATO airstrikes and the Bosnian Serbs' retaliation by taking U.N. peacekeepers hostage. Arnett is answering questions for the host and audience of CNN's interactive "Talk Back Live." Some of that audience is in cyberspace, sending in questions via CompuServe. At the top of the hour, Bacon will escort a "senior Defense Department official" to the podium of the Pentagon briefing room to explain to skeptical reporters why the Clinton administration's latest apparent policy change toward Bosnia is not a change at all.

Here it is, the nexus of media power and foreign policy, where television's instantly transmitted images fire public opinion, demanding instant responses from government officials, shaping and reshaping foreign policy at the whim of electrons. It's known as the CNN Effect.

It's a catchall phrase that has been used to describe a number of different phenomena. Perhaps the best definition, used by Professor Steven Livingston of George Washington University, is a loss of policy control on the part of policy makers because of the power of the media, a power that they can do nothing about.

Or is it the best definition? I'm here to ask Bacon that question. Bacon, a former journalist, is a precise man. He wears a bow tie and wire rim glasses, and looks like he doesn't get ruffled easily. On a day like today, his response is telling. "Policy makers," he says, "are becoming more adept at dealing with the CNN factor."

Bacon's opinion is one heard, in one form or another, over and over in the course of nearly 100 interviews during [1995 and 1996] with secretaries of state, spokespersons and everyone in between. I talked with officials from the Bush and Clinton administrations, the United Nations, and relief agencies; military officers who have been in Bosnia, Somalia, Haiti, and Rwanda; and journalists who have reported from those places. It is possible, of course, that they are all lying (the officials, that is). After all, who would want to admit that their authority has been usurped, their important jobs made redundant? To paraphrase legendary diplomat George Kennan's almost plaintive diary entry from the day U.S. troops landed in Somalia: If CNN determines foreign policy, why do we need administrators and legislators?

But the closer one looks at those incidents that supposedly prove a CNN Effect, where dramatic and/or real-time images appear to have forced policy makers into making sudden changes, the more the Effect shrinks. It is like a shimmering desert mirage, disappearing as you get closer.

A growing body of academic research is casting doubt on the notion that CNN in particular, or television in general, determines U.S. foreign policy the way it might seem from a quick glance at the live broadcasts from Tiananmen Square in 1989 or the image of the U.S. soldier being dragged through the streets of Mogadishu, Somalia, in October 1993. . . . What officials told me closely parallels the findings of Nik Gowing, diplomatic editor for Britain's Independent Television Network, who interviewed dozens of British and American officials for a Harvard University study. Even many military officers, who might be expected to criticize media performance, have found the CNN Effect to be less than it is billed. But no one is arguing that CNN has had no effect on journalists, government officials, and the way both conduct their business.

> Virtually every official interviewed agrees that the rise of Cable News Network has radically altered the way U.S. foreign policy is conducted. Information is everywhere, not just because of CNN, but through other developments, such as the increasingly sophisticated media systems in developing nations and the explosive growth of the Internet. "It's part and parcel of governing," says Margaret Tutwiler, assistant secretary of state for public affairs under James A. Baker III. During her days at the State Department podium, Tutwiler knew that the most important audience was not the reporters asking the questions, but the array of cameras at the back of the briefing room, which sent her descriptions of U.S. policy to leaders, journalists, and the public the globe over.

Baker says CNN has destroyed the concept of a "news cycle." In his days as a political campaign director, the news cycle was much longer, which meant the candidate had more time to respond to an opponent's charges. Now officials must respond almost instantly to developments. Because miniaturized cameras and satellite dishes can go virtually anywhere, policy makers no longer have the luxury of ignoring faraway crises.

These changes also affect modern U.S. military operations, which increasingly involve peacekeeping or humanitarian activities, and in which there is no vital U.S. interest at stake and thus less rationale for controlling the news media. The journalist-military debate over news media pools and other restrictions that date from Grenada and the Persian Gulf War has been eclipsed by the Somalias and Haitis, where the news media were so pervasive that reporters were often providing information to the military rather than vice versa. U.S. Army Maj. David Stockwell and Col. Barry Willey, the chief military spokesmen in Somalia and Haiti, both described this media presence as alternately helpful and annoying, but in the end an inevitable piece of what the military calls the "operating environment."

But to say that CNN changes governance, shrinks decision making time, and opens up military operations to public scrutiny is not the same as saying that it determines policy. Information indeed has become central to international affairs, but whether officials use this or are used by it depends largely on them. The stakes are higher for those who must make policy, but the tools at their command are also more powerful.

How, then, does the CNN Effect really work? One way to answer that question is to look at some common myths about the network, and at what government officials who must deal with it on a daily basis say really happens.

## MYTH NO. 1

*CNN makes life more difficult for foreign policy makers.*

For those government officials who know how to use it, Ted Turner's round-the-clock video wire service can in fact be an immense boon. This was seen most vividly during the Persian Gulf War, when the Bush White House, knowing that Iraqi President Saddam Hussein's top aides were reluctant to bring him bad news, got into Saddam's living room via CNN. And because CNN carried Pentagon briefings in Saudi Arabia and Washington live, officials were talking directly to the American public for hours on end. A study of commentators featured on the network during the gulf war found that the majority of them were retired military officers or other "elites" who by and large supported the administration's view of the crisis. Saddam, of course, used CNN too, as illustrated by the controversy over Peter Arnett's reporting from Iraq. This challenged the administration—but also provided a useful window into what the man in Baghdad was thinking.

It doesn't take a massive confrontation and half a million U.S. troops in the desert for CNN to perform this favor for officials. "Everybody talks about the CNN factor being bad," Pentagon spokesman Bacon says. "But in fact, a lot of it is good." If the Pentagon [disagreed] with a report by CNN Pentagon correspondent Jamie McIntyre, [then] Defense Secretary William Perry [could] and [would] call him to try to put his spin on events. In the good old days of the 6 o'clock evening news, officials would have to wait 24 hours. By then it was usually too late. With CNN, they get many chances throughout the day to try to shape public perceptions.

Because of its speed, CNN also provides a convenient way for administration officials to leak new policies in the hope that they'll define the debate before political opponents do. Many a White House reporter knows that CNN's Wolf Blitzer is a frequent recipient of such leaks. Blitzer is on the White House lawn, repeating to the camera what he's just been told by unnamed officials, while newspaper reporters are still fretting over their leads.

The images of strife and horror abroad that are displayed on CNN and other television outlets also help foreign policy officials explain the need for U.S. intervention. CNN may be the last defense against isolationism. The press "makes the case of the need to be involved sometimes more than we can," says Richard Boucher, State Department spokesman under Baker and former Secretary of State Lawrence Eagleburger.

## MYTH NO. 2

*CNN dictates what's on the foreign policy agenda.*

Somalia, of course, is the prime example cited. There was equal suffering in southern Sudan in 1992, the common wisdom goes, but the Bush administration was forced to pay attention to Somalia because the TV cameras were there.

While journalists undoubtedly were drawn to the drama of the famine in Somalia, they had a lot of help getting there. Much of this came from international relief agencies that depend on TV images to move governments to respond and the public to open its wallets. "We need the pictures. Always the pictures," says on official who works with the U.N. High Commissioner for Refugees (UNHCR). There isn't anything sinister about this. These private and intergovernmental agencies do good work under dangerous conditions. But for that very reason they are seen by many journalists as lacking the motives that most other sources are assumed to have. In the case of Somalia, these organizations were joined by U.S. government relief agencies and members of Congress interested in Africa in a campaign to generate media attention and government action.

One of the leaders of that campaign was Andrew Natsios, then an assistant administrator of the U.S. Agency for International Development, known for his rapport with reporters. Natsios and his aides gave numerous media interviews and held news conferences in Africa and in Washington in early 1992. "I deliberately used the news media as a medium for educating policy makers in Washington and in Europe" about how to address the crisis, Natsios says. And he says he used the media "to drive policy." Once reporters got to Somalia—sometimes with the UNHCR, the International Committee of the Red Cross, and others—they of course sent back graphic reports of the famine that increased the pressure on President Bush to do something.

"It started with government manipulating press," says Herman Cohen, former assistant secretary of state for African affairs, "and then changed to press manipulating the government."

A quick look at the patterns of television reporting on Somalia also raises questions about the media's agenda-setting powers. There were very few television reports on Somalia (15 on the three networks to be exact) prior to Bush's August 1992 decision to begin an airlift. That decision resulted in a burst of reporting. The pattern was repeated later in the year when Bush ordered 25,000 U.S. troops to safeguard humanitarian aid. When they weren't following the actions of relief officials or members of Congress, the cameras were following the troops. CNN, in fact, was less likely than the networks to do independent reporting when Somalia was not on the Washington agenda.

## MYTH NO. 3

*Pictures of suffering force officials to intervene.*

Televised images of humanitarian suffering do put pressure on the U.S. government to act, as was seen in northern Iraq following the gulf war, in Somalia and in Rwanda. Part of the reason for this, officials say, is because the costs of lending a hand are presumed to be low. (The U.S. foreign policy establishment was disabused of this notion in Somalia, an experience that probably permanently shrunk this facet of the CNN Effect.)

But something interesting happens when the pictures suggest an intervention that is potentially high in costs, especially the cost of American casualties. Images of civil wars, no matter how brutal, simply don't have the same effects as those of lines of refugees or malnourished children at a feeding station.

In the summer and fall of 1992 the Bush administration was under intense pressure from Congress and the U.N. to do something to stop the outrages perpetrated against Bosnia's Muslims. In August, *Newsday* reported the existence of a string of detention camps where Bosnian Serbs were torturing, raping, and killing. Within a few days, Britain's ITN confirmed the worst when it broadcast images of emaciated men trapped behind barbed wire. Yet by this time President Bush and his aides had concluded that intervening in the Bosnian civil war would take thousands of troops who might be mired down for years. CNN and its brethren did not change this calculation.

"It wouldn't have mattered if television was going 24 hours around the clock with Serb atrocities. Bush wasn't going to get in," says Warren Zimmermann, the last U.S. ambassador to Yugoslavia. Former Secretary of State Eagleburger confirmed this, saying: "Through all the time we were there, you have to understand that we had largely made a decision we were not going to get militarily involved. And nothing, including those stories, pushed us into it. . . . It made us damn uncomfortable. But this was a policy that wasn't going to get changed no matter what the press said."

The pressures that Eagleburger spoke of were very real. But rather than alter firmly held policy, in Bosnia and many other places, officials, in essence, pretended to. They took minimal steps designed to ease the pressure while keeping policy intact. These responses probably account for much of the perception that CNN and television in general change policy. Bush administration concern with the media "only extended to the appearance of maintaining we were behaving responsibly," says Foreign Service officer George Kenney, who resigned publicly to protest the lack of real U.S. action to save Bosnia. Roy Gutman, who won the Pulitzer Prize for his reporting from Bosnia for *Newsday*, concurs. "What you had is a lot of reaction to reports, but never any policy change."

Images of the brutal slaughter of half a million people in Rwanda in 1994 did not move governments to intervene with force. This was true despite the fact that there was more television coverage of the slaughter than there was of Somalia at any time in 1992 until Bush actually sent the troops. According to officials at the Pentagon and elsewhere, once the slaughter in Rwanda ended and the massive exodus of refugees began, what had seemed like an intervention nightmare became a relatively simple logistical and humanitarian problem that the U.S. military was well-equipped to solve.

Interestingly, the public reacted the same way as the Pentagon did. According to a top relief representative, private relief agencies "got virtually no money whatsoever" from the viewing public when television was broadcasting images of Rwandans who had been hacked to death. Contributions began to pour in when refugees flooded across Rwanda's borders and there were "pictures of women and children . . . innocents in need."

# MYTH NO. 4

*There is nothing officials can do about the CNN Effect.*

To the contrary, whether or not the CNN Effect is real depends on the actions of government officials themselves. As ABC News' Ted Koppel puts it, "To the degree . . . that U.S. foreign policy in a given region has been clearly stated and adequate, accurate information has been provided, the influence of television coverage diminishes proportionately." In other words, the news media fill a vacuum, and CNN, by its reach and speed, can do so powerfully and quickly.

But this gives officials a lot more sway than Kennan thinks they have. The officials I interviewed did not identify a single instance when television reports forced them to alter a strongly held and/or well-communicated policy. Rather, the media seemed to have an impact when policy was weakly held, was already in the process of being changed, or was lacking public support.

There is little doubt that the image of a dead U.S. soldier being desecrated in October 1993 forced President Clinton to come up with a rapid response to calls in Congress for the withdrawal of U.S. troops from Somalia. Often forgotten, however, is that by September 1993 the Clinton administration already was making plans to extract U.S. troops. Just days before the images of the dead soldier were aired, Secretary of State Warren Christopher had told U.N. Secretary General Boutros Boutros-Ghali of Washington's desire to pull out. Congress had withdrawn its approval, and public support for the mission, documented in opinion polls, began falling well before the gruesome video started running on CNN.

What was most important about the imagery, however, was that it could not be explained by U.S. foreign policy makers. The Clinton administration had casually allowed the mission in Somalia to evolve from humanitarian relief to nation-building without explaining to the public and Congress the new costs, risks, and goals. The images were the coup de grace. "The message was not handled properly from the administration," says one U.S. military officer who served in Somalia. The images were "a graphic illustration of the futility of what we were doing."

This ability of CNN to alter a policy that is in flux was graphically demonstrated again just a few months later in February 1994 when a mortar shell slammed into a marketplace in Sarajevo, killing 68 people and wounding many more. The images of the "market massacre" caused outrage around the world. The United States abandoned a year-old hands-off policy toward the Balkans and, a few days later, persuaded NATO to declare a zone around Sarajevo free of Bosnian Serb heavy weapons.

But what looks like a simple cause-effect relationship looked different to those making the policy. Here again, just days before, Christopher had presented to his senior government colleagues a plan for more aggressive U.S. action in Bosnia. He and others had become alarmed at the way U.S.–European disputes over Bosnia were debilitating NATO.

A senior State Department official was in a meeting on the new Bosnia policy when the mortaring occurred. He recalls worrying that the new policy would be seen, incorrectly, as a response to the massacre. The images did force the Clinton administration to respond quickly in public and ensured that an internal policy debate that might have lasted for months was tele-scoped into a few days. But the episode also provides additional evidence that CNN helps officials explain actions they already want to take. The images provided a moment of increased attention to Bosnia that could help justify the administration's policy response. "It was a short window. We took advantage of it. We moved the policy forward. And it was successful," then-White House spokeswoman Dee Dee Myers recalls.

## MYTH NO. 5

*The CNN Effect is on the rise.*

Sadly, there is at least preliminary evidence that the public and officials are becoming inoculated against pictures of tragedy or brutality coming across their television screens. "We are developing an ability now to see incomprehensible human tragedy on television and understand no matter how horrible it is, we can't get involved in each and every instance," says White House spokesman Michael McCurry. "We are dulling our senses."

When a mortar again struck the Sarajevo marketplace in August 1995, the images were familiar: pools of blood and shredded limbs. For that reason, McCurry says, they had less impact. The policy response—bombing Bosnian Serbs—was driven instead by NATO's pledge a few weeks earlier to use air power to protect remaining U.N.-declared safe areas. NATO knew it had to make good on the pledge if it was to have any credibility left at all. McCurry's point about the dulling of our senses can be heard in what a viewer told an NBC audience researcher: "If I ever see a child with flies swarming around it one more time, I'm not going to watch that show again."

As with any new technology, people are learning over time to adapt to real-time television. While the danger remains that officials will respond to instant reports on CNN that later turn out to be wrong, several current and former spokespeople say that governments are becoming more sophisti-cated in dealing with time pressures. "As often as not, we buy ourselves time when things happen," Boucher says. "If we think we need the time to decide, we take the time to decide."

Pentagon spokesman Bacon says, "We do not have a big problem with saying, 'Yeah, this looks really awful, but let's find out what the facts really are.' " . . .

On that day [in May 1995] when I interviewed Bacon, media images had not pushed the United States further into the Balkan tangle. Rather, NATO bombing and the prospect that U.S. troops might go to Bosnia to rescue U.N. peacekeepers had sent journalists scurrying back to Sarajevo. The story was heating up again.

The CNN Effect is narrower and far more complex than the conventional wisdom holds. In a more perfect world, the news media—especially television—would be a more independent force, pointing out problems and helping set the public agenda. In reality, CNN and its brethren follow newsmakers at least as frequently as they push them or make them feel uncomfortable. The struggle between reporters and officials continues as before—just at a faster pace.

# 11 Three Historical Stages of Ethnic Group Influence

## TONY SMITH

The influence of ethnically based lobbies and interest groups on American foreign policy can be significant. The foreign attachments maintained by a nation of immigrants often remain strong, translating into specific foreign policy interests and goals. Americans of Irish, Cuban, Jewish, Mexican, and other ancestries have become organized and active, with the result that their voices are often heard and responded to in American foreign policy debates.

Tony Smith argues that this phenomenon has changed since the end of the Cold War, giving ethnic lobbies greater access to policy-making elites than ever before. During the Cold War, he argues, virtually all American ethnic groups concerned about foreign policy shared common goals, supporting the American effort to combat the Soviet Union and contain communism, while promoting the maintenance or creation of self-government in their respective homelands. These goals cut across most ethnicities—Western and Eastern European, Jewish, African American, and Latin American. After the Cold War, a host of new international problems—failed states, ethnic wars, the

Reprinted by permission of the publisher from *Foreign Attachments: The Power of Ethnic Groups in the Making of American Foreign Policy* by Tony Smith, pp. 47–48, 64–73, 76. Cambridge, Mass.: Harvard University Press, Copyright © 2000 by the President and Fellows of Harvard College.

transition from communism, the Oslo Accords on Middle East peace, expansion of NATO—presented themselves at the same time that the common thread linking the foreign policy agendas of different ethnic groups disappeared. In addition to these developments, there was, at least before September 11, no clear threat to U.S. national security, and a rise in the legitimacy of multiculturalism. The result of all these factors has been that ethnic interest groups have attained greater prominence in policymaking, and their goals are less likely to coincide with broader American foreign policy interests.

One important effect of these developments, Smith argues, is that American foreign policy is "increasingly being defined by organized social groups." In the most extreme cases, such as that involving Cuban Americans, ethnic lobbies have been able to "capture" their small corner of American foreign policy, making U.S. policy conform quite closely to their own wishes. Though Smith wrote this book before September 11, his analysis still describes the political dynamic involving ethnic groups quite accurately. A strong presidency and an assertive foreign policy have diminished the visibility and prominence of many ethnic lobbies, but such groups continue to be vocal and intently focused on their specific areas of concern, often achieving great success.

---

Ethnic groups have long exerted influence on U.S. foreign policy. The history of that influence in the twentieth century can be divided into three periods. In the first stage, from the 1910s through the 1930s, the most active ethnic groups—German, Scandinavian, and Irish, and later Italian—acted as a drag on American involvement in world affairs. These groups may not have been primarily responsible for U.S. neutralism at the onset of World War I, the failure to enter the League of Nations thereafter, and the isolationism of the 1930s, but they were of more than marginal importance to the positions Washington took on the world stage.

During the Cold War, or stage two, by contrast, virtually all American ethnic groups concerned about foreign policy were internationalists, backing an assertive American effort to stand up to Soviet communism, most often by promoting national self-government abroad. Americans of West European, East European, or Balkan ancestry feared Soviet communism. Jewish Americans supported the creation of Israel. African Americans called for the decolonization of Africa. Later other groups—such as Cuban or Armenian Americans—would be added to the list. In contrast to the first stage, when ethnic and national loyalties could stand in stark contrast, during the Cold War ethnic and national identities tended to coincide. While an exception should be made in this generalization for African Americans, here too, during the Carter years, there was a blending of ethnic activism with policy decisions taken in Washington with regard to America's role in world affairs.

Since the end of the Cold War, we have entered what might be called a third stage, in which ethnic group internationalism has remained pronounced. The creation of new states abroad following the implosion of the Soviet empire and the Soviet Union itself has called forth a sympathetic response among their American kinfolk. Moreover, all ethnic groups are more than ever aware of the extent of American power in world affairs. At the same time, the decline of a sense of clear U.S. national interests since the disintegration of Soviet communism has engendered an erosion of bipartisanship on foreign policy. The lack of consensus on foreign policy priorities, combined with the reassertion of the power of society relative to the state ("the era of big government is over," as President Bill Clinton twice put it in his January 1996 State of the Union address), has facilitated the access of American ethnic lobbies to policymaking in Washington to an unprecedented degree. Today more than ever is the ethnic group moment in the making of American foreign policy.

## STAGE III

Since the end of the Cold War, the influence of American ethnic lobbies on foreign policy may be said to have entered a third stage. Its most important feature is the continued commitment to internationalism. If American public opinion remains committed to an active role in world affairs, one may assume that communities that are ethnically organized are even more committed, at percentages that may equal those of the political elite.[1] Greek American organizations keep a sharp eye out for events in the Balkans and the Aegean; Jewish Americans remain attentive to the Middle East and the fate of their kinfolk in Russia; African Americans are involved in monitoring the occupation of Haiti and the future of democratic government in and U.S. economic relations with Africa; Armenian Americans closely follow events in the Caucasus; Irish Americans worry about the peace process in Northern Ireland; East European Americans work for the enlargement of NATO; and new groups, of which the most prominent is Mexican American but which include Asian Americans as well, are active regarding immigration legislation, adding an important new dimension to ethnic group politicking with respect to America's role in world affairs.

The end of the Cold War has given rise to two interrelated developments so far as the influence of American ethnic groups in Washington is concerned: the rise of ethnonationalist conflict abroad stemming from the collapse of Soviet power and the withdrawal of American support has alerted American kinfolk to the need for action; and the decline of any obvious threat to U.S. security has weakened the American state relative to social forces at home, which in turn has increased the openness of our political system to interest group influence.

Of course, in important ways, Washington and ethnic groups can act together for related ends. The post–Cold War call by the Clinton administration to replace containment by efforts to enlarge the number of democratic states worldwide well suited a host of ethnic groups, giving them the right to champion their kinfolk abroad by appeals to America's democratic and human rights traditions. For instance, in Africa and Latin America the end of the superpower contest created a new opportunity to make the effort to create democratic governments, often favored by American ethnic communities. In addition, the creation of new states from the disintegration of the Soviet empire, the Soviet Union, and Yugoslavia meant a new source of demands in foreign capitals to which American ethnic groups have been responding.

But an identity of purpose between Washington and ethnic activists is not always apparent. The end of the Cold War has contributed to a change in the domestic American political process that has served to increase ethnic group influence. In a situation where the country is under no threat to its vital security interests, where the once "imperial presidency" is in retreat before Congress, and where the Congress itself is increasingly subject to partisan rivalries, social forces have correspondingly more power to influence foreign policy than they did during the Cold War. Given the rising legitimacy of multiculturalism in domestic American life, it seems fair to conclude that, powerful as ethnic sentiment may have been in shaping U.S. foreign policy during the Cold War, it is even more influential today.

As the debate over the enlargement of NATO showed in 1998–99, the end of the Cold War did not stop some Americans of East European descent from mobilizing to influence the fate of their ancestral homelands. In 1994 the Central and East European Coalition was formed by members of various American ethnicities whose ancestral homelands had once been under Soviet domination. To underscore their political clout, they pointed out that for the 1996 election their fellow ethnics represented at least 10 percent of the vote in North Dakota, Nebraska, Minnesota, Wisconsin, Illinois, Michigan, Ohio, New York, Massachusetts, New Jersey, Delaware, Maryland, and (the highest, at over 18 percent of the total) Connecticut and Pennsylvania.[2]

It should thus come as no surprise that President Clinton delivered all his major addresses in 1996–97 on NATO enlargement in cities like Detroit, Chicago, and Milwaukee, where large ethnic communities would be attentive to the message and likely to rally in support.[3] In my opinion, it was not Americans of East European origin alone, or even principally, who were driving the decision to expand NATO; instead, long-standing decisions to combine as much of Europe as possible in ways favorable to American interests dictated Washington's policy. Still, the perception that Clinton was angling for votes was widespread, as was illustrated in the comment by Canadian Prime Minister Jean Chrétien (who thought his microphone was turned off) to the Belgian Prime Minister about NATO's three new candidate members in August 1997: "All this for short-term political reasons, to win elections. In fact [American politicians] are selling their votes, they are selling their votes . . . It's incredible. In your country or in mine, all the politicians would be in prison."[4]

With East European governments now free of Moscow's control, leaders of these countries have become more active in soliciting the support of American ethnic communities to whom they are culturally related. Much as Masaryk or Paderewski visited the United States to encourage both the American government and their kinfolk here to come to the aid of the ancestral homeland, so the leaders of the Czech Republic and Poland come today, to be entertained at the White House and to address Congress, while at less publicized moments also meeting with Czech or Polish American groups to coordinate their positions on world affairs.

The result has been a triple alliance involving the Clinton administration (with its activist Secretary of State Madeleine Albright, of Czech birth), East European governments, and American ethnic constituencies in a common cause to bring the new countries of this region into Western-dominated economic institutions and NATO. The success of these ambitions with respect to Poland, the Czech Republic, and Hungary in March 1999 crowned more than eighty years of effort, beginning with the activism of East European Americans, East European political leaders, and Woodrow Wilson during World War I. Nothing could have been more Wilsonian than Albright's speech at Harvard University in June 1997, on the fiftieth anniversary of the announcement of the Marshall Plan, in which she declared that "American security and prosperity are linked to economic and political health abroad":

> We must take advantage of the historic opportunity that now exists to bring the world together in an international system based on democracy, open markets, law and a commitment to peace. Today the greatest danger to America is not some foreign enemy; it is the possibility that we will fail to heed the example of [the postwar] generation; that we will allow the momentum toward democracy to stall, take for granted the institutions and principles upon which our own freedom is based, and forget what the history of this century reminds us: that problems, if left unattended, will all too often come home to America. A decade or two from now, we will be known as the neo-isolationists, who allowed tyranny and lawlessness to rise again, or as the generation that solidified the global triumph of democratic principles.[5]

Yet in the spring of 1999 the easy association of those who were now calling themselves Central (no longer Eastern) European American groups with the expansion of NATO ran into opposition from other Orthodox Americans, who were alarmed at Washington's attempts to curtail Serbian power first in Bosnia then in Kosovo. When bombing runs on Serbia began at the end of March 1999, the first to protest were Serbian Americans, located in many eastern cities but especially in Chicago (where some 250,000 of them make up the largest Serbian community outside Serbia proper). By April other Orthodox communities in the United States began to criticize the attacks, as the Serbian Americans were joined by U.S. communities of Greek and Russian descent. The ethnic patchwork quilt of the Balkans, where Western Christianity and Islam were in conflict with the world of Orthodox Christianity, suddenly revealed itself to be present in the United States as well, where congregations of Muslim (and not only Albanian) Americans could be seen mobilizing in favor of the war effort. "President Clinton, why do you ignore the suffering of Orthodox Christians," ran a full-page ad in the *New York Times* on May 2, 1999, which recounted oppression against the Orthodox in Cyprus, Southern Albania, Croatia, and Turkey, before concluding: "Why is Washington more tolerant when the victims are Orthodox Christians? Why is American foreign policy slanted against Orthodox Christians wherever we turn?"[6]

Similarly, the end of the Cold War opened up new possibilities for peace in the Middle East, which Jewish Americans working with the government of Yitzhak Rabin in Israel were vital in promoting. With the eclipse of Soviet power and the defeat of Iraq in the Gulf War in 1991, radical Arab rejectionists had been weakened to such a point that it appeared that a process could finally begin of exchanging recognition of Israel for the independence of occupied Arab territories on the West Bank of the Jordan River. The result in domestic American politics was for the first time a collaboration between mainstream Arab and Jewish Americans for a goal they all shared.[7]

Of course, it was also necessary that Israel and the Palestine Liberation Organization be willing to exchange territory for peace. The coming to power of a Labour government under Rabin in Israel (in 1992) and a Democratic administration in the United States (in 1993) facilitated the task that the Bush administration had begun, leading to the signature of a peace settlement between Israel and the PLO in September 1993 and its extension to Israel and Jordan a year later.

What neither Rabin nor Clinton nor the end of the Cold War could bring about, however, was the acceptance of the peace process by Iran and certain Arab states and movements. As a result, the United States sponsored a "double containment" of Iran and Libya (which was actually "triple" because of an embargo on Iraq). The American Jewish community was basic to the U.S. decision in August 1996 to extend a full commercial embargo on Iran, with penalties on third parties investing more than $40 million in that country. In addition, the American Israel Public Affairs Committee (AIPAC) played a leading role in seeing that Russian firms were penalized if they helped Iran to improve its missile technology.[8]

The end of the Cold War also facilitated efforts by the World Jewish Congress, in alliance with the U.S. government, to pursue claims on behalf of victims of the Holocaust against the Swiss banking system. Tens of millions of dollars in accounts once belonging to European Jews had in effect been confiscated by Swiss banks. Prominent Jewish Americans like Stuart Eizenstadt and others in the Clinton administration assembled the evidence, which was brought to the Senate floor by the head of the Senate Banking Committee, Alfonse D'Amato, with the implied threat that Swiss banks in the United States might be closed if the matter were not satisfactorily addressed (a threat that was first realized in October 1997, when the Union Bank of Switzerland was barred from participation in a New York state bond project because of the negative attitude of its leadership toward the investigations).[9]

An equally impressive example of ethnic group lobbying for a trade embargo came when Cuban Americans allied in the Cuban American National Foundation (CANF) persuaded Congress to pass, and President Clinton to sign, the Helms-Burton bill in February 1996, extending the jurisdiction of American courts over suits brought by American citizens to defend property rights that the Castro government had nullified after 1959. To be sure, the Cuban American sponsors of this bill were working closely with powerful Cold Warriors like Senate Foreign Relations chairman Jesse Helms, who were determined to complete the American triumph against the Soviet Union by destroying the Castro government, and by economic interests that wanted either compensation or protection from competition from Cuba. And they were fortunate in that Castro proved once again to be his own worst enemy, easing the task of his American opponents by shooting down unarmed Cuban American planes that were dropping anti-Fidelista pamphlets over Cuba while a Cuban human rights organization in Havana was holding its first meeting, which Castro then shut down.

The result of Helms-Burton was a major row in U.S. relations with its best trading partners, including not only all the members of the European Union but Canada and Mexico as well. Perhaps these countries should agree with the United States, as conservative Americans often say, maintaining that a regime like Castro's would only be emboldened if relations with it were normalized. Perhaps Castro would be better "killed with kindness," as more liberal Americans argue, claiming that his government could not withstand the upsurge of confidence Cuban society would experience if its isolation were ended. For our purposes, the point is rather that CANF demonstrated real power over American foreign policy in these debates, and that through the trade bill's impact on U.S. relations with all its trading partners in the World Trade Organization, this ethnic group has had an impact on matters far beyond the Caribbean.[10]

While the internationalism of Jewish and East European Americans is now several generations old, and that of Cuban Americans begins with the Bay of Pigs in 1961, the end of the Cold War has allowed other ethnic communities a new role in American foreign policy. Thus Armenian Americans gained critical influence on U.S. policy in the Caucasus by virtue of the creation in 1991 for the first time of an Armenian Republic. It is widely agreed that the high level of U.S. aid to Armenia (the second highest per capita in the world, after Israel) and the embargo of official assistance to Azerbaijan (which sits alongside massive amounts of oil in the Caspian Sea) would be inconceivable American policy were it not for this ethnic American community and its determination that the Armenian population of Nagorno Karabakh, a province of Azerbaijan, be given home rule if not united with Armenia itself. By Section 907 of the Freedom Support Act of 1992, Armenian American lobbyists managed to exclude Azerbaijan from receiving aid intended to support newly independent former Soviet states, despite the fact that the Armenian government was highly authoritarian, that it was an aggressor state, and that it was friendly with Iran and Russia, the two rivals of the United States in the region.[11]

In their efforts, the Armenians have been aided by Greek Americans, who for over two decades have successfully mitigated what would otherwise surely be, in the minds of most observers, a much more pro-Turkish policy on the part of Washington. While all ethnic lobbies have an understandable tendency to exaggerate their strength in order to increase their membership and their clout in Washington, the assessment of the 104th Congress by Aram Hamparian, the executive director of the Armenian National Committee of America, was probably close to the mark: "The Armenian lobby enjoyed unprecedented success during the 104th Congress. The Radanovich-Bonior, Visclosly, and Porter Amendments sanctioning Turkey for their ongoing denial of the Armenian Genocide, continued blockade of Armenia and human rights abuses—each passed by an overwhelming margin. At the same time, U.S. aid to Armenia steadily increased . . . We owe these successes to the tireless efforts of countless Armenian Americans."[12]

To be sure, the Armenian lobby could make only limited gains as the oil industry rallied to break its hold on U.S. policy in the Caucasus for the sake of getting access to the estimated 50–200 billion barrels of oil under the Caspian Sea. In late 1997 these reserves were estimated to be worth some $4 trillion at current prices, not counting another $4 trillion in gas reserves (making the area second only to the Persian Gulf, which has at least three times more energy resources underground).[13] As I indicated in the Introduction, the Armenian lobby also had to contend with the American Jewish community, which rallied to the side of Turkey in the petroleum dispute in its ambition to defend the growing Turkish–Israeli relationship. Still, it is well worth noting that for years the Armenian lobby has had a remarkable degree of control over American policy in this region, and that in September 1998, even as the tide was turning against this lobby over the direction of U.S. policy in the Caucasus, the Congress approved $100 million in aid to Armenia and Nagorno Karabakh.

The end of the Cold War has also seen a continuation of African American involvement in the formulation of U.S. foreign policy. Black Americans were critical in determining a policy toward Haiti that ultimately led in October 1994 to that country's military occupation by the United States, with the expressed purpose of restoring it to democratic government under its duly elected president Jean-Baptiste Aristide. Perhaps the United States would have acted without this pressure, for there was opposition to the arrival of Haitian refugees, and the government of Raoul Cedras had repeatedly humiliated the Clinton administration by reneging on its commitments. But given widespread public opposition to military intervention there (polls showed 80 percent in opposition at one point), the principal force behind the U.S. occupation was the demand by black Americans (the political elite especially) on a president whom they had done much to elect that decisive action be taken to restore Aristide.[14]

Subsequently, black Americans became leaders in defining administration policy toward sub-Saharan Africa. A particular ambition of TransAfrica was the restoration of democratic government in Nigeria, as well as the promotion of human rights elsewhere on the continent. In December 1997 Jesse Jackson visited Kenya to back the idea of democratic processes there in light of upcoming elections. At the same time, black entrepreneurs, apparently working through the Congressional Black Caucus (CBC), were influential in persuading legislative forces and the administration to combine behind new initiatives for trade and investment throughout the region, which were announced in June 1997 (and passed in the House in March 1998 under the name Africa Growth and Opportunity Bill).

This recital of events should not obscure the complexity of black involvement in American foreign policy. Apparently, Nigerian pressure eventually forced TransAfrica to back off from its campaign to promote democracy there. Disagreements between the CBC and Randall Robinson over trade with and aid to Africa ultimately stymied the legislation. Still, the importance of promoting the participation of African Americans in the making of U.S. foreign policy—and not just toward the Caribbean and Africa—can be seen by Minister Louis Farrakhan's attacks on America's role in the world. In a trip through the Middle East and Africa in 1996, Farrakhan was reported to have called for the destruction of this country by the Muslim world and to have accepted $1 billion from the Libyan leader Muammar Qadaffi for his political activities within the United States. Better by far the role played by the Reverend Jesse Jackson in world affairs, most Americans would agree, than that played by Minister Farrakhan.[15]

As in Haiti, so in Northern Ireland, the end of the Cold War allowed the Clinton administration to take initiatives at the behest of an American ethnic community. Late in 1968 "the Troubles" began in Northern Ireland, as police attacked a Catholic civil rights march. The following summer riots escalated and British troops arrived; by 1970 the IRA had split and the Provisional IRA, using the threat of force, was renewing a traditional effort to get the British out of the six provinces and reunify the island. The IRA effort was backed in the United States by NORAID, the Irish Northern Aid Committee, which formed the same year. Shortly thereafter prominent Irish Americans like Chicago Mayor Richard Daley and Senator Edward Kennedy called for withdrawal of British troops and unification of the island, but denounced the use of violence to achieve these goals.[16]

In the 1992 election Clinton sought to gain the Irish vote by promising to encourage a peace process in Ulster. Given British objections to American involvement, it seems unlikely that he would have undertaken this initiative had he not been advised by the Irish American Senators Daniel Patrick Moynihan and Edward Kennedy that it would aid the return of so-called Reagan Democrats (largely blue collar, white Catholics) to the Democratic party.[17] In the event, it appears the initiative paid off; for the first time a presidential candidate pledged to try to end the sectarian struggle in Northern Ireland and set out to do so. According to the polls for the 1992 and 1996 elections, the only groups of white Americans who voted more for Clinton than for his rivals were Jews and Catholics, the Catholics returning to the Democratic party in a presidential election for the first time since 1977 and presumably including many Irish and East European Americans (the latter pleased by the prospects for NATO's expansion as the former were by his positions on Northern Ireland).

Well before the signing of the Good Friday peace accord on April 10, 1998, there was general agreement—even among those British who at first deplored Clinton's invitation to Sinn Fein leader Gerry Adams to visit the United States and Clinton's follow-up trip to Ireland late in 1995—that the American role in the peace process, under George Mitchell's leadership, had been positive and substantive. Had it not been for the activism of Irish Americans, little of this might have happened—neither direct presidential involvement, nor participation in the International Fund for Ireland, which funnels nearly $20 million yearly from the United States to the North to assist investments in areas that might otherwise be shunned or in companies that agree to abide by the MacBride Principles, designed to promote equality for Catholics in the country. During his involvement, Clinton changed from an apparently opportunistic to a seriously committed partisan of a just peace in Ulster. He said on his visit to Belfast on November 30, 1995: "Because [America's] greatness flows from the wealth of our diversity as well as the strength of the ideals we share in common, we feel bound to support others around the world who seek to bridge their own divides. This is an important part of our country's mission on the eve of the twenty-first century, because we know that the chain of peace that protects us grows stronger with every new link that is forged."

In a more general sense, the change in the ethnoracial structure of the United States caused by large-scale immigration since the late 1960s may eventually have a dramatic impact on this country's foreign policy by realigning domestic concerns about foreign affairs. "The immigration process is the single most important determinant of American foreign policy," declared Daniel Patrick Moynihan and Nathan Glazer in 1975, and if the statement is surely exaggerated, the point is nonetheless well taken:

> It is odd how little this phenomenon figures in American public discussion; it is neither hailed nor challenged, but simply ignored . . . This process regulates the ethnic composition of the American electorate. Foreign policy responds to that ethnic composition. It responds to other things as well, but probably *first of all* to the primal facts of ethnicity . . . Foreign policy will be affected in diverse and profound ways. Yet oddly, the United States Department of State almost wholly ignores the immigration process. The fact that immigration policy is foreign policy is a seemingly inexplicable thought in Foggy Bottom.[18]

## Notes

1. Jack Citrin et al., "Is American Nationalism Changing? Implications for Foreign Policy," *International Studies Quarterly*, 38, 1, 1994; John E. Rielly, ed., "American Public Opinion and U.S. Foreign Policy, 1999" (Chicago Council on Foreign Relations, 1999), 4, finds support for an active role at 61 percent among the public at large, but at 96 percent among policy leaders.

2. Dick Kirschten, "Ethnic Resurging," *National Journal*, 2/25/95.
3. *Detroit News*, 11/23/96; *Chicago Tribune*, 1/28/97.
4. *New York Times*, 8/11/97.
5. Ibid., 6/6/97; on Albright's enthusiasm over the expansion of NATO, see ibid., 3/13/99.
6. Reports on the growing political solidarity of Orthodox Americans appeared in the *New York Times*, 3/25/99, 4/4/99; and on the *Lehrer NewsHour*; 3/26/99. But presumably undercutting this sentiment, on July 4, 1999, the *New York Times* reported that the Patriarch of the Serbian Orthodox church in Serbia was denouncing crimes of the Serbian army in Kosovo.
7. Shain, ch. 3.
8. *Wall Street Journal*, 6/18/96; *New York Times*, 5/1/96; 8/6/96; *Journal of Commerce*, 12/15/98.
9. Frontline, "Nazi Gold," 6/17/97; Gordon A. Craig, "How to Think about the Swiss," *New York Review of Books*, 6/11/98; *New York Times*, 7/23/97, 7/31/97, 10/10/97, 12/2/97. In December 1999 Germany announced a related settlement on the claims of Nazi forced laborers amounting to $5.1 billion.
10. Patrick J. Haney and Walt Vanderbush, "The Role of Ethnic Groups in U.S. Foreign Policy: The Case of the Cuban American National Foundation," *International Studies Quarterly*, 43, 2, 1999; Patrick J. Kiger, "Squeeze Play: The United States, Cuba, and the Helms-Burton Act" (Washington: Center for Public Integrity, 1997); Peter H. Stone, "Cuban Clout," *National Journal*, 2/20/95; *International Herald Tribune*, 7/12/96; *New York Times*, 10/23/96.
11. Carroll J. Doherty, "Armenia's Special Relationship with U.S. Is Showing Strain," *Congressional Quarterly*, 5/31/97; *Washington Post*, 8/1/96.
12. ANCA web page, dated 11/1/96, retrieved 11/5/97.
13. *Boston Globe*, 11/13/97.
14. *New York Times*, 7/14/94; Thernstrom and Thernstrom, 304f; Peter J. Boyer, "The Rise of Kweisi Mfume," *New Yorker*, 8/1/94; Shain, 70ff. Georges A. Fauriol, ed., *Haitian Frustrations: Dilemmas for U.S. Policy* (Washington: Center for Strategic and International Studies, 1995).
15. *New York Times*, 2/21/96; *Washington Post*, 2/26/96; Karin L. Stanford, *Beyond the Boundaries: Reverend Jesse Jackson in International Affairs* (Albany: State University of New York Press, 1997); Robert Singh, *The Farrakhan Phenomenon: Race, Reaction, and the Paranoid Style in American Politics* (Washington: Georgetown University Press, 1997); Thernstrom and Thernstrom, 304f; Shain, 70ff.
16. Tim Pat Coogan, *The Troubles: Ireland's Ordeal 1966–1996 and the Search for Peace* (Niwot, CO: Roberts Rinehart, 1996).
17. Joseph O'Grady, "An Irish Policy Born in the U.S.A.," *Foreign Affairs*, 75, 3, 1996; Karen Donfried, "Northern Ireland: Fair Employment and the MacBride Principles," Congressional Research Service, Library of Congress, 4/18/96; Adrian Guelke, "The United States, Irish Americans and the Northern Ireland Peace Process," *International Affairs*, 72, 3, 1996; Ray O'Hanlon, *The New Irish Americans* (Niwot, CO: Roberts Rinehart, 1998).
18. Daniel Patrick Moynihan and Nathan Glazer, eds., *Ethnicity: Theory and Experience* (Cambridge, MA: Harvard University Press, 1975), 23f.

# 12

## Extending the Theory of Public Opinion in American Foreign Policy: Public Opinion as Intervention Constraint

### RICHARD SOBEL

The American public, in general, tends not to pay much attention to foreign policy. The details and intricacies of most American efforts overseas do not usually rise to a high level of interest among the public, and news organizations usually focus on a narrow set of foreign policy topics for any sustained time. This apparent lack of interest does not mean, however, that Americans are entirely withdrawn from foreign policy concerns. Rather, the American public can be quite informed and engaged when issues involve the broad contours of U.S. foreign policy, war and intervention, or crisis moments. In such instances, public opinion can be quite influential in the formulation of American foreign policy.

Richard Sobel considers the effects of public opinion on foreign policy, and finds that they are most pronounced when it comes to questions of war and intervention. Looking at a variety of cases, Sobel examines how public opinion has served to influence foreign policy during wartime. He suggests that public attitudes are an "unavoidable and consistent factor in [the] decision-making processes" of government leaders, and that as the public becomes increasingly vocal, the American government becomes more sensitive to public opinion. In other words, the policymaking process can be quite democratic at times, and public opinion can impose considerable restraints upon government action.

This observation has considerable relevance for current American policies. The U.S. government has seen domestic support for the military presence in Iraq slip considerably as the war has continued over a period of years. President Bush has repeatedly vowed to "stay the course," and he has not cut troop levels in Iraq. The president has, in fact, increased the number of American troops in Iraq in the "surge," but this action actually reflects attention to the impatience and dissatisfaction of the America public. This action lends credence to Sobel's argument, which speaks to the president's ability

to maintain the American commitment to an American military presence in Iraq, as well as limitations on further military actions in the
war on terror and in combating nuclear proliferation.

---

*The Impact of Public Opinion on U.S. Foreign Policy Since Vietnam* examines
the role that public attitudes have played over the last generation in the
making of U.S. foreign policy. The study explains the place of opinion in
the policy process, particularly decisions about U.S. interventions, both
on a theoretical level and from the perspective of actual decision-makers.
In pursuing its goals, the book focuses on four of the most prominent
foreign interventions of the last generation: the Vietnam War, the
Nicaraguan contra funding controversy, the Gulf War, and the war in
Bosnia. By demonstrating how public opinion affected policy, the cases
provide the basis for the building of an overall theory of public opinion in
foreign policymaking.

This concluding chapter summarizes and reflects on the insights the
book provides into the relationship between public opinion and foreign
policymaking. In particular, it draws conclusions from comparisons across
the cases about how public opinion actually entered into the foreign policy
decision-making process in military interventions. Further, it explores the
impact of national public opinion on administration policymakers, and for
the Nicaragua case, the influence of national and constituent opinion on
congressional decision-makers. In short, it evaluates the actual roles of
public opinion in the foreign policy of our democracy.

Through the combination of analytic approaches, the investigation of
these four controversies advances the knowledge of and the theories about
public opinion in foreign interventions. Reviews of the major empirical theories of the influence of public opinion set the basis for Key's system of
dikes theory, which generally holds that public opinion sets limits or constraints on the discretion that policymakers have in choosing from among
possible policy options. The decline of public support established, for
instance, how long the United States could continue intervention in
Vietnam. Protest as a type of public opinion set limits on how extreme, for
example, could be the options from which the Johnson and Nixon administration policymakers could choose.

In developing general insights about opinion's impact on foreign policy,
the study explores foreign policy attitudes as shaped by the climate of
opinion, overall presidential approval, and public preferences for specific
policies. The examination of the actual role of public opinion in foreign
intervention policy shows that both administration and congressional policymakers saw themselves more typically as trustees of good government
than as delegates of the people. Despite minimizing the importance of

public opinion, officials were aware of public attitudes and recognized the central importance of public support for their policies. Both recognized existing or anticipated constraints in public opinion on their decisions.

To set a larger historical context for the particular cases, the book also investigates how current public opinion interacts with longer-term trends or cycles in interventionist or isolationist sentiments. Rather than having unique meanings, particular levels of opinion occur within the general climate of attitudes of interventionism or noninterventionism. In particular, contemporary attitudes toward involvement in Vietnam, against intervention in Nicaragua, and for and against actions in the Persian Gulf and Bosnia fit with long-term trends in attitudes toward intervention or nonintervention. Each era was both influenced by and contributed to the adjacent cycles in internationalism and noninterventionism.

Though the Vietnam War began during an interventionist era, it soon contributed to and was influenced by sentiments toward withdrawal. The contra funding controversy was constrained by the "post-Vietnam syndrome." Attitudes during the Gulf War and war in Bosnia were both influenced by the post-Vietnam syndrome and contributed to attitudes more supportive of later successful interventions. Anticommunism and humanitarianism drove interventionism, while isolationism, the post-Vietnam syndrome, costs, and casualties drove anti-interventionism. Generally, opinion influenced policy, though policymakers also affected opinion, particularly through the media.

The significance of this study appears in several guises. First, the research bases its conclusions on careful evaluation of prominent cases, pertinent evidence, and appropriate multiple and mutually reinforcing sources of information. The analysis is based on the words by the major decision-makers themselves in speeches, public statements, memos, memoirs, minutes, and interviews. Because they are given public scrutiny and reflect sensitivity to public sentiment, public statements often reveal more than private papers, although private papers reveal personal thoughts and concerns often kept from the public. Leaders may not think about public opinion explicitly in their daily decisions or may try to deny any influence, but they find that public attitudes are an unavoidable and consistent factor in their decision-making processes. Second, the study demonstrates not only that public opinion influences policy but also that the major effects of public opinion typically manifest themselves in constraint rather than in policy setting.

Third, the study shows the generally increasing role of public opinion in, if not always on, foreign policymaking and how that change has occurred over time. For better or worse, the public voice grows louder, and sensitivity to that volume increases, though not always more responsively. The exploration of the implications for policymakers and citizens in a democracy suggests that knowledge of the role of public opinion on policy might assist efforts to move the American foreign policy process in a more democratic direction. The coincidence of empirical evidence of how public opinion affects foreign policymaking with normative ideas about how public opinion should affect policy may create more effective decision making.

## REVIEW OF THE CASES

In focusing on the relationship of public opinion to foreign policy in the four central military interventions in recent history, the book draws insights from the words of principal decision-makers. Major cabinet officers, confirmed by the Senate, in the State Department and Department of Defense (as well as the National Security Council) inform the president, who ultimately decides policy. To fill out the historical record, the Nicaragua chapter explores other prominent decision-makers, particularly representatives and senators for the contra funding controversy when Congress was central to funding decisions, as it was for the vote to go to war in the Gulf.

In short, for each major crisis and decision-maker, the study identifies, from the decision-maker's own words, to what extent he was aware of public opinion at key benchmarks during the controversy. Then it attempts to ascertain whether public opinion, and in the case of Vietnam, protest, influenced the policymaker's decisions.

### The Vietnam War

The opening case examines the complexities of the Vietnam War and how public opinion and protest affected the development of U.S. escalatory and de-escalatory policies from the 1960s to the early 1970s. It focuses on U.S. policy at the specific benchmarks of the Johnson decision to escalate the war in 1964 after the Tonkin Gulf incident, the period after the Tet offensive, and the 1969 moratorium and the Nixon administration's planned Duck Hook escalation and the 1970 Cambodia invasion. During the war, support dropped and opposition rose, though presidential approval depended on the perceived success of current policy. Yet opinion and policy were generally consistent because, as opinion changed, so did the policy. The Vietnam case shows that both opinion influenced policy and policy influenced opinion. Johnson was the consummate poll reader who cited the polls he kept in his pocket when they favored him and tried to ignore them when they opposed him. Johnson's decisions to escalate in 1965 were abetted by conservative pressure, while his post-Tet decisions to de-escalate in 1968 were constrained by both declining public support and increasing protest. Dean Rusk underestimated the extent to which the American public was impatient to end the war, while Robert McNamara felt, and perhaps later accepted, the constraints of protest and declining public support against his rational evaluation of policy options. When it was clear the public and elite opposed further involvement in Vietnam, McNamara's successor, Clark Clifford, overturned Johnson's opposition to beginning to de-escalate the war.

Aware of public opposition in the ongoing moratorium protests, Richard Nixon's strategies in 1969 were constrained to Vietnamization rather than escalation by declining public support and increasing protest, especially around the time of the moratoriums. But his "silent majority" speech in November 1969 created leeway for continuing the war, and the threat and actuality of protests as intense forms of public expression constrained the extremity of policy options away from intensive bombing or even invasion of the North. The surge in protest on campuses after the Cambodia invasions accelerated the exit of allied forces.

First as national security adviser, and then as secretary of state, Henry Kissinger was hamstrung by public opposition to his policy. Though he railed against the antiwar movement, he ultimately had to accommodate to it. (William Rogers' role as secretary of state was largely focused elsewhere.) As a former congressman and practicing politician, Melvin Laird recognized the declining public support in his advocacy of Vietnamization as a way of de-escalating the war and reducing public pressure for a quick end. The decline of the antiwar movement permitted the escalatory bombings in 1972 that led to an armistice in 1973. The U.S. role in the war ended when the public's patience ultimately ran out.

## The Contra Funding Controversy

The examination of the Nicaraguan case flows from the Vietnam study because it focuses on the first major, albeit indirect, post-Vietnam intervention during the 1980s. Nicaragua was a case of both nonintervention and intervention constrained by public opposition. Although U.S. combat forces were not directly involved, U.S. funding sustained the contras. Interviews with high-level decision-makers in both the Reagan administration and Congress reveal influences at the top unknown to previous exploration of the issues (Sobel, 1993). The post-Vietnam syndrome, public opposition, and congressional resistance circumscribed what policymakers could do in Nicaragua. As at the end of the Vietnam War, despite continuing anticommunist sentiment, the public opposed intervention in Central America.

Specifically, public opinion constraints appeared in limits to the amount of money or potential personnel the administration could allocate to the contras. The failure of President Reagan to persuade the public to support administration policy demonstrates the limits of leadership even for a popularly perceived president who attempts to change public opinion on a controversial issue. Administration policymakers acknowledged that opinion limited the scope of their contra aid policy, but they largely attempted to ignore public opposition. Recognizing that they lacked general public support, the leaders were unwilling to change their goals to meet the public preference for nonintervention. Instead they sought public approval as a potential "tool" with which they could act as trustees of the people in choosing a different foreign policy direction from that which the American public preferred.

Ronald Reagan was well aware of public opinion and that it forced his administration to ask for less funding for the contras than he would have liked. Yet he continued to press for a policy that the public rejected. George Shultz was also aware of public opposition, but he felt that correct and successful policy would produce its own constituency. Taking lessons from Vietnam, and recognizing public opposition Caspar Weinberger took into account public attitudes and felt that the support of the Congress and the public was essential to carrying out intervention policy. The Shultz-Weinberger debate in November 1984 on the bases for U.S. intervention policy set the terms for discussions of the role of opinion in this and later foreign interventions. Shultz's deputies Elliot Abrams and Ed Fox revealed how opinion was a tool toward a chosen policy. Reagan pollster Richard Wirthlin reveals how extensively poll evidence entered the policy process.

Public opinion also loosely influenced the Congress, which represented public preferences by voting largely according to ideology, partisanship, and presidential popularity. Public opinion influenced members of Congress, but not particularly how they voted on contra aid. Legislators were not especially worried about public opinion in their districts but were afraid of what public sentiment might become, particularly during an election campaign. Representatives carefully monitored public opinion to be sure that their voting decisions were not too directly constrained. Despite consistent public opposition to the Reagan policy of aiding the contras, Congress typically reflected district public opinion in voting for only limited assistance and opposing direct involvement. Senators Lugar and Pell acknowledged that electoral consequences sensitized them to the public attitudes. Congressmen Skelton and Spratt felt they were trusted by their constituencies but they carefully monitored public support in their districts to make sure that they were not more clearly constrained. Presidential lobbying of Congress ultimately provided the few swing votes on close funding decisions.

## The Gulf War

The Gulf War was the first major post-Vietnam direct U.S. intervention. In response to Iraq's invasion of Kuwait in August 1990, the United States led coalition forces into the Middle East and ultimately initiated an air and ground war in January and February 1991. Strong initial public support of Desert Shield indicated a decline of the post-Vietnam syndrome. But decreasing and divided support and increasing congressional questioning as the buildup to war continued during a recession began to restrict the Bush administration's options in the direction of negotiations. Administration attention and communication that reflected sensitivity to domestic political support also sent mixed messages to Mideast leaders. The potential for a sharp decline in public support for a prolonged Desert Storm campaign constrained the administration to a "100-hour war." Protest against the war grew quickly but had little effect on the administration and was poorly received by a public largely supportive of the U.S.'s role in the conflict.

George Bush was aware that there was more public support for the war than there was in Congress, but he promised that politics would not affect his policies. The lessons of Vietnam encouraged his undertaking a massive but short intervention to circumvent the dynamics of potentially dropping public support. James Baker recognized at the start of the war that there was not yet public support for an intervention, but he contributed to its rise as the war approached. Like Melvin Laird, Dick Cheney, a former congressman and later White House chief of staff, knowledgeable about public opinion, revealed little in his public statements about his own awareness of public opinion or its impact on his decisions; but in interviews both men acknowledged the public's constraining role in interventions. Cheney's deft use of the media suggested an awareness of the need to keep the public on the administration's side.

## Bosnia

Bosnia was the first extended post–Cold War conflict. In a sense, it was both an example of nonintervention, during most of the Bush and the early Clinton administration, and of more forceful intervention that began during the middle of the Clinton presidency. The public opposed unilateral U.S. intervention but supported humanitarian, indirect, and multilateral involvement. Because of their perceptions of public opposition, U.S. leaders consistently refused to send ground troops to fight but offered to send peacekeepers once the war was settled. Eventually the United States became involved in fairly popular multilateral air strikes that brought the fighting to an end.

Perceptions of public opposition, first in the Bush administration and then in the Clinton administration, restrained Bosnia policy. U.S. involvement was limited and reluctant for three years across both administrations. At first, the United States provided humanitarian aid and patrolled the no-fly zone, for both of which there was strong support. Eventually it took part in aggressive allied air strikes of which the public approved in a multilateral context. Finally, it sent peacekeeping troops, a measure for which there had been strong public support earlier. As deployment approached, this support gradually reduced to minority levels until it became clear to a majority again that the involvement was relatively riskless and successful.

George Bush was aware of public opposition but promised not to let politics interfere with his concerns for humanitarian intervention. Always the political animal, James Baker felt there was not enough U.S. public support to intervene more forcefully. Lawrence Eagleburger was little aware of public sentiments and felt little constrained by them. Dick Cheney held his counsel in public on this issue but later revealed his sensitivity to public sentiment.

Bill Clinton indicated some awareness of more forceful public sentiment in his interventionist campaign statements. When in office, he weakened his policy as he felt the constraint of public opposition. Though Warren Christopher was aware of public opinion and felt it should have a role in policymaking, he perceived the public to be more opposed to involvement than it really was. William Perry indicated less awareness or influence by public opinion, and he was generally opposed to intervention for pragmatic reasons.

## SOME REFLECTIONS

Aggressive conservative pressures and general anticommunism permitted U.S. involvement in Vietnam until casualties and costs that contrasted with administration promises of success destroyed public support. Despite continuing anticommunist sentiments and approval of a communicative president who strongly supported Nicaragua involvement, during the early post-Vietnam era the American public generally preferred to avoid interventions. Those specific attitudes on policy contributed to the climate of opinion that constrained the administration's efforts. Both administration members and congressional representatives were aware of public opposition, and even when they sought to avoid it, they acknowledged its apparent or potential effects. What is "effective" public opinion that actually influences policy depends on the opinion context and the centrality of groups holding specific attitudes (Kull and Destler, 1999).

In short, decision-makers were constantly aware of public opinion and were by necessity constrained in the timing, extent, and direction of their actions. Presidents follow the polls for both governing and electoral purposes. Secretaries of state are often more aggressive than the public would require and typically less aware of public opinion until it runs counter to their policies. Secretaries of defense tend, in general, to be less aware of and less constrained by public attitudes, yet often less interventionist than their state department counterparts.

Even four compelling cases do not make a theory, but the consistencies in research findings suggest that constraint is the revealing theoretical model. The testimony of principal decision-makers through interviews, memoirs, and public statements advances empirical theory for public opinion that also emphasizes constraint and indirect control. Rather than constraint being the maximum effect that opinion may have on policy, public opinion increasingly influences the nature and presentation of policy (Nacos, Shapiro, and Isernia, 2000). When intensely focused, public opinion may essentially set policy (Graham, 1989). That its influence extends further into the different stages of development of policy actions is increasingly apparent.

## CONCLUSION: BEYOND CONSTRAINT

In short, public opinion has constrained the U.S. foreign policy decision-making process over the last generation. By delving into theory, events, and interpretations of the Vietnam, Nicaragua, Gulf, and Bosnia interventions and obtaining the views of active decision-makers, this analysis provides valuable insights about public opinion's influences in U.S. foreign relations for scholars, policymakers, and citizens engaged by the historical material and policy recommendations illuminating these complex processes.

The issues of public support and opposition to U.S. interventions remain pressing ones for American domestic politics and foreign policy. Public opinion is increasingly recognized as a central factor in the decisions about U.S. foreign relations. The voice of the people speaks during intervention debates, and, in this collision of public attitudes with national security, policy continues to be of fundamental concern for citizens and policymakers. The reality that public opinion constrains foreign intervention policy contributes both to the development of theory about opinion in foreign interventions and to the advance of democracy in the realm of foreign affairs.

Public opinion may constrain policy, but policymakers need not always be constrained by public attitudes. There are times when leaders should heed opinion, times when they should lead opinion, and times when they should proceed despite opinion. Those times depend on American norms and history, because U.S. policy needs to follow the fundamental principles of the nation and the goals of democracy and world peace. The history of the United States before the two world wars suggests that when presidents delay in entering the world stage at crucial times, the costs of such dalliance may be far more devastating than the price of earlier action. When America's fundamental goals are in evidence or in peril, policymakers should educate the public; but leadership may need to risk the public's opprobrium temporarily to pursue enlightened policies and develop public support for the longer term.

The beginning of the new century, a decade after the Cold War's end, is an auspicious time to examine in detail a central issue of democratic governance and international affairs: how public opinion influences U.S. foreign policy. In providing evidence about how opinion affected past foreign interventions in the context of our normative ideals, this study helps readers to comprehend how America makes its foreign policy and also to evaluate how well democracy works here in the realm of foreign affairs.

# PART III

# An Emerging Power at the Turn of the Century: Creating a Global American Foreign Policy

Part III looks to the formation of an American foreign policy at the turn of the 20th century, when the United States became a global power. In this period, the United States had consolidated control across a continent, experienced strong economic growth fueled by rapid industrialization, and had become a more powerful, confident nation. The result was a broader outlook—a global outlook—and a more assertive foreign policy. Spain, Britain, and other European powers increasingly found themselves confronting the United States in places such as Latin America, the Caribbean, East Asia and the Pacific, and the United States eventually found itself in possession of new territories—from Puerto Rico to Hawaii to the Philippines.

The readings in this part look at how this situation evolved, and how American attitudes toward territorial expansion, economic interests, and ideological reach emerged in response to growing American power. As the readings illustrate, American policymakers were optimistic about the potential of American power. Only a few years after the United States had won the Spanish-American War, President Theodore Roosevelt informed the world that the United States would act as an international police power in the Western Hemisphere. Senator Albert Beveridge went much further, asserting the right of the United States to conquer new territories to build an "empire of liberty." Woodrow Wilson extended America's attempted reach beyond this, seeking to build a world that was safe for democracy. Each of these formulations reflected that the United States was a rising power in the world, and that its leaders intended to capitalize on this circumstance. In the latter half of 20th century, Otto von Bismarck, the Chancellor of Germany, commenting on the great fortunes and successes of the United States, said that God had a special providence for fools, drunks, and the United States of America. As the 20th century progressed, American leaders appeared to act as if they believed this too, and expansion across a continent turned into expansion (both territorial and ideological) beyond the continent. As Robert Kagan points out in "Cowboy Nation," this aggressiveness was not unusual, as it has been a consistent feature of U.S. foreign policy, from the first Indian wars right up to the Iraq War.

The selections by LaFeber and Mead speak to this same phenomenon of a rising United States, but from a different angle, by examining the economic foundations that lay at the heart of the country's growing national strength. Precisely because the United States' economic interests had expanded and advanced over time, American leaders could subsequently project American power with confidence. By the end of this era, American power eclipsed that of all other rivals, including Britain, which it eventually replaced as a global hegemon.

# 13 The Roosevelt Corollary to the Monroe Doctrine

## THEODORE ROOSEVELT

The first three selections in this part of the book come from Theodore Roosevelt, Albert Beveridge, and Woodrow Wilson, each of whom advocated an activist, robust policy of American engagement with other parts of the world. The thinking of each, however, was informed by a somewhat different understanding of American motivations, needs, and goals. And indeed, the foreign policy traditions that each gave voice to have all played important roles in the development and implementation of American foreign policy.

In the first of these selections, President Teddy Roosevelt describes his policy with regard to the Western Hemisphere in what became known as The Roosevelt Corollary to the Monroe Doctrine. The Monroe Doctrine sought to prohibit further European colonization and interference in the Western Hemisphere, but Roosevelt extended the idea in the early 1900s. Concerned that a financial crisis in the Dominican Republic would prompt an invasion by European powers, Roosevelt stated in his annual address to Congress in December of 1904 that the United States would intervene if needed as an international police power to maintain order, in effect to make certain that nations in the Western Hemisphere paid their debts to international creditors. In practice, the Roosevelt Corollary served as a justification for the United States to frequently intervene in places such as Cuba, Nicaragua, Haiti, and the Dominican Republic in order to restore internal stability (an effort that often failed or was, at best, temporary) and maintain U.S. influence.

Roosevelt's extension of the Monroe Doctrine is informed very much by the Realist school of thought. Roosevelt's words, and the deeds he carried out, involved seeking stability in Central America and the Caribbean, denying access and influence to strategic rivals (or at least potential rivals), and developing a U.S. sphere of influence by projecting power into a region that was considered "America's backyard." In this formulation, the United States would protect its own interests and security by imposing order where it did not exist, largely to keep foreign influence out and American influence in.

Theodore Roosevelt, "The Roosevelt Corollary to the Monroe Doctrine" from President Theodore Roosevelt's Annual Message to Congress, December 6, 1904.

In treating of our foreign policy and of the attitude that this great Nation should assume in the world at large, it is absolutely necessary to consider the Army and the Navy, and the Congress, through which the thought of the Nation finds its expression, should keep ever vividly in mind the fundamental fact that it is impossible to treat our foreign policy, whether this policy takes shape in the effort to secure justice for others or justice for ourselves, save as conditioned upon the attitude we are willing to take toward our Army, and especially toward our Navy. It is not merely unwise, it is contemptible, for a nation, as for an individual, to use high-sounding language to proclaim its purposes, or to take positions which are ridiculous if unsupported by potential force, and then to refuse to provide this force. If there is no intention of providing and keeping the force necessary to back up a strong attitude, then it is far better not to assume such an attitude.

The steady aim of this Nation, as of all enlightened nations, should be to strive to bring ever nearer the day when there shall prevail throughout the world the peace of justice. There are kinds of peace which are highly undesirable, which are in the long run as destructive as any war. Tyrants and oppressors have many times made a wilderness and called it peace. Many times peoples who were slothful or timid or shortsighted, who had been enervated by ease or by luxury, or misled by false teachings, have shrunk in unmanly fashion from doing duty that was stern and that needed self-sacrifice, and have sought to hide from their own minds their shortcomings, their ignoble motives, by calling them love of peace. The peace of tyrannous terror, the peace of craven weakness, the peace of injustice, all these should be shunned as we shun unrighteous war.

The goal to set before us as a nation, the goal which should be set before all mankind, is the attainment of the peace of justice, of the peace which comes when each nation is not merely safe-guarded in its own rights, but scrupulously recognizes and performs its duty toward others. Generally peace tells for righteousness; but if there is conflict between the two, then our fealty is due first to the cause of righteousness. Unrighteous wars are common, and unrighteous peace is rare; but both should be shunned. The right of freedom and the responsibility for the exercise of that right can not be divorced. One of our great poets has well and finely said that freedom is not a gift that tarries long in the hands of cowards. Neither does it tarry long in the hands of those too slothful, too dishonest, or too unintelligent to exercise it. The eternal vigilance which is the price of liberty must be exercised, sometimes to guard against outside foes; although of course far more often to guard against our own selfish or thoughtless shortcomings.

If these self-evident truths are kept before us, and only if they are so kept before us, we shall have a clear idea of what our foreign policy in its larger aspects should be. It is our duty to remember that a nation has no more right to do injustice to another nation, strong or weak, than an individual has to do injustice to another individual; that the same moral law applies in one case as in the other. But we must also remember that it is as much the duty of the Nation to guard its own rights and its own interests as it is the duty of the individual so to do. Within the Nation the individual has now delegated this right to the State, that is, to the representative of all the individuals, and it is a maxim of the law that for every wrong there is a remedy. But in international law we have not advanced by any means as far as we have advanced in municipal law. There is as yet no judicial way of enforcing a right in international law. When one nation wrongs another or wrongs many others, there is no tribunal before which the wrongdoer can be brought. Either it is necessary supinely to acquiesce in the wrong, and thus put a premium upon brutality and aggression, or else it is necessary for the aggrieved nation valiantly to stand up for its rights. Until some method is devised by which there shall be a degree of international control over offending nations, it would be a wicked thing for the most civilized powers, for those with most sense of international obligations and with keenest and most generous appreciation of the difference between right and wrong, to disarm. If the great civilized nations of the present day should completely disarm, the result would mean an immediate recrudescence of barbarism in one form or another. Under any circumstances a sufficient armament would have to be kept up to serve the purposes of international police; and until international cohesion and the sense of international duties and rights are far more advanced than at present, a nation desirous both of securing respect for itself and of doing good to others must have a force adequate for the work which it feels is allotted to it as its part of the general world duty.

Therefore it follows that a self-respecting, just, and far-seeing nation should on the one hand endeavor by every means to aid in the development of the various movements which tend to provide substitutes for war, which tend to render nations in their actions toward one another, and indeed toward their own peoples, more responsive to the general sentiment of humane and civilized mankind; and on the other hand that it should keep prepared, while scrupulously avoiding wrongdoing itself, to repel any wrong, and in exceptional cases to take action which in a more advanced stage of international relations would come under the head of the exercise of the international police. A great free people owes it to itself and to all mankind not to sink into helplessness before the powers of evil.

## POLICY TOWARD OTHER NATIONS OF THE WESTERN HEMISPHERE

It is not true that the United States feels any land hunger or entertains any projects as regards the other nations of the Western Hemisphere save such as are for their welfare. All that this country desires is to see the neighboring countries stable, orderly, and prosperous. Any country whose people conduct themselves well can count upon our hearty friendship. If a nation shows that it knows how to act with reasonable efficiency and decency in social and political matters, if it keeps order and pays its obligations, it need fear no interference from the United States. Chronic wrongdoing, or an impotence which results in a general loosening of the ties of civilized society, may in America, as elsewhere, ultimately require intervention by some civilized nation, and in the Western Hemisphere the adherence of the United States to the Monroe Doctrine may force the United States, however reluctantly, in flagrant cases of such wrongdoing or impotence, to the exercise of an international police power.

If every country washed by the Caribbean Sea would show the progress in stable and just civilization which with the aid of the Platt Amendment Cuba has shown since our troops left the island, and which so many of the republics in both Americas are constantly and brilliantly showing, all question of interference by this Nation with their affairs would be at an end. Our interests and those of our southern neighbors are in reality identical. They have great natural riches, and if within their borders the reign of law and justice obtains, prosperity is sure to come to them. While they thus obey the primary laws of civilized society they may rest assured that they will be treated by us in a spirit of cordial and helpful sympathy. We would interfere with them only in the last resort, and then only if it became evident that their inability or unwillingness to do justice at home and abroad had violated the rights of the United States or had invited foreign aggression to the detriment of the entire body of American nations. It is a mere truism to say that every nation, whether in America or anywhere else, which desires to maintain its freedom, its independence, must ultimately realize that the right of such independence can not be separated from the responsibility of making good use of it.

In asserting the Monroe Doctrine, in taking such steps as we have taken in regard to Cuba, Venezuela, and Panama, and in endeavoring to circumscribe the theater of war in the Far East, and to secure the open door in China, we have acted in our own interest as well as in the interest of humanity at large. There are, however, cases in which, while our own interests are not greatly involved, strong appeal is made to our sympathies. Ordinarily it is very much wiser and more useful for us to concern ourselves with striving for our own moral and material betterment here at home than to concern ourselves with trying to better the condition of things in other nations. We have plenty of sins of our own to war against, and under ordinary circumstances we can do more for the general uplifting of humanity by striving with heart and soul to put a stop to civic corruption, to brutal lawlessness and violent race prejudices here at home than by passing resolutions and wrongdoing elsewhere. Nevertheless there are occasional crimes committed on so vast a scale and of such peculiar horror as to make us doubt whether it is not our manifest duty to endeavor at least to show our disapproval of the deed and our sympathy with those who have suffered by it. The cases must be extreme in which such a course is justifiable. There must be no effort made to remove the mote from our brother's eye if we refuse to remove the beam from our own. But in extreme cases action may be justifiable and proper. What form the action shall take must depend upon the circumstances of the case; that is, upon the degree of the atrocity and upon our power to remedy it. The cases in which we could interfere by force of arms as we interfered to put a stop to intolerable conditions in Cuba are necessarily very few. Yet it is not to be expected that a people like ours, which in spite of certain very obvious shortcomings, nevertheless as a whole shows by its consistent practice its belief in the principles of civil and religious liberty and of orderly freedom, a people among whom even the worst crime, like the crime of lynching, is never more than sporadic, so that individuals and not classes are molested in their fundamental rights—it is inevitable that such a nation should desire eagerly to give expression to its horror on an occasion like that of the massacre of the Jews in Kishenef, or when it witnesses such systematic and long-extended cruelty and oppression as the cruelty and oppression of which the Armenians have been the victims, and which have won for them the indignant pity of the civilized world.

## 14 In Support of American Empire
### ALBERT J. BEVERIDGE

As an expanding nation in the 19th century, the United States grew significantly from a small country on the Eastern seaboard to a continental power. This success was considered by many to be the result of American ideals and institutions, which were often regarded in this country as superior to those found in other countries. When the United States defeated Spain in war in 1898, and the United States acquired control over Cuba, Puerto Rico, and the Philippines, there were calls throughout the United States for the country to annex new territories and establish an empire.

Albert Beveridge, "In Support of an American Empire," *Congressional Record*, U.S. Senate, 56th Congress, 1st Session, pp. 704–712, 1900.

Senator Albert Beveridge, one of the great advocates of American expansion at the turn of the 20th century, was a firm believer in the idea that the United States was a unique country that possessed great blessings and capabilities. As such, he argued in a floor speech in the U.S. Senate that the United States had an obligation to other peoples and nations: it should extend its rule over other, less advanced societies to bring them the blessings of liberty and democracy. This formulation goes much further than that of President Roosevelt, who sought stability and order in Central America and the Caribbean, if necessary with the assistance of U.S. leadership and troops. Beveridge, by contrast, sought the extension of American political control—involving American ideals, governance, and institutions—into an extended American empire that would bring (at least according to advocates of an imperial policy) enlightened civilization to those had no experience with such a thing. In Beveridge's time, this empire reached into the Caribbean at one end, and all the way across the Pacific to Hawaii and the Philippines, but he saw no natural boundary to this empire.

Senator Beveridge was informed by the idea of American exceptionalism, which suggests that the United States is fundamentally different from all other nations (all nations are in some way unique, but exceptionalism involves the idea that the United States is uniquely unique). For Beveridge, exceptionalism carried with it certain goals to expand the ideals, institutions, and practices of American democracy. At the same time, however, the expansionist goal was also seen as an obligation—one that seemed to require the United States to pursue a policy of imperialism and extend its rule. While Beveridge's zeal for a formal empire is no longer espoused by U.S. policymakers, the exceptionalism that informed Beveridge, as well as the inclination to extend and promote American democracy around the globe, continue to play an important role in American foreign policy.

---

Mr. President, the times call for candor. The Philippines are ours forever, "territory belonging to the United States," as the Constitution calls them. And just beyond the Philippines are China's illimitable markets. We will not retreat from either. We will not repudiate our duty in the archipelago. We will not abandon our opportunity in the Orient. We will not renounce our part in the mission of our race, trustee, under God, of the civilization of the world. And we will move forward to our work, not howling out regrets like slaves whipped to their burdens but with gratitude for a task worthy of our strength and thanksgiving to Almighty God that He has marked us as His chosen people, henceforth to lead in the regeneration of the world . . .

Let men beware how they employ the term "self-government." It is a sacred term. It is the watchword at the door of the inner temple of liberty, for liberty does not always mean self-government. Self-government is a method of liberty—the highest, simplest, best—and it is acquired only after centuries of study and struggle and experiment and instruction and all the elements of the progress of man. Self-government is no base and common thing to be bestowed on the merely audacious. It is the degree which crowns the graduate of liberty, not the name of liberty's infant class, who have not yet mastered the alphabet of freedom. Savage blood, Oriental blood, Malay blood, Spanish example—are these the elements of self-government?

Mr. President, self-government and internal development have been the dominant notes of our first century; administration and the development of other lands will be the dominant notes of our second century. And administration is as high and holy a function as self-government, just as the care of a trust estate is as sacred an obligation as the management of our own concerns. Cain was the first to violate the divine law of human society which makes of us our brother's keeper. And administration of good government is the first lesson in self-government, that exalted estate toward which all civilization tends.

Administration of good government is not denial of liberty. For what is liberty? It is not savagery. It is not the exercise of individual will. It is not dictatorship. It involves government, but not necessarily self-government. It means law. First of all, it is a common rule of action, applying equally to all within its limits. Liberty means protection of property and life without price, free speech without intimidation, justice without purchase or delay, government without favor or favorites. What will best give all this to the people of the Philippines—American administration, developing them gradually toward self-government, or self-government by a people before they know what self-government means?

Senators in opposition are estopped from denying our constitutional power to govern the Philippines as circumstances may demand, for such power is admitted in the case of Florida, Louisiana, Alaska. How, then, is it denied in the Philippines? Is there a geographical interpretation to the Constitution? Do degrees of longitude fix constitutional limitations? Does a thousand miles of ocean diminish constitutional power more than a thousand miles of land?

The ocean does not separate us from the field of our duty and endeavor—it joins us, an established highway needing no repair and landing us at any point desired. The seas do not separate the Philippine Islands from us or from each other. The seas are highways through the archipelago, which would cost hundreds of millions of dollars to construct if they were land instead of water. Land may separate men from their desire; the ocean, never. Russia has been centuries in crossing Siberian wastes; the Puritans cross the Atlantic in brief and flying weeks.

If the Boers must have traveled by land, they would never have reached the Transvaal; but they sailed on liberty's ocean; they walked on civilization's untaxed highway, the welcoming sea. Our ships habitually sailed round the Cape and anchored in California's harbors before a single trail had lined the desert with the whitening bones of those who made it. No! No! The ocean unites us; steam unites us; electricity unites us; all the elements of nature unite us to the region where duty and interest call us.

There is in the ocean no constitutional argument against the march of the flag, for the oceans, too, are ours. With more extended coastlines than any nation of history; with a commerce vaster than any other people ever dreamed of, and that commerce as yet only in its beginnings; with naval traditions equaling those of England or of Greece, and the work of our Navy only just begun; with the air of the ocean in our nostrils and the blood of a sailor ancestry in our veins; with the shores of all the continents calling us, the Great Republic before I die will be the acknowledged lord of the world's high seas. And over them the republic will hold dominion, by virtue of the strength God has given it, for the peace of the world and the betterment of man.

No; the oceans are not limitations of the power which the Constitution expressly gives Congress to govern all territory the nation may acquire. The Constitution declares that "Congress shall have power to dispose of and make all needful rules and regulations respecting the territory belonging to the United States." Not the Northwest Territory only; not Louisiana or Florida only; not territory on this continent only but any territory anywhere belonging to the nation.

The founders of the nation were not provincial. Theirs was the geography of the world. They were soldiers as well as landsmen, and they knew that where our ships should go our flag might follow. They had the logic of progress, and they knew that the republic they were planting must, in obedience to the laws of our expanding race, necessarily develop into the greater republic which the world beholds today, and into the still mightier republic which the world will finally acknowledge as the arbiter, under God, of the destinies of mankind. And so our fathers wrote into the Constitution these words of growth, of expansion, of empire, if you will, unlimited by geography or climate or by anything but the vitality and possibilities of the American people: "Congress shall have power to dispose of and make all needful rules and regulations respecting the territory belonging to the United States."

Mr. President, this question is deeper than any question of party politics; deeper than any question of the isolated policy of our country even; deeper even than any question of constitutional power. It is elemental. It is racial.

God has not been preparing the English-speaking and Teutonic peoples for a thousand years for nothing but vain and idle self-contemplation and self-admiration. No! He has made us the master organizers of the world to establish system where chaos reigns. He has given us the spirit of progress to overwhelm the forces of reaction throughout the earth. He has made us adepts in government that we may administer government among savage and senile peoples. Were it not for such a force as this the world would relapse into barbarism and night. And of all our race He has marked the American people as His chosen nation to finally lead in the regeneration of the world. This is the divine mission of America, and it holds for us all the profit, all the glory, all the happiness possible to man. We are trustees of the world's progress, guardians of its righteous peace. The judgment of the Master is upon us: "Ye have been faithful over a few things; I will make you ruler over many things."

What shall history say of us? Shall it say that we renounced that holy trust, left the savage to his base condition, the wilderness to the reign of waste, deserted duty, abandoned glory, forget our sordid profit even, because we feared our strength and read the charter of our powers with the doubter's eye and the quibbler's mind? Shall it say that, called by events to captain and command the proudest, ablest, purest race of history in history's noblest work, we declined that great commission? Our fathers would not have had it so. No! They founded no paralytic government, incapable of the simplest acts of administration. They planted no sluggard people, passive while the world's work calls them. They established no reactionary nation. They unfurled no retreating flag.

That flag has never paused in its onward march. Who dares halt it now—now, when history's largest events are carrying it forward; now, when we are at last one people, strong enough for any task, great enough for any glory destiny can bestow? How comes it that our first century closes with the process of consolidating the American people into a unit just accomplished, and quick upon the stroke of that great hour presses upon us our world opportunity, world duty, and world glory, which none but the people welded into an invisible nation can achieve or perform?

Blind indeed is he who sees not the hand of God in events so vast, so harmonious, so benign. Reactionary indeed is the mind that perceives not that this vital people is the strongest of the saving forces of the world; that our place, therefore, is at the head of the constructing and redeeming nations of the earth; and that to stand aside while events march on is a surrender of our interests, a betrayal of our duty as blind as it is base. Craven indeed is the heart that fears to perform a work so golden and so noble; that dares not win a glory so immortal.

Do you tell me that it will cost us money? When did Americans ever measure duty by financial standards? Do you tell me of the tremendous toil required to overcome the vast difficulties of our task? What mighty work for the world, for humanity, even for ourselves has ever been done with ease? Even our bread must we eat by the sweat of our faces. Why are we charged with power such as no people ever knew if we are not to use it in a work such as no people ever wrought? Who will dispute the divine meaning of the fable of the talents?

Do you remind me of the precious blood that must be shed, the lives that must be given, the broken hearts of loved ones for their slain? And this is indeed a heavier price than all combined. And, yet, as a nation, every historic duty we have done, every achievement we have accomplished has been by the sacrifice of our noblest sons. Every holy memory that glorifies the flag is of those heroes who have died that its onward march might not be stayed. It is the nation's dearest lives yielded for the flag that makes it dear to us; it is the nation's most precious blood poured out for it that makes it precious to us. That flag is woven of heroism and grief, of the bravery of men and women's tears, of righteousness and battle, of sacrifice and anguish, of triumph and of glory. It is these which make our flag a holy thing.

# 15 War Message to Congress
## WOODROW WILSON

The American entry into World War I marked an important milestone in the evolution of U.S. foreign policy. American participation in the war made a decisive difference that led to the defeat of Germany, while at the same time, during the war, the United States became a creditor nation and a more influential actor in global politics. In addition, American participation in the war allowed for President Woodrow Wilson to proclaim and act upon a distinct doctrine of U.S. foreign policy, which he did in his message to Congress asking for a declaration of war against Germany. In contrast to the ideas offered by Theodore Roosevelt and Albert Beveridge, Wilson offered yet another rationale behind an activist, interventionist foreign policy. This doctrine, which later became known as Wilsonian idealism, saw U.S. intervention in the war not as an exercise in self-interest such as protecting American security or achieving imperial expansion, but in terms of the spread of liberal democratic practices and institutions around the world as a way of making global politics more peaceful.

Woodrow Wilson, "War Message to Congress," April 2, 1917.

The idea that Wilson advocated was not to extend American rule (as Beveridge sought) but American rules. As Wilson communicated to Congress, the goal to be sought was a noble one, in which the United States would not act to achieve its own gain. It would instead serve as a disinterested party, seeking only, as Wilson said in what became his most famous phrase, to "make the world safe for democracy."

Wilson was not the first to enunciate such ideas (and he was far from the last), but he was the first to do so when the American role in global affairs had become quite substantial, and when the stakes of that involvement had become remarkably high. The result is that Wilsonian idealism has had a hold on American foreign policy ever since Wilson himself announced it. American power, joined by American ideals, have offered presidents, policymakers, pundits, scholars, and other Wilsonians not only a rationale and an opportunity to influence the political development of other countries, but also a temptation to seek to impose change overseas—everywhere from Germany to Mexico to Iran to Cuba to Iraq and Afghanistan. America's global role therefore suggests that the United States remains, at least in part, under the sway of President Wilson. The man has never entirely left office.

---

Gentlemen of the Congress:

I have called the Congress into extraordinary session because there are serious, very serious, choices of policy to be made, and made immediately, which it was neither right nor constitutionally permissible that I should assume the responsibility of making.

On the third of February last I officially laid before you the extraordinary announcement of the Imperial German Government that on and after the first day of February it was its purpose to put aside all restraints of law or of humanity and use its submarines to sink every vessel that sought to approach either the ports of Great Britain and Ireland or the western coasts of Europe or any of the ports controlled by the enemies of Germany within the Mediterranean.

That had seemed to be the object of the German submarine warfare earlier in the war, but since April of last year the Imperial Government had somewhat restrained the commanders of its undersea craft in conformity with its promise then given to us that passenger boats should not be sunk and that due warning would be given to all other vessels which its submarines might seek to destroy, when no resistance was offered or escape attempted, and care taken that their crews were given at least a fair chance to save their lives in their open boats.

The precautions taken were meager and haphazard enough, as was proved in distressing instance after instance in the progress of the cruel and unmanly business, but a certain degree of restraint was observed. The new policy has swept every restriction aside. Vessels of every kind, whatever their flag, their character, their cargo, their destination, their errand, have been ruthlessly sent to the bottom without warning and without thought of help or mercy for those on board, the vessels of friendly neutrals along with those of belligerents. Even hospital ships and ships carrying relief to the sorely bereaved and stricken people of Belgium, though the latter were provided with safe conduct through the proscribed areas by the German Government itself and were distinguished by unmistakable marks of identity, haven been sunk with the same reckless lack of compassion or of principle.

I was for a little while unable to believe that such things would in fact be done by any government that hitherto subscribed to the humane practices of civilized nations. International law had its origin in the attempt to set up some law which would be respected and observed upon the seas, where no nation had right of dominion and where lay the free highways of the world. By painful stage after stage has that law been built up, with meager enough results, indeed, after all was accomplished that could be accomplished, but always with a clear view, at least, of what the heart and conscience of mankind demanded.

This minimum of right the German Government has swept aside under the plea of retaliation and necessity and because it had no weapons which it could use at sea except these which it is impossible to employ as it is employing them without throwing to the winds all scruples of humanity or of respect for the understandings that were supposed to underlie the intercourse of the world.

I am not now thinking of the loss of property involved, immense and serious as that is, but only of the wanton and wholesale destruction of the lives of non-combatants, men, women, and children, engaged in pursuits which have always, even in the darkest periods of modern history, been deemed innocent and legitimate. Property can be paid for; the lives of peaceful and innocent people cannot be.

The present German submarine warfare against commerce is a warfare against mankind.

It is war against all nations.

American ships have been sunk, American lives taken, in ways which it has stirred us very deeply to learn of, but the ships and people of other neutral and friendly nations have been sunk and overwhelmed in the waters in the same way. There has been no discrimination. The challenge is to all mankind.

Each nation must decide for itself how it will meet it. The choice we make for ourselves must be made with a moderation of counsel and temperateness of judgment befitting our character and our motives as a nation.

We must put excited feeling away. Our motive will not be revenge or the victorious assertion of the physical might of the nation, but only the vindication of right, of human right, of which we are only a single champion . . .

With a profound sense of the solemn and even tragical character of the step I am taking and of the grave responsibilities which it involves, but in unhesitating obedience to what I deem my constitutional duty, I advise that the Congress declare the recent course of the Imperial German Government to be in fact nothing less than war against the government and people of the United States; that it formally accept the status of belligerent which has thus been thrust upon it; and that it take immediate steps not only to put the country in a more thorough state of defense but also to exert all its power and employ all its resources to bring the Government of the German Empire to terms and end the war . . .

While we do these things, these deeply momentous things, let us be very clear, and make very clear to all the world what our motives and our objects are. Our object now, as then, is to vindicate the principles of peace and justice in the life of the world as against selfish and autocratic power and to set up amongst the really free and self-governed peoples of the world such a concert of purpose and of action as will henceforth ensure the observance of those principles.

Neutrality is no longer feasible or desirable where the peace of the world is involved and the freedom of its peoples, and the menace to that peace and freedom lies in the existence of autocratic governments backed by organized force which is controlled wholly by their will, not by the will of their people. We have seen the last of neutrality in such circumstances. We are at the beginning of an age in which it will be insisted that the same standards of conduct and responsibility for wrong done shall be observed among nations and their governments that are observed among the individual citizens of civilized states.

We have no quarrel with the German people. We have no feeling towards them but one of sympathy and friendship. It was not upon their impulse that their government acted in entering this war. It was not with their previous knowledge or approval. It was a war determined upon as wars used to be determined upon in the old, unhappy days when peoples were nowhere consulted by their rulers and wars were provoked and waged in the interest of dynasties or of little groups of ambitious men who were accustomed to use their fellow men as pawns and tools.

Self-governed nations do not fill their neighbor states with spies or set the course of intrigue to bring about some critical posture of affairs which will give them an opportunity to strike and make conquest. Such designs can be successfully worked out only under cover and where no one has the right to ask questions. Cunningly contrived plans of deception or aggression, carried, it may be, from generation to generation, can be worked out and kept from the light only within the privacy of courts or behind carefully guarded confidences of a narrow and privileged class. They are happily impossible where public opinion commands and insists upon full information concerning all the nation's affairs.

A steadfast concert for peace can never be maintained except by a partnership of democratic nations. No autocratic government could be trusted to keep faith within it or observe its covenants. It must be a league of honor, a partnership of opinion. Intrigue would eat its vitals away; the plottings of inner circles who could plan what they would and render account to no one would be a corruption seated at its very heart. Only free peoples can hold their purpose and their honor steady to a common end and prefer the interests of mankind to any narrow interest of their own . . .

We are glad, now that we see the facts with no veil of false pretense about them, to fight thus for the ultimate peace of the world and for the liberation of its peoples, the German peoples included: for the rights of nations great and small and the privilege of men everywhere to choose their way of life and of obedience. The world must be made safe for democracy. Its peace must be planted upon the tested foundations of political liberty. We have no selfish ends to serve.

We desire no conquest, no dominion. We seek no indemnities for ourselves, no material compensation for the sacrifices we shall cheerfully make. We are but one of the champions of the rights of mankind. We shall be satisfied when those rights have been made as secure as the faith and the freedom of nations can make them.

Just because we fight without rancor and without selfish object, seeking nothing for ourselves but what we shall wish to share with all free peoples, we shall, I feel confident, conduct our operations as belligerents without passion and ourselves observe with proud punctilio the principles of right and fair play we profess to be fighting for . . .

We enter this war only where we are clearly forced into it because there are no other means of defending our rights.

It will be all the easier for us to conduct ourselves as belligerents in a high spirit of right and fairness because we act without animus, not in enmity towards a people or with the desire to bring any injury or disadvantage upon them, but only armed opposition to an irresponsible government which has thrown aside all considerations of humanity and of right and is running amuck.

We are, let me say again, the sincere friends of the German people, and shall desire nothing so much as the early reestablishment of intimate relations of mutual advantage between us—however hard it may be for them, for the time being, to believe that this is spoken from our hearts . . .

It is a distressing and oppressive duty, Gentlemen of the Congress, which I have performed in thus addressing you. There are, it may be, many months of fiery trial and sacrifice ahead of us. It is a fearful thing to lead this great peaceful people into war, into the most terrible and disastrous of all wars, civilization itself seeming to be in the balance.

But the right is more precious than peace, and we shall fight for the things which we have always carried nearest our hearts, for democracy, for the right of those who submit to authority to have a voice in their own governments, for the rights and liberties of small nations, for a universal dominion of right by such a concert of free peoples as shall bring peace and safety to all nations and make the world at last free.

To such a task we can dedicate our lives and our fortunes, everything that we are and everything that we have, with the pride of those who know that the day has come when America is privileged to spend her blood and her might for the principles that gave her birth and happiness and the peace which she has treasured. God helping her, she can do no other.

# 16 Cowboy Nation
## ROBERT KAGAN

The perspectives offered by Roosevelt, Beveridge, and Wilson each provide a different strain of thought regarding American engagement and intervention around the world. Alongside these traditions, however, there is also an understanding that these views and the actions they spawned represent an aberration—that most of the time, the United States is a somewhat reluctant actor in global politics, a country that has generally preferred its historic isolationist tendencies, going to war or taking on the responsibilities of global leadership only when such roles have been thrust upon it.

Robert Kagan considers these contrasting views, which seem especially relevant in light of contemporary concerns over the wisdom of American intervention in Iraq. While the current debate reflects a sense that the United States has made a historic departure from past practices, Kagan suggests instead that the war in Iraq reflects a consistency that has characterized the United States for centuries. Considering the perspectives and policies of Roosevelt, Beveridge, and Wilson to be only variations on the same theme, Kagan offers a brief analysis of American history and the liberal ideology that has informed and justified American behavior since the country's founding.

He posits that the United States, far from being an unambitious or disinterested global actor, has been "consistently expanding its participation and influence in the world …The impulse to involve ourselves in the affairs of others is neither a modern phenomenon nor a deviation from the American spirit. It is embedded in the American DNA." Any denial of such an orientation, says Kagan, amounts to a fundamentally inaccurate understanding of America's past.

---

These days, we are having a national debate over the direction of foreign policy. Beyond the obvious difficulties in Iraq and Afghanistan, there is a broader sense that our nation has gone astray. We have become too militaristic, too idealistic, too arrogant; we have become an "empire." Much of the world views us as dangerous. In response, many call for the United States to return to its foreign policy traditions, as if that would provide the answer.

What exactly are those traditions? One tradition is this kind of debate, which we've been having ever since the birth of the nation, when Patrick Henry accused supporters of the Constitution of conspiring to turn the young republic into a "great and mighty empire." Today, we are mightier than Henry could have ever imagined. Yet we prefer to see ourselves in modest terms—as a reluctant hegemon, a status quo power that seeks only ordered stability in the international arena. James Schlesinger captured this perspective several years ago, when he said that Americans have "been thrust into a position of lonely preeminence." The United States, he added, is "a most unusual, not to say odd, country to serve as international leader." If, at times, we venture forth and embroil ourselves in the affairs of others, it is either because we have been attacked or because of the emergence of some dangerous revolutionary force—German Nazism, Japanese imperialism, Soviet communism, radical Islamism. Americans do not choose war; war is thrust upon us. As a recent presidential candidate put it, "The United States of America never goes to war because we want to; we only go to war because we have to. That is the standard of our nation."

But that self-image, with its yearning for some imagined lost innocence, is based on myth. Far from the modest republic that history books often portray, the early United States was an expansionist power from the moment the first pilgrim set foot on the continent; and it did not stop expanding—territorially, commercially, culturally, and geopolitically— over the next four centuries. The United States has never been a status quo power; it has always been a revolutionary one, consistently expanding its participation and influence in the world in ever-widening arcs. The impulse to involve ourselves in the affairs of others is neither a modern phenomenon nor a deviation from the American spirit. It is embedded in the American DNA.

Long before the country's founding, British colonists were busy driving the Native American population off millions of acres of land and almost out of existence. From the 1740s through the 1820s, and then in another burst in the 1840s, Americans expanded relentlessly westward from the Alleghenies to the Ohio Valley and on past the Rocky Mountains to the Pacific, southward into Mexico and Florida, and northward toward Canada—eventually pushing off the continent not only Indians, but the great empires of France, Spain, and Russia as well. (The United Kingdom alone barely managed to defend its foothold in North America.) This often violent territorial expansion was directed not by redneck "Jacksonians" but by eastern gentlemen expansionists like George Washington, Thomas Jefferson, and John Quincy Adams.

It would have been extraordinary had early Americans amassed all this territory and power without really wishing for it. But they did wish for it. With 20 years of peace, Washington predicted in his valedictory, the United States would acquire the power to "bid defiance, in a just cause, to any earthly power whatsoever." Jefferson foresaw a vast "empire of liberty" spreading west, north, and south across the continent. Hamilton believed the United States would, "erelong, assume an attitude correspondent with its great destinies—majestic, efficient, and operative of great things. A noble career lies before it." John Quincy Adams considered the United States "destined by God and nature to be the most populous and powerful people ever combined under one social compact." And Americans' aspirations only grew in intensity over the decades, as national power and influence increased. In the 1850s, William Seward predicted that the United States would become the world's dominant power, "the greatest of existing states, greater than any that has ever existed." A century later, Dean Acheson, present at the creation of a U.S.-dominated world order, would describe the United States as "the locomotive at the head of mankind" and the rest of the world as "the caboose." More recently, Bill Clinton labeled the United States "the world's indispensable nation."

From the beginning, others have seen Americans not as a people who sought ordered stability but as persistent disturbers of the status quo. As the ancient Corinthians said of the Athenians, they were "incapable of either living a quiet life themselves or of allowing anyone else to do so." Nineteenth-century Americans were, in the words of French diplomats, "numerous," "warlike," and an "enemy to be feared." In 1817, John Quincy Adams reported from London, "The universal feeling of Europe in witnessing the gigantic growth of our population and power is that we shall, if united, become a very dangerous member of the society of nations." The United States was dangerous not only because it was expansionist, but also because its liberal republicanism threatened the established conservative order of that era. Austria's Prince Metternich rightly feared what would happen to the "moral force" of Europe's conservative monarchies when "this flood of evil doctrines" was married to the military, economic, and political power Americans seemed destined to acquire.

What Metternich understood, and what others would learn, was that the United States was a nation with almost boundless ambition and a potent sense of national honor, for which it was willing to go to war. It exhibited the kind of spiritedness, and even fierceness, in defense of home, hearth, and belief that the ancient Greeks called thumos. It was an uncommonly impatient nation, often dissatisfied with the way things were, almost always convinced of the possibility of beneficial change and of its own role as a catalyst. It was also a nation with a strong martial tradition. Eighteenth- and nineteenth-century Americans loved peace, but they also believed in the potentially salutary effects of war. "No man in the nation desires peace more than I," Henry Clay declared before the war with Great Britain in 1812. "But I prefer the troubled ocean of war, demanded by the honor and independence of the country, with all its calamities, and desolations, to the tranquil, putrescent pool of ignominious peace." Decades later, Oliver Wendell Holmes Jr., the famed jurist who had fought—and been wounded three times—in the Civil War, observed, "War, when you are at it, is horrible and dull. It is only when time has passed that you see that its message was divine."

Modern Americans don't talk this way anymore, but it is not obvious that we are very different in our attitudes toward war. Our martial tradition has remained remarkably durable, especially when compared with most other democracies in the post-World War II era. From 1989 to 2003, a 14-year period spanning three very different presidencies, the United States deployed large numbers of combat troops or engaged in extended campaigns of aerial bombing and missile attacks on nine different occasions: in Panama (1989), Somalia (1992), Haiti (1994), Bosnia (1995–1996), Kosovo (1999), Afghanistan (2001), and Iraq (1991, 1998, 2003). That is an average of one significant military intervention every 19 months—a greater frequency than at any time in our history. Americans stand almost alone in believing in the utility and even necessity of war as a means of obtaining justice. Surveys commissioned by the German Marshall Fund consistently show that 80 percent of Americans agree with the proposition that "[u]nder some conditions, war is necessary to obtain justice." In France, Germany, Italy, and Spain, less than one-third of the population agrees.

How do we reconcile the gap between our preferred self-image and this historical reality? With difficulty. We are, and have always been, uncomfortable with our power, our ambition, and our willingness to use force to achieve our objectives. What the historian Gordon Wood has called our deeply rooted "republicanism" has always made us suspicious of power, even our own. Our enlightenment liberalism, with its belief in universal rights and self-determination, makes us uncomfortable using our influence, even in what we regard as a good cause, to deprive others of their freedom of action. Our religious conscience makes us look disapprovingly on ambition—both personal and national. Our modern democratic worldview conceives of "honor" as something antiquated and undemocratic. These misgivings rarely stop us from pursuing our goals, any more than our suspicion of wealth stops us from trying to accumulate it. But they do make us reluctant to see ourselves as others see us. Instead, we construct more comforting narratives of our past. Or we create some idealized foreign policy against which to measure our present behavior. We hope that we can either return to the policies of that imagined past or approximate some imagined ideal to recapture our innocence. It is easier than facing the hard truth: America's expansiveness, intrusiveness, and tendency toward political, economic, and strategic dominance are not some aberration from our true nature. That is our nature.

Why are we this way? In many respects, we share characteristics common to all peoples through history. Like others, Americans have sought power to achieve prosperity, independence, and security as well as less tangible goals. As American power increased, so, too, did American ambitions, both noble and venal. Growing power changes nations, just as it changes people. It changes their perceptions of the world and their place in it. It increases their sense of entitlement and reduces their tolerance for obstacles that stand in their way. Power also increases ambition. When Americans acquired the unimaginably vast territory of Louisiana at the dawn of the nineteenth century, doubling the size of their young nation with lands that would take decades to settle, they did not rest content but immediately looked for still more territory beyond their new borders. As one foreign diplomat observed, "Since the Americans have acquired Louisiana, they appear unable to bear any barriers round them."

But, in addition to the common human tendency to seek greater power and influence over one's surroundings, Americans have been driven outward into the world by something else: the potent, revolutionary ideology of liberalism that they adopted at the nation's birth. Indeed, it is probably liberalism, more than any other factor, that has made the United States so energetic, expansive, and intrusive over the course of its history.

Liberalism fueled the prodigious territorial and commercial expansion in the eighteenth and nineteenth centuries that made the United States, first, the dominant power in North America and, then, a world power. It did so by elevating the rights of the individual over the state—by declaring that all people had a right to life, liberty, property, and the pursuit of happiness and by insisting it was the government's primary job to safeguard those rights. American political leaders had little choice but to permit, and sometimes support, territorial and commercial claims made by their citizens, even when those claims encroached on the lands or waters of foreigners. Other eighteenth- and nineteenth-century governments, ruled by absolute monarchs, permitted national expansion when it served personal or dynastic interests—and, like Napoleon in the New World, blocked it when it did not. When the king of England tried to curtail the territorial and commercial expansionism of his Anglo-American subjects, they rebelled and established a government that would not hold them back. In this respect, the most important foreign policy statement in U.S. history was not George Washington's farewell address or the Monroe Doctrine but the Declaration of Independence and the enlightenment ideals it placed at the heart of American nationhood. Putting those ideals into practice was a radical new departure in government, and it inevitably produced a new kind of foreign policy.

Liberalism not only drove territorial and commercial expansion; it also provided an overarching ideological justification for such expansion. By expanding territorially, commercially, politically, and culturally, Americans believed that they were bringing both modern civilization and the "blessings of liberty" to whichever nations they touched in their search for opportunity. As Jefferson told one Indian leader: "We desire above all things, brother, to instruct you in whatever we know ourselves. We wish to learn you all our arts and to make you wise and wealthy." In one form or another, Americans have been making that offer of instruction to peoples around the world ever since.

Americans, from the beginning, measured the world exclusively according to the assumptions of liberalism. These included, above all, a belief in what the Declaration of Independence called the "self-evident" universality of certain basic truths—not only that all men were created equal and endowed by God with inalienable rights, but also that the only legitimate and just governments were those that derived their powers "from the consent of the governed." According to the Declaration, "whenever any Form of Government becomes destructive of these ends, it is the Right of the People to alter or to abolish it." Such a worldview does not admit the possibility of alternative truths. Americans, over the centuries, accepted the existence of cultural distinctions that influenced other peoples to rule themselves differently. But they never really accepted the legitimacy of despotic governments, no matter how deeply rooted in culture. As a result, they viewed them as transitory. And so, wherever Americans looked in the world, they saw the possibility and the desirability of change.

The notion of progress is a central tenet of liberalism. More than any other people, Americans have taken a progressive view of history, evaluating other nations according to where they stood on the continuum of progress. The Russians, Theodore Roosevelt believed, were "below the Germans just as the Germans are below us . . . [but] we are all treading the same path, some faster, some slower." If Roosevelt's language sounds antiquated, our modern perspective is scarcely different. Although we may disagree among ourselves about the pace of progress, almost all Americans believe that it is both inevitable and desirable. We generally agree on the need to assist other nations in their political and economic development. But development toward what, if not toward the liberal democratic ideal that defines our nationalism? The "great struggle of the epoch," Madison declared in the 1820s, is "between liberty and despotism." Because the rights of man were written "by the hand of the divinity itself," as Hamilton put it, that struggle could ultimately have only one outcome.

It was a short step from that conviction to the belief that the interests of the United States were practically indistinguishable from the interests of the world. "The cause of America is in a great measure the cause of all mankind," Thomas Paine argued at the time of the revolution. Herman Melville would later write that, for Americans, "national selfishness is unbounded philanthropy; for we cannot do a good to America but we give alms to the world." It was another short step to the belief that the United States had a special, even unique, role to play in serving as a catalyst for the evolution of mankind. "The rights asserted by our forefathers were not peculiar to themselves," Seward declared, "they were the common rights of mankind." Therefore, he said, the United States had a duty "to renovate the condition of mankind" and lead the way to "the universal restoration of power to the governed" everywhere in the world. Decades earlier, John Quincy Adams had noted with pride that the United States was the source of ideas that made "the throne of every European monarch rock under him as with the throes of an earthquake." Praising the American Revolution, he exhorted "every individual among the sceptered lords of mankind: 'Go thou and do likewise!'"

A Russian minister, appalled at this "appeal to the nations of Europe to rise against their Governments," noted the hypocrisy of Adams's message, asking, "How about your two million black slaves?" Indeed. The same United States that called for global revolution on behalf of freedom was, throughout its first eight decades, also the world's great defender of racial despotism. The slaveholding South was itself a brutal tyranny, almost totalitarian in its efforts to control the speech and personal behavior of whites as well as blacks. Much of the U.S. territorial expansion in the nineteenth century—including the Mexican War, which garnered today's American Southwest and California—was driven by slaveholders, insisting on new lands to which they could spread their despotic system.

In the end, the violent abolition of slavery in the United States was a defining moment in the country's foreign policy: It strengthened the American tendency toward liberal moralism in foreign affairs. The Northern struggle against slavery, culminating in the Civil War, was America's first moral crusade. The military defeat of the Southern slaveholders was America's first war of ideological conquest. And what followed was America's first attempt at occupation and democratic nation-building (with the same mixed results as later efforts). The effect of the whole struggle was to intensify the American dedication to the universality of rights and to reaffirm the Declaration of Independence, rather than the Constitution with its tacit acceptance of slavery, as the central document of American nationhood. The Civil War fixed in the American mind, or at least in the Northern mind, the idea of the just war—a battle, fought for moral reasons, whose objectives can be achieved only through military action.

Such thinking led to the Spanish-American War of 1898. One of the most popular wars in U.S. history, it enjoyed the support of both political parties, of William Jennings Bryan and Andrew Carnegie, of eastern Brahmin Republicans like Henry Cabot Lodge, radical prairie populists, and labor leaders. Although one would not know it from reading most histories today, the war was motivated primarily by humanitarian concerns. Civil strife in Cuba and the brutal policies of the Spanish government—in particular the herding of the civilian population into "reconcentration" camps—had caused some 300,000 deaths, one-fifth of Cuba's population. Most of the victims were women, children, and the elderly. Lodge and many others argued that the United States had a responsibility to defend the Cuban people against Spanish oppression precisely because it had the power to do so. "Here we stand motionless, a great and powerful country not six hours away from these scenes of useless bloodshed and destruction," he said, imploring that, if the United States "stands for humanity and civilization, we should exercise every influence of our great country to put a stop to that war which is now raging in Cuba and give to that island once more peace, liberty, and independence." The overwhelming majority of the nation agreed. The U.S. intervention put an end to that suffering and saved untold thousands of lives. When John Hay called it a "splendid little war," it was not because of the smashing military victory—Hay was no militarist. It was the lofty purposes and accomplishments of the war that were splendid.

It was also true that the United States had self-interested reasons for going to war: commercial interests in Cuba, as well as the desire to remove Spain from the hemisphere and establish our preeminence in the region. Most of Europe condemned the United States as selfish and aggressive, failing to credit it with humanitarian impulses. Moreover, the war produced some unintended and, for many who idealistically supported it, disillusioning consequences. It led to the acquisition of the Philippines and a most unsplendid war against independence-minded Filipinos. It also produced a well-intentioned, but ultimately disappointing, multiyear occupation of Cuba that would haunt Americans for another century. And it reignited an old debate over the course of U.S. foreign policy—similar to the one that consumes us today.

Now, as then, the projection of U.S. power for liberal purposes faces its share of domestic criticism—warnings against arrogance, hubris, excessive idealism, and "imperialism." Throughout the eighteenth and nineteenth centuries, conservatives in the republican tradition of Patrick Henry worried about the effect at home of expansive policies abroad. They predicted, correctly, that a big foreign policy generally meant a big federal government, which—in their eyes—meant impingements on the rights and freedoms of the individual. The conservatives of the slaveholding South were the great realists of the nineteenth century. They opposed moralism, rightly fearing it would be turned against the institution of slavery. As Jefferson Davis put it, "We are not engaged in a Quixotic fight for the rights of man. Our struggle is for inherited rights. . . . We are conservative." At the end of the century, when Americans were enthusiastically pushing across the Pacific, critics like Grover Cleveland's long-forgotten secretary of state, Walter Q. Gresham, warned that "[e]very nation, and especially every strong nation, must sometimes be conscious of an impulse to rush into difficulties that do not concern it, except in a highly imaginary way. To restrain the indulgence of such a propensity is not only the part of wisdom, but a duty we owe to the world as an example of the strength, the moderation, and the beneficence of popular government."

But, just as progressivism and big government have generally triumphed in domestic affairs, so, too, has the liberal approach to the world beyond our shores. Henry failed to defeat the Constitution. Southern realism lost to Northern idealism. The critics of liberal foreign policy—whether conservative, realist, or leftist—have rarely managed to steer the United States on a different course.

The result has been some accomplishments of great historical importance—the defeat of German Nazism, Japanese imperialism, and Soviet communism—as well as some notable failures and disappointments. But it was not as if the successes were the product of a good America and the failures the product of a bad America. They were all the product of the same America. The achievements, as well as the disappointments, derived from the very qualities that often make us queasy: our willingness to accumulate and use power; our ambition and sense of honor; our spiritedness in defense of both our interests and our principles; our dissatisfaction with the status quo; our belief in the possibility of change. And, throughout, whether succeeding or failing, we have remained a "dangerous" nation in many senses—dangerous to tyrannies, dangerous to those who do not want our particular brand of liberalism, dangerous to those who fear our martial spirit and our thumos, dangerous to those, including Americans, who would prefer an international order not built around a dominant and often domineering United States.

Whether a different kind of international system or a different kind of America would be preferable is a debate worth having. But let us have this debate about our future without illusions about our past.

# 17 Epilogue

## WALTER LAFEBER

The antecedents of an engaged, internationalist foreign policy have clearly been informed by American security interests and the spread of democratic practices and ideologies, as the previous readings indicate. But these are not the only sources of American action. Economic considerations have also been of great importance to understanding American policies abroad, and in fact may be of greater significance in understanding U.S. engagement with other countries. The expansion of U.S. business opportunities, the search for new markets, and the continually evolving characteristics of the global economy have all served as drivers of American foreign policy.

Walter LaFeber examines this idea in *The New Empire*, looking at how the economic interests of the United States in the second half of the 19th century changed. Driven by industrialization, American economic needs and objectives evolved, leading to a commercial expansion that sought opportunities and markets overseas, rather than territorial acquisition in North America. This change, from a quest for land to a quest for markets, led to a rapid growth in American economic interests, and this subsequently led to numerous political and military entanglements and responsibilities in Latin America and the Caribbean, in the Pacific, and in Asia. One result is that places such as Hawaii, Samoa, and Guam became seen as important holdings in order to extend American reach and acquire markets in Asia, where the United States both encouraged and forced China and Japan into open trading relationships.

LaFeber argues the critical importance of these developments in creating a new orientation and a changed American foreign policy. His assessment of this evolution, and the changing nature of American engagement with a great number of foreign lands, not only highlights the economic sources of U.S. foreign policy. It also points to how the policies and practices of this era laid the foundation for the globally oriented foreign policy of the United States in the 20th century.

In less than a century and a quarter the United States developed from thirteen states strung along a narrow Atlantic coastline into a great world power with possessions in the far Pacific.

Until the middle of the nineteenth century this had been, for the most part, a form of landed expansion which had moved over a large area of the North American continent. The Louisiana Purchase in 1803 had been followed by further important acquisitions in 1819, 1848, 1853, and 1867. But when William H. Seward entered the State Department in 1861, the nature of American expansion had begun to change. Under the impact of the industrial revolution Americans began to search for markets, not land. Sometimes the State Department seized the initiative in making the search, as in the Harrison administration. Frequently the business community pioneered in extending the interests of the United States into foreign areas, as in Mexico in the 1870s and in China in the 1890s. Regardless of which body led the expansionist movement, the result was the same: the growth of economic interests led to political entanglements and to increased military responsibilities.

Americans attempted to build a new empire, an empire which differed fundamentally from the colonial holdings of European powers. Until 1898 the United States believed that its political institutions were suitable only for the North American continent. Many policy makers and important journalists warned that extra-continental holdings would wreck the American republic just as they had ruined the Roman republic. Such sentiment helped to prevent the acquisition of Hawaii in 1893.

In 1898, however, the United States annexed Hawaii and demanded the Philippines from Spain. These acquisitions were not unheralded. Seward had pushed his nation's claims far out into the Pacific with the purchase of Alaska and the Midway islands. Fish, Evarts, Bayard, Blaine, and Cleveland had maintained a tight hold on Pago Pago in Samoa, although they strongly disliked the political entanglements with England and Germany which were necessarily part of the bargain.

One striking characteristic tied these acquisitions to the new territory brought under American control in 1898 and 1899, immediately after the war with Spain. The United States obtained these areas not to fulfill a colonial policy, but to use these holdings as a means to acquire markets for the glut of goods pouring out of highly mechanized factories and farms.

The two acquisitions which might be considered exceptions to this statement are Alaska and Hawaii. It is most difficult, however, to understand the purchase of "Seward's Icebox" without comprehending the Secretary of State's magnificent view of the future American commercial empire. This view did not premise a colonial policy, but assumed the necessity of controlling the Asian markets for commercial, not political, expansion. As the chairman of the

House Foreign Affairs Committee commented in 1867, Alaska was the "draw-bridge" between the North American continent and Asia.

Hawaii had become an integral part of the American economy long before Harrison attempted to annex it in 1893. Missionaries had forged strong religious and secular links between the islands and the mainland, but of much more importance were the commercial ties. After the reciprocity treaty of 1875 the United States possessed a virtual veto power over Hawaii's relations with foreign powers. American capital, especially attracted by the islands' fertility during the depression years that plagued the mainland in the 1870's and 1880's, developed sugar plantations whose prosperity depended upon the American consumer. Exports of finished industrial goods left United States ports in increasing amounts for Hawaiian consumers. When the 1890 tariff severely retarded the export of Hawaiian sugar, American exports moved without abatement into the islands. The economic expansion of the United States, in terms of both capital and goods, had tied Hawaii irrevocably to the mainland.

By 1893 only the political tie remained to be consummated. The United States enjoyed the benefits of Hawaiian trade without the burdens of governmental responsibilities. But in five years the situation changed. Regaining confidence in American political institutions as the depression lessened in severity, and fearful of Japanese control, the McKinley administration attempted to annex the islands in 1897–1898. But one other factor was also of prime importance. American interests in Asia suddenly assumed much significance. And in this new framework, the Isthmian canal project gained added importance and support, for many expansionists believed the canal to be absolutely necessary if the eastern and Gulf states hoped to compete in Asian markets. As Senator John T. Morgan, Alfred Thayer Mahan, and Senator Cushman Davis noted, Hawaii was essential if the United States was to safeguard the Pacific approaches to the canal. When the Senate Foreign Relations Committee issued its majority report in March, 1898, which advocated annexation by joint resolution, the committee argued that the strategic position of Hawaii was "the main argument in favor of the annexation" plan. This, the report explained, meant not only the shielding of the western coast of the United States, but the "efficient protection" of American commerce as well. This report also noted the irrelevance of one of the antiannexationist arguments, then combined the strategic factor with the fear of Japanese encroachment as reasons for annexation: "The issue in Hawaii is not between monarchy and the Republic. That issue has been settled. . . . The issue is whether, in that inevitable struggle, Asia or America shall have the vantage ground of the control of the naval 'Key of the Pacific', the commercial 'Cross-roads of the Pacific.'"[1]

The administration forces finally won their objective during the summer of 1898. By July both the business community and policy makers had fully realized the value of Asia as a potential area for American financial and commercial expansion. The operations of Admiral George Dewey in the Philippines had, moreover, taught Americans that Hawaii was absolutely essential as a coaling station and naval base if the United States hoped to become a dominant force in the Far East.

The Philippines marked the next step westward. In 1899 the Secretary of the American Asiatic Association analyzed the reason for the annexation of these islands in a single sentence: "Had we no interests in China, the possession of the Philippines would be meaningless." Mark Hanna, a somewhat more objective observer of the Far East than the gentleman just quoted, also desired "a strong foothold in the Philippine Islands," for then "we can and will take a large slice of the commerce of Asia. That is what we want. We are bound to share in the commerce of the Far East, and it is better to strike for it while the iron is hot." The interests of missionaries and of investors who believed the islands had great natural wealth no doubt encouraged McKinley to demand the Philippines. But it should be noted that, when the President first formulated his peace terms, he wanted the islands to "remain with Spain, except a port and necessary appurtenances to be selected by the United States." He changed this view only when convinced that Manila would be insecure and indefensible unless the United States annexed the remainder of the islands. Mahan had followed similar reasoning to reach the same conclusion. The key to the Philippine policy of both men was their view of Manila as a way station to the Orient.[2]

Throughout the 1890s, debate had raged around the desirability of annexing yet another outlying possession. The growing desire for an American-controlled Isthmian canal partially explains the interest Hawaii held for some Americans. But it should be emphasized that in the 1890s, at least, Americans did not define their interests in a future canal as military; they termed these interests as economic. Policy makers viewed the control of strategic areas such as Hawaii or Guantanamo Bay in the same light as they viewed the Philippines, that is, as strategic means to obtaining and protecting objectives which they defined as economic. Few persons discussed the military aspects of the canal, and to interpret American expansion into the Pacific and the Caribbean as expansion for *merely* strategic objectives distorts the true picture. Most of those who were concerned with a canal agreed with McKinley's statement in his annual message of 1897: the Nicaragua canal would be of "utility and value to American commerce." The foremost advocate of a Central American passageway, Senator Morgan, constantly discussed the canal's value in economic terms.[3]

American control of these areas followed logically if two assumptions were granted: first, the general consensus reached by the American business community and policy makers in the mid-1890s that additional foreign markets would solve the economic, social, and political problems created by the industrial revolution; and, second, the growing belief that, however great its industrial prowess, the United States needed strategic bases if it hoped to compete successfully with government-supported European enterprises in Asia and Latin America. The *Journal of Commerce* summarized opinion on the first point when it remarked in early 1895 that "within the last half century" the industrial and transportation revolutions had made it a fact that "we are a part of 'abroad.'" Commenting upon one aspect of the frontier thesis, this journal warned that the nation was no longer "a vast public domain awaiting agriculture"; as a result of this transformation, Americans could not afford "to imagine that we can maintain ourselves in isolation from the rest of the commercial world."[4]

The principal antiannexationist argument, that the Constitution and traditional American society would be ruined by expanding to noncontiguous areas, was, in fact, quite irrelevant granted the common assumption of the need for commercial expansion. By agreeing that a constantly expanding trade was also vital to the economic and political well-being of the nation, the antiannexationists had opened themselves to the devastating counterargument that this trade could not find the crucial markets in Asia and Latin America without the security which the Philippines and Hawaii would provide.[5]

As for the annexationist forces, Lodge could espouse "large policies," but correctly argue, "I do not mean that we should enter on a widely extended system of colonization." When Alfred Thayer Mahan urged the State Department to demand only Manila in the summer of 1898, he differed little from many antiannexationists. His studies had convinced him, however, that a naval base could be strong and secure only when the hinterland of the base was strong and secure. He would accept the political burdens of the hinterland if this was necessary in order to safeguard the naval base and the trade which depended upon that base. McKinley apparently arrived at the same conclusion in much the same way. The President actually occupied a middle-of-the-road position on the issue, for by the early summer of 1898 some business periodicals, military experts, and such politicians as "Fire Alarm Joe" Foraker of Ohio urged the annexation of other Pacific islands and wanted to renege on the Teller Amendment in order to annex Cuba.[6] The administration's Cuban policy is one of the best examples of the new empire approach. Not wanting the political burdens or the economic competition inherent in annexation, the problem was neatly solved by the Platt Amendment, which gave the Cubans their independence; but the measure also gave to the United States the Guantanamo Naval Base as a safeguard for American interests in the Caribbean, created a Cuban tariff which opened the island to American agricultural and industrial products, and recognized the right of American military intervention in the event that Cuban political life became too chaotic.

By 1899 the United States had forged a new empire. American policy makers and businessmen had created it amid much debate and with conscious purpose. The empire progressed from a continental base in 1861 to assured pre-eminence in the Western Hemisphere in 1895. Three years later it was rescued from a growing economic and political dilemma by the declaration of war against Spain. During and after this conflict the empire moved past Hawaii into the Philippines, and, with the issuance of the Open-Door Notes, enunciated its principles in Asia. The movement of this empire could not be hurried. Harrison discovered this to his regret in 1893. But under the impetus of the effects of the industrial revolution and, most important, *because of the implications for foreign policy which policy makers and businessmen believed to be logical corollaries of this economic change*, the new empire reached its climax in the 1890's. At this point those who possessed a sense of historical perspective could pause with Henry Adams and observe that one hundred and fifty years of American history had suddenly fallen into place. Those who preferred to peer into the dim future of the twentieth century could be certain only that the United States now dominated its own hemisphere and, as Seward had so passionately hoped, was entering as a major power into Asia, "the chief theatre of events in the world's great hereafter."

## Notes

1. Senate Report No. 681, 55th Cong., 2nd Sess. (serial 3627), 1–119, especially 31; Stevens, *American Expansion in Hawaii*, 297–299; James Harrison Wilson, "America's Interests in China," *North American Review*, CLXVI (February, 1898), 140; *Commercial Advertiser*, Feb. 8, 1898, 6:3; clipping of London *Times*, June 17, 1897, enclosed in Hay to Sherman, June 17, 1897, Great Britain, Despatches, NA, RG 59.
2. Campbell, *Special Business Interests*, 16; memorandum of McKinley's terms, Day to Hay, June 4, 1898, copy in Box 185, and Hay to Day, May 18, 1898, Box 185, J. B. Moore MSS; *Economist*, June 11, 1898, 877; F. F. Hilder, "The Philippine Islands," *Forum*, XXV (July, 1898), 534–545; Truxtun Beale, "Strategical Value of the Philippines," *North American Review*, CLXVI (June, 1898), 759–760; Livermore, "American Naval-Base Policy in the Far East, 1850–1914," 116–117; Philadelphia *Press*, June 29, 1898, 6: 3.
3. *Public Opinion*, May 26, 1898, 646; *Congressional Record*, 55th Cong., 2nd Sess., 6 and 3222; Melville, "Our Future on the Pacific," 293–294. There is a good discussion of the canal issue in Campbell, *Special Business Interests*, 14–15.
4. *Journal of Commerce*, Jan. 22, 1895, 4: 2–3.
5. Fred Harvey Harrington, "The Anti-Imperialist Movement in the United States, 1898–1900," *Mississippi Valley Historical Review*, XXII (September, 1935), 211–212; *House Report No. 1355*, part 2, 55th Cong., 2nd Sess. (serial 3721), 1–2; *Senate Report No. 681*, 55th Cong., 2nd Sess. (serial 3627), 1–119. *Congressional Record*, 55th Cong., 3rd Sess., 20, contains Vest's resolution.
6. Lodge's statement is given in Stevens, *American Expansion in Hawaii*, 279; on Mahan, see Chapter II, above; on the business views, see Pratt, *Expansionists of 1898*, 274–275.

# 18 Changing the Paradigms
## WALTER RUSSELL MEAD

The foreign policy of the United States has consistently been shaped by its interests in the international economic environment, from the founding of the country to the present day, argues Walter Russell Mead. From this economic context has arisen the critical strategic questions and concerns that the United States has either chosen or been forced to address. The previous selection from LaFeber looks at one period in American history to make this point. Mead adds to this understanding by looking at the large sweep of American interests and global engagement.

Mead suggests that the United States' relationship to Great Britain has effectively defined and determined the course of America's relationship to the rest of the world. Whether this involved participating as a junior partner in a British-led system that maintained the balance of power and managed a global trade and financial system, or refusing to accept greater responsibility for the world system as British power waned, or eventually supplanting Britain as the "gyroscope" of world order, Mead argues that the United States' role in the world has been closely related to the strength and then decline of British power and influence.

This selection clearly elucidates not only the historical antecedents of contemporary American foreign policy, but also the continuities in American actions over the centuries, speaking to the close association between American economic interests and American strategic thinking. The crucial link between these two areas encompasses what we today call globalization, which Mead argues "has been at the heart of American strategic thinking and policy making for virtually all of our history." America's goals have been to maintain a relatively open global economic order, while maintaining a balance of power such that no rival country could ever dominate global politics and threaten American safety and prosperity. To that extent, notes Mead, the basic strategic posture of U.S. foreign policy has not changed since the 1800s.

The basic shape of American foreign policy throughout American history has been determined by the nation's interest in the international, largely maritime trading and financial order that over the last few centuries has gradually spread over the earth and integrated the economies of many nations and continents. What we now call globalization—the growth of an international economic system—is one of the most important historical developments of the last five centuries. Indeed, the colonization of what became the United States was an episode in this long process.

For most of American history the global economic order was centered on Great Britain, and therefore our key national dependency on and concern about this order implied a close if sometimes conflicted relationship with Great Britain. This British-based international system affected both the political and economic interests of the United States. Economically we were concerned to have opportunities for our trade and to control the impact on our domestic order of the international economic system. Politically the United States always had to think about whether Britain would wield the power of its global system in ways that would benefit us, or at least not impose unacceptable risks and costs. In the worst case Americans had to think about what to do if a clash of interests with Great Britain led to war. (Contingency planning for a war against the British Empire was an important activity for American military strategists well into the twentieth century.) Increasingly, as British power declined, the United States had to think about whether Britain could maintain this system, and what the United States should do if and when Britain failed.

Although the word *globalization* is new, and although the process has accelerated and deepened in recent years, globalization has been the most important fact of world history during the entire history of the United States. Because of our geographical situation and the commercial and enterprising nature of American society, globalization has been at the heart of American strategic thinking and policy making for virtually all of our history.

The history of American foreign policy divides into four eras based on our changing relationship to Great Britain and the emerging global order. The first era, lasting from 1776 to 1823, saw the United States win its political independence from the British Empire, and then immediately begin to work out the question of its relations with the British economic system and imperial power. Both Britain and the United States had to grapple with questions about the relationship. On the British side: Should the mother country try to strangle the infant Union, or was Britain better off with a strong and stable trading partner? From the American side, another set of questions had to be addressed. Was the United States better off undermining Britain by forming alliances with strong Continental powers, or was it wiser policy to side with British attempts to maintain a balance of power in Europe? Should we have stood ready to help Britain keep the continental scorpions stuffed in their bottle, or would it have been safer to help one of the scorpions out, thus ensuring that Britain never had the leisure or resources to turn on the United States?

Opinion in both countries seesawed on these issues, but ultimately each side reached a consensus. The British acknowledged that Britain was better off trading with the United States than adding the dangers and expenses of an anti-American foreign policy to all the worries of maintaining a balance of power in Europe and building a growing global system. The United States for its part decided that having Britannia rule the waves was better than letting the rest of the scorpions out of the bottle. For its own selfish reasons, Britain would do its best to keep the European empires bottled up in Europe. The United States decided that it would not only not stab Britain in the back, but it also hinted that, if one of the scorpions got too strong, the United States as an absolutely last resort might come to Britain's assistance and help keep the bottle firmly corked.

We can and should say now what policy makers knew but lacked the time to say earlier in the century. Franklin Roosevelt was technically right that the Monroe Doctrine was not so formal or clear even as an "unwritten agreement." But Walter Lippmann was also right to say that there was a tacit understanding. The myth of isolation was wrong. The Monroe Doctrine was not only not isolationist, it was anti-isolationist. It amounted to the recognition that American safety depended on the balance of power in Europe. With that doctrine's promulgation, the first era in American foreign policy came to a close. The strategic principles of the Monroe Doctrine have continued without interruption to shape American foreign policy from that day to this. American interventions in the world wars as well as the Cold War were not a series of revolutionary departures from Monroe's statecraft; they were examples of the same thinking that led Monroe to proclaim it. Just as Monroe and his talented secretary of state, John Quincy Adams, were prepared in the last analysis to help Britain prevent the French or the Spanish from reestablishing dynastic empires in the Americas in 1823, twentieth-century American presidents were prepared to step in to keep Germany and the Soviet Union from overturning the European power balance and spreading their power through the rest of the world. If another antidemocratic power should threaten to unite all Europe under its dominion tomorrow, we would step in and resist it again. We would do the same thing in Asia, and for the same reason. Our policies have changed over the decades and centuries to reflect changing circumstances; our basic strategic posture has not changed since 1823.

The second era in American foreign policy lasted from 1823 through 1914. During this time the United States existed in a Britain-centered global order. Britain's power, and therefore the world order, were secure during most of these years. There was no need to think about helping to prop up the system; Britain seemed perfectly capable of handling that on its own. Instead the United States concentrated on getting the best deal for itself within the British system, while staying on guard against the danger that Britain might be tempted by its strength to crush or divide it. The Republic wanted to ensure that the economic structure of the emerging and developing economic system would be favorable to both its long- and its short-term economic development. The United States believed that over time American power and influence within the British system would grow, and looked forward to the day when it would surpass Great Britain as what today is called a global superpower.

The uneasy balance between the two powers was largely in Britain's favor early in the period. The Union victory in the Civil War marked the beginning of a period when the United States moved steadily toward equality, and more, with Britain, increasingly asserting influence over Britain's global policies as Britain's awareness grew of its dependence on good relations with the United States. Perhaps the 1871 Treaty of Washington marked the true turning point: It provided for international arbitration of all outstanding issues between the two nations, and under it the United States was ultimately awarded $15.5 million for damage to Union shipping during the Civil War by British-built Confederate raiders. It was the first treaty between the two nations that clearly favored the American side.

During this period the United States first began to think seriously about its future when and if the Pax Britannica ended. One response was American imperialism; if Britain fell, it would be necessary for the United States to follow a more active world strategy. The acquisition of bases and coaling stations (fuel depots to allow the coal-fired navies of the day to project power in distant waters) throughout the Pacific was part of a process by which American policy makers prepared for the end of the Pax Britannica.

The third era of American foreign policy encompassed the two world wars and saw the rapid decline and fall of the British world system. In the years between 1914 and 1947 the United States was forced to wrestle again with some of the basic strategic questions it had examined in the first, pre-Monroe era. With the old mother country visibly in decline, should the United States supplement British power as it waned, propping up Britain as it propped up the global order? Should the United States instead stand back and let the world order look after itself? Or should the United States replace Great Britain as the gyroscope of world order, with all the political, military, and economic costs, benefits, and responsibilities that role would entail?

Between the start of World War I and the winter of 1947, the United States experimented with all of these approaches. Slowly it became unpleasantly apparent that there was no middle way: The United States had to choose between filling Britain's old role in its own way or living in a world in which no power took responsibility for the kind of world order in which we had always existed. This was no choice at all.

The third era in the history of American foreign policy ended with the decision that opened the fourth, in which we still live. In 1947 as in 1823, Americans concluded that the national interest required a strong maritime power able to uphold the balance of power in Europe and to maintain an international economic and political order in the rest of the world. By 1947 that power could no longer be Great Britain; it would have to be the United States. Atlas shrugged, and the United States would shoulder the sky. Since World War II, that choice has been and remains the cornerstone of American foreign policy. The Cold War, large though it loomed at the time, and vital as it was to win, was less of a milestone in American history than many assume. The real decision, whose implications and consequences are still with us today, was to take on Britain's old role. The Cold War was an incident in American foreign policy, not an epoch, and its end left the United States with essentially the same set of responsibilities, interests, and tasks that we had when it began.

# PART IV

# The Cold War: The Foreign Policy of a Superpower

In the years between 1914 and 1945, the United States responded to a drastically changing world system. As Walter Russell Mead pointed out in Part III, the United States had the choice in this era of either propping up the declining British Empire, ignoring British decline and allowing an international system without a hegemonic power, or taking over the British role. In fact, the United States tried all three of these, though by the late 1940s, the United States had established itself as the successor to the British. The end of World War II also gave rise to a bipolar international system dominated by two superpowers, the United States and the Soviet Union. As the world's richest and most powerful country, and as the undisputed leader of the noncommunist world, the United States at this time emerged into a new global role, one unlike any other it had previously carried out. The readings in Part IV look at the era of the Cold War, when the United States took the lead in fashioning a new world order.

The order that the United States sought to build was based on the dual strategies of containing the Soviet Union and fostering a liberal international economic order. Containment was offered as a strategy by George Kennan. The policies that followed, as enunciated by President Truman in the Truman Doctrine, possessed an internal logic and a simple formula for action: pushing back against the Soviets wherever they threatened noncommunist governments, be they in Italy or South Vietnam or Cuba, and challenging governments around the world that had aligned with the Soviet Union. The mechanisms and rationales for building a liberal international economic order, which are explained in the reading by Stephen Cohen, were crafted at Bretton Woods, where postwar planning brought forth institutions such as the General Agreement on Tariffs and Trade (now more commonly known as the World Trade Organization or WTO), the World Bank, the International Monetary Fund, and a new currency exchange standard.

Both of these strategies were revised over time in response to how the Cold War unfolded and to stresses in the international economic system. The selection by Robert Gilpin describes the changes in global political economy and how the United States was impacted. The other readings look at the U.S. policy of containment and some of the key occurrences during the Cold War such as the Cuban Missile Crisis, the War in Vietnam, détente, reassertion under President Reagan, and the end of the Cold War. These articles do not address one another directly, but what they do is provide analyses that explain how and why American policy evolved and changed throughout the Cold War, while still maintaining continuity in the larger strategy of containment.

The seemingly straightforward nature of American actions during these years has yielded a wide range of assessments, and the readings in Part I speak to this divergence of opinion. Joshua Muravchik describes American actions during the Cold War as producing sublime results, and John Ikenberry argues that the American-led system worked because the United States embedded itself in a larger, institution and rule-based international system. By contrast, Noam Chomsky represents a critical view, arguing that American foreign policy constituted a drive for global dominance—political, economic, and military.

# 19 The Sources of Soviet Conduct
## GEORGE KENNAN

The outset of the Cold War marks the beginning of the American role as a global superpower. Until this time, Americans had historically turned inward after war, generally preferring not to seek a global leadership role like the British and the French. Americans had chosen a policy of isolationism between the two world wars, and its leaders during and after World War II had decided not to allow that to happen again, believing that American abdication of global responsibility for order and peace had in part contributed to the rise of chaos and conflict in the 1930s. When confronted with the Soviet challenge in a Europe devastated by war, the American government began what became a long-term effort to confront the threat.

George Kennan was working in the U.S. embassy in Moscow when the Cold War began. He was asked to reply to a State Department query regarding how the United States should interpret and react to Soviet behavior in Eastern Europe. Cooperation was fast turning into confrontation in a number of places, and the United States was looking for an effective way to respond. Kennan replied with what became known as "The Long Telegram," a detailed explanation of the evolution of Soviet power within the context of Russian history and Marxist-Leninist ideology. He was encouraged to share his assessment and recommendations with the public, and in 1947 he submitted "The Sources of Soviet Conduct" to *Foreign Affairs*, still today a leading journal of U.S. foreign policy. Since he was about to become the head of a new policy planning unit of the State Department, Kennan did not want to publish under his own name, and so he signed the article simply as "X," though this did little to hide his identity.

Kennan argued that Soviet behavior was a product of both Communist ideology and historical circumstance, and he offered "containment" as a policy that could be employed to combat Soviet aggressive tendencies by making the cost of expansion too high for the Soviets to bear. He also suggested, rather prophetically, that a successful containment policy could eventually lead to the break up or mellowing of Soviet power, a prediction that led him to be hailed as something of a genius when the Soviet Union collapsed and the Cold War ended.

X (George F. Kennan), "The Sources of Soviet Conduct." Reprinted with permission from *Foreign Affairs*, 25.4, July 1947. Copyright 1947 by the Council on Foreign Relations, Inc.

Kennan's analysis is useful and interesting in that it did more than help set the stage for America's role in the Cold War. Kennan offers one of the first examples describing an American effort to create and sustain a global order based on American power. His analysis and prescription for action begins to spell out the logic and the justification of an American imposed order, one that is centered around American military might and the creation of a liberal international economic system. This American project, which was begun in Kennan's era, has lived beyond the experience of the Cold War and continues to this day.

---

The political personality of Soviet power as we know it today is the product of ideology and circumstances: ideology inherited by the present Soviet leaders from the movement in which they had their political origin, and circumstances of the power which they now have exercised for nearly three decades in Russia. There can be few tasks of psychological analysis more difficult than to try to trace the interaction of these two forces and the relative role of each in the determination of official Soviet conduct, yet the attempt must be made if that conduct is to be understood and effectively countered.

It is difficult to summarize the set of ideological concepts with which the Soviet leaders came into power. Marxian ideology, in its Russian-Communist projection, has always been in process of subtle evolution. The materials on which it bases itself are extensive and complex. But the outstanding features of Communist thought as it existed in 1916 may perhaps be summarized as follows: (a) that the central factor in the life of man, the factor which determines the character of public life and the "physiognomy of society," is the system by which material goods are produced and exchanged; (b) that the capitalist system of production is a nefarious one which inevitable leads to the exploitation of the working class by the capital-owning class and is incapable of developing adequately the economic resources of society or of distributing fairly the material good produced by human labor; (c) that capitalism contains the seeds of its own destruction and must, in view of the inability of the capital-owning class to adjust itself to economic change, result eventually and inescapably in a revolutionary transfer of power to the working class; and (d) that imperialism, the final phase of capitalism, leads directly to war and revolution.

The rest may be outlined in Lenin's own words: "Unevenness of economic and political development is the inflexible law of capitalism. It follows from this that the victory of Socialism may come originally in a few capitalist countries or even in a single capitalist country. The victorious proletariat of that country, having expropriated the capitalists and having organized Socialist production at home, would rise against the remaining capitalist world, drawing to itself in the process the oppressed classes of other countries." It must be noted that there was no assumption that capitalism would perish without proletarian revolution. A final push was needed from a revolutionary proletariat movement in order to tip over the tottering structure. But it was regarded as inevitable that sooner of later that push be given.

For 50 years prior to the outbreak of the Revolution, this pattern of thought had exercised great fascination for the members of the Russian revolutionary movement. Frustrated, discontented, hopeless of finding self-expression—or too impatient to seek it—in the confining limits of the Tsarist political system, yet lacking wide popular support or their choice of bloody revolution as a means of social betterment, these revolutionists found in Marxist theory a highly convenient rationalization for their own instinctive desires. It afforded pseudo-scientific justification for their impatience, for their categoric denial of all value in the Tsarist system, for their yearning for power and revenge and for their inclination to cut corners in the pursuit of it. It is therefore no wonder that they had come to believe implicitly in the truth and soundness of the Marxist-Leninist teachings, so congenial to their own impulses and emotions. Their sincerity need not be impugned. This is a phenomenon as old as human nature itself. It is has never been more aptly described than by Edward Gibbon, who wrote in *The Decline and Fall of the Roman Empire*: "From enthusiasm to imposture the step is perilous and slippery; the demon of Socrates affords a memorable instance of how a wise man may deceive himself, how a good man may deceive others, how the conscience may slumber in a mixed and middle state between self-illusion and voluntary fraud." And it was with this set of conceptions that the members of the Bolshevik Party entered into power.

Now it must be noted that through all the years of preparation for revolution, the attention of these men, as indeed of Marx himself, had been centered less on the future form which Socialism would take than on the necessary overthrow of rival power which, in their view, had to precede the introduction of Socialism. Their views, therefore, on the positive program to be put into effect, once power was attained, were for the most part nebulous, visionary and impractical, beyond the nationalization of industry and the expropriation of large private capital holdings there was no agreed program. The treatment of the peasantry, which, according to the Marxist formulation was not of the proletariat, had always been a vague spot in the pattern of Communist thought: and it remained an object of controversy and vacillation for the first ten years of Communist power.

The circumstances of the immediate post-revolution period—the existence in Russia of civil war and foreign intervention, together with the obvious fact that the Communists represented only a tiny minority of the Russian people—made the establishment of dictatorial power a necessity. The experiment with "war Communism" and the abrupt attempt to eliminate private production and trade had unfortunate economic consequences and caused further bitterness against the new revolutionary regime. While the temporary relaxation of the effort to communize Russia, represented by the New Economic Policy, alleviated some of this economic distress and thereby served its purpose, it also made it evident that the "capitalistic sector of society" was still prepared to profit at once from any relaxation of governmental pressure, and would, if permitted to continue to exist, always constitute a powerful opposing element to the Soviet regime and a serious rival for influence in the country. Somewhat the same situation prevailed with respect to the individual peasant who, in his own small way, was also a private producer.

Lenin, had he lived, might have proved a great enough man to reconcile these conflicting forces to the ultimate benefit of Russian society, though this is questionable. But be that as it may, Stalin, and those whom he led in the struggle for succession to Lenin's position of leadership, were not the men to tolerate rival political forces in the sphere of power which they coveted. Their sense of insecurity was too great. Their particular brand of fanaticism, unmodified by any of the Anglo-Saxon traditions of compromise, was too fierce and too jealous to envisage any permanent sharing of power. From the Russian-Asiatic world out of which they had emerged they carried with them a skepticism as to the possibilities of permanent and peaceful coexistence of rival forces. Easily persuaded of their own doctrinaire "rightness," they insisted on the submission or destruction of all competing power. Outside the Communist Party, Russian society was to have no rigidity. There were to be no forms of collective human activity or association which would not be dominated by the Party. No other force in Russian society was to be permitted to achieve vitality or integrity. Only the Party was to have structure. All else was to be an amorphous mass.

And within the Party the same principle was to apply. The mass of Party members might go through the motions of election, deliberation, decision and action; but in these motions they were to be animated not by their own individual wills but by the awesome breath of the Party leadership and the overbrooding presence of "the word."

Let it be stressed again that subjectively these men probably did not seek absolutism for its own sake. They doubtless believed—and found it easy to believe—that they alone knew what was good for society and that they would accomplish that good once their power was secure and unchallengeable. But in seeking that security of their own rule they were prepared to recognize no restrictions, either of God or man, on the character of their methods. And until such time as that security might be achieved, they placed far down on their scale of operational priorities the comforts and happiness of the peoples entrusted to their care.

Now the outstanding circumstance concerning the Soviet regime is that down to the present day this process of political consolidation has never been completed and the men in the Kremlin have continued to be predominantly absorbed with the struggle to secure and make absolute the power which they seized in November 1917. They have endeavored to secure it primarily against forces at home, within Soviet society itself. But they have also endeavored to secure it against the outside world. For ideology, as we have seen, taught them that the outside world was hostile and that it was their duty eventually to overthrow the political forces beyond their borders. Then powerful hands of Russian history and tradition reached up to sustain them in this feeling. Finally, their own aggressive intransigence with respect to the outside world began to find its own reaction; and they were soon forced, to use another Gibbonesque phrase, "to chastise the contumacy" which they themselves had provoked. It is an undeniable privilege of every man to prove himself right in the thesis that the world is his enemy; for if he reiterates it frequently enough and makes it the background of his conduct he is bound eventually to be right.

Now it lies in the nature of the mental world of the Soviet leaders, as well as in the character of their ideology, that no opposition to them can be officially recognized as having any merit or justification whatsoever. Such opposition can flow, in theory, only from the hostile and incorrigible forces of dying capitalism. As long as remnants of capitalism were officially recognized as existing in Russia, it was possible to place on them, as an internal element, part of the blame for the maintenance of a dictatorial form of society. But as these remnants were liquidated, little by little, this justification fell away, and when it was indicated officially that they had been finally destroyed, it disappeared altogether. And this fact created one of the most basic of the compulsions which came to act upon the Soviet regime: since capitalism no longer existed in Russia and since it could not be admitted that there could be serious or widespread opposition to the Kremlin springing spontaneously from the liberated masses under its authority, it became necessary to justify the retention of the dictatorship by stressing the menace of capitalism abroad.

This began at an early date. In 1924 Stalin specifically defended the retention of the "organs of suppression," meaning, among others, the army and the secret police, on the ground that "as long as there is a capitalistic encirclement there will be danger of intervention with all the consequences that flow from that danger." In accordance with that theory, and from that time on, all internal opposition forces in Russia have consistently been portrayed as the agents of foreign forces of reaction antagonistic to Soviet power.

By the same token, tremendous emphasis has been placed on the original Communist thesis of a basic antagonism between the capitalist and Socialist worlds. It is clear, from many indications, that this emphasis is not founded in reality. The real facts concerning it have been confused by the existence abroad of genuine resentment provoked by Soviet philosophy and tactics and occasionally by the existence of great centers of military power, notably the Nazi regime in Germany and the Japanese Government of the late 1930s, which did indeed have aggressive designs against the Soviet Union. But there is ample evidence that the stress laid in Moscow on the menace confronting Soviet society from the world outside its borders is founded not in the realities of foreign antagonism but in the necessity of explaining away the maintenance of dictatorial authority at home.

Now the maintenance of this pattern of Soviet power, namely, the pursuit of unlimited authority domestically, accompanied by the cultivation of the semi-myth of implacable foreign hostility, has gone far to shape the actual machinery of Soviet power as we know it today. Internal organs of adminis-tration which did not serve this purpose withered on the vine. Organs which did serve this purpose became vastly swollen. The security of Soviet power came to rest on the iron discipline of the Party, on the severity and ubiquity of the secret police, and on the uncompromising economic monop-olism of the state. The "organs of suppression," in which the Soviet leaders had sought security from rival forces, became in large measures the masters of those whom they were designed to serve. Today the major part of the structure of Soviet power is committed to the perfection of the dictatorship and to the maintenance of the concept of Russia as in a state of siege, with the enemy lowering beyond the walls. And the millions of human beings who form that part of the structure of power must defend at all costs this concept of Russia's position, for without it they are themselves superfluous.

As things stand today, the rulers can no longer dream of parting with these organs of suppression. The quest for absolute power, pursued now for nearly three decades with a ruthlessness unparalleled (in scope at least) in modern times, has again produced internally, as it did externally, its own reaction. The excesses of the police apparatus have fanned the potential opposition to the regime into something far greater and more dangerous than it could have been before those excesses began.

But least of all can the rulers dispense with the fiction by which the maintenance of dictatorial power has been defended. For this fiction has been canonized in Soviet philosophy by the excesses already committed in its name; and it is now anchored in the Soviet structure of thought by bonds far greater than those of mere ideology.

# II

So much for the historical background. What does it spell in terms of the political personality of Soviet power as we know it today?

Of the original ideology, nothing has been officially junked. Belief is maintained in the basic badness of capitalism, in the inevitability of its destruction, in the obligation of the proletariat to assist in that destruction and to take power into its own hands. But stress has come to be laid primarily on those concepts which relate most specifically to the Soviet regime itself: to its position as the sole truly Socialist regime in a dark and misguided world, and to the relationships of power within it.

The first of these concepts is that of the innate antagonism between capitalism and Socialism. We have seen how deeply that concept has become imbedded in foundations of Soviet power. It has profound implications for Russia's conduct as a member of international society. It means that there can never be on Moscow's side a sincere assumption of a community of aims between the Soviet Union and powers which are regarded as capitalist. It must inevitably be assumed in Moscow that the aims of the capitalist world are antagonistic to the Soviet regime, and therefore to the interests of the peoples it controls. If the Soviet government occasionally sets it signature to documents which would indicate the contrary, this is to be regarded as a tactical maneuver permissible in dealing with the enemy (who is without honor) and should be taken in the spirit of *caveat emptor*. Basically, the antagonism remains. It is postulated. And from it flow many of the phenomena which we find disturbing in the Kremlin's conduct of foreign policy: the secretiveness, the lack of frankness, the duplicity, the wary suspiciousness, and the basic unfriendliness of purpose. These phenomena are there to stay, for the foreseeable future. There can be variations of degree and of emphasis. When there is something the Russians want from us, one or the other of these features of their policy may be thrust temporarily into the background; and when that happens there will always be Americans who will leap forward with gleeful announcements that "the Russians have changed," and some who will even try to take credit for having brought about such "changes." But we should not be misled by tactical maneuvers. These characteristics of Soviet policy, like the postulate from which they flow, are basic to the internal nature of Soviet power, and will be with us, whether in the foreground or the background, until the internal nature of Soviet power is changed.

This means we are going to continue for a long time to find the Russians difficult to deal with. It does not mean that they should be considered as embarked upon a do-or-die program to overthrow our society by a given date. The theory of the inevitability of the eventual fall of capitalism has the fortunate connotation that there is no hurry about it. The forces of progress can take their time in preparing the final *coup de grâce*. Meanwhile, what is vital is that the "Socialist fatherland"—that oasis of power which has already been won for Socialism in the person of the Soviet Union—should be cherished and defended by all good Communists at home and abroad, its fortunes promoted, its enemies badgered and confounded. The promotion of premature, "adventuristic" revolutionary projects abroad which might embarrass Soviet power in any way would be an inexcusable, even a counter-revolutionary act. The cause of Socialism is the support and promotion of Soviet power, as defined in Moscow.

This brings us to the second of the concepts important to contemporary Soviet outlook. That is the infallibility of the Kremlin. The Soviet concept of power, which permits no focal points of organization outside the Party itself, requires that the Party leadership remain in theory the sole repository of truth. For if truth were to be found elsewhere, there would be justification for its expression in organized activity. But it is precisely that which the Kremlin cannot and will not permit.

The leadership of the Communist Party is therefore always right, and has been always right ever since in 1929 Stalin formalized his personal power by announcing that decisions of the Politburo were being taken unanimously.

On the principle of infallibility there rests the iron discipline of the Communist Party. In fact, the two concepts are mutually self-supporting. Perfect discipline requires recognition of infallibility. Infallibility requires the observance of discipline. And the two go far to determine the behaviorism of the entire Soviet apparatus of power. But their effect cannot be understood unless a third factor be taken into account: namely, the fact that the leadership is at liberty to put forward for tactical purposes any particular thesis which it finds useful to the cause at any particular moment and to require the faithful and unquestioning acceptance of that thesis by the members of the movement as a whole. This means that truth is not a constant but is actually created, for all intents and purposes, by the Soviet leaders themselves. It may vary from week to week, from month to month. It is nothing absolute and immutable—nothing which flows from objective reality. It is only the most recent manifestation of the wisdom of those in whom the ultimate wisdom is supposed to reside, because they represent the logic of history. The accumulative effect of these factors is to give to the whole subordinate apparatus of Soviet power an unshakable stubbornness and steadfastness in its orientation. This orientation can be changed at will by the Kremlin but by no other power. Once a given party line has been laid down on a given issue of current policy, the whole Soviet governmental machine, including the mechanism of diplomacy, moves inexorably along the prescribed path, like a persistent toy automobile wound up and headed in a given direction, stopping only when it meets with some unanswerable force. The individuals who are the components of this machine are unamenable to argument or reason, which comes to them from outside sources. Their whole training has taught them to mistrust and discount the glib persuasiveness of the outside world. Like the white dog before the phonograph, they hear only the "master's voice." And if they are to be called off from the purposes last dictated to them, it is the master who must call them off. Thus the foreign representative cannot hope that his words will make any impression on them. The most that he can hope is that they will be transmitted to those at the top, who are capable of changing the party line. But even those are not likely to be swayed by any normal logic in the words of the bourgeois representative. Since there can be no appeal to common purposes, there can be no appeal to common mental approaches. For this reason, facts speak louder than words to the ears of the Kremlin; and words carry the greatest weight when they have the ring of reflecting, or being backed up by, facts of unchallengeable validity.

But we have seen that the Kremlin is under no ideological compulsion to accomplish its purposes in a hurry. Like the Church, it is dealing in ideological concepts which are of long-term validity, and it can afford to be patient. It has no right to risk the existing achievements of the revolution for the sake of vain baubles of the future. The very teachings of Lenin himself require great caution and flexibility in the pursuit of Communist purposes. Again, these precepts are fortified by the lessons of Russian history: of centuries of obscure battles between nomadic forces over the stretches of a vast unfortified plain. Here caution, circumspection, flexibility and deception are the valuable qualities; and their value finds a natural appreciation in the Russian or the oriental mind. Thus the Kremlin has no compunction about retreating in the face of superior forces. And being under the compulsion of no timetable, it does not get panicky under the necessity for such retreat. Its political action is a fluid stream which moves constantly, wherever it is permitted to move, toward a given goal. Its main concern is to make sure that it has filled every nook and cranny available to it in the basin of world power. But if it finds unassailable barriers in its path, it accepts these philosophically and accommodates itself to them. The main thing is that there should always be pressure, unceasing constant pressure, toward the desired goal. There is no trace of any feeling in Soviet psychology that that goal must be reached at any given time.

These considerations make Soviet diplomacy at once easier and more difficult to deal with than the diplomacy of individual aggressive leaders like Napoleon and Hitler. On the one hand it is more sensitive to contrary force, more ready to yield on individual sectors of the diplomatic front when that force is felt to be too strong, and thus more rational in the logic and rhetoric of power. On the other hand it cannot be easily defeated or discouraged by a single victory on the part of its opponents. And the patient persistence by which it is animated means that it can be effectively countered not by sporadic acts which represent the momentary whims of democratic opinion but only be intelligent long-range policies on the part of Russia's adversaries—policies no less steady in their purpose, and no less variegated and resourceful in their application, than those of the Soviet Union itself.

In these circumstances it is clear that the main element of any United States policy toward the Soviet Union must be that of long-term, patient but firm and vigilant containment of Russian expansive tendencies. It is important to note, however, that such a policy has nothing to do with outward histrionics: with threats or blustering or superfluous gestures of outward "toughness." While the Kremlin is basically flexible in its reaction to political realities, it is by no means unamenable to considerations of prestige. Like almost any other government, it can be placed by tactless and threatening gestures in a position where it cannot afford to yield even though this might be dictated by its sense of realism. The Russian leaders are keen judges of human psychology, and as such they are highly conscious that loss of temper and of self-control is never a source of strength in political affairs. They are quick to exploit such evidences of weakness. For these reasons it is a *sine qua non* of successful dealing with Russia that the foreign government in question should remain at all times cool and collected and that its demands on Russian policy should be put forward in such a manner as to leave the way open for a compliance not too detrimental to Russian prestige.

## III

In the light of the above, it will be clearly seen that the Soviet pressure against the free institutions of the western world is something that can be contained by the adroit and vigilant application of counter-force at a series of constantly shifting geographical and political points, corresponding to the shifts and maneuvers of Soviet policy, but which cannot be charmed or talked out of existence. The Russians look forward to a duel of infinite duration, and they see that already they have scored great successes. It must be borne in mind that there was a time when the Communist Party represented far more of a minority in the sphere of Russian national life than Soviet power today represents in the world community.

But if the ideology convinces the rulers of Russia that truth is on their side and they can therefore afford to wait, those of us on whom that ideology has no claim are free to examine objectively the validity of that premise. The Soviet thesis not only implies complete lack of control by the west over its own economic destiny, it likewise assumes Russian unity, discipline and patience over an infinite period. Let us bring this apocalyptic vision down to earth, and suppose that the western world finds the strength and resourcefulness to contain Soviet power over a period of ten to fifteen years. What does that spell for Russia itself?

The Soviet leaders, taking advantage of the contributions of modern techniques to the arts of despotism, have solved the question of obedience within the confines of their power. Few challenge their authority; and even those who do are unable to make that challenge valid as against the organs of suppression of the state.

The Kremlin has also proved able to accomplish its purpose of building up Russia, regardless of the interests of the interests of the inhabitants, and industrial foundation of heavy metallurgy, which is, to be sure, not yet complete but which is nevertheless continuing to grow and is approaching those of the other major industrial countries. All of this, however, both the maintenance of internal political security and the building of heavy industry, has been carried out at a terrible cost in human life and in human hopes and energies. It has necessitated the use of forced labor on a scale unprecedented in modern times under conditions of peace. It has involved the neglect or abuse of other phases of Soviet economic life, particularly agriculture, consumers' goods production, housing and transportation.

To all that, the war has added its tremendous toll of destruction, death and human exhaustion. In consequence of this, we have in Russia today a population which is physically and spiritually tired. The mass of the people are disillusioned, skeptical and no longer as accessible as they once were to the magical attraction which Soviet power still radiates to its followers abroad. The avidity with which people seized upon the slight respite accorded to the Church for tactical reasons during the war was eloquent testimony to the fact that their capacity for faith and devotion found little expression in the purposes of the regime.

In these circumstances, there are limits to the physical and nervous strength of people themselves. These limits are absolute ones, and are binding even for the cruelest dictatorship, because beyond them people cannot be driven. The forced labor camps and the other agencies of constraint provide temporary means of compelling people to work longer hours than their own volition or mere economic pressure would dictate; but if people survive them at all they become old before their time and must be considered as human casualties to the demands of dictatorship. In either case their best powers are no longer available to society and can no longer be enlisted in the service of the state.

Here only the younger generations can help. The younger generation, despite all vicissitudes and sufferings, is numerous and vigorous; and the Russians are a talented people. But it still remains to be seen what will be the effects on mature performance of the abnormal emotional strains of childhood which Soviet dictatorship created and which were enormously increased by the war. Such things as normal security and placidity of home environment have practically ceased to exist in the Soviet Union outside of the most remote farms and villages. And observers are not yet sure whether that is not going to leave its mark on the overall capacity of the generation now coming into maturity.

In addition to this, we have the fact that Soviet economic development, while it can list certain formidable achievements, has been precariously spotty and uneven. Russian Communists who speak of the "uneven development of capitalism" should blush at the contemplation of their own national economy. Here certain branches of economic life, such as the metallurgical and machine industries, have been pushed out of all proportion to other sectors of economy.

Here is a nation striving to become in a short period one of the great industrial nations of the world while it still has no highway network worthy of the name and only a relatively primitive network of railways. Much has been done to increase efficiency of labor and to teach primitive peasants something about the operation of machines. But maintenance is still a crying deficiency of all Soviet economy. Construction is hasty and poor in quality. Depreciation must be enormous. And in vast sectors of economic life it has not yet been possible to instill into labor anything like that general culture of production and technical self-respect which characterizes the skilled worker of the west.

It is difficult to see how these deficiencies can be corrected at an early date by a tired and dispirited population working largely under the shadow of fear and compulsion. And as long as they are not overcome, Russia will remain economically as vulnerable, and in a certain sense an impotent, nation, capable of exporting its enthusiasms and of radiating the strange charm of its primitive political vitality but unable to back up those articles of export by the real evidences of material power and prosperity.

Meanwhile, a great uncertainty hangs over the political life of the Soviet Union. That is the uncertainty involved in the transfer of power from one individual or group of individuals to others.

This is, of course, outstandingly the problem of the personal position of Stalin. We must remember that his succession to Lenin's pinnacle of pre-eminence in the Communist movement was the only such transfer of individual authority which the Soviet Union has experienced. That transfer took 12 years to consolidate. It cost the lives of millions of people and shook the state to its foundations. The attendant tremors were felt all through the international revolutionary movement, to the disadvantage of the Kremlin itself.

It is always possible that another transfer of pre-eminent power may take place quietly and inconspicuously, with no repercussions anywhere. But again, it is possible that the questions involved may unleash, to use some of Lenin's words, one of those "incredibly swift transitions" from "delicate deceit" to "wild violence" which characterize Russian history, and may shake Soviet power to its foundations.

But this is not only a question of Stalin himself. There has been, since 1938, a dangerous congealment of political life in the higher circles of Soviet power. The All-Union Congress of Soviets, in theory the supreme body of the Party, is supposed to meet not less often than once in three years. It will soon be eight full years since its last meeting. During this period membership in the Party has numerically doubled. Party mortality during the war was enormous; and today well over half of the Party members are persons who have entered since the last Party congress was held meanwhile, the same small group of men has carried on at the top through an amazing series of national vicissitudes. Surely there is some reason why the experiences of the war brought basic political changes to every one of the great governments of the west. Surely the causes of that phenomenon are basic enough to be present somewhere in the obscurity of Soviet political life, as well. And yet no recognition has been given to these causes in Russia.

It must be surmised from this that even within so highly disciplined an organization as the Communist Party there must be a growing divergence in age, outlook and interest between the great mass of Party members, only so recently recruited into the movement, and the little self-perpetuating clique of men at the top, whom most of these Party members have never met, with whom they have never conversed, and with whom they can have no political intimacy.

Who can say whether, in these circumstances, the eventual rejuvenation of the higher spheres of authority (which can only be a matter of time) can take place smoothly and peacefully, or whether rivals in the quest for higher power will not eventually reach down into these politically immature and inexperienced masses in order to find support for their respective claims? If this were ever to happen, strange consequences could flow for the Communist Party: for the membership at large has been exercised only in the practices of iron discipline and obedience and not in the arts of compromise and accommodation. And if disunity were ever to seize and paralyze the Party, the chaos and weakness of Russian society would be revealed in forms beyond description. For we have seen that Soviet power is only concealing an amorphous mass of human beings among whom no independent organizational structure is tolerated. In Russia there is not even such a thing as local government. The present generation of Russians have never known spontaneity of collective action. If, consequently, anything were ever to occur to disrupt the unity and efficacy of the Party as a political instrument, Soviet Russia might be changed overnight from one of the strongest to one of the weakest and most pitiable of national societies.

Thus the future of Soviet power may not be by any means as secure as Russian capacity for self-delusion would make it appear to the men of the Kremlin. That they can quietly and easily turn it over to others remains to be proved. Meanwhile, the hardships of their rule and the vicissitudes of international life have taken a heavy toll of the strength and hopes of the great people on whom their power rests. It is curious to note that the ideological power of Soviet authority is strongest today in areas beyond the frontiers of Russia, beyond the reach of its police power. This phenomenon brings to mind a comparison used by Thomas Mann in his great novel *Buddenbrooks*. Observing that human institutions often show the greatest outward brilliance at a moment when inner decay is in reality farthest advanced, he compared one of those stars whose light shines most brightly on this world when in reality it has long since ceased to exist. And who can say with assurance that the strong light still cast by the Kremlin on the dissatisfied peoples of the western world is not the powerful afterglow of a constellation which is in actuality on the wane? This cannot be proved. And it cannot be disproved. But the possibility remains (and in the opinion of this writer it is a strong one) that Soviet power, like the capitalist world of its conception, bears within it the seeds of its own decay, and that the sprouting of these seeds is well advanced.

## IV

It is clear that the United States cannot expect in the foreseeable future to enjoy political intimacy with the Soviet regime. It must continue to regard the Soviet Union as a rival, not a partner, in the political arena. It must continue to expect that Soviet policies will reflect no abstract love of peace and stability, no real faith in the possibility of a permanent happy coexistence of the Socialist and capitalist worlds, but rather a cautious, persistent pressure toward the disruption and, weakening of all rival influence and rival power.

Balanced against this are the facts that Russia, as opposed to the western world in general, is still by far the weaker party, that Soviet policy is highly flexible, and that Soviet society may well contain deficiencies which will eventually weaken its own total potential. This would of itself warrant the United States entering with reasonable confidence upon a policy of firm containment, designed to confront the Russians with unalterable counterforce at every point where they show signs of encroaching upon the interests of a peaceful and stable world.

But in actuality the possibilities for American policy are by no means limited to holding the line and hoping for the best. It is entirely possible for the United States to influence by its actions the internal developments, both within Russia and throughout the international Communist movement, by which Russian policy is largely determined. This is not only a question of the modest measure of informational activity which this government can conduct in the Soviet Union and elsewhere, although that, too, is important. It is rather a question of the degree to which the United States can create among the peoples of the world generally the impression of a country which knows what it wants, which is coping successfully with the problem of its internal life and with the responsibilities of a world power, and which has a spiritual vitality capable of holding its own among the major ideological currents of the time. To the extent that such an impression can be created and maintained, the aims of Russian Communism must appear sterile and quixotic, the hopes and enthusiasm of Moscow's supporters must wane, and added strain must be imposed on the Kremlin's foreign policies. For the palsied decrepitude of the capitalist world is the keystone of Communist philosophy. Even the failure of the United States to experience the early economic depression which the ravens of the Red Square have been predicting with such complacent confidence since hostilities ceased would have deep and important repercussions throughout the Communist world.

By the same token, exhibitions of indecision, disunity and internal disintegration within this country have an exhilarating effect on the whole Communist movement. At each evidence of these tendencies, a thrill of hope and excitement goes through the Communist world; a new jauntiness can be noted in the Moscow tread; new groups of foreign supporters climb on to what they can only view as the bandwagon of international politics; and Russian pressure increases all along the line in international affairs.

It would be an exaggeration to say that American behavior unassisted and alone could exercise a power of life and death over the Communist movement and bring about the early fall of Soviet power in Russia. But the United States has it in its power to increase enormously the strains under which Soviet policy must operate, to force upon the Kremlin a far greater degree of moderation and circumspection than it has had to observe in recent years, and in this way to promote tendencies which must eventually find their outlet in either the breakup or the gradual mellowing of Soviet power. For no mystical, Messianic movement—and particularly not that of the Kremlin—can face frustration indefinitely without eventually adjusting itself in one way or another to the logic of that state of affairs.

Thus the decision will really fall in large measure in this country itself. The issue of Soviet-American relations is in essence a test of the overall worth of the United States as a nation among nations. To avoid destruction the United States need only measure up to its own best traditions and prove itself worthy of preservation as a great nation.

Surely, there was never a fairer test of national quality than this. In the light of these circumstances, the thoughtful observer of Russian-American relations will find no cause for complaint in the Kremlin's challenge to American society. He will rather experience a certain gratitude to a Providence which, by providing the American people with this implacable challenge, has made their entire security as a nation dependent on their pulling themselves together and accepting the responsibilities of moral and political leadership that history plainly intended them to bear.

# 20 The Content of International Economic Policy

## STEPHEN D. COHEN

During the Cold War, the American-led global order rested on two pillars. One of these pillars involved the maintenance of a policy of containment, as outlined by George Kennan in the previous article, which served to curb the spread of Soviet power and influence around the globe. The second pillar of this global order was a liberal international economic order comprised of a system of global institutions and rules. These included, most importantly, the General Agreement on Tariffs and Trade (GATT), the International Monetary Fund (IMF), the World Bank, and a system of currency exchanges based on a gold standard and later on free-floating, market-based exchange rates.

This second pillar of the American international system complemented the first, though neither element of this U.S. foreign policy framework depended upon the existence of the other in order to serve America's international goals. These goals involved not only an obligation to further American prosperity, but also a responsibility for the larger, general interest of global economic stability and peace. As Stephen Cohen explains, throughout much of the Cold War, American international economic measures were often explicitly placed in the service of larger geopolitical interests, and as such, the United States paid a disproportionate cost for the maintenance of the international economic order. This was by design. As World War II came to a close, American leaders, along with their allied counterparts, sought to produce an international economic system that would not lead to the type of protectionist, nationalist economic policies of the 1930s. Such policies were seen to have produced and exacerbated a worldwide depression and the resultant political chaos and conflict that followed.

Cohen explains the formation and goals of a liberal international economic order that emerged in the aftermath of the Second World War. He describes the evolution of the system and how it changed over the course of a generation in response to financial crises, rising oil prices, and the speedy economic recovery of Western Europe and Japan. These changes, along with American responses, produced great instability in the global economy. U.S. policy, however, adapted to the changes, allowing the liberal American-led system to continue to dominate global economic relations. This system has now withstood the end of the Cold War and a new reorientation of U.S. foreign policy focusing on terror and weapons of mass destruction. Operating rather independently of global or American security policy, this economic order seems to have in fact become more attractive, as evidenced by the number of new countries that have joined the GATT/WTO since the end of the Cold War.

---

U.S. international economic policy is different in scope from that of other countries because the American role in world affairs is extraordinary. There are three principal reasons for this. One is the simple quantitative involvement of the U.S. private sector in the world economy via trade, finance, and investment. The second reason is qualitative, devolving from the possession by the United States of the world's principal reserve and transactions currency (i.e., the U.S. dollar). The final factor is the unusually frequent subordination of international commercial priorities to national security concerns, a fallout of the United States' role as the world's only bona fide political and military superpower. Specifically, this role deters government officials from looking at international relations primarily through an economic lens. The United States is no longer obsessed with being the chief military protector of the free world against communist incursions from the former Soviet Union. However, it is now fascinated with the prospects for positive international political adjustments, such as a resolution of the Arab-Israeli conflict, a scenario that was suddenly enhanced by the disappearance of its rival superpower. The U.S. government has a broad, geographically wide-ranging political view of how it wants the so-called new world order to evolve. As proved in Kuwait, it has a sense of obligation strong enough to utilize massive military force to crush anyone who would significantly threaten this foreign policy blueprint. Furthermore, as proved in its recent relations with China, Haiti, Libya, and elsewhere, the United States is in a class by itself in its readiness to accept the economic costs of imposing export restrictions designed to force a foreign government to change its policy.

The international economic policies of most other countries can be based on a more straightforward concern with promoting exports, fostering the growth of favored domestic industries, minimizing unemployment, attracting foreign investment capital, ameliorating the grosser excesses of multinational corporations, and placating the demands of countries who are principal suppliers of critical raw materials.

The perspective of a country with the global objectives of the United States perforce must be broader. Policy reflects purposes. "Our purpose is not simply to defend but to construct, not simply to react to events in a world which others shape but to initiate so as ourselves to shape a world order in which we can live peaceably and prosper," Anthony Solomon has stated.[1]

A comprehensive, activist U.S. international economic policy is a post–World War II phenomenon. Prior to its birth in the Bretton Woods Agreement of 1944, this policy had been a blend of economic isolationism and economic nationalism. "Before the mid-1930s the United States paid little attention to international economic problems; on the occasions when it was forced to do so, it played a lone hand without much regard for the interests of other countries."[2] However, abstinence was by no means total. For example, the United States government was heavily involved in the financial aftermath of World War I: renegotiations of foreign debts owed to it and German reparations agreements. In the main, however, the executive branch did little more than articulate attitudes; there was little vigorous pursuit of specific policy objectives across the foreign economic spectrum.

A systematic, clearly articulated U.S. international economic policy emerged only after structural shifts had occurred in the world economy following World War II and the United States had emerged as a political-military superpower. Prior to 1945, the dollar was not the linchpin of the international monetary system; the U.S. balance of payments experienced the same constraints as other countries. The poor countries were mainly colonies of European nations, and there was no formal U.S. foreign aid program. Multinational corporations existed, but not in a number large enough to cause any meaningful repercussions or controversy.

World War II brought many irrevocable changes. One was the emergence of an activist, comprehensive U.S. international economic policy. Superpower status had been thrust upon the United States, initially because of its comparative economic strength. Americans fruitfully used this status in the construction of the Bretton Woods Agreement, which effectively designed the rules and structures of the postwar international economy. The main impetus at Bretton Woods was the need to prepare for economic reconstruction and the desire to avoid repetition of the absurd beggar-thy-neighbor economic policies of the 1930s, as manifested in exchange rate depreciations. Then came the advent of the cold war and the perceived need to urgently strengthen the free world and contain the spread of communist aggression. The traditional isolationist posture of the United States was discarded. The country's new course was clearly set: the bountiful productivity of its large, strong, and undamaged economy would be used, in part, to finance the establishment of a first line of defense in Western Europe and Japan.

Postwar U.S. international economic policy passed through two distinct stages before entering a third stage at the onset of the 1990s. For upwards of 20 years after 1945, U.S. policy was solely designed to maximize and accommodate national security needs. Widespread economic destruction in Europe and Asia meant that in the initial postwar period, the U.S. economy would suffer no significant disruption from import competition. However, it also meant that U.S. export opportunities would be limited in overseas markets that were either struggling to regain their competitiveness or emerging from colonial rule into the uncertainties of political independence. The U.S. economy, a veritable colossus in a world of economic weakness, could easily afford to accept temporary foreign discrimination against U.S. goods. Moreover, it could easily tolerate the moderately adverse trade impact caused by other countries devaluing their currencies against the dollar. There was only a very small economic price to be paid for the larger political benefits of encouraging the restoration of economic prosperity in noncommunist countries. The ensuing American sense of magnanimity was strongly reinforced by a growing trade surplus.

Furthermore, in the U.S. government's mode of thinking, its efforts to foster recovery abroad were fully compatible with assuring the long-term success of the multilateral economic institutions it had helped to design in 1944. All were designed to promote a liberal, market-based international economic system and to discourage a repeat of the disastrous nationalistic economic policies of the 1930s. Financed principally by the United States, the International Monetary Fund (IMF) was created to prevent a resurrection of the competitive devaluation policies of the 1930s. Similarly, the General Agreement on Tariffs and Trade (GATT) was formulated to provide an impetus to multilateral trade liberalization.

International economic policy, in short, served foreign policy. Since national security priorities caused no real damage to the U.S. economy through the mid-1960s, there simply was no conflict between "good" foreign policy and "good" international economic policy. Consequently, the U.S. national interest in this time period was unambiguous.

By the onset of the 1970s, however, long-simmering, underlying changes in political and economic fundamentals had surfaced with a vengeance, fomenting the dawn of an entirely new era of modern U.S. international economic policy. Undisputed U.S. hegemony and the very skewed balance of power in the immediate post–World War II period were transitory phenomena. They were neither a natural nor a permanent state of affairs. The vigor and speed with which Western Europe and Japan

recovered their economic strength, however, was completely unanticipated. The gold-buying spree at the expense of the U.S. Treasury, begun
by President Charles de Gaulle in the mid-1960s, signified the beginning
of a new era in international economic relations. The real problem was
that the international economic system was ill-equipped to react to the
unfolding structural changes, which at first were imperceptible. By the
time they had become clearly evident (by the shrinking U.S. trade surplus,
for example) the United States was experiencing the reappearance of
isolationist feelings, mainly because of the war in Vietnam. The burden of
acting as the world's "policeman" had brought considerable disenchant-
ment within the United States about its role in world affairs and at the
same time had further reduced the United States' relative international
competitiveness.

The international monetary system was being stretched to its breaking
point by the chronic balance-of-payments surpluses of the European
Community countries and Japan and the corresponding U.S. external
deficits. The very success and dynamism of the international economic
order, which the United States had sponsored and led, had done much to
undermine American economic strength. In the words of a special report
submitted to President Richard Nixon in 1971 by the first head of the
Council on International Economic Policy (CIEP), Peter Peterson: "The
international institutions created after World War II were simply not
equipped to deal with these changes, and governments were either disin-
clined or thought themselves unable to cope effectively with the rapidly
changing realities."[3]

For the United States, these "realities" were a trade account moving from
the black into the red, increases in domestic consumption coming increasingly at the expense of incremental exports, and growing unemployment
attributable to foreign competition. Slowly but steadily, the suspicion spread
that the existing international economic order was working against the
United States. Many Americans felt that their country was no longer able to
"hold its own" in global competition. Edward Fried eloquently described
the resulting sense of malaise:

> The United States grappled with a stubborn inflation, a deteriorating
> position in foreign trade, high defense costs, and, beginning in 1969, seri-
> ous unemployment. Its balance-of-payments deficit, chronic though rea-
> sonably stable for two decades, suddenly grew much larger and became
> subject to alarmist interpretations. Western Europe and Japan, on the
> other hand, were characterized by prosperity, continuing balance-of-
> payments surpluses, strong foreign trade positions, and comparatively
> low defense costs.... Did not this contrast between the United States
> and its once economically prostrate industrial partners mean that there
> was something "unfair" about the ground rules governing our foreign

economic relations and something misguided about our foreign economic policy? Was the United States not over-emphasizing the importance of foreign relations in foreign economic policy and thereby paying a heavy economic price?[4]

These questions were all answered in the affirmative when, on August 15, 1971, President Nixon announced the new economic policy. His administration's concern with domestic politics and economics, momentarily at least, had seized control of international economic policy. National security priorities were put aside as dollar-gold convertibility was terminated and a 10 percent import surcharge was initiated. On a de facto basis, the postwar monetary system of fixed exchange rates was ended. The trading system was given a severe jolt and was set up for a major new round of trade negotiations to deal with the full range of outstanding trade issues. The first historic shift in modern U.S. international economic policy produced monumental effects on the global order.

The era of the "foreign policy imperative" in U.S. international economic policy had ended. The policy center of gravity shifted inward, away from the immediate post–World War II priority of transferring U.S. wealth to Western Europe and Japan as a means of accelerating their economic and political recoveries. As U.S. international competitiveness sagged under the burdens of inflation and an overvalued exchange rate, and as the threat of communism to Western Europe and Japan receded, senior U.S. policymakers became committed to tilting the benefits of global economic relations back toward the United States. The need for internal economic adjustment ascended in importance relative to foreign policy considerations associated with alliance leadership.

The inward turn of U.S. international economic policy was tempered by an unprecedented onslaught of international crises and strains so severe as to put the global economic order at risk. Too many distractions materialized to allow for a simple U.S. shift to unilateralism. Along with all other countries, the United States had to innovate and experiment with new multilateral responses to one challenge after another. In 1973, the Bretton Woods system of fixed exchange rates suddenly collapsed and was replaced by a regime of unregulated floating rates; in addition, that year saw the first phase of an oil shock in which, ultimately, prices would approximately quadruple. Just as the world order had grown accustomed to history's greatest international transfer of purchasing power (from oil importers to oil exporters), a second, more severe oil price shock occurred in 1979 and 1980.

The resulting double-digit inflation that plagued the industrialized countries led to a nearly universal tightening of monetary policy, which by 1981 had produced the worst global recession since the Great Depression of the

1930s. No sooner had business cycle recovery gotten underway than two new shocks developed. First, changes in U.S. macroeconomic policy led to an overvalued exchange rate for the dollar, which in turn triggered the biggest national trade deficits the world had ever seen. Second, a number of important less developed countries (LDCs), mainly in Latin America, found themselves unable to repay their skyrocketing external obligations, an event that triggered an international debt crisis that threatened to unleash financial chaos in the international banking system.

Normalcy in international economic relations had all but disappeared.

## Notes

1. Anthony M. Solomon, "Administration of a Multipurpose Economic Diplomacy," *Public Administration Review* 24 (November–December 1969): 585.
2. Richard S. Gardner, *Sterling-Dollar Diplomacy* (New York: McGraw-Hill, 1969), p. 1.
3. Peter G. Peterson, *The United States in the Changing World Economy* (Washington, D.C.: U.S. Government Printing Office, 1971), p. iii.
4. Edward Fried, "Foreign Economic Policy: The Search for a Strategy," in *The Next Phase in Foreign Policy,* Henry Owen and Morton Halperin, eds. (Washington, D.C.: Brookings Institution, 1973), p. 161.

# 21   The Cuban Missile Crisis

### RICHARD CROCKETT

The Cuban Missile Crisis was the conflict that brought the United States and the Soviet Union closest to a direct military confrontation involving nuclear weapons. At no other time did the superpowers come this close to fighting a nuclear war, though exactly how close this was continues to be a subject of debate. If the United States had sought, through policies of containment and liberal

Richard Crockatt, from *The Fifty Years War: The United States and the Soviet Union in World Politics, 1941–1991.* Copyright 1995, published by Routledge. Reproduced by permission of Taylor & Francis Books UK.

economic internationalism, to produce a relatively stable global setting, the Soviet Union and other countries continually provided a series of challenges.

The success of Fidel Castro in Cuba and his subsequent turn to the Soviet Union presented the United States with an adversary who challenged the United States on two fronts. Castro had exceeded the bounds of what had historically been permissible for a Caribbean country, expropriating U.S. property and eliminating American influence from the country. In addition to this, he went Communist as well, creating a Marxist-Leninist dictatorship and aligning his government with the Soviet Union in the 1960s. American efforts to oust Castro were unsuccessful, and in the wake of such efforts the Soviets and Cubans agreed to install nuclear missiles in Cuba. The resolution of this crisis, which lasted 13 days, resulted in a deal between the United States and the Soviets: The United States pledged never to invade Cuba and the Soviets pledged to never install nuclear weapons in Cuba.

The end of the crisis resulted in two significant developments, one involving the conduct of the Cold War, the other involving the study of international relations. When the crisis had ended, a shift in the dynamics of the Cold War began to take place. From this point on, the United States and the Soviet Union avoided direct confrontation with their military forces, and indeed, took several steps to try and reduce the chances of similar crises recurring. There were a number of 'hotspots' around the globe from the time of the Cuban Missile Crisis until the end of the Cold War, but in all these places—Vietnam, Angola, the Middle East, Nicaragua, Afghanistan, and many others—American and Soviet military forces were not directly engaged against one another. In spite of the seemingly endless succession of crises and conflicts, the Cold War was in fact a much more predictable, stable standoff than it had been before the Cuban Missile Crisis.

The study of international relations also was affected. No sooner had the crisis ended when analysts began dissecting the events and the decision making that led to a successful resolution of the crisis. While many of the post-mortems discussed the event as an example of skillful crisis management by the Americans, suggesting models for future crises, Graham Allison offered what was a novel critique. He suggested that traditional analyses explaining American and Soviet actions were incomplete. These types of analyses attempt to understand foreign policies as the results of rational, unified governments whose actions are based on concerns involving power, threats, security, and the capabilities and intentions of international actors. Allison highlighted certain courses of action during the missile crisis and came to the conclusion that traditional views did not adequately explain the U.S. response to the Soviet Union—much of America's response seemed irrational.

In order to understand American behavior, it was necessary to view it from an alternative perspective, grounded in a clear understanding of bureaucratic politics and organizational behavior.

In this article, Richard Crockett discusses the events of the crisis and the effects of the agreement that ended it. He also revisits Allison's assessment in light of new information that became available as the Cold War came to a close. His analysis confirms that Allison was in large part correct. The Cuban Missile Crisis was not a 'masterpiece of crisis management'. He also suggests, however, that drawing the opposite conclusion—that the world was at the brink of a nuclear war—is also inaccurate.

---

The Cuban missile crisis embodied all the dynamics which had characterized the development of the arms race in the previous decade: its competitive nature, the uncertainties inherent in the nuclear stand-off, the fear that conflict 'on the periphery' might trigger war at the centre, and not least the significance of individual leadership and of domestic factors influencing decision-making. But the missile crisis also crystallized these tensions in a peculiarly stark fashion, making it an event to which analysts have returned again and again in seeking clues to the nuclear danger in the superpower relationship, and above all to the behaviour of the superpower leaderships in moments of crisis. Here the debates can only be touched on. A brief outline of the events of October 1962 will serve to introduce the main issues involved.

The Cuban revolution was close to four years old in October 1962. Fidel Castro had consolidated his power internally, having within a year of his victory over the Batista dictatorship resolved any ambiguity about his relation to communism. Mutual hostility between Castro and the Americans, signalled by expropriation of American assets in Cuba and an American trade embargo on Cuba, soon removed any basis for accommodation. A Cuban economy almost entirely dependent on American trade prior to 1959, within three years of the revolution was effectively integrated into the Soviet bloc. By the beginning of 1962 the Soviet Union and Eastern Europe accounted for 80 per cent of Cuba's trade. Soviet arms defended Cuban soil which, as the Americans hardly needed reminding, lay a mere 90 miles off the Florida coast.

It was, of course, Soviet arms which triggered the missile crisis. During the summer of 1962 enough Soviet hardware and personnel arrived in Cuba to produce calls from Senator Goldwater and others for an immediate invasion. Kennedy moved cautiously—there was as yet no evidence of 'offensive' missiles—gaining an assurance from Khrushchev as late as 17 October that he had no intention of installing offensive missiles in Cuba.

The date is significant. The previous day American photographic intelligence had confirmed the existence of intermediate and medium-range ballistic (IRBM and MRBM) missile sites in Cuba. Kennedy moved quickly to set up a crisis team, formally designated as the 'Ex-Comm' (or Executive Committee of the National Security Council), which met almost continuously until the crisis was resolved.

The bare facts of the crisis can be quickly summarized. Relatively little debate took place about the goal of seeking the removal of the missiles. Their deployment was considered to be a provocative and aggressive threat to American security, an unacceptable unilateral change in the military and political *status quo*. The Ex-Comm swiftly narrowed down the range of possible options to two: an air strike or a blockade (more precisely a 'quarantine', since technically a blockade could be considered an act of war). By Saturday 20 October Kennedy had firmly decided upon a quarantine, which was publicly announced on the evening of Monday the 22nd and over the next five days produced the desired effect of checking the flow of missiles to Cuba. Several Soviet ships bound for Cuba, including one which was known to be carrying nuclear warheads, turned back to Soviet ports. The quarantine, however, was only one of the potential flash-points. In Cuba itself work on the missile sites was continuing, with the likelihood that they might soon be operational. It could not be assumed that no warheads had got through. Plans for an American invasion of Cuba were prepared and US bases around the world put on a high state of alert in the expectation that an American move in Cuba might produce a Soviet response, most probably in Berlin.

The resolution of the crisis was as tense as the operation of the blockade had been. On the evening of Friday the 26th a letter was received from Khrushchev, containing the seeds of a solution acceptable to the United States—removal of Soviet offensive weapons from Cuba in return for lifting the quarantine and an American pledge not to invade Cuba. As the Ex-Comm considered its reply, however, a second letter was received from the Kremlin which was markedly less conciliatory than the first. It also raised the stakes, demanding as a quid pro quo for the removal of Soviet missiles from Cuba the removal of recently installed American Jupiter and Thor missiles in Turkey. Tension reached a peak on the evening of Saturday 27 October as the Ex-Comm deliberated, heightened by news of the shooting down of an American U-2 spy plane over Cuba with the death of the pilot. After much agonizing the solution adopted was to reply positively to the first letter as if the second had not been received, coupled with a strong warning of the consequences should the Soviet Union continue on its present course. The ploy paid off. On Sunday morning Khrushchev communicated his agreement on the basis of the terms set out in his first letter. The Americans for their part let the Soviets know that the missiles in Turkey would be removed, though this was not included as part of the formal agreement between the governments. Though implementation of the agreement took some months, the immediate crisis was over by the morning of 28 October.

The crisis has proved a magnet for theorists of international relations and for historians. Among the theorists, Graham Allison employed the missile crisis as a means of studying decision-making processes. Of course he was also concerned to elucidate the facts of the crisis, and, despite the mass of recent research, his study remains an important starting point for knowledge of the events. The theoretical purpose, however, remains primary. Factual knowledge of the events has received a great boost in recent years from the revelations which have emerged from joint US–Soviet study groups on the crisis, made possible by the climate of *glasnost* in the Soviet Union. It may be that we can use this new knowledge to reflect back on the questions raised by Allison.

In essence, Allison's question is: what can the missile crisis tell us about the relationship between particular policies—the Soviet emplacement of missiles in Cuba, for example—and their outcomes? In seeking explanations of the origins and consequences of foreign policy initiatives, what interpretative frameworks are most likely to yield the most adequate results? Allison elaborates three conceptual schemes, the first being the 'common sense' approach employed by most analysts and laymen alike. He terms this the 'rational actor model' (or Model I). Those employing this model 'attempt to understand happenings in foreign affairs as the more or less purposive acts of unified national governments' (Allison 1971: 4–5).

Models II and III dispense with the notion of a unitary decision-making body in different ways, arguing instead that analysts must confront the 'intra-national mechanisms from which governmental actions emerge'. Model II, termed the 'organizational process model', replaces Model I's assumption of purposive acts and choices with a focus on the 'outputs of large organizations functioning according to regular patterns of behaviour', the question being: 'from what organizational context and pressures did this decision emerge?' (Allison 1971: 6). Model III, termed the 'bureaucratic decision-making model', bears a close relation to Model II, in that it emphasizes intra-governmental processes, but explains events, not in terms of choices or outputs, but as the 'resultant of various bargaining games among players in the national government'. Politics rather than organizational processes are thus conceived by the Model III analyst to be the central explanatory concept (Allison 1971: 6–7).

As Allison is aware, the test of an explanatory scheme lies in how much of reality it is capable of explaining. Here we can examine only one of the many questions posed by Allison, the question of why the Soviet Union installed the missiles in Cuba. Even limiting ourselves to this one area, only a sketch of Allison's richly detailed account can be given. With reference to Model I, in examining the various reasons for the Soviet decision to place missiles in Cuba, Allison settles on the view that it was primarily designed to rectify the imbalance in missile capacity between the superpowers and more specifically to enhance the Soviet capacity to reach American soil with its missiles (and thus compensate for the Soviet Union's relative weakness in ICBMs). Such a hypothesis, he writes, 'permits an understanding of the Cuban venture as another application of the strategy that the Soviets had been pursuing for the previous five years: the strategy of bluff and deception designed to rectify the adverse strategic balance' (Allison 1971: 55). There are several puzzles, however, which are not resolved by the Model I approach. The method and the timing of the installation of the missiles does not square with the assumption of a planned and purposive strategy. Among the puzzles Allison cites are that surface-to-air anti-aircraft batteries (SAMs) were installed after rather than before work on the MRBM sites was finished, the reverse of what one would expect; there was no attempt made to camouflage the missile sites, nor did the Soviets apparently take account of American U-2 flights; furthermore, the Soviets ignored Kennedy's repeated warnings about the consequences of placing offensive missiles in Cuba (Allison 1971: 55–6).

What can Model II do to clarify some of the problems not solved by Model I? 'Many pieces of this maze of seeming contradictions', writes Allison, 'become considerably less puzzling if one assumes the perspective of an observer of the outputs of Soviet organizations.' Standard Soviet operating procedures, most notably the premium on secrecy in Soviet decision-making in general and nuclear policy in particular, can account for some of the anomalies: 'each organization's tendency to "do what it knows how to do" was reinforced by a lack of information about the activity of other organizations and the impossibility of an overview of the whole operation'. Shipping, unloading, and transport to the missile sites was under the eye of military intelligence and the KGB, but once on site the personnel of the Strategic Rocket Services took over. Never having installed missiles outside the Soviet Union, they chose the deployment format they were familiar with (and which was familiar to American intelligence), and felt no need to camouflage the missiles because it had never been done in the Soviet Union. Besides, that would take time and risk failure to meet the schedule for completion. The SAM batteries in turn were under another command—the Air Defence Command—which proceeded according to its familiar pattern, independently of the IRBM and MRBM installations (Allison 1971: 109–11). In short, however clear cut the decision may have been in the mind of Khrushchev himself, implementation of policy was subject to pressures which substantially affected outcomes.

What of Model III? Allison concedes that assessment of the internal political background to the decision to install missiles must be largely speculative, since so little is known about Soviet decision-making processes. In the light of the Model III approach Allison begins by noting that American public response to the Soviet buildup of arms in Cuba during the summer of 1962 was sufficiently ambiguous to leave some doubt as to how seriously its warnings to the Soviet Union should be taken. Into this grey area it was possible for various Soviet leaders possessing very different motives to come to agreement on a policy which served not a single purpose but several. From the Model III perspective, writes Allison, 'it seems likely that the decision emerged not from global grand planning—the Soviet government (or Khrushchev) standing back and considering, for example, where to probe the United States—but rather from a process in which a number of different individuals' quite distinct perceptions of separable problems snow-balled into a solution' (Allison 1971: 237). These could range from Party leaders who had been urging specific Soviet security guarantees to Cuba for two years, to military leaders anxious to close the missile gap, and to economic planners attracted to the missile emplacement as a cheaper way of meeting Soviet strategic needs (Allison 1971: 238–44).

The differences between these three approaches lie not in the fact that they give different answers to the same question but that they yield differently formulated questions. While Model I, for example, asks the question 'why were the missiles placed in Cuba?' and answers that 'Khrushchev' or 'Moscow' or 'the Kremlin', acting with calculated rationality, believed that it was a useful means of rectifying the strategic imbalance, Models II and III shift the ground by asking respectively 'what kinds of processes led to the missile decision?' and 'whose interests did the decision serve?' Doubtless, as Allison points out, 'the best analysts of foreign policy manage to weave strands of each of the three conceptual models into their explanations', but while they may be complementary in some respects, in other respects their implications may be incompatible (Allison 1971: 258–9). Allison's broad aim indeed is to question the common assumption that Model I is an adequate all-purpose approach. What Model I does best is analysis of long-term policy trends, for which the assumption of rationality is a useful shorthand (Allison 1971: 257–8). In analysing the details of events, however, Models II and III represent a marked gain because they give more attention to the institutional contexts of events and processes. Perhaps the differences between the models are most obviously revealed in assessments of the lessons of the missile crisis drawn by the three models. The Model I lesson is that nuclear crises are 'manageable'; leaders will have little difficulty in thinking through alternative courses of action and arriving at satisfactory limited policies. The lessons of Models II and III, however, are that 'nuclear crises between machines as large as the United States and

Soviet governments are inherently chancy', making the process of crisis management 'obscure and terribly risky' (Allison 1971: 259–60).

Much of the new information which has been published about the missile crisis tends to confirm Allison's assessment of the significance of Models II and III for an understanding of the events, though it has by no means displaced Model I. As one would expect, the most important new revelations refer to Soviet decision-making, though there are some important new findings about American policy too. Much of the evidence is complex and contradictory and, since it is still appearing, will take years to digest. It is sufficient, however, to suggest that both sides made decisions which were based on scanty information, guesswork, or misinterpretation of each other's actions and motives.

In the first place, it seems clear from the record of the sequence of conferences held since 1987—attended by participants in the crisis from both sides—that Soviet motives for installing the missiles were mixed, and that even now Soviet individuals disagree on whether the prime reason was to protect Cuba (as Khrushchev stated in his memoirs, 1971: 494) or to right the strategic imbalance (Blight and Welch 1990: 238–43; Lebow 1988: 15–16). On the other hand, much greater emphasis is now given to the Soviet aim of protecting Cuba, as research on American attempts to destabilize Cuba has proceeded. Even Robert McNamara, while protesting that the Kennedy administration had no intention of invading Cuba, conceded that 'if I was a Cuban and read the evidence of covert American action against their government, I would be quite ready to believe that the U.S. intended to mount an invasion' (Blight and Welch 1990: 329–30). One historian has taken this same point further and argued, on the basis of the United States' efforts 'to harrass, isolate, and destroy the radical government in Havana', that without these 'there would not have been a Cuban missile crisis'. 'The origins of the crisis, then,' it is concluded 'derived largely from the concerted campaign to quash the Cuban revolution' (Paterson 1990: 256). An argument which began as an attempt to understand the source of the crisis in Soviet policy thus ends by locating it in American policy. A later analysis concluded that 'the new evidence suggests that Moscow and Havana were justified in suspecting that Washington was considering an invasion of Cuba, although it does not confirm that a decision to order an invasion was, in fact, ever made' (Hershberg 1992: 238). At the very least, however, this line of argument has redirected attention to the Cuban factor in the crisis, a point to which we shall return.

Secondly, an interview conducted with Sergo Mikoyan (son of deputy Prime Minister Anastas Mikoyan at the time of the crisis) confirms Allison's hypothesis about the method and timing of emplacement of the missiles and the absence of camouflage. The technicians, Mikoyan states, 'were military men and they only knew the order to build it, and they were used to building these sites at home. They acted in Cuba as if they were in the USSR' (Greiner: 1990: 214). Model II, with its emphasis on standard operating procedures in defiance of changed conditions, yields positive results here.

Thirdly, there were far more Soviet troops deployed in Cuba during 1962 than American intelligence had known at the time. Its highest estimate during the crisis was 12,000–16,000, upped to 22,000 in a retrospective estimate made in 1963. In fact the number was 42,000 in October 1962 (Garthoff 1988: 67). If, as Garthoff notes, the American government had known the true number, the troop issue 'would have stretched tension still tighter' (Garthoff 1989: 121).

Fourthly, much new information has been revealed about the shooting down of the American U-2 plane. On the basis of somewhat inconclusive evidence, one claim is that the finger on the trigger of the SAM missile battery in question was Cuban rather than Soviet. The SAM site, it is said, had been forcibly seized by Cuban troops, with the implication that Castro's determination to press the Soviets into the strongest possible response to the Americans was an important and dangerous factor in the crisis. This view has been firmly rejected by other scholars on the basis of statements by Soviet officials, who confirm that the order to shoot down the U-2 was given by the local Soviet commander (Trachtenberg 1990: 244–5). Differences of opinion exist also on the significance of this apparent loss of control between the decision-making centre in Moscow and the Soviet commander on the ground. Some scholars suggest that, since the Americans assumed the order came from Moscow and that it therefore represented a 'conscious provocation and escalation by Khrushchev', this incident was among the most inflammatory of the crisis. A different reading of the evidence, however, indicates that the Ex-Comm made no categorical assumption about where the order to shoot down the U-2 came from. In any case, not only did the Ex-Comm choose to respond in a moderate fashion but the Americans were assured by the Soviets at the time that 'it had been an accident and that it would not be repeated' (Trachtenberg 1990: 245, 246).

This incident, of course, took place at a critical juncture in the crisis: at the moment when the Ex-Comm was puzzling over how to respond to the two letters which had been received from Khrushchev. Until recently it had been thought that the first more moderate letter was the work of Khrushchev himself, while the second bore the stamp of hardliners in the Kremlin, a view which would seem to illustrate the dynamics of Model III. In fact, it now appears, the difference in tone and substance of the letters reflected a change in Soviet intelligence estimates of the likelihood of an American attack on Cuba. The first was written when it was believed that an American attack was imminent, leaving no time for diplomatic bargaining, the second when it appeared that the danger of an immediate attack was past, in which case the Soviet leadership could now afford to up the ante and spin out the bargaining process (Blight and Welch 1990: 342). In this they were forestalled by the American decision to ignore the second letter. One could perhaps, then, interpret this particular incident in the light of Model I with its assumption that policy is based on a rational calculation of advantage.

Among the most contentious issues raised by new evidence concerns the role of short-range Soviet nuclear missiles designed for use in a possible American invasion of Cuba. The debate is not about whether they were present in Cuba—it seems clear that they were—but whether, as some scholars claim, the local Soviet commander had authority to use them without reference to Moscow. The debate is highly technical and cannot be rehearsed here, but the question bears on assessments of the level of risk in the crisis. Indeed, this particular debate is the clearest case of a divide which has always existed in studies of the missile crisis but which has widened considerably since 1987 between those who tend to point up the risk of nuclear war in the crisis and those who are more inclined to downplay such dangers. On balance, on the particular issue of authority to order the use of tactical nuclear missiles in Cuba the weight of evidence and argument would seem to lie with Mark Kramer's view that the local commander was specifically prohibited from firing the missiles on his own authority (Kramer 1993: 40, 42–6; cf. Blight *et al.* 1993: 41, 47–50). This conclusion seems warranted, however, not merely on technical–historical grounds but because it is more consistent with the overall patterns of interaction during the crisis.

As it happens, the most important piece of new evidence regarding American policy tends to confirm the view that there were important forces at work making for restraint. It had always been assumed that Kennedy was unwilling to trade the American missiles in Turkey for the Soviet missiles in Cuba, since this would have been visibly to back down under Soviet pressure, indeed to legitimize the Soviet action by equating their Cuban missiles with the American missiles in Turkey. The chosen tactic, as mentioned above, was to convey to the Soviets that the Turkish missiles would be removed but that this was not to be considered part of the Cuban deal. It has now emerged that Kennedy held in reserve a message to be passed to the UN Secretary-General, U Thant, which proposed the removal of the missiles in Turkey and in Cuba. As Dean Rusk (Kennedy's Secretary of State) remarked in retrospect, 'I think this . . . ploy would have been used before we landed troops in Cuba, because landing those troops in Cuba with thirty thousand or more Russian troops in there and Russian missiles there would have been a major escalation from the Soviet point of view' (Blight and Welch 1990: 173–4). In the event, of course, the Soviets accepted Kennedy's offer of the 27th October which left the removal of the Turkish missiles as an informal verbal assurance. The UN ploy therefore was never activated. It does show, however, that Kennedy was prepared to go to greater lengths than was previously believed to check a possible escalation of the crisis beyond control. To this evidence of positive moves for restraint one could add negative instances—such as Khrushchev's decision not to respond aggressively to an American U-2 flight which strayed into Siberian airspace on the 27th or to the action of American naval vessels forcing a Soviet submarine to the surface near the quarantine line around Cuba. These cases are comparable with the Ex-Comm's decision not to allow the downing of the U-2 over Cuba to arrest the moves towards a resolution of the crisis.

Numerous other details have emerged from recent studies, but the above points will serve to show the kinds of issues which they raise. The 'what-ifs' multiply as more evidence appears, suggesting that in many respects Allison's call for a reorientation of international relations scholarship towards study of foreign policy processes was salutary. So much of the evidence points towards the significance of procedures and bureaucratic processes, of personalities, perceptions, and misperceptions. The simple assumption that policy was unitary, rational, and purposive in character cannot stand as a catch-all explanation. Nevertheless, as we have seen, the evidence points in several directions, and much of it tends to support the view that, despite the many incalculable elements in the decision-making processes, in crucial instances the leaders on both sides chose courses of action which were both non-provocative and allowed room for retreat from exposed positions.

We might think of the decision-making process as composed of a core around which much peripheral and often random activity took place which might tend to distract attention from the core and even threaten to disintegrate it. If we picture the core as control, the integrity of the decision-making process itself, then little conclusive evidence has so far been produced to indicate that either side was prepared deliberately to pursue actions which would provoke a loss of control. On the contrary, in the main the reverse was true. Intentions, of course, were not everything. Indeed, even at the time and without access to the knowledge we now have, the decision-makers could hardly have been unaware that they were walking on a knife edge between maintenance of control and catastrophe. This awareness was enough to stimulate efforts in the aftermath of the crisis to find ways of reducing the force of the incalculable, of misperceptions, and the role of potentially dangerous contingencies. The institution of a 'hot-line' connection between the White House and the Kremlin, the move towards conclusion of the Limited Test Ban Treaty, the joint US–Soviet agreement to support a UN resolution banning the placing of nuclear weapons in space, and even the resolve to seek a Nuclear Non-Proliferation Treaty (not signed until 1969) all owed much to the shock of the missile crisis (Garthoff 1989: 134–5). *Détente* itself showed the impress of the missile crisis.

In sum, if it is no longer adequate to picture the crisis as a masterpiece of crisis management, it is equally wrong to exaggerate the risks of a breakdown of control—of nuclear war itself.

There is an important twist in the tale. Neither Castro nor his revolution was unseated by the crisis. Indeed for this reason Khrushchev had some justification for his claim that the Soviet Union had 'achieved . . . a spectacular success without having to fire a single shot!' (Khrushchev 1971: 504). The Cuban revolution remained a substantial breach in the wall of the Monroe Doctrine which the United States was never able to plug. In 1970 and again in 1979 mini-Cuban crises erupted, both arising from apparent attempts by the Soviet Union to increase its military presence in Cuba, and in both cases the United States invoked what might be called the 'spirit of '62' to check these moves. The military stalemate over Cuba, however, did not prevent Castro from dispatching troops to Angola in 1975 to support the revolutionary regime there following Portugal's withdrawal from Africa. The implication of these points is that missile crisis must be viewed within the context of revolutionary change in the Third World and not merely of the arms race.

## 22 Misadventure Revisited
### RICHARD K. BETTS

The war in Vietnam entailed the largest commitment of American resources for any single "battle" in the Cold War. When the United States withdrew its forces from South Vietnam in 1973, unable to achieve its goals, the failed venture prompted a great deal of reexamination of American foreign policy—its aims, its methods, its implementation, its wisdom. The failure of American policy was not merely a problem of battlefield strategy and tactics. Vietnam represented the logical conclusion of America's containment policy and the commitment to "pay any price," in order to stop communist

Richard K. Betts, "Misadventure Revisited," *The Wilson Quarterly*, Summer 1983. Reprinted by permission of the author.

expansion. In other words, as one analyst pointed out at the time, the irony of Vietnam was that the system worked as intended.

In this article, Richard Betts advances such an argument, suggesting that the manner by which the United States pursued containment in Vietnam was bound to fail because the way the system worked, the United States was only committed to paying the lowest possible price necessary to avoid defeat. While the United States could escalate the conflict and commit greater resources to stave off defeat, the larger choice faced by American policymakers provided little hope for success. The United States could either quit and withdraw, cutting its losses while ensuring the defeat of South Vietnam, or it could commit more troops, and hope that North Vietnam would grow weary and eventually negotiate an end to the war. This choice between certain defeat versus uncertain victory was routinely decided in favor of the latter until the commitment became too costly.

In the end, the war in Vietnam fractured the Cold War bipartisan consensus on containment. Though the goal of containment itself continued to be supported across party lines, sharp differences emerged with respect to how the United States should achieve this goal. From this time forward, up until the present day, the United States has continued to be divided over how, when, to what level, and under what circumstances it should use military force and intervene in foreign lands.

---

Each November 22nd, representatives of the U.S. Army Special Forces—the Green Berets—join members of the Kennedy family at a memorial ceremony at President John F. Kennedy's grave. This joint tribute symbolizes the ambiguous legacy of the U.S. venture in Vietnam. Kennedy had personally championed the Green Berets as an elite vanguard combating Communism revolution and subversion in the Third World. But just four years after the President's assassination, his brothers Robert and Edward had moved into the vanguard of congressional opposition to this commitment.

Last autumn, there was an added irony; the Reagan administration had recently moved, as Kennedy did two decades ago, to re-emphasize the role of the Special Forces. The United States was once again speaking as if it would "pay any price, bear any burden" to oppose challenges to the free world.

To the extent that Ronald Reagan's assertive policy in El Salvador recalls that early period of U.S. involvement in Vietnam, it is useful to re-examine the White House assumptions, deliberations, and expectations of the 1960s. One finds lessons and nonlessons.

The U.S. commitment to South Vietnam was impelled by the overarching post-1945 goal of "containing" Communist expansion, first in Europe, then, with the Korean War, in Asia.

In the case of Vietnam, a few critics in Washington and in academe quarreled with applying "containment" to a theater low in priority to the West. Indeed, scholar-diplomat George F. Kennan, the Soviet affairs specialist who had coined the term, was an early critic of the Johnson administration's involvement in Indochina. But not until late 1965, after Lyndon Baines Johnson started bombing North Vietnam and sent 184,000 troops to the South, did many in Congress, the press, the universities, or the politically sensitive public begin to doubt that South Vietnam was a vital testing ground in the global East-West struggle to keep the world safe for democracy.

By the time Richard Nixon and Henry Kissinger gained the White House in 1969, the war had become a political fiasco; the whole notion of containment was under heavy attack. Disillusionment over Vietnam, Sino-American rapprochement, and high hopes for détente and arms control soon eroded the bipartisan constituency for maintaining a strong U.S. military presence overseas, even outside the Third World.[1] But the reaction proved more transient than the consensus that led to Vietnam. As the Soviets or their allies advanced in Angola, Ethiopia, and Yemen, as revolutionary Iran humiliated the United States, and as Soviet troops went into Afghanistan, assertiveness slowly became popular again.

The U.S. experience in Vietnam will not inevitably repeat itself elsewhere, despite all the recent hue and cry over Central America. But it is worth examining what circumstances, beliefs, and judgments make Presidents and their advisers in Washington decide that in certain cases they have only one choice, and that they are better off enduring high costs rather than backing off from further engagement.

The United States became gradually involved in Indochina after 1950. Even before the outbreak of the Korean War, President Harry S. Truman began to take on the financial burden of the vain struggle of America's NATO ally, France, to defeat Ho Chi Minh's Viet Minh, which was assisted by Communist China, America's foe in Korea. Dwight D. Eisenhower continued and increased that support, and committed the United States to the new regime in South Vietnam after French withdrawal. South Vietnam did not become a high U.S. priority until Kennedy's Presidency, and it did not become the highest overseas priority until the Johnson era.

The 1960s were, of course, a turning point, but not because Washington's goals changed. Ever since the Korean War, U.S. policy in Indochina had vacillated between contrary objectives—preventing a Communist takeover while avoiding American participation in a major war in Asia. Yet the contradiction between these two aims did not become acute until 1965.

The efforts of Kennedy and Johnson differed in scale—the 1961 decision to increase the number of U.S. advisers (from 948 in November 1961 to 2,646 in January 1962) pales beside the 1965 decisions to bomb the North and to dispatch combat troops to the South. But in both cases, U.S. involvement grew dramatically in order to prevent imminent South Vietnamese collapse under Communist pressure and to shift momentum to the anti-Communist side. What was required to do this in 1961 was far less than what was required four years later.

All in all, Kennedy was less willing to disengage than later apologists suggested, and Johnson less deceptive about his goals and less anxious to escalate than later detractors believed. The notion that Kennedy intended to extricate the United States from South Vietnam after the 1964 U.S. election is belied by his actions right up to his death: a continuing build-up of aid and advisers, presidential reaffirmations[2] that would have been gratuitous if he were looking forward to withdrawal, and prior endorsement of the 1963 Saigon coup against President Ngo Dinh Diem. Johnson's campaign rhetoric against Barry Goldwater in 1964 exploited public fears of war, but he never suggested that defeat would be an acceptable alternative.[3] And, although Johnson ordered contingency planning for direct U.S. military action before November 1964, he continued to search for alternatives *after* the election.

## LOSING AND WINNING

Indeed, LBJ was a most reluctant warrior. Like his predecessor, he refused to accept any radical options proposed by subordinates that promised *victory*. Early in 1965, he authorized the bombing of North Vietnam, but only in limited, gradually increasing doses—not the quick and overwhelming effort sought by the Air Force. In July 1965, he ordered a buildup to 125,000 men in South Vietnam, despite the lack of promises of a long-term solution from Army leaders. In late 1965, Defense Secretary Robert S. McNamara privately estimated that 600,000 U.S. troops (10 percent more than the highest level ever reached during the war) might be needed by 1967 and admitted that even that number "will not guarantee success."

Once the air strikes against the North began, Johnson abstemiously expanded them (rejecting military protests that such gradualism vitiated their effect) in consonance with his civilian advisers' hopes that mounting pressure might induce Hanoi to negotiate on U.S. terms.

As U.S. troop strength grew, General William C. Westmoreland's ground operations in the South expanded too, and soon, after Hanoi's spectacular but costly 1968 Tet Offensive, their cumulative effect—even if blunt and wasteful—forced the Communists, both regulars and guer-rillas, onto the defensive and rolled back many of their earlier gains. But, in most circumstances, guerrillas win as long as they do not lose, and government forces lose as long as they do not win. And Hanoi, with its sanctuaries at home and its bases and routes of reinforcement in Laos and Cambodia, could keep from "losing" indefinitely. Colonel Harry G. Summers ruefully described his encounter in 1973, during negotiations on American MIAs (Missing-in-Action) in Hanoi, with a North Vietnamese officer who, confronted with the assertion that the Communists had never beaten U.S. troops in a major battle, replied, "That is correct. It is also irrelevant."

In March 1967, Westmoreland told LBJ and McNamara that unless his forces were allowed to cut off Hanoi's infiltration of men and supplies, the war could continue indefinitely. Later in the year, despite their public opti-mism, Westmoreland and General Earle Wheeler, Chairman of the Joint Chiefs of Staff, told the President that with current U.S. troop levels, the war would continue as an indecisive "meat-grinder"; with a reinforcement of 95,000, it could drag on for three years; and with one of 195,000 (to a total of 665,000), it could last two years. Yet Johnson authorized an increase of only 55,000.

## A QUEST FOR COMPROMISE

Like JFK, LBJ chose a *limited* strategy. He chose to nibble the bullet rather than bite it. He feared provoking Chinese intervention and undertaking a full-scale war (or withdrawal) that could wreck his primary ambition: to build the Great Society.

Most important was his unwillingness to provoke a domestic political assault from either the Right (for "selling out" Vietnam) *or* the Left (for going too far militarily). In effect, he preferred to compromise on the battle-field and to suffer limited attacks at home from both ends of the political spectrum rather than face the full fury of either—although until the Tet Offensive, he feared the hawks more than the doves. A consensus-seeking, centrist political strategy drove the White House military policy. In this, too, Johnson's approach reflected that of his predecessors.

Nixon also sought to follow a middle path between his own instincts (more hawkish than Johnson's) and the growing opposition in Congress and the broader public. He successfully appealed to the "Silent Majority"—who, polls indicated, wanted to withdraw but not to lose—by combining "re-escalations" (secretly bombing Communist bases in Cambodia in 1969, briefly invading Cambodia in 1970, supporting a short-lived Army of the Republic of Vietnam [ARVN] invasion into Laos in 1971, renewing the bombing of North Vietnam and mining Haiphong harbor in 1972) with peace talks, the phased withdrawal of U.S. troops, and "Vietnamization."

Actually, Nixon's approach was no less contradictory than that of his predecessors. Like Kissinger, Nixon overestimated his ability to solve the problem through the negotiations at Paris that Johnson had initiated in 1968. Nixon milked his "madman" theory—that the Communists would quail before the threat of his irrational behavior—but his hopes (like those of LBJ) of enlisting Moscow's aid to sway Hanoi did not materialize, and Nixon, not the enemy, made the crucial negotiating concession in May 1971 by implicitly accepting the presence of North Vietnamese troops in the South after any cease-fire.[4]

Under Kennedy, Johnson, and Nixon, senior policy-makers in Washington were seldom deluded that the odds of routing the Communists in Vietnam were high. Indeed, in most cases, they increased U.S. deployments of men and/or firepower simply to stave off defeat, with no real expectation of victory. What made the men in Washington believe that they were making efforts that with luck might pan out, rather than marching *inevitably* toward defeat?

## THE IRON COMBINATION

The answer lies between hubris and hope. During the early 1960s, both civilian and military theorists of "counterinsurgency" promoted the fateful illusion that American tutelage could reshape the fragile, war-battered South Vietnamese political system, creating a new nationalism among the South Vietnamese that could confront Marxist revolutionary élan with some sort of vigorous Asian Jeffersonianism—through land reform, free elections, better government.

Some U.S. "pacification" techniques proved successful—in the short term. For all their much-publicized deficiencies, the sheer weight of allied manpower and economic resources produced major gains in rural prosperity, population control, and road security during the years between Tet and the 1972 Easter Offensive. Increasingly unable to enlist new recruits, the southern Communist guerrillas (Viet Cong) were ground down by attrition; North Vietnamese forces took over the chief burden of combat. Large-scale *conventional* North Vietnamese attacks, with bases in Laos and Cambodia, rather than Viet Cong guerrilla insurgency, brought on the 1975 collapse of the Saigon regime.

Even more important was limited war theory,[5] an outgrowth of opposition to the Eisenhower administration's post-Korea "massive retaliation" policy. The focus was on using measured doses of force to induce an adversary to negotiate and to compromise. The 1965–67 air war against North Vietnam exposed the holes in some versions of the theory. The Pentagon civilians who had designed the air war originally expected to "calibrate" the U.S. response to each enemy provocation and to use incremental pressure to convince Hanoi to desist. This aim was inevitably subverted by practical difficulties—targeting, timing, communications—that derailed Washington's "orchestration" of words and deeds.

Most of all, the theory foundered because its proponents vastly underestimated Hanoi's determination and overestimated the basis for a negotiated compromise. The Vietnam War was primarily a civil war, and, overall, a struggle involving *incompatible* ideologies and visions of society, not just a proxy conflict between great powers over influence in a third area. Both American leaders and their critics in Congress and the press found this reality hard to understand. As Kissinger reflected with hindsight,

> Because the United States had become great by assimilating men and women of different beliefs, we had developed an ethic of tolerance; having had little experience with unbridgeable schisms, our mode of settling conflicts was to seek a solution somewhere between the contending positions. But to the Vietnamese this meant that we were not serious about what we put forward and that we treated them as frivolous. They had not fought for forty years to achieve a compromise. [Kissinger, *White House Years*, p. 259.]

Professional military men never agreed with the civilians' game-theory logic. Yet, with few exceptions, until 1968 both military and civilian leaders in Washington assumed that South Vietnam *had* to be saved. The United States could not just walk out on its ally. The disputes, seldom publicized, were over means, not ends.

Only if President Johnson, McNamara, and Secretary of State Dean Rush had known for *sure* in early 1965 that "graduated pressure" would fail and that the most pessimistic military estimates of what would be required to bend Hanoi's will were correct would there have been a chance for a White House decision to disengage. Like Kennedy, Johnson distrusted the Joint Chiefs of Staff (JCS). Some of his civilian lieutenants viewed bleak JCS estimates or pleas for "decisive" strategies as "worst-case" ploys designed to maximize their options and to protect their reputations in case of failure.

This tragic misjudgment aside, the fact remains that LBJ & Co. knew that gradually building up U.S. strength in Vietnam offered no assurance of victory. Yet at each juncture until Tet 1968, they saw no alternative to pressing on, *hoping* that the Politburo in Hanoi would grow weary and negotiate.

The air war strategy was flawed, but the details of its rationale fade in significance beside the overarching White House decision in 1965 to keep the war effort, as a whole, limited. Except for the military, who did not protest in public, there were virtually no officials in the executive branch—and few newspaper editors or legislators—who in 1965 questioned the premise of limitation.

The tragedy stemmed from the iron combination of this consensus with the premise that the war still had to be fought.

The one high-ranking official who opposed escalation was Under Secretary of State George W. Ball. Beginning in 1963, he argued that Vietnam was of secondary importance, and that our commitment there drained resources away from NATO. LBJ's negative reaction was ironic, since the initial U.S. involvement in Indochina was spurred by the priority of NATO—to support France in the early 1950s even though Washington had no love for colonialism. But not until 1965, after the first Marines went ashore at Da Nang in March, did Ball recommend outright withdrawal.

In 1964–65, Congress was quite complaisant; only Senate mavericks like Wayne L. Morse (D.-Ore.) and Ernest H. Gruening (D.-Alaska) opposed crucial decisions of the mid-1960s. When J. W. Fulbright, chairman of the Senate Foreign Relations Committee, turned against the war in 1966, he was still countered by colleagues of equal rank such as John C. Stennis, chairman of the Armed Services Committee.

There was little early active support for Johnson administration policy on Capitol Hill, but, contrary to myth, even well after Tet, nearly all congressional war foes, from Edward M. Kennedy (D.-Mass.) to George S. McGovern (D.-S.D.) issued calls for faster troop withdrawals and greater concessions in peace talks, *not* for unconditional U.S. withdrawal. Though opposition on Capitol Hill mounted with time, it was not until *after* U.S. troops had been withdrawn and the POWs returned in 1973 that the raft of legislation was passed constraining both presidential war powers and aid to the South Vietnamese ally.

## RUNNING OUT OF TIME

In short, the remarkable American consensus behind the initial intervention, from 1961 to the 1968 Tet Offensive, has been obscured in retrospect by the force of later disillusionment. Only *after* it became clear that the cost of prolonged U.S. intervention in Vietnam was prohibitive did it begin to seem to large segments of Congress, the media, and academe that the alternative, a Communist victory in South Vietnam, was not so grave a disaster (for America). But by that time, compromises that had seemed radical during the Johnson administration seemed insufficient. As Kissinger recounts:

> By August of 1969 we had offered or undertaken unilaterally all of the terms of the 1968 *dove* plank of the Democrats (which had been defeated in Chicago). We had exceeded the promises of the Republican platform, expecting by our demonstration of flexibility to foster moderation in Hanoi and unity at home. We were naively wrong in both expectations. [Kissinger, *White House Years*, p. 256.]

The American effort in 1965–72 was not subverted by moral objections (such objections remained those of a minority even to the end), but by a gradually building public perception that all the blood and treasure was simply being *wasted* to no visible end. The United States may be able to fight a major limited war again, say, in the Persian Gulf, but only if it is not long and inconclusive. As Harvard's Samuel P. Huntington observed: "The most crucial limitation . . . is not the limitation on weapons or geographical scope or goals, but rather the limitation on *time*."

Wide recognition of such U.S. political realities reinforces the military's argument against limitations on the use of conventional forces. But this recognition provides no guarantee against future mistakes. The necessary scale and duration of successful military operations can never be known for sure in advance. What the Vietnam record shows is that Washington's top decision-makers knew in 1964–65 that, given the limits they imposed on U.S. strategy, victory would not come quickly, if it came at all. A similar prognosis by the White House in a future case, with the Vietnam experience in mind, could produce a presidential choice between a decisive hard-hitting use of force or no military intervention at all.

## HINDSIGHT IS EASIER

Should future U.S. ventures overseas be undertaken only if a cut-off point is decided in advance? Political scientist Richard Neustadt has criticized the White House National Security Council staff in 1964–65 for not seriously addressing "the option of getting out of Vietnam. . . . It was always taken to be unacceptable on the face of it." Doing this, however, is politically dangerous; any leak to the press about such a study would surely subvert the commitment's support and credibility.

White House decisions on what is vital to U.S. interests abroad are affected by limited information and by official perceptions that may not be known to be—or may not *be*—incorrect until later. For example, as Rusk was wont to explain, part of the rationale for sending U.S. troops to South Vietnam was to prevent Chinese advances further into Southeast Asia. The problem was not simply an obtuse U.S. failure to recognize the Sino-Soviet split. Despite their dispute, Moscow and Beijing were seen in Washington as having parallel interests in promoting violent Communist revolution. Because a Sino-American rapprochement occurred during the 1970s does not mean that it could have happened during the 1960s—before the 1969 Soviet-Chinese border clashes and before Soviet hints of a future preventive attack on China's new nuclear facilities pushed Beijing toward accommodation with Washington.

## A YEARNING IN WASHINGTON

Moreover, the President does not act in a vacuum. Had North Korea, armed by the Soviets, not attacked South Korea in 1950 (shaking Washington into revision of judgments about whether Communist leaders would resort to armed conquest), Truman might have felt no urge to become more involved in support of the French in Indochina. Had Eisenhower not just concluded the Korean War and scored anti-Communist successes in Iran and Guatemala, he might not have felt secure enough in 1954 to accept the partition of Vietnam (though his acceptance resulted in a U.S. commitment to the new regime in the South). Had Kennedy not experienced the unsettling Vienna summit with Nikita Khrushchev, the Bay of Pigs, a new Berlin crisis, and setbacks in Laos—all in 1961—he might have felt he had more leeway in avoiding a major increase in the U.S. advisory effort in South Vietnam later that year.

The crucial phase of any overseas commitment is the formative period, when presidential rhetoric becomes mortgaged and initial costs are sunk. Yet during this early phase, the long-range consequences are least certain and the commitment is a secondary matter, rather than the centerpiece it may become later as U.S. involvement and costs accumulate. When costs are still limited, the alternative seems bleaker than when the commitment burgeons into full-blown national sacrifice.

John F. Kennedy, Lyndon B. Johnson, and lesser policymakers during the 1960s faced these pressures and ambiguities and decided that a gamble in South Vietnam was preferable to the alternative; uncertain prospects of victory were better than certain prospects of defeat. The results make clear the folly of this judgment.

By 1975, the dominant "lesson" was that Washington should take no risks, that it should not begin messy involvements in the Third World if there is *any* danger that they cannot be concluded without considerable sacrifice. Despite President Jimmy Carter's creation of a much-publicized Rapid Deployment Force in 1978–80, the lesson still has a powerful hold. In 1983, Congress has shown little enthusiasm for the Reagan administration's modest efforts to counter Marxist guerrillas in Central America, and none at all for direct combat involvement of U.S. military men, even as advisers. Yet "containment," in theory at least, has been reinvigorated. Reagan's rhetoric recalls the staunchness of the New Frontier. The Pentagon speaks of a global "maritime strategy."

What has not rebounded to the same degree is the bipartisan consensus among politicians and in the press behind containment. If anything, there seems to be a yearning in Reagan's Washington for the containment of the Eisenhower years, to bestride the globe and confront Soviet power without spilling blood, to be strong but at peace, to support anti-Communist allies or clients with money and arms but not men, all without raising the spectre of war.

Dwight Eisenhower could accomplish all that because the predicament that his successors faced—imminent collapse of the whole row of Indochina dominoes—did not develop while he was in office. We know more now, but we still do not know how a disastrous war could have been avoided except at the price foreseen in 1961 as in 1965—apparently disastrous defeat. John Kennedy and Lyndon Johnson were wrong in moving into Vietnam on so grand a scale, but neither was wrong in thinking that his failure to do so could produce unpleasant reactions at home and abroad. Now, as then, neither containment nor disengagement is risk-free.

## Notes

1. In May 1971, Senate Majority Leader Mike Mansfield (D.-Mont.) offered an amendment to a military draft bill that would have required the United States to withdraw one-half of its 300,000 troops in Europe as of December 31, 1971. After intense White House lobbying, the Senate defeated that amendment by a margin of 61–36.
2. E.g., on September 12, 1963: "In some ways I think the Vietnamese people and ourselves agree: we want the war to be won, the Communists to be contained, and the Americans to go home. . . . But we are not there to see a war lost, and we will follow the policy which I have indicated today of advancing those causes and issues which help win the war."
3. In Akron, Ohio, on October 21, 1964, Johnson stated: "[We] are not about to send American boys 9 or 10,000 miles away from home to do what Asian boys ought to be doing for themselves." But Johnson added that "we are going to assist them [the South Vietnamese] against attack as we have" in the past and "[we] will not permit the independent nations of the East to be swallowed up by Communist conquest."
4. Henry A. Kissinger, *White House Years* (Boston: Little, Brown, 1979), p. 1,018.
5. Its chief academic proponents were Robert Osgood and Thomas Schelling; their views found many echoes in the Army, notably in writings by Generals Maxwell Taylor (*The Uncertain Trumpet*, 1959) and James Gavin (*War and Peace in the Space Age*, 1959).

# 23 Commencement Address at the University of Notre Dame

## JIMMY CARTER

President Carter came to office determined to put a new face on American foreign policy. In his view, the disastrous war in Vietnam had in part resulted from an inordinate fear of possible Soviet expansionism, a fear that had caused the United States to overlook the divide between rich and poor nations. In addition, the amoral realism of his predecessors was considered to be inappropriate in that it often divorced American policies from American values of democracy and human rights. Upon taking office, Carter continued the policy of détente that he had inherited from Nixon, Kissinger, and Ford, but he also broke with his predecessors in two significant ways. First, he made human rights a centerpiece of his foreign policy, stating that the United States would no longer "embrace any dictator" simply because of a shared interest in anticommunism. The result was that a number of dictatorships that had benefited from American military and economic aid were cut off from U.S. assistance because of their violations of basic human rights. This move away from a strictly realist point of view toward a liberal internationalist policy meant that America would support friends and allies that shared more than adversaries, but also values. It also reflected a return to what has been the norm in U.S. foreign policy. This has involved, both in the past and the present, a combination of realist and liberal elements.

Second, Carter believed that the Cold War—the conflict between east and west—could no longer be considered the only major conflict affecting the course of global politics. The rise of China, the strength of OPEC, the Arab-Israeli conflict, the emergence of newly independent nations, and the changing global economy all presented problems that had to be considered independently of Cold War considerations. These developments had sufficiently changed the international setting, necessitating the formulation of new priorities and policies by the United States. In particular, Carter sought to address the problems resulting from the poverty and lack of development in most of the world. Highlighting this "north-south" divide, Carter asserted that the world could not be at peace with, "one-third rich and two-thirds hungry."

---

Jimmy Carter, Commencement Address delivered at the University of Notre Dame, May 22, 1977. Reprinted by permission of The Carter Center on behalf of Jimmy Carter.

In the address that follows, Carter outlines his priorities at the beginning of his presidency. Like many presidents (and secretaries of state) before him, Carter chose to make a major foreign policy speech in a venue that had historically been used for delivering major foreign policy speeches: in a commencement address at a major university.

---

Thank you very much. To Father Hesburgh and the great faculty of Notre Dame, to those who have been honored this afternoon with the degree from your great university, to the graduate and undergraduate group who I understand is the largest in the history of this great institution, friends and parents:

Thank you for that welcome. I'm very glad to be with you. You may have started a new graduation trend which I don't deplore; that is, throwing peanuts on graduation day. [*Laughter*] The more that are used or consumed, the higher the price goes. [*Laughter*]

I really did appreciate the great honor bestowed upon me this afternoon. My other degree is blue and gold from the Navy, and I want to let you know that I do feel a kinship with those who are assembled here this afternoon. I was a little taken aback by the comment that I had brought a new accent to the White House. In the minds of many people in our country, for the first time in almost 150 years, there is no accent. [*Laughter*]

I tried to think of a story that would illustrate two points simultaneously and also be brief, which is kind of a difficult assignment. I was sitting on the Truman Balcony the other night with my good friend, Charles Kirbo, who told me about a man who was arrested and taken in to court for being drunk and for setting a bed on fire. When the judge asked him how he pleaded, he said, "not guilty." He said, "I was drunk but the bed was on fire when I got in it." [*Laughter*]

I think most of the graduates can draw the parallel between that statement and what you are approaching after this graduation exercise. But there are two points to that, and I'll come to the other one in just a few minutes.

In his 25 years as president of Notre Dame, Father Hesburgh has spoken more consistently and more effectively in the support of the rights of human beings than any other person I know. His interest in the Notre Dame Center for Civil Rights has never wavered. And he played an important role in broadening the scope of the center's work—and I visited there last fall—to see this work include, now, all people in the world, as shown by last month's conference here on human rights and American foreign policy.

And that concern has been demonstrated again today in a vivid fashion by the selection of Bishop Donal Lamont, Paul Cardinal Arns, and Stephen Cardinal Kim, to receive honorary degrees. In their fight for human freedoms in Rhodesia, Brazil, and South Korea, these three religious leaders typify all that is best in their countries and in our church. I'm honored to join you in recognizing their dedication, their personal sacrifice, and their supreme courage.

Quite often, brave men like these are castigated and sometimes punished, sometimes even put to death, because they enter the realm where human rights is a struggle. And sometimes, they are blamed for the very circumstance which they helped to dramatize, but it's been there for a long time. And the flames which they seek to extinguish concern us all and are increasingly visible around the world.

Last week, I spoke in California about the domestic agenda for our Nation: to provide more efficiently for the needs of our people, to demonstrate—against the dark faith of our times—that our Government can be both competent and more humane.

But I want to speak to you today about the strands that connect our actions overseas with our essential character as a nation. I believe we can have a foreign policy that is democratic, that is based on fundamental values, and that uses power and influence, which we have, for humane purposes. We can also have a foreign policy that the American people both support and, for a change, know about and understand.

I have a quiet confidence in our own political system. Because we know that democracy works, we can reject the arguments of those rulers who deny human rights to their people.

We are confident that democracy's example will be compelling, and so we seek to bring that example closer to those from whom in the past few years we have been separated and who are not yet convinced about the advantages of our kind of life.

We are confident that democratic methods are the most effective, and so we are not tempted to employ improper tactics here at home or abroad.

We are confident of our own strength, so we can seek substantial mutual reductions in the nuclear arms race.

And we are confident of the good sense of American people, and so we let them share in the process of making foreign policy decisions. We can thus speak with the voices of 215 million, and not just of an isolated handful.

Democracy's great recent successes—in India, Portugal, Spain, Greece—show that our confidence in this system is not misplaced. Being confident of our own future, we are now free of that inordinate fear of communism which once led us to embrace any dictator who joined us in that fear. I'm glad that that's being changed.

For too many years, we've been willing to adopt the flawed and erroneous principles and tactics of our adversaries, sometimes abandoning our own values for theirs. We've fought fire with fire, never thinking that fire is better quenched with water. This approach failed, with Vietnam the best example of its intellectual and moral poverty. But through failure, we have now found our way back to our own principles and values, and we have regained our lost confidence.

By the measure of history, our Nation's 200 years are very brief, and our rise to world eminence is briefer still. It dates from 1945 when Europe and the old international order lay in ruins. Before then America was largely on the periphery of world affairs, but since then we have inescapably been at the center of world affairs.

Our policy during this period was guided by two principles: a belief that Soviet expansion was almost inevitable but that it must be contained, and the corresponding belief in the importance of an almost exclusive alliance among non-Communist nations on both sides of the Atlantic. That system could not last forever unchanged. Historical trends have weakened its foundation. The unifying threat of conflict with the Soviet Union has become less intensive even though the competition has become more extensive.

The Vietnamese war produced a profound moral crisis sapping worldwide faith in our own policy and our system of life, a crisis of confidence made even more grave by the covert pessimism of some of our leaders.

In less than a generation, we've seen the world change dramatically. The daily lives and aspirations of most human beings have been transformed. Colonialism is nearly gone. A new sense of national identity now exists in almost 100 new countries that have been formed in the last generation. Knowledge has become more widespread; aspirations are higher. As more people have been freed from traditional constraints, more have been determined to achieve for the first time in their lives social justice.

The world is still divided by ideological disputes, dominated by regional conflicts, and threatened by danger that we will not resolve the differences of race and wealth without violence or without drawing into combat the major military powers. We can no longer separate the traditional issues of war and peace from the new global questions of justice, equity, and human rights.

It is a new world—but America should not fear it. It is a new world—and we should help to shape it. It is a new world that calls for a new American foreign policy—a policy based on constant decency in its values and on optimism in our historical vision.

We can no longer have a policy solely for the industrial nations as the foundation of global stability, but we must respond to the new reality of a politically awakening world.

We can no longer expect that the other 150 nations will follow the dictates of the powerful, but we must continue–confidently— our efforts to inspire, to persuade, and to lead.

Our policy must reflect our belief that the world can hope for more than simple survival and our belief that dignity and freedom are fundamental spiritual requirements. Our policy must shape an international system that will last longer than secret deals.

We cannot make this kind of policy by manipulation. Our policy must be open; it must be candid; it must be one of constructive global involvement, resting on five cardinal principles.

I've tried to make these premises clear to the American people since last January. Let me review what we have been doing and discuss what we intend to do.

First, we have reaffirmed America's commitment to human rights as a fundamental tenet of our foreign policy. In ancestry, religion, color, place of origin, and cultural background, we Americans are as diverse a nation as the world has ever seen. No common mystique of blood or soil unites us. What draws us together, perhaps more than anything else, is a belief in human freedom.

We want the world to know that our Nation stands for more than financial prosperity. This does not mean that we can conduct our foreign policy by rigid moral maxims. We live in a world that is imperfect and which will always be imperfect—a world that is complex and confused and which will always be complex and confused.

I understand fully the limits of moral suasion. We have no illusion that changes will come easily or soon. But I also believe that it is a mistake to undervalue the power of words and of the ideas that words embody. In our own history, that power has ranged from Thomas Paine's *Common Sense* to Martin Luther King, Jr.'s "I Have a Dream."

In the life of the human spirit, words are action, much more so than many of us may realize who live in countries where freedom of expression is taken for granted. The leaders of totalitarian nations understand this very well. The proof is that words are precisely the action for which dissidents in those countries are being persecuted.

Nonetheless, we can already see dramatic, worldwide advances in the protection of the individual from the arbitrary power of the state. For us to ignore this trend would be to lose influence and moral authority in the world. To lead it will be to regain the moral stature that we once had.

The great democracies are not free because we are strong and prosperous. I believe we are strong and influential and prosperous because we are free.

Throughout the world today, in free nations and in totalitarian countries as well, there is a preoccupation with the subject of human freedom, human rights. And I believe it is incumbent on us in this country to keep that discussion, that debate, that contention alive. No other country is as well-qualified as we to set an example. We have our own shortcomings and faults, and we should strive constantly and with courage to make sure that we are legitimately proud of what we have.

Second, we've moved deliberately to reinforce the bonds among our democracies. In our recent meetings in London, we agreed to widen our economic cooperation, to promote free trade, to strengthen the world's monetary system, to seek ways of avoiding nuclear proliferation. We prepared constructive proposals for the forthcoming meetings on North-South problems of poverty, development, and global well-being, and we agreed on joint efforts to reinforce and to modernize our common defense.

You may be interested in knowing that at this NATO meeting, for the first time in more than 25 years, all members are democracies. Even more important, all of us reaffirmed our basic optimism in the future of the democratic system. Our spirit of confidence is spreading. Together, our democracies can help to shape the wider architecture of global cooperation.

Third, we've moved to engage the Soviet Union in a joint effort to halt the strategic arms race. This race is not only dangerous, it's morally deplorable. We must put an end to it.

I know it will not be easy to reach agreements. Our goal is to be fair to both sides, to produce reciprocal stability, parity, and security. We desire a freeze on further modernization and production of weapons and a continuing, substantial reduction of strategic nuclear weapons as well. We want a comprehensive ban on all nuclear testing, a prohibition against all chemical warfare, no attack capability against space satellites, and arms limitations in the Indian Ocean.

We hope that we can take joint steps with all nations toward a final agreement eliminating nuclear weapons completely from our arsenals of death. We will persist in this effort.

Now, I believe in détente with the Soviet Union. To me, it means progress toward peace. But the effects of détente should not be limited to our own two countries alone. We hope to persuade the Soviet Union that one country cannot impose its system of society upon another, either through direct military intervention or through the use of a client state's military force, as was the case with Cuban intervention in Angola.

Cooperation also implies obligation. We hope that the Soviet Union will join with us and other nations in playing a larger role in aiding the developing world, for common aid efforts will help us build a bridge of mutual confidence in one another.

Fourth, we are taking deliberate steps to improve the chances of lasting peace in the Middle East. Through wide-ranging consultation with leaders of the countries involved—Israel, Syria, Jordan, and Egypt—we have found some areas of agreement and some movement toward consensus. The negotiations must continue.

Through my own public comments, I've also tried to suggest a more flexible framework for the discussion of the three key issues which have so far been so intractable: the nature of a comprehensive peace—What is peace? What does it mean to the Israelis? What does it mean to their Arab neighbors? Secondly, the relationship between security and borders—How can the dispute over border delineations be established and settled with a feeling of security on both sides? And the issue of the Palestinian homeland.

The historic friendship that the United States has with Israel is not dependent on domestic politics in either nation; it's derived from our common respect for human freedom and from a common search for permanent peace.

We will continue to promote a settlement which all of us need. Our own policy will not be affected by changes in leadership in any of the countries in the Middle East. Therefore, we expect Israel and her neighbors to continue to be bound by United Nations Resolutions 242 and 338, which they have previously accepted.

This may be the most propitious time for a genuine settlement since the beginning of the Arab-Israeli conflict almost 30 years ago. To let this opportunity pass could mean disaster not only for the Middle East but, perhaps, for the international political and economic order as well.

And fifth, we are attempting, even at the risk of some friction with our friends, to reduce the danger of nuclear proliferation and the world-wide spread of conventional weapons.

At the recent summit, we set in motion an international effort to determine the best ways of harnessing nuclear energy for peaceful use while reducing the risks that its products will be diverted to the making of explosives.

We've already completed a comprehensive review of our own policy on arms transfers. Competition in arms sales is inimical to peace and destructive of the economic development of the poorer countries.

We will, as a matter of national policy now in our country, seek to reduce the annual dollar volume of arms sales, to restrict the transfer of advanced weapons, and to reduce the extent of our co-production arrangements about weapons with foreign states. And, just as important, we are trying to get other nations, both free and otherwise, to join us in this effort.

But all of this that I've described is just the beginning. It's a beginning aimed towards a clear goal: to create a wider framework of international cooperation suited to the new and rapidly changing historical circumstances.

We will cooperate more closely with the newly influential countries in Latin America, Africa, and Asia. We need their friendship and cooperation in a common effort as the structure of world power changes.

More than 100 years ago, Abraham Lincoln said that our Nation could not exist half slave and half free. We know a peaceful world cannot long exist one-third rich and two-thirds hungry.

Most nations share our faith that in the long run, expanded and equitable trade will best help the developing countries to help themselves. But the immediate problems of hunger, disease, illiteracy, and repression are here now.

The Western democracies, the OPEC nations, and the developed Communist countries can cooperate through existing international institutions in providing more effective aid. This is an excellent alternative to war.

We have a special need for cooperation and consultation with other nations in this hemisphere—to the north and to the south. We do not need another slogan. Although these are our close friends and neighbors, our links with them are the same links of equality that we forge for the rest of the world. We will be dealing with them as part of a new, worldwide mosaic of global, regional, and bilateral relations.

It's important that we make progress toward normalizing relations with the People's Republic of China. We see the American and Chinese relationship as a central element of our global policy, and China as a key force for global peace. We wish to cooperate closely with the creative Chinese people on the problems that confront all mankind, and we hope to find a formula which can bridge some of the difficulties that still separate us.

Finally, let me say that we are committed to a peaceful resolution of the crisis in southern Africa. The time has come for the principle of majority rule to be the basis for political order, recognizing that in a democratic system the rights of the minority must also be protected.

To be peaceful, change must come promptly. The United States is determined to work together with our European allies and with the concerned African States to shape a congenial international framework for the rapid and progressive transformation of southern African society and to help protect it from unwarranted outside interference.

Let me conclude by summarizing: Our policy is based on an historical vision of America's role. Our policy is derived from a larger view of global change. Our policy is rooted in our moral values, which never change. Our policy is reinforced by our material wealth and by our military power. Our policy is designed to serve mankind. And it is a policy that I hope will make you proud to be Americans.

Thank you.

# 24 Dictatorships and Double Standards

## JEANNE KIRKPATRICK

The policy of the Carter administration involving the promotion of human rights attempted to hold countries to a particular standard of conduct or they would risk the loss of American aid and support. This policy came under increasing fire from a number of critics who claimed it was undermining American power and influence around the globe. The most notable of these critics was Jeanne Kirkpatrick, who argued that the Carter administration had not only failed to achieve greater respect for human rights around the world, it had also allowed the Soviet Union to gain an advantage in the Cold War competition.

Kirkpatrick argued that American policy under Carter had the effect of hurting only those countries that had historically been on the American side in the Cold War. Highlighting the cases of Iran and Nicaragua, she argued that the use of American leverage to force democratic changes upon dictatorial regimes only hastened their demise. In their wake, new regimes came to power that were decidedly worse and openly hostile to the United States. At the same time, Kirkpatrick noted, the United States was pursuing a policy of détente with the Soviet Union and the communist bloc, with an aim of achieving a "peaceful coexistence." Thus, she argued, the United States maintained a double standard when it came to dealing with dictatorships. Even worse was that this double standard had the effect of punishing America's friends while doing nothing to undermine or inflict costs upon America's enemies.

Kirkpatrick's article became notable and its ideas cited by others for a number of reasons. It not only presented a strong critique of U.S. policy, it also offered a way to understand American relations with nondemocratic governments of both the right and left. It provided an analytical distinction between "authoritarian" dictators on the right and the "totalitarian" dictatorships of communist countries. While this was not a new idea, Kirkpatrick's argument popularized it. In fact, the publication of this article brought Kirkpatrick's thinking to the attention of presidential candidate Ronald Reagan. When he was elected, he appointed Kirkpatrick as his ambassador to the United Nations and moved away from Carter's policy of linking American support to human rights. Instead, Reagan returned to the Cold War

Jeanne Kirkpatrick, from "Dictatorships and Double Standards," *Commentary*, November 1979. Reprinted by permission of Commentary.

practice that had been, and continues to be, quite common in American foreign policy: supporting "authoritarian" dictatorships that side with the United States in its foreign policy, regardless of their human rights records.

---

The failure of the Carter administration's foreign policy is now clear to everyone except its architects, and even they must entertain private doubts, from time to time, about a policy whose crowning achievement has been to lay the groundwork for a transfer of the Panama Canal from the United States to a swaggering Latin dictator of Castroite bent. In the thirty-odd months since the inauguration of Jimmy Carter as President there has occurred a dramatic Soviet military build-up, matched by the stagnation of American armed forces, and a dramatic extension of Soviet influence in the Horn of Africa, Afghanistan, Southern Africa, and the Caribbean, matched by a declining American position in all these areas. The U.S. has never tried so hard and failed so utterly to make and keep friends in the Third World.

As if this were not bad enough, in the current year the United States has suffered two other major blows—in Iran and Nicaragua—of large and strategic significance. In each country, the Carter administration not only failed to prevent the undesired outcome, it actively collaborated in the replacement of moderate autocrats friendly to American interests with less friendly autocrats of extremist persuasion. It is too soon to be certain about what kind of regime will ultimately emerge in either Iran or Nicaragua, but accumulating evidence suggests that things are as likely to get worse as to get better in both countries. The Sandinistas in Nicaragua appear to be as skillful in consolidating power as the Ayatollah Khomeini is inept, and leaders of both revolutions display an intolerance and arrogance that do not bode well for the peaceful sharing of power or the establishment of constitutional governments, especially since those leaders have made clear that they have no intention of seeking either.

It is at least possible that the SALT debate may stimulate new scrutiny of the nation's strategic position and defense policy, but there are no signs that anyone is giving serious attention to this nation's role in Iranian and Nicaraguan developments—despite clear warnings that the U.S. is confronted with similar situations and options in El Salvador, Guatemala, Morocco, Zaire, and elsewhere. Yet no problem of American foreign policy is more urgent than that of formulating a morally and strategically acceptable, and politically realistic, program for dealing with non-democratic governments who are threatened by Soviet-sponsored subversion. In the absence of such a policy, we can expect that the same reflexes that guided Washington in Iran and Nicaragua will be permitted to determine American actions from Korea to Mexico—with the same disastrous effects on the U.S.

strategic position. (That the administration has not called its policies in Iran and Nicaragua a failure—and probably does not consider them such—complicates the problem without changing its nature.)

There were, of course, significant differences in the relations between the United States and each of these countries during the past two or three decades. Oil, size, and proximity to the Soviet Union gave Iran greater economic and strategic import than any Central American "republic," and closer relations were cultivated with the Shah, his counselors, and family than with President Somoza, his advisers, and family. Relations with the Shah were probably also enhanced by our approval of his manifest determination to modernize Iran regardless of the effects of modernization on traditional social and cultural patterns (including those which enhanced his own authority and legitimacy). And, of course, the Shah was much better looking and altogether more dashing than Somoza; his private life was much more romantic, more interesting to the media, popular and otherwise. Therefore, more Americans were more aware of the Shah than of the equally tenacious Somoza.

But even though Iran was rich, blessed with a product the U.S. and its allies needed badly, and led by a handsome king, while Nicaragua was poor and rocked along under a long-tenure president of less striking aspect, there were many similarities between the two countries and our relations with them. Both these small nations were led by men who had not been selected by free elections, who recognized no duty to submit themselves to searching tests of popular acceptability. Both did tolerate limited opposition, including opposition newspapers and political parties, but both were also confronted by radical, violent opponents bent on social and political revolution. Both rulers, therefore, sometimes invoked martial law to arrest, imprison, exile, and occasionally, it was alleged, torture their opponents. Both relied for public order on police forces whose personnel were said to be too harsh, too arbitrary, and too powerful. Each had what the American press termed "private armies," which is to say, armies pledging their allegiance to the ruler rather than the "constitution" or the "nation" or some other impersonal entity.

In short, both Somoza and the Shah were, in central ways, traditional rulers of semi-traditional societies. Although the Shah very badly wanted to create a technologically modern and powerful nation and Somoza tried hard to introduce modern agricultural methods, neither sought to reform his society in the light of any abstract idea of social justice or political virtue. Neither attempted to alter significantly the distribution of goods, status, or power (though the democratization of education and skills that accompanied modernization in Iran did result in some redistribution of money and power there).

Both Somoza and the Shah enjoyed long tenure, large personal fortunes (much of which were no doubt appropriated from general revenues), and good relations with the United States. The Shah and Somoza were not only anti-Communist, they were positively friendly to the U.S., sending their sons and others to be educated in our universities, voting with us in the United Nations, and regularly supporting American interests and positions even when these entailed personal and political cost. The embassies of both governments were active in Washington social life, and were frequented by powerful Americans who occupied major roles in this nation's diplomatic, military, and political life. And the Shah and Somoza themselves were both welcome in Washington, and had many American friends.

Though each of the rulers was from time to time criticized by American officials for violating civil and human rights, the fact that the people of Iran and Nicaragua only intermittently enjoyed the rights accorded to citizens in the Western democracies did not prevent successive administrations from granting—with the necessary approval of successive Congresses—both military and economic aid. In the case of both Iran and Nicaragua, tangible and intangible tokens of U.S. support continued until the regime became the object of a major attack by forces explicitly hostile to the United States.

But once an attack was launched by opponents bent on destruction, everything changed. The rise of serious, violent opposition in Iran and Nicaragua set in motion a succession of events which bore a suggestive resemblance to one another and a suggestive similarity to our behavior in China before the fall of Chiang Kai-shek, in Cuba before the triumph of Castro, in certain crucial periods of the Vietnamese war, and, more recently, in Angola. In each of these countries, the American effort to impose liberalization and democratization on a government confronted with violent internal opposition not only failed, but actually assisted the coming to power of new regimes in which ordinary people enjoy fewer freedoms and less personal security than under the previous autocracy—regimes, moreover, hostile to American interests and policies.

The pattern is familiar enough: an established autocracy with a record of friendship with the U.S. is attacked by insurgents, some of whose leaders have long ties to the Communist movement, and most of whose arms are of Soviet, Chinese, or Czechoslovak origin. The "Marxist" presence is ignored and/or minimized by American officials and by the elite media on the ground that U.S. support for the dictator gives the rebels little choice but to seek aid "elsewhere." Violence spreads and American officials wonder aloud about the viability of a regime that "lacks the support of its own people." The absence of an opposition party is deplored and civil-rights violations are reviewed. Liberal columnists question the morality of continuing aid to a "rightist dictatorship" and provide assurances concerning the essential moderation of some insurgent leaders who "hope" for some sign that the U.S. will remember its own revolutionary origins. Requests for help from the beleaguered autocrat go unheeded, and the argument is increasingly voiced that ties should be established with rebel leaders "before it is too late." The President, delaying U.S. aid, appoints a special emissary who confirms the deterioration of the government position and its diminished capacity to control the situation and recommends various measures for "strengthening" and "liberalizing" the regime, all of which involve diluting its power.

The emissary's recommendations are presented in the context of a growing clamor for American disengagement on grounds that continued involvement confirms our status as an agent of imperialism, racism, and reaction; is inconsistent with support for human rights; alienates us from the "forces of democracy"; and threatens to put the U.S. once more on the side of history's "losers." This chorus is supplemented daily by interviews with returning missionaries and "reasonable" rebels.

As the situation worsens, the President assures the world that the U.S. desires only that the "people choose their own form of government"; he blocks delivery of all arms to the government and undertakes negotiations to establish a "broadly based" coalition headed by a "moderate" critic of the regime who, once elevated, will move quickly to seek a "political" settlement to the conflict. Should the incumbent autocrat prove resistant to American demands that he step aside, he will be readily overwhelmed by the military strength of his opponents, whose patrons will have continued to provide sophisticated arms and advisers at the same time the U.S. cuts off military sales. Should the incumbent be so demoralized as to agree to yield power, he will be replaced by a "moderate" of American selection. Only after the insurgents have refused the proffered political solution and anarchy has spread throughout the nation will it be noticed that the new head of government has no significant following, no experience at governing, and no talent for leadership. By then, military commanders, no longer bound by loyalty to the chief of state, will depose the faltering "moderate" in favor of a fanatic of their own choosing.

In either case, the U.S. will have been led by its own misunderstanding of the situation to assist actively in deposing an erstwhile friend and ally and installing a government hostile to American interests and policies in the world. At best we will have lost access to friendly territory. At worst the Soviets will have gained a new base. And everywhere our friends will have noted that the U.S. cannot be counted on in times of difficulty and our enemies will have observed that American support provides no security against the forward march of history.

The Carter administration brought to the crises in Iran and Nicaragua several common assumptions each of which played a major role in hastening the victory of even more repressive dictatorships than had been in place before. These were, first, the belief that there existed at the moment of crisis a democratic alternative to the incumbent government: second, the belief that the continuation of the status quo was not possible; third, the belief that any change, including the establishment of a government headed by self-styled Marxist revolutionaries, was preferable to the present government. Each of these beliefs was (and is) widely shared in the liberal community generally. Not one of them can withstand close scrutiny.

Although most governments in the world are, as they always have been, autocracies of one kind or another, no idea holds greater sway in the mind of educated Americans than the belief that it is possible to democratize governments, anytime, anywhere, under any circumstances. This notion is belied by an enormous body of evidence based on the experience of dozens of countries which have attempted with more or less (usually less) success to move from autocratic to democratic government. Many of the wisest political scientists of this and previous centuries agree that democratic institutions are especially difficult to establish and maintain—because they make heavy demands on all portions of a population and because they depend on complex social, cultural, and economic conditions.

Two or three decades ago, when Marxism enjoyed its greatest prestige among American intellectuals, it was the economic prerequisites of democracy that were emphasized by social scientists. Democracy, they argued, could function only in relatively rich societies with an advanced economy, a substantial middle class, and a literate population, but it could be expected to emerge more or less automatically whenever these conditions prevailed. Today, this picture seems grossly oversimplified. While it surely helps to have an economy strong enough to provide decent levels of well-being for all, and "open" enough to provide mobility and encourage achievement, a pluralistic society and the right kind of political culture—and time—are even more essential.

In the relatively few places where they exist, democratic governments have come into being slowly, after extended prior experience with more limited forms of participation during which leaders have reluctantly grown accustomed to tolerating dissent and opposition, opponents have accepted the notion that they may defeat but not destroy incumbents, and people have become aware of government's effects on their lives and of their own possible effects on government. Decades, if not centuries, are normally required for people to acquire the necessary disciplines and habits. In Britain, the road from the Magna Carta to the Act of Settlement, to the great Reform Bills of 1832, 1867, and 1885, took seven centuries to traverse. American history gives no better grounds for believing that democracy comes easily, quickly, or for the asking. A war of independence, an unsuccessful constitution, a civil war, a long process of gradual enfranchisement marked our progress toward constitutional democratic government. The French path was still more difficult. Terror, dictatorship, monarchy, instability, and incompetence followed on the revolution that was to usher in a millennium of brotherhood. Only in the 20th century did the democratic principle finally gain wide acceptance in France and not until after World War II were the principles of order and democracy, popular sovereignty and authority, finally reconciled in institutions strong enough to contain conflicting currents of public opinion.

Although there is no instance of a revolutionary "socialist" or Communist society being democratized, right-wing autocracies do sometimes evolve into democracies—given time, propitious economic, social, and political circumstances, talented leaders, and a strong indigenous demand for representative government. Something of the kind is in progress on the Iberian peninsula and the first steps have been taken in Brazil. Something similar could conceivably have also occurred in Iran and Nicaragua if contestation and participation had been more gradually expanded.

But it seems clear that the architects of contemporary American foreign policy have little idea of how to go about encouraging the liberalization of an autocracy. In neither Nicaragua nor Iran did they realize that the only likely result of an effort to replace an incumbent autocrat with one of his moderate critics or a "broad-based coalition" would be to sap the foundations of the existing regime without moving the nation any closer to democracy. Yet this outcome was entirely predictable. Authority in traditional autocracies is transmitted through personal relations: from the ruler to his close associates (relatives, household members, personal friends) and from them to people to whom the associates are related by personal ties resembling their own relation to the ruler. The fabric of authority unravels quickly when the power and status of the man at the top are undermined or eliminated. The longer the autocrat has held power, and the more pervasive his personal influence, the more dependent a nation's institutions will be on him. Without him, the organized life of the society will collapse, like an arch from which the keystone has been removed. The blend of qualities that bound the Iranian army to the Shah or the national guard to Somoza is typical of the relationships—personal, hierarchical, non-transferable—that support a traditional autocracy. The speed with which armies collapse, bureaucracies abdicate, and social structures dissolve once the autocrat is removed frequently surprises American policy-makers and journalists accustomed to public institutions based on universalistic norms rather than particularistic relations.

The failure to understand these relations is one source of the failure of U.S. policy in this and previous administrations. There are others. In Iran and Nicaragua (as previously in Vietnam, Cuba, and China) Washington overestimated the political diversity of the opposition—especially the strength of "moderates" and "democrats" in the opposition movement; underestimated the strength and intransigence of radicals in the movement; and misestimated the nature and extent of American influence on both the government and the opposition.

When U.S. policy-makers and large portions of the liberal press interpret insurgency as evidence of widespread popular discontent and a will to democracy, the scene is set for disaster. For if civil strife reflects a popular demand for democracy, it follows that a "liberalized" government will be more acceptable to "public opinion."

Thus, in the hope of strengthening a government, U.S. policy-makers are led, mistake after mistake, to impose measures almost certain to weaken its authority. Hurried efforts to force complex and unfamiliar political practices on societies lacking the requisite political culture, tradition, and social structures not only fail to produce desired outcomes; if they are undertaken at a time when the traditional regime is under attack, they actually facilitate the job of the insurgents.

Vietnam presumably taught us that the United States could not serve as the world's policeman; it should also have taught us the dangers of trying to be the world's midwife to democracy when the birth is scheduled to take place under conditions of guerrilla war.

If the administration's actions in Iran and Nicaragua reflect the pervasive and mistaken assumption that one can easily locate and impose democratic alternatives to incumbent autocracies, they also reflect the equally pervasive and equally flawed belief that change *per se* in such autocracies is inevitable, desirable, and in the American interest. It is this belief which induces the Carter administration to participate actively in the toppling of non-Communist autocracies while remaining passive in the face of Communist expansion.

At the time the Carter administration came into office it was widely reported that the President had assembled a team who shared a new approach to foreign policy and a new conception of the national interest. The principal elements of this new approach were said to be two: the conviction that the cold war was over, and the conviction that, this being the case, the U.S. should give priority to North-South problems and help less developed nations achieve their own destiny.

More is involved in these changes than originally meets the eye. For, unlikely as it may seem, the foreign policy of the Carter administration is guided by a relatively full-blown philosophy of history which includes, as philosophies of history always do, a theory of social change, or, as it is currently called, a doctrine of modernization. Like most other philosophies of history that have appeared in the West since the 18th century, the Carter administration's doctrine predicts progress (in the form of modernization for all societies) and a happy ending (in the form of a world community of developed, autonomous nations).

Although the modernization paradigm has proved a sometimes useful as well as influential tool in social science, it has become the object of searching critiques that have challenged one after another of its central assumptions. Its shortcomings as an analytical tool pale, however, when compared to its inadequacies as a framework for thinking about foreign policy, where its principal effects are to encourage the view that events are manifestations of deep historical forces which cannot be controlled and that the best any government can do is to serve as a "midwife" to history, helping events to move where they are already headed.

This perspective on contemporary events is optimistic in the sense that it foresees continuing human progress; deterministic in the sense that it perceives events as fixed by processes over which persons and policies can have but little influence; moralistic in the sense that it perceives history and U.S. policy as having moral ends; cosmopolitan in the sense that it attempts to view the world not from the perspective of American interests or intentions but from the perspective of the modernizing nation and the "end" of history. It identifies modernization with both revolution and morality, and U.S. policy with all three.

The idea that it is "forces" rather than people which shape events recurs each time an administration spokesman articulates or explains policy. The President, for example, assured us in February of this year:

> The revolution in Iran is a product of deep social, political, religious, and economic factors growing out of the history of Iran itself.

And of Asia he said:

> At this moment there is turmoil or change in various countries from one end of the Indian Ocean to the other; some turmoil as in Indochina is the product of age-old enmities, inflamed by rivalries for influence by conflicting forces. Stability in some other countries is being shaken by the process of modernization, the search for national significance, or the desire to fulfill legitimate human hopes and human aspirations.

So what if the "deep historical forces" at work in such diverse places as Iran, the Horn of Africa, Southeast Asia, Central America, and the United Nations look a lot like Russians or Cubans? Having moved past what the President calls our "inordinate fear of Communism," identified by him with the cold war, we should, we are told, now be capable of distinguishing Soviet and Cuban "machinations," which anyway exist mainly in the minds of cold warriors and others guilty of oversimplifying the world, from evolutionary changes, which seem to be the only kind that actually occur.

What *is* the function of foreign policy under these conditions? It is to understand the processes of change and then, like Marxists, to align ourselves with history, hoping to contribute a bit of stability along the way. And this, administration spokesmen assure us, is precisely what we are doing. The Carter administration has defined the U.S. national interest in the Third World as identical with the putative end of the modernization process. Vance put this with characteristic candor in a recent statement when he explained that U.S. policy vis-à-vis the Third World is "grounded in the conviction that we best serve our interest there by supporting the efforts of developing nations to advance their economic well-being and preserve their political independence." Our "commitment to the promotion of constructive change worldwide" (Brzezinski's words) has been vouchsafed in every conceivable context.

But there is a problem. The conceivable contexts turn out to be mainly those in which non-Communist autocracies are under pressure from revolutionary guerrillas. Since Moscow is the aggressive, expansionist power today, it is more often than not insurgents, encouraged and armed by the Soviet Union, who challenge the status quo. The American commitment to "change" in the abstract ends up by aligning us tacitly with Soviet clients and irresponsible extremists like the Ayatollah Khomeini or, in the end, Yasir Arafat.

So far, assisting "change" has not led the Carter administration to undertake the destabilization of a *Communist* country. The principles of self-determination and nonintervention are thus both selectively applied. We seem to accept the status quo in Communist nations (in the name of "diversity" and national autonomy), but not in nations ruled by "right-wing" dictators or white oligarchies. Concerning China, for example, Brzezinski has observed: "We recognize that the PRC and we have different ideologies and economic and political systems. . . . We harbor neither the hope nor the desire that through extensive contacts with China we can remake that nation into the American image. Indeed, we accept our differences." Of Southeast Asia, the President noted in February:

> Our interest is to promote peace and the withdrawal of outside forces and not to become embroiled in the conflict among Asian nations. And, in general, our interest is to promote the health and the development of individual societies, not to a pattern cut exactly like ours in the United States but tailored rather to the hopes and the needs and desires of the peoples involved.

But the administration's position shifts sharply when South Africa is discussed. For example, Anthony Lake asserted in late 1978:

> . . . We have indicated to South Africa the fact that if it does not make significant progress toward racial equality, its relations with the international community, including the United States, are bound to deteriorate.

Over the years, we have tried through a series of progressive steps to demonstrate that the U.S. cannot and will not be associated with the continued practice of apartheid.

As to Nicaragua, Hodding Carter III said in February 1979:

The unwillingness of the Nicaraguan government to accept the [OAS] group's proposal, the resulting prospects for renewal and polarization, and the human-rights situation in Nicaragua . . . unavoidably affect the kind of relationships we can maintain with that government. . . .

And Carter commented on Latin American autocracies:

My government will not be deterred from protecting human rights, including economic and social rights, in whatever ways we can. We prefer to take actions that are positive, but where nations persist in serious violations of human rights, we will continue to demonstrate that there are costs to the flagrant disregard of international standards.

Something very odd is going on here. How does an administration that desires to let people work out their own destinies get involved in determined efforts at reform in South Africa, Zaire, Nicaragua, El Salvador, and elsewhere? How can an administration committed to nonintervention in Cambodia and Vietnam announce that it "will not be deterred" from righting wrongs in South Africa? What should be made of an administration that sees the U.S. interest as identical with economic modernization and political independence and yet heedlessly endangers the political independence of Taiwan, a country whose success in economic modernization and egalitarian distribution of wealth is unequaled in Asia? The contrast is as striking as that between the administration's frenzied speed in recognizing the new dictatorship in Nicaragua and its continuing refusal to recognize the elected government of Zimbabwe Rhodesia, or its refusal to maintain any presence in Zimbabwe Rhodesia while staffing a U.S. Information Office in Cuba. Not only are there ideology and a double standard at work here, the ideology neither fits nor explains reality, and the double standard involves the administration in the wholesale contradiction of its own principles.

Inconsistencies are a familiar part of politics in most societies. Usually, however, governments behave hypocritically when their principles conflict with the national interest. What makes the inconsistencies of the Carter administration noteworthy are, first, the administration's moralism—which renders it especially vulnerable to charges of hypocrisy; and, second, the administration's predilection for policies that violate the strategic and economic interests of the United States. The administration's conception of national interest borders on doublethink: it finds friendly powers to be guilty representatives of the status quo and views the triumph of unfriendly groups as beneficial to America's "true interests."

This logic is quite obviously reinforced by the prejudices and preferences of many administration officials. Traditional autocracies are, in general and in their very nature, deeply offensive to modern American sensibilities. The notion that public affairs should be ordered on the basis of kinship, friendship, and other personal relations rather than on the basis of objective "rational" standards violates our conception of justice and efficiency. The preference for stability rather than change is also disturbing to Americans whose whole national experience rests on the principles of change, growth, and progress. The extremes of wealth and poverty characteristic of traditional societies also offend us, the more so since the poor are usually *very* poor and bound to their squalor by a hereditary allocation of role. Moreover, the relative lack of concern of rich, comfortable rulers for the poverty, ignorance, and disease of "their" people is likely to be interpreted by Americans as moral dereliction pure and simple. The truth is that Americans can hardly bear such societies and such rulers. Confronted with them, our vaunted cultural relativism evaporates and we become as censorious as Cotton Mather confronting sin in New England.

But if the politics of traditional and semi-traditional autocracy is nearly antithetical to our own—at both the symbolic and the operational level—the rhetoric of progressive revolutionaries sounds much better to us; their symbols are much more acceptable. One reason that some modern Americans prefer "socialist" to traditional autocracies is that the former have embraced modernity and have adopted modern modes and perspectives, including an instrumental, manipulative, functional orientation toward most social, cultural, and personal affairs; a profession of universalistic norms; an emphasis on reason, science, education, and progress; a deemphasis of the sacred; and "rational," bureaucratic organizations. They speak our language.

Because socialism of the Soviet/Chinese/Cuban variety is an ideology rooted in a version of the same values that sparked the Enlightenment and the democratic revolutions of the 18th century; because it is modern and not traditional; because it postulates goals that appeal to Christian as well as to secular values (brotherhood of man, elimination of power as a mode of human relations), it is highly congenial to many Americans at the symbolic level. Marxist revolutionaries speak the language of a hopeful future while traditional autocrats speak the language of an unattractive past. Because left-wing revolutionaries invoke the symbols and values of democracy—emphasizing egalitarianism rather than hierarchy and privilege, liberty rather than order, activity rather than passivity—they are again and again accepted as partisans in the cause of freedom and democracy.

Nowhere is the affinity of liberalism, Christianity, and Marxist socialism more apparent than among liberals who are "duped" time after time into supporting "liberators" who turn out to be totalitarians, and among Left-leaning clerics whose attraction to a secular style of "redemptive community" is stronger than their outrage at the hostility of socialist regimes to religion. In Jimmy Carter—egalitarian, optimist, liberal, Christian—the tendency to be repelled by frankly non-democratic rulers and hierarchical societies is almost as strong as the tendency to be attracted to the idea of popular revolution, liberation, and progress. Carter is, *par excellence*, the kind of liberal most likely to confound revolution with idealism, change with progress, optimism with virtue.

Where concern about "socialist encirclement," Soviet expansion, and traditional conceptions of the national interest inoculated his predecessors against such easy equations, Carter's doctrine of national interest and modernization encourages support for all change that takes place in the name of "the people," regardless of its "superficial" Marxist or anti-American content. Any lingering doubt about whether the U.S. should, in case of conflict, support a "tested friend" such as the Shah or a friendly power such as Zimbabwe Rhodesia against an opponent who despises us is resolved by reference to our "true," our "long-range" interests.

Stephen Rosenfeld of the Washington *Post* described the commitment of the Carter administration to this sort of "progressive liberalism":

> The Carter administration came to power, after all, committed precisely to reducing the centrality of strategic competition with Moscow in American foreign policy, and to extending the United States' association with what it was prepared to accept as legitimate wave-of-the-future popular movements around the world—first of all with the victorious movement in Vietnam.
>
> ... Indochina was supposed to be the state on which Americans could demonstrate their "post-Vietnam" intent to come to terms with the progressive popular element that Kissinger, the villain, had denied.

In other words, the Carter administration, Rosenfeld tells us, came to power resolved not to assess international developments in the light of "cold-war" perspectives but to accept at face value the claim of revolutionary groups to represent "popular" aspirations and "progressive" forces—regardless of the ties of these revolutionaries to the Soviet Union. To this end, overtures were made looking to the "normalization" of relations with Vietnam, Cuba, and the Chinese People's Republic, and steps were taken to cool relations with South Korea, South Africa, Nicaragua, the Philippines, and others. These moves followed naturally from the conviction that the U.S. had, as our enemies said, been on the wrong side of history in supporting the status quo and opposing revolution.

One might have thought that this perspective would have been under-mined by events in Southeast Asia since the triumph of "progressive" forces there over the "agents of reaction." To cite Rosenfeld again:

> In this administration's time, Vietnam has been transformed for much of American public opinion, from a country wronged by the U.S. to one revealing a brutal essence of its own.
>
> This has been a quiet but major trauma to the Carter people (as to all liberals) scarring their self-confidence and their claim on public trust alike.

Presumably, however, the barbarity of the "progressive" governments in Cambodia and Vietnam has been less traumatic for the President and his chief advisers than for Rosenfeld, since there is little evidence of changed predispo-sitions at crucial levels of the White House and the State Department. The President continues to behave as before—not like a man who abhors autocrats but like one who abhors only right-wing autocrats.

To be sure, neither the President, nor Vance, nor Brzezinski *desires* the proliferation of Soviet-supported regimes. Each has asserted his disap-proval of Soviet "interference" in the modernization process. But each, nev-ertheless, remains willing to "destabilize" friendly or neutral autocracies without any assurance that they will not be replaced by reactionary totali-tarian theocracies, totalitarian Soviet client states, or worst of all, by mur-derous fanatics of the Pol Pot variety.

The foreign policy of the Carter administration fails not for lack of good intentions but for lack of realism about the nature of traditional versus revo-lutionary autocracies and the relation of each to the American national inter-est. Only intellectual fashion and the tyranny of Right/Left thinking prevent intelligent men of good will from perceiving the *facts* that traditional author-itarian governments are less repressive than revolutionary autocracies, that they are more susceptible of liberalization, and that they are more compati-ble with U.S. interests. The evidence on all these points is clear enough.

Surely it is now beyond reasonable doubt that the present governments of Vietnam, Cambodia, Laos are much more repressive than those of the despised previous rulers; that the government of the People's Republic of China is more repressive than that of Taiwan, that North Korea is more repressive than South Korea, and so forth. This is the most important lesson of Vietnam and Cambodia. It is not new but it is a gruesome reminder of harsh facts.

From time to time a truly bestial ruler can come to power in either type of autocracy—Idi Amin, Papa Doc Duvalier, Joseph Stalin, Pol Pot are examples—but neither type regularly produces such moral monsters (though democracy regularly prevents their accession to power). There are, however, *systemic* differences between traditional and revolutionary autocracies that have a predictable effect on their degree of repressiveness. Generally speaking, traditional autocrats tolerate social inequities, brutality, and poverty while revolutionary autocracies create them.

Traditional autocrats leave in place existing allocations of wealth, power, status, and other resources which in most traditional societies favor an affluent few and maintain masses in poverty. But they worship traditional gods and observe traditional taboos. They do not disturb the habitual rhythms of work and leisure, habitual places of residence, habitual patterns of family and personal relations. Because the miseries of traditional life are familiar, they are bearable to ordinary people who, growing up in the society, learn to cope, as children born to untouchables in India acquire the skills and attitudes necessary for survival in the miserable roles they are destined to fill. Such societies create no refugees.

Precisely the opposite is true of revolutionary Communist regimes. They create refugees by the million because they claim jurisdiction over the whole life of the society and make demands for change that so violate internalized values and habits that inhabitants flee by the tens of thousands in the remarkable expectation that their attitudes, values, and goals will "fit" better in a foreign country than in their native land.

The former deputy chairman of Vietnam's National Assembly from 1976 to his defection early in August 1979, Hoang Van Hoan, described recently the impact of Vietnam's ongoing revolution on that country's more than one million Chinese inhabitants:

> They have been expelled from places they have lived in for generations. They have been dispossessed of virtually all possessions—their lands, their houses. They have been driven into areas called new economic zones, but they have not been given any aid.
>
> How can they eke out a living in such conditions reclaiming new land? They gradually die for a number of reasons—diseases, the hard life. They also die of humiliation.

It is not only the Chinese who have suffered in Southeast Asia since the "liberation," and it is not only in Vietnam that the Chinese suffer. By the end of 1978 more than six million refugees had fled countries ruled by Marxist governments. In spite of walls, fences, guns, and sharks, the steady stream of people fleeing revolutionary utopias continues.

There is a damning contrast between the number of refugees created by Marxist regimes and those created by other autocracies: more than a million Cubans have left their homeland since Castro's rise (one refugee for every nine inhabitants) as compared to about 35,000 each from Argentina, Brazil, and Chile. In Africa more than five times as many refugees have fled Guinea and Guinea Bissau as have left Zimbabwe Rhodesia, suggesting that civil war and racial discrimination are easier for most people to bear than Marxist-style liberation.

Moreover, the history of this century provides no grounds for expecting that radical totalitarian regimes will transform themselves. At the moment there is a far greater likelihood of progressive liberalization and democratization in the governments of Brazil, Argentina, and Chile than in the government of Cuba; in Taiwan than in the People's Republic of China; in South Korea than in North Korea; in Zaire than in Angola; and so forth.

Since many traditional autocracies permit limited contestation and participation, it is not impossible that U.S. policy could effectively encourage this process of liberalization and democratization, provided that the effort is not made at a time when the incumbent government is fighting for its life against violent adversaries, and that proposed reforms are aimed at producing gradual change rather than perfect democracy overnight. To accomplish this, policy-makers are needed who understand how actual democracies have actually come into being. History is a better guide than good intentions.

A realistic policy which aims at protecting our own interest and assisting the capacities for self-determination of less developed nations will need to face the unpleasant fact that, if victorious, violent insurgency headed by Marxist revolutionaries is unlikely to lead to anything but totalitarian tyranny. Armed intellectuals citing Marx and supported by Soviet-bloc arms and advisers will almost surely not turn out to be agrarian reformers, or simple nationalists, or democratic socialists. However incomprehensible it may be to some, Marxist revolutionaries are not contemporary embodiments of the Americans who wrote the Declaration of Independence, and they will not be content with establishing a broad-based coalition in which they have only one voice among many.

It may not always be easy to distinguish between democratic and totalitarian agents of change, but it is also not too difficult. Authentic democratic revolutionaries aim at securing governments based on the consent of the governed and believe that ordinary men are capable of using freedom, knowing their own interest, choosing rulers. They do not, like the current leaders in Nicaragua, assume that it will be necessary to postpone elections for three to five years during which time they can "cure" the false consciousness of almost everyone.

If, moreover, revolutionary leaders describe the United States as the scourge of the 20th century, the enemy of freedom-loving people, the perpetrator of imperialism, racism, colonialism, genocide, war, then they are not authentic democrats or, to put it mildly, friends. Groups which define themselves as enemies should be treated as enemies. The United States is not in fact a racist, colonial power, it does not practice genocide, it does not threaten world peace with expansionist activities. In the last decade especially we have practiced remarkable forbearance everywhere and undertaken the "unilateral restraints on defense spending" recommended by Brzezinski as appropriate for the technetronic era. We have also moved further, faster, in eliminating domestic racism than any multiracial society in the world or in history.

For these reasons and more, a posture of continuous self-abasement and apology vis-à-vis the Third World is neither morally necessary nor politically appropriate. No more is it necessary or appropriate to support vocal enemies of the United States because they invoke the rhetoric of popular liberation. It is not even necessary or appropriate for our leaders to forswear unilaterally the use of military force to counter military force. Liberal idealism need not be identical with masochism, and need not be incompatible with the defense of freedom and the national interest.

# 25 Address to the British Parliament
## RONALD REAGAN

Ronald Reagan delivered a speech to the British Parliament in 1982 that has remained noteworthy to this day for many reasons. First of all, it embodied Reagan's ideological outlook. It fully captured his view of the future of freedom and democracy, of the force of American and Western power, while offering his assessment of the prospects for communism, which he considered bleak. Citing the unrest in Poland, the comparison between East and West Germany, and the streams of refugees fleeing communist rule, Reagan declared that communism had failed and that it was the job of the Western powers to help hasten its demise through a reassertion of American power. He said that his policies represented a plan and a hope for the long term that would "leave Marxism-Leninism on the ash heap of history." While no one at the time, including Reagan, would have suspected that in nine years there would be no more Soviet Union, his words seem eerily prophetic today. At the time, however, such words were seen as provocative and inflammatory.

Reagan's speech also expressed the idea that would later become known as the "Reagan Doctrine," a commitment to arm and support rebel groups and armies around the world seeking to

Ronald Reagan, Address to the British Parliament, June 8, 1982.

overthrow governments aligned with the Soviets. Though Reagan claimed that such support would further the cause of democracy, it involved helping nondemocratic groups to weaken their governments and perhaps attain power through non-democratic means. The logic was that opposing totalitarian dictatorships, no matter the means, was of benefit to the cause of spreading democracy. This logic was larger than the Reagan Doctrine; it was inherent in the type of thinking that became known as neoconservatism. As Joshua Muravchik described it in Part I, neoconservative doctrine favors the assertion of American power and military force if necessary to help bring democratic governments into existence. While Reagan never referred to himself with this label, his policies and the thinking behind them helped provide practical justification for the use of American military power in the direct service of eradicating dictatorship to foster democratic change. While controversial, especially in light of recent American military action in Iraq and Afghanistan, this view of the world expressed so forcefully by Reagan continues to resonate and possess a great hold over American foreign policy.

---

My Lord Chancellor, Mr. Speaker:

We're approaching the end of a bloody century plagued by a terrible political invention—totalitarianism. Optimism comes less easily today, not because democracy is less vigorous, but because democracy's enemies have refined their instruments of repression. Yet optimism is in order because day by day democracy is proving itself to be a not at all fragile flower. From Stettin on the Baltic to Varna on the Black Sea, the regimes planted by totalitarianism have had more than thirty years to establish their legitimacy. But none—not one regime—has yet been able to risk free elections. Regimes planted by bayonets do not take root.

The strength of the Solidarity movement in Poland demonstrates the truth told in an underground joke in the Soviet Union. It is that the Soviet Union would remain a one-party nation even if an opposition party were permitted because everyone would join the opposition party.

America's time as a player on the stage of world history has been brief. I think understanding this fact has always made you patient with your younger cousins—well not always patient. I do recall that on one occasion, Sir Winston Churchill said in exasperation about one of our most distinguished diplomats: "He is the only case I know of a bull who carries his china shop with him."

But witty as Sir Winston was, he also had that special attribute of great statesmen—the gift of vision, the willingness to see the future based on the experience of the past. It is this sense of history, this understanding of the past that I want to talk with you about today, for it is in remembering what we share of the past that our two nations can make common cause for the future.

We have not inherited an easy world. If developments like the Industrial Revolution, which began here in England, and the gifts of science and technology have made life much easier for us, they have also made it more dangerous. There are threats now to our freedom, indeed to our very existence, that other generations could never even have imagined.

There is first the threat of global war. No president, no congress, no prime minister, no parliament can spend a day entirely free of this threat. And I don't have to tell you that in today's world the existence of nuclear weapons could mean, if not the extinction of mankind, then surely the end of civilization as we know it. That's why negotiations on intermediate-range nuclear forces now under way in Europe and the START talks—Strategic Arms Reduction Talks—which will begin later this month, are not just critical to American or Western policy; they are critical to mankind. Our commitment to early success in these negotiations is firm and unshakable, and our purpose is clear: reducing the risk of war by reducing the means of waging war on both sides.

At the same time there is a threat posed to human freedom by the enormous power of the modern state. History teaches the dangers of government that overreaches—political control taking precedence over free economic growth, secret police, mindless bureaucracy, all combining to stifle individual excellence and personal freedom.

Now, I'm aware that among us here and throughout Europe there is legitimate disagreement over the extent to which the public sector should play a role in a nation's economy and life. But on one point all of us are united—our abhorrence of dictatorship in all its forms, but most particularly totalitarianism and the terrible inhumanities it has caused in our time—the great purge, Auschwitz and Dachau, the gulag, and Cambodia.

Historians looking back at our time will note the consistent restraint and peaceful intentions of the West. They will note that it was the democracies who refused to use the threat of their nuclear monopoly in the forties and early fifties for territorial or imperial gain. Had that nuclear monopoly been in the hands of the Communist world, the map of Europe—indeed, the world—would look very different today. And certainly they will note it was not the democracies that invaded Afghanistan or suppressed Polish Solidarity or used chemical and toxic warfare in Afghanistan and Southeast Asia.

If history teaches anything, it teaches self-delusion in the face of unpleasant facts is folly. We see around us today the marks of our terrible dilemma—predictions of doomsday, antinuclear demonstrations, an arms race in which the West must, for its own protection, be an unwilling participant. At the same time we see totalitarian forces in the world who seek subversion and conflict around the globe to further their barbarous assault on the human spirit. What, then, is our course? Must civilization perish in a hail of fiery atoms? Must freedom wither in a quiet, deadening accommodation with totalitarian evil?

Sir Winston Churchill refused to accept the inevitability of war or even that it was imminent. He said, "I do not believe that Soviet Russia desires war. What they desire is the fruits of war and the indefinite expansion of their power and doctrines. But what we have to consider here today while time remains is the permanent prevention of war and the establishment of conditions of freedom and democracy as rapidly as possible in all countries."

Well, this is precisely our mission today: to preserve freedom as well as peace. It may not be easy to see; but I believe we live now at a turning point.

In an ironic sense Karl Marx was right. We are witnessing today a great revolutionary crisis, a crisis where the demands of the economic order are conflicting directly with those of the political order. But the crisis is happening not in the free, non-Marxist West, but in the home of Marxism-Leninism, the Soviet Union. It is the Soviet Union that runs against the tide of history by denying human freedom and human dignity to its citizens. It also is in deep economic difficulty. The rate of growth in the national product has been steadily declining since the fifties and is less than half of what it was then.

The dimensions of this failure are astounding: A country which employs one-fifth of its population in agriculture is unable to feed its own people. Were it not for the private sector, the tiny private sector tolerated in Soviet agriculture, the country might be on the brink of famine. These private plots occupy a bare 3 percent of the arable land but account for nearly one-quarter of Soviet farm output and nearly one-third of meat products and vegetables. Overcentralized, with little or no incentives, year after year the Soviet system pours its best resources into the making of instruments of destruction. The constant shrinkage of economic growth combined with the growth of military production is putting a heavy strain on the Soviet people. What we see here is a political structure that no longer corresponds to its economic base, a society where productive forces are hampered by political ones.

The decay of the Soviet experiment should come as no surprise to us. Wherever the comparisons have been made between free and closed societies—West Germany and East Germany, Austria and Czechoslovakia, Malaysia and Vietnam—it is the democratic countries that are prosperous and responsive to the needs of their people. And one of the simple but overwhelming facts of our time is this: Of all the millions of refugees we've seen in the modern world, their flight is always away from, not toward the Communist world. Today on the NATO line, our military forces face east to prevent a possible invasion. On the other side of the line, the Soviet forces also face east to prevent their people from leaving.

The hard evidence of totalitarian rule has caused in mankind an uprising of the modern intellect and will. Whether it is the growth of the new schools of economics in America and England or the appearance of the so-called new philosophers in France, there is one unifying thread running through the intellectual work of these groups—rejection of the arbitrary power of the state, the refusal to subordinate the rights of the individual to the super-state, the realization that collectivism stifles all the best human impulses.

Since the exodus from Egypt, historians have written of those who sacrificed and struggled for freedom—the stand at Thermopylae, the revolt of Spartacus, the storming of the Bastille, the Warsaw uprising in World War II. More recently we've seen evidence of this same human impulse in one of the developing nations in Central America. For months and months the world news media covered the fighting in El Salvador. Day after day we were treated to stories and film slanted toward the brave freedom fighters battling oppressive government forces in behalf of the silent, suffering people of that tortured country.

And then one day those silent, suffering people were offered a chance to vote, to choose the kind of government they wanted. Suddenly the freedom fighters in the hills were exposed for what they really are—Cuban-backed guerrillas who want power for themselves, and their backers, not democracy for the people. They threatened death to any who voted, and destroyed hundreds of buses and trucks to keep the people from to the polling places. But on election day, the people of El Salvador, an unprecedented 1.4 million of them, braved ambush and gun-fire, and trudged for miles to vote for freedom.

They stood for hours in the hot sun waiting for their turn to vote. Members of our Congress who went there as observers told me of a women who was wounded by rifle fire on the way to the polls, who refused to leave the line to have her wound treated until after she had voted. A grandmother, who had been told by the guerrillas she would be killed when she returned from the polls, told the guerrillas, "You can kill me, you can kill my family, kill my neighbors, but you can't kill us all." The real free-dom fighters of El Salvador turned out to be the people of that country—the young, the old, the in-between . . .

Around the world today, the democratic revolution is gather-ing new strength. In India a critical test has been passed with the peaceful change of governing political parties. In Africa, Nigeria is moving in remarkable and unmistakable ways to build and strengthen its democratic institutions. In the Caribbean and Central America, sixteen of twenty-four countries have freely elected governments. And in the United Nations, eight of the ten developing nations which have joined that body in the past five years are democracies.

In the Communist world as well, man's instinctive desire for freedom and self-determination surfaces again and again. To be sure, there are grim reminders of how brutally the police state attempts to snuff out this quest for self-rule—1953 in East Germany, 1956 in Hungary, 1968 in Czechoslovakia, 1981 in Poland. But the struggle continues in Poland. And we know that there are even those who strive and suffer for freedom within the confines of the Soviet Union itself. How we conduct our-selves here in the Western Hemisphere will determine whether this trend continues.

No, democracy is not a fragile flower. Still it needs cultivat-ing. If the rest of this century is to witness the gradual growth of freedom and democratic ideals, we must take actions to assist the campaign for democracy.

Some argue that we should encourage democratic change in right-wing dictatorships, but not in Communist regimes. Well, to accept this preposterous notion—as some well-meaning peo-ple have—is to invite the argument that once countries achieve a nuclear capability, they should be allowed an undisturbed reign of terror over their own citizens. We reject this course.

As for the Soviet view, Chairman Brezhnev repeatedly has stressed that the competition of ideas and systems must continue and that this is entirely consistent with relaxation of tensions and peace.

Well, we ask only that these systems begin by living up to their own constitutions, abiding by their own laws, and complying with the international obligations they have undertaken. We ask only for a process, a direction, a basic code of decency, not for an instant transformation.

We cannot ignore the fact that even without our encouragement there has been and will continue to be repeated explosions against repression and dictatorships. The Soviet Union itself is not immune to this reality. Any system is inherently unstable that has no peaceful means to legitimize its leaders. In such cases, the very repressiveness of the state ultimately drives people to resist it, if necessary, by force.

While we must be cautious about forcing the pace of change, we must not hesitate to declare our ultimate objectives and to take concrete actions to move toward them. We must be staunch in our conviction that freedom is not the sole prerogative of a lucky few, but the inalienable and universal right of all human beings. So states the United Nations Universal Declaration of Human Rights, which, among other things, guarantees free elections.

The objective I propose is quite simple to state: to foster the infrastructure of democracy, the system of a free press, unions, political parties, universities, which allows a people to choose their own way to develop their own culture, to reconcile their own differences through peaceful means.

This is not cultural imperialism, it is providing the means for genuine self-determination and protection for diversity. Democracy already flourishes in countries with very different cultures and historical experiences. It would be cultural condescension, or worse, to say that any people prefer dictatorship to democracy. Who would voluntarily choose not to have the right to vote, decide to purchase government propaganda handouts instead of independent newspapers, prefer government worker-controlled unions, opt for land to be owned by the state instead of those who till it, want government repression of religious liberty, a single political party instead of a free choice, a rigid cultural orthodoxy instead of democratic tolerance and diversity?

Since 1947 the Soviet Union has given covert political training and assistance to Marxists-Leninists in many countries. Of course, it also has promoted the use of violence and subversion by these same forces. Over the past several decades, West

European and other Social Democrats, Christian Democrats, and leaders have offered open assistance to fraternal, political, and social institutions to bring about peaceful and democratic progress. Appropriately, for a vigorous new democracy, the Federal Republic of Germany's political foundations have become a major force in this effort.

We in America now intend to take additional steps, as many of our allies have already done; toward realizing this same goal. The chairman and other leaders of the national Republican and Democratic Party organizations are initiating a study with the bipartisan American Political Foundation to determine how the United States can best contribute as a nation to the global campaign for democracy now gathering force. They will have the cooperation of congressional leaders of both parties, along with representatives of business, labor, and other major institutions in our society. I look forward to receiving their recommendations and to working with these institutions and the Congress in the common task of strengthening democracy throughout the world.

It is time that we committed ourselves as a nation—in both the public and private sectors—to assisting democratic development . . .

At the same time, we invite the Soviet Union to consider with us how the competition of ideas and values—which it is committed to support—can be conducted on a peaceful and reciprocal basis. For example, I am prepared to offer President Brezhnev an opportunity to speak to the American people on our television if he will allow me the same opportunity with the Soviet people. We also suggest that panels of our newsmen periodically appear on each other's television to discuss major events.

Now, I don't wish to sound overly optimistic, yet the Soviet Union is not immune from the reality of what is going on in the world. It has happened in the past—a small ruling elite either mistakenly attempts to ease domestic unrest through greater repression and foreign adventure, or it chooses a wiser course. It begins to allow its people a voice in their own destiny. Even if this latter process is not realized soon, I believe the renewed strength of the democratic movement, complemented by a global campaign for freedom, will strengthen the prospects for arms control and a world at peace.

I have discussed on other occasions, including my address on May 9th, the elements of Western policies toward the Soviet Union to safeguard our interests and protect the peace. What I am describing now is a plan and a hope for the long term—the march of freedom and democracy which will leave Marxism-Leninism on the ash heap of history as it has left other tyrannies which stifle the freedom and muzzle the self-expression of the people. And that's why we must continue our efforts to strengthen NATO even as we move forward with our Zero-Option initiative in the negotiations on intermediate-range forces and our proposal for a one-third reduction in strategic ballistic missile warheads.

Our military strength is a prerequisite to peace, but let it be clear we maintain this strength in the hope it will never be used, for the ultimate determinant in the struggle that's now going on in the world will not be bombs and rockets, but a test of wills and ideas, a trial of spiritual resolve, the values we hold, the beliefs we cherish, the ideals to which we are dedicated.

The British people know that, given strong leadership, time, and a little bit of hope, the forces of good ultimately rally and triumph over evil. Here among you is the cradle of self-government, the mother of parliaments. Here is the enduring greatness of the British contribution to mankind, the great civilized ideas: individual liberty, representative government, and the rule of law under God.

I've often wondered about the shyness of some of us in the West about standing for these ideals that have done so much to ease the plight of man and the hardships of our imperfect world. This reluctance to use those vast resources at our command reminds me of the elderly lady whose home was bombed in the Blitz. As the rescuers moved about, they found a bottle of brandy she'd stored behind the staircase, which was all that was left standing. And since she was barely conscious, one of the workers pulled the cork to give her a taste of it. She came around immediately and said, "Here now—there now, put it back. That's for emergencies."

Well, the emergency is upon us. Let us be shy no longer. Let us go to our strength. Let us offer hope. Let us tell the world that a new age is not only possible but probable.

During the dark days of the Second World War, when this island was incandescent with courage, Winston Churchill exclaimed about Britain's adversaries, "What kind of a people do they think we are?" Well, Britain's adversaries found out what kind extraordinary people the British are. But all the democracies paid a terrible price for allowing the dictators to underestimate us. We dare not make that mistake again. So, let us ask ourselves, "What kind of people do we think we are?" And let us answer, "Free people, worthy of freedom and determined not only to remain so but to help others gain their freedom as well."

Sir Winston led his people to great victory in war and then lost an election just as the fruits of victory were about to be enjoyed. But he left office honorably, and as it turned out, temporarily, knowing that the liberty of his people was more important than the fate of any single leader. History recalls his greatness in ways no dictator will ever know. And he left us a message of hope for the future, as timely now as when he first uttered it, as opposition leader in the Commons nearly twenty-seven years ago, when he said, "When we look back on all the perils through which we have passed and at the mighty foes that we have laid low and all the dark and deadly designs that we have frustrated, why should we fear for our future? We have," he said, "come safely through the worst."

Well, the task I've set forth will long outlive our own generation. But together, we too have come through the worst. Let us now begin a major effort to secure the best—a crusade for freedom that will engage the faith and fortitude of the next generation. For the sake of peace and justice, let us move toward a world in which all people are at least free to determine their own destiny.

Thank you.

## 26 Japanese Subsidization of American Hegemony

### ROBERT GILPIN

During the Reagan administration, the United States was pursuing a military buildup and reasserting its power to challenge the Soviet Union around the world. At the same time, the economic position of the United States was changing. One of the most important developments was that the United States had lost its dominant position in the international economy. In the 1970s, the move off

---

From Gilpin, Robert; *The Political Economy of International Relations.* ©1987 Princeton University Press. Reprinted by permission of Princeton University Press.

of the gold standard, deficit spending, inflation, oil price shocks, and the growing economic strength and vitality of Japan and Europe all contributed to a decline in American economic might. When Ronald Reagan came to office, his economic policies (known as Reaganomics) involved increased government spending and borrowing to pay for military programs and spur economic growth. The economy grew considerably, but the government also assumed massive amounts of debt. This occurred at the same time that the Japanese economy was booming and Japanese companies were increasingly investing profits and surplus capital in American markets.

As Robert Gilpin explains, this confluence of events had significant results, the most important of which was that the Japanese were financing America and helping to maintain its global hegemony. Japanese investments in U.S. securities were one of the primary sources of funds that paid for America's added debt and government spending. The downside of this was that the United States went from being the world's largest creditor nation to being the world's largest debtor nation. In addition, Gilpin explains, the United States acquired a huge trade deficit and saw many of its own industries irreparably weakened. In particular, American manufacturing, which had enjoyed a comparative advantage over other countries around the world for decades, experienced a decline.

Gilpin's argument not only explained the economic position of the United States, his work is also notable in that it reflects the American concern at the time over Japan's increasing influence over America's economic policies and choices. Throughout the late 1980s and early 1990s, Japan was seen by the United States not only as a strategic ally in the Cold War, but also as a strong rival in the economic realm. The country's economic strength fed fears in the United States that it would someday be outmatched by an economically superior Japan. Japanese acquisition of Rockefeller Center in New York City and Universal Studios in Hollywood only exacerbated the concern and led to increased efforts by the United States to restore a trade balance by opening up Japan's market to more American goods and restricting Japanese imports.

The Japanese economy soon went into a prolonged recession, diminishing the perceived threat to America, but American economic vulnerability continues. As the United States presently pursues economic policies involving massive spending and borrowing, a similar dynamic has emerged in which China now contributes to the subsidization of the American economy. This relationship with China presents perhaps an even greater challenge for the United States. While Japan was an economic competitor in the 1980s, it was a strategic ally. China, by contrast, is today both an economic and strategic competitor.

Along with the rise of the Eurocurrency market and the onset of the global debt problem, the third extraordinary development in international finance during the postwar period has been the historic reversal of the financial positions of the United States and Japan. This financial turnabout has transformed the political and economic relations of the two dominant capitalist powers. Each for its own reasons entered into a relationship in which the Japanese became the principal underwriters of American hegemony.

By the end of the First World War, the United States had displaced Great Britain as the world's foremost creditor nation. This financial supremacy was consolidated in the interwar period, and at the end of the Second World War the United States became the hegemonic financial power. Although its financial status diminished during the 1970s, the United States retained its dominant financial position until the Reagan Administration. Then, in the 1980s, Japan supplanted the United States as the dominant creditor nation and financial power. Never before in the history of international finance has such a dramatic shift taken place in such a relatively short time.

In 1981, Japan became the world's most important capital exporter. Its huge trade surplus, which rose from about $35 billion in 1983 to over $53 billion in 1985, enabled it to rise rapidly as a financial power. In 1983, Japan's net capital outflow was only $17.7 billion; a year later it had jumped dramatically to $49.7 billion and to an astonishing $64.5 billion in 1985 (*The New York Times*, April 27, 1986, p. 16). This last figure was more than all the OPEC countries at the height of their wealth (Ibid., August 31, 1986, p. F7). By 1986, Japan's net assets abroad had risen to $129.8 billion, making it the world's largest creditor nation. Great Britain's net assets abroad were $90 billion and West Germany's, $50 billion at that time (*The Japan Economic Journal*, June 7, 1986, p. 1). In the same period, the net asset position of the United States was approaching zero.

Although it is true that total OPEC foreign investment in the mid-1980s was substantially larger, it was primarily placed in bank deposits and thus was recycled through the market by Western commercial banks. Japanese overseas investment, however, was heavily in bonds and, as one Japanese bank official put it, "we have direct control over our money" (*Globe and Mail, Report on Business Magazine*, April 1986, p. 28). The four largest banks and six of the top ten in the world are Japanese. These banks as well as other financial institutions and the Japanese government have a significant influence over the disposition of Japan's vast savings, and their power over international finance and the allocation of capital has become formidable indeed. In the mid-1980s the leaders of Japanese finance chose to place a substantial portion of their overseas investments in United States Treasury bonds.[1]

This remarkable transformation of Japan's trading and financial position had begun in the early 1970s when, responding to the OPEC price increase, Japan drastically cut its oil consumption, expanded its exports to pay for the increased cost of energy, and accelerated the speed at which it scaled the technology ladder. In addition, several important features of Japan's economy contributed to its massive trade and payments surplus. They include its high savings rate (about 18 percent in the mid-1980s) in combination with reduced domestic investment, the high productivity of Japanese industry, and the shift in the mid-1970s to a policy of economic contraction and export-led growth (Yoshitomi, 1985). The unusual structure of Japanese trade—the exporting of high value-added manufactured products and the importing of unprocessed commodities—meant that Japan was ultimately the principal beneficiary of the glut and price collapse of food, oil, and other commodities that occurred in the 1980s. These developments produced a "structural" surplus in Japan's trade and payments balances.

Using Marxist language, one could say that Japan in the mid-1980s had become a mature capitalist economy afflicted by the classic problems of underconsumption and surplus capital. It could not absorb the huge quantity of goods its factories turned out, nor could it find productive uses at home for its accumulating capital surplus. The causes of this underconsumption and falling rate of profit on domestic investment, however, had much more to do with internal Japanese politics than with the inevitable laws of the motion of capitalism. If the interests of the ruling Liberal Democratic Party had been different, Japan could easily have used the capital to improve the quality of Japanese life. Unwilling to make the needed domestic reforms, Japanese capitalism therefore required a "colony" to rid itself of these financial surpluses. The Japanese found this "vent for surplus" in an America experimenting with Reaganomics; the new "Japanese Co-Prosperity Sphere" was to be located across the Pacific Ocean in Ronald Reagan's America.[2]

At the same time that Japan was becoming a creditor nation, the United States was becoming a debtor nation. In 1981, the United States had succeeded in arresting the post-Vietnam deterioration of its international economic position; it had a surplus in its current account ($6.3 billion) and its repatriated net earnings on foreign investments had reached their zenith ($34 billion); this was to be, however, the last year of an American surplus in the current account (Council of Economic Advisers, 1986, p. 366). By 1985, this favorable situation had been reversed and the United States had become a net debtor for the first time since 1914. Between 1982 and 1984, foreign lending by American banks dropped dramatically, from $111 billion to approximately $10 billion (Emminger, 1985, p. 9). In 1984, the United States borrowed approximately $100 billion

(Ibid., p. 7). In that same year it had an historically unprecedented trade deficit of $108.3 billion, of which $34 billion was with Japan! By the end of 1985, the United States had become the world's largest debtor and had borrowed abroad over $100 billion in that year alone, a sum larger than the total Brazilian debt. In the mid-1980s, the United States was borrowing approximately $100–120 billion net each year and foreign holdings of American government securities soared. Projections of future borrowing indicated that by the end of the decade, the American foreign debt could reach $1 trillion. The world's richest country in less than five years had reversed a century-long trend and become the world's most indebted nation (Drobnik, 1985, p. 1).

The immediate cause of this historic shift in the financial position of the United States was located in the tax and fiscal policies of the Reagan Administration. A massive tax cut without a complementary reduction of the expenditures of the federal government had resulted in a huge and continuing budget deficit. This deficit subsequently gave a powerful fiscal or Keynesian stimulus to the American and, to a lesser extent, the world economy. Inadequate American savings, however, meant that the United States had to finance the budget deficit through borrowing heavily in world capital markets. From 1981 on, the resulting overvalued dollar and the increase in world interest rates led to the gigantic American trade deficit and greatly aggravated the global debt crisis.

What Reaganomics Phase Two (i.e., following its induced recession) actually entailed was an economic recovery financed by foreign creditors. As pointed out by E. Gerald Corrigan, President of the Federal Reserve Bank of New York, "we are vitally dependent on foreign savings flows" that directly or indirectly are "financing half or more of the budget deficit" (quoted in *The New York Times*, November 7, 1985, p. D1). The expansionary economic policies, domestic albeit reduced investment, and the unprecedented defense buildup of the Reagan Administration were possible because they were financed by other nations.

The three largest sources of this capital were the world's surplus savers: certain Arab OPEC producers (mainly Saudi Arabia), West Germany and, in particular, Japan. Whereas the Japanese gross purchases of Treasury bonds amounted to only $197 million in 1976, in April 1986 alone the figure was $138 billion (*The New York Times*, July 28, 1986, p. D6). Of the $81.8 billion that Japan invested abroad in 1985, $53.5 billion went into bonds, particularly U.S. Treasury issues (Ibid., April 27, 1986, p. 16). In the mid-1980s, the Japanese were supplying a substantial fraction of the $100–120 billion borrowed annually by the United States government and were investing heavily in all types of American assets. Without this immense flow of Japanese capital into the American economy, the Reagan Administration could not have simultaneously stimulated American domestic consumption and commenced the largest military expansion in peacetime American history. If there had been no flow of foreign capital into the economy, the Administration would have either had to decrease defense expenditures sharply or permit the increase in the domestic interest rate to cut short the economic recovery.

The importance of Japanese finance to the success of President Reagan's economic and defense program may be appreciated by contrasting it with an earlier event. In October 1979, West German unwillingness to support the dollar and to import American inflation was a vital factor in causing the United States to change its domestic economic policy and to shift to a tight monetary policy. The Federal Reserve contracted the money supply and caused the recession that helped elect Ronald Reagan. This was the first time in the postwar era that the United States made a major change in its domestic economic policy in response to foreign pressures. In the economic realm, this policy reversal was the end of American hegemony. Henceforth, the United States required the financial backing of the Japanese.[3]

By the mid-1980s, Japan had replaced West Germany as America's principal economic ally and the financial backer of the continued economic and political hegemony of the United States. Japanese investment of their savings and of the nation's huge payments surplus in the United States supported the dollar, helped finance the defense buildup, and contributed to American prosperity. More importantly it masked the relative economic decline of the United States. Japanese financial assistance enabled the American people to postpone, at least for a time, the difficult task of coming to terms with the classic problem that faces every declining power, that is, determining how to bring its power and commitments back into a state of economic and political equilibrium (Gilpin, 1981, p. 187).

Thus, by the mid-1980s, the world monetary and financial system based on the dollar had become largely underwritten by Japanese capital. The greatly overvalued dollar would have declined and perhaps collapsed in value as a consequence of the Reagan Administration's economic policies had it not been for this Japanese financial backing. The title of a monograph, *The Dollar's Borrowed Strength* (1985), by Otmar Emminger, a distinguished German central banker, portrayed the situation only too accurately.

The principal reason for this flow of Japanese capital into American Treasury bills was the sharp increase in the difference between American and Japanese real interest rates; the Japanese had opened and liberalized their capital nearly simultaneously with the American tax cuts and budget deficit (Calder, 1985, pp. 607–608). Differential interest rates, however, do not tell the whole story. The intensifying political relationship between Ronald Reagan's America and Yasuhiro Nakasone's Japan was certainly an important factor in the eagerness of the Japanese to invest in the United States. This developing global partnership was reinforced by the symbiotic interests of a United States living far beyond its means and a Japan in dire need of foreign markets and outlets for surplus capital.

The special American-Japanese financial relationship had been codified in the May 1984 report of the Japan-U.S. Yen-Dollar Committee on the liberalization and internationalization of the Japanese financial system (Yoshitomi, 1985, p. 18). The committee had been established at the time of President Reagan's visit to Tokyo in November 1983. Although the ostensible purpose of the committee and its recommendations was to correct the misalignment of the yen, the core and significance of the agreement was to open up Japanese financial markets and give the United States and other foreigners greater access to Japanese capital. It also increased the international role of the yen and thus accelerated Tokyo's emergence as a major financial center and the movement toward a tripartite monetary system based on the dollar, the yen, and the Deutschmark.[4]

This agreement, comparable to the Tripartite Monetary Agreement of 1936, which laid the basis for the postwar financial cooperation of the United States and Great Britain, resulted from American pressures on the Japanese to open their financial markets and make certain reforms within their economy (Fukushima, 1985, pp. 30–31). The United States appears to have had several motives in pressuring Japan to deregulate and open up its financial system: the belief that greater international use of the yen would cause the yen to appreciate and thereby decrease Japanese exports, the expectation that Japanese business would lose the competitive advantage provided by low interest rates and capital costs, and the desire to open up the vast reservoir of Japanese domestic savings to American financial institutions.[5] The Reagan Administration believed that the United States had a comparative advantage in financial services (as Japan did in manufacturing) and that American competition in financial and related services would enable the United States to reestablish the economic balance between the two countries (McRae, 1985, pp. 21–22). Thus, the agreement was a key element in the Reagan Administration policies toward Japan and for managing the American financial deficit.

The agreement was effective in stabilizing U.S.-Japanese relations as American pressures on Japan to increase its military role were muted and the Reagan Administration intensified its resistance to protectionist legislation. Japan and the United States had established a special relationship that reflected their respective strengths and political concerns. As Peter Drucker has pointed out, the American-Japanese economic relationship in the mid-1980s was extraordinary (*The Wall Street Journal*, Oct. 11, 1985,

p. 28). One key element was that the United States borrowed its own currency from the Japanese as well as from others. The scale and significance of this situation were unprecedented in international finance. "For the first time a debtor nation stands to benefit both on its capital account and on its trading account from devaluing its currency" (Ibid.). With the devaluation of the dollar the United States would in effect expropriate and wipe out a substantial fraction of its debt; the drop of the dollar between March 1985 and March 1986, in fact, may have reduced the debt by as much as one third. Simultaneously, the devaluation of the dollar would regain markets that the United States had lost because of the greatly overvalued dollar.

The Japanese, by loaning dollars back to the United States, were maintaining their most valuable export market and preventing domestic unemployment; over 10 percent of Japanese jobs are tied to exports. Domestic demand in Japan has been weak because of the reluctance to stimulate the economy by increasing the already huge budget deficit. Losing the American market would have severe repercussions in strategic and high-technology industries. The actual and potential losers in this curious form of mercantilism have been both American producers, who lose their markets to Japanese exporters, and frugal Japanese savers, who will receive devalued dollars.

Despite the short-term benefits of this symbiotic American-Japanese relationship, its long-term prospects are problematic. It is doubtful that the United States and the other advanced countries will be able to support the pressures placed on them by Japan's mammoth trade and capital surplus. Previously, Great Britain and the United States had graduated from debtor to creditor status through a generally low rate of capital accumulation over a period of decades (except for the impact of World War One on the American position). Moreover, as creditor economies, they were also major importers of the industrial exports of other economies. However, Japan's rapidity of change from debtor to creditor and the immense scale of Japan's capital outflow have been extraordinary, forcing equally rapid and large changes on other economies. In addition, the structure of Japanese trade as an importer of raw materials and an exporter of industrial products has placed a further burden of adjustment on the United States and Western Europe. Although successful adjustment by the other industrial economies to Japan's new international economic role will ultimately depend on a return to a high rate of world economic growth, the pace set by Japan's rapid advances in comparative advantage and the structure of its trade will continue to cause a severe strain under any circumstances.

The alarm, especially in the American Rustbelt, over Japan's increasing trading and financial strength greatly intensified in the 1980s. Americans became concerned over the fact, as one business economist quipped, "not only are our cars made in Japan, but increasingly so are our interest rates" (quoted in *The Wall Street Journal*, February 24, 1986, p. 1). Others took note of the fact that a growing segment of American securities, real estate, and other tangible assets were in Japanese or other foreign hands. In the words of U.S. Secretary of State George Shultz, "I think one could say that, if the world were content to let the Japanese provide a major share of the savings and wind up owning more and more, it's O.K. But that is not the way the United States, at least, is oriented" (quoted in *The New York Times*, February 12, 1986, p. D2). The Secretary failed to add that it was the policies of the Reagan Administration that had created this unfortunate situation.

Nevertheless, although some concern was expressed over the budget and trade deficits in the mid-1980s, the general consensus in the United States was one of optimism. The stock market was bullish and the Reagan Administration announced that the scourge of inflation had been eliminated. As for the long-term problem of the vast accumulated debt to the Japanese and other foreign creditors, optimistic sentiment was well expressed in the view of one former high official that we simply "run the clock backwards," that is, the United States would devalue the dollar and achieve a trade surplus with which to repay the debt. According to the former Chairman of the Council of Economic Advisers, Martin Feldstein (1986, p. 4), the United States would require a balance-of-trade surplus of about $100 billion per year for a number of years to retire the accumulated foreign debt.

The problems that such a turnaround in the American trading position would cause for other nations would be considerable. Such a reversal in world trade would necessitate a considerable devaluation of the dollar along with an appreciation of other currencies. Past experience has taught both the Japanese and the West Europeans to resist strongly any large appreciations of their currencies because of its consequences for domestic levels of unemployment. At the least, considerable international cooperation over macroeconomic policy will be required if a devastating mercantilistic conflict over trade is to be avoided.

The notion that policies can be reversed and the clock can be turned back betrays the great faith that American economists and policy makers have in the liberal conception of market equilibrium. In the abstract world of American economists, equations run both ways; they believe that by changing the sign of a variable from plus to minus or from minus to plus or the price and quantity of $x$ or $y$, the direction of historical movement can be reversed. Similarly, many believe that the damage to the international economy done by the Reagan Administration budget deficit can be set right simply by changing one price, the price of the dollar.

This overly sanguine view of the predicament of the United States in the latter part of the 1980s ignores a number of structural changes that have taken place in the American and world economies. Suffice it to say here that the importation of huge amounts of foreign capital and the consequently overvalued dollar have had profound and long-lasting effects on the American economy. First, the competitive position of important sectors of the American economy has been permanently damaged and the structure of the entire economy has been distorted (Emminger, 1985, p. 17). Second, repayment of the immense external debt and the associated interest payments will absorb a large share of America's productive resources for many years to come; these costs will substantially lower the standard of living for a considerable period, even if defense expenditures are considerably curtailed. And, third, the newly acquired preference of Americans for foreign goods and the expansion of productive capacity abroad have decimated many industries in which the United States once had a strong comparative advantage; America will be required to develop new products and industries if it is to regain even part of its former competitive position in world markets. The task of reversing the trends toward deindustrialization will be difficult and very costly.[6]

## Notes

1. Although it is certainly the case that Japanese financial institutions invested in the United States because of interest rate differentials and other market considerations, the discretionary power of the Japanese, as revealed by past experience, is not to be denied.
2. Calder (1985) presents an excellent summary of the developing economic ties across the Pacific.
3. The specific change was a shift away from efforts to control interest rates to the setting of monetary growth targets in order to achieve tighter discipline over the money supply and inflation rate. Former Secretary of the Treasury Michael Blumenthal has suggested that the appropriate date for the change in the American economic position is a year earlier, in November 1978. The fear of a run on the dollar led to a rise in the discount rate and a slowing of the economy.
4. Frankel (1984) is a good analysis of this agreement.
5. Why important members of the Reagan Administration believed that an increased capital outflow from Japan would cause the yen to rise was a mystery to most economists.
6. Feldstein (1986) provides a frank appraisal of the damage to capital formation and other aspects of the American economy caused by the economic policies of the Administration.

# 27 Retrospect and Prospect
## RAYMOND L. GARTHOFF

The end of the Cold War, after 45 years of conflict between the United States and the Soviet Union, came about rather abruptly, surprising most of the world when it happened. Though there was (and is) substantial agreement around the globe that the Soviet system had failed horribly in political and economic terms, there is no consensus on the reasons for the Soviet collapse and why it happened when it did. Contending arguments tend to fall into two camps (a fitting circumstance, indeed). The first suggests that the United States won the Cold War by virtue of its longstanding policy of containment, which placed such costs and strains on the Soviet Union that it was ultimately forced to capitulate. A variation on this idea suggests that in particular, the policies of Ronald Reagan—a massive military buildup and the Reagan Doctrine—were the direct cause of the Soviet collapse in the late 1980s. This interpretation is widely accepted in the United States, especially among partisan supporters of former President Reagan.

The second explanation places greater responsibility with the Soviets, pointing out that the Cold War ended when Mikhail Gorbachev and the rest of the Soviet leadership realized how badly their system had failed and began to change Soviet policies. Though they did not anticipate the breakup of the Soviet Union or the collapse of communism in Eastern Europe, they did seek fundamental change in their society and a new relationship with both their Warsaw Pact allies and their NATO adversaries. In the end, Gorbachev's reforms—glasnost, perestroika, democratization, and new thinking in foreign policy—escaped the control of the Soviet government and resulted in the end of the Cold War, European communism, and the USSR itself.

Raymond Garthoff, one of the preeminent scholars of the Cold War, considers these perspectives and arrives at a conclusion that equitably and accurately describes the role of each country in ending the Cold War. He notes that the American part in ending the Cold War was necessary, but not primary. The United States, over four decades, kept Soviet power in check, precluding "any temptations by Moscow to advance Soviet hegemony by military means."

Nonetheless, it was Mikhail Gorbachev and the Soviets, who by design and by chance, brought the Cold War to a close.

The selection from Garthoff succinctly explains the resolution of the Cold War, but his assessment, while not explicitly addressing other topics, speaks to subsequent challenges in American foreign policy. The implication of his argument is that the robust projection of American power has an important, but limited effect. He thus provides a mild warning that the use of American power to extend democracy and free markets may not be as effective as expected by proponents of such a policy. Rather, the internal characteristics and political dynamics of a country may be paramount in allowing for a transformation toward democracy and/or capitalism.

---

# LOOKING BACK: THE COLD WAR IN RETROSPECT

The fundamental underlying cause of the Cold War was the belief in both the Soviet Union and the United States that confrontation was unavoidable, imposed by history. Soviet leaders believed that Communism would ultimately triumph in the world and that the Soviet Union was the vanguard socialist-communist state. They also believed that the Western "imperialist" powers were historically bound to pursue a hostile course against them. For their part, American and other Western leaders assumed that the Soviet Union was determined to enhance its power and to pursue expansionist policies by all expedient means to achieve a Soviet-led communist world. Each side thought that it was compelled by the very existence of the other to engage in zero-sum competition, and each saw the unfolding history of the Cold War as confirming its views.

The prevailing Western view was wrong in attributing a master plan to the Kremlin, in believing that communist ideology impelled Soviet leaders to expand their power, in exaggerating communist abilities to subvert a Free World, and in thinking that Soviet officials viewed military power as an ultimate recourse. But the West was not wrong in believing that Soviet leaders were committed to a historically driven struggle between two worlds until, in the end, theirs would triumph. To be sure, other motivations and interests, including national aims, institutional interests, and even personal psychological considerations, played a part. These influences, however, tended to enhance the ideological framework rather than weaken it. Moreover, the actions of each side were sufficiently consistent with the ideological expectations of the other side to sustain their respective worldviews for many years.

Within the framework of ideological conflict, the Americans and the Soviets waged the Cold War as a geopolitical struggle, based more realistically on traditional balance-of-power politics than on world class struggle or global containment and deterrence theory. If ideology was the only thing driving the superpowers in the Cold War, why is the conflict seen as arising from the ashes of World War II rather than as stemming from the October Revolution of 1917? The answer is clear. In 1917 and during the next twenty-five years the Soviet Union was relatively weak and only one of several great powers in a multipolar world. By the end of World War II, however, Germany and Japan had been crushed, Britain, France, and China were weakened, and the enlarged Soviet Union, even though much weaker than the United States, seemed to pose an unprecedented threat by virtue of its massive armies and their presence deep in Central Europe. Under these circumstances, Josef Stalin's reassertion in 1946 and 1947 of the division of the world into two contending camps seemed more valid and more threatening than ever before.

So the Cold War had essential ideological and geopolitical dimensions. A Manichean communist worldview spawned a Manichean anticommunist worldview. Each side imputed unlimited objectives, ultimately world domination, to the other. Each side looked to the realization of its ambitions (or its historical destiny) over the long term and thus posited an indefinite period of conflict. But even though both sides envisioned a conflict of indefinite duration, and even though policy decisions were pragmatic and based on calculation of risk, cost, and gain, the hazard of a miscalculation always existed. And that could be fatally dangerous, given the historical coincidence of the Cold War and the first half-century of the nuclear age. Nuclear weapons, by threatening the existence of world civilization, added significantly to the tension of the epoch; the stakes were utterly without precedent and beyond full comprehension.

Nuclear weapons also helped to keep the Cold War cold, to prevent a third world war in the twentieth century. Nonetheless, in the final analysis and despite their awesome power, nuclear weapons did not cause, prevent, or end the Cold War, which would have been waged even if such weapons had never existed. The arms race and other aspects of the superpower rivalry were, however, driven in part by ideological assumptions. As a result, while the Cold War and the nuclear arms race could be attenuated when opportunities or constraints led both sides to favor a relaxation of tensions, neither could be ended until the ideological underpinnings of the confrontation had also been released. This occurred under Mikhail Gorbachev's leadership, which saw a fundamental reevaluation in Moscow of the processes at work in the real world, a basic reassessment of threats, and finally a deep revision of aims and political objectives. The United States and the West in general were cautious but eventually recognized this fundamental change and reciprocated.

The West did not, as is widely believed, win the Cold War through geopolitical containment and military deterrence. Still less was the Cold War won by the Reagan military buildup and the Reagan Doctrine, as some have suggested. Instead, "victory" came when a new generation of Soviet leaders realized how badly their system at home and their policies abroad had failed. What containment did do was to successfully preclude any temptations by Moscow to advance Soviet hegemony by military means. It is doubtful that any postwar Soviet leadership would have deliberately resorted to war. That was not, however, so clear to many at the time. Deterrence may have been redundant, but at the least it was highly successful in providing reassurance to the peoples of Western Europe. For over four decades it performed the historic function of holding Soviet power in check, or being prepared to do so, until the internal seeds of destruction in the Soviet Union and its empire could mature. At that point, however, Mikhail Gorbachev and the transformation of Soviet policy brought the Cold War to an end.

Despite the important differences among them, all Soviet leaders from Lenin until Gorbachev had shared a belief in an ineluctable conflict between socialism and capitalism. Although Gorbachev remained a socialist, and in his own terms even a communist, he renounced the Marxist-Leninist-Stalinist idea of inevitable world conflict. His avowed acceptance of the interdependence of the world, of the priority of all-human values over class values, and of the indivisibility of common security marked a revolutionary ideological change. That change, which Gorbachev publicly declared as early as February 1986 (though it was then insufficiently noted), manifested itself in many ways during the next five years, in deeds as well as words, including policies reflecting a drastically reduced Soviet perception of the Western threat and actions to reduce the Western perception of a Soviet threat.

In 1986, for example, Gorbachev made clear his readiness to ban all nuclear weapons. In 1987 he signed the INF Treaty, eliminating not only the Soviet and American missiles deployed since the late 1970s but also the whole of the Soviet strategic theater missile forces that had faced Europe and Asia for three decades. What is more, the treaty instituted an intrusive and extensive system of verification. In 1988 Gorbachev proposed conventional arms reductions in Europe under a plan that would abandon the Soviet Union's numerical superiority, and he also launched a substantial unilateral force reduction. In 1988–89 he withdrew all Soviet forces from Afghanistan. At about the same time, he encouraged the ouster of the old communist leadership in Eastern Europe and accepted the transition of the former Soviet-allied states into noncommunist neutral states. By 1990 Gorbachev had signed the CFE Treaty accepting Soviet conventional arms levels in Europe to the Urals that were much lower than the levels for NATO. By that time he had not only accepted Germany's reunification but also the membership of a unified Germany in NATO. Within another year he had jettisoned the Warsaw Pact and the socialist bloc and agreed in START I to verified deep cuts in strategic nuclear forces.

Although Gorbachev had not expected the complete collapse of communism (and Soviet influence) in Eastern Europe that occurred in 1989 and 1990, he had made clear to the Twenty-seventh Congress of the Soviet Communist Party as early as February 1986 that a new conception of security had to replace the previous one, and that the confrontation of the Cold War had to end. No longer speaking in Leninist terms of contending socialist and capitalist words, Gorbachev spoke instead of one world, an "interdependent and in many ways integral world." He denied that any country could find security in military power, either for defense or deterrence. Security, he said, could only be found through political means, and only on a mutual basis. The goal, he asserted, should be the "creation of a comprehensive system of international security" that embraced economic, ecological, and humanitarian, as well as political and military, elements. Hence, the Soviet decision to give new support to the United Nations, including collective peacekeeping, and to join the world economic system. Hence, the cooperative Soviet efforts to resolve regional conflicts in Central America, Southern Africa, the Horn of Africa, Cambodia, Afghanistan, and the Middle East, not to mention the Soviet Union's support for the collective UN-endorsed action against Iraq in 1991. And hence Moscow's willingness to countenance the dissolution of the Eastern European alliance and socialist commonwealth, which had been fashioned to meet security requirements and ideological imperatives that had now been abandoned. These moves were all prefigured in the new approach that Gorbachev laid down in early 1986.

In the final analysis, only a Soviet leader could have ended the Cold War because it rested on the Marxist-Leninist assumption of a struggle to the end of two social-economic-political systems, the capitalist world and the socialist (communist) world. Gorbachev set out deliberately to end the Cold War. Although earlier Soviet leaders had understood the impermissibility of war in the nuclear age, Gorbachev was the first to recognize that reciprocal political accommodation, rather than military power for deterrence or "counterdeterrence," was the defining core of the Soviet Union's relationship with the rest of the world. He accepted the idea of building relations on the basis of a "balance of interests" among nations, rather than pursuing maximization of the power of one state or bloc on the basis of a "correlation of forces," a balance of power. The conclusions that Gorbachev drew from this recognition, and consequent Soviet actions, finally permitted the Iron Curtain to be dismantled and the global confrontation of the Cold War to be ended.

Gorbachev, to be sure, seriously underestimated the task of changing the Soviet Union, and this led to policy errors that contributed to the failure of his program for the transformation of Soviet society and polity. His vision of a resurrected socialism built on the foundation of successful *perestroika* and *demokratizatsiya* was never a realistic possibility. He knew deep economic reform was necessary, and he tried; he did not find the solution. A revitalized Soviet political union was perhaps beyond realization as well. The reasons for Gorbachev's failure were primarily objective, not subjective; that is, they were real obstacles he was unable to overcome—internal opposition, powerful inertia, intractable problems of economic transformation, and the politically charged problem of redefining a democratic relationship between a traditional imperial center and the rest of the country, *not* unwillingness or inability to give up or modify his ideological presuppositions and predispositions.

In the external political arena, however, Gorbachev both understood and successfully charted the course that led to the end of the Cold War, even though in this area, too, at first he had an exaggerated expectation of the capacity for reform on the part of the communist governments in Eastern Europe.

As the preceding discussion suggests, the American role in ending the Cold War was necessary but not primary. There are several reasons for this conclusion, but the basic one is that the American worldview was derivative of the communist worldview. Containment was hollow without an expansionist power to contain. In this sense, it was the Soviet threat, partly real and partly imagined, that generated the American dedication to waging the Cold War, regardless of what revisionist American historians have to say. These historians point to Washington's atomic diplomacy and to its various overt and covert political, economic, paramilitary, and military campaigns. Supposedly designed to counter a Soviet threat, they argue, these initiatives actually entailed an expansion of American influence and dominion.

The revisionist interpretation errs in attributing imperial initiative and design to American diplomacy, but it is not entirely wrong. American policymakers were guilty of accepting far too much of the communist worldview in constructing an anticommunist antipode, and of being too ready to fight fire with fire. Indeed, once the Cold War became the dominant factor in global politics (and above all in American and Soviet perceptions), each side viewed every development around the world in terms of its relationship to that great struggle, and each was inclined to act according to a self-fulfilling prophecy. The Americans, for example, often viewed local and regional conflicts of indigenous origins as Cold War battles and acted on that assumption. Like the Soviets, they distrusted the neutral and nonaligned nations and were always more comfortable when countries around the world were either their allies or the satellites and surrogates of the other side. Thus, many traditional diplomatic relationships not essentially attendant on the superpower rivalry were swept into the vortex of the Cold War, at least in the eyes of the protagonists—and partly in fact as a result of their actions.

It is true that the Cold War led in some instances to constructive American involvements. The Marshall Plan is a prime example, not to mention American support for some democratic political movements, and for the Congress for Culture Freedom and the liberal journal *Encounter*. But other overt and covert involvements were more frequently less constructive, and often subversive, of real liberalism and democracy. Apart from the loss of American lives and treasure in such misplaced ventures as the Vietnam War and in the massive overinvestment in weaponry, one of the worst effects of forcing all world developments onto the procrustean bed of the Cold War was the distortion of America's understanding and values. By dividing the globe into a communist Evil Empire controlled by Moscow and a Free World led by Washington, American policymakers promoted numerous antidemocratic regimes into rewarded members of the Free World as long as they were anti-communist (or even rhetorically anticommunist). Washington also used the exigencies of the Cold War to justify assassination plots, to negotiate deals with war lords, drug lords, and terrorists, and to transform anticommunist insurgents, however corrupt or antidemocratic, into "freedom fighters." Alliance ties, military basing rights, and support for insurgencies were routinely given priority over such other American objectives as the promotion of nuclear nonproliferation, economic development, human rights, and democracy.

Parallel Soviet sins were at least as great. While Soviet foreign assistance to socialist and "progressive" countries was sometimes constructive (building of the Aswan Dam, for example, or economic assistance to India), it was also skewed by the ideological expectation of moving the world toward communism and by expectations of Soviet geopolitical advantage in the Cold War. Often dictatorial regimes, "marxist" or "socialist" only according to the cynical claims of their leaders, provided the basis for Soviet support, as with Siad Barre in Somalia, for example, or Mengistu in Ethiopia. The Soviet Union also engaged in many covert political operations and lent support to national liberation movements (some authentic, others less so) that sometimes included elements engaged in terrorism. On both sides, then, ideological beliefs combined with geopolitical considerations to fuel a Cold War struggle that left many victims in its wake.

Although the decisive factor in the end of the Cold War was a change in these beliefs, it is worth repeating that the Soviet leaders could discard a long-encrusted and familiar ideology only because of a powerful transformation in the way Gorbachev and some colleagues perceived reality, and because they were ready to adapt domestic and foreign policies to the new perception. Over time, the extent and depth of these changes became inescapable and their validity compelling. Earlier I noted some of the cumulative changes in Soviet foreign policy that brought the Cold War to an end. The critical culminating event was the Revolution of '89.

The year between the destruction of the Berlin Wall in November 1989 and the European conference in Paris in November 1990 saw the removal of the most important concrete manifestation of the Cold War—the division of Germany and Europe. The division of Europe had symbolized the global battle between the two ideological and geopolitical camps in the years immediately after World War II. When that division came to an end, the consequences for the international balance of power were so substantial that even the most hardened cold warriors in the West were forced to acknowledge that the Cold War had ended—even before the collapse of communist rule in the Soviet Union or of the Soviet Union itself. Moreover, the Revolution of '89 in Eastern Europe was decisive not only in demonstrating that the ideological underpinnings of the Cold War had been removed but also in shifting the actual balance of power. The removal of Soviet military power from Eastern Europe dissolved the threat to Western Europe and also restored a reunified Europe to the center of the world political state. Russia and even the United States, though still closely linked to Europe, have now become less central.

## 28  The Long Peace: Elements of Stability in the Postwar International System

### JOHN LEWIS GADDIS

The Cold War saw a great buildup of armaments, numerous civil wars, revolution, ethnic and religious violence, intense ideological rivalry, and a global divide among the superpowers. Yet despite all the reasons that might have prompted a major war between the United States and the Soviet Union, none ever occurred. This fact, in and of itself, is worthy of attention. The absence of war is perhaps even more remarkable when it is considered that the end of the Second World War was not followed by a formal peace settlement as World War I had been. Rather, upon achieving success, the victors immediately began to clash among themselves and soon came to regard each other as their principal enemy.

In the following article, which was written three years before the Berlin Wall fell, John Lewis Gaddis provides what could be considered a counterintuitive analysis of the Cold War, maintaining that the previous 40 years were to be more accurately characterized as a time of peace than as a time of war, albeit Cold War. He explains why this great war between the United States and the Soviet Union did not happen, and why it appeared that it would not in the future, positing several factors, such as deterrence and bipolarity, that contributed to global stability between the superpowers.

Gaddis suggests that this long peace produced a number of unwritten "rules" that informed the conduct of the superpowers and helped to keep the peace. This recognition, though a product of a historical perspective that had the luxury of 40 years of Cold War experience to look at, highlights one of the concerns of contemporary U.S. foreign policy. American leaders and scholars have little idea of what the "rules" are that govern and inform international conflict in a world where terrorism and WMD proliferation represent the greatest fears and vulnerabilities of the United States.

---

I should like to begin this essay with a fable. Once upon a time, there was a great war that involved the slaughter of millions upon millions of people. When, after years of fighting, one side finally prevailed over the other and the war ended, everyone said that it must go down in history as the last great war ever fought. To that end, the victorious nations sent all of their wisest men to a great peace conference, where they were given the task of drawing up a settlement that would be so carefully designed, so unquestionably fair to all concerned, that it would eliminate war as a phenomenon of human existence. Unfortunately, that settlement lasted only twenty years.

There followed yet another great war involving the slaughter of millions upon millions of people. When, after years of fighting, one side finally prevailed over the other and the war ended, everyone said that it must go down in history as the last great war ever fought. To everyone's horror, though, the victors in that conflict immediately fell to quarreling among themselves, with the result that no peace conference ever took place. Within a few years each of the major victors had come to regard each other, and not their former enemies, as the principal threat to their survival; each sought to ensure that survival by developing weapons capable, at least in theory, of ending the survival of everyone on earth. Paradoxically, that arrangement lasted twice as long as the first one, and as the fable ended showed no signs of coming apart anytime soon.

It is, of course, just a fable, and as a general rule one ought not to take fables too seriously. There are times, though, when fables can illuminate reality more sharply than conventional forms of explanation are able to do, and this may well be one of them. For it is the case that the post-World War II system of international relations, which nobody designed or even thought could last for very long, which was based not upon the dictates of morality and justice but rather upon an arbitrary and strikingly artificial division of the world into spheres of influence, and which incorporated within it some of the most bitter and persistent antagonisms short of war in modern history, has now survived twice as long as the far more carefully designed World War I settlement, has approximately equaled in longevity the great 19th-century international systems of Metternich and Bismarck, and unlike those earlier systems after four decades of existence shows no perceptible signs of disintegration. It is, or ought to be, enough to make one think.

To be sure, the term "peace" is not the first that comes to mind when one recalls the history of the Cold War. That period, after all, has seen the greatest accumulation of armaments the world has ever known, a whole series of protracted and devastating limited wars, an abundance of revolutionary, ethnic, religious, and civil violence, as well as some of the deepest and most intractable ideological rivalries in human experience. Nor have those more ancient scourges—famine, disease, poverty, injustice—by any means disappeared from the face of the earth. Is it not stretching things a bit, one might well ask, to take the moral and spiritual desert in which the nations of the world conduct their affairs, and call it "peace"?

It is, of course, but that is just the point. Given all the conceivable reasons for having had a major war in the past four decades—reasons that in any other age would have provided ample justification for such a war—it seems worthy of comment that there has not in fact been one; that despite the unjust and wholly artificial character of the post-World War II settlement, it has now persisted for the better part of half a century. That may not be grounds for celebration, but it is at least grounds for investigation: for trying to comprehend how this great power peace has managed to survive for so long in the face of so much provocation, and for thinking about what might be done to perpetuate that situation. For, after all, we could do worse.

## II

Any such investigation should begin by distinguishing the structure of the international system in question from the behavior of the nations that make it up.[1] The reason for this is simple: behavior alone will not ensure stability if the structural prerequisites for it are absent, but structure can under certain circumstances impose stability even when its behavioral prerequisites are unpromising.

Now, bipolarity may seem to many today—as it did forty years ago—an awkward and dangerous way to organize world politics.[2] Simple geometric logic would suggest that a system resting upon three or more points of support would be more stable than one resting upon two. But politics is not geometry: the passage of time and the accumulation of experience has made clear certain structural elements of stability in the bipolar system of international relations that were not present in the multipolar systems that preceded it:

(1) The postwar bipolar system realistically reflected the facts of where military power resided at the end of World War II—and where it still does today, for that matter. In this sense, it differed markedly from the settlement of 1919, which made so little effort to accommodate the interests of Germany and Soviet Russia. It is true that in other categories of power—notably the economic—states have since arisen capable of challenging or even surpassing the Soviet Union and the United States in the production of certain specific commodities. But as the *political* position of nations like West Germany, Brazil, Japan, South Korea, Taiwan, and Hong Kong suggests, the ability to make video recorders, motorcycles, even automobiles and steel efficiently has yet to translate into anything approaching the capacity of Washington or Moscow to shape events in the world as a whole.

(2) The post-1945 bipolar structure was a simple one that did not require sophisticated leadership to maintain it. The great multipolar systems of the 19th century collapsed in large part because of their intricacy: they required a Metternich or a Bismarck to hold them together, and when statesmen of that calibre were no longer available, they tended to come apart.[3] Neither the Soviet nor the American political system has been geared toward identifying statesmen of comparable prowess and entrusting them with responsibility; demonstrated skill in the conduct of foreign policy has hardly been a major prerequisite for leadership in either country. And yet, a bipolar structure of international relations—because of the inescapably high stakes involved for its two major actors—tends, regardless of the personalities involved, to induce in them a sense of caution and restraint, and to discourage irresponsibility. "It is not," Kenneth Waltz notes, "that one entertains the utopian hope that all future American and Russian rules will combine in their persons ... nearly perfect virtues, but rather that the pressures of a bipolar world strongly encourage them to act internationally in ways better than their characters may lead one to expect."[4]

(3) Because of its relatively simple structure, alliances in this bipolar system have tended to be more stable than they had been in the 19th century and in the 1919–39 period. It is striking to consider that the North Atlantic

Treaty Organization has now equaled in longevity the most durable of the pre-World War I alliances, that between Germany and Austria-Hungary; it has lasted almost twice as long as the Franco-Russian alliance, and certainly much longer than any of the tenuous alignments of the interwar period. Its principal rival, the Warsaw Treaty Organization, has been in existence for almost as long. The reason for this is simple: alliances, in the end, are the product of insecurity;[5] so long as the Soviet Union and the United States each remain for the other and for their respective clients the major source of danger in the world, neither super-power encounters very much difficulty in maintaining the coalitions it controls. In a multipolar system, sources of insecurity can vary in much more complicated ways; hence it is not surprising to find alliances shifting to accommodate these variations.[6]

(4) At the same time, though, and probably because of the overall stability of the basic alliance systems, defections from both the American and Soviet coalitions—China, Cuba, Vietnam, Iran, and Nicaragua, in the case of the Americans; Yugoslavia, Albania, Egypt, Somalia, and China again in the case of the Russians—have been tolerated without the major disruptions that might have attended such changes in a more delicately balanced multipolar system. The fact that a state the size of China was able to reverse its alignment twice during the Cold War without any more dramatic effect upon the position of the super-powers says something about the stability bipolarity brings; compare this record with the impact, prior to 1914, of such apparently minor episodes as Austria's annexation of Bosnia and Herzegovina, or the question of who was to control Morocco. It is a curious consequence of bipolarity that although alliances are more durable than in a multipolar system, defections are at the same time more tolerable.[7]

In short, without anyone's having designed it, and without any attempt whatever to consider the requirements of justice, the nations of the postwar era lucked into a system of international relations that, because it has been based upon realities of power, has served the cause of order—if not justice—better than one might have expected.

## III

But if the structure of bipolarity in itself encouraged stability, so too did certain inherent characteristics of the bilateral Soviet-American relationship.

It has long been an assumption of classical liberalism that the more extensive the contacts that take place between nations, the greater are the chances for peace. Economic interdependence, it has been argued, makes war unlikely because nations who have come to rely upon one another for vital commodities cannot afford it. Cultural exchange, it has been suggested, causes peoples to become more sensitive to each other's concerns, and hence reduces the likelihood of misunderstandings. "People to people" contacts, it has been assumed, make it possible for nations to "know" one another better; the danger of war between them is, as a result, correspondingly reduced.[8]

These are pleasant things to believe, but there is remarkably little historical evidence to validate them. As Kenneth Waltz has pointed out, "the fiercest civil wars and the bloodiest international ones are fought within arenas populated by highly similar people whose affairs are closely knit."[9] Consider, as examples, the costliest military conflicts of the past century and a half, using the statistics conveniently available now through the University of Michigan "Correlates of War" project: of the ten bloodiest interstate wars, every one of them grew out of conflicts between countries that either directly adjoined one another, or were involved actively in trade with one another.[10] Certainly economic interdependence did little to prevent Germany, France, Britain, Russia, and Austria-Hungary from going to war in 1914; nor did the fact that the United States was Japan's largest trading partner deter that country from attacking Pearl Harbor in 1941. Since 1945, there have been more civil wars than interstate wars; that fact alone should be sufficient to call into question the proposition that interdependence necessarily breeds peace.

The Russian-American relationship, to a remarkable degree for two nations so extensively involved with the rest of the world, has been one of mutual *in*dependence. The simple fact that they occupy opposite sides of the earth has had something to do with this: geographical remoteness from one another has provided little opportunity for the emergence of irredentist grievances comparable in importance to historic disputes over, say, Alsace-Lorraine, or the Polish Corridor, or the West Bank, the Gaza Strip and Jerusalem. In the few areas where Soviet and American forces—or their proxies—have come into direct contact, they have erected artificial barriers like the Korean demilitarized zone, or the Berlin Wall, perhaps in unconscious recognition of an American poet's rather chilly precept that "good fences make good neighbors."

Nor have the two nations been economically dependent upon one another in any critical way. Certainly the United States requires nothing in the form of imports from the Soviet Union that it cannot obtain elsewhere. The situation is different for the Russians, to be sure, but even though the Soviet Union imports large quantities of food from the United States—and would like to import advanced technology as well—it is far from being wholly dependent upon these items, as the failure of recent attempts to change Soviet behavior by denying them has shown. The relative invulnerability of Russians and Americans to one another in the economic sphere may be frustrating to their respective policy-makers, but it is probably fortunate, from the standpoint of international stability, that the two most powerful nations in the world are also its two most self-sufficient.

It may well be, then, that the extent to which the Soviet Union and the United States have been independent of one another rather than interdependent—the fact that there have been so few points of economic leverage available to each, the fact that two such dissimilar people have had so few opportunities for interaction—has in itself constituted a structural support for stability in relations between the two countries, whatever their respective governments have actually done.

## V

Stability in international systems is only partly a function of structure, though; it depends as well upon the conscious behavior of the nations that make them up. Even if the World War II settlement had corresponded to the distribution of power in the world, even if the Russian-American relationship had been one of minimal interdependence, even if domestic constraints had not created difficulties, stability in the postwar era still might not have resulted if there had been, among either of the dominant powers in the system, the same willingness to risk war that has existed at other times in the past.

For whatever reason, it has to be acknowledged that statesmen of the post-1945 super-powers have, compared to their precedessors, been exceedingly cautious in risking war with one another.[11] In order to see this point, one need only run down the list of crises in Soviet-American relations since the end of World War II: Iran, 1946; Greece, 1947; Berlin and Czechoslovakia, 1948; Korea, 1950; the East Berlin riots, 1953; the Hungarian uprising, 1956; Berlin again, 1958–59; the U-2 incident, 1960; Berlin again, 1961; the Cuban missile crisis, 1962; Czechoslovakia again, 1968; the Yom Kippur war, 1973; Afghanistan, 1979; Poland, 1981; the Korean airliner incident, 1983—one need only run down this list to see how many occasions there have been in relations between Washington and Moscow that in almost any other age, and among almost any other antagonists, would sooner or later have produced war.

That they have not cannot be chalked up to the invariably pacific temperament of the nations involved: the United States participated in eight international wars involving a thousand or more battlefield deaths between 1815 and 1980; Russia participated in nineteen.[12] Nor can this restraint be attributed to any unusual qualities of leadership on either side: the vision and competency of postwar Soviet and American statesmen does not appear to have differed greatly from that of their precedessors. Nor does weariness growing out of participation in two world wars fully explain this unwillingness to resort to arms in their dealings with one another: during the postwar era both nations have employed force against third parties—in the case of the United States in Korea and Vietnam; in the case of the Soviet Union in Afghanistan—for protracted periods of time, and at great cost.

It seems inescapable that what has really made the difference in inducing this unaccustomed caution has been the workings of the nuclear deterrent.[13] Consider, for a moment, what the effect of this mechanism would be on a statesman from either super-power who might be contemplating war. In the past, the horrors and costs of wars could be forgotten with the passage of time. Generations like the one of 1914 had little sense of what the Napoleonic Wars—or even the American Civil War—had revealed about the brutality, expense, and duration of military conflict. But the existence of nuclear weapons—and, more to the point, the fact that we have direct evidence of what they can do when used against human beings[14]—has given this generation a painfully vivid awareness of the realities of war that no previous generation has had. It is difficult, given this awareness, to generate the optimism that historical experience tells us prepares the way for war; pessimism, it appears, is a permanent accompaniment to our thinking about war, and that, as Blainey reminds us, is a cause of peace.

That same pessimism has provided the super-powers with powerful inducements to control crises resulting from the risk-taking of third parties. It is worth recalling that World War I grew out of the unsuccessful management of a situation neither created nor desired by any of the major actors in the international system. There were simply no mechanisms to put a lid on escalation: to force each nation to balance the short-term temptation to exploit opportunities against the long-term danger that things might get out of hand.[15] The nuclear deterrent provides that mechanism today, and as a result the United States and the Soviet Union have successfully managed a whole series of crises—most notably in the Middle East—that grew out of the actions of neither but that could have involved them both.

None of this is to say, of course, that war cannot occur: if the study of history reveals anything at all it is that one ought to expect, sooner or later, the unexpected. Nor is it to say that the nuclear deterrent could not function equally well with half, or a fourth, or even an eighth of the nuclear weapons now in the arsenals of the super-powers. Nor is it intended to deprecate the importance of refraining from steps that might destabilize the existing stalemate, whether through the search for technological breakthroughs that might provide a decisive edge over the other side, or through so mechanical a duplication of what the other side has that one fails to take into account one's own probably quite different security requirements, or through strategies that rely upon the first use of nuclear weapons in the interest of achieving economy, forgetting the far more fundamental systemic interest in maintaining the tradition, dating back four decades now, of never actually employing these weapons for military purposes.

I am suggesting, though, that the development of nuclear weapons has had, on balance, a stabilizing effect on the postwar international system. They have served to discourage the process of escalation that has, in other eras, too casually led to war. They have had a sobering effect upon a whole range of statesmen of varying degrees of responsibility and capability. They have forced national leaders, every day, to confront the reality of what war is really like, indeed to confront the prospect of their own mortality, and that, for those who seek ways to avoid war, is no bad thing.

## VI

But although nuclear deterrence is the most important behavioral mechanism that has sustained the post-World War II international system, it is by no means the only one. Indeed, the very technology that has made it possible to deliver nuclear weapons anywhere on the face of the earth has functioned also to lower greatly the danger of surprise attack, thereby supplementing the self-regulating features of deterrence with the assurance that comes from knowing a great deal more than in the past about adversary capabilities. I refer here to what might be called the "reconnaissance revolution," a development that may well rival in importance the "nuclear revolution" that preceded it, but one that rarely gets the attention it deserves.

The point was made earlier that nations tend to start wars on the basis of calculated assessments that they have the power to prevail. But it was suggested as well that they have often been wrong about this: they either have failed to anticipate the nature and the costs of war itself, or they have misjudged the intentions and capabilities of the adversary they have chosen to confront.[16]

Now, it would be foolish to argue that Americans and Russians have become anymore skillful than they ever were at discerning the other's *intentions:* clearly the United States invasion of Grenada surprised Moscow as much as the Soviet invasion of Afghanistan surprised Washington. The capacity of each nation to behave in ways that seem perfectly logical to it but quite unfathomable to the other remains about what it has been throughout the entire Cold War. But both sides are able—and indeed have been able for at least two decades—to evaluate each other's *capabilities* to a degree that is totally unprecedented in the history of relations between great powers.

What has made this possible, of course, has been the development of the reconnaissance satellite, a device that if rumors are correct allows the reading of automobile license plates or newspaper headlines from a hundred or more miles out in space, together with the equally important custom that has evolved among the super-powers of allowing these objects to pass unhindered over their territories.[17] The effect has been to give each side a far more accurate view of the other's military capabilities—and, to some degree, economic capabilities as well—than could have been provided by an entire phalanx of the best spies in the long history of espionage. The resulting intelligence does not rule out altogether the possibility of surprise attack, but it does render it far less likely, at least as far as the super-powers are concerned. And that is no small matter, if one considers the number of wars in history—from the Trojan War down through Pearl Harbor—in the origins of which deception played a major role.[18]

The "reconnaissance revolution" also corrects, at least to an extent, the asymmetry imposed upon Soviet-American relations by the two countries' sharply different forms of political and social organization. Throughout most of the early Cold War years the Soviet Union enjoyed all the advantages of a closed society in concealing its capabilities from the West; the United States and its allies, in turn, found it difficult to keep anything secret for very long.[19] That problem still exists, but the ability now to see both visually and electronically into almost every part of the Soviet Union helps to compensate for it. And, of course, virtually none of the limited progress the two countries have made in the field of arms control would have been possible had Americans and Russians not tacitly agreed to the use of reconnaissance satellites and other surveillance techniques to monitor compliance[20]; clearly any future progress in that field will depend heavily upon these devices as well.

## VII

The relationship between the Soviet Union and the United States has not been free from ideological rivalries; it could be argued, in fact, that these are among the most ideological nations on the face of the earth.[21] Certainly their respective ideologies could hardly have been more antithetical, given the self-proclaimed intention of one to overthrow the other.[22] And yet, since their emergence as super-powers, both nations have demonstrated an impressive capacity to subordinate antagonistic ideological interests to a common goal of preserving international order. The reasons for this are worth examining.

If there were ever a moment at which the priorities of order overcame those of ideology, it would appear to be the point at which Soviet leaders decided that war would no longer advance the cause of revolution. That clearly had not been Lenin's position: international conflict, for him, was good or evil according to whether it accelerated or retarded the demise of capitalism.[23] Stalin's attitude on this issue was more ambivalent: he encouraged talk of an "inevitable conflict" between the "two camps" of communism and capitalism in the years immediately following World War II, but he also appears shortly before his death to have anticipated the concept of "peaceful coexistence."[24] It was left to Georgii Malenkov to admit publicly, shortly after Stalin's death, that a nuclear war would mean "the destruction of world civilization"; Nikita Khrushchev subsequently refined this idea (which he had initially condemned) into the proposition that the interests of world revolution, as well as those of the Soviet state, would be better served by working within the existing international order than by trying to overthrow it.[25]

The proliferation of nuclear capabilities on both sides had confirmed Malenkov's conclusion that in any future war between the great powers there would be no victors at all, whether capitalist or communist. "[T]he atomic bomb," Soviet leaders reminded their more militant Chinese comrades in 1963, "does not observe the class principle."[26]

The effect was to transform a state which, if ideology alone had governed, should have sought a complete restructuring of the existing international system, into one for whom that system now seemed to have definite benefits, within which it now sought to function, and for whom the goal of overthrowing capitalism had been postponed to some vague and indefinite point in the future. Without this moderation of ideological objectives, it is difficult to see how the stability that has characterized great power relations since the end of World War II could have been possible.

It is no easy matter to explain why Americans did not commit themselves to the eradication of Soviet "totalitarianism" with the same single-minded determination they had earlier applied to German and Japanese "totalitarianism." One reason, of course, would have been the daunting prospect of attempting to occupy a country the size of the Soviet Union, when compared with the more manageable adversaries of World War II.[27] Another was the fact that, despite the hostility that had developed since 1945, American officials did not regard their Russian counterparts as irredeemable: the very purpose of "containment" had been to change the *psychology* of the Soviet leadership; but not as had been the case with Germany and Japan, the leadership itself.[28]

But Washington's aversion to an "unconditional surrender" doctrine for the Soviet Union stemmed from yet another less obvious consideration: it had quickly become clear to American policy-makers, after World War II, that insistence on the total defeat of Germany and Japan had profoundly destabilized the postwar balance of power. Only by assuming responsibility for the rehabilitation of these former enemies as well as the countries they had ravaged had the United States been able to restore equilibrium, and even then it had been clear that the American role in this regard would have to be a continuing one. It was no accident that the doctrine of "unconditional surrender" came under severe criticism, after 1945, from a new school of "realist" geopoliticians given to viewing international stability in terms of the wary toleration of adversaries rather than, as a point of principle, their annihilation.[29]

Largely as a result of such reasoning, American officials at no point during the history of the Cold War seriously contemplated, as a deliberate political objective, the elimination of the Soviet Union as a major force in world affairs.

All of this would appear to confirm, then, the proposition that systemic interests tend to take precedence over ideological interests.[30] Both the Soviet ideological aversion to capitalism and the American ideological aversion to totalitarianism could have produced policies—and indeed had produced policies in the past—aimed at the complete overthrow of their respective adversaries. That such ideological impulses could be muted to the extent they have been during the past four decades testifies to the stake both Washington and Moscow have developed in preserving the existing international system: the moderation of ideologies must be considered, then, along with nuclear deterrence and reconnaissance, as a major self-regulating mechanism of postwar politics.

## VIII

The question still arises, though: how can order emerge from a system that functions without any superior authority?

These "rules" are, of course, implicit rather than explicit: they grow out of a mixture of custom, precedent, and mutual interest that takes shape quite apart from the realm of public rhetoric, diplomacy, or international law. They require the passage of time to become effective; they depend, for that effectiveness, upon the extent to which successive generations of national leadership on each side find them useful. They certainly do not reflect any agreed-upon standard of international morality: indeed they often violate principles of "justice" adhered to by one side or the other. But these "rules" have played an important role in maintaining the international system that has been in place these past four decades: without them the correlation one would normally anticipate between hostility and instability would have become more exact than it has in fact been since 1945.

No two observers of super-power behavior would express these "rules" in precisely the same way; indeed it may well be that their very vagueness has made them more acceptable than they otherwise might have been to the nations that have followed them. What follows is nothing more than my own list, derived from an attempt to identify *regularities* in the postwar Soviet-American relationship whose pattern neither side could now easily disrupt.

(1) *Respect spheres of influence.* Neither Russians nor Americans officially admit to having such "spheres," but in fact much of the history of the Cold War can be written in terms of the efforts both have made to consolidate and extend them. But what is important from the standpoint of super-power "rules" is the fact that, although neither side has ever publicly endorsed the other's right to a sphere of influence, neither has ever directly challenged it either.

Thus, despite publicly condemning it, the United States never attempted seriously to undo Soviet control in Eastern Europe; Moscow reciprocated by tolerating, though never openly approving of, Washington's influence in Western Europe, the Mediterranean, the Near East, and Latin America. A similar pattern held up in East Asia, where the Soviet Union took no more action to oppose United States control over occupied Japan than the Truman administration did to repudiate the Yalta agreement, which left the Soviet Union dominant, at least for the moment, on the Northeast Asian mainland.[31]

(2) *Avoid direct military confrontation.* It is remarkable, in retrospect, that at no point during the long history of the Cold War have Soviet and American military forces engaged each other directly in sustained hostilities. The super-powers have fought three major limited wars since 1945, but in no case with each other: the possibility of direct Soviet-American military involvement was greatest—although it never happened—during the Korean War; it was much more remote in Vietnam and has remained so in Afghanistan as well. In those few situations where Soviet and American military units have confronted one another directly—the 1948 Berlin blockade, the construction of the Berlin Wall in 1961, and the Cuban missile crisis the following year—great care was taken on both sides to avoid incidents that might have triggered hostilities.[32]

Where the super-powers have sought to expand or to retain areas of control, they have tended to resort to the use of proxies or other indirect means to accomplish this: examples would include the Soviet Union's decision to sanction a North Korean invasion of South Korea, and its more recent reliance on Cuban troops to promote its interests in sub-Saharan Africa; on the American side covert intervention has been a convenient (if not invariably successful) means of defending spheres of influence. In a curious way, clients and proxies have come to serve as buffers, allowing Russians and Americans to pursue their competition behind a facade of "deniability" that minimizes the risks of open—and presumably less manageable—confrontation.

The two super-powers have also been careful not to allow the disputes of third parties to embroil them directly: this pattern has been most evident in the Middle East, which has witnessed no fewer than five wars between Israel and its Arab neighbors since 1948; but it holds as well for the

India-Pakistan conflicts of 1965 and 1971, and for the more recent—and much more protracted—struggle between Iran and Iraq. The contrast between this long tradition of restraint and the casualness with which great powers in the past have allowed the quarrels of others to become their own could hardly be more obvious.[33]

(3) *Use nuclear weapons only as an ultimate resort.* One of the most significant—though least often commented upon—of the super-power "rules" has been the tradition that has evolved, since 1945, of maintaining a sharp distinction between conventional and nuclear weapons, and of reserving the military use of the latter only for the extremity of total war.

This pattern of caution in the use of nuclear weapons did not develop solely, as one might have expected, from the prospect of retaliation. As early as 1950, at a time when the Soviet Union had only just tested an atomic bomb and had only the most problematic methods of delivering it, the United States had nonetheless ruled out the use of its own atomic weapons in Korea because of the opposition of its allies, the fear of an adverse reaction in the world at large, and uncertainty as to whether they would produce the desired military effect. And despite his public position favoring such use, Eisenhower would repeatedly, in the years that followed, reject recommendations to resort to them in limited war situations.[34]

It was precisely this sense that nuclear weapons were qualitatively different from other weapons[35] that most effectively deterred their employment by the United States during the first decade of the Cold War, a period in which the tradition of "non-use" had not yet taken hold, within which ample opportunities for their use existed, and during which the possibility of Soviet retaliation could not have been great. The idea of a discrete "threshold" between nuclear and conventional weapons, therefore, may owe more to the moral—and public relations—sensibilities of Washington officials than to any actual fear of escalation. By the time a credible Soviet retaliatory capability was in place, at the end of the 1950s, the "threshold" concept was equally firmly fixed: one simply did not cross it short of all-out war.

(4) *Prefer predictable anomaly over unpredictable rationality.* One of the most curious features of the Cold War has been the extent to which the super-powers—and their respective clients, who have had little choice in the matter—have tolerated a whole series of awkward, artificial, and, on the surface at least, unstable regional arrangements: the division of Germany is, of course, the most obvious example; others would include the Berlin Wall, the position of West Berlin itself within East Germany, the arbitrary and ritualized partition of the Korean peninsula, the existence of an avowed Soviet satellite some ninety miles off the coast of Florida, and, not least, the continued functioning of an important American naval base

within it. There is to all of these arrangements an appearance of wildly illogical improvisation: none of them could conceivably have resulted, it seems, from any rational and premeditated design.

And yet, at another level, they have had a kind of logic after all: the fact that these jerry-built but rigidly maintained arrangements have lasted for so long suggests an unwillingness on the part of the super-powers to trade familiarity for unpredictability. To try to rationalize the German, Korean, or Cuban anomalies would, it has long been acknowledged, create the unnerving possibility of an uncertain result; far better, Soviet and American leaders have consistently agreed, to perpetuate the anomalies rather than to risk the possibilities for destabilization inherent in trying to resolve them. For however unnatural and unjust these situations may be for the people whose lives they directly affect, it seems nonetheless incontestable that the super-powers' preference for predictability over rationality has, on the whole, enhanced more than it has reduced prospects for a stable relationship.

(5) *Do not seek to undermine the other side's leadership.* The death of Stalin, in March, 1953, set off a flurry of proposals within the United States government for exploiting vulnerabilities inside the Soviet Union that were thought certain to result, and yet, by the following month President Eisenhower was encouraging Stalin's successors to join in a major new effort to control the arms race and reduce the danger of war.[36]

There have been repeated leadership crises in both the United States and the Soviet Union since Stalin's death: one thinks especially of the decline and ultimate deposition of Khrushchev following the Cuban Missile Crisis, of the Johnson administration's all-consuming fixation with Vietnam, or the collapse of Nixon's authority as a result of Watergate, and of the recent paralysis in the Kremlin brought about by the illness and death of three Soviet leaders within less than three years. And yet, in none of these instances can one discern a concerted effort by the unaffected side to exploit the other's vulnerability.

# IX

The Cold War, with all of its rivalries, anxieties, and unquestionable dangers, has produced the longest period of stability in relations among the great powers that the world has known in this century; it now compares favorably as well with some of the longest periods of great power stability in all of modern history. We may argue among ourselves as to whether or not we can legitimately call this "peace": it is not, I daresay, what most of us have in mind when we use that term. But I am not at all certain that the contemporaries of Metternich or Bismarck would have regarded their eras as "peaceful" either, even though historians looking back on those eras today clearly do.

Who is to say, therefore, how the historians a century from now—if there are any left by then—will look back on us? Is it not at least plausible that they will see our era, not as "the Cold War" at all, but rather, like those ages of Metternich and Bismarck, as a rare and fondly remembered "Long Peace"? Wishful thinking? Speculation through a rose-tinted word processor? Perhaps. But would it not behoove us to give at least as much attention to the question of how this might happen—to the elements in the contemporary international system that might make it happen—as we do to the fear that it may not?

## Notes

1. Waltz, *Theory of International Politics*, pp. 73–78; Gilpin, *War and Change in World Politics*, pp. 85–88.
2. Among those who have emphasized the instability of bipolar systems, are Morgenthau, *Politics Among Nations*, pp. 350–54; Wright, *A Study of War*, pp. 763–64. See also Blainey, *The Causes of War*, pp. 110–11.
3. Henry Kissinger has written two classic accounts dealing with the importance of individual leadership in sustaining international systems. See his *A World Restored* (New York: 1957), on Metternich; and, on Bismarck, "The White Revolutionary: Reflections on Bismarck," *Daedalus*, XCVII (Summer, 1968), pp. 888–924. For a somewhat different perspective on Bismarck's role, see George F. Kennan, *The Decline of Bismarck's European Order: Franco-Russian Relations, 1875–1890* (Princeton: 1979), especially pp. 421–22.
4. Waltz, *Theory of International Politics*, p. 176. On the tendency of unstable systemic structures to induce irresponsible leadership, see Ludwig Dehio, *The Precarious Balance: Four Centuries of the European Power Struggle*, translated by Charles Fullman (New York: 1962), pp. 257–58.
5. See, on this point, Roger V. Dingman, "Theories of, and Approaches to, Alliance Politics," in Lauren, ed., *Diplomacy*, pp. 246–47.
6. My argument here follows that of Snyder and Diesing, *Conflict Among Nations*, pp. 429–45.
7. Waltz, *Theory of International Politics*, pp. 167–69.
8. The argument is succinctly summarized in Nelson and Olin, *Why War?*, pp. 35–43.
9. Waltz, *Theory of International Politics*, p. 138. For Waltz's general argument against interdependence as a necessary cause of peace, see *ibid.*, pp. 138–60.
10. Small and Singer, *Resort to Arms*, p. 102. The one questionable case is the Crimean War, which pitted Britain and France against Russia, but that conflict began as a dispute between Russia and Turkey.
11. See Michael Howard's observations on the absence of a "bellicist" mentality among the great powers in the postwar era, in his *The Causes of War*, pp. 271–73.
12. Small and Singer, *Resort to Arms*, pp. 167, 169.

13. For a persuasive elaboration of this argument, with an intriguing comparison of the post-1945 "nuclear" system to the post-1815 "Vienna" system, see Michael Mandelbaum, *The Nuclear Revolution: International Politics Before and After Hiroshima* (New York: 1981), pp. 58–77; also Morgan, *Deterrence*, p. 208; Craig and George, *Force and Statecraft*, pp. 117–20; Howard, *The Causes of War*, pp. 22, 278–79.

14. See, on this point, Mandelbaum, *The Nuclear Revolution*, p. 109; also the discussion of the "crystal ball effect" in Albert Carnesale, *et al.*, *Living with Nuclear Weapons* (New York: 1983), p. 44.

15. For a brief review of the literature on crisis management, together with an illustrative comparison of the July, 1914, crisis with the Cuban missile crisis, see Ole R. Holsti, "Theories of Crisis Decision Making," in Lauren, ed., *Diplomacy*, pp. 99–136; also Craig and George, *Force and Statecraft*, pp. 205–19.

16. Gilpin, *War and Change in World Politics*, pp. 202–3.

17. For the historical evolution of reconnaissance satellites, see Chapter Seven, above.

18. The most recent assessment, but one whose analysis does not take into account examples prior to 1940, is Richard K. Betts, *Surprise Attack: Lessons for Defense Planning* (Washington: 1982). See also, on the problem of assessing adversary intentions, Ernest R. May, ed., *Knowing One's Enemies: Intelligence Assessment Before the Two World Wars* (Princeton: 1984).

19. For a summary of what the open literature reveals about the difficulties faced by American intelligence in the first decade after World War II, see Thomas Powers, *The Man Who Kept the Secrets: Richard Helms and the CIA* (New York: 1979), pp. 43–58; and John Prados, *The Soviet Estimate: U.S. Intelligence and Russian Military Strength* (New York: 1982), pp. 24–30.

20. On this point, see Michael Krepon, *Arms Control: Verification and Compliance* (New York: 1984), especially pp. 8–13.

21. See, on this point, Halle, *The Cold War as History*, pp. 157–60.

22. Adam B. Ulam, *Expansion and Coexistence: The History of Soviet Foreign Policy, 1917–73*, Second Edition (New York: 1974), pp. 130–31.

23. See, on this point, E. H. Carr, *The Bolshevik Revolution, 1917–1923* (New York: 1953), pp. 549–66; and Marshall D. Shulman, *Stalin's Foreign Policy Reappraised* (New York: 1969), p. 82.

24. For Stalin's mixed record on this issue, see Shulman, *Stalin's Foreign Policy Reappraised, passim.*; also Taubman, *Stalin's American Policy*, pp. 128–227; and Adam B. Ulam, *Stalin: The Man and His Era* (New York: 1973), especially pp. 641–43, 654.

25. Herbert Dinerstein, *War and the Soviet Union: Nuclear Weapons and the Revolution in Soviet Military and Political Thinking* (New York: 1959), pp. 65–90; William Zimmerman, *Soviet Perspectives on International Relations, 1956–1967* (Princeton: 1969), pp. 251–52.

26. *Ibid.*, pp. 5, 255–59. See also *Khrushchev Remembers*, p. 530; and Bialer, *The Soviet Paradox*, pp. 270–71.

27. Kennan made the point explicitly in NSC 20/I, "U.S. Objectives with Respect to Russia," August 18, 1948, in Etzold and Gaddis, eds., *Containment*, p. 191; also in *The Realities of American Foreign Policy* (Princeton: 1954), p. 80.

28. On changing Soviet psychology as the ultimate goal of containment, see Gaddis, *Strategies of Containment*, pp. 48–51, 71–83, 98–99, 102–6.

29. See, for example, Hans J. Morgenthau, *In Defense of the National Interest: A Critical Examination of American Foreign Policy* (New York: 1951), pp. 31–33, 142–46. The critique of "unconditional surrender" can best be followed in Armstrong, *Unconditional Surrender*, pp. 248–62; and in Hanson W. Baldwin, *Great Mistakes of the War* (New York: 1950), pp. 14–25.

30. See, on this point, John Spanier, *Games Nations Play: Analyzing International Politics*, Fifth Edition (New York: 1984), p. 91.

31. For a good overview of this process of consolidation, see Keal, *Unspoken Rules and Superpower Dominance*, pp. 87–115.

32. Coral Bell, *The Conventions of Crisis: A Study in Diplomatic Management* (London: 1971): Phil Williams, *Crisis Management: Confrontation and Diplomacy in the Nuclear Age* (New York: 1976). They have also managed successfully to control incidents at sea; see Sean M. Lynn-Jones, "A Quiet Success for Arms Control: Preventing Incidents at Sea," *International Security*, IX (Spring, 1985), pp. 154–84.

33. The classic case, of course, is the amply documented July, 1914, crisis, the implications of which have most recently been reassessed in a special edition of *International Security*, IX (Summer, 1984). But see also Richard Smoke's essays on how the Seven Years War and the Crimean War grew out of a comparable failure of the major powers to limit the escalation of quarrels they did not initiate, in *War: Controlling Escalation*, pp. 147–236; also Richard Ned Lebow, *Between Peace and War: The Nature of International Crisis* (Baltimore: 1981).

34. These points are more fully developed in Chapter Five, but see also Richard Ned Lebow, "Windows of Opportunity: Do States Jump Through Them?" *International Security*, IX (Summer, 1984), 147–86.

35. For the importance of this distinction, see Thomas C. Schelling, *Arms and Influence* (New Haven: 1966), pp. 132–34.

36. Eisenhower speech to the American Society of Newspaper Editors, April 16, 1953, *Eisenhower Public Papers: 1953* (Washington: 1960), pp. 179–88. For the origins of this speech, see Emmet John Hughes, *The Ordeal of Power: A Political Memoir of the Eisenhower Years* (New York: 1963), pp. 100–112.

# After the Cold War: A New World Order

The end of the Cold War ushered in a new and rare era in global politics. It was characterized by a unipolar system in which the United States was the sole superpower, operating in the world without a major strategic rival. This unusual historical circumstance offered the United States the opportunity to try and modify the global system—toward its own ends and, at best, in its own image, by fostering or forcing transitions to democracy, market capitalism, and greater globalization. The readings in Part V explore this period, between the end of the Cold War and September 11, 2001 (when yet another strategic change occurred in U.S. foreign policy), and look at how the United States both shaped and responded to the international system.

Over the course of the 1990s, American dominance in the world seemed to loom larger and larger, though at the outset, it was unclear what direction the United States would pursue. The first two articles in the section directly address this question, with different answers. While Charles Krauthammer called for the United States to recognize the new opportunities and threats, and use its power to challenge "rogue" states to craft a much more orderly international order, Ronald Steel suggested that America's Cold War victory was ambiguous, whose results had yet to unfold.

The United States did actively try to create a more liberal world order—it expanded NATO, it encouraged globalization and the expansion of the European Union, it helped bring into existence the WTO, it imposed on debtor countries a set of economic policies based on the "Washington Consensus." The strategy was called "democratic enlargement," which is addressed in the readings by the The White House and Douglas Brinkley, and while it seemed a new strategy, it was also a continuation of the

American project begun after World War II, albeit an intensified effort. It relied on fostering liberalization while keeping disorder and threats to the system at bay. Such threats continually appeared, however, such as nuclear proliferation, failed states, ethnic conflict, and violence in the Middle East, among others. As the world's superpower, the United States involved itself in all these problems, extending its reach further and further as the decade progressed.

To those commenting on global politics at the end of the decade, as the readings by President Clinton and Samuel Huntington do, the international landscape looked very much as if it had a "made in America" stamp on it. The global imbalance of power evident in 1991 had only widened by 2000. President Clinton observed this and spoke to America's success—and the world's successes—in an increasingly interconnected world, but Huntington observed the downsides, which entailed a superpower hovering above all others, pushing its weight around, and causing resentment and an erosion in American legitimacy. To the extent that America "bestrode the world like a colossus," as *The Economist* put it at the time, the question remained what the United States would do with its power and influence.

# 29 The Unipolar Moment

## CHARLES KRAUTHAMMER

The end of the Cold War left the United States in a preeminent position in the world, without a major strategic rival. This meant that the United States had great freedom of action to carry out its policies and achieve its international goals. Charles Krauthammer called this period "The Unipolar Moment," and speculated that this era of American dominance could last anywhere from 10 to 40 years, depending upon the wisdom of American actions.

Krauthammer argues for a robust American internationalism, claiming that it would be necessary to preserve peace, prosperity, and order around the world. His argument reflects a neoconservative perspective, and his call for an assertive U.S. foreign policy is based upon his understanding of global politics and the balance of power in the post–Cold War world. Krauthammer states that in spite of the increasing cohesiveness of the European Union, German and Japanese economic strength, Russian military power, and the rise of China, the world was not becoming multipolar, as many analysts had speculated. Rather, it had become unipolar, with the United States as the only power with the capacity to be a decisive player in any conflict around the world. Moreover, any foreseeable alternative to a unipolar world dominated by American power would be chaos. This is because, as Krauthammer states, the most significant threat to world peace was emerging in the form of the proliferation of WMD and the rise of the "Weapon State," countries such as Iraq or North Korea whose development of WMD would represent the single greatest threat to world security for a generation. While marshalling the will and resources of the United States to combat chaos might seem "a rather subtle call to greatness," according to Krauthammer it would be both necessary and just.

When one considers America's substantial global power and influence since the end of the Cold War, as well as its focus on stopping weapons proliferation, Krauthammer's words appear to have accurately captured much of what the future would hold.

Charles Krauthammer, "The Unipolar Moment," *Foreign Affairs*, Winter 1990/91, adapted from the author's Henry M. Jackson Memorial Lecture delivered September 18, 1990. Reprinted by permission of Charles Krauthammer.

Ever since it became clear that an exhausted Soviet Union was calling off the Cold War, the quest has been on for a new American role in the world. Roles, however, are not invented in the abstract; they are a response to a perceived world structure. Accordingly, thinking about post-Cold War American foreign policy has been framed by several conventionally accepted assumptions about the shape of the post-Cold War environment.

First, it has been assumed that the old bipolar world would beget a multipolar world with power dispersed to new centers in Japan, Germany (and/or "Europe"), China and a diminished Soviet Union/Russia. Second, that the domestic American consensus for an internationalist foreign policy, a consensus radically weakened by the experience in Vietnam, would substantially be restored now that policies and debates inspired by "an inordinate fear of communism" could be safely retired. Third, that in the new post-Soviet strategic environment the threat of war would be dramatically diminished.

All three of these assumptions are mistaken. The immediate post-Cold War world is not multipolar. It is unipolar. The center of world power is the unchallenged superpower, the United States, attended by its Western allies. Second, the internationalist consensus is under renewed assault. The assault this time comes not only from the usual pockets of post-Vietnam liberal isolationism (e.g., the churches) but from a resurgence of 1930s-style conservative isolationism. And third, the emergence of a new strategic environment, marked by the rise of small aggressive states armed with weapons of mass destruction and possessing the means to deliver them (what might be called Weapon States), makes the coming decades a time of heightened, not diminished, threat of war.

## II

The most striking feature of the post-Cold War world is its unipolarity. No doubt, multipolarity will come in time. In perhaps another generation or so there will be great powers coequal with the United States, and the world will, in structure, resemble the pre-World War I era. But we are not there yet, nor will we be for decades. Now is the unipolar moment.

There is today no lack of second-rank powers. Germany and Japan are economic dynamos. Britain and France can deploy diplomatic and to some extent military assets. The Soviet Union possesses several elements of power—military, diplomatic and political—but all are in rapid decline. There is but one first-rate power and no prospect in the immediate future of any power to rival it.

Only a few months ago it was conventional wisdom that the new rivals, the great pillars of the new multipolar world, would be Japan and Germany (and/or Europe). How quickly a myth can explode. The notion that economic power inevitably translates into geopolitical influence is a materialist illusion. Economic power is a necessary condition for great power status. But it certainly is not sufficient, as has been made clear by the recent behavior of Germany and Japan, which have generally hidden under the table since the first shots rang out in Kuwait. And while a unified Europe may sometime in the next century act as a single power, its initial disarray and disjointed national responses to the crisis in the Persian Gulf again illustrate that "Europe" does not yet qualify even as a player on the world stage.

Which leaves us with the true geopolitical structure of the post-Cold War world, brought sharply into focus by the gulf crisis: a single pole of world power that consists of the United States at the apex of the industrial West. Perhaps it is more accurate to say the United States and behind it the West, because where the United States does not tread, the alliance does not follow. That was true for the reflagging of Kuwaiti vessels in 1987. It has been all the more true of the world's subsequent response to the invasion of Kuwait.

American preeminence is based on the fact that it is the only country with the military, diplomatic, political and economic assets to be a decisive player in any conflict in whatever part of the world it chooses to involve itself. In the Persian Gulf, for example, it was the United States, acting unilaterally and with extraordinary speed, that in August 1990 prevented Iraq from taking effective control of the entire Arabian Peninsula.

Iraq, having inadvertently revealed the unipolar structure of today's world, cannot stop complaining about it. It looks at allied and Soviet support for American action in the gulf and speaks of a conspiracy of North against South. Although it is perverse for Iraqi leader Saddam Hussein to claim to represent the South, his analysis does contain some truth. The unipolar moment means that with the close of the century's three great Northern civil wars (World War I, World War II and the Cold War) an ideologically pacified North seeks security and order by aligning its foreign policy behind that of the United States. That is what is taking shape now in the Persian Gulf. And for the near future, it is the shape of things to come.

The Iraqis are equally acute in demystifying the much celebrated multilateralism of this new world order. They charge that the entire multilateral apparatus (United Nations resolutions, Arab troops, European Community pronouncements, and so on) established in the gulf by the United States is but a transparent cover for what is essentially an American challenge to Iraqi regional hegemony.

But of course. There is much pious talk about a new multilateral world and the promise of the United Nations as guarantor of a new post-Cold War order. But this is to mistake cause and effect, the United States and the United Nations. The United Nations is guarantor of nothing. Except in a formal sense, it can hardly be said to exist. Collective security? In the gulf, without the United States leading and prodding, bribing and blackmailing, no one would have stirred. Nothing would have been done: no embargo, no "Desert Shield," no threat of force. The world would have written off Kuwait the way the last body pledged to collective security, the League of Nations, wrote off Abyssinia.

There is a sharp distinction to be drawn between real and apparent multilateralism. True multilateralism involves a genuine coalition of coequal partners of comparable strength and stature—the World War II Big Three coalition, for example. What we have today is pseudo-multilateralism: a dominant great power acts essentially alone, but, embarrassed at the idea and still worshiping at the shrine of collective security, recruits a ship here, a brigade there, and blessings all around to give its unilateral actions a multilateral sheen. The gulf is no more a collective operation than was Korea, still the classic case study in pseudo-multilateralism.

Why the pretense? Because a large segment of American opinion doubts the legitimacy of unilateral American action but accepts quite readily actions undertaken by the "world community" acting in concert. Why it should matter to Americans that their actions get a Security Council nod from, say, Deng Xiaoping and the butchers of Tiananmen Square is beyond me. But to many Americans it matters. It is largely for domestic reasons, therefore, that American political leaders make sure to dress unilateral action in multilateral clothing. The danger, of course, is that they might come to believe their own pretense.

But can America long sustain its unipolar preeminence? The spectacle of secretaries of state and treasury flying around the world rattling tin cups to support America's Persian Gulf deployment exposed the imbalance between America's geopolitical reach and its resources. Does that not imply that the theorists of American decline and "imperial overstretch" are right and that unipolarity is unsustainable?

It is, of course, true that if America succeeds in running its economy into the ground, it will not be able to retain its unipolar role for long. In which case the unipolar moment will be brief indeed (one decade, perhaps, rather than, say, three or four). But if the economy is run into the ground it will not be because of imperial overstretch, i.e., because America has overreached abroad and drained itself with geopolitical entanglements. The United States today spends 5.4 percent of its GNP on defense. Under John F. Kennedy, when the United States was at its economic and political apogee, it spent almost twice as much. Administration plans have U.S. defense spending on a trajectory down to four percent by 1995, the lowest since Pearl Harbor.

An American collapse to second-rank status will be not for foreign but for domestic reasons. This is not the place to engage in extended debate about the cause of America's economic difficulties. But the notion that we have spent ourselves into penury abroad is simply not sustainable. America's low savings rate, poor educational system, stagnant productivity, declining work habits, rising demand for welfare state entitlements and new taste for ecological luxuries have nothing at all to do with engagement in Europe, Central America or the Middle East. Over the last thirty years, while taxes remained almost fixed (rising from 18.3 percent to 19.6 percent) and defense spending declined, domestic entitlements nearly doubled. What created an economy of debt unrivaled in American history is not foreign adventures but the low tax ideology of the 1980s, coupled with America's insatiable desire for yet higher standards of living without paying any of the cost.

One can debate whether America is in true economic decline. Its percentage of world GNP is roughly where it has been throughout the twentieth century (between 22 and 26 percent), excepting the aberration of the immediate post-World War II era when its competitors were digging out from the rubble of war. But even if one does argue that America is in economic decline, it is simply absurd to imply that the road to solvency is to, say, abandon El Salvador, evacuate the Philippines or get out of the gulf. There may be other good reasons for doing all of these. But it is nonsense to suggest doing them as a way to get at the root of America's economic problems.

It is, moreover, a mistake to view America's exertions abroad as nothing but a drain on its economy. As can be seen in the gulf, America's involvement abroad is in many ways an essential pillar of the American economy. The United States is, like Britain before it, a commercial, maritime, trading nation that needs an open, stable world environment in which to thrive. In a world of Saddams, if the United States were to shed its unique superpower role, its economy would be gravely wounded. Insecure sea lanes, impoverished trading partners, exorbitant oil prices, explosive regional instability are only the more obvious risks of an American abdication. Foreign entanglements are indeed a burden. But they are also a necessity. The cost of ensuring an open and safe world for American commerce—5.4 percent of GNP and falling—is hardly exorbitant.

# III

Can America support its unipolar status? Yes. But will Americans support such unipolar status? That is a more problematic question. For a small but growing chorus of Americans this vision of a unipolar world led by a dynamic America is a nightmare. Hence the second major element of the post-Cold War reality: the revival of American isolationism.

I have great respect for American isolationism. First, because of its popular appeal and, second, because of its natural appeal. On the face of it, isolationism seems the logical, God-given foreign policy for the United States. It is not just geography that inclines us to it—we are an island continent protected by two vast oceans, bordered by two neighbors that could hardly be friendlier—but history. America was founded on the idea of cleansing itself of the intrigues and irrationalities, the dynastic squabbles and religious wars, of the Old World. One must have respect for a strain of American thinking so powerful that four months before Pearl Harbor the vote to extend draft enlistments passed the House of Representatives by a single vote.

Isolationists say rather unobjectionably that America should confine its attentions in the world to defending vital national interests. But the more extreme isolationists define vital national interests to mean the physical security of the United States, and the more elusive isolationists take care never to define them at all.

Isolationists will, of course, say that this is unfair, that they do believe in defending vital national interests beyond the physical security of the United States. We have a test case. Iraq's invasion of Kuwait and hegemonic designs on Arabia posed as clear a threat to American interests as one can imagine—a threat to America's oil-based economy, to its close allies in the region, and ultimately to American security itself. The rise of a hostile power, fueled by endless oil income, building weapons of mass destruction and the means to deliver them regionally and eventually intercontinentally (Saddam has already tested a three-stage rocket) can hardly be a matter of indifference to the United States.

If under these conditions a cadre of influential liberals and conservatives finds that upon reflection (and in contradiction to the doctrine enunciated by the most dovish president of the postwar era, Jimmy Carter) the Persian Gulf is not, after all, a vital American interest, then it is hard to see what "vital interest" can mean. If the Persian Gulf is not a vital interest, then nothing is. All that is left is preventing an invasion of the Florida Keys. And for that you need a Coast Guard—you do not need a Pentagon and you certainly do not need a State Department.

Isolationism is the most extreme expression of the American desire to return to tend its vineyards. But that desire finds expression in another far more sophisticated and serious foreign policy school: not isolationism but realism, the school that insists that American foreign policy be guided solely by interests and that generally defines these interests in a narrow and national manner.

Many of realism's practitioners were heroic in the heroic struggles against fascism and communism. Now, however, some argue that the time for heroism is passed. For example, Jeane J. Kirkpatrick wrote, to be sure before the gulf crisis, that "It is time to give up the dubious benefits of superpower status," time to give up the "unusual burdens" of the past and "return to 'normal' times." That means taking "care of pressing problems of education, family, industry and technology" at home. That means that we should not try to be the balancer of power in Europe or in Asia, nor try to shape the political evolution of the Soviet Union. We should aspire instead to be "a normal country in a normal time."[1]

This is a rather compelling vision of American purpose. But I am not sure there is such a thing as normal times. If a normal time is a time when there is no evil world empire on the loose, when the world is in ideological repose, then even such a time is not necessarily peacetime. Saddam has made this point rather emphatically. If a normal time is a time when the world sorts itself out on its own, leaving America relatively unmolested— say, for America, the nineteenth century—then I would suggest that there are no normal times. The world does not sort itself out on its own. In the nineteenth century, for example, international stability was not achieved on its own but, in large part, as the product of Britain's unrelenting exertions on behalf of the balance of power. America tended her vineyards, but only behind two great ocean walls patrolled by the British navy. Alas, the British navy is gone.

International stability is never a given. It is never the norm. When achieved, it is the product of self-conscious action by the great powers, and most particularly of the greatest power, which now and for the foreseeable future is the United States. If America wants stability, it will have to create it. Communism is indeed finished; the last of the messianic creeds that have haunted this century is quite dead. But there will constantly be new threats disturbing our peace.

# IV

What threats? Everyone recognizes one great change in the international environment, the collapse of communism. If that were the only change, then this might be a normal time and the unipolar vision I have outlined would seem at once unnecessary and dangerous.

But there is another great change in international relations. And here we come to the third and most crucial new element in the post-Cold War world: the emergence of a new strategic environment marked by the proliferation of weapons of mass destruction. It is a certainty that in the near future there will be a dramatic increase in the number of states armed with biological, chemical and nuclear weapons and the means to deliver them anywhere on earth. "By the year 2000," estimates Defense Secretary Dick Cheney, "more than two dozen developing nations will have ballistic missiles, 15 of those countries will have the scientific skills to make their own, and half of them either have or are near to getting nuclear capability, as well. Thirty countries will have chemical weapons and ten will be able to deploy biological weapons."[2]

It is of course banal to say that modern technology has shrunk the world. But the obvious corollary, that in a shrunken world the divide between regional superpowers and great powers is radically narrowed, is rarely drawn. Missiles shrink distance. Nuclear (or chemical or biological) devices multiply power. Both can be bought at market. Consequently the geopolitical map is irrevocably altered. Fifty years ago, Germany—centrally located, highly industrial and heavily populated—could pose a threat to world security and to the other great powers. It was inconceivable that a relatively small Middle Eastern state with an almost entirely imported industrial base could do anything more than threaten its neighbors. The central truth of the coming era is that this is no longer the case: relatively small, peripheral and backward states will be able to emerge rapidly as threats not only to regional, but to world, security.

Iraq, which (unless disarmed by Desert Storm) will likely be in possession of intercontinental missiles within the decade, is the prototype of this new strategic threat, what might be called the "Weapon State." The Weapon State is an unusual international creature marked by several characteristics:

- It is not much of a nation state. Iraq, for example, is a state of recent vintage with arbitrary borders whose ruling party explicitly denies that Iraq is a nation. (It refers to Iraq and Syria as regions, part of the larger Arab nation for which it reserves the term.)
- In the Weapon State, the state apparatus is extraordinarily well developed and completely dominates civil society. The factor that permits most Weapon States to sustain such a structure is oil. Normally a state needs some kind of tacit social contract with the civil society because ultimately the state must rely on society to support it with taxes. The oil states are in an anomalous

position: they do not need a social contract because national wealth comes from oil and oil is wholly controlled by the state. Oil states are peculiarly distributive states. Government distributes goods to society rather than the other way around. It is therefore the source not only of power but of wealth. This makes possible an extraordinary degree of social control exercised by a powerful, often repressive state apparatus.

- The current Weapon States have deep grievances against the West and the world order that it has established and enforces. They are therefore subversive of the international status quo, which they see as a residue of colonialism. These resentments fuel an obsessive drive to high-tech military development as the only way to leapfrog history and to place themselves on a footing from which to challenge a Western-imposed order.

The Weapon State need not be an oil state. North Korea, hard at work on nuclear technology, is a candidate Weapon State: it has about as much legitimacy as a nation-state as the German Democratic Republic; its state apparatus totally dominates civil society by virtue not of oil but of an exquisitely developed Stalinism; its anti-Western grievances run deep.

The danger from the Weapon State is posed today by Iraq, tomorrow perhaps by North Korea or Libya. In the next century, however, the proliferation of strategic weapons will not be restricted to Weapon States. Windfall wealth allows oil states to import high-technology weapons in the absence of a mature industrial base. However, it is not hard to imagine maturer states—say, Argentina, Pakistan, Iran, South Africa—reaching the same level of weapons development by means of ordinary industrialization. (Today most of these countries are friendly, but some are unstable and potentially hostile.)

The post-Cold War era is thus perhaps better called the era of weapons of mass destruction. The proliferation of weapons of mass destruction and their means of delivery will constitute the greatest single threat to world security for the rest of our lives. That is what makes a new international order not an imperial dream or a Wilsonian fantasy but a matter of the sheerest prudence. It is slowly dawning on the West that there is a need to establish some new regime to police these weapons and those who brandish them.

In parliamentary debate on the gulf crisis even British Labour Party leader Neil Kinnock has emphasized that it is not enough to get Iraq out of Kuwait. Iraq's chemical stocks, he said, must be destroyed and its nuclear program internationally controlled. When the Labour Party, hardly a home for hawks, speaks thus, we have the makings, the beginnings, of a new Western consensus.

To do what exactly? There is no definitive answer, but any solution will have to include three elements: denying, disarming, and defending. First, we will have to develop a new regime, similar to COCOM (Coordinating Committee on Export Controls) to deny yet more high technology to such states. Second, those states that acquire such weapons anyway will have to submit to strict outside control or risk being physically disarmed. A final element must be the development of antiballistic missile and air defense systems to defend against those weapons that do escape Western control or preemption.

There might be better tactics, but the overall strategy is clear. With the rise of the Weapon State, there is no alternative to confronting, deterring and, if necessary, disarming states that brandish and use weapons of mass destruction. And there is no one to do that but the United States, backed by as many allies as will join the endeavor.

The alternative to such robust and difficult interventionism—the alternative to unipolarity—is not a stable, static multipolar world. It is not an eighteenth-century world in which mature powers like Europe, Russia, China, America, and Japan jockey for position in the game of nations. The alternative to unipolarity is chaos.

I do not mean to imply that weapons of mass destruction are the only threat facing the post-Cold War world. They are only the most obvious. Other threats exist, but they are more speculative and can be seen today only in outline: the rise, for example, of intolerant aggressive nationalism in a disintegrating communist bloc (in one extreme formulation, the emergence of a reduced but resurgent, xenophobic and resentful "Weimar" Russia). And some threats to the peace of the 21st century are as invisible today as was, say, Nazism in 1920. They will make themselves known soon enough. Only a hopeless utopian can believe otherwise.

We are in for abnormal times. Our best hope for safety in such times, as in difficult times past, is in American strength and will—the strength and will to lead a unipolar world, unashamedly laying down the rules of world order and being prepared to enforce them. Compared to the task of defeating fascism and communism, averting chaos is a rather subtle call to greatness. It is not a task we are any more eager to undertake than the great twilight struggle just concluded. But it is just as noble and just as necessary.

## Notes

1. "A Normal Country in a Normal Time," *National Interest*, Fall 1990, pp. 40–44.
2. Address to the Conservative Leadership Conference, Washington, D.C., Nov. 9, 1990.

# 30 An Ambiguous Victory
## RONALD STEEL

The end of the Cold War produced an irony, according to Ronald Steel. The United States, after the fall of the Soviet Union, had gotten everything it had asked for: no more Soviet Union, communism discredited, the spread of democracy, and free market capitalism. Yet the United States seemed to be living the curse of those who get what they ask for. For American victory in the Cold War was an ambiguous one. It left America triumphant and unrivaled, yet without direction and, in spite of its superior power, without the ability to achieve some of its important political goals. Somalia, Yugoslavia, and Iraq all seemed to elude satisfying solutions, while disorder itself seemed to be the new enemy of the United States.

The problem confronting America, however, was greater than this, according to Steel. It was not merely political; it was existential. It is in this characterization that Ronald Steel accurately and thoughtfully voices the spirit of the times in the early 1990s. As the whole edifice of international relations was dismantled, Americans were somewhat adrift. The Cold War had offered a structure for understanding the world, and its disappearance eliminated satisfying notions of certainty, predictability, and simplicity. Global problems became more complex, and also less compelling. Amidst numerous commentaries and analyses about why the world would soon miss the Cold War, the United States embarked upon a world no longer defined by black and white, but by shades of gray and ambiguities. Steel alludes to this Cold War nostalgia, suggesting that it demonstrates the hold that the Cold War had over American politics and society. It was America's central focus for generations, defining not only foreign policy but domestic life as well—the economy, education, movies, literature, and academic research all reflected the politics of the Cold War. Letting go and finding a new purpose, one that was commensurate with America's power and promise, would now be the task of a new post–Cold War generation of leaders, and it would not be a simple one.

History plays strange jokes on nations, as it does on people. We are now living the curse of those who get what they ask for. Only a few years ago we yearned for the disappearance of what Ronald Reagan called the "evil empire" and for victory in the Cold War. We got our wish. The Soviet Union is no more, communism is discredited, and free market capitalism is trumpeted in the corridors of the Kremlin.

By the standards of the Cold War we should be in a triumphant mood. With the demise of the Soviet Union, the United States stands in magnificent splendor as the world's only remaining superpower. Our fleets and air squadrons roam the world unimpeded by any rival force. No nation has the means to challenge us. We can exert overwhelming power virtually anywhere we choose and in whatever cause we see fit.

Yet this is an ambiguous victory. Although our military power is unchallenged, it cannot easily be translated into the political goals we seek. We destroyed the Iraqi army in 1991, yet Saddam Hussein remained in power. We fed the hungry in Somalia, but retreated in disorder after interfering in the power struggle of rival clans. We deplored the ethnic violence in the former Yugoslavia, but had no solution for a conflict rooted in ancient enmities.

What the end of the Cold War taught us is that the weapons we forged to fight it are virtually irrelevant once the battle is over. We are facing a problem we had not anticipated: that of translating military might into political power. We can bomb or blockade such places as Serbia, or Haiti, or North Korea. But we cannot impose our political will so easily.

The Cold War was dangerous, wasteful, obsessive, and at times irrational. Tens of thousands of lives were sacrificed in battles that we can hardly understand, let alone justify, today. Yet at least we could define what the Cold War was ostensibly about. The United States sought to restrain, and ultimately reverse, the military reach and political influence of the Soviet Union. Officials told us that if this were done, the major cause of violence in the world would be removed.

But the world after the Cold War is even more violent, yet without a single cause. We were no more prepared for this than we were for the abrupt and unexpected end of the Cold War. Although we devoted an enormous part of our national resources, as well as our emotional and intellectual energies, into fighting the Soviets, we never seriously thought about what the political landscape might be after battle. Many of us simply assumed that the world would return to something like normal.

But of course there was no normal. Europe had not been normal since 1914. War, revolution, depression, then war again had obliterated the boundaries and the common civilization of the self-confident societies that had existed before World War I. When communist authority collapsed in 1990, with it went the whole structure of postwar Europe. In the east, the former communist states were no longer sullen and orderly, but fearful and disorderly. Whereas they had once blamed distant "imperialists" for their troubles, they now turned on ethnic minorities in their own midst. In the west of the continent, where the wealthy and secure had built a European "community," the dream of unity was shaken by the realization that the very notion of Europe, as it had been understood for half a century, was a creation of the Cold War. That conception would have to be redefined—and in a way that threatened long-cherished assumptions.

In Asia, too, there was no normal. Before the Cold War set the stage for new alliances, Japan was a defeated imperial nation and China an impoverished and exploited colony. Today Japan has become rich and economically powerful, and China has embarked on a path of industrialization and militarization that is making it a major global player.

While the end of the Cold War has resolved some problems, it has unleashed others we had not anticipated—problems that have no simple military solution.

The "captive nations" of Eastern Europe, whose liberation we ritualistically demanded in Congressional resolutions, are now our problem—and that of the West Europeans—rather than Moscow's. Our NATO allies, who used to berate us for being domineering and "hegemonic," now complain even more loudly that we do not care about them anymore. Whereas we once protected them from the Soviets, they now want us to protect them from one another. And Russia—our Cold War nemesis—is today a problem not because of its strength but because of its weakness. A weak Russia cannot provide stability or prosperity for its citizens. It cannot impose order on the violent tribes along its frontiers. And it cannot ensure the strong centralized control over nuclear weapons on which our own security depends. Ironically, a Russian threat to commit suicide today seems more dangerous than an earlier one to commit aggression.

The Third World, where we fought the most vicious battles of the Cold War—sometimes with proxy armies, as in Angola, Nicaragua, and Afghanistan—has now become politically irrelevant. The communist country whose unification we fought so hard, and destroyed so much to prevent—Vietnam—has traded the teachings of Karl Marx for those of Adam Smith. And after viewing it as a willing tool of Chinese imperialism, we now have come to appreciate it as a useful counter to China.

Finally, Japan, whose economy we restored so that it could play its role in the integrated global market that our policymakers were intent on creating, has succeeded all too well. It has today achieved by commerce what it tried to do half a century ago by war: its Greater East Asian Co-prosperity Sphere. It has done this with our help. We spared it the expense of paying for its own defense against its communist neighbors, and we provided the lucrative markets for it to service our military operations in Korea and

Vietnam. We now hold contentious summit conferences with the Japanese, just as we used to do with the Russians. And Americans tell pollsters that, with the Soviet Union gone, they consider Japan to be our most formidable rival.

It is not surprising that there are those, particularly in the foreign policy elite, who actually miss the Cold War. It gave us a cause to defend, allies that paid deference, and a role as undisputed boss of the realm we called the "free world." No wonder that we do not celebrate its end, as we do that of earlier wars.

Soviet communism, for all its evils, held in check the explosive nationalism of Eastern Europe and the old Soviet republics. It also enabled the superpowers to control their more unruly Third World clients. The Soviet Union almost certainly would not have allowed its client, Saddam Hussein, to have attacked Kuwait, thus provoking the Americans to send an army to the Gulf. Nor would Washington have tolerated the banditry that led to mass starvation in its former "strategically located" Cold War base in Somalia.

In its perverted way, the Cold War was a force for stability. By dividing Germany it resolved, for a time, the perennial problem of preventing it from dominating Europe. It smothered the ethnic rivalries of the old Romanov, Ottoman, and Hapsburg empires that have now emerged with such fury. It slowed down the dispersion of nuclear weapons to ambitious states. And it ensured the status of the superpowers.

The Cold War also offered a structure for understanding the world. It was a struggle not only for power and influence, but for the minds of men everywhere. As an alternative to our own messianic ideology of market democracy, communism posed a challenge to what we were and what we espoused.

The Cold War world seemed neatly divided between democracy and totalitarianism, with the shades of gray wiped out. To the sordid and self-serving politics of statecraft, and to alliances of convenience, it provided a comforting note of moral certainty.

Now, with the battle over, the lines between good and evil are once again fuzzy. It used to be that a regime had only to invoke the specter of communism to be showered with American aid and protection. But without communism the issues are more complex, and also less compelling.

Should we become involved if a government founders? Why? Because a state is democratic? Capitalist? A good market? A source of supplies? Or simply needy? We espouse principles like democracy and freedom. But where should we apply them? Can we apply them? And if so, at what price?

During the Cold War it was all so easy. Whatever was wrong in the world was the fault of communism. We had an enemy and we had a crusade. Now we are alone: a superpower without a challenger, a crusader without a mission.

What happened to our enemy? For decades our leaders warned that this evil, yet somehow seductive, force was poised to take over the world. They led us to wars in remote and seemingly insignificant places for reasons that were often as difficult for them to explain as for us to understand. Yet in the end there was no colossus: only an inept, strife-ridden, and impoverished regime—a gigantic Potemkin village.

What were we so afraid of? Indeed, were our leaders really afraid of the power of the Soviets to seduce and intimidate the entire world? Or did they find it to be a useful enemy that allowed them to build up the military and economic power that created what has been justly called the American Century?

Future historians will ask why we felt so vulnerable—far more so than the Europeans, who were within walking distance of the Red Army. The answer lies partly in our long history of geographic invulnerability. The protection of vast oceans produced an exaggerated sense of security that we came to take as a birthright. The answer also lies in the struggle with an ideology so alien to our own, yet seemingly so seductive to many.

Unlike World War II, which for the United States was a four-year state of emergency with a clear beginning and a triumphant military conclusion, the Cold War was a permanent crisis. With the nuclear stalemate, it could not be resolved in military battle, and it was hard to foresee how or when it would ever end. Generations came and went, while the Cold War continued.

Inevitably the Cold War came to dominate our thinking, just as it did the national agenda. It defined our government and how we lived our lives. We even used it to justify our own domestic activities to ourselves. When the government provided aid to school children, it called the program the "National Defense Education Act." When it built the interstate highway system, it labeled it the "National Defense Highway Act."

Until the inauguration of Bill Clinton in 1993, every president since Franklin Roosevelt has been preoccupied with foreign policy. Some—like John Kennedy, Richard Nixon, and George Bush—seemed to view the nation's domestic problems as annoying distractions from the excitement and dangers of global crises. Foreign policy always came first. How we lived with each other—whether we were rich or poor, segregated or integrated, united or divided—always came second. This, too, we came to take as natural and proper.

Now, with the Cold War behind us, the old clarity has given way to confusion and doubt. In part this contributes to what has been called Cold War nostalgia.

The Cold War was many things: a deadly struggle, an obsession, a vocation. It was also a competition in economic bankruptcy. In this the Soviets, being poorer, gave out first. But if the struggle destroyed them, it also weakened us: in our ability to compete with our allies, in meeting the needs of our people, in honoring our political values.

It will be difficult to find a way back from the Cold War. For it was more than merely an appendage to our society. It was its central focus for three generations. The American economy, its work force, its education and training, its films and literature, its myths and its dreams all focused on the Cold War. Whole professions and even states have been dependent on it.

The contest is over and the Cold War world has receded into the already-dim past. Yet it cannot be so easily exorcised. For the Cold War was only in part about America's contest with the Soviet Union. It was also about a role of dominance that the foreign policy elite sought to exert, and to which it is still committed even though the old foe is vanquished.[1]

Today we are at a turning point in our foreign policy in some ways comparable to that of 1946–1947. At that time, in the flush of victory—with Japan and Germany in ruins, Britain and France reduced to dependency, and the wartime alliance with the Soviet Union falling apart—the nation redefined its relationship with the world. The prewar policy of isolationism had become irrelevant, the old balance of power could not be reconstituted, and Moscow seemed threatening. From the foundation of American power, officials crafted a policy of sweeping scope.

Its twin anchors were containment and expansion: containment of Soviet territorial temptations through military and economic power; expansion through alliances, bases, investments, and bribes. This policy restrained Soviet ambitions and ushered in an era of dominance from Washington justly called the Pax Americana.

That era is now behind us, a casualty of the very success of containment and the economic recovery of Europe and Asia. Containment has become obsolete, and with it the enormous military apparatus constructed in its name. We are left with a doctrine deprived of its logic, and with a military force—capable of wiping out whole countries—without an objective commensurate with its power.

As the architects of the American Century did nearly half a century ago, we must reinvent American foreign policy for another postwar world. This means forging not only the mechanics and the superstructure, but the very terms of our relationship with other states—and beyond that, with ourselves.

Perhaps most crucial is the restructuring of the compact we Americans have with one another—our sense of who we are as a people, what we stand for, and how we can best live among others. For as long as most of us can remember, foreign policy has dominated our national agenda.

Our domestic needs have consistently been sacrificed to it. We have turned security against foreign challengers into a shibboleth. But we have neglected the threats to our own security that come from within.

## Note

1. For the argument pro and con, see *International Security* 17, no. 4 (Spring 1993), with articles by Christopher Layne, Robert Jervis, and Samuel P. Huntington.

# 31   A National Security Strategy of Engagement and Enlargement
## THE WHITE HOUSE

The development of an American grand strategy that could replace containment emerged during the Clinton administration. As the first post–Cold War president, Clinton agreed that, despite a single major adversary, there remained a struggle in the world between the forces of democracy and market capitalism on the one hand and those of tyranny, disorder, and isolation on the other. The challenges to the security and stability of democratic, capitalist development would be many—regional aggressors, the spread of WMD, financial and economic chaos, ethnic and religious war, pariah states, terrorism, tyrannical governments that abuse human rights, drug trafficking, organized crime. By contrast, the ends that would promote American interests would be the spread of democracy and market capitalism. Therefore, the American national security strategy, as stated by the White House, would be based on "enlarging the community of market democracies while deterring and limiting a range of threats to our nation, our allies and our interests." The United States of America would unabashedly pursue a strategy grounded firmly in the tradition of liberal internationalism, whereby peace and prosperity would be the fruits of political and economic liberalization. It would also seek to actively engage all of the challenges to this goal in order to keep it from being threatened.

The National Security Council, "A National Security Strategy of Engagement and Enlargement," February 1996.

This document was produced by the National Security Council, and as such it had to pay homage to all the potential threats and opportunities that characterized a world without the Soviet Union. This apparent evenhandedness sometimes tends to mask the significance of particular elements within the text. In this case two of the features that came to define U.S. foreign policy thinking in the 1990s—the centrality of economics and the increasing level of globalization—are not highlighted in such a way that this significance stands out. Instead, they are embedded in the document as part of the larger project of engagement and enlargement. This is by no means an inaccuracy. A national security strategy is expected to be comprehensive in scope. The result, however, is the failure to fully capture some of the key features, which involve focusing on an economic strategy emphasizing free trade, global economic integration, intervention in the global economy to stabilize weak countries, and the aggressive promotion of a "Washington consensus" on how countries should reform their economies to adopt free market principles. All of these economic elements have strongly influenced American foreign policy in the post–Cold War era.

## INTRODUCTION

When this Administration assumed office, the United States and its allies faced a radically transformed security environment. The primary security imperative of the past half century—containing communist expansion while preventing nuclear war—was gone. Instead, we confronted a complex array of new and old security challenges America had to meet as we approached the 21st century.

The Administration outlined a national security strategy that assessed America's role in this new international context and described a strategy to advance our interests at home and abroad.

The strategy recognized that the United States was facing a period of great promise but also great uncertainty. We stand as the world's preeminent power. America's core value of freedom, as embodied in democratic governance and market economics, has gained ground around the world. Hundreds of millions of people have thrown off communism, dictatorship or apartheid. Former adversaries now work with us in diplomacy and global problem solving. Both the threat of a war among great powers and the specter of nuclear annihilation have receded dramatically. The dynamism of the global economy is transforming commerce, culture and global politics, promising greater prosperity for America and greater cooperation among nations.

At the same time, troubling uncertainties and clear threats remain. The new, independent states that replaced the Soviet Union continue to experience wrenching economic and political transitions, while the progress of the many new democracies of Central and Eastern Europe is still fragile. While our relations with the other great powers are as constructive as at any point in this century, Russia's historic transformation will face difficult challenges, and China maintains an authoritative regime even as that country assumes a more important economic and political role in global affairs. The spread of weapons of mass destruction poses serious threats, and rogue states still threaten regional aggression. Violent extremists threaten fragile peace processes in many parts of the world. Worldwide, there is a resurgence of militant nationalism as well as ethnic and religious conflict. This has been demonstrated by the upheavals in Bosnia, Rwanda and Somalia, where the United States has participated in peacekeeping and humanitarian missions.

The strategy also recognized that a number of transnational problems which once seemed quite distant, like environmental degradation, natural resource depletion, rapid population growth and refugee flows, now pose threats to our prosperity and have security implications for both present and long-term American policy. In addition, the emergence of the information and technology age presents new challenges to U.S. strategy even as it offers extraordinary opportunities to build a better future. This technology revolution brings our world closer together as information, money and ideas move around the globe at record speed; but it also makes possible for the violence of terrorism, organized crime and drug trafficking to challenge the security of our borders and that of our citizens in new ways.

It is a world where clear distinctions between threats to our nation's security from beyond our borders and the challenges to our security from within our borders are being blurred; where the separation between international problems and domestic ones is evaporating; and where the line between domestic and foreign policy is eroding. The demise of communism not only lifted the lid on age-old conflicts but it opened the door to new dangers, such as the spread of weapons of mass destruction to non-state, as well as state, forces. And it did so at a time when these forces can now try to threaten our security from within our borders because of their access to modern technology. We must therefore assess these forces for what they are, with our response based on the nature of their threat, not just where they occur.

Because problems that start beyond our borders can now much more easily become problems within them, American leadership and engagement in the world has never been more important. There is also a simple truth about this new world: the same idea that was under attack three times in this century—first by imperialism and then by fascism and communism—remains under attack today, but on many fronts at once. It is an idea that comes under many names—democracy, liberty, civility, pluralism—but which together are the values of a society where leaders and governments preserve individual freedoms and ensure opportunity and human dignity. As the President has said, "We face a contest as old as history—a struggle between freedom and tyranny; between tolerance and isolation. It is a fight between those who would build free societies governed by laws and those who would impose their will by force. Our struggle today, in a world more high-tech, more fast-moving, more chaotically diverse than ever, is the age-old fight between hope and fear." Just as surely as fascism and communism once did, so, too, are our freedom, democracy, security and prosperity now threatened by regional aggressors and the spread of weapons of mass destruction; ethnic, religious and national rivalries; and the forces of terrorism, drug trafficking and international organized crime. Today, addressing these threats demands American leadership.

The victors of World War I squandered their triumph in this age-old struggle when they turned inward, bringing on a global depression and allowing fascism to rise, and reigniting global war. After World War II, we remembered the lessons of the past. In the face of a new totalitarian threat, this great nation did not walk away from the challenge of the moment. Instead, it chose to reach out, to rebuild international security structures and to lead. This determination of previous generations to prevail over communism by shaping new international structures left us a world stronger, safer and freer. It is this example and its success that now inspire us to continue the difficult task of a new stage in this old struggle: to secure the peace won in the Cold War against those who would still deny people their human rights, terrorists who threaten innocents and pariah states who choose repression and extremism over openness and moderation.

By exerting our leadership abroad, we make America safer and more prosperous—by deterring aggression, by fostering the peaceful resolution of dangerous conflicts, by opening foreign markets, by helping democratic regimes and by tackling global problems. Without our active leadership and engagement abroad, threats will fester and our opportunities will narrow. We seek to be as creative and constructive—in the literal sense of that word—as the generation of the late 1940's. For all its dangers, this new world presents an immense opportunity—the chance to adapt and construct global institutions that will help to provide security and increase economic growth for America and the world.

At issue is whether our efforts at this construction can continue to succeed in the face of shifting threats to the ideals and habits of democracy. It is therefore in our interest that democracy be at once the foundation and the purpose of the international structures we build through this constructive diplomacy: the foundation, because the institutions will be a reflection of their shared values and norms; the purpose, because if political and economic institutions are secure, democracy will flourish.

Promoting democracy does more than foster our ideals. It advances our interests because we know that the larger the pool of democracies, the better off we, and the entire community of nations, will be. Democracies create free markets that offer economic opportunity, make for more reliable trading partners and are far less likely to wage war on one another. While democracy will not soon take hold everywhere, it is in our interest to do all that we can to enlarge the community of free and open societies, especially in areas of greatest strategic interest, as in Central and Eastern Europe and the new independent states of the former Soviet Union.

Our national security strategy is therefore based on enlarging the community of market democracies while deterring and limiting a range of threats to our nation, our allies and our interests. The more that democracy and political and economic liberalization take hold in the world, particularly in countries of strategic importance to us, the safer our nation is likely to be and the more our people are likely to prosper.

To that broad end, the three central components of our strategy of engagement and enlargement are: (1) our efforts to enhance our security by maintaining a strong defense capability and employing effective diplomacy to promote cooperative security measures; (2) our work to open foreign markets and spur global economic growth; and (3) our promotion of democracy abroad. It also explains how we are pursuing these elements of our strategy in specific regions by adapting and constructing institutions that will help to provide security and increase economic growth throughout the world.

In a democracy, however, the foreign policy and security strategy of the nation must serve the needs of the people. The preamble of the Constitution sets out the basic objectives: provide for the common defence, promote the general welfare, and secure the blessings of liberty to ourselves and our posterity.

The end of the Cold War does not alter these fundamental purposes. Nor does it reduce the need for active American efforts, here and abroad, to pursue those goals. Our efforts to advance the common good at home depend upon our efforts to advance our interests around the world. Therefore, we must judge the success of our security strategy by its impact on the domestic lives of our citizens: has it made a real difference in the day to day lives of Americans? Consider just a few examples:

Every American today is safer because we are stepping back from the nuclear precipice. Russian missiles are no longer targeted at the United States; we have convinced Ukraine, Kazakstan and Belarus to give up nuclear weapons left on their land when the Soviet Union collapsed. American leadership secured the indefinite and unconditional extension of the Nuclear Proliferation Treaty. We also convinced North Korea to freeze its nuclear program. Our strategy continues to ensure the safeguarding of more nuclear materials so they do not fall into the hands of terrorists or international criminals and endanger our citizens.

In a world where the boundaries between threats outside our borders and the challenges from within are diminishing, Americans are safer because our counterterrorism strategy promoted closer cooperation with foreign governments and sanctions against states that sponsor terrorism, while increasing the resources for our own law enforcement agencies.

Large-scale migration from Haiti has been stemmed because we gave democracy another chance in that nation. In the month before we forced the military rulers to step down, 16,000 Haitians fled their country for our shores and elsewhere in the region. Three months after the intervention, the refugee flow was practically zero.

Our strategy to help the nations of Central Europe consolidate democracy, find lasting security and build strong economics makes it much less likely that Americans might have to fight another war on the battlegrounds of Europe. By supporting democratic reform and the transition to free markets in the new independent states of the former Soviet Union and in Central Europe, our strategy promoted stability and prosperity in an area that will become a vast market for the United States, creating jobs in America. In Bosnia, diplomatic determination combined with military muscle to create an opportunity to secure a peace rather than permit instability to undermine this fragile region and U.S. interests.

Our strategy's trade initiatives, from NAFTA and the Uruguay Round of GATT to over 80 separate trade agreements, have created more than two million American jobs. With the Summit of the Americas and the APEC process, U.S. exports—and jobs—will continue to grow. Because of our emergency assistance to Mexico during its financial crisis, economic growth—although fragile—has returned and exports now exceed pre-NAFTA levels. Mexico has begun repaying its debt to the United States ahead of schedule, protecting the 340,000 American jobs NAFTA has already created because of exports to our partners.

From Iraq to Haiti, South Africa to the Korean Peninsula, the Middle East to Northern Ireland, our strategy has stopped or prevented war and brought former adversaries together in peace because it is in our interest. These efforts, combined with assisting developing nations who are fighting overpopulation, AIDS, drug smuggling and environmental degradation, ensure that future generations of Americans will not have to contend with the consequences of neglecting these threats to our security and prosperity.

Many of these decisions were made in the face of significant disagreement over what needed to be done at the moment. But the alternatives bore unacceptable costs to our citizens: tariffs and barriers would still cripple the world trading system if not for GATT and NAFTA; the Persian Gulf region would be very different today if the rapid response of the United States and its allies had not deterred Iraq's threatened aggression against Kuwait in 1994; the flood of Haitian refugees at our borders would have continued had we not intervened in that country; Latin America would have seen financial and economic chaos affecting its fragile democracies, and U.S. trade would have been harmed, had we not moved to help stabilize Mexico's economy; and the dangers to our people from weapons of mass destruction would be much greater had our strategy not reduced the threat of nuclear arms, curbed the spread of chemical and biological weapons around the world and countered the terrorists and criminals who would endanger us if they possessed these weapons. The money we devoted to development, peace-keeping or disaster relief helped to avert future crises whose cost would have been far greater in terms of lives lost and resources spent.

We can continue to engage actively abroad to achieve these results only if the American people and the Congress are willing to bear the costs of that leadership—in dollars, political energy and, at times, American lives. U.S. security, prosperity and freedom are neither cost- nor risk-free; resources must be spent and casualties may be incurred. One purpose of this report is to help foster the broad, bipartisan understanding and sup-port necessary to sustain our international engagement. A coalition of the center through bipartisan congressional participation is critical to this commitment. Some decisions must be made in the face of opposition; these decisions must ultimately be judged as to whether they benefited the American people by advancing their interests of security, prosperity and democracy in the long run.

# 32  Democratic Enlargement: The Clinton Doctrine

## Douglas Brinkley

The strategy of "democratic enlargement" by President Clinton offered a blueprint for engaging a world that seemed increasingly dis-orderly after the end of the Cold War. This strategy, which Douglas Brinkley dubs, "The Clinton Doctrine," placed the promotion of

Douglas Brinkley, from "Democratic Enlargement: The Clinton Doctrine." Reproduced with permission from *Foreign Policy*, March 22, 1997. www.foreignpolicy.com. Permission conveyed through Copyright Clearance Center, Inc.

market capitalism and democratic governance at the center of U.S. foreign policy. As Brinkley points out in this article, it took the Clinton administration some time to arrive at this policy. The president came to office inheriting crises from his predecessor in the Balkans, Somalia, and Haiti. Moreover, he was relatively inexperienced in foreign policy. In fact, the new president was often criticized for getting foreign policy wrong and lurching from crisis to crisis without a plan or a vision with which to guide America's actions. Brinkley argues, however, that the critics were missing the point: these interventions were not central to Clinton's strategic goals. They were the challenges that had to be contained so that the goal of fostering strong market democracies in Central Europe, Latin America, and Asia could be realized.

The Clinton administration decided upon a policy of enlargement in 1994. While the term never gained wide acceptance, the strategy did provide a guide for the conduct of American foreign policy. Clinton expanded the NATO alliance to cement the community of democracies together. The United States also provided assistance and aid to democratizing countries. The core of this strategy, however, was free trade and globalization. Pursuing both of these ends was seen as serving American prosperity and power as well as world order and economic development. Increased exports, reduced trade barriers, and the widespread acceptance of an American global agenda would all enhance the American-led global system of trade and finance, while allowing for the spread of American values and even cultural influence. The product of a liberal international perspective, it was designed to expand trade and integration, which would serve to diminish tendencies toward conflict among nations. In this sense, Clinton was a direct descendant of the political and economic policies of Alexander Hamilton, who also sought to achieve American goals through an emphasis on economic strategies and the maintenance of an open trading system in the world.

The Clinton strategy about the virtues of democratization and free markets was pursued through multilateral institutions and initiatives dealing with economic integration and cooperation, as well as political coalitions to combat disorder and threats to the global system. This means of pursuing policy would be in contrast to the current administration of George W. Bush. The current president has also pursued a foreign policy of democracy promotion, but it has been more assertive in the use of military force, especially in Iraq, to achieve these ends. It has also placed less emphasis on working with and through multilateral institutions to achieve international coalitions to pursue strategic goals. Though the two presidencies have in general agreed on a set of goals for American action, they have pursued divergent strategies to achieve them.

Ever since *Foreign Affairs* published George Kennan's seminal article, "The Sources of Soviet Conduct," which outlined what was to become President Harry Truman's strategy of "containment," succeeding administrations have sought to coin a phrase that encapsulates their foreign and defense policies. From the Eisenhower-Dulles "New Look" to Bush-Baker's multi-national "new world order," foreign policy monikers have been concocted for the purpose of convincing both America's overseas allies and its domes-tic electorate that the current administration, far from being caught in the shifting tides of ad hoc diplomacy, had a long-range grand plan. Thus it came as no surprise when on September 27, 1993, in a speech to the United Nations General Assembly, President Bill Clinton tried to elucidate his for-eign policy agenda by offering up the concept of "democratic enlargement."

While campaigning in 1992, Clinton had outlined what he considered to be the three foreign policy priorities that the next commander in chief would confront: updating and restructuring American military and secu-rity capabilities, elevating the role of economics in international affairs, and promoting democracy abroad.

From the very outset of his presidency it was obvious that, in addition to traditional national security concerns, U.S. economic interests would attain high priority in Clinton foreign policy. He spoke again and again of the need for global integration-technology-sharing, and in July 1993 he spent a fruitful week in Asia cementing trade pacts with Japan and South Korea. After only a few months under his administration the nation was spouting economic acronyms like GATT, NAFTA, APEC (Asia-Pacific Economic Cooperation forum), and G-7 (Group of Seven). Many international affairs experts, however, fretted that Clinton seemed to think that trade policy could substitute for a coherent foreign policy. "A foreign economic policy is not a foreign policy and it is not a national security strategy," lamented Council on Foreign Relations president Leslie Gelb when talk arose of expanding NAFTA to create a pan-American Free Trade Area by the year 2005 and a trans-Pacific one by 2020.

U.S. foreign policy during Clinton's first months in office was the product of crisis management rather than strategic doctrine. In many ways this was to be expected. Clinton was America's first post-Cold War president, so if he had no comprehensive strategy like "containment" it was because America had no single enemy like the Soviet Union against which to rally a national consensus. Elastic foreign policymaking appealed to Clinton; it allowed him the freedom to maneuver as the day's headlines dictated and to be an expo-nent of realpolitik one week and of Eleanor Roosevelt's idealism the next. While this sort of reactive diplomacy fit a politician famous for his ability to avoid being painted into a corner, Clinton's Yale Law/Georgetown School of Foreign Service side apparently realized that a larger vision would be needed if he was to enter the ranks of the great presidents. America was now the world's only superpower, and that reality demanded that global leadership emanate from the Oval Office. Great foreign policy, Clinton understood, did not only respond to situations; it created them.

It was in this climate of criticism and confusion in August 1993 that the president asked his pragmatic and unassuming national security adviser, Anthony Lake, to organize a study group to select a single word or slogan—like "containment"—that would embrace the three foreign policy priorities Clinton had articulated during the campaign. (The new compass word was ultimately featured in a major policy speech the president delivered before the U.N. General Assembly in late September.) If the Cold War had focused the United States on containing global threats to democracy and open markets, Clinton advised his NSC, its end freed him to find ways to expand the community of market democracies.

Clinton embraced the enlargement concept almost immediately, according to Lake; the president understood that it signified the notion that as free states grew in number and strength the international order would become both more prosperous and more secure. As Lake explained in his SAIS speech, the successor to containment "must be a strategy of enlargement . . . of the world's free community of market democracies." The blueprint focused on four points: 1) to "strengthen the community of market democracies"; 2) to "foster and consolidate new democracies and market economies where possible"; 3) to "counter the aggression and support the liberalization of states hostile to democracy"; and 4) to "help democracy and market economies take root in regions of greatest humanitarian concern."

These strategies of enlargement rejected the more expansive view that the United States was duty-bound to promote constitutional democracy and human rights everywhere; as a politically viable concept, enlargement had to be aimed at primary U.S. strategic and economic interests. For example, Asians in general took a vastly different view of what constituted democracy, preferring to emphasize social order over individual rights. Under enlargement, America's chief concern in Asia would therefore be free market access—the rest, for the most part, would be left to sort itself out.

## ENLARGEMENT IN ACTION

Clinton likened enlargement to the old anticommunist "domino theory" in reverse: It posited that where communist command economies collapsed, free markets would eventually arise and flourish. "Now the age of geopolitics has given way to an age of what might be called geo-economics," journalist Martin Walker wrote in the October 1, 1996, New Yorker. "The new virility symbols are exports and productivity and growth rates and the great international encounters are the trade pacts of the economic superpowers." Or, as Clinton himself put it in his 1994 budget message to Congress, "We have put our economic competitiveness at the heart of our foreign policy."

As for the emerging democracies, Clinton believed that if they developed consumer-oriented middle classes with the desired appetites for American products, peace and prosperity could become a reality. Relations with countries with bright economic futures such as Mexico and South Korea would thus be placed on the front burner in his administration; poor, blighted nations, particularly in sub-Saharan Africa and Central America, would receive back-burner attention, at best. Only when the international clamor for humanitarian aid rang too loudly to ignore would the administration focus on other nations. By the same token, the United States would no longer concern itself with the bloody, unprofitable civil and religious wars that raged from Angola to the Caucasus to Kashmir. Only when anarchy reigned in a major trade pact region—Bosnia or Northern Ireland, for example—would Clinton play global peacemaker. Likewise, the continuation of the Middle East peace process was considered to be important to the global economy.

Simply put, to the Clinton administration economic policy was the means to global leverage. "Information, ideas and money now pulse across the planet at light speed," enthused Lake. "This borderless global economy has generated an entrepreneurial boom and a demand for political openness." There were even trade pact precedents that fit nicely into enlargement's worldview: the GATT Uruguay Round and NAFTA—two international economic regimes inherited from the Bush administration that required bipartisan congressional support for passage. These tied domestic growth to a foreign policy that promotes U.S. exports and global free trade. In fact, what Clinton liked best about Lake's enlargement policy was the way it was inextricably linked to domestic renewal, with its emphasis on making sure the United States remained the world's largest exporter. The area of greatest export expansion has been services, with the U.S. trade surplus in that sector rising from $5 billion in 1986 to $58 billion in 1992. By the time Clinton began his second term, exports of services exceeded imports by $80 billion. Unlike many of his critics, Clinton was quick to understand that in the post-Cold War era good trade policy was the sine qua non of sound foreign policy, as the presence of market-based democracies plausibly would render the world a safer, richer place. If the Cold War enemy was communism, the post-Cold War villain was protectionism.

Clinton's NSC staff accepted that enlargement would have to begin with nations that were well on the way to becoming open-market democracies: the countries of Central and Eastern Europe and the Asia-Pacific region. Rogue or terrorist regimes—like Iran or Iraq—would be dealt with firmly if they tried to undermine the new order. The vision of democratic enlargement was econocentric: Only countries with free-spending middle classes, it was believed, could become democratic and adopt the Western values of embracing ethnic diversity, protecting citizens' rights, and cooperating with the world community to stop terrorism.

Thus by September 27, 1993, when Clinton delivered his address to the General Assembly, the NSC had reason to hope that enlargement would replace containment as America's grand strategy. "During the Cold War we sought to contain a threat to [the] survival of free institutions," Clinton told the U.N. "Now we seek to enlarge the circle of nations that live under those free institutions." Or, as Lake put it in a speech to the Council on Foreign Relations on December 14, 1993, "I believe that in the best tradition of twentieth-century American diplomacy, enlargement . . . marries our interests and our ideals."

Unfortunately for the administration, "enlargement" proved to be a public relations dud; few liked it or even took a passing interest. The foreign policy community greeted the Clinton and Lake speeches with indifference and even derision. Critics called enlargement uninspired, the predictable byproduct of Lake—a former professor—perusing arcane geopolitical textbooks. While some allowed that enlargement could make for an interesting white paper, most of the priests of geopolitics complained that this policy had no connection to reality and that it was an aspiration rather than a strategy. That charge was difficult to refute after October 3, 1993, when 18 U.S. Army soldiers were killed in an ill-planned operation in Mogadishu. It was even more difficult to refute after October 12, when anti-American demonstrations broke out in Haiti following the president's decision to recall a U.S. Navy ship carrying American and Canadian military personnel en route to Port-au-Prince in response to the junta there. The deaths in Somalia so affected Lake that he offered to resign, but Clinton would not allow it. A lesson had been learned: Seven months later Lake recommended against sending any peacekeepers to Rwanda.

What the administration's critics failed to see was that the events in both Somalia and Haiti were holdovers from President Bush's multinational "new world order." The Clinton administration's enlargement strategy suggested that both Somalia and Haiti—because they were incapable of developing middle-class consumer markets in the foreseeable future—should be on the periphery of U.S. foreign policy interests. There were to be no more blind humanitarian interventions under the Clinton administration, and the likes of Haiti would be handled not in terms of U.S. national security, economic policy, or humanitarian aid, but mostly in response to domestic pressures. In 1994, for example, it was relentless pressure from the Cuban' American community in Florida and the Congressional Black Caucus that persuaded Clinton to intervene in Haiti, forcing the junta's ouster.

Regardless of how well Clinton maneuvers through crises, free trade remains the heart of enlargement and the core of his foreign policy.

In July 1994, Clinton tried to weave the enlargement theme into the so-called En-En document: the National Security Strategy of Engagement and Enlargement. At the center of that policy paper is the belief that "the line between our domestic and foreign policies has increasingly disappeared—that we must revitalize our economy if we are to sustain our military forces, foreign initiatives and global influence, and that we must engage actively abroad if we are to open foreign markets and create jobs for our people." When two subsequent En-En policy papers were released by the White House—in February 1995 and February 1996—domestic renewal was portrayed as the linchpin of U.S. foreign policy.

Another important example of how Lake's enlargement concept took hold can be seen in then U.S. ambassador to the U.N. Madeleine Albright's abrupt conversion from a multinational moralist worried about genocidal wars to a realpolitik maverick who, with Senator Jesse Helms (R-North Carolina) cheering her on, became an archcritic of the U.N. Most commentators attributed Albright's turnabout to the Republican takeover of Congress in 1994. There, conservatives were all too happy to scapegoat the U.N. for any number of global woes, from Bosnia to Somalia. Instead of challenging the Republicans' anti-U.N. premise, Albright essentially joined their ad hominem chorus, denouncing U.N. secretary-general Boutros-Boutros Ghali and his slow pace of reform.

But electoral politics played only a partial role in her change of heart. The White House made it clear that the enlargement doctrine was official policy. U.N. peacekeeping, which flourished under Bush, was in disrepute, and under the strategy of enlargement it will continue to be eclipsed, even with Ghana's pro-American Kofi Annan serving as the new secretary-general. "We live in an era without power blocs in which old assumptions must be re-examined, institutions modernized and relationships transformed," Albright, now the secretary of state, noted in December 1996. The new blocs are an enlarged NATO and America's trade alliances, with the United States serving as locomotive for them all.

Of course, not everybody in the Clinton administration cottoned to enlargement the way Albright did. The State Department, for instance, worried that enlargement's emphasis on trade policy would mean massive cuts in its embassy operating budgets as corporations took the lead in trade disputes. [Secretary of State Warren] Christopher in particular wanted nothing to do with Lake's "grand strategy"—to his eyes a trade policy masquerading as foreign policy, according to a former top State Department official.

Although the secretary of state reportedly dismissed "democratic enlargement" as a self-aggrandizing gimmick on the part of Lake, the concept in fact became the president's general framework for dealing with global issues on a day-to-day basis. One of the main things Clinton liked about the concept by 1996 was how well it jibed with circumstances: NATO replaced the U.N. and curtailed fighting in Bosnia; nuclear weapons were on their way out of Belarus, Kazakhstan, and Ukraine; and democratic elections were being held in Russia. At last the president acquired the breathing room he would need to make the enlargement of NATO the top foreign policy priority of his second term.

That priority first emerged at the January 1994 NATO summit in Brussels, not long after Clinton's U.N. address. Clinton called on the NATO allies to "enlarge" the transatlantic military alliance to include the new free market democracies of Central and Eastern Europe, with most foreign policy experts believing that this meant the Czech Republic, Hungary, and Poland (the Visegrad states). Encouraged by the United States' bold lead, the heads of the NATO countries agreed in principle to a process of enlargement that "would reach to democratic states to our East as part of an evolutionary process, taking into account political and security developments in the whole of Europe." Clinton also led the way in creating the alliance's Partnership for Peace (PFP) in 1994, an agreement among NATO's current members intended to facilitate an orderly process of enlargement that will admit new members while modernizing the organization. "Partnership will serve one of the most important goals in our enlargement strategy . . . building a stable environment in which the new democracies and free markets of Eastern and Central Europe and the former USSR can flourish," Lake said.

Clinton and Lake saw NATO enlargement and PFP as important to achieving the larger objective of European integration. Reagan is remembered for ending the Cold War and Bush for reunifying Germany; Clinton saw a chance for a lasting legacy as the president who united Europe. If Washington had its way, NATO would enlarge, and the European Union (EU) would quickly follow suit. The Czech-born Albright will undoubtedly be an enthusiastic promoter of NATO enlargement, which will be spotlighted at NATO'S July 1997 "Supersummit" in Madrid. The outcome of that meeting—where NATO expansion to include the Visegrad states is supposed to be approved—will set the tone for Clinton's foreign policy in his second term.


## FREE TRADE AT THE CORE

A New York Times/CBS News opinion poll taken in September 1996 found that Clinton's foreign policy approval rating was a solid 53 per cent. *The New York Times'* R. W. Apple, Jr., concluded that Clinton had "escaped any significant damage from crises overseas." Apple also suggested that the polls showed how little foreign policy had to do with Clinton's odds of re-election; again, it was "the economy, stupid." What Apple failed to take into account was that Clinton viewed domestic renewal as partially dependent upon foreign trade policy: From 1993 to 1996, more than 200 new market opening agreements helped to create 1.6 million American jobs, Christopher proudly noted in a farewell address at Harvard University. During Clinton's first administration, the dollar grew stronger largely due to a combination of trade and fiscal policy, and from there it is not hard to understand one major reason why Michigan and Ohio voted for Clinton: Automobile exports increased dramatically during his first term. All over the world the United States was negotiating trade pacts. If John Foster Dulles had been accused of "pactomania" for engineering so many security treaties, Clinton was practicing pactomania for free trade.

With the possible exception of splitting his own party in Congress to push through NAFTA and GATT, nowhere has Clinton executed his enlargement strategy of free trade so boldly as in the Asia-Pacific region. In office only one year, Clinton decided to convene the 15 heads of state of the Pacific region at an APEC conference in Seattle to galvanize the creation of a giant free trade zone. A year later, in Jakarta, at the second APEC conference, its members signed an accord pledging to develop a free-trading Pacific Rim by 2010.

After trade talks between Tokyo and Washington collapsed in February 1994, Clinton decided the time for toughness had come. The administration's subsequent moves were unprecedented in post-war U.S.-Japanese relations. U.S. trade representative Mickey Kantor threatened Tokyo with trade sanctions for violating a 1989 agreement to open its market to American cellular phones. "America for 10 years tried 30 different trade agreements," Clinton announced, "and nothing ever happened. . . . The trade deficit just got bigger and bigger. So we're going to try to pursue a more aggressive policy now which will actually open markets." Over the ensuing years, the threat worked well—as several of Japan's key markets were pried open.

Ignoring trade policy in the recent campaign, Republicans contended that Clinton's foreign policy was weak and visionless. "My biggest criticism is that this administration lacks a conceptual framework to shape the world going into the next century and [to] explain what threatens that vision," Senator John McCain of Arizona, a Dole adviser, complained. "Without that global strategy, we keep getting ourselves involved in peripheral matters such as Northern Ireland and Haiti."

What McCain failed to realize was that both Northern Ireland and Haiti were on the periphery of the Clinton administration's foreign policy agenda for the past two years, despite all the media attention they had attracted. On the Democratic side, pro-U.N. forces berated Clinton for refusing to pay America's bills to the organization and for scapegoating Boutros-Ghali over Somalia and Bosnia. Ignoring enlargement, McCain and other critics dismissed Clinton as an amateur juggler in the realm of foreign policy. They were half right. Clinton, after a rough beginning, slowly overcame his proclivity for procrastination and developed into an able practitioner of Band-Aid diplomacy. By 1995, he demonstrated the flexibility and decisiveness necessary to deal adroitly with such trouble spots as Bosnia, Haiti, North Korea, the Persian Gulf, and the Taiwan Strait. "U.S. foreign policy has been increasingly successful precisely because Bill Clinton has refused to embrace chimerical visions," Jacob Heilbrunn observed in the November 11, 1996, New Republic. "As a result, he has skillfully piloted the U.S. through a sea of new world disorder."

Regardless of how well Clinton maneuvers through crises, free trade remains the heart of enlargement and the core of his foreign policy—not that Clinton was the first postwar American leader to lead the way in the establishment of free trade zones. A number of presidents, from Truman to Richard Nixon—all devoted to the vision of Jean Monnet—pushed for Atlantic community trade agreements that eventually led to the Kennedy Round, where the GATT was jump-started. When Clinton went to Madrid in December 1995 to launch a new transatlantic agenda with EU leaders, he was giving credence to a half-century of noble attempts to integrate North America and Western Europe economically. Nor should it be forgotten that Reagan was chiefly responsible for engineering the free trade pact with Canada and that Bush brought Mexico into the NAFTA framework. But it was Clinton who advanced the view that democracy would prevail in the post-Cold War world through trade pacts as much as ballot boxes.

Put another way, enlargement was about spreading democracy through promoting the gospel of geoeconomics. "The elegance of the Clinton strategy was that the Pacific, the European, and Western Hemisphere blocs should all have one thing in common; Clinton's America was locking itself steadily into the heart of each one," Martin Walker has observed. Some critics prefer a more militarily activist approach, even a new sort of gunboat diplomacy,[1] but Clinton favors enlargement; he is more interested in helping Toys "R" Us and Nike to flourish in Central Europe and Asia than in dispatching Marines to quell unrest in economically inconsequential nations. "With our help, the forces of reform in Europe's newly free nations have laid the foundations of democracy," Clinton boasted at an October 1996 campaign rally in

Detroit. "We've helped them to develop successful market economies, and now are moving from aid to trade and investment." *The New York Times'* Thomas Friedman identified one key tenet of Clinton's enlargement strategy in a December 8, 1996, column titled "Big Mac 1": "No two countries that both have a McDonald's have ever fought a war against each other."

But many emerging democracies would have preferred U.S. dollars to "deterrent" hamburgers—Russia in particular. The U.S. budget deficit prevents Clinton from devising some sort of grandiose Marshall Plan for Russia, but his administration has come up with $43 billion in bilateral assistance for Yeltsin's government since 1993. This aid in the name of enlargement has helped to facilitate economic reform in Russia by curbing inflation and stabilizing the ruble—with the net result being that more than 60 per cent of Russia's gross domestic product is now generated by its private sector. In fact, the Clinton administration's assistance has helped Russia to privatize more property in less time than any other foreign-development venture in history: As of September 1996, more than 120,000 Russian enterprises large and small had been transferred to private hands, with U.S.-Russian trade up 65 per cent since Clinton took office.

Meanwhile, again thanks to enlargement, the United States became Russia's largest foreign investor, with the U.S. Export-Import Bank, the Overseas Private Investment Corporation, and the Trade and Development Agency supporting commercial transactions with Moscow valued at more than $4 billion. This expansion of the global free market, coupled with Russia's 1995 parliamentary elections and 1996 presidential contest, indicates that democracy may finally be taking root there. With Russia becoming more stabilized economically and politically—and with U.S.-Russian relations "normalized" for the first time since the First World War—the Clinton administration is eager to push the enlargement of NATO.

Far into the next century, various trade agreements—APEC, the Free Trade Agreement of the Americas, GATT, NAFTA, the Trans Atlantic Free Trade Area, and the World Trade Organization—will advance Washington's global agenda while promoting American domestic renewal. Critics like former secretary of state Lawrence Eagleburger—who complains about a lack of "hard strategic thinking about how we want to see the world in the first part of the next century"—fail to recognize that Clinton's enlargement policy is already catapulting America into the next millennium, even if the word "enlargement" itself has been largely ignored. In light of the unilateralism of the Helms-Burton act, which seeks to isolate Cuba economically, and given administration support for

Republican senator Alfonse D'Amato's Iran and Libya Sanctions Act, which seeks to reinforce the pariah status of those countries, it should be clear that enlargement means free trade on American terms. By adopting the strategy of enlargement, Clinton hopes to be remembered by historians as the free trade president and the leading architect of a new world economic order.

More than any other Clinton administration figure, it was Lake who set the course for the first term's foreign policy. His enlargement strategy will dominate the second term, whether he remains a major player or not. "There are very few times that [Tony's position] ultimately is reversed or changed or modified," then White House chief of staff Leon Panetta told the *New York Times*. Then undersecretary of commerce for international trade Stuart Eizenstat added, "Tony's enlargement strategy makes perfect sense. In the Cold War the concept was containment; now it's to enlarge the scope of democracy. It's all about widening market access." By the end of 1995, four years after the USSR's collapse, 117 countries—nearly two of every three independent nations—had chosen their leaders in open elections. They are anxious for the McDonalds of this world to open shop.

Even more than Lake, Sandy Berger—Lake's former deputy and successor as NSC adviser—has a long history of smashing protectionist barriers as the former director of the international trade group of his Washington law firm, Hogan & Hartson. Berger's expertise lies in global monetary transactions, and in the Clinton White House he is known as the "trade troubleshooter"—the public official best suited to confront Japanese protectionist tendencies and Chinese closed markets. Meanwhile, even at the Pentagon, trade desks are being created, causing career military officers to scratch their heads in puzzlement.

The second-term Clinton administration foreign policy team of Albright, Berger, and Lake—grounded in the modern realist school, with hints of neo-Wilsonian idealism popping up from time to time—will continue trying to enlarge the "blue blob" of democracy. "The American people want their country's foreign policy rooted in idealpolitik as well as realpolitik," Deputy Secretary of State Strobe Talbott recently asserted. Lake essentially concurs; pragmatic realism first, idealism always a close second. Democratic enlargement, a concept drawn from geoeconomics, follows this principle and could well be remembered by future historians as the Clinton Doctrine.

## Note

1. See William Kristol and Robert Kagan, "Toward a Neo-Reaganite Foreign Policy," *Foreign Affairs* 75:4 (July/August 1996).

# 33 Avoiding Nuclear Anarchy

## GRAHAM ALLISON, OWEN COTE JR., RICHARD FALKENRATH, AND STEVEN MILLER

The collapse of the Soviet Union and the end of the Cold War shaped the subsequent international environment in a multitude of ways, well beyond the larger, often abstract concerns about unipolarity, America's role in the world, and the development of a new grand strategy. One of the most significant issues of the post–Cold War period involves the proliferation of nuclear weapons. This concern, which has only grown in importance and continues to be a central feature of American foreign policy, centers around the development of nuclear weapons by allies such as Japan and Germany, so-called "orphans" such as Pakistan and India, and most particularly, "rogue states" such as North Korea and Iran. Even more troublesome has been the concern over non-state actors. While terrorist organizations or other groups seeking to upset the status quo might not be able to develop their own technologies, they can still purchase technology or weapons. Since non-state actors cannot be deterred in the same way as states, the likelihood that such weapons will be used once acquired is much greater.

Russia is the country that represents the greatest potential threat regarding the "leakage" of nuclear materials, as the country has had great difficulty controlling and accounting for fissile materials within its own borders. The capacity of the Russian government and military to maintain tight control over the huge stockpile of Soviet nuclear resources diminished significantly in the years following the Cold War, and there have been several incidents involving theft or smuggling of these materials. This lack of certainty regarding the security of the Russian stockpile became especially worrisome in a world that in the 1990s was characterized by increasing disorder in the form of regional conflict, ethnic and religious wars, failed states, and terrorism. The dangers of the Cold War had been immense, but the conflict did also have a restraining influence on other actors and lesser conflicts around the world, as the superpowers could not afford to let small conflicts get out of control. Once the international system changed, this restraint disappeared, and it seemed that a number of grievances, old and new,

Coté, Owen R., Jr., Graham T. Allison, Steven E. Miller, and Richard A. Falkenrath, *Avoiding Nuclear Anarchy: Containing the Threat of Loose Russian Nuclear Weapons and Fissile Material*, excerpt from pp. 3-17. © 1996 BCSIA. By permission of The MIT Press.

emerged with a fury. Thus at a time when the ability to control limited conflicts diminished, the attractiveness of nuclear weapons to states and non-state actors seemed to be on the rise.

Allison and Cote discuss the fact that the United States has responded to the threat, engaging in a variety of efforts to secure Russia's nuclear materials. The United States has provided assistance to dismantle Russian nuclear weapons, buy enriched uranium, pay salaries for Russian nuclear scientists, and dismantle old Soviet "nuclear cities," where weapons had been produced. This assistance amounted to almost $400 million a year throughout most of the 1990s. The authors argue, however, that while this aid has been helpful, it comes nowhere near addressing the full measure of the potential threat. America and Russia have not addressed this problem "in a manner that is commensurate with their stakes in the issue." They strongly suggest that the United States acknowledge this fact and strengthens its efforts, and they have continued to make the same argument since the time this article appeared. Allison and Cote, however, expect little to be done until after a nuclear detonation by terrorists, when it will be too late.

---

With the end of the Cold War, a new conventional wisdom declares that the United States faces "no direct threat" to its security. Despite repeated assertions of this proposition by government officials, those who have come to understand the nuclear leakage threat—including many in the intelligence and policy communities—generally accept the judgment that the risk of a nuclear detonation on American soil has increased. But because this new threat comes in the form so unfamiliar, indeed so radically different from prior experience, and because the instruments and policies to address it are so unlike the familiar Cold War approaches that the U.S. defense establishment pursued successfully for decades, Americans have had difficulty awakening to this fact.

## COPING WITH NEW NUCLEAR CHALLENGES

The collapse of the former Soviet Union presented American policy-makers with three major new nuclear challenges. The first was to secure and consolidate the Soviet Union's far-flung arsenal of tactical nuclear weapons, the type which would be most useful to a terrorist group or rogue state in search of an instant nuclear capability. The second challenge was to cope with the fact that Soviet strategic nuclear weapons—principally its nuclear-armed intercontinental ballistic missiles (ICBMs)—were located in four of the Soviet successor states, raising the prospect that the demise of the Soviet Union might result in the emergence of several states with intercontinental nuclear forces. Finally, the third post-Soviet nuclear challenge was and remains to prevent the leakage of nuclear weapons or weapons-usable material from Russia and the rest of the former Soviet Union. Assessing U.S. and Russian performance in addressing these three challenges over the past several years: there has been great success in rapidly consolidating the tactical nuclear arsenal into Russia; high prospects for great success in removing the Soviet strategic arsenal from Belarus, Kazakstan, and Ukraine; but distressingly little progress in securing the remnants of the Soviet nuclear legacy now located principally in Russia. Reducing the threat of nuclear leakage remains the great unanswered challenge of the post-Cold War nuclear agenda.

## Tactical Nuclear Weapons

The total size of the Soviet tactical nuclear weapons arsenal has never been precisely known, but it is believed that some 15,000–30,000 tactical nuclear weapons were stationed in 14 of the Soviet Union's 15 constituent republics in 1991. In the context of increasing turmoil within the ranks of the Soviet military and rising instability along the Soviet periphery, especially in the conflict-ridden republics such as Armenia, Azerbaijan, Georgia, and Tajikistan, the Soviet Union's tactical nuclear weapons arsenal presented an acute risk of diversion. Scores of weapons could have come loose. If they had, could they have found their way into international black markets? Diamonds, precious metals, and virtually everything else of great value in the former Soviet Union do, so it seems unlikely that nuclear weapons would have been different. If available in international arms bazaars, would there have been buyers? Certainly, including in all likelihood both rogue states and terrorist groups. Recognizing this risk, the U.S. government undertook two unprecedented initiatives in 1991. First, in September 1991, President George Bush announced the unilateral withdrawal of tactical nuclear weapons from U.S. forces around the world, a sweeping and historic initiative that vitiated in a stroke decades of U.S. military planning. President Bush successfully challenged the Soviet government (soon to be succeeded by the Russian government) to undertake a reciprocal withdrawal of tactical nuclear weapons from its military forces abroad, a process which in fact Moscow had already begun, albeit on a modest scale. Before the end of 1992, more than 10,000 tactical nuclear weapons previously stationed beyond Russia's border had been returned to Russia.

The second historic U.S. initiative was the Soviet Nuclear Threat Reduction Act of 1991, better known as the "Nunn-Lugar program" after its two principal sponsors, Senators Sam Nunn and Richard Lugar. In its first year, the Nunn-Lugar program allowed the U.S. government to spend up to $400 million from the defense budget on initiatives designed to offer technical assistance to the Soviet Union (soon to be the Soviet successor states) directed toward the safe and secure transportation and dismantlement of nuclear weapons and their delivery systems, and toward the implementation of other important arms control and nonproliferation objectives. For example, one of the first Nunn-Lugar projects to yield practical results was a 1992 program in Ukraine to deliver transportation equipment that was needed to move the tactical nuclear weapons (which were in the process of being withdrawn) from their storage depots to the rail heads from which they could be shipped to Russia. Responsibility for managing the Nunn-Lugar program was assigned to the Office of the Secretary of Defense, while the process of actually negotiating Nunn-Lugar agreements with the Soviet successor states was carried out under the auspices of a specially created Safe and Secure Dismantlement (SSD) delegation. Congress has authorized the Nunn-Lugar program to spend about $300–400 million each year during 1991–96, but these authorizations have been subject to an array of problematic restrictions and requirements that have tended to reduce the effectiveness of the program as a whole. Nonetheless, the Nunn-Lugar program has played a pivotal, though often controversial, role in the U.S. government's efforts to cope with the new nuclear challenges of the immediate post-Soviet period.

## Strategic Nuclear Weapons

The second major challenge of the post-Soviet period concerned the ownership of the Soviet Union's strategic nuclear forces. When the Soviet Union expired, the former Soviet strategic arsenal was left in four successor states: Russia, Ukraine, Kazakstan, and Belarus. The Bush administration and the Congress wasted no time in deciding that the United States could accept only one nuclear successor state to the Soviet Union—Russia; this was a view shared by most other states on the planet, importantly including (at least at first) the newly sovereign governments of former Soviet republics. In practice, however, the process of denuding Belarus, Kazakstan, and Ukraine of the strategic nuclear weapons they had inherited proved to be no simple matter, particularly in the case of Ukraine. Belarus was never a serious concern because of its subservience to Moscow. Kazakstan wavered only briefly before the pragmatic policies of President Nursultan Nazerbayev set Kazakstan on a firm course toward total denuclearization, a status it achieved when the last nuclear warhead was removed from Kazak territory in April 1995.

In its most consequential national security initiative, the Clinton administration moved in 1993 to establish a multidimensional relationship with Ukraine aimed at securing its prompt and complete denuclearization. The two central strands of this strategy were an intense engagement of Russia and Ukraine designed to resolve, or at least smooth over, many of the most serious differences between Moscow and Kiev, and the extensive use of Nunn-Lugar assistance to coax Ukraine into fulfilling its own commitments to relinquish its nuclear warheads. Much of this diplomacy was carried out in the context of the Gore-Chernomyrdin Commission (GCC), a biannual forum convened by Russian Prime Minister Victor Chernomyrdin and U.S. Vice President Al Gore that brings together senior Russian and American officials for high-profile, and often highly technical, negotiations. Vice President Gore brokered the deal that restarted the denuclearization of Ukraine at the end of 1993, an arrangement which was set forth in the "trilateral statement" issued by U.S. President Bill Clinton, Russian President Boris Yeltsin, and Ukrainian President Leonid Kravchuk at the January 1994 summit in Moscow.

## Nuclear Leakage

The third nuclear challenge of the post-Soviet era is qualitatively different—and orders of magnitude more difficult—than the first two. Solutions to the first two problems have succeeded in concentrating the former Soviet nuclear arsenal—some 30,000–40,000 nuclear weapons—into, Russia, which also contains the components and bulk fissile material for tens of thousands more weapons. Thus, the geographic expanse of the former Soviet nuclear arsenal has been reduced from one-sixth to one-seventh of the earth's landmass. The trouble, of course, arises from the fact that this one-seventh of the earth's landmass into which the Soviet nuclear legacy has been consolidated is a profoundly troubled society, one marked by political instability, economic distress, and rampant crime and corruption. Thousands of nuclear weapons and hundreds of thousands of pounds of weapons-usable fissile material are being held at scores of sites scattered across Russia—a fact that will hold true indefinitely. What makes this situation an international security problem without precedent, however, is that these nuclear weapons and materials are being stored in installations that lack adequate security, which are themselves located inside a highly unstable country.

The risk is that the former Soviet nuclear weapons and materials will leak out of Russia, finding their way into the hands of rogue states or terrorist groups. American and Russian policy have not yet begun to address this problem in a manner that is commensurate with their stakes in the issue. During 1992–94, most of the U.S. initiatives designed to combat the threat of nuclear leakage were carried out in the context of the Nunn-Lugar program within the Department of Defense. The effectiveness of this early effort suffered from an array of legal restrictions and bureaucratic obstacles, making the Nunn-Lugar program a problematic vehicle for improving the security of Russian fissile material quickly or comprehensively. Responsibility for implementing the various U.S. anti-leakage programs was broadened in 1994–95, but although this bureaucratic adaptation began to show a few promising results in 1995, the overall U.S. government effort was still moving too slowly. Indeed, on the current track, U.S. and Russian policies will not fully address the nuclear leakage problem for years to come, leaving U.S. interests unacceptably jeopardized for a protracted period of time.

## NUCLEAR LEAKAGE: OCCURRING AND LIKELY TO GET WORSE

Since 1991, the press has been filled with stories about the theft and illicit trafficking of nuclear materials and weapons from the former Soviet Union. Literally hundreds of incidents have been reported, but the vast majority of the known incidents have been hoaxes or have not involved weapons-usable materials. Nevertheless, the available facts are grounds for grave concern, for at least four reasons. First, the large number of real or fraudulent efforts to sell things nuclear suggests a widespread appreciation within the former Soviet Union that such materials have market value. Second, these facts suggest a considerable effort to fill the supply side of an emerging nuclear black market. Third, it is unlikely that every attempt at nuclear smuggling is detected and reported; by definition, successful transactions on black markets are covert and unnoticed. Finally, and perhaps most tellingly, buried in the large number of alleged cases are a small number of very serious incidents.

### Six Known Incidents

Since 1992, there have been six known cases of theft or illicit trafficking in fissile material. An employee stole approximately 3.7 pounds of HEU [highly enriched uranium] from the Luch Scientific Production Association at Podolsk, Russia, in mid-1992. A captain in the Russian Navy stole approximately 10 pounds of HEU from a submarine fuel storage facility in Murmansk in November 1993. German police accidentally discovered 5.6 grams of super-grade plutonium in the garage of a suspected counterfeiter in Tengen, Germany, in May 1994. In June 1994, Bavarian police in Landshut seized 0.8 grams of HEU in a sting operation. A sting operation also resulted in the seizure of almost a pound of near-weapons-grade plutonium at the Munich airport in August 1994. And approximately six pounds of HEU were seized in Prague in December

1994. To put this into historical perspective, more fissile material is known to have been stolen from the former Soviet Union than the United States managed to produce in the first three years of the Manhattan Project.

### Why Leakage Is Likely to Grow Worse

Though any leakage is worrisome, a catastrophic rupture of the Russian nuclear complex, which could release a vast quantity of nuclear weapons or fissile material into international black markets, has not yet taken place. Unfortunately, there are a number of reasons to believe that nuclear leakage from Russia is likely to continue and could easily get worse: Russian society suffers from profound disorder, the result of social and economic hardship, political opportunism, and rampant criminalization; Russia's sprawling nuclear complex is in the midst of a seemingly terminal economic decline; the oppressive internal security system developed during the Soviet era has largely collapsed, and the integrity of what remains is questionable; Russia lacks a national or even a site-specific inventory system for its fissile material; Russia's nuclear installations have inadequate security against theft, particularly against insider threats; and the process of dismantling Russia's excess nuclear warheads is overwhelming Russia's capacity to store the resulting excess weapons components. Given this situation, more nuclear leakage is likely, serious incidents involving weapons quantities of fissile material are a distinct possibility, and the risk of a catastrophic rupture of the Russian custodial system remains distressingly high.

## NUCLEAR LEAKAGE: THE SINGLE GREATEST THREAT TO U.S. NATIONAL SECURITY INTERESTS

Nuclear leakage constitutes the most serious direct threat to vital U.S. interests today and for the foreseeable future. The new threat of nuclear leakage caused by the Soviet collapse has transformed the nature of the proliferation problem for the United States (and for other states seriously concerned with proliferation). To appreciate this threat, four pervasive myths about nuclear weapons and fissile material must be jettisoned: first, that building a nuclear weapon is hard to do; second, that fissile materials are too hazardous or too heavy to smuggle; third, that the delivery of a nuclear weapon against the United States is a challenge; and fourth, that there is no demand for illicitly acquired nuclear weapons or fissile material. All four assumptions are dead wrong, and deeply pernicious to the extent that they inform or guide the national security policies of any state.

# THE U.S. RESPONSE TO THE NUCLEAR LEAKAGE THREAT: INADEQUATE

The U.S. response to this new threat of nuclear leakage has not begun to equal the U.S. stakes in the matter. During the first three years after the collapse of the Soviet Union, virtually no progress was made toward reducing the likelihood that a nuclear weapon or a quantity of fissile material would leak out of Russia. In 1995, a few hopeful steps were taken in a few areas of the post-Soviet nuclear archipelago. Yet most of the relevant facilities are no more secure by the end of 1995 than they were when the Soviet Union disappeared. And although several important individual successes of U.S. policy can now be identified, not enough has been done to reverse the broad-based vulnerability of Russia's nuclear custodial system.

## Many U.S. Programs, But Progress Too Slow

Within the confines of current political constraints, the Clinton administration has pursued a broad range of innovative programs designed to deal with many different nuclear issues in the former Soviet Union. These programs fall into three basic categories: those that seek to directly improve the security of nuclear weapons and materials in the former Soviet Union; those that seek permanent disposition of fissile materials; and those that seek to "build confidence through openness" by enhancing the transparency of the Russian and American nuclear establishments. With respect to improving the security of nuclear materials, there have been a few important achievements, but in general the U.S. effort in this area has proceeded at a slow pace and on a small scale, and stands little chance of effecting a near-term reduction in the severity of the nuclear leakage threat. Similarly, the long-term disposition and transparency negotiations have proceeded extremely slowly. While there have been some modest achievements on the long-term disposition question, the transparency negotiations have largely been stymied by Russian intransigence.

## Why Progress Has Been Slow

The U.S. effort to reduce the nuclear leakage threat has been obstructed by Russia's reluctance to cooperate, financial limits, political conditions, and legal restrictions imposed by Congress, the competing priorities of the Clinton administration itself, and the meagerness of the contributions of the U.S. allies. The basic weakness in the Clinton administration's response to the nuclear leakage threat has been the absence of a concerted high-level effort to overcome these obstacles, especially by inducing cooperation from the Russian government and convincing the Congress, the U.S. public, and the other advanced industrial nations of the need for a more ambitious and better financed campaign against the nuclear leakage threat.

# RECOMMENDATIONS

To combat the threat of nuclear leakage, the leaders of Russia, the United States, and the other major industrial powers must find a way to overcome the obstacles to faster progress that they have encountered over the past four years. At the broadest level, the president and his senior deputies should devote more time and energy to creating the political latitude that the administration must have if it is to succeed in safeguarding the United States against future nuclear threats. Since the political constraints noted above emanate principally from Moscow and Capitol Hill, the Clinton administration should aim its efforts toward these two audiences. The United States should also focus more intensely on securing the cooperation and support of its friends and allies in this effort. Assuming that such an effort does increase the political latitude needed to combat nuclear leakage, the United States should pursue programs that can contribute to the following three objectives.

## Promote Programs That Directly Improve Nuclear Security

The highest priority of U.S. nonproliferation policy must be to persuade Russia to take immediate concrete steps that reduce the near-term likelihood of nuclear leakage. To meet the urgent aim of achieving the greatest possible reduction in the nuclear leakage threat in the shortest possible time, there are at least four programs that the United States should either initiate or pursue with greater urgency. First, the United States should expand and accelerate the U.S. purchase of Russian HEU. Second, the U.S. government should offer to purchase Russia's excess weapons-grade plutonium. Third, the United States should do whatever is necessary to implement or accelerate security enhancement at all nuclear installations in the former Soviet Union. Finally, the U.S. government should propose to Moscow a high-priority joint inventory and site-by-site security analysis of all U.S. and Russian nuclear installations.

## Build a Constructive Relationship with the Russian Government, Especially Minatom

Rapid progress on major programs designed to reduce the threat of nuclear leakage is possible only in the context of a strong, cooperative relationship with the Russian government and, most importantly, the custodian of Russia's far-flung nuclear stockpiles. Therefore, the U.S. government should put greater emphasis on defining and advancing nuclear security programs that serve the institutional interests of key Russian actors along with U.S. national security interests. Hence, the United States should: (1) restructure the U.S. plan to purchase Russian HEU in a way that gives Minatom [the Ministry of Atomic Energy] better economic incentives to cooperate with the United States; (2) finance joint nuclear technology projects between Minatom and Western firms; (3) fund the joint environmental cleanup of key nuclear-weapons installations in both countries; (4) expand the Industrial Partnering Program (IPP), the most successful of the U.S. programs aimed at reorienting Russian nuclear weapons enterprises toward non-military commercial activities; and (5) provide a near-term alternative energy source to the two Russian cities where weapons-grade plutonium is still being produced, so that the Russian government can shut down its three remaining plutonium-production reactors.

### Promote and Implement a Long-term Fissile Material Management Plan

Finally, the United States should, in cooperation with Russia and the other key nuclear states, define a long-term plan for coping with the global surplus of excess fissile materials, and must commit the resources needed to implement this plan. Long-term fissile material management is a task of global proportions that should be carried out on the basis of close international cooperation and consultation; given their unique roles as nuclear superpowers, the United States and Russia must take the lead in this area. Given the urgency of the nuclear leakage threat, a long-term strategy for coping with surplus fissile materials should be designed to reinforce near-term efforts to prevent nuclear leakage from the former Soviet Union. In this respect, the United States should (1) define and implement a staged international monitoring regime for fissile materials, beginning on a bilateral basis with Russia and gradually assuming multilateral characteristics; (2) establish an international plutonium bank, or "depository," as an interim plutonium disposition solution; and (3) take the lead in a concerted effort by the world's key law enforcement and intelligence agencies to develop the skills, procedures, and equipment needed to combat the illicit trafficking in nuclear materials effectively and systematically—an effort referred to in shorthand as the establishment of a "nuclear Interpol."

## ACT NOW, NOT THE MORNING AFTER

Despite the serious threat of loose nuclear weapons and fissile material, and despite the existence of a panoply of measures that could help reduce the likelihood of leakage from the deadly arsenal of former Soviet weapons and fissile materials, at present there appears to be little prospect that

America's leaders—whether President Clinton, or Senator [Robert] Dole, or Speaker [Newt] Gingrich—will take the lead in crafting a more ambitious and potentially more effective anti-leakage effort. And the reason why is clear. The "political realities," as knowing Washingtonians say, make this infeasible. No new initiative, however vital to the interests of the United States, has much prospect of getting a serious hearing in the climate of massive deficits, deep budget cuts, partisan rivalry, electoral calculations, and shrinking imagination.

Difficult as it is, identifying a new challenge is the easier part of the problem. Summoning the will and wherewithal to act effectively is harder still. This is especially so where the response requires significant changes in behavior and major exertion over a sustained period.

On the morning after the first act of nuclear terrorism, what will the president of the United States wish he had done earlier? What will the leaders of Congress be willing to support in the aftermath? What will the administration do then? What prevents us from pausing, reflecting, and summoning the wisdom to act now?

## 34 Nation Building: The Inescapable Responsibility of the World's Only Superpower

### JAMES DOBBINS

The rise of ethnic conflict and failed states in the 1990s prompted the United States to intervene in a number of places around the globe. The spread of disorder and violence occurred in Somalia, Bosnia, Kosovo, Haiti, Rwanda, and several other places. The specific circumstances of each case were quite different, but each of these spots had a common element: they all represented humanitarian crises. In four of these places—Somalia, Haiti, Bosnia, and Kosovo—the United States intervened, usually with its allies, in order to stop humanitarian disasters from becoming even greater. As James

James Dobbins, excerpt from "Nation Building: The Inescapable Responsibility of the World's Only Superpower," *Rand Review,* Summer 2003. Copyright 2003 by Rand Corporation. Figures from *America's Guide to Nation-Building: From Germany to Iraq* by James Dobbins et al. Copyright 2003 by Rand Corporation. Reproduced by permission of Rand Corporation in the format textbook via Copyright Clearance Center.

Dobbins discusses, in each of these instances the United States and its allies came to pursue the ambitious goal known as "nation building," which involved intervening in order to establish an enduring transition to democracy so that withdrawal of American and allied troops would not result in a renewed outbreak of violence.

Dobbins looks at the record of American nation-building efforts, examining the factors behind success and failure. He points out that the cases of Germany and Japan set a standard for nation building that has never been matched, and then goes on to look at American efforts in the post–Cold War era. Dobbins examines the major factors leading to a successful nation building effort, arguing that the level of commitment made by the United States and its allies in the form of time, money, and troops have been the most significant elements. The greater the level of commitment, the more successful the effort, with the greatest success occurring in Kosovo. In each subsequent intervention, Dobbins argues, the United States learned from past practices and applied the lessons it had learned.

This article focuses to a great extent on American interventions during the 1990s, and for that reason it is included in this section. Humanitarian intervention and nation building were important elements of America's foreign policy in the decade after the collapse of communism. Dobbins, however, also offers an analysis of American actions in Afghanistan and Iraq. He suggests that nation building will continue to be the responsibility of the United States, and provides a comparative analysis to see if current American efforts in these countries are sufficient to produce a success similar to Kosovo. He finds that the "positive learning curve has not been sustained" in either place, and that in Iraq, the level of commitment by the United States is most likely to lead to "lower levels of security, higher casualties sustained and inflicted, lower economic growth rates, and slower, less thoroughgoing political transformation."

---

We at the RAND Corporation have compiled what we have found to be the most important lessons learned by the United States in its nation-building efforts since World War II. Not all these hard-won lessons have yet been fully applied to America's most recent nation-building efforts in Afghanistan and Iraq.

We define nation-building as "the use of armed force in the aftermath of a conflict to underpin an enduring transition to democracy." We have compared the levels of progress toward this goal among seven historical cases: Germany, Japan, Somalia, Haiti, Bosnia, Kosovo, and Afghanistan. These are the most important instances in which American military power has been used in the aftermath of a conflict to underpin democratization elsewhere around the world since World War II.

# FROM GERMANY TO AFGHANISTAN

The cases of Germany and Japan set a standard for postconflict nation-building that has not been matched since. Both were comprehensive efforts at social, political, and economic reconstruction. These successes demonstrated that democracy was transferable, that societies could be encouraged to transform themselves, and that major transformations could endure.

For the next 40 years, there were few attempts to replicate these early successes. During the cold war with the Soviet Union, America employed its military power to preserve the status quo, not to alter it; to manage crises, not to resolve the underlying problems; to overthrow unfriendly regimes and reinstall friendly ones, not to bring about fundamental societal change.

After 1989, a policy of global containment of the Soviet Union no longer impelled the United States to preserve the status quo. Washington was now free to overlook regional instability in places like Yugoslavia and Afghanistan as long as the instability did not directly threaten American interests. At the same time, though, the United States had the unprecedented opportunity of using its unrivaled power to resolve, not just to manage or to contain, international problems of strategic importance. In addition, the United States could secure broader international support for such efforts than ever before.

Throughout the 1990s, each successive post-cold war effort became wider in scope and more ambitious in intent than its predecessor had been. In Somalia, the original objective was purely humanitarian but was subsequently expanded to democratization. In Haiti, the objective was to reinstall a president and to conduct elections according to an existing constitution. In Bosnia, the objective was to create a multiethnic state out of a former Yugoslav republic. In Kosovo, the objective was to establish a democratic polity and market economy virtually from scratch.

From Somalia in 1992 to Kosovo in 1999, each nation-building effort was somewhat better managed than the previous one (see table below). Somalia was the nadir. Everything that could go wrong did. The operation culminated in the withdrawal of U.S. troops in 1994 after a sharp tactical setback that had resulted in 18 American deaths in October 1993. This reverse, which became memorialized in the book and film "Black Hawk Down," was largely the result of an unnecessarily complicated U.S. and United Nations command structure that had three distinct forces operating with three distinct chains of command. Despite its failure, the Somalia mission taught America crucial lessons for the future. One was the importance of unity of command in peace operations as well as in war. Second was the need to scale mission objectives to available resources in troops, money, and staying power. A third lesson was the importance of deploying significant numbers of international police alongside international military forces to places where the local law enforcement institutions had disappeared or become illegitimate.

America applied these lessons to Haiti in the mid-1990s. We had unity of command throughout the operation. We did not have parallel American and allied forces. We had a single force under a single command with a clear hierarchy of decisionmaking. We deployed a large number of police within weeks of the military deployment, and the police were armed with both weapons and arrest authority. Unfortunately, we were obsessed with exit strategies and exit deadlines in the wake of the Somalia debacle. So we pulled out of Haiti with the job at best half done.

The Bosnia experience of the late 1990s was more successful. We set an exit deadline but wisely ignored it when the time came. On the negative side, there was a lack of coordination between the military stabilization efforts of NATO and those organizations responsible for civilian recon-struction. Consequently, the authority for implementing the civilian reconstruction projects became fragmented among numerous competing institutions. To complicate the situation further, the international police who had been deployed were armed with neither weapons nor arrest authority.

By the time of the Kosovo conflict in 1999, we and our allies had absorbed most of these lessons. We then made smarter choices in Kosovo. We achieved unity of command on both the civil and military sides. As in Bosnia, NATO was responsible for military operations. On the civil side, we established a clear hierarchical structure under a United Nations repre-sentative. Leadership was shared effectively between Europe and the United States. Working together, we deployed nearly 5,000 well-armed police alongside military peacekeepers. Although far from perfect, the arrangement was more successful than it had been in Bosnia.

During his presidential campaign in 2000, George W. Bush criticized the Clinton administration for this expansive nation-building agenda. As pres-ident, Bush adopted a more modest set of objectives when faced with a comparable challenge in Afghanistan. Nevertheless, the attempt to reverse the trend toward ever larger and more ambitious U.S.-led nation-building operations has proven short-lived. In Iraq, the United States has taken on a task comparable in its vast scope to the transformational efforts still under way in Bosnia and Kosovo and comparable in its enormous scale to the ear-lier American occupations of Germany and Japan. Nation-building, it appears, is the inescapable responsibility of the world's only superpower.

## QUANTITATIVE COMPARISONS OF CASES

For each of the seven historical cases of nation-building, we at RAND com-pared quantitative data on the "inputs" (troops, money, and time) and "outputs." The outputs included casualties (or lack thereof), democratic elections, and increases in per capita gross domestic product (GDP).

Troop levels varied widely across the cases. The levels ranged from 1.6 million U.S. troops in the American sector in Germany at the end of World War II to 14,000 U.S. and international troops currently in Afghanistan. Gross numbers, however, are not the most useful numbers for comparison, because the size and populations of the nations being built have been so disparate. We chose instead to compare the numbers of U.S. and foreign soldiers per thousand inhabitants in each occupied territory. We then compared the proportional force levels at specified times after the conflict ended (or after the U.S. rebuilding efforts began).

Figure 5.1 shows the number of international troops (or in the German and Japanese cases, U.S. troops) per thousand inhabitants in each territory at the outset of the intervention and at various intervals thereafter. As the data illustrate, even the proportional force levels vary immensely across the operations. (The levels vary so tremendously that they require a logarithmic, or exponential, scale for manageable illustration.)

Bosnia, Kosovo, and particularly the U.S.-occupied sector of Germany started with substantial proportions of military forces, whereas the initial levels in Japan, Somalia, Haiti, and especially Afghanistan were much more modest. The levels generally decreased over time. In Germany, the

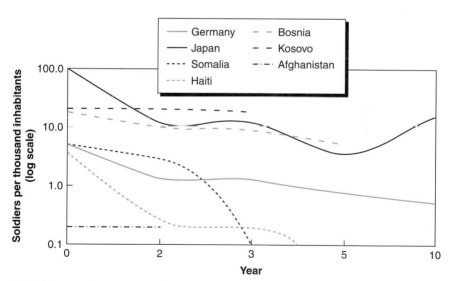

**FIGURE 5.1** Higher Force Levels for Longer Time Periods Promote Successful Nation-Building

*Source:* America's Role in Nation Building, 2003.

*Note:* Year 0 represents the end of the conflict. The numbers for Germany include only those troops in the U.S. sector. The data for the other nations include all participants.

level then rose again for reasons having to do with the Cold War. Overall, the differences in force levels across the cases had significant implications for other aspects of the operations.

Figure 5.2 compares the amount of foreign economic aid per capita (in constant 2001 U.S. dollars) provided to six of the territories during the first two years. Although Germany received the most aid in raw dollar terms ($12 billion), the country did not rank high on a per capita basis. Per capita assistance there ran a little over $200. Kosovo, which ranked fourth in terms of total assistance, received over $800 per resident. With the second-highest level of economic assistance per capita, Kosovo enjoyed the most rapid recovery in levels of per capita GDP. In contrast, Haiti, which received much less per capita than Kosovo, has experienced little growth in per capita GDP.

Germany and Japan both stand out as unequaled success stories. One of the most important questions is why both operations fared so well compared with the others. The easiest answer is that Germany and Japan were already highly developed and economically advanced societies. This certainly explains why it was easier to reconstruct their economies than it was to reconstruct those in the other territories. But economics is not a sufficient answer to explain the transition to democracy. The spread of democracy to poor countries in Latin America, Asia, and parts of Africa suggests that this form of government is not unique to advanced industrial economies.

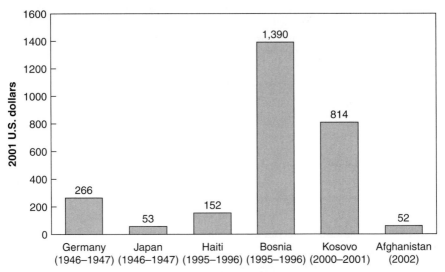

**FIGURE 5.2** Foreign Aid per Capita During the First Two Years

*Source*: America's Role in Nation Building, 2003.

Indeed, democracy can take root in countries where neither Western culture nor significant economic development exists. Nation-building is not principally about economic reconstruction, but rather about political transformation.

Because Germany and Japan were also ethnically homogeneous societies, some people might argue that homogeneity is the key to success. We believe that homogeneity helps greatly but that it is not essential, either. It is true that Somalia, Haiti, and Afghanistan are divided ethnically, socio-economically, or tribally in ways that Germany and Japan were not. However, the kinds of communal hatred that mark Somalia, Haiti, and Afghanistan are even more pronounced in Bosnia and Kosovo, where the process of democratization has nevertheless made some progress.

What principally distinguishes Germany, Japan, Bosnia, and Kosovo from Somalia, Haiti, and Afghanistan is not their levels of Western culture, democratic history, economic development, or ethnic homogeneity. Rather, the principal distinction is the level of effort that the United States and the international community have put into the democratic transformations. Among the recent operations, the United States and its allies have put 25 times more money and 50 times more troops on a per capita basis into post-conflict Kosovo than into post-conflict Afghanistan. These higher levels of input account in significant measure for the higher levels of output in terms of democratic institution building and economic growth.

The seven historical cases have differed in terms of duration. The record suggests that although staying long does not guarantee success, leaving early assures failure. To date, no effort at enforced democratization has been brought to a successful conclusion in less than seven years.

## UNITY OF COMMAND

Throughout the 1990s, the United States wrestled with the challenge of gaining wider participation in its nation-building endeavors while also preserving adequate unity of command. In Somalia and Haiti, the United States experimented with sequential arrangements in which it initially managed and funded the operations but then quickly turned responsibility over to the United Nations. In Bosnia, the United States succeeded in achieving both broad participation and unity of command on the military side of the operation through NATO. But in Bosnia the United States resisted the logic of achieving a comparable and cohesive arrangement on the civil side. In Kosovo, the United States achieved broad participation and unity of command on both the military and civil sides by working through NATO and the United Nations.

None of these models proved entirely satisfactory. However, the arrangements in Kosovo seem to have provided the best amalgam to date of American leadership, European and other participation, financial burden-sharing, and unity of command. Every international official in Kosovo works ultimately for either the NATO commander or the Special Representative of the U.N. Secretary General. Neither of these is an American. But by virtue of America's credibility in the region and America's influence in NATO and on the U.N. Security Council, the United States has been able to maintain a satisfactory leadership role while fielding only 16 percent of the peacekeeping troops and paying only 16 percent of the reconstruction costs.

The efficacy of the Bosnia and Kosovo models has depended on the ability of the United States and its principal allies to attain a common vision of the objectives and then to coordinate the relevant institutions—principally NATO, the Organization for Security and Cooperation in Europe, the European Union, and the United Nations—to meet the objectives. These two models offer a viable fusion of burden-sharing and unity of command.

In Afghanistan, in contrast, the United States opted for parallel arrangements on the military side and even greater divergence on the civil side. An international force—with no U.S. participation—operates in the capital of Kabul, while a national and mostly U.S. force operates everywhere else. The United Nations has responsibility for promoting political transformation, while individual donors coordinate economic reconstruction—or, more often, fail to do so.

The arrangement in Afghanistan is a marginal improvement over that in Somalia, because the separate U.S. and international forces are at least not operating in the same physical space. But the arrangement represents a clear regression from what we achieved in Haiti, Bosnia, or, in particular, Kosovo. It is therefore not surprising that the overall results achieved to date in Afghanistan are better than in Somalia, not yet better than in Haiti, and not as good as in Bosnia or Kosovo. The operation in Afghanistan, though, is a good deal less expensive than those in Bosnia or Kosovo.

## APPLYING THE LESSONS TO IRAQ

The challenges facing the United States in Iraq today are formidable. Still, it is possible to draw valuable lessons from America's previous experiences with nation-building. There are four main lessons to be learned for Iraq.

The first lesson is that democratic nation-building can work given sufficient inputs of resources. These inputs, however, can be very high. Regarding military forces, Figure 5.3 takes the numbers of troops used in

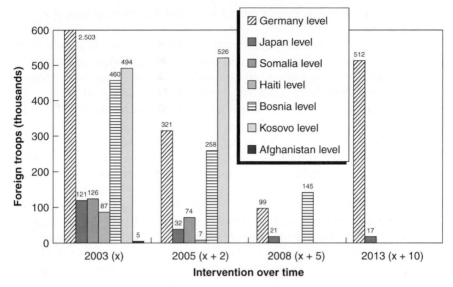

**FIGURE 5.3** Based on Kosovo Standards, Iraq Would Need 526,000 Foreign Troops Through 2005

*Source*: America's Role in Nation Building, 2003.

*Note*: Year x = 2003, the year of intervention in Iraq.

the previous cases of nation-building and projects, for each, a proportion- ally equivalent force for the Iraqi population over the next decade. For example, if Kosovo levels of troop commitments were deployed to Iraq, the number would be some 500,000 U.S. and coalition troops through 2005. (There are roughly 150,000 coalition troops stationed in Iraq today.) To pro- vide troop coverage at Bosnia levels, the requisite troop figures would be 460,000 initially, falling to 258,000 by 2005 and 145,000 by 2008.

In addition to military forces, it is often important to deploy a significant number of international civil police. To achieve a level comparable to the nearly 5,000 police deployed in Kosovo, Iraq would need an infusion of 53,000 international civil police officers through 2005 (in addition to the forces represented in Figure 5.3).

It is too early to predict with accuracy the required levels of foreign aid, but we can draw comparisons with the previous historical cases. If Bosnia levels of foreign aid per capita were provided to Iraq, the country would require some $36 billion in aid from now through 2005. Conversely, aid at the same level as Afghanistan would total $1 billion over the next two years.

According to the lessons learned, the ultimate consequences for Iraq of a failure to generate adequate international manpower and money are likely to be lower levels of security, higher casualties sustained and inflicted, lower economic growth rates, and slower, less thoroughgoing political transformation.

The second lesson for Iraq is that short departure deadlines are incompatible with nation-building. The United States will succeed only if it makes a long-term commitment to establishing strong democratic institutions and does not beat a hasty retreat tied to artificial deadlines. Moreover, setting premature dates for early national elections can be counterproductive.

Third, important hindrances to nation-building include both internal fragmentation (along political, ethnic, or sectarian lines) and a lack of external support from neighboring states. Germany and Japan had homogeneous societies. Bosnia and Kosovo had neighbors that, following the democratic transitions in Croatia and Serbia, collaborated with the international community. Iraq could combine the worst of both worlds, lacking both internal cohesion and regional support. The United States should consider putting a consultative mechanism in place, on the model of the Peace Implementation Council in the Balkans or the "Two Plus Six" group that involved Afghanistan's six neighbors plus Russia and the United States, as a means of consulting with the neighboring countries of Iraq.

Fourth, building a democracy, a strong economy, and long-term legitimacy depends in each case on striking the balance between international burden-sharing and unity of command. As noted above, the United States is unlikely to be able to generate adequate levels of troops, money, or endurance as long as it relies principally upon the limited coalition with which it fought the war. On the other hand, engaging a broader coalition, to include major countries that will expect to secure influence commensurate with their contributions, will require either new institutional arrangements or the extension of existing ones, such as NATO.

Throughout the 1990s, the management of each major stabilization and reconstruction mission represented a marginal advance over its predecessor, but in the past several years this modestly positive learning curve has not been sustained.

Over the past decade, the United States has made major investments in the combat efficiency of its forces. The return on investment has been evident in the dramatic improvements demonstrated from one campaign to the next, from Desert Storm to the Kosovo air campaign to Operation Iraqi Freedom. But there has been no comparable increase in the capacity of U.S. armed forces, or of U.S. civilian agencies for that matter, to conduct post-combat stabilization and reconstruction operations.

Nation-building has been a controversial mission over the past decade, and the extent of this controversy has undoubtedly curtailed the investments needed to do these tasks better. So has institutional resistance in both the state and defense departments, neither of which regards nation-building among its core missions. As a result, successive administrations tend to treat each new such mission as if it were the first and, more importantly, the last.

This expectation is unlikely to be realized any time soon. In the 1990s, the Clinton administration conducted a major nation-building intervention, on the average, every two years. The current administration, despite a strong disinclination to engage American armed forces in these activities, has launched two major such enterprises in a period of eighteen months.

Post-conflict stabilization and reconstruction with the objective of promoting a transition to democracy appear to be the inescapable responsibility of the world's only superpower. Therefore, in addition to securing the major resources that will be needed to carry through the current operation in Iraq to success, the United States ought to make the smaller long-term investments in its own institutional capacity to conduct such operations. In this way, the ongoing improvements in combat performance of American forces could be matched by improvements in the postconflict performance of our government as a whole.

## 35 Sharm El-Sheik Fact-Finding Committee Report

### GEORGE MITCHELL ET AL.

One of the most difficult issues for American policymakers, both during and after the Cold War, involved the problem of curtailing violence, or at best achieving peace, in the Middle East. During President Clinton's first year in office, Israeli and Palestinian negotiators reached an agreement in Oslo to achieve Palestinian self-rule in the West Bank and Gaza. The Accords detailed a step-by-step plan to allow confidence-building measures to be implemented. The Israeli government recognized the PLO as the legitimate representative of the Palestinian people and allowed a new Palestinian Authority to govern in the occupied territories. At the same time, the PLO recognized the right of the state of Israel to exist and renounced terrorism, violence, and its desire for the destruction of

George Mitchell et al., "Sharm El-Sheikh Fact Finding Report," U.S. Department of State, April 30, 2001.

Israel. After five years, a final settlement would be negotiated. The understanding among the parties was that this final negotiation would include not only a permanent peace settlement in Israel, the West Bank, and Gaza, but an independent Palestinian state.

The United States provided its backing for the undertaking, but continued violence in the region and provocative actions by both parties resulted in diminished enthusiasm for the Accords, causing implementation to be delayed or reversed. In his final months in office, President Clinton made an effort to achieve a lasting peace that put everything on the negotiating table, including the most difficult issues involving the status of Jerusalem and the right of return for Palestinians. Clinton invited Israeli Prime Minister Ehud Barak and P.L.O. Chairman Yassir Arafat to Camp David to secure a deal. While the two sides came as close as they ever have to reaching a peace settlement, the summit ultimately ended in failure. Within a few months of this failure, violence between Israel and the Palestinians engulfed the region.

The fact finding report of the Sharm El-Sheik Committee looks at this peace effort and its violent aftermath in order to explain why negotiations failed and violence erupted. The report, offering an explanation of what occurred and why, examines the divergent interests, views, and expectations of both sides regarding the Oslo Accords, pointing out how such divergence made lasting peace a difficult prospect. In characterizing these views, the report offers a clear understanding of how far apart the two parties remain.

The failure of the peace process (including one last ditch effort in December 2000 at Taba, Egypt) set the stage for the violence and recriminations that have occurred since. The subsequent elections of George W. Bush and Ariel Sharon solidified the positions of all the involved parties, and over the next several years, there was little chance to achieve peace in the region. At this writing, the death of Yassir Arafat, the pursuit of a unilateral withdrawal strategy by Sharon and his successor Ehud Olmert, and the election of Hamas to the Palestinian parliament, all in a period of about two years, have significantly changed the situation in the area, leading to even greater uncertainty about the prospects for peace.

---

# INTRODUCTION

Despite their long history and close proximity, some Israelis and Palestinians seem not to fully appreciate each other's problems and concerns. Some Israelis appear not to comprehend the humiliation and frustration that Palestinians must endure every day as a result of living with the continuing effects of occupation, sustained by the presence of Israeli military forces and settlements in their midst, or the determination of the Palestinians to achieve independence and genuine self-determination. Some Palestinians appear not to comprehend the extent to which terrorism creates fear among the Israeli people and undermines their belief in the possibility of co-existence, or the determination of the GOI (Government of Israel) to do whatever is necessary to protect its people.

Fear, hate, anger, and frustration have risen on both sides. The greatest danger of all is that the culture of peace, nurtured over the previous decade, is being shattered. In its place there is a growing sense of futility and despair, and a growing resort to violence.

Political leaders on both sides must act and speak decisively to reverse these dangerous trends; they must rekindle the desire and the drive for peace. That will be difficult. But it can be done and it must be done, for the alternative is unacceptable and should be unthinkable.

Two proud peoples share a land and a destiny. Their competing claims and religious differences have led to a grinding, demoralizing, dehumanizing conflict. They can continue in conflict or they can negotiate to find a way to live side-by-side in peace.

## WHAT HAPPENED?

In late September 2000, Israeli, Palestinian, and other officials received reports that Member of the Knesset (now Prime Minister) Ariel Sharon was planning a visit to the Haram al-Sharif/Temple Mount in Jerusalem. Palestinian and U.S. officials urged then Prime Minister Ehud Barak to prohibit the visit. Mr. Barak told us that he believed the visit was intended to be an internal political act directed against him by a political opponent, and he declined to prohibit it.

Mr. Sharon made the visit on September 28 accompanied by over 1,000 Israeli police officers. Although Israelis viewed the visit in an internal political context, Palestinians saw it as highly provocative to them. On the following day, in the same place, a large number of unarmed Palestinian demonstrators and a large Israeli police contingent confronted each other. According to the U.S. Department of State, "Palestinians held large demonstrations and threw stones at police in the vicinity of the Western Wall. Police used rubber-coated metal bullets and live ammunition to disperse the demonstrators, killing 4 persons and injuring about 200." According to the GOI, 14 Israeli policemen were injured.

Similar demonstrations took place over the following several days. Thus began what has become known as the "Al-Aqsa Intifada" (Al-Aqsa being a mosque at the Haram al-Sharif/Temple Mount).

The GOI asserts that the immediate catalyst for the violence was the breakdown of the Camp David negotiations on July 25, 2000 and the "widespread appreciation in the international community of Palestinian responsibility for the impasse." In this view, Palestinian violence was planned by the PA leadership, and was aimed at "provoking and incurring Palestinian casualties as a means of regaining the diplomatic initiative."

The Palestine Liberation Organization (PLO) denies the allegation that the intifada was planned. It claims, however, that "Camp David represented nothing less than an attempt by Israel to extend the force it exercises on the ground to negotiations," and that "the failure of the summit, and the attempts to allocate blame on the Palestinian side only added to the tension on the ground . . ."

From the perspective of the PLO, Israel responded to the disturbances with excessive and illegal use of deadly force against demonstrators; behavior which, in the PLO's view, reflected Israel's contempt for the lives and safety of Palestinians. For Palestinians, the widely seen images of the killing of 12-year-old Muhammad al Durra in Gaza on September 30, shot as he huddled behind his father, reinforced that perception.

From the perspective of the GOI, the demonstrations were organized and directed by the Palestinian leadership to create sympathy for their cause around the world by provoking Israeli security forces to fire upon demonstrators, especially young people. For Israelis, the lynching of two military reservists, First Sgt. Vadim Novesche and First Cpl. Yosef Avrahami, in Ramallah on October 12, reflected a deep-seated Palestinian hatred of Israel and Jews.

What began as a series of confrontations between Palestinian demonstrators and Israeli security forces, which resulted in the GOI's initial restrictions on the movement of people and goods in the West Bank and Gaza Strip (closures), has since evolved into a wider array of violent actions and responses.

From the Palestinian perspective, the decision of Israel to characterize the current crisis as "an armed conflict short of war" is simply a means "to justify its assassination policy, its collective punishment policy, and its use of lethal force." From the Israeli perspective, "The Palestinian leadership have instigated, orchestrated and directed the violence. It has used, and continues to use, terror and attrition as strategic tools."

## WHY DID IT HAPPEN?

The roots of the current violence extend much deeper than an inconclusive summit conference. Both sides have made clear a profound disillusionment with the behavior of the other in failing to meet the expectations arising from the peace process launched in Madrid in 1991 and then in Oslo in 1993. Each side has accused the other of violating specific undertakings and undermining the spirit of their commitment to resolving their political differences peacefully.

Divergent Expectations: We are struck by the divergent expectations expressed by the parties relating to the implementation of the Oslo process. Results achieved from this process were unthinkable less than 10 years ago. During the latest round of negotiations, the parties were closer to a permanent settlement than ever before.

Nonetheless, Palestinians and Israelis alike told us that the premise on which the Oslo process is based—that tackling the hard "permanent status" issues be deferred to the end of the process—has gradually come under serious pressure. The step-by-step process agreed to by the parties was based on the assumption that each step in the negotiating process would lead to enhanced trust and confidence. To achieve this, each party would have to implement agreed-upon commitments and abstain from actions that would be seen by the other as attempts to abuse the process in order to predetermine the shape of the final outcome. If this requirement is not met, the Oslo road map cannot successfully lead to its agreed destination. Today, each side blames the other for having ignored this fundamental aspect, resulting in a crisis in confidence. This problem became even more pressing with the opening of permanent status talks.

The GOI has placed primacy on moving toward a Permanent Status Agreement in a nonviolent atmosphere, consistent with commitments contained in the agreements between the parties. "Even if slower than was initially envisaged, there has, since the start of the peace process in Madrid in 1991, been steady progress towards the goal of a Permanent Status Agreement without the resort to violence on a scale that has characterized recent weeks." The "goal" is the Permanent Status Agreement, the terms of which must be negotiated by the parties.

The PLO view is that delays in the process have been the result of an Israeli attempt to prolong and solidify the occupation. Palestinians "believed that the Oslo process would yield an end to Israeli occupation in five years," the timeframe for the transitional period specified in the Declaration of Principles. Instead there have been, in the PLO's view, repeated Israeli delays culminating in the Camp David summit, where, "Israel proposed to annex about 11.2% of the West Bank (excluding Jerusalem) . . ." and offered unacceptable proposals concerning Jerusalem, security and refugees. "In sum, Israel's proposals at Camp David provided for Israel's annexation of the best Palestinian lands, the perpetuation of Israeli control over East Jerusalem, a continued Israeli military presence on Palestinian territory, Israeli control over Palestinian natural resources, airspace and borders, and the return of fewer than 1% of refugees to their homes."

Both sides see the lack of full compliance with agreements reached since the opening of the peace process as evidence of a lack of good faith. This conclusion led to an erosion of trust even before the permanent status negotiations began.

Divergent Perspectives: During the last seven months, these views have hardened into divergent realities. Each side views the other as having acted in bad faith; as having turned the optimism of Oslo into the suffering and grief of victims and their loved ones. In their statements and actions, each side demonstrates a perspective that fails to recognize any truth in the perspective of the other.

The Palestinian Perspective: For the Palestinian side, "Madrid" and "Oslo" heralded the prospect of a State, and guaranteed an end to the occupation and a resolution of outstanding matters within an agreed time frame. Palestinians are genuinely angry at the continued growth of settlements and at their daily experiences of humiliation and disruption as a result of Israel's presence in the Palestinian territories. Palestinians see settlers and settlements in their midst not only as violating the spirit of the Oslo process, but also as an application of force in the form of Israel's overwhelming military superiority, which sustains and protects the settlements.

The Interim Agreement provides that "the two parties view the West Bank and Gaza as a single territorial unit, the integrity and status of which will be preserved during the interim period." Coupled with this, the Interim Agreement's prohibition on taking steps which may prejudice permanent status negotiations denies Israel the right to continue its illegal expansionist settlement policy. In addition to the Interim Agreement, customary international law, including the Fourth Geneva Convention, prohibits Israel (as an occupying power) from establishing settlements in occupied territory pending an end to the conflict.

The PLO alleges that Israeli political leaders "have made no secret of the fact that the Israeli interpretation of Oslo was designed to segregate the Palestinians in non-contiguous enclaves, surrounded by Israeli military-controlled borders, with settlements and settlement roads violating the territories' integrity." According to the PLO, "In the seven years since the [Declaration of Principles], the settler population in the West Bank, excluding East Jerusalem and the Gaza Strip, has doubled to 200,000, and the settler population in East Jerusalem has risen to 170,000. Israel has constructed approximately 30 new settlements, and expanded a number of existing ones to house these new settlers."

The PLO also claims that the GOI has failed to comply with other commitments such as the further withdrawal from the West Bank and the release of Palestinian prisoners. In addition, Palestinians expressed frustration with the impasse over refugees and the deteriorating economic circumstances in the West Bank and Gaza Strip.

The Israeli Perspective: From the GOI perspective, the expansion of settlement activity and the taking of measures to facilitate the convenience and safety of settlers do not prejudice the outcome of permanent status negotiations.

Israel understands that the Palestinian side objects to the settlements in the West Bank and the Gaza Strip. Without prejudice to the formal status of the settlements, Israel accepts that the settlements are an outstanding issue on which there will have to be agreement as part of any permanent status resolution between the sides. This point was acknowledged and agreed upon in the Declaration of Principles of 13 September 1993 as well as in other agreements between the two sides. There has in fact been a good deal of discussion on the question of settlements between the two sides in the various negotiations toward a permanent status agreement.

Indeed, Israelis point out that at the Camp David summit and during subsequent talks the GOI offered to make significant concessions with respect to settlements in the context of an overall agreement.

Security, however, is the key GOI concern. The GOI maintains that the PLO has breached its solemn commitments by continuing the use of violence in the pursuit of political objectives. "Israel's principal concern in the peace process has been security. This issue is of overriding importance . . . [S]ecurity is not something on which Israel will bargain or compromise. The failure of the Palestinian side to comply with both the letter and spirit of the security provisions in the various agreements has long been a source of disturbance in Israel."

According to the GOI, the Palestinian failure takes several forms: institutionalized anti-Israel, anti-Jewish incitement; the release from detention of terrorists; the failure to control illegal weapons; and the actual conduct of violent operations, ranging from the insertion of riflemen into demonstrations to terrorist attacks on Israeli civilians. The GOI maintains that the PLO has explicitly violated its renunciation of terrorism and other acts of violence, thereby significantly eroding trust between the parties. The GOI perceives "a thread, implied but nonetheless clear, that runs throughout the Palestinian submissions. It is that Palestinian violence against Israel and Israelis is somehow explicable, understandable, legitimate."

## RECOMMENDATIONS

The GOI and the Palestinian Authority must act swiftly and decisively to halt the violence. Their immediate objectives then should be to rebuild confidence and resume negotiations. What we are asking is not easy. Palestinians and Israelis—not just their leaders, but two publics at large— have lost confidence in one another. We are asking political leaders to do, for the sake of their people, the politically difficult: to lead without knowing how many will follow.

# 36 Remarks at a Democratic Leadership Council Gala

## WILLIAM JEFFERSON CLINTON

As President Clinton neared the final year of his presidency, the full extent of his global economic policies had taken shape and they were producing results. NAFTA and the WTO had been launched; new trade liberalization talks were about to begin; numerous countries were applying to join the WTO; the "Washington consensus" regarding international finance and development was widely adopted; and the spread of globalization, coupled with a revolution in information technology, had allowed America to excel in the global marketplace while producing greater economic integration throughout the world. These economic developments were not only considered significant in and of themselves, the president believed that global economic concerns were a central feature of U.S. foreign policy.

In this speech to fellow Democrats, which thoroughly embodies Clinton's views on the potential of trade and globalization, the president provides his understanding of what had been accomplished and what remained to be done. He points out that there is great agreement in the United States regarding the virtues of free markets, expanded trade opportunities, the explosive growth in the information technology sector, and globalization. The benefits of such developments are evident around the world. His praise for these policies and their results is emblematic of the enduring nature of America's liberal orientation regarding the global economic policies that were begun after World War II.

The president, however, also highlighted a significant point of contention regarding free trade and globalization, one that foresaw the kinds of conflicts that were soon to emerge in protests, demonstrations, and violence. He stated that it was essential to "put a human face on the global economy," so that it worked for everyone. Economic competition and the broadening of free trade, he said, should not become "a race to the bottom in labor standards and environmental pollution." This problem—reconciling economic strategies with environmental, labor, and human right concerns—soon led to great divisiveness, especially within the president's own party. Although President Clinton tried to address it, the issue has ultimately not been resolved.

---

William Jefferson Clinton, "Remarks at a Democratic Leadership Council Gala," October 13, 1999.

Tonight I ask you not to think about our differences with the Republicans but to think about the one remaining issue on which we have not forged a consensus within our party. And that is how we're going to respond to globalization, to the global economy, the information age, and the whole nature of how we relate to other countries in terms of economics, the environment, and trade.

I believe a strong, properly constructed global trading system is good for all the nations of the world. I know it's good for America because of the evidence of what has happened here. Today, the worst of the global financial crisis is behind us, and I think the time has come to take an important step forward. I believe we can make our economy even stronger and make open trade an even greater force for peace and prosperity in the new century.

How are we going to do it, and how are we going to begin? In a little more than a month's time, in Seattle, Washington, our Nation will host a gathering of leaders from government, business, labor, and civil society. That meeting of the World Trade Organization will launch a new round of global trade talks that I called for in my State of the Union Address last January.

We've had eight such rounds in the last 50 years, helping trade to grow fifteen-fold worldwide. It's no coincidence that this period has seen the most rapid sustained economic growth ever recorded. Every trade round in this half-century has served to expand frontiers of opportunity, to expand the circle of prosperity and the rule of law and the spread of peace. I want the round we launch in Seattle to do the same.

But I also want it to be a new kind of trade round for a new century, a round that is about jobs and development, a round about broadly shared prosperity, about improving the quality of life and work around the world. I want to ensure that the global trading system of the 21st century honors our values and meets our goals . . .

We can lift living standards worldwide if we level the playing field for goods and services. Manufacturing remains a powerful engine of our own economic growth; it generates nearly a fifth of our GDP and two-thirds of our exports. It employs more than 18 million Americans in good jobs. This sector has grown since 1992, accelerated greatly by expanded trade, boosted by agreements made at previous trade rounds. If the Asian crisis has hurt our manufacturers—and it certainly has—it's because expanded trade is vital to their economic health, and it will remain so.

Since 1948, we have cut major industrial nations' tariffs on manufactured goods by 90 percent. Where they remain too high, we can do better, beginning in Seattle where we'll join other nations in pressing to lower barriers even further, some entirely and immediately.

Eight key industries, from an environmental technology to medical instruments to chemicals to toys, stand ready to take this step now. They account for nearly a third of our exports. So let's take that step at Seattle and set ambitious goals for other manufacturing sectors.

We should set equally ambitious goals for services. Trade is no longer just agricultural and manufactured goods. It's construction and distribution and entertainment. America is the world's largest exporter of services, in quantity and quality. And though we've made really important advances in agreements on financial and communication services, too many markets remain closed to us. In Seattle, I want to open those markets more fully and unlock the full creative and entrepreneurial potential of our people.

Third, we have to have a trading system that taps the full potential of the information age. The revolution in information technology can be the greatest global force for prosperity in this century. Last year, in the U.S. alone, electronic commerce totaled about $50 billion. That number may reach $1.4 trillion in 3 years. Three years later almost half our work force will either be employed by the new information industries or rely on their services and products.

Around the world, the number of Internet users may reach 1 billion in 5 years. Now, currently, no country charges customs duties on telephone calls, fax transmissions, E-mail, or computer links when they cross borders. That's the way it should be. The lines of communication should not crackle with interference.

Last year the world's nations joined the U.S. in placing a moratorium on tariffs on E-commerce. In Seattle, we should pledge to extend that ban and reach a second agreement to eliminate remaining tariffs on the tools of the high-tech revolution.

Fourth, as I have often said, in the immortal words of Sam Fried, we must put a human face on the global economy. We're Democrats; we've got to make sure this deal works for ordinary people. We need to ensure working people everywhere feel they have a stake in global trade, that it gives them a chance for a better life, that they know that spirited economic competition will not become a race to the bottom in labor standards and environmental pollution.

I know to some people in some nations open trade seems at odds with these basic human goals, but I think the opposite is true. A strong system of trade and a dialog like the one we'll begin in Seattle are our best means to achieve those goals.

For those of us who believe the global economy can be a force for good, our defining mission must be to spread its benefits more broadly and to make rules for trade that support our values. It is nothing more than an international commitment to doing what we're trying to do here with the new markets agenda and with the empowerment zones. I really believe, if we work it right, we can bring the benefits of enterprise to the people and the places in America that have not yet felt it, from Appalachia to the Mississippi Delta to the Indian reservations to the inner cities. And I feel that way about the rest of the world.

So I ask you to support our efforts to have international organizations work to protect and enhance the environment while expanding trade and to have a decent regard for the need to have basic labor standards so that people who work receive the dignity and reward of work.

The American agenda in Seattle includes a thorough review of the round's environmental impact, as well as win-win opportunities that benefit both the economy and the environment. We will continue to ensure that WTO rules recognize our right to take science-based health, safety, and environmental measures even when they are higher than international standards.

In Seattle, the WTO should also create a working group on trade and labor. And I know you're going to have some labor people here tomorrow, and I congratulate you on that. We have got to keep working on this and banging our heads together until we reach a consensus that is consistent with the reality of the modern world and its opportunities and consistent with the values that we both share.

How can we deny the legitimacy or the linking of these issues, trade and labor, in a global economy? I think the WTO should commit to collaborate more closely with the International Labor Organization, which has worked so hard to protect human rights and to ban child labor, and with the International Environmental Organization. To facilitate this process, in the last year or so, I have gone to Geneva twice, once to talk about new trade rules for the global economy and once to meet with the ILO to talk about the necessity of banning child labor everywhere in the world.

This organization needs to be on the forefront of integrating our objectives and trying to build a global economy that will promote open trade and open prosperity and lift the standards of living and the quality of life for people throughout the world. They should be reinforcing efforts, not efforts in conflict.

I also believe that the WTO itself has got to become more open and accessible. You know, every NGO, just about, with an environmental or a labor ax to grind is going to be outside the meeting room in Seattle, demonstrating against us, telling us what a terrible thing world trade is. Now, I think they're dead wrong about that. But all over the world, when issues come up, a lot of people representing these groups have some legitimate question or legitimate interest in being heard in the debate. And the WTO has been treated for too long like some private priesthood for experts, where we know what's right, and we pat you on the head and tell you to just go right along and play by the rules that we preach.

The world doesn't work that way anymore. This open world we're trying to build, where anybody can get on the Internet and say anything, is a rowdy, raucous place. And if we want the world trading system to have legitimacy, we have got to allow every legitimate group with any kind of beef, whether they're right or wrong, to have some access to the deliberative process of the WTO. And I hope you will support that.

Finally, let me say, we have got to expand the family of nations that benefit from trade and play by the rules. In Seattle and beyond, we have to be guided by Franklin Roosevelt's vision, a basic essential to a permanent peace is a decent standard of living for all individual men and women and children in the world. Freedom from fear is eternally linked with freedom from want.

It was this understanding that led the generation of postwar leaders to embrace what was still a revolutionary idea: that freedom, not just of commerce but of governments and ideas and human transit, was the surest route to prosperity for the greatest number of people. This new round should promote development in places where poverty and hunger still stoke despair.

We just went over, I think in the last 24 hours, 6 billion people on the face of the Earth. Half of them live on $2 a day or less; 1.3 billion live on $1 a day or less. One of the reasons that I want to expand the reach of global trade is because I want more people to be able to lift themselves up. One of the reasons I want to expand the reach of global technology is that I believe if we work to bridge the digital divide here at home and around the world, we can help poor people in poor countries skip 20 or 30 or 40 years in the ordinary pace of development because of the explosion of technology. And I believe we can prove to them that they can grow a middle class and grow a wealthy country without having to pollute the atmosphere, as their forebears did in the industrial era. I believe that.

But for those who share our views and our party, we must make clear there is no easy way to this. We can't get this done if we're not willing to build a global economic system and tear down these trade barriers and trade with people more and give them access to our markets and try to get our technology and our investments into their markets and build the right kind of partnership.

We can't just say we want all these things and then always find some reason to be against whatever trade agreement is worked out. We have got to have a global trading system, and we're either going to keep pushing it forward, or we're going to fall behind.

I hope we will bring more countries into the WTO in Seattle. Thirty-three nations are applying for WTO membership today. Two-thirds once had communist command and control economies. It is remarkable and hopeful to all the [countries]—listen to this—Albania, Estonia, Georgia, Kyrgyzstan, and Mongolia wanting to enter the world trading system.

This is not charity. This is an economic and political imperative. It is good for us because we want more trading partners. Never forget, your country has 4 percent of the world's people and 22 percent of its wealth. We've go to sell something to the other 96 percent if we want to hold on to our standard of living. And the more people we bring into our network of possibility, the better they do, the better we'll do. It is very, very important to remember this.

It's also important to remember that as these countries that are new to the experience of freedom and the rule of law and cooperation with other nations that has no element of coercion in it—they are new to all this—the more they have a chance to be a part of it, the more they will like it and the more they will become a part of an international system of democracy and law that is so important to the future of our children.

In that same spirit, I am still determined to pursue an agreement for China to join the WTO on viable, commercial terms again, not as a favor but to reinforce China's efforts to open, to reform its markets, to subscribe to the rules of the global trading system, and, inevitably, as more and more people have access to more and more information, more and more contacts, to feel that stability comes from openness and not repression of thought or religion or political views.

What is at stake here is more than the spread of free markets or the strength of the global economy, even more than the chance to lift billions of people into a worldwide middle class. It is a chance to move the world closer toward genuine interdependence rooted in shared commitments to peace and reconciliation.

Good luck, and God bless you. Thank you.

## The Lonely Superpower

**3 7** *SAMUEL HUNTINGTON*

As a new century was dawning, the United States was as rich and powerful as any country had ever been in the history of the world, and it operated in a world where no other single country could

Samuel Huntington, from "The Lonely Superpower." Reprinted with permission from *Foreign Affairs*, 78.2, March/April 1999. Copyright 1999 by the Council on Foreign Relations, Inc.

rival its power and influence. This circumstance remains, but in spite of such differences, the United States is not always able to achieve its political goals. As Samuel Huntington argues, this is because the world is characterized by a global system that is neither unipolar nor multipolar. Rather it is a "uni-multipolar" system with one superpower and several major powers. In order to achieve its goals, the United States has to gain acceptance and cooperation from some combination of major powers. American leaders, however, do not fully seem to understand this, and behave as if the United States were a unipolar power. The result is that the United States, while continually speaking of its benign hegemony and the universal validity of its institutions and economic practices, is actually becoming increasingly alone in the world. Huntington points out that the United States often finds itself acting unilaterally, opposing most of the rest of the world on a number of issues: payment of U.N. dues; sanctions against Cuba, Iran, and several other countries; the land mine treaty; global warming; and the use of force against Iraq, to name but a few. Consequently, America is often seen by other countries as something of a "rogue" superpower.

Huntington makes the case that it is unhelpful and self-defeating for the United States to act in an increasingly unilateral manner. Military preeminence can only accomplish so much. Imposing order in the world requires a constant process of negotiation, communication, and mutual help. Standing alone, by contrast, only seems to diminish American influence, not enhance it.

Huntington's analysis, which was published in 1999, highlights a couple of interesting points regarding contemporary political debates. First, in spite of the characterization of U.S. foreign policy as unilateral during the George W. Bush administration, this criticism was being leveled at the United States before he came to office. The term *hyperpower*, which was used to criticize American hegemony, was coined by the French in the 1990s. Second, this article provided a glimpse into the future, highlighting what has become one of the most significant issues in American foreign policy.

---

## THE NEW DIMENSION OF POWER

There is now only one superpower. But that does not mean that the world is unipolar. A unipolar system would have one superpower, no significant major powers, and many minor powers. As a result, the superpower could effectively resolve important international issues alone, and no combination of other states would have the power to prevent it from doing so. For several centuries the classical world under Rome, and at times East Asia under China, approximated this model. A bipolar system like the Cold

War has two superpowers, and the relations between them are central to international politics. Each superpower dominates a coalition of allied states and competes with the other superpower for influence among non-aligned countries. A multipolar system has several major powers of comparable strength that cooperate and compete with each other in shifting patterns. A coalition of major states is necessary to resolve important international issues. European politics approximated this model for several centuries.

Contemporary international politics does not fit any of these three models. It is instead a strange hybrid, a uni-multipolar system with one superpower and several major powers. The settlement of key international issues requires action by the single superpower but always with some combination of other major states; the single superpower can, however, veto action on key issues by combinations of other states. The United States, of course, is the sole state with preeminence in every domain of power—economic, military, diplomatic, ideological, technological, and cultural—with the reach and capabilities to promote its interests in virtually every part of the world. At a second level are major regional powers that are preeminent in areas of the world without being able to extend their interests and capabilities as globally as the United States. They include the German-French condominium in Europe, Russia in Eurasia, China and potentially Japan in East Asia, India in South Asia, Iran in Southwest Asia, Brazil in Latin America, and South Africa and Nigeria in Africa. At a third level are secondary regional powers whose interests often conflict with the more powerful regional states. These include Britain in relation to the German-French combination, Ukraine in relation to Russia, Japan in relation to China, South Korea in relation to Japan, Pakistan in relation to India, Saudi Arabia in relation to Iran, and Argentina in relation to Brazil.

## NOT SO BENIGN

American officials quite naturally tend to act as if the world were unipolar. They boast of American power and American virtue, hailing the United States as a benevolent hegemon. They lecture other countries on the universal validity of American principles, practices, and institutions. At the 1997 G-7 summit in Denver, President Clinton boasted about the success of the American economy as a model for others. Secretary of State Madeleine K. Albright has called the United States "the indispensable nation" and said that "we stand tall and hence see further than other nations." This statement is true in the narrow sense that the United States is an indispensable participant in any effort to tackle major global problems. It is false in also implying that other nations are dispensable—the United States needs the cooperation of some major countries in handling any issue—and that American indispensability is the source of wisdom.

Addressing the problem of foreign perceptions of American "hegemonism," Deputy Secretary of State Strobe Talbott set forth this rationale: "In a fashion and to an extent that is unique in the history of Great Powers, the United States defines its strength—indeed, its very greatness—not in terms of its ability to achieve or maintain dominance over others, but in terms of its ability to work with others in the interests of the international community as a whole. . . . American foreign policy is consciously intended to advance *universal values* [his italics]." The most concise statement of the "benign hegemon" syndrome was made by Deputy Secretary of the Treasury Lawrence H. Summers when he called the United States the "first nonimperialist superpower"—a claim that manages in three words to exalt American uniqueness, American virtue, and American power.

American foreign policy is in considerable measure driven by such beliefs. In the past few years the United States has, among other things, attempted or been perceived as attempting more or less unilaterally to do the following: pressure other countries to adopt American values and practices regarding human rights and democracy; prevent other countries from acquiring military capabilities that could counter American conventional superiority; enforce American law extraterritorially in other societies; grade countries according to their adherence to American standards on human rights, drugs, terrorism, nuclear proliferation, missile proliferation, and now religious freedom; apply sanctions against countries that do not meet American standards on these issues; promote American corporate interests under the slogans of free trade and open markets; shape World Bank and International Monetary Fund policies to serve those same corporate interests; intervene in local conflicts in which it has relatively little direct interest; bludgeon other countries to adopt economic policies and social policies that will benefit American economic interests; promote American arms sales abroad while attempting to prevent comparable sales by other countries; force out one U.N. secretary-general and dictate the appointment of his successor; expand NATO initially to include Poland, Hungary, and the Czech Republic and no one else; undertake military action against Iraq and later maintain harsh economic sanctions against the regime; and categorize certain countries as "rogue states," excluding them from global institutions because they refuse to kowtow to American wishes.

In the unipolar moment at the end of the Cold War and the collapse of the Soviet Union, the United States was often able to impose its will on other countries. That moment has passed. The two principal tools of coercion that the United States now attempts to use are economic sanctions and military intervention. Sanctions work, however, only when other countries also support them, and that is decreasingly the case. Hence, the United States either applies them unilaterally to the detriment of its economic interests and its relations with its allies, or it does not enforce them, in which case they become symbols of American weakness.

At relatively low cost the United States can launch bombing or cruise missile attacks against its enemies. By themselves, however, such actions achieve little. More serious military interventions have to meet three conditions: They have to be legitimated through some international organization, such as the United Nations where they are subject to Russian, Chinese, or French veto; they also require the participation of allied forces, which may or may not be forthcoming; and they have to involve no American casualties and virtually no "collateral" casualties. Even if the United States meets all three conditions, it risks stirring up not only criticism at home but widespread political and popular backlash abroad.

American officials seem peculiarly blind to the fact that often the more the United States attacks a foreign leader, the more his popularity soars among his countrymen who applaud him for standing tall against the greatest power on earth. The demonizing of leaders has so far failed to shorten their tenure in power, from Fidel Castro (who has survived eight American presidents) to Slobodan Milosevic and Saddam Hussein. Indeed, the best way for a dictator of a small country to prolong his tenure in power may be to provoke the United States into denouncing him as the leader of a "rogue regime" and a threat to global peace.

Neither the Clinton administration nor Congress nor the public is willing to pay the costs and accept the risks of unilateral global leadership. Some advocates of American leadership argue for increasing defense expenditures by 50 percent, but that is a nonstarter. The American public clearly sees no need to expend effort and resources to achieve American hegemony. In one 1997 poll, only 13 percent said they preferred a preeminent role for the United States in world affairs, while 74 percent said they wanted the United States to share power with other countries. Other polls have produced similar results. Public disinterest in international affairs is pervasive, abetted by the drastically shrinking media coverage of foreign events. Majorities of 55 to 66 percent of the public say that what happens in Western Europe, Asia, Mexico, and Canada has little or no impact on their lives. However much foreign policy elites may ignore or deplore it, the United States lacks the domestic political base to create a unipolar world. American leaders repeatedly make threats, promise action, and fail to deliver. The result is a foreign policy of "rhetoric and retreat" and a growing reputation as a "hollow hegemon."

## THE ROGUE SUPERPOWER

In acting as if this were a unipolar world, the United States is also becoming increasingly alone in the world. American leaders constantly claim to be speaking on behalf of "the international community." But whom do they have in mind? China? Russia? India? Pakistan? Iran? The Arab world? The Association of Southeast Asian Nations? Africa? Latin America? France? Do any of these countries or regions see the United States as the spokesman for a community of which they are a part? The community for which the United States speaks includes, at best, its Anglo-Saxon cousins (Britain, Canada, Australia, New Zealand) on most issues, Germany and some smaller European democracies on many issues, Israel on some Middle Eastern questions, and Japan on the implementation of U.N. resolutions. These are important states, but they fall far short of being the global international community.

On issue after issue, the United States has found itself increasingly alone, with one or a few partners, opposing most of the rest of the world's states and peoples. These issues include U.N. dues; sanctions against Cuba, Iran, Iraq, and Libya; the land mines treaty; global warming; an international war crimes tribunal; the Middle East; the use of force against Iraq and Yugoslavia; and the targeting of 35 countries with new economic sanctions between 1993 and 1996. On these and other issues, much of the international community is on one side and the United States is on the other. The circle of governments who see their interests coinciding with American interests is shrinking. This is manifest, among other ways, in the central lineup among the permanent members of the U.N. Security Council. During the first decades of the Cold War, it was 4:1—the United States, the United Kingdom, France, and China against the Soviet Union. After Mao's communist government took China's seat, the lineup became 3:1:1, with China in a shifting middle position. Now it is 2:1:2, with the United States and the United Kingdom opposing China and Russia, and France in the middle spot.

While the United States regularly denounces various countries as "rogue states," in the eyes of many countries it is becoming the rogue superpower. One of Japan's most distinguished diplomats, Ambassador Hisashi Owada, has argued that after World War II, the United States pursued a policy of "unilateral globalism," providing public goods in the form of security, opposition to communism, an open global economy, aid for economic development, and stronger international institutions. Now it is pursuing a policy of "global unilateralism," promoting its own particular interests with little reference to those of others. The United States is unlikely to become an isolationist country, withdrawing from the world. But it could become an isolated country, out of step with much of the world.

If a unipolar world were unavoidable, many countries might prefer the United States as the hegemon. But this is mostly because it is distant from them and hence unlikely to attempt to acquire any of their territory. American power is also valued by the secondary regional states as a constraint on the dominance of other major regional states. Benign hegemony, however, is in the eye of the hegemon. "One reads about the world's desire for American leadership only in the United States," one British diplomat observed. "Everywhere else one reads about American arrogance and unilateralism."

Political and intellectual leaders in most countries strongly resist the prospect of a unipolar world and favor the emergence of true multipolarity. At a 1997 Harvard conference, scholars reported that the elites of countries comprising at least two-thirds of the world's people—Chinese, Russians, Indians, Arabs, Muslims, and Africans—see the United States as the single greatest external threat to their societies. They do not regard America as a military threat but as a menace to their integrity, autonomy, prosperity, and freedom of action. They view the United States as intrusive, interventionist, exploitative, unilateralist, hegemonic, hypocritical, and applying double standards, engaging in what they label "financial imperialism" and "intellectual colonialism," with a foreign policy driven overwhelmingly by domestic politics. For Indian elites, an Indian scholar reported, "the United States represents the major diplomatic and political threat. On virtually every issue of concern to India, the United States has 'veto' or mobilizational power, whether it is on nuclear, technological, economic, environmental, or political matters. That is, the United States can deny India its objectives and can rally others to join it in punishing India." Its sins are "power, hubris, and greed." From the Russian perspective, a Moscow participant said, the United States pursues a policy of "coercive cooperation." All Russians oppose "a world based on a dominant U.S. leadership which would border on hegemony." In similar terms, the Beijing participant said Chinese leaders believe that the principal threats to peace, stability, and China are "hegemonism and power politics," meaning U.S. policies, which they say are designed to undermine and create disunity in the socialist states and developing countries. Arab elites see the United States as an evil force in world affairs, while the Japanese public rated in 1997 the United States as a threat to Japan second only to North Korea.

Such reactions are to be expected. American leaders believe that the world's business is their business. Other countries believe that what happens in their part of the world is their business, not America's, and quite explicitly respond. As Nelson Mandela said, his country rejects another state's having "the arrogance to tell us where we should go or which countries should be our friends. . . . We cannot accept that a state assumes the role of the world's policeman." In a bipolar world, many countries welcomed the United States as their protector against the other superpower. In a uni-multipolar world, in contrast, the world's only superpower is automatically a threat to other major powers. One by one, the major regional powers are making it clear that they do not want the United States messing around in regions where their interests are predominant. Iran, for instance, strongly opposes the U.S. military presence in the Persian Gulf. The current bad relations between the United States and Iran are the product of the Iranian revolution. If, however, the Shah or his son now ruled Iran, those relations would probably be deteriorating because Iran would see the American presence in the Gulf as a threat to its own hegemony there.

## FLEXIBLE RESPONSES

Countries respond in various ways to American superpowerdom. At a relatively low level are widespread feelings of fear, resentment, and envy. These ensure that when at some point the United States suffers a humiliating rebuff from a Saddam or a Milosevic, many countries will think, "They finally got what they had coming to them!" At a somewhat higher level, resentment may turn into dissent, with other countries, including allies, refusing to cooperate with the United States on the Persian Gulf, Cuba, Libya, Iran, extraterritoriality, nuclear proliferation, human rights, trade policies, and other issues. In a few cases, dissent has turned into outright opposition as countries attempt to defeat U.S. policy. The highest level of response would be the formation of an antihegemonic coalition involving several major powers. Such a grouping is impossible in a unipolar world because the other states are too weak to mount it. It appears in a multipolar world only when one state begins to become strong and troublesome enough to provoke it. It would, however, appear to be a natural phenomenon in a uni-multipolar world. Throughout history, major powers have tended to balance against the attempted domination by the strongest among them.

Some antihegemonic cooperation has occurred. Relations among non-Western societies are in general improving. Gatherings occur from which the United States is conspicuously absent, ranging from the Moscow meeting of the leaders of Germany, France, and Russia (which also excluded America's closest ally, Britain) to the bilateral meetings of China and Russia and of China and India. There have been recent rapprochements between Iran and Saudi Arabia and Iran and Iraq. The highly successful meeting of the Organization of the Islamic Conference hosted by Iran coincided with the disastrous Qatar meeting on Middle Eastern economic development sponsored by the United States. Russian Prime Minister Yevgeni Primakov has promoted Russia, China, and India as a "strategic triangle" to counterbalance the United States, and the "Primakov doctrine" reportedly enjoys substantial support across the entire Russian political spectrum.

Undoubtedly the single most important move toward an antihegemonic coalition, however, antedates the end of the Cold War: the formation of the European Union and the creation of a common European currency. As French Foreign Minister Hubert Vedrine has said, Europe must come together on its own and create a counterweight to stop the United States from dominating a multipolar world. Clearly the euro could pose an important challenge to the hegemony of the dollar in global finance.

## THE LONELY SHERIFF

What are the implications of a uni-multipolar world for American policy? First, it would behoove Americans to stop acting and talking as if this were a unipolar world. It is not. To deal with any major global issue, the United States needs the cooperation of at least some major powers. Unilateral sanctions and interventions are recipes for foreign policy disasters. Second, American leaders should abandon the benign-hegemon illusion that a natural congruity exists between their interests and values and those of the rest of the world. It does not. At times, American actions may promote public goods and serve more widely accepted ends. But often they will not, in part because of the unique moralistic component in American policy but also simply because America is the only superpower, and hence its interests necessarily differ from those of other countries. This makes America unique but not benign in the eyes of those countries.

Third, while the United States cannot create a unipolar world, it is in U.S. interests to take advantage of its position as the only superpower in the existing international order and to use its resources to elicit cooperation from other countries to deal with global issues in ways that satisfy American interests. This would essentially involve the Bismarckian strategy recommended by Josef Joffe, but it would also require Bismarckian talents to carry out, and, in any event, cannot be maintained in definitely.

Fourth, the interaction of power and culture has special relevance for European-American relations. The dynamics of power encourage rivalry; cultural commonalities facilitate cooperation. The achievement of almost any major American goal depends on the triumph of the latter over the former. The relation with Europe is central to the success of American foreign policy, and given the pro- and anti-American outlooks of Britain and France, respectively, America's relations with Germany are central to its relations with Europe. Healthy cooperation with Europe is the prime antidote for the loneliness of American superpowerdom.

# PART VI

# September 11 and Beyond: Contemporary American Foreign Policy

September 11 has been characterized as a day that "changed everything." Clearly, the refocusing of American foreign policy on global terrorism and the spread of weapons of mass destruction has marked a shift in emphasis and action. And it can plausibly be argued that the United States has entered into a new era of foreign relations, some yet-to-be-named period following the post–Cold War period defined by a war on terrorism, on counterproliferation, on global disorder, on threats from non-state actors, and on American unilateralism and alienation from the international community. However, as has been consistently argued throughout this book, continuity is also a prominent feature of U.S. foreign policy. American goals of spreading democracy and advocating market capitalism, of supporting increased trade, and maintaining U.S. global leadership and military strength all continue to exemplify American behavior, and are likely to do so for quite some time.

Part VI looks at the current evolution and possible futures of U.S. foreign policy, examining first of all America's response to September 11 and its invasion of Iraq, and what these policies may portend for the future. These actions do indeed take the lion's share of American attention, but there are also a number of other important issues presenting challenges for the United States. Nuclear proliferation, the rise of China, growing authoritarianism in Russia, global warming, looming financial crises, a potentially divided Western Hemisphere, and the opportunities and threats posed by globalization all demand attention, but it is not always clear how the United States will react to many of these developments, and less clear what the outcomes of U.S. actions will be. Like those dissecting American foreign policy in the late 1940s, looking for trends and patterns in the early Cold War years, today's foreign policy analysts are telling a story that may have scarcely begun. They may very well be missing what turns out to be the real story. September 11 could turn out to be the day that changed very little, or the opening round of an entirely new epoch in global politics.

Yogi Berra used to say, "I hate to make predictions, especially about the future," but the readings included in this section exhibit no such hesitancy. President Bush's speech to Congress following the attacks on the Twin Towers and the Pentagon points to a long, protracted struggle. The National Security Strategy of 2002 seems to promise an indefinite period of American hegemony, as well as intolerance for rival powers. James Chace analyzes the possible impacts of America's decision to invade Iraq, while Pete Peterson considers a looming financial crunch that can bring great harm to the American economy, and Lee Lane and Samuel Thernstrom look to the long-term environmental and economic impacts of global warming. And these challenges don't even begin to address the ongoing regional concerns involving Russia, China, Latin America, and other places. As was noted in the introduction to the book, the United States has a big foreign policy that deals with a myriad of issues, and no one knows which of these will soon become big problems or crises that demand attention. Therefore, unlike previous sections of the book, the articles here talk a little bit less to each other, and a bit more past each other. Each looks ahead by extrapolating from the past, wondering what the next great set of problems and challenges will be. The opportunities and threats, indeed, seem almost unlimited.

# 38

## Address to a Joint Session of Congress and the American People

### GEORGE W. BUSH

On September 11, 2001, the United States was attacked by terrorists from al-Qaeda, resulting in the death of 3,000 people and the destruction of the World Trade Center and part of the Pentagon. The attacks fundamentally changed the context and the focus of American foreign policy. Americans had spent the previous decade growing into a role as the sole superpower, one that faced no great or imminent threats to its national security. U.S. foreign policy had centered around globalization, economic liberalization, and responding to failed states and ethnic conflicts. After September 11, the United States reoriented its foreign policy, making the fight against terrorism its number one priority. It responded by fighting back against al-Qaeda and their Taliban allies on a great many fronts—going to war in Afghanistan, creating a new Department of Homeland Security, passing new laws such as the PATRIOT Act, invigorating police and intelligence operations, and targeting financial resources of terrorist organizations.

Just as importantly, a new sense of mission was injected into U.S. foreign policy. This was best captured by President Bush, who gave an address to Congress nine days after the attacks. In this address, which has been considered by many to be the best speech of his presidency, Bush expressed that the United States would wage a new war, one that would be longstanding and look like no other war America had fought in the past. He also said that the United States would not only pursue terrorists, but countries that provided aid or harbored them. In what became the most quoted line in the speech, the president put all nations on notice, stating that "either you are with us, or you are with the terrorists."

This speech represented the beginning of a new direction in American foreign policy. At the same time, however, it represented great continuity with the past. The sense of mission established at this time greatly resembled that of an earlier era, at the outset of the Cold War. That conflict too, was characterized as a long struggle, across many battlefields, on many fronts, against an adversary described as an enemy of freedom itself. Though what soon became known as "The War on Terror" involved new rivals, as well as new strategies and tactics, it did not represent a break with longstanding American foreign policy goals involving the promotion of democracy,

---

George W. Bush, Address to Congress, September 20, 2001.

the maintenance of a liberal economic order, and the continuation
of American preponderance in global politics.

---

Mr. Speaker, Mr. President Pro Tempore, members of Congress,
and fellow Americans:

In the normal course of events, Presidents come to this chamber
to report on the state of the Union. Tonight, no such report is
needed. It has already been delivered by the American people.

We have seen it in the courage of passengers, who rushed
terrorists to save others on the ground—passengers like an
exceptional man named Todd Beamer. And would you please
help me to welcome his wife, Lisa Beamer, here tonight.

We have seen the state of our Union in the endurance of rescuers, working past exhaustion. We have seen the unfurling of
flags, the lighting of candles, the giving of blood, the saying of
prayers—in English, Hebrew, and Arabic. We have seen the
decency of a loving and giving people who have made the grief
of strangers their own.

My fellow citizens, for the last nine days, the entire world has
seen for itself the state of our Union—and it is strong.

Tonight we are a country awakened to danger and called to
defend freedom. Our grief has turned to anger, and anger to
resolution. Whether we bring our enemies to justice, or bring
justice to our enemies, justice will be done.

I thank the Congress for its leadership at such an important
time. All of America was touched on the evening of the tragedy
to see Republicans and Democrats joined together on the steps
of this Capitol, singing "God Bless America." And you did more
than sing; you acted, by delivering $40 billion to rebuild our
communities and meet the needs of our military.

Speaker Hastert, Minority Leader Gephardt, Majority Leader
Daschle and Senator Lott, I thank you for your friendship, for
your leadership and for your service to our country.

And on behalf of the American people, I thank the world for
its outpouring of support. America will never forget the sounds
of our National Anthem playing at Buckingham Palace, on the
streets of Paris, and at Berlin's Brandenburg Gate.

We will not forget South Korean children gathering to pray
outside our embassy in Seoul, or the prayers of sympathy offered
at a mosque in Cairo. We will not forget moments of silence and
days of mourning in Australia and Africa and Latin America.

Nor will we forget the citizens of 80 other nations who died with our own: dozens of Pakistanis; more than 130 Israelis; more than 250 citizens of India; men and women from El Salvador, Iran, Mexico and Japan; and hundreds of British citizens. America has no truer friend than Great Britain. Once again, we are joined together in a great cause—so honored the British Prime Minister has crossed an ocean to show his unity of purpose with America. Thank you for coming, friend.

On September the 11th, enemies of freedom committed an act of war against our country. Americans have known wars—but for the past 136 years, they have been wars on foreign soil, except for one Sunday in 1941. Americans have known the casualties of war—but not at the center of a great city on a peaceful morning. Americans have known surprise attacks—but never before on thousands of civilians. All of this was brought upon us in a single day—and night fell on a different world, a world where freedom itself is under attack.

Americans have many questions tonight. Americans are asking: Who attacked our country? The evidence we have gathered all points to a collection of loosely affiliated terrorist organizations known as al Qaeda. They are the same murderers indicted for bombing American embassies in Tanzania and Kenya, and responsible for bombing the USS Cole.

Al Qaeda is to terror what the mafia is to crime. But its goal is not making money; its goal is remaking the world—and imposing its radical beliefs on people everywhere.

The terrorists practice a fringe form of Islamic extremism that has been rejected by Muslim scholars and the vast majority of Muslim clerics—a fringe movement that perverts the peaceful teachings of Islam. The terrorists' directive commands them to kill Christians and Jews, to kill all Americans, and make no distinction among military and civilians, including women and children.

This group and its leader—a person named Osama bin Laden—are linked to many other organizations in different countries, including the Egyptian Islamic Jihad and the Islamic Movement of Uzbekistan. There are thousands of these terrorists in more than 60 countries. They are recruited from their own nations and neighborhoods and brought to camps in places like Afghanistan, where they are trained in the tactics of terror. They are sent back to their homes or sent to hide in countries around the world to plot evil and destruction.

The leadership of al Qaeda has great influence in Afghanistan and supports the Taliban regime in controlling most of that country. In Afghanistan, we see al Qaeda's vision for the world.

Afghanistan's people have been brutalized—many are starving and many have fled. Women are not allowed to attend school. You can be jailed for owning a television. Religion can be practiced only as their leaders dictate. A man can be jailed in Afghanistan if his beard is not long enough.

The United States respects the people of Afghanistan—after all, we are currently its largest source of humanitarian aid—but we condemn the Taliban regime. It is not only repressing its own people, it is threatening people everywhere by sponsoring and sheltering and supplying terrorists. By aiding and abetting murder, the Taliban regime is committing murder.

And tonight, the United States of America makes the following demands on the Taliban: Deliver to United States authorities all the leaders of al Qaeda who hide in your land. Release all foreign nationals, including American citizens, you have unjustly imprisoned. Protect foreign journalists, diplomats and aid workers in your country. Close immediately and permanently every terrorist training camp in Afghanistan, and hand over every terrorist, and every person in their support structure, to appropriate authorities. Give the United States full access to terrorist training camps, so we can make sure they are no longer operating.

These demands are not open to negotiation or discussion. The Taliban must act, and act immediately. They will hand over the terrorists, or they will share in their fate.

I also want to speak tonight directly to Muslims throughout the world. We respect your faith. It's practiced freely by many millions of Americans, and by millions more in countries that America counts as friends. Its teachings are good and peaceful, and those who commit evil in the name of Allah blaspheme the name of Allah. The terrorists are traitors to their own faith, trying, in effect, to hijack Islam itself. The enemy of America is not our many Muslim friends; it is not our many Arab friends. Our enemy is a radical network of terrorists, and every government that supports them.

Our war on terror begins with al Qaeda, but it does not end there. It will not end until every terrorist group of global reach has been found, stopped and defeated.

Americans are asking, why do they hate us? They hate what we see right here in this chamber—a democratically elected government. Their leaders are self-appointed. They hate our freedoms—our freedom of religion, our freedom of speech, our freedom to vote and assemble and disagree with each other.

They want to overthrow existing governments in many Muslim countries, such as Egypt, Saudi Arabia, and Jordan. They want to drive Israel out of the Middle East. They want to drive Christians and Jews out of vast regions of Asia and Africa.

These terrorists kill not merely to end lives, but to disrupt and end a way of life. With every atrocity, they hope that America grows fearful, retreating from the world and forsaking our friends. They stand against us, because we stand in their way.

We are not deceived by their pretenses to piety. We have seen their kind before. They are the heirs of all the murderous ideologies of the 20th century. By sacrificing human life to serve their radical visions—by abandoning every value except the will to power—they follow in the path of fascism, and Nazism, and totalitarianism. And they will follow that path all the way, to where it ends: in history's unmarked grave of discarded lies.

Americans are asking: How will we fight and win this war? We will direct every resource at our command—every means of diplomacy, every tool of intelligence, every instrument of law enforcement, every financial influence, and every necessary weapon of war—to the disruption and to the defeat of the global terror network.

This war will not be like the war against Iraq a decade ago, with a decisive liberation of territory and a swift conclusion. It will not look like the air war above Kosovo two years ago, where no ground troops were used and not a single American was lost in combat.

Our response involves far more than instant retaliation and isolated strikes. Americans should not expect one battle, but a lengthy campaign, unlike any other we have ever seen. It may include dramatic strikes, visible on TV, and covert operations, secret even in success. We will starve terrorists of funding, turn them one against another, drive them from place to place, until there is no refuge or no rest. And we will pursue nations that provide aid or safe haven to terrorism. Every nation, in every region, now has a decision to make. Either you are with us, or you are with the terrorists. From this day forward, any nation that continues to harbor or support terrorism will be regarded by the United States as a hostile regime.

Our nation has been put on notice: We are not immune from attack. We will take defensive measures against terrorism to protect Americans. Today, dozens of federal departments and agencies, as well as state and local governments, have responsibilities affecting homeland security. These efforts must be coordinated at the highest level. So tonight I announce the creation of a Cabinet-level position reporting directly to me—the Office of Homeland Security.

And tonight I also announce a distinguished American to lead this effort, to strengthen American security: a military veteran, an effective governor, a true patriot, a trusted friend—Pennsylvania's Tom Ridge. He will lead, oversee and coordinate a comprehensive national strategy to safeguard our country against terrorism, and respond to any attacks that may come.

These measures are essential. But the only way to defeat terrorism as a threat to our way of life is to stop it, eliminate it, and destroy it where it grows.

Many will be involved in this effort, from FBI agents to intelligence operatives to the reservists we have called to active duty. All deserve our thanks, and all have our prayers. And tonight, a few miles from the damaged Pentagon, I have a message for our military: Be ready. I've called the Armed Forces to alert, and there is a reason. The hour is coming when America will act, and you will make us proud.

This is not, however, just America's fight. And what is at stake is not just America's freedom. This is the world's fight. This is civilization's fight. This is the fight of all who believe in progress and pluralism, tolerance and freedom.

We ask every nation to join us. We will ask, and we will need, the help of police forces, intelligence services, and banking systems around the world. The United States is grateful that many nations and many international organizations have already responded—with sympathy and with support. Nations from Latin America, to Asia, to Africa, to Europe, to the Islamic world. Perhaps the NATO Charter reflects best the attitude of the world: An attack on one is an attack on all.

The civilized world is rallying to America's side. They understand that if this terror goes unpunished, their own cities, their own citizens may be next. Terror, unanswered, can not only bring down buildings, it can threaten the stability of legitimate governments. And you know what—we're not going to allow it.

Americans are asking: What is expected of us? I ask you to live your lives, and hug your children. I know many citizens have fears tonight, and I ask you to be calm and resolute, even in the face of a continuing threat.

I ask you to uphold the values of America, and remember why so many have come here. We are in a fight for our principles, and our first responsibility is to live by them. No one should be singled out for unfair treatment or unkind words because of their ethnic background or religious faith.

I ask you to continue to support the victims of this tragedy with your contributions. Those who want to give can go to a central source of information, libertyunites.org, to find the names of groups providing direct help in New York, Pennsylvania, and Virginia.

The thousands of FBI agents who are now at work in this investigation may need your cooperation, and I ask you to give it.

I ask for your patience, with the delays and inconveniences that may accompany tighter security; and for your patience in what will be a long struggle.

I ask your continued participation and confidence in the American economy. Terrorists attacked a symbol of American prosperity. They did not touch its source. America is successful because of the hard work, and creativity, and enterprise of our people. These were the true strengths of our economy before September 11th, and they are our strengths today.

And, finally, please continue praying for the victims of terror and their families, for those in uniform, and for our great country. Prayer has comforted us in sorrow, and will help strengthen us for the journey ahead.

Tonight I thank my fellow Americans for what you have already done and for what you will do. And ladies and gentlemen of the Congress, I thank you, their representatives, for what you have already done and for what we will do together.

Tonight, we face new and sudden national challenges. We will come together to improve air safety, to dramatically expand the number of air marshals on domestic flights, and take new measures to prevent hijacking. We will come together to promote stability and keep our airlines flying, with direct assistance during this emergency.

We will come together to give law enforcement the additional tools it needs to track down terror here at home. We will come together to strengthen our intelligence capabilities to know the plans of terrorists before they act, and find them before they strike.

We will come together to take active steps that strengthen America's economy, and put our people back to work.

Tonight we welcome two leaders who embody the extraordinary spirit of all New Yorkers: Governor George Pataki and Mayor Rudolph Giuliani. As a symbol of America's resolve, my administration will work with Congress, and these two leaders, to show the world that we will rebuild New York City.

After all that has just passed—all the lives taken, and all the possibilities and hopes that died with them—it is natural to wonder if America's future is one of fear. Some speak of an age of terror. I know there are struggles ahead, and dangers to face. But this country will define our times, not be defined by them. As long as the United States of America is determined and strong, this will not be an age of terror; this will be an age of liberty, here and across the world.

Great harm has been done to us. We have suffered great loss. And in our grief and anger we have found our mission and our moment. Freedom and fear are at war. The advance of human freedom—the great achievement of our time, and the great hope of every time—now depends on us. Our nation—this generation—will lift a dark threat of violence from our people and our future. We will rally the world to this cause by our efforts, by our courage. We will not tire, we will not falter, and we will not fail.

It is my hope that in the months and years ahead, life will return almost to normal. We'll go back to our lives and routines, and that is good. Even grief recedes with time and grace. But our resolve must not pass. Each of us will remember what happened that day, and to whom it happened. We'll remember the moment the news came—where we were and what we were doing. Some will remember an image of a fire, or a story of rescue. Some will carry memories of a face and a voice gone forever.

And I will carry this: It is the police shield of a man named George Howard, who died at the World Trade Center trying to save others. It was given to me by his mom, Arlene, as a proud memorial to her son. This is my reminder of lives that ended, and a task that does not end.

I will not forget this wound to our country or those who inflicted it. I will not yield; I will not rest; I will not relent in waging this struggle for freedom and security for the American people.

The course of this conflict is not known, yet its outcome is certain. Freedom and fear, justice and cruelty, have always been at war, and we know that God is not neutral between them.

Fellow citizens, we'll meet violence with patient justice—assured of the rightness of our cause, and confident of the victories to come. In all that lies before us, may God grant us wisdom, and may He watch over the United States of America.

Thank you.

## 39 The National Security Strategy of the United States of America
### THE WHITE HOUSE

One year after the attacks of September 11, the White House developed a new national security strategy, providing a blueprint for American engagement in a world with a "security environment more complex and dangerous" than existed during the Cold War. This environment, it was argued, was characterized by threats to global order and peace from rogue states and terrorist organizations, as well as the spread of weapons of mass destruction among such states and non-state actors. These concerns, above all else, came to dominate the foreign policy of the United States and, of course, continue to do so into the present.

The document was in some ways similar to previous national security strategies. It addressed the need for maintaining security by advancing democracy, working with allies, promoting trade and economic growth, and finding solutions for troubled parts of the world. The sections that dealt with these challenges reflected a degree of continuity with previous such documents, often seeking multilateral solutions to global problems. These sections attracted little more than the usual attention devoted to such policy statements. At the same time, however, this national security strategy was notable for two important points that received widespread attention and criticism. These points involved maintaining American security by means of preemption and American military supremacy. Preemption was based on the idea that some enemies could not be deterred from taking hostile action against American interests. The threat posed by rogue states willing to take risks, and stateless terrorists whose goals are characterized as wanton destruction

The National Security Council, "The National Security Strategy of the United States of America," September 2002.

and martyrdom, meant that "to forestall or prevent such hostile acts by our adversaries, the United States will, if necessary, act preemptively." The strategy also called for American military supremacy—a level of superiority so far beyond the capability of other countries, it would dissuade them from even attempting to build their military forces up to a level that would equal or surpass the United States.

Both of these elements provoked strong reaction, domestically and internationally. The document seems to discuss these issues in a way that suggested only a difference in emphasis or degree from past policy. In light of subsequent U.S. action in Iraq, however, they were more often regarded as a difference in kind, signaling a more aggressive international posture. The Bush administration argued that this strategy represented a logical response to a set of dangerous new circumstances. Critics, however, suggested that it demonstrated little regard for America's longstanding alliances, flouted international law and norms by turning the principle of self-defense upside-down, reflected a degree of arrogance and hubris by suggesting no other countries could ever rival American military forces, and set a dangerous precedent in international relations—after all, the logic of preemption could be used to justify aggression by any country. Whether or not these criticisms turn out to be justified in the long term, President Bush has applied the logic of this strategy and has carried out, especially during his first term, a foreign policy that in large part conforms to this assessment.

---

## PREVENT OUR ENEMIES FROM THREATENING US, OUR ALLIES, AND OUR FRIENDS WITH WEAPONS OF MASS DESTRUCTION

The nature of the Cold War threat required the United States—with our allies and friends—to emphasize deterrence of the enemy's use of force, producing a grim strategy of mutual assured destruction. With the collapse of the Soviet Union and the end of the Cold War, our security environment has undergone profound transformation.

But new deadly challenges have emerged from rogue states and terrorists. None of these contemporary threats rival the sheer destructive power that was arrayed against us by the Soviet Union. However, the nature and motivations of these new adversaries, their determination to obtain destructive powers hitherto available only to the world's strongest states, and the greater likelihood that they will use weapons of mass destruction against us, make today's security environment more complex and dangerous.

In the 1990s we witnessed the emergence of a small number of rogue states that, while different in important ways, share a number of attributes. These states:

- brutalize their own people and squander their national resources for the personal gain of the rulers;
- display no regard for international law, threaten their neighbors, and callously violate international treaties to which they are party;
- are determined to acquire weapons of mass destruction, along with other advanced military technology, to be used as threats or offensively to achieve the aggressive designs of these regimes;
- sponsor terrorism around the globe; and
- reject basic human values and hate the United States and everything for which it stands.

At the time of the Gulf War, we acquired irrefutable proof that Iraq's designs were not limited to the chemical weapons it had used against Iran and its own people, but also extended to the acquisition of nuclear weapons and biological agents. In the past decade North Korea has become the world's principal purveyor of ballistic missiles, and has tested increasingly capable missiles while developing its own WMD arsenal. Other rogue regimes seek nuclear, biological, and chemical weapons as well. These states' pursuit of, and global trade in, such weapons has become a looming threat to all nations.

We must be prepared to stop rogue states and their terrorist clients before they are able to threaten or use weapons of mass destruction against the United States and our allies and friends. Our response must take full advantage of strengthened alliances, the establishment of new partnerships with former adversaries, innovation in the use of military forces, modern technologies, including the development of an effective missile defense system, and increased emphasis on intelligence collection and analysis.

Our comprehensive strategy to combat WMD includes:

- *Proactive counterproliferation efforts.* We must deter and defend against the threat before it is unleashed. We must ensure that key capabilities—detection, active and passive defenses, and counterforce capabilities—are integrated into our defense transformation and our homeland security systems. Counterproliferation must also be integrated into the doctrine, training, and equipping of our forces and those of our allies to ensure that we can prevail in any conflict with WMD-armed adversaries.

- *Strengthened nonproliferation efforts to prevent rogue states and terrorists from acquiring the materials, technologies, and expertise necessary for weapons of mass destruction.* We will enhance diplomacy, arms control, multilateral export controls, and threat reduction assistance that impede states and terrorists seeking WMD, and when necessary, interdict enabling technologies and materials. We will continue to build coalitions to support these efforts, encouraging their increased political and financial support for nonproliferation and threat reduction programs. The recent G-8 agreement to commit up to $20 billion to a global partnership against proliferation marks a major step forward.
- *Effective consequence management to respond to the effects of WMD use, whether by terrorists or hostile states.* Minimizing the effects of WMD use against our people will help deter those who possess such weapons and dissuade those who seek to acquire them by persuading enemies that they cannot attain their desired ends. The United States must also be prepared to respond to the effects of WMD use against our forces abroad, and to help friends and allies if they are attacked.

It has taken almost a decade for us to comprehend the true nature of this new threat. Given the goals of rogue states and terrorists, the United States can no longer solely rely on a reactive posture as we have in the past. The inability to deter a potential attacker, the immediacy of today's threats, and the magnitude of potential harm that could be caused by our adversaries' choice of weapons, do not permit that option. We cannot let our enemies strike first.

In the Cold War, especially following the Cuban missile crisis, we faced a generally status quo, risk-averse adversary. Deterrence was an effective defense. But deterrence based only upon the threat of retaliation is less likely to work against leaders of rogue states more willing to take risks, gambling with the lives of their people, and the wealth of their nations.

- In the Cold War, weapons of mass destruction were considered weapons of last resort whose use risked the destruction of those who used them. Today, our enemies see weapons of mass destruction as weapons of choice. For rogue states these weapons are tools of intimidation and military aggression against their neighbors. These weapons may also allow these states to attempt to blackmail the United States and our allies to prevent us from deterring or repelling the aggressive behavior of rogue states. Such states also see these weapons as their best means of overcoming the conventional superiority of the United States.

- Traditional concepts of deterrence will not work against a terror-ist enemy whose avowed tactics are wanton destruction and the targeting of innocents; whose so-called soldiers seek martyrdom in death and whose most potent protection is statelessness. The overlap between states that sponsor terror and those that pursue WMD compels us to action.

For centuries, international law recognized that nations need not suffer an attack before they can lawfully take action to defend themselves against forces that present an imminent danger of attack. Legal scholars and inter-national jurists often conditioned the legitimacy of preemption on the exis-tence of an imminent threat—most often a visible mobilization of armies, navies, and air forces preparing to attack.

We must adapt the concept of imminent threat to the capabilities and objectives of today's adversaries. Rogue states and terrorists do not seek to attack us using conventional means. They know such attacks would fail. Instead, they rely on acts of terror and, potentially, the use of weapons of mass destruction—weapons that can be easily concealed, delivered covertly, and used without warning.

The targets of these attacks are our military forces and our civilian popu-lation, in direct violation of one of the principal norms of the law of warfare. As was demonstrated by the losses on September 11, 2001, mass civilian casualties is the specific objective of terrorists and these losses would be exponentially more severe if terrorists acquired and used weapons of mass destruction.

The United States has long maintained the option of preemptive actions to counter a sufficient threat to our national security. The greater the threat, the greater is the risk of inaction— and the more compelling the case for taking anticipatory action to defend ourselves, even if uncertainty remains as to the time and place of the enemy's attack. To forestall or prevent such hostile acts by our adversaries, the United States will, if necessary, act preemptively.

The United States will not use force in all cases to preempt emerging threats, nor should nations use preemption as a pretext for aggression. Yet in an age where the enemies of civilization openly and actively seek the world's most destructive technologies, the United States cannot remain idle while dangers gather. We will always proceed deliberately, weighing the conse-quences of our actions. To support preemptive options, we will:

- build better, more integrated intelligence capabilities to provide timely, accurate information on threats, wherever they may emerge;
- coordinate closely with allies to form a common assessment of the most dangerous threats; and

- continue to transform our military forces to ensure our ability to conduct rapid and precise operations to achieve decisive results.

The purpose of our actions will always be to eliminate a specific threat to the United States or our allies and friends. The reasons for our actions will be clear, the force measured, and the cause just.

## TRANSFORM AMERICA'S NATIONAL SECURITY INSTITUTIONS TO MEET THE CHALLENGES AND OPPORTUNITIES OF THE TWENTY-FIRST CENTURY

The major institutions of American national security were designed in a different era to meet different requirements. All of them must be transformed.

It is time to reaffirm the essential role of American military strength. We must build and maintain our defenses beyond challenge. Our military's highest priority is to defend the United States. To do so effectively, our military must:

- assure our allies and friends;
- dissuade future military competition;
- deter threats against U.S. interests, allies, and friends; and
- decisively defeat any adversary if deterrence fails.

The unparalleled strength of the United States armed forces, and their forward presence, have maintained the peace in some of the world's most strategically vital regions. However, the threats and enemies we must confront have changed, and so must our forces. A military structured to deter massive Cold War-era armies must be transformed to focus more on how an adversary might fight rather than where and when a war might occur. We will channel our energies to overcome a host of operational challenges.

The presence of American forces overseas is one of the most profound symbols of the U.S. commitments to allies and friends. Through our willingness to use force in our own defense and in defense of others, the United States demonstrates its resolve to maintain a balance of power that favors freedom. To contend with uncertainty and to meet the many security challenges we face, the United States will require bases and stations within and beyond Western Europe and Northeast Asia, as well as temporary access arrangements for the long-distance deployment of U.S. forces.

Before the war in Afghanistan, that area was low on the list of major planning contingencies. Yet, in a very short time, we had to operate across the length and breadth of that remote nation, using every branch of the armed forces. We must prepare for more such deployments by developing assets such as advanced remote sensing, long-range precision strike capabilities, and transformed maneuver and expeditionary forces. This broad portfolio of military capabilities must also include the ability to defend the homeland, conduct information operations, ensure U.S. access to distant theaters, and protect critical U.S. infrastructure and assets in outer space.

Innovation within the armed forces will rest on experimentation with new approaches to warfare, strengthening joint operations, exploiting U.S. intelligence advantages, and taking full advantage of science and technology. We must also transform the way the Department of Defense is run, especially in financial management and recruitment and retention. Finally, while maintaining near-term readiness and the ability to fight the war on terrorism, the goal must be to provide the President with a wider range of military options to discourage aggression or any form of coercion against the United States, our allies, and our friends.

We know from history that deterrence can fail; and we know from experience that some enemies cannot be deterred. The United States must and will maintain the capability to defeat any attempt by an enemy—whether a state or non-state actor—to impose its will on the United States, our allies, or our friends. We will maintain the forces sufficient to support our obligations, and to defend freedom. Our forces will be strong enough to dissuade potential adversaries from pursuing a military build-up in hopes of surpassing, or equaling, the power of the United States.

# 40 Keeping Saddam Hussein in a Box

## JOHN J. MEARSHEIMER AND STEPHEN M. WALT

The first test of the Bush administration's new national security strategy came in Iraq. President Bush had declared in his State of the Union Address in 2002 that the regimes of Iraq, Iran, and North Korea constituted an "axis of evil," and that he intended to address the threats that these countries posed to American and global security. The president specifically cited Iraqi connections to al-Qaeda and the development of weapons of mass destruction as the justifications for war. A secondary benefit would be to end a brutal dictatorship and establish a democratic government, which ideally would serve as a catalyst for democratic change in the region. As the United

John Mearsheimer and Stephen Walt, "Keeping Saddam Hussein in a Box," *The New York Times*, February 2, 2003. © 2003 The New York Times Co. Reprinted by permission.

States began a military buildup around Iraq, the policy generated heated controversy around the world. Iraq had not attacked the United States, and an American invasion would constitute a preventive war to counter what might become a significant threat in the future, not an imminent threat.

Prior to the American invasion that ousted Saddam Hussein's regime, John Mearsheimer and Stephen Walt offered an analysis of why the United States did not need to launch a preventive war against Hussein, but could instead achieve its security objectives by containing Iraq. They argued that Hussein was not as reckless as suggested by the president. He had, after all, refrained from using chemical weapons against America in 1991 and in the years afterward due to fears of retaliation. The same logic, that of deterrence, would continue to apply into the future. Moreover, the nuclear weapons capacity of Iraq had been dismantled as a result of U.N. inspections, and Iraq was nowhere near rebuilding it. In addition, the authors point out that no evidence has been found connecting Hussein to al-Qaeda, while arguing that a connection to the group involving the transfer of weapons of mass destruction is unlikely.

The authors concluded that containment is a far better alternative to war, and their argument is based on more than an alternative interpretation of the facts regarding Iraq. It is also rooted in a rejection of the national security strategy offered by President Bush. The result, they suggest, of pursuing such a strategy, would be ironic: war to stop nuclear proliferation would actually encourage other states, especially Iran and North Korea, to develop nuclear weapons in order to deter a potential war with the United States in the future.

---

The United States faces a clear choice on Iraq: containment or preventive war. President Bush insists that containment has failed and we must prepare for war. In fact, war is not necessary. Containment has worked in the past and can work in the future, even when dealing with Saddam Hussein.

The case for preventive war rests on the claim that Mr. Hussein is a reckless expansionist bent on dominating the Middle East. Indeed, he is often compared to Adolf Hitler, modern history's exemplar of serial aggression. The facts, however, tell a different story.

During the 30 years that Mr. Hussein has dominated Iraq, he has initiated two wars. Iraq invaded Iran in 1980, but only after Iran's revolutionary government tried to assassinate Iraqi officials, conducted repeated border raids and tried to topple Mr. Hussein by fomenting unrest within Iraq. His decision to attack was not reckless, because Iran was isolated and widely seen as militarily weak. The war proved costly, but it ended Iran's regional ambitions and kept Mr. Hussein in power.

Iraq's invasion of Kuwait in 1990 arose from a serious dispute over oil prices and war debts and occurred only after efforts to court Mr. Hussein led the first Bush administration unwittingly to signal that Washington would not oppose an attack. Containment did not fail the first time around—it was never tried.

Thus, Mr. Hussein has gone to war when he was threatened and when he thought he had a window of opportunity. These considerations do not justify Iraq's actions, but they show that Mr. Hussein is hardly a reckless aggressor who cannot be contained. In fact, Iraq has never gone to war in the face of a clear deterrent threat.

But what about the Iraqi regime's weapons of mass destruction? Those who reject containment point to Iraq's past use of chemical weapons against the Kurds and Iran. They also warn that he will eventually get nuclear weapons. According to President Bush, a nuclear arsenal would enable Mr. Hussein to "blackmail the world." And the real nightmare is that he will give chemical, biological or nuclear weapons to Al Qaeda.

These possibilities sound alarming, but the dangers they pose do not justify war.

Mr. Hussein's use of poison gas was despicable, but it tells us nothing about what he might do against the United States or its allies. He could use chemical weapons against the Kurds and Iranians because they could not retaliate in kind. The United States, by contrast, can retaliate with overwhelming force, including weapons of mass destruction. This is why Mr. Hussein did not use chemical or biological weapons against American forces or Israel during the 1991 Persian Gulf war. Nor has he used such weapons since, even though the United States has bombed Iraq repeatedly over the past decade.

The same logic explains why Mr. Hussein cannot blackmail us. Nuclear blackmail works only if the blackmailer's threat might actually be carried out. But if the intended target can retaliate in kind, carrying out the threat causes the blackmailer's own destruction. This is why the Soviet Union, which was far stronger than Iraq and led by men of equal ruthlessness, never tried blackmailing the United States.

Oddly enough, the Bush administration seems to understand that America is not vulnerable to nuclear blackmail. For example, Condoleezza Rice, the national security adviser, has written that Iraqi weapons of mass destruction "will be unusable because any attempt to use them will bring national obliteration." Similarly, President Bush declared last week in his State of the Union address that the United States "would not be blackmailed" by North Korea, which administration officials believe has nuclear weapons. If Iraq's chemical, biological and nuclear arsenal is "unusable" and North Korea's weapons cannot be used for blackmail, why do the president and Ms. Rice favor war?

But isn't the possibility that the Iraqi regime would give weapons of mass destruction to Al Qaeda reason enough to topple it? No—unless the administration isn't telling us something. Advocates of preventive war have made Herculean efforts to uncover evidence of active cooperation between Iraq and Al Qaeda, and senior administration officials have put great pressure on American intelligence agencies to find convincing evidence. But these efforts have borne little fruit, and we should view the latest reports of alleged links with skepticism. No country should weave a case for war with such slender threads.

Given the deep antipathy between fundamentalists like Osama bin Laden and secular rulers like Saddam Hussein, the lack of evidence linking them is not surprising. But even if American pressure brings these unlikely bedfellows together, Mr. Hussein is not going to give Al Qaeda weapons of mass destruction. He would have little to gain and everything to lose since he could never be sure that American surveillance would not detect the handoff. If it did, the United States response would be swift and devastating.

The Iraqi dictator might believe he could slip Al Qaeda dangerous weapons covertly, but he would still have to worry that we would destroy him if we merely suspected that he had aided an attack on the United States. He need not be certain we would retaliate, he merely has to think that we might.

Thus, logic and evidence suggest that Iraq can be contained, even if it possesses weapons of mass destruction. Moreover, Mr. Hussein's nuclear ambitions—the ones that concern us most—are unlikely to be realized in his lifetime, especially with inspections under way. Iraq has pursued nuclear weapons since the 1970's, but it has never produced a bomb. United Nations inspectors destroyed Iraq's nuclear program between 1991 and 1998, and Iraq has not rebuilt it. With an embargo in place and inspectors at work, Iraq is further from a nuclear capacity than at any time in recent memory. Again, why the rush to war?

War may not be necessary to deny Iraq nuclear weapons, but it is likely to spur proliferation elsewhere. The Bush administration's contrasting approaches to Iraq and North Korea send a clear signal: we negotiate with states that have nuclear weapons, but we threaten states that don't. Iran and North Korea will be even more committed to having a nuclear deterrent after watching the American military conquer Iraq. Countries like Japan, South Korea and Saudi Arabia will then think about following suit. Stopping the spread of nuclear weapons will be difficult in any case, but overthrowing Mr. Hussein would make it harder.

Preventive war entails other costs as well. In addition to the lives lost, top-pling Saddam Hussein would cost at least $50 billion to $100 billion, at a time when our economy is sluggish and huge budget deficits are predicted for years. Because the United States would have to occupy Iraq for years, the actual cost of this war would most likely be much larger. And because most of the world thinks war is a mistake, we would get little help from other countries.

Finally, attacking Iraq would undermine the war on terrorism, diverting manpower, money and attention from the fight against Al Qaeda. Every dollar spent occupying Iraq is a dollar not spent dismantling terrorist net-works abroad or improving security at home. Invasion and occupation would increase anti-Americanism in the Islamic world and help Osama bin Laden win more followers. Preventive war would also reinforce the grow-ing perception that the United States is a bully, thereby jeopardizing the international unity necessary to defeat global terrorism.

Although the Bush administration maintains that war is necessary, there is a better option. Today, Iraq is weakened, its pursuit of nuclear weapons has been frustrated, and any regional ambitions it may once have cherished have been thwarted. We should perpetuate this state of affairs by maintain-ing vigilant containment, a policy the rest of the world regards as prefer-able and effective. Saddam Hussein needs to remain in his box—but we don't need a war to keep him there.

## 41 The Folly of Containment
### ROBERT LIEBER

The war in Iraq was preceded by a long and strenuous debate over sev-eral months regarding the wisdom of such a war. In contrast to the idea that Saddam Hussein could be contained, the counterargument was advanced that it was not certain at all that he could be contained—his actions were too reckless and unpredictable—and that this was exactly the reason the United States should take military action to remove him from power and disarm Iraq.

In the weeks just before the war began, Robert Lieber offered a clear and succinct case for war. Responding to Mearsheimer and

Robert Lieber, from "The Folly of Containment," *Commentary*, April 2003. Reprinted by per-mission of Commentary.

Walt, as well as many others, he critiques the policy of containment, refuting their conclusions and explaining in detail why proponents of containing Iraq are misguided in their assessment. Lieber's argument is that Saddam Hussein is simply not containable. Containment requires an aversity to risk, as well as careful, rational calculation among both parties to the conflict. Hussein, Lieber states, displays neither of these qualities. Iraq's wars against Iran and Kuwait, its deception with regard to weapons inspections over the years, Hussein's links and potential for greater links to terrorist organizations, his use of chemical weapons, his refusal to countenance the idea that his grand designs will fail, and his sheer brutality all support the idea that Hussein cannot ultimately be contained. Rather, they clearly suggest that he is pursuing weapons of mass destruction and is likely to use them to attack or blackmail his enemies.

What informs this argument is the logic of the national security strategy of 2002: The United States should act now to remove a menace and a threat before it is a much bigger threat at some point in the future. The analogy of World War II was often invoked in this debate. Had the Allies acted sooner to block Hitler, war could have been avoided, or at least been much shorter and less costly. While critics of the administration suggested that it was unclear that Hussein would build or use nuclear weapons one day, National Security Advisor Condoleeza Rice stated that this was exactly the reason the United States should and would act, because, "we don't want the smoking gun to be a mushroom cloud."

---

No matter what finally happens in our confrontation with Iraq, the use of force against Saddam Hussein is a subject that is bound to be debated for years to come. Any proposed resort to war carries great risks and entails unforeseeable consequences; this particular resort to war, having occasioned months of impassioned and often bitter discussion at home and abroad, and having run up against determined resistance on the part of some of America's democratic allies, invites repeated reassessment.

Beyond the fever swamps of the far Left and the far Right, beyond the serried ranks of the earnest demonstrators for "peace," with their incantations of no-blood-for-oil, beyond the delusional rantings about an "axis of oil and Jews" and the claims that the crisis with Iraq was manufactured by Israel and a cabal of its American supporters, it has been possible from the beginning to discern a more measured cluster of arguments opposing military action. These arguments have been advanced by people who are neither reflexively anti-American nor blind to Saddam's tyranny, his programs to acquire weapons of mass destruction (WMD), and his calculated defiance of the United Nations. Instead, their opposition to the use of force has proceeded through an appeal to an alternative and, in their view, superior approach: containment.

In many ways, indeed, it is the future of that venerable cold-war doctrine that has been on the line in the debate over Iraq. Whatever the outcome of this particular engagement, the real question being decided is what containment means in the world we have entered since September 11, 2001.

There are various schools of thought among these critics, and differences of nuance and terminology when it comes to what they think we ought to do. Some, for instance, have called for "coercive inspections" in Iraq (the term favored in a report of the Carnegie Endowment for International Peace), others for something called "vigilant containment" (urged by a group of scholars of international relations led by John Mearsheimer of the University of Chicago and Stephen Walt of Harvard). In propounding their alternative to war, many have raised dire warnings about the terrible risks of battlefield conflict, including Saddam's likely use of his weapons of mass destruction; others have predicted chaos and internecine bloodshed in a post-Saddam Iraq, held out the threat of a total breakdown in the machinery of international diplomacy, and the like. One distinguished advocate of containment, Stanley Hoffmann of Harvard, has urged that we concentrate on the conflict between Israel and the Palestinians "before we turn on Iraq"—and he is not alone.

Still, the bottom line on which the argument rests is that a policy of containment—"the adroit and vigilant application of counterforce at a series of constantly shifting . . . political points," to quote the words of George F. Kennan in the 1947 article that gave the doctrine its name—has all along been sufficient to deal with the situation in Iraq, and that the Bush administration, in its determination to go to war, has never given it a fair chance to show that it could work. In building their case, the critics appeal to history and to experience. They contend that we have in fact been able to contain Saddam in the past, that we are doing so in the present, and that we can continue to do so in the future.

Looking to the past, for example, Mearsheimer and Walt write that Saddam has shown himself to be "neither mindlessly aggressive nor particularly reckless," citing as evidence the fact that over the last 30 years Iraq has started "only" two wars. Moreover, Saddam's decision to attack Iran in 1980 was, they assert, taken for essentially defensive reasons, and even his August 1990 invasion of Kuwait amounted to "an attempt to deal with Iraq's continued vulnerability" in the aftermath of the war with Iran. To the objection that, in the case of Kuwait. Saddam was in fact not contained either by a UN Security Council resolution demanding his withdrawal from that country or by the massing of an American-led army on his doorstep, Mearsheimer and Walt have answered by invoking the Iraqi dictator's belief that the U.S. would back off from open conflict rather than risk the casualties that Iraqi forces were certain to inflict on it.

Other authors examining Iraq's record point to the decade after the Gulf war as offering additional evidence for the success of containment. Here the contention is that at least up until 1998, when the first UN inspection team, UNSCOM, was forced to withdraw from the country, the combination of inspections and economic sanctions had significantly reduced Saddam's missile capabilities, degraded his nuclear program, and left his armed forces seriously weakened.

As for Saddam's disposition in the run-up to the current confrontation, he has been, according to proponents of containment, in a box. What has kept him in that box is, first of all, his own rationality. In the words of Shibley Telhami of the University of Maryland, Saddam's is "a ruthless regime, but it isn't suicidal." The same calculation has been applied to his possession of weapons of mass destruction: "Iraq remains constrained from using such weapons," writes the activist Todd Gitlin—"which is the point of containment."

This idea was elaborated upon by a group of 33 professors who signed an ad in the New York Times last September. Although, they conceded, "war is sometimes necessary to insure our national security or other vital interests," it was not called for against Iraq. Among their reasons: there was no proof that Iraq had been collaborating with al Qaeda; a war with Iraq would distract us from the fight against terrorism; and, most crucially, even if Saddam were to add a nuclear capability to his already formidable array of chemical and biological weapons, we could nevertheless successfully deter him from using it. Although the ad did not spell out how exactly we were to accomplish this, its main authors, who were once again Mearsheimer and Walt, have since written that "the United States can contain Iraq effectively—even if Saddam has nuclear weapons—just as it contained the Soviet Union during the cold war." In support of this proposition they note that Saddam has "never used weapons of mass destruction against an adversary who could retaliate in kind."

And there is, according to the critics, still another inhibiting factor—namely, the new United Nations inspection regime, UNMOVIC, headed by Hans Blix. To the proponents of containment, what is needed is simply to strengthen that regime. In the words of Jessica Tuchman Mathews, president of the Carnegie Endowment, "The idea is to disarm Iraq, and that can be done by truly muscular inspections backed by a multinational military force." The recommended steps include putting inspectors in the field who are "the most qualified and experienced experts available," getting our U-2 spy planes flying again, toughening our enforcement of "no-fly" zones and creating "no-drive" zones, destroying weapons sites that are being "sanitized" by the Iraqis, and putting UN bases on the ground if inspectors find they need additional support. Pushing these ideas still further, two Carnegie authors have suggested that the Security Council "compel" Iraq to answer remaining questions about its nuclear program and that the world body "establish a permanent monitoring system to keep Saddam under house arrest for the rest of his life."

Is there anything to these arguments? Let us return to the past, and specifically to our twelve-year experience with UN sanctions and weapons inspections, which the critics hail as a success. In fact, it was anything but.

In 1991, following Iraq's ouster from Kuwait and the end of the Gulf war, the UN Security Council passed Resolution 687, issued under Chapter VII of the UN Charter and therefore considered binding. This required Iraq to relinquish all existing weapons of mass destruction, to abandon its programs for the further development of biological, chemical, and nuclear weapons as well as of missiles with a range beyond 150 kilometers, and to cooperate with UN inspectors in identifying and eliminating these weapons. In addition, economic sanctions that had been imposed in the aftermath of Iraq's August 1990 invasion of Kuwait were to be kept in place until the disarmament was completed. Finally, the U.S., Britain, and—for a time—France imposed no-fly zones that ultimately covered northern Iraq above the 36th parallel and southern Iraq below the 33rd parallel.

It is hardly a secret that this system failed. Accounts by leaders of UNSCOM (Ralf Ekeus, Richard Butler, David Kay, and others) have painstakingly corroborated Iraq's record of systematic deception and non-compliance. Initially, it is true, the Iraqis did reveal large stocks of chemical warheads—many of them dangerously unstable—and these were duly destroyed. But henceforth and in virtually every other area it dragged its feet or actively subverted the efforts of the inspectors; as the latter consistently came up empty, Iraq's apologists on the Security Council, especially France and Russia, pushed for easing or lifting the sanctions, thus further hobbling the inspectors in their task.

The weaker the international pressures grew, the more Saddam obstructed the work of the teams. Ultimately, in 1998, it became impossible to carry on, and the UNSCOM inspectors were removed. The United States, supported by Britain, launched four days of retaliatory air strikes; they had little effect.

But it was not until after September 11, 2001, and after it had become clear that the Bush administration was preparing to use force against Iraq, that inspectors were finally allowed to return. The enabling act was Resolution 1441, unanimously approved by the Security Council on November 8, 2002. This resolution, the seventeenth in the UN's long history of futile demands that Saddam comply with the obligation to disarm, was explicit in stating that Iraq had been in "material breach" of previous resolutions, that it was being offered a "final opportunity" to comply, that it had to deliver within 30 days a "full, and complete declaration of all aspects of its programs," that "false statements or omissions . . . [would] constitute a further material breach," and that in such an eventuality Iraq would face "serious consequences as a result of its continued violations of its obligations."

Sure enough, 30 days later, Iraq delivered a 12,000-page report that falsely claimed its WMD programs no longer existed. On January 27 of this year, Blix testified that "Iraq appears not to have come to a genuine acceptance, not even today, of the disarmament which was demanded of it"; under the rubric of "unaccounted for," he cited 6,500 chemical bombs, stocks of VX nerve agents and anthrax, 3,000 tons of precursor chemicals, 360 tons of bulk agents for chemical weapons, and thousands of munitions for delivering such agents. Then, on February 5, Secretary of State Colin Powell delivered a comprehensive and utterly damning account of Saddam's record of defiance and deception and of his relentless drive to acquire and develop weapons of mass destruction.

To all this, Saddam's response, so breathtakingly cynical that it ought to have evoked the UN's wrath and scorn—but of course did not—was to issue an edict prohibiting the manufacture of weapons of mass destruction in Iraq.

In sum, the record is long, dreary, and unmistakable. As Secretary Powell reminded his colleagues, Resolution 1441 was about disarmament, not about inspections; and disarmament has not occurred. The supposition that strengthened or "coercive" inspections would succeed in inducing Saddam to disarm where "regular" inspections failed is pointless. In the United Nations itself, no consensus could be expected to form behind such a proposal, and if such intrusive inspections were actually attempted, Saddam would deflect them in the same manner as before, lifting his skirt to show a little leg (that is, pretending to comply) and thereby inveigling members of the Security Council as well as the inspectors themselves into downplaying or disregarding the requirements of their mandate and its threatened consequences. Nor is the sine qua non for coercive inspections— a long-term, massive military presence in the region exerting a credible threat of force—in the least conceivable.

There is no reason to believe that Saddam would ever give up the goods. How could he? The possession of weapons of mass destruction is the keystone of his power, allowing him to intimidate his own populace, menace and dominate his neighbors, and in his own mind—as soon as he can acquire nuclear weapons—deter the United States from interfering with his ambitions.

But, critics say, the Soviet Union was successfully deterred; why not Saddam? The comparison is far from reassuring. Cold-war-style deterrence required careful, rational calculation on both sides, plus the permanent deployment in Europe of large-scale American forces. Saddam's calculations are rather different from the Soviet Union's, and much less predictable—and in any case we are hardly about to keep massive amounts of men and materiel in the Persian Gulf indefinitely. But what critics also forget is that during the cold war we had no choice. In the early days of that conflict, we ourselves were deterred by the exhaustion of World War II and fears of a Soviet conquest of Western Europe; once the Soviets' nuclear arsenal had become highly developed, any all-out effort to disarm the USSR would have entailed the prospect of mass death and destruction on both sides. With Iraq, there are other options, and—for the moment—still time to exercise them.

Where the arguments put forward by advocates of containment veer into outright denial is on the subject of who, exactly, Saddam Hussein is. Their analyses give little significant weight to how this heedless gambler has launched wars of aggression against two of his neighbors (Iran and Kuwait), fired missiles at Iran as well as at Israel and Saudi Arabia, employed chemical weapons against Iran and against his own Kurdish population, and oppressed, brutalized, and committed mass murder against his own countrymen. As a leader, Saddam has repeatedly ignored his picked inner circle of advisers when their counsel has conflicted with his fixed preconceptions, to the point of initiating military actions that have hugely damaged his own interests.

An early example was the 1974 series of attacks on the Kurdish population in northern Iraq; when these brought fierce retaliation from Iran, Saddam was forced to sign a humiliating agreement ceding control of portions of the Iraqi border along the Shatt-al-Arab and adjacent waterways—thus setting the stage for his catastrophic war with Iran beginning in September 1980. That conflict, in which Saddam relied primarily on the poor advice of former Iranian military officers and attacked without any real planning, lasted eight years. From early 1984 on, Iraq used chemical weapons in every major battle. Despite the fact that it was easier for Iran to hit Baghdad and Basra than it was for Iraqi missiles to reach Iran's major cities, Saddam did not hesitate to bomb Iranian centers of population. In the end, the war cost the lives of at least 200,000 Iraqis and 400,000 Iranians, nearly resulted in Iraq's defeat and ruin, and left the country traumatized and deeply in debt.

But no sooner did the dust settle than Saddam launched another campaign against the Kurds, leveling villages, using poison gas, and murdering some 180,000 people. Then, in August 1990, he invaded Kuwait, determined to seize its oil, its territory, and its financial reserves. This too was a debacle. In the ensuing war, Saddam's army was decimated, and he himself escaped being ousted from power only because of the ill-fated decision by the elder President Bush to halt the ground war after just 100 hours and because the victorious allied forces permitted the Iraqi military to use its surviving helicopters and armor to slaughter rebelling Kurds and Shiites.

In short, both Saddam's character and the record of his behavior are another reason why containment—i.e., some structured way, short of war, of reliably preventing him from dominating or attacking his neighbors—is not viable. In January 1991, on the eve of the Gulf war, Iraq's foreign minister, Tariq Aziz, was handed a letter by Secretary of State James Baker at a meeting in Geneva. The letter warned of devastating consequences should Iraq use chemical or biological weapons in any military hostilities. The fact that the Gulf war passed without the employment of such weapons is often cited by critics as evidence that Saddam can be deterred. But it is no less significant that the same letter included two other warnings—against Iraqi support for terrorist acts, and against the destruction of Kuwait's oil fields and installations—that he simply ignored.

Shrewd but reckless—and, as Baram wryly notes, an "incurable optimist" who believes he will prevail no matter what the odds. Such is the man who has openly proclaimed his ambition to dominate his region, threatened to "burn half of Israel," and declared his readiness to take on the United States. This is not exactly the model of the risk-calculating, value-maximizing, rational actor posited by theorists of containment or inhabiting the imagination of critics of administration policy.

Misreading history and misunderstanding the character and conduct of Saddam Hussein, the critics have also turned a blind eye to larger realities.

In a single morning in September 2001, simultaneous attacks on the World Trade Center and the Pentagon propelled the United States and its allies into a new and lethal strategic environment. Not only are we no longer fighting the cold war, we are no longer in the realm of contingent scenarios, that catch-all term of the post-cold-war decade that loosely incorporated any number of potential dangers (including global warming, epidemics, overpopulation, drought, mass migration, and ethnic conflict) without any clear consensus as to whether or when any of them might erupt. Instead, the threats we face are at once unique and ominously conjoined: terrorism, weapons of mass destruction, and the complicity of failed or rogue states.

Vis-à-vis Iraq, the implication is plain: Saddam Hussein and his regime must be disarmed and deposed before they are in a position definitively to dominate the Gulf region and the wider Middle East or otherwise threaten the vital interests of the United States, whether directly or in complicity with terrorists.

This is why critics who question the "links" between Saddam and terrorism have missed the point. At issue is not just the matter of direct links—though these are easy enough to establish. Terrorists, including al Qaeda, require some kind of base. They do not dwell on abandoned offshore oil rigs or in outer space, but operate from the territory of national states. The full extent of the links between Saddam and al Qaeda remains in dispute, but the administration has provided convincing evidence that a top al Qaeda leader, Abu Musab Zarqawi, and other operatives have taken shelter in Iraq and received training there in the use of chemical weapons. In addition, Iraq's embassy in Islamabad (Pakistan) has coordinated contacts between Iraqi biochemists and members of al Qaeda, and other Iraqi embassies abroad have been in periodic contact with Islamist terrorists.

It is routinely claimed by advocates of containment that the use of force against Iraq puts in jeopardy, and distracts us from, the campaign against al Qaeda. The opposite is more likely to be the case. The downfall of Saddam will not only put an end to Iraq's military, financial, and political support of al Qaeda and other terrorist groups; it will send a graphic warning to the remaining states that support terrorism. On this point, it is again worth quoting no less an authority than Osama bin Laden: "When people see a strong horse and a weak horse, by nature they will like the strong horse."

In the world we have inherited since September 11, 2001, the long-term prospects for reliably containing terrorists and rogue regimes are poor. Although the use of force should never be undertaken lightly, the weight of the evidence suggests that it is far better to confront a Saddam Hussein before rather than after he acquires nuclear weapons. Failing to act in time entails costs that can be measured not only regionally but globally: in this case, such costs would include a still more aggressive and emboldened Iraq, the likelihood of more rather than less worldwide terrorism, the certainty of a later and wider war when Baghdad's actions become impossible to appease or ignore, and the further withering-away of the United Nations into impotence and irrelevance.

On the other side of the ledger, the use of force brings not only risks but opportunities. Dislodging the Iraqi regime will deal a serious blow to Arab and Muslim rejectionists who have opposed any realistic proposal for peace and coexistence with Israel. Beyond that, as Fouad Ajami has eloquently written, the successful application of American power and prestige can stimulate change in the Arab world by strengthening those who seek to turn away at long last from the "belligerence and self-pity in Arab life, its retreat from modernist culture, and its embrace of conspiracy theories."

In the end, the search for alternatives to the use of force bespeaks a failure of imagination—a stark unwillingness, even after September 11, to conceive of what it means for weapons of mass destruction to fall into the hands of monstrous figures like Saddam Hussein and Osama bin Laden.

In the light of this unfolding and ever more perilous reality, to choose to avoid force at all costs is to choose not the lesser but the greater evil. As one self-described reluctant hawk, Bill Keller of the *New York Times*, has put it, "In the short run, war is perilous. In the long run, peace can be a killer too." This is a fitting epitaph for the lost, and not soon to be recovered, world that gave rise to the doctrine of containment.

# 42 Present at the Destruction: The Death of American Internationalism

## JAMES CHACE

The tendency toward unilateralism in American foreign policy has prompted strong critiques arguing that such an orientation is counterproductive to American and global interests. While the neoconservative argument says that multilateralism limits the United States, the liberal internationalist response is that by embedding itself in international institutions and abiding by norms, laws, customs, and treaties, the United States has made its power and hegemony legitimate, less threatening, and therefore acceptable to other countries, who have generally preferred to join the international institutions that the United States created in the 1940s rather than oppose American power.

James Chace provides an analysis supporting this internationalist view. He suggests that, regardless of the outcome of war in Iraq, American policies and actions are resulting in reversal of the American internationalist commitment begun after World War II. This commitment involved creation of the U.N., IMF, World Bank, GATT, and of course, NATO, all of which have contributed greatly to global order and prosperity. Chace points to American withdrawal from the Kyoto Protocol, the ABM treaty, and the International Criminal Court, as evidence of a reversal, not merely from the internationalism of the Clinton years, but from the entire previous 50 years of American foreign policy. American policy, he argues, is now suffering from overstretch and hubris, resulting in a "crusader mentality" to impose democracy in Iraq and a huge increase in American debt, which is largely being financed by foreign lenders. He argues that this is counterproductive, as the United States has

James Chace, "Present at the Destruction: The Death of American Internationalism," *World Policy Journal*, 20.1 (Spring 2003), pp. 1–6. © 2003 by the World Policy Institute. Reprinted by permission of MIT Press Journals.

alienated the allies it needs to fight terrorism and manage the global economy, which are worthy goals that serve not only U.S. interests, but also the common good.

Chace's interpretation of American behavior was part of a large number of critiques written at the time arguing that a unilateralist policy, while claiming to serve the common good, did not actually do so at all. This is because it did not in practice maintain respect for the concerns of the larger international community, and this undermines American foreign policy—both its legitimacy and its effectiveness.

---

No matter what the ultimate outcome of the war with Iraq, the assault on international institutions and the bullying language leveled at America's allies by the president and his closest advisers signaled a robust rebirth of American unilateralism. This reverses the American internationalist commitment that came out of the Second World War and that lasted throughout the 45 years of the Cold War. It is surely the most significant detour in U.S. foreign policy since Franklin D. Roosevelt met with Winston Churchill on the British battleship Prince of Wales near the harbor of Argentia, Newfoundland, in August 1941. The result of that meeting was the commitment of the United States to a policy of collective security, freedom of the seas, and liberal trading practices—the Atlantic Charter. The Americans, in particular, insisted on a statement calling for "access, on equal terms, to the trade and to the raw materials of the world which are needed for economic prosperity." By accepting "the establishment of a wider and permanent system of general security," Roosevelt laid the ground for the founding of the United Nations that was to vest in the great powers—Britain, China, Russia, and America (and later France)—the responsibility for keeping the peace.

It was FDR, the president who best combined the idealistic aspirations of the Founders to create a republic of virtue with their realist appraisal of the need to accept temporary alliances, who provided the post-war vision for the Western world. With the world war still underway, a series of conferences, mostly initiated by Washington, began to shape the international environment we have lived in for the past half century—Bretton Woods (which, through the establishment of the International Monetary Fund and the World Bank, provided for currency stabilization); Dumbarton Oaks (where plans for the United Nations were drawn up); Hot Springs (for food and agriculture); Washington (for relief and rehabilitation); and Chicago (for civil aviation).

With the advent of the Cold War, Harry Truman, George Marshall, and Dean Acheson deepened and extended the new internationalism—with the Truman Doctrine to contain the expansion of the Soviet Union in the eastern

Mediterranean, the economic rebuilding of Europe spurred on by the Marshall Plan, and the creation of NATO.

The Bush administration, even before the terrorist attack on the World Trade Center and the Pentagon on September 11, 2001, had already begun to dismantle or reject treaties that would bind the United States to a larger international community. The United States rejected the Kyoto Protocol to curb the emission of noxious gases in the atmosphere, withdrew from the Anti-Ballistic Missile Treaty, scuttled the Land Mine Treaty and the Comprehensive Test Ban Treaty, and refused to back the International Criminal Court.

As the rifts between America and Europe deepened in the months and weeks prior to the American-led attack on Iraq, Secretary of Defense Donald Rumsfeld referred to France and Germany, the most vocal opponents of military action against Iraq without U.N. endorsement, as "old Europe," and the newer potential members of the European Union, such as Poland, Hungary, and the Czech Republic, as "new Europe." In thus choosing to divide Europe, Rumsfeld may well have succeeded in exacerbating the tensions within the European Union, as well as straining to a breaking point the ties of a more unified Europe to America. (His most egregious remark in this context was to bracket Germany with Cuba and Libya for refusing to support the use of force against Iraq.)[1]

All this points to a renewal of the unilateralist behavior that had so often marked the United States during much of the nineteenth and the first half of the twentieth centuries. This impulse carried with it an implicit, though absolute, goal: to prevent America's security from being undermined by constraints imposed by other powers, including—and perhaps most especially—those of America's traditional allies. Americans have never shied away from using force unilaterally, either in defense of their own borders or on behalf of foreign regimes whose security Washington viewed as vital. In this respect, the United States has never been truly isolationist. We fought or threatened wars against Britain, Spain, and Mexico to enable us to expand across a continent. In the twentieth century, even putting aside the two world wars, we intervened militarily in Mexico, Honduras, Nicaragua, the Dominican Republic, Guatemala, Haiti, Grenada, and Panama. But apart from the Korean and Vietnam Wars, we have been reluctant to use military force outside the Western Hemisphere without allies, as witness Bush senior's insistence on putting together a substantial coalition to fight the Gulf War, and Clinton's hesitation to use force unilaterally in Bosnia and Kosovo.

## A DIFFERENT APPROACH

With the end of the Cold War, however, the neoconservatives, who were already coming to the fore during the first Bush administration, proposed a different approach to the world. In 1992, a draft of a Pentagon planning document that has been called "Dick Cheney's masterwork" (it appeared when Cheney was secretary of defense) argued that the United States must "discourage the advanced industrial nations from challenging our leadership or even aspiring to a larger regional or global role." Instead, America should "retain the preeminent responsibility for addressing . . . those wrongs which threaten not only our interests, but those of our allies or friends, or which could seriously unsettle international relations."[2]

A second document, written ten years later, the now-famous National Security Strategy issued by the White House in September 2002, echoes in somewhat more muted language the previous one. It promises to maintain whatever military capability is needed to defeat any attempt by any state to oppose the will of the United States or its allies, and to discourage or prevent any potential adversaries from building up their own forces to equal or surpass ours. Together, these two documents assert a doctrine of U.S. global domination.[3]

No power will be allowed to challenge American leadership or, to repeat, even "to aspire to a larger regional or global role"—surely this is the authentic voice of American neo-imperialism. Under this reading, America seeks satellites, not allies. We are to be imperialists with good intentions, the benevolent hegemon who is prepared to wage preventive wars, or launch preemptive strikes at any presumed enemy.

When George W. Bush and Vice President Dick Cheney talk of a preventive war against Iraq, this recalls a very different period in American history when, in the early years of the Cold War, cries for preventive military action against the Soviet Union reverberated—not in the White House, but in the press and Congress. Unlike George W., however, Truman and Acheson stood firmly against the idea of a preventive war.

This was no easy task in the winter and spring of 1950. The shocks of the preceding year—the successful testing of a Soviet atomic bomb in August 1949, years ahead of the predictions of many scientists and military advisers, and the victory of Mao Zedong's Communists over the Chinese Nationalists in October—along with Moscow's military strength on the ground as well as its program of building an atomic force capable of striking the United States, led to calls for a preemptive attack against Stalinist Russia while America still possessed an overwhelming lead in atomic weaponry.

On a number of occasions in early 1950, in press conferences, at universities, and before business groups, Acheson spoke out strongly against the notion of any unprovoked military action against Russia. The secretary of state argued instead that "the only way to deal with the Soviet Union," was "to create situations of strength." Negotiating from strength meant, in this period, building up America's conventional forces in order to avoid having no other choice but to respond to a Soviet attack with U.S. atomic weapons.

Echoing his predecessor at State, General Marshall, Acheson declared that it was the policy of the United States to be the "first to attend international conferences and the last to retire."[4] Today, such a statement seems inconceivable coming from any member of the foreign policy inner circle of the Bush administration (except perhaps from Colin Powell).

In 1950, the ability of the Soviet air force to target the United States with atomic weapons was far greater than Iraq's ability to launch an intercontinental missile against the United States today. Containing the Soviet Union aggressively through a coalition of European states and Canada (which later became NATO) effectively stopped the Soviet Union from expanding on the ground or thinking of launching a nuclear attack against the United States.

Robert Byrd, the dean of the Senate, declared from the Senate floor on February 12, 2003, that the "doctrine of preemption—the idea that the United States or any other nation can legitimately attack a nation that is not imminently threatening but may be threatening in the future—is a radical new twist on the traditional idea of self-defense. It appears in contravention of international law and the U.N. Charter."[5] Most bizarre of all, as Harvard's Stanley Hoffmann has pointed out, is the claim put forth by American neo-imperialists that "the United States Constitution allows no bowing to a superior law, such as international law, and no transfer, pooling or delegation of sovereignty to any international organization."[6]

## OVERSTRETCH AND HUBRIS

One can understand any U.S. administration's disgust with a United Nations whose Human Rights Commission is headed by Libya and in which Iraq was until recently supposed to chair its Conference on Disarmament. But this begs the question: Is the United States prepared to work with the international organizations it did so much to create? Or does it expect to act as a global policeman simply because Washington believes it has the power to do so?

We may have massive military might, but it is nearly impossible to fight terrorism without the cooperation of other nations (most notably France and Germany). In addition, there is the danger of what the historian Paul Kennedy has called "imperial overstretch." According to Senator Byrd, the "war in Afghanistan has cost us $37 billion so far, yet there is evidence that terrorism may already be starting to regain its hold on that region."[7] We are now not only training Filipino soldiers to root out Muslim insurrectionists, but we may also be preparing to send our own troops into that conflict—and this in addition to expenditures that might total $95 billion for the war against Iraq.[8]

According to the nonpartisan Congressional Budget Office, the government shortfall for fiscal year 2003 could rise to $287 billion, and for fiscal year 2004 to $338 billion. The budget office calculates that over the next five years Bush's economic program would raise the deficit by about $800 billion. In addition to the budget deficit, America is also running massive current account deficits—by importing more than it exports—that have now reached an annual rate of $500 billion. To cover this debt, America borrows from foreign lenders. The profligacy of these policies will almost certainly lead to the weakening of the dollar, higher taxes, and reductions in domestic social programs, or an inflated currency that will have to be contained by high interest rates. This will then likely result in economic stagnation at best, or a severe recession at worst. In short, the costs of unilateralism could prove devastating.[9]

One of the reasons the Bush administration put forth for military action against Iraq is the favorable demonstration effect this is likely to have in the Middle East. In a revealing interview with Nicholas Lemann in the *New Yorker*, Douglas Feith, the Undersecretary of Defense for Policy, said, "If we help the Iraqis, and if the Iraqis show an ability to create a humane representative government for themselves—will that have beneficial spillover effects on the politics of the whole region? The answer, I think is yes."[10] President Bush made somewhat the same point on at least two occasions. In June 2002, he argued that "a new regime in Iraq would serve as a dramatic and inspiring example of freedom for other nations in the region."[11] And in a speech at the American Enterprise Institute this past February, he defined an ambitious role for America and (as he put it) "the civilized world" in the transformation of the Middle East."[12]

Feith's words are in line with Deputy Secretary of Defense Paul Wolfowitz's expressed belief that the war in Iraq could help to bring about democracy to the Arab Middle East. President Bush, in his 2003 State of the Union address, made somewhat the same point when he said that "all people have a right to choose their own government, and determine their own destiny—and the United States supports their aspirations to live in freedom."

The neo-Wilsonian ring to these statements points to the crusader mentality that now inhabits the minds of some of the closest advisers to the president. The realist perspective is apparently being supplanted by a more evangelical approach to replacing tyrannical regimes with democratic ones. America's values are thus seen as universal values. In this respect, it is dangerous to compare the Bush administration's plan to "democratize" Iraq and other parts of the Middle East with the remaking of Nazi Germany and imperial Japan after the traumatic carnage of the Second World War. Both countries had had democratic norms and practices in the 1920s; just as their industrial capacity could be fully restored in a relatively short time through American aid, so, too, could the United States hope to resuscitate their democratic traditions. In the Arab Middle East, such a task would be Herculean, and, I suspect, quixotic. But it is a task that the crusader often welcomes, and, if necessary, is willing to do alone.

While it is true that the United States cannot pursue a successful foreign policy without a moral component, as Franklin Roosevelt well understood, that component today needs to be linked to a range of international institutions. To seek to promote the common good implies respect for the concerns of the larger international community. It is in fact the height of realism not only to advance the nation's interests, but also to seek allies among other governments and peoples who share those interests.

As Americans we would do well to heed Alexander Hamilton, who urged nations to avoid policies that were "absolutely selfish" and rather to pursue "a policy regulated by their own interest, as far as justice and good faith permit."[13] These are not evangelical concepts nor are they those of a lone crusader. They require a commitment to internationalism, not a rejection of it. They are the practical goals of a realistic American foreign policy for the twenty-first century.

## Notes

1. See Gerard Baker, "Tartuffe and the Shock-Jock Gird for War," *Financial Times*, February 13, 2003.
2. See Patrick E. Tyler, "U.S. Strategy Plan Calls for Insuring No Rivals Develop," *New York Times*, March 8, 1992.
3. See Stanley Hoffmann, "The High and the Mighty," *American Prospect*, January 23, 2003.
4. See James Chace, Acheson: *The Secretary of State Who Created the American World* (New York: Simon and Schuster, 1998), pp. 270–71.
5. Senator Byrd's remarks are available at www.commondreams.org.
6. Hoffmann, "The High and the Mighty."
7. See note 5.
8. Eric Schmitt, "Military Spending: Pentagon Contradicts General on Iraq Occupation Force's Size," *New York Times*, February 28, 2003; and Seth Mydans, "Asian Front: Filipinos Awaiting U.S. Troops with Skepticism," *New York Times*, February 28, 2003.
9. See Paul Krugman, "On the Second Day, Atlas Waffled," *New York Times*, February 14, 2003; Edmund L. Andrews, "U.S. Budget Deficit Seen Rising Fast," *New York Times*, March 5, 2003; David E. Rosenbaum, "Cost of War: Troop Movement Alone Could Cost $25 Billion, Congressional Office Finds," *New York Times*, March 8, 2003; and Clyde V. Prestowitz, Jr., "The Unmighty Dollar," *International Newsweek*, March 24, 2003.
10. Nicholas Lemann, "After Iraq," *New Yorker*, February 17–24, 2003.
11. As quoted in "Birth of a Bush Doctrine?" *The Economist*, March 1, 2003.

12. "In the President's Words: 'Free People Will Keep the Peace of the World, '"
    *New York Times*, February 27, 2003.
13. Alexander Hamilton, *Pacificus*, no. 4, July 10, 1793.

# 43

# Assessment of the Current Situation in Iraq

*JAMES A. BAKER, LEE H. HAMILTON ET AL. (THE IRAQ STUDY GROUP)*

The debate over the possible impacts of the U.S.-led invasion of Iraq was quickly influenced by events happening on the ground in Iraq. While the American and coalition forces had rapidly defeated the Iraqi army, forcing Saddam Hussein and other government leaders to flee, the United States was not able to pacify the country and bring peace, security, and order. The collapse of the Iraqi state, the de-Baathification of the country, the lack of sufficient troop strength by the United States to prevent chaos and maintain security, and the lack of a coherent post-war reconstruction plan all contributed to a situation in which an insurgency developed, consisting of both Iraqi nationals and foreign "jihadists." The insurgency prevented the establishment of basic security in many parts of the country, leading to a situation in which the United States may have won the war, but it could not win the peace.

As the situation continued to deteriorate, Congress and President Bush convened a blue ribbon panel called The Iraq Study Group, which prepared a report on what the United States should do to change the direction of the war. Saying that "the situation . . . is dire," and that "the ability of the United States to shape outcomes is diminishing," the report provided an assessment of the challenges that confront Iraq and the United States, looking at American military operations, the country's political divisions and governance, the lack of security, the politics of oil, and economic issues. The report reflected the idea that there is no military solution to ending the war in Iraq; any hope for success must involve a political and diplomatic solution. As such, the report offered dozens of recommendations, including the opening of a regional dialogue with Iran and Syria, reversing de-Baathifaction, and drawing down the number of U.S.

James Baker, Lee Hamilton et al., (The Iraq Study Group), from "Assessment of the Current Situation in Iraq," *The Iraq Study Group Report*. The United States Institute of Peace, December 2006. www.usip.org.

combat troops while placing more troops in an advisory and support role within Iraqi units.

Released after the 2006 elections, when President Bush and the Republican party suffered a significant defeat due to the unpopularity of the war (Republicans lost control of both houses of Congress), there was some thought that this report offered a way out of the war. President Bush, however, rejected most of The Iraq Study Group's recommendations, and instead increased the number of U.S. troops in Iraq to try and stabilize the country. This effort is currently underway at the time of this writing.

American efforts in Iraq are by no means doomed to fail. Elections have taken place in Iraq with millions of Iraqis participating, and a new government has been established. There are, however, few indications that the insurgency and the ineffectiveness of the Iraqi government will be substantially reversed anytime soon. Even among many who supported the idea of going to war against Iraq, there is a growing sense in the United States that the war represents the greatest American foreign policy failure since Vietnam.

---

There is no guarantee for success in Iraq. The situation in Baghdad and several provinces is dire. Saddam Hussein has been removed from power and the Iraqi people have a democratically elected government that is broadly representative of Iraq's population, yet the government is not adequately advancing national reconciliation, providing basic security, or delivering essential services. The level of violence is high and growing. There is great suffering, and the daily lives of many Iraqis show little or no improvement. Pessimism is pervasive.

U.S. military and civilian personnel, and our coalition partners, are making exceptional and dedicated efforts—and sacrifices—to help Iraq. Many Iraqis have also made extraordinary efforts and sacrifices for a better future. However, the ability of the United States to influence events within Iraq is diminishing. Many Iraqis are embracing sectarian identities. The lack of security impedes economic development. Most countries in the region are not playing a constructive role in support of Iraq, and some are undercutting stability.

Iraq is vital to regional and even global stability, and is critical to U.S. interests. It runs along the sectarian fault lines of Shia and Sunni Islam, and of Kurdish and Arab populations. It has the world's second-largest known oil reserves. It is now a base of operations for international terrorism, including al Qaeda.

Iraq is a centerpiece of American foreign policy, influencing how the United States is viewed in the region and around the world. Because of the gravity of Iraq's condition and the country's vital importance, the United

States is facing one of its most difficult and significant international challenges in decades. Because events in Iraq have been set in motion by American decisions and actions, the United States has both a national and a moral interest in doing what it can to give Iraqis an opportunity to avert anarchy.

An assessment of the security, political, economic, and regional situation follows (all figures current as of publication), along with an assessment of the consequences if Iraq continues to deteriorate, and an analysis of some possible courses of action.

# 1. SECURITY

Attacks against U.S., Coalition, and Iraqi security forces are persistent and growing. October 2006 was the deadliest month for U.S. forces since January 2005, with 102 Americans killed. Total attacks in October 2006 averaged 180 per day, up from 70 per day in January 2006. Daily attacks against Iraqi security forces in October were more than double the level in January. Attacks against civilians in October were four times higher than in January. Some 3,000 Iraqi civilians are killed every month.

## Sources of Violence

Violence is increasing in scope, complexity, and lethality. There are multiple sources of violence in Iraq: the Sunni Arab insurgency, al Qaeda and affiliated jihadist groups, Shiite militias and death squads, and organized criminality. Sectarian violence—particularly in and around Baghdad—has become the principal challenge to stability.

Most attacks on Americans still come from the Sunni Arab insurgency. The insurgency comprises former elements of the Saddam Hussein regime, disaffected Sunni Arab Iraqis, and common criminals. It has significant support within the Sunni Arab community. The insurgency has no single leadership but is a network of networks. It benefits from participants' detailed knowledge of Iraq's infrastructure, and arms and financing are supplied primarily from within Iraq. The insurgents have different goals, although nearly all oppose the presence of U.S. forces in Iraq. Most wish to restore Sunni Arab rule in the country. Some aim at winning local power and control.

Al Qaeda is responsible for a small portion of the violence in Iraq, but that includes some of the more spectacular acts: suicide attacks, large truck bombs, and attacks on significant—religious or political targets. Al Qaeda in Iraq is now largely Iraqi-run and composed of Sunni Arabs. Foreign fighters—numbering an estimated 1,300—play a supporting role or carry out suicide operations. Al Qaeda's goals include instigating a wider sectarian war between Iraq's Sunni and Shia, and driving the United States out of Iraq.

Sectarian violence causes the largest number of Iraqi civilian casualties. Iraq is in the grip of a deadly cycle: Sunni insurgent attacks spark large-scale Shia reprisals, and vice versa. Groups of Iraqis are often found bound and executed, their bodies dumped in rivers or fields. The perception of unchecked violence emboldens militias, shakes confidence in the government, and leads Iraqis to flee to places where their sect is the majority and where they feel they are in less danger. In some parts of Iraq—notably in Baghdad—sectarian cleansing is taking place. The United Nations estimates that 1.6 million are displaced within Iraq, and up to 1.8 million Iraqis have fled the country.

Shiite militias engaging in sectarian violence pose a substantial threat to immediate and long-term stability. These militias are diverse. Some are affiliated with the government, some are highly localized, and some are wholly outside the law. They are fragmenting, with an increasing breakdown in command structure. The militias target Sunni Arab civilians, and some struggle for power in clashes with one another. Some even target government ministries. They undermine the authority of the Iraqi government and security forces, as well as the ability of Sunnis to join a peaceful political process. The prevalence of militias sends a powerful message: political leaders can preserve and expand their power only if backed by armed force.

The Mahdi Army, led by Moqtada al-Sadr, may number as many as 60,000 fighters. It has directly challenged U.S. and Iraqi government forces, and it is widely believed to engage in regular violence against Sunni Arab civilians. Mahdi fighters patrol certain Shia enclaves, notably northeast Baghdad's teeming neighborhood of 2.5 million known as "Sadr City." As the Mahdi Army has grown in size and influence, some elements have moved beyond Sadr's control.

The Badr Brigade is affiliated with the Supreme Council for the Islamic Revolution in Iraq (SCIRI), which is led by Abdul Aziz al-Hakim. The Badr Brigade has long-standing ties with the Iranian Revolutionary Guard Corps. Many Badr members have become integrated into the Iraqi police, and others play policing roles in southern Iraqi cities. While wearing the uniform of the security services, Badr fighters have targeted Sunni Arab civilians. Badr fighters have also clashed with the Mahdi Army, particularly in southern Iraq.

Criminality also makes daily life unbearable for many Iraqis. Robberies, kidnappings, and murder are commonplace in much of the country. Organized criminal rackets thrive, particularly in unstable areas like Anbar province. Some criminal gangs cooperate with, finance, or purport to be part of the Sunni insurgency or a Shiite militia in order to gain legitimacy.

As one knowledgeable American official put it, "If there were foreign forces in New Jersey, Tony Soprano would be an insurgent leader."

Four of Iraq's eighteen provinces are highly insecure—Baghdad, Anbar, Diyala, and Salah ad Din. These provinces account for about 40 percent of Iraq's population of 26 million. In Baghdad, the violence is largely between Sunni and Shia. In Anbar, the violence is attributable to the Sunni insurgency and to al Qaeda, and the situation is deteriorating.

In Kirkuk, the struggle is between Kurds, Arabs, and Turkmen. In Basra and the south, the violence is largely an intra-Shia power struggle. The most stable parts of the country are the three provinces of the Kurdish north and parts of the Shia south. However, most of Iraq's cities have a sectarian mix and are plagued by persistent violence.

## U.S., Coalition, and Iraqi Forces

Confronting this violence are the Multi-National Forces–Iraq under U.S. command, working in concert with Iraq's security forces. The Multi-National Forces–Iraq were authorized by UN Security Council Resolution 1546 in 2004, and the mandate was extended in November 2006 for another year.

Approximately 141,000 U.S. military personnel are serving in Iraq, together with approximately 16,500 military personnel from twenty-seven coalition partners, the largest contingent being 7,200 from the United Kingdom. The U.S. Army has principal responsibility for Baghdad and the north. The U.S. Marine Corps takes the lead in Anbar province. The United Kingdom has responsibility in the southeast, chiefly in Basra.

Along with this military presence, the United States is building its largest embassy in Baghdad. The current U.S. embassy in Baghdad totals about 1,000 U.S. government employees. There are roughly 5,000 civilian contractors in the country.

Currently, the U.S. military rarely engages in large-scale combat operations. Instead, counterinsurgency efforts focus on a strategy of "clear, hold, and build"—"clearing" areas of insurgents and death squads, "holding" those areas with Iraqi security forces, and "building" areas with quick-impact reconstruction projects.

Nearly every U.S. Army and Marine combat unit, and several National Guard and Reserve units, have been to Iraq at least once. Many are on their second or even third rotations; rotations are typically one year for Army units, seven months for Marine units. Regular rotations, in and out of Iraq or within the country, complicate brigade and battalion efforts to get to know the local scene, earn the trust of the population, and build a sense of cooperation.

Many military units are under significant strain. Because the harsh conditions in Iraq are wearing out equipment more quickly than anticipated, many units do not have fully functional equipment for training when they redeploy to the United States. An extraordinary amount of sacrifice has been asked of our men and women in uniform, and of their families. The American military has little reserve force to call on if it needs ground forces to respond to other crises around the world.

A primary mission of U.S. military strategy in Iraq is the training of competent Iraqi security forces. By the end of 2006, the Multi-National Security Transition Command–Iraq under American leadership is expected to have trained and equipped a target number of approximately 326,000 Iraqi security services. That figure includes 138,000 members of the Iraqi Army and 188,000 Iraqi police. Iraqis have operational control over roughly one-third of Iraqi security forces; the U.S. has operational control over most of the rest. No U.S. forces are under Iraqi command.

## The Iraqi Army

The Iraqi Army is making fitful progress toward becoming a reliable and disciplined fighting force loyal to the national government. By the end of 2006, the Iraqi Army is expected to comprise 118 battalions formed into 36 brigades under the command of 10 divisions. Although the Army is one of the more professional Iraqi institutions, its performance has been uneven. The training numbers are impressive, but they represent only part of the story.

Significant questions remain about the ethnic composition and loyalties of some Iraqi units—specifically, whether they will carry out missions on behalf of national goals instead of a sectarian agenda. Of Iraq's 10 planned divisions, those that are even-numbered are made up of Iraqis who signed up to serve in a specific area, and they have been reluctant to redeploy to other areas of the country. As a result, elements of the Army have refused to carry out missions.

The Iraqi Army is also confronted by several other significant challenges:

*Units lack leadership.* They lack the ability to work together and perform at higher levels of organization the brigade and division level. Leadership training and the experience of leadership are the essential elements to improve performance.

*Units lack equipment.* They cannot carry out their missions without adequate equipment. Congress has been generous in funding requests for U.S. troops, but it has resisted fully funding Iraqi forces. The entire appropriation for Iraqi defense forces for FY 2006 ($3 billion) is less than the United States currently spends in Iraq every two weeks.

*Units lack personnel.* Soldiers are on leave one week a month so that they can visit their families and take them their pay. Soldiers are paid in cash because there is no banking system. Soldiers are given leave liberally and face no penalties for absence without leave. Unit readiness rates are low, often at 50 percent or less.

*Units lack logistics and support.* They lack the ability to sustain their operations, the capability to transport supplies and troops, and the capacity to provide their own indirect fire support, close-air support, technical intelligence, and medical evacuation. They will depend on the United States for logistics and support through at least 2007.

## The Iraqi Police

The state of the Iraqi police is substantially worse than that of the Iraqi Army. The Iraqi Police Service currently numbers roughly 135,000 and is responsible for local policing. It has neither the training nor legal authority to conduct criminal investigations, nor the firepower to take on organized crime, insurgents, or militias. The Iraqi National Police numbers roughly 25,000 and its officers have been trained in counterinsurgency operations, not police work. The Border Enforcement Department numbers roughly 28,000.

Iraqi police cannot control crime, and they routinely engage in sectarian violence, including the unnecessary detention, torture, and targeted execution of Sunni Arab civilians. The police are organized under the Ministry of the Interior, which is confronted by corruption and militia infiltration and lacks control over police in the provinces.

The United States and the Iraqi government recognize the importance of reform. The current Minister of the Interior has called for purging militia members and criminals from the police. But he has little police experience or base of support. There is no clear Iraqi or U.S. agreement on the character and mission of the police. U.S. authorities do not know with precision the composition and membership of the various police forces, nor the disposition of their funds and equipment. There are ample reports of Iraqi police officers participating in training in order to obtain a weapon, uniform, and ammunition for use in sectarian violence. Some are on the payroll but don't show up for work. In the words of a senior American general, "2006 was supposed to be 'the year of the police' but it hasn't materialized that way."

## Facilities Protection Services

The Facilities Protection Service poses additional problems. Each Iraqi ministry has an armed unit, ostensibly to guard the ministry's infrastructure. All together, these units total roughly 145,000 uniformed Iraqis under arms.

However, these units have questionable loyalties and capabilities. In the ministries of Health, Agriculture, and Transportation controlled by Moqtada al-Sadr the Facilities Protection Service is a source of funding and jobs for the Mahdi Army. One senior U.S. official described the Facilities Protection Service as "incompetent, dysfunctional, or subversive." Several Iraqis simply referred to them as militias.

The Iraqi government has begun to bring the Facilities Protection Service under the control of the Interior Ministry. The intention is to identify and register Facilities Protection personnel, standardize their treatment, and provide some training. Though the approach is reasonable, this effort may exceed the current capability of the Interior Ministry.

## 2. POLITICS

The composition of the Iraqi government is basically sectarian, and key players within the government too often act in their sectarian interest. Iraq's Shia, Sunni, and Kurdish leaders frequently fail to demonstrate the political will to act in Iraq's national interest, and too many Iraqi ministries lack the capacity to govern effectively. The result is an even weaker central government than the constitution provides.

There is widespread Iraqi, American, and international agreement on the key issues confronting the Iraqi government: national reconciliation, including the negotiation of a "political deal" among Iraq's sectarian groups on Constitution review, de-Baathification, oil revenue sharing, provincial elections, the future of Kirkuk, and amnesty; security, particularly curbing militias and reducing the violence in Baghdad; and governance, including the provision of basic services and the rollback of pervasive corruption. Because Iraqi leaders view issues through a sectarian prism, we will summarize the differing perspectives of Iraq's main sectarian groups.

### Sectarian Viewpoints

The Shia, the majority of Iraq's population, have gained power for the first time in more than 1,300 years. Above all, many Shia are interested in preserving that power. However, fissures have emerged within the broad Shia coalition, known as the United Iraqi Alliance. Shia factions are struggling for power—over regions, ministries, and Iraq as a whole. The difficulties in holding together a broad and fractious coalition have led several observers in Baghdad to comment that Shia leaders are held "hostage to extremes." Within the coalition as a whole, there is a reluctance to reach a political accommodation with the Sunnis or to disarm Shiite militias.

Sunni Arabs feel displaced because of the loss of their traditional position of power in Iraq. They are torn, unsure whether to seek their aims through political participation or through violent insurgency. They remain angry about U.S. decisions to dissolve Iraqi security forces and to pursue the "de-Baathification" of Iraq's government and society. Sunnis are confronted by paradoxes: they have opposed the presence of U.S. forces in Iraq but need those forces to protect them against Shia militias; they chafe at being governed by a majority Shia administration but reject a federal, decentralized Iraq and do not see a Sunni autonomous region as feasible for themselves.

Iraqi Kurds have succeeded in presenting a united front of two main political blocs—the Kurdistan Democratic Party (KDP) and the Patriotic Union of Kurdistan (PUK). The Kurds have secured a largely autonomous Kurdish region in the north, and have achieved a prominent role for Kurds within the national government. Barzani leads the Kurdish regional government, and Talabani is president of Iraq.

Leading Kurdish politicians told us they preferred to be within a democratic, federal Iraqi state because an independent Kurdistan would be surrounded by hostile neighbors. However, a majority of Kurds favor independence. The Kurds have their own security forces the peshmerga—which number roughly 100,000. They believe they could accommodate themselves to either a unified or a fractured Iraq.

## 3. CONCLUSIONS

The United States has made a massive commitment to the future of Iraq in both blood and treasure. As of December 2006, nearly 2,900 Americans have lost their lives serving in Iraq. Another 21,000 Americans have been wounded, many severely.

To date, the United States has spent roughly $400 billion on the Iraq War, and costs are running about $8 billion per month. In addition, the United States must expect significant "tail costs" to come. Caring for veterans and replacing lost equipment will run into the hundreds of billions of dollars. Estimates run as high as $2 trillion for the final cost of the U.S. involvement in Iraq.

Despite a massive effort, stability in Iraq remains elusive and the situation is deteriorating. The Iraqi government cannot now govern, sustain, and defend itself without the support of the United States. Iraqis have not been convinced that they must take responsibility for their own future. Iraq's neighbors and much of the international community have not been persuaded to play an active and constructive role in supporting Iraq. The ability of the United States to shape outcomes is diminishing. Time is running out.

# 44 Contemplating the Ifs

## PATRICK LANG AND LARRY JOHNSON

While the war on terror and the war in Iraq have dominated American foreign policy, numerous other challenges remain. One of the most significant is the proliferation of nuclear weapons, especially in Iran and North Korea. North Korea already appears to have a limited nuclear capability, but Iran does not yet possess such weapons, leaving open the question of how to stop the country's progress toward this goal. The government of Iran has represented a longstanding challenge to the United States since the Iranian revolution in 1979, and its burgeoning nuclear program has become a particularly pressing issue for the United States, as well as many of its allies and other states in the Middle East. President George W. Bush labeled Iran as part of the "axis of evil" in 2002, and he has stated that the United States and the international community "will not tolerate the construction of a nuclear weapon" by Iran. Though Iran's government has repeatedly stated that it seeks only peaceful uses of nuclear power, and not military applications, such statements have not been convincing. Moreover, Iran has made clear that it seeks to continue its efforts to develop nuclear technology. Therefore, absent major concessions or changes by either the United States or Iran, the two countries appear to be headed toward a serious crisis.

Patrick Lang and Larry Johnson discuss the options that the United States has in dealing with Iran, and find that all options involving the use of force have significant costs and drawbacks, and may not even be viable at all. Large-scale military assaults, limited strikes involving special forces and air raids, and relying on the Israelis all represent scenarios to be avoided, as does allowing Iran to possess nuclear weapons. In addition, the authors point out, the Iranians can strike back effectively if the United States uses military force against Iran—by fomenting violence in Iraq, sponsoring terror, and/or withholding oil.

It appears that the United States may have no good options with Iran. Seeking a negotiated settlement has been the focus of the United States and the European Union. However, talks have been unsuccessful thus far, leading to concerns that Iran will be content to talk for years, making no concessions while it simultaneously develops a nuclear capability that becomes even more difficult, if not

Patrick Lang and Larry Johnson, "Contemplating the Ifs," *The National Interest*, Spring 2006. Reprinted by permission of The National Interest.

impossible, to stop. Should the EU, Russia, China, India, and other countries come to fear an Iranian nuclear weapon as much as the United States, there remains the possibility of enacting broad economic sanctions against Iran, which could possibly effect a change in policy. A more worrisome outcome is that the development of an Iranian nuclear capability will further erode, and perhaps fatally undermine, the nuclear nonproliferation regime that has been in place since 1970.

---

The war drums are reverberating while warnings about an Iranian nuclear threat are becoming more frequent and dire. The 2005 National Intelligence Estimate (NIE) concludes that Iran, if left to its own devices, is about a decade away from manufacturing the key ingredient for a nuclear weapon. In making a judgment about the soundness of that estimate, it would be prudent to recall the October 2002 NIE on Iraq's WMD capability. That estimate proved to be altogether wrong in alleging the existence of such programs in Iraq. Should we wager that the estimate on Iran is more accurate?

In contrast to the claims made in the run-up to the war in Iraq, the Bush Administration will prove to be fully justified by the facts in the case of Iran. Iran continues to provide direct operational support both to Al-Qaeda and a congeries of other Islamic terrorist groups. Moreover, the regime has carried out mass-casualty terrorist attacks against the United States. Iran played a direct role in the 1996 attack on the U.S. military base in Dharan, Saudi Arabia, and, regardless of how accurate the NIE is, Iran is seriously pursuing the development of the only real weapon of mass destruction: a nuclear bomb. The extensive reporting in the *New York Times* on the contents of a laptop computer obtained in Iran by U.S. intelligence bears directly on the subject. The computer is reputed to have contained a mass of details pointing to Iranian intentions to produce a miniaturized weapon that could be mated with a guided missile. U.S. intelligence officials believe, according to their own sources, that the ongoing Iranian ballistic missile program has now produced a vehicle that has a 2,000-kilometer range and is geared towards developing a ballistic missile with a 6,000-kilometer range. There is a very real and gathering threat from Iran—but the United States needs a viable policy, not sloganeering or wishful thinking, for dealing with Tehran.

The Bush Administration has warned Iran that it will suffer dire consequences if it fails to cease and desist from its nefarious nuclear activities. But Iran's leaders apparently see our warnings as mostly bark rather than bite— and they are probably correct in doing so. An all-out conventional military assault seems implausible to most people, unless all other measures fail. This is why the media, the blogosphere and the think-tank community are rife with rumors about plans to deal with Iran's nuclear program by using commandos or surgically targeted air strikes.

Friends in the intelligence community tell us that civilian officials at the Department of Defense have been pushing aggressively for almost two years to "do something violent" in Iran. But before we embark on another military operation, we must reckon the costs; we must ensure that we are willing to pay those costs; and we should ensure that neoconservative enthusiasts would not be tempted to say—if venturing into Iran becomes a misadventure—that it was impossible to foresee negative consequences. There are a lot of bad things that could happen if we launch a pre-emptive war with Iran. Before we act, we must thoroughly consider what our viable military options are.

A conventional military invasion is out of the question. The war in Iraq has fully committed and stretched our ground military capability. Even the announced "drawdown" from Iraq would still leave us short of the numbers we would need. We do not have the resources, in terms of troops or airlift, to go it alone in Iran. Iran is almost twice the size of Iraq and slightly larger than Alaska. Iranians number over 68 million. A ground invasion would require at least a half-million troops. The number of troops needed for such an operation would dwarf the numbers that we have seen employed in Afghanistan and Iraq. In order to meet the ever-hungry appetite of our commitments in Afghanistan and Iraq, we are already rotating active Army and Marine Corps troops from far distant continents. Brigade Combat Teams of the divisions in Europe and Korea have already served rotational tours of combat duty. The ability of the National Guard and Marine Reserve to sustain deployments is rapidly being exhausted both institutionally and politically.

Realistically, a conventional invasion would require a large ground force requiring many new brigade-sized units. The administration could try to use leadership cadres from existing forces to command new private soldiers, but obtaining that mass of soldiers would require bringing back the draft. In our opinion, that requirement effectively cancels out the possibility of a ground invasion of Iran. Unless John Bolton, the U.S. ambassador to the United Nations, persuades his Russian and Chinese colleagues at the UN to call for a blue-helmeted invasion or NATO decides to take part, count out the option of a ground operation. Public opinion in Europe, which fails to account for the gathering Iranian threat, would almost certainly preclude military action by NATO.

## COMMANDOS AND AIR RAIDS

What about the much-discussed commando-attack option? Such an approach might entail simultaneous Army Ranger, Special Forces and airborne troop raids on Iran's nuclear facilities. In addition, Marine units that could be helicoptered in from ships in the Persian Gulf could presumably attack targets close to sea. This would involve perhaps a thousand men and many aircraft.

With such an attack, we should not include visions of anything like The Guns of Navarone or Where Eagles Dare. Iran's nuclear program involves a large complex of facilities scattered over an immense area, deep within a country that would not welcome our men. A commando option might sound good at first glance, ignoring the fact that Iran is a large, hostile country. The recent elections demonstrate convincingly that there are literally millions of people in Iran just waiting for an opportunity to help the "authorities" hunt down a commando force. There is no equivalent of the French Maquis waiting to act as guides and provide shelter.

Moreover, the United States does not possess the assets needed to conduct a true attack by infiltration on these targets, since we have nothing like the needed number of Special Forces soldiers or CIA operatives with the language, regional or cultural training needed to successfully operate behind Iranian lines. We haven't exactly been producing large numbers of commandos with a perfect command of Farsi, and this type of mission is too risky and complicated to be entrusted to hastily recruited bands of Iranian exiles.

Complicating matters is the fact that Iran's many nuclear facilities spread around the country are hardened and defended against attack. Commando and light forces could, conceivably, at least partially destroy those targets, but there is also the looming possibility that the raids would fail to significantly impair Iran's nuclear capability and that we would encounter difficulties in extracting our forces. This is not a suitable target set for special-operations forces. Iran might gain leverage by seizing U.S. troops; moreover, the probability of large numbers of casualties make this an unsuitable mission for Special Forces, Rangers or airborne troops.

A worthwhile air campaign would require a massive Air Force and Navy effort, involving about a thousand aircraft and cruise-missile strike sorties (one trip by one aircraft for the use of one missile), launched from platforms redeployed all over the planet. Air strikes come with the risk of downed pilots. Although combat search and rescue units would be deployed, their ability to operate may be constrained by Iran's defenses. Iran still has an air force and has had more than 15 years to study U.S. air-warfare tactics from its ringside seat on the border of Iraq.

More positively, America's technically oriented intelligence agencies are well suited to draw on existing data to target Iran's nuclear facilities. The United States could attack facilities with nuclear weapons at a fraction of the effort and cost of conventional raids, but the rational among us know that option will not be exercised. In attacking the Iranian nuclear program, we would be seeking to prevent the destabilizing use of nuclear weapons.

The last thing we would want to do is use them ourselves and contribute to the destabilization.

## THE ISRAELI MIRAGE

Faced with these questions, some are advocating an Israeli solution to the Iranian threat—that is, to stand aside and let Israel launch air action or commando strikes. Those proposals are hardly viable. The 1981 Israeli air attack against Iraqi nuclear facilities in Osirak involved a target much closer to Israel, one set of above-ground and essentially unguarded buildings, and half a dozen aircraft. The 1976 Israeli commando raid at Entebbe, Uganda, involved one aircraft-load of troops in a very primitive setting. The differences in scale and distance between those operations and what would have to be done in Iran are impressive.

Analysts that propose the Israeli option seem to be envisioning imaginary assets. An Israeli operation might achieve little more than angering the Iranians. Their air force lacks the strength, range, tanker capability and targeting capability to conduct such massive and distant operations. The Iranian nuclear target set would require numerous waves of restrike missions after bomb damage assessments were made.

In addition, the Israelis would have to fly over Jordan, Iraq, the Gulf states and Saudi Arabia. All of these countries would object loudly, and they are all allies of the United States. Would the Shi'a-run government of Iraq assent to Israeli overflight for such a mission or allow Israel to use Iraqi air bases? Ignoring the Iraqi government is not an option. After all, the current Iraqi government is the sovereign authority. We made it that way. The government becomes more entrenched in power by the day, thanks in large measure both to strenuous U.S. efforts and Iran's maneuvering.

## IRAN'S RECOURSE

In this atmosphere of building tension, Iran is not going to sit idly by and wait for America to crush it. Tehran has nearly achieved the installation of a friendly government on its western border. While U.S. bases in Iraq could potentially be used to infiltrate Iran with spies and commandos and, more importantly, to support and launch air strikes, those bases are vulnerable politically, not to mention logistically. The supply lines of food, water, fuel and bullets to U.S. bases run from Kuwait to the north and through the Iraqi Shi'a heartland. Iranian intelligence agencies have given Iraqi Shi'a massive support since the U.S. invasion. The Shi'a are well organized and control the country through which U.S. supplies are moved. Islamic militants loyal to the likes of Ali al-Sistani and Moqtada al-Sadr could easily cut vital supply lines.

Iran can also play the oil card. If Iran were attacked, Iran could halt its oil exports and thereby immediately impact the global price. It would be unwise to hope that Iran, as part of its national security plan, is not willing to shut down Persian Gulf oil exports. Iran is well equipped to shower Persian Gulf states and oil fields with missiles, or to shut down exports with a variety of other military, terrorist or political methods. At a minimum, a U.S. military air campaign, even if successful in wrecking the Iranian nuclear program, would severely disrupt oil markets for at least six months. Such a disruption would hurt the world economy, not just that of the United States. In addition, there are countries sympathetic to Iran, such as Venezuela, that have indicated they are more than willing to cut off their oil supply to the United States. The United States could find itself facing a 20–30 percent shortfall in oil imports (and that estimate assumes that the Saudi fields are untouched and that oil imports continue to flow unimpeded).

Finally, Iran can play the global terror card. Unlike Al-Qaeda, groups tied directly to Iran continue to have robust capabilities and could cause a lot of trouble over the short term. Hizballah in particular has a significant presence in South America. U.S. commercial and transportation assets there would certainly be targeted, further inflicting damage to the U.S. economy.

The latter point raises an even more intriguing question—what would the Chinese do? They hold a substantial amount of U.S. debt. What happens if they decide to find some other currency to hold instead of the dollar? This could add an entirely new and dangerous dimension to an attack on Iran. Put simply, the United States spends too much and saves too little, and Asia saves too much and spends too little. The Chinese would view a disruption in the flow of oil out of the Persian Gulf as a damaging blow to the U.S. economy. Although the dollar traditionally has been the currency people seek during a crisis, the growing imbalance with China creates new dynamics that could convince the Chinese that holding dollars no longer made economic sense. Under such a scenario, dumping dollars on the international market would trigger an inflationary spiral in the United States.

The scenario of an inflationary spike triggered by China's dumping of dollars may strike some as fanciful. The point for U.S. planners and policy-makers, though, is to recognize that war brings unintended consequences that go well beyond the tactical realities on the ground where the fighting occurs. At a minimum, we should contemplate how a pre-emptive military strike in Iran could harm other U.S. foreign policy interests. A crisis in Iran would not occur in a vacuum.

We wish there were a simple, painless, guaranteed solution for persuading Iran not to go nuclear. Iran, for its part, is going to pursue its national interest, and its leaders believe that Iran is in a stronger position if it has nuclear weapons. Unless the world community comes together to isolate and condemn Iran for pursuing this goal, there is little likelihood that Iran will wilt in the face of sanctions.

China's role in this regard is critical. If China continues to do business as usual with Iran, then Iran is likely to continue its efforts to develop a nuclear weapon capability. If that happens, we will face the stark choice of accepting a nuclear Iran or pursuing a military option.

## NUCLEAR ARMED AND DANGEROUS

With nuclear weapons in hand, Iran will become the dominant local power in the Persian Gulf. They will have no pressing need to use these weapons, because their mere possession will ensure that everyone in the region, including Israel, will have to deal with them as a major power. We, too, would probably have to learn to deal with them on this basis.

A nuclear-armed Iran would not pose so large a threat to the region if it lacks dependable, long-range delivery platforms. As an interim strategy, the United States ought to consider stepping up efforts to ensure that North Korean or Chinese missiles do not find their way into Iran's inventory. An Iran equipped with nuclear weapons it could not deliver would pose less of a threat. If Iran acquires weapons that it can deliver via a No Dong missile, for example, then Iran's Middle East neighbors, particularly Saudi Arabia, would face a substantive concern requiring a reassessment of regional power alignments.

The impending crisis of Shi'a nuclear power may have at least one beneficial outcome, in that it may create an opportunity to rebuild bridges to the Sunni Islamic world that were destroyed by our misadventure in Iraq. Iran would love for the dispute over nuclear weapons to be cast as a conflict between the "crusading infidels" and God's faithful. This makes it doubly important that our diplomatic effort to contain Iran would draw on the help of Turkey, Jordan, Saudi Arabia, Pakistan, Afghanistan and Egypt.

An Iran armed with nuclear weapons would bolster both the supply source and morale of jihadi forces. The possession of such power by Iran would greatly undercut the goals of modernism and democracy, which the United States has promoted in the Islamic world. The probability of a major war in the region would be greatly increased.

What would be the posture of the United States if the Iranians gain nuclear weapons? Would we maintain forces in the Persian Gulf and in Iraq? How safe would Europe feel, given the ranges of ballistic missiles

Iran is developing, plus those that the Chinese have previously sold to Middle Eastern countries (Saudi Arabia for example)? In the end, it may become necessary to confront Iran militarily over its emergent nuclear power status, but the costs would be so high that all diplomatic resources should be exhausted before such measures are adopted.

# 45  Riding for a Fall
## PETER PETERSON

The question of how to pursue an American foreign policy that secures American interests while promoting global peace, prosperity, order, and democracy involves assessing not only the political and military elements of policy, but the economic dimensions as well. American actions have a cost, and a substantial one at that. Former Secretary of Commerce Peter Peterson examines America's current financial health and resources and finds that the United States is setting itself up for a financial crisis in the not-too-distant future, one that will affect this country's ability to act in the world and meet its commitments at home.

Peterson argues that the United States is spending itself into disaster and refusing to own up to it. Moreover, America's political leaders, from both political parties, are silent when it comes to facing the long-term fiscal and economic future of this country. Peterson identifies three developments that will put an increasing strain on America's financial resources: 1) the war on terrorism, which will involve large amounts of new spending to secure the homeland and fight abroad; 2) the growing indebtedness of the United States, which not only threatens economic growth, but risks a crash in the U.S. economy, especially if foreign investors, who hold massive amounts of American debt, divest in American dollars and securities; and 3) the aging of America, which will soon result in huge expenditures from Social Security and Medicare and cause further American debt. The combination of these three elements, Peterson argues, is likely to cause a "day of reckoning."

Peterson highlights what is an often overlooked aspect of American foreign policy. The great concerns over terrorism and WMD have tended to obscure the fact that the United States is the world's largest debtor nation and that this indebtedness is increasing. This circumstance, he points out, is unsustainable. "Leading nations cannot indefinitely borrow massively from those they intend to lead." Markets will eventually correct themselves as investors lose confidence in American securities and the dollar (which has lost a great deal of its value in recent years), and American power and credibility will likely erode with these developments. The only way to avoid such a future is to realistically address the issue and decide what trade-offs have to be made among national security and economic security priorities.

## COSTS OF BEING A SUPERPOWER

President George W. Bush has called terrorism the United States' greatest national security threat since World War II and has declared that the war on terrorism must be waged "for years and decades, not weeks or months." Most Americans agree with this assessment and with the need to pay whatever price is necessary to wage this war. But what is the price? And how will the United States pay for it?

It now seems nearly certain that the aging of America's population—which would pose a massive fiscal challenge over the next few decades itself—will unfold in an era of large additional commitments to our national security agenda. Two other issues, in addition to security costs, require attention because of their profound connections both to U.S. national security and to U.S. fiscal and economic performance: the United States' growing financial dependence on foreigners, and the extreme aging overtaking the rest of the developed world.

To paraphrase the poet John Donne, no nation is an island, least of all a superpower with such manifest responsibilities as the United States has in a newly dangerous world. But to commit America to a broader role while remaining blindly ignorant of the ultimate cost of doing so is sheer folly. Clearly, there are long-term tradeoffs to be faced: between economic security and national security, between retirement security and national security, and between today's taxpayers and tomorrow's taxpayers. As yet, however, the leaders of the two major political parties have hardly mentioned these trade-offs, much less discussed them seriously. When it comes to the long-term fiscal and economic future, U.S. leaders are mute not only on domestic challenges but on global challenges too.

# FIRST GLOBAL CHALLENGE: THE WAR ON TERRORISM

In September 2003, with bombs still raining down on Baghdad, President Bush made an emergency war-spending request for $87 billion. It was the largest such request since the opening months of World War II. The cost details arriving from the battlefield were riveting. For patrolling the "Sunni Triangle" in Iraq, the Army wanted 595 extra Humvees, at a price tag of $250,000 each. Another 60,000 troops needed three-piece body-armor suits: $5,000 each. Every day, the logistical needs of the forces in Iraq required dozens of 30-truck convoys from Kuwait and Turkey, carrying everything from half a million bottles of spring water to countless electronic modules, all provided by 6,000 civilian contractors. Sun and sand, meanwhile, did more damage to the equipment than did ambushes by insurgents. Every Bradley fighting vehicle in Iraq needed new tracks every 60 days, at $22,576 each. Apache attack helicopters, in perpetual need of maintenance, single-handedly devoured an amazing $1.3 billion in spare parts in fiscal year 2003. Engineering and construction costs were (and still are) billions of dollars over their original estimates.

In short, the stunning effectiveness of the U.S. armed forces has come with an equally stunning price tag. For most of U.S. history, going to war was like organizing a large federal jobs program, with most of the work done by inexpensive, quickly trained recruits. Today, it is more like a NASA moon launch, entailing a massive logistical tail supporting a professionally managed and swiftly depreciating body of high-tech physical capital. Just keeping two divisions engaged in "stability operations" in Iraq for one week costs $1 billion; keeping them engaged for a full year would cost the entire GDP of New Zealand.

Since September 11, moreover, the U.S. military has been planning to invest even more in its war machine to overcome some of the remaining weaknesses: slow reaction time to crises in remote regions and inexperience in dealing with unconventional, so-called "asymmetrical," threats, such as terrorism, guerrilla war, and weapons of mass destruction (WMD). Even after scrapping certain old weapons plans (such as the Crusader artillery system) and scaling back some other purchases, the total net cost of this military transformation will be large.

Weapons procurement, which fell to a post-Cold War low of about $50 billion a year in the mid-1990s, is scheduled to rise to over $100 billion a year by 2010—more than its previous (real dollar) peak in the mid-Reagan years. On the drawing board are lightweight Stryker brigades, state-of-the-art stealth warships, super-fast low-profile watercraft for coastline combat, and all the science-fiction paraphernalia of the Army's next-generation "Objective Force." These weapons will include non-line-of-sight cannons, electromagnetic "rail guns," robotic mules and assault vehicles, long-endurance unmanned tactical aircraft, loitering attack missiles, and total digital integration of fire and sensor systems.

Although the Bush administration incorporates an estimate of these new costs into its projections for defense outlays, most budget experts believe that it seriously underestimates the total future cost of the war on terrorism. To begin with, the administration refuses to make any projections for future military operations; it plans to procure all such funds through emergency appropriations. Also, much of the new technology is still under development and thus sure to experience cost overruns.

The Congressional Budget Office recently recalculated the administration's projections assuming, first, ongoing but diminishing operations in Iraq, Afghanistan, and elsewhere; and second, a historical rate of cost overruns for all new procurement. The results are eye-opening: total defense outlays over the next decade may cost 18 percent more than the administration's official projection. Including interest costs, this excess amounts to $1.1 trillion in new spending, a budgetary surcharge higher than the cost of the first decade of the new Medicare drug benefit.

Even this number does not reflect the cost of any new military operations abroad, which three of every four Americans believe are "very likely" in "the next few years," according to a Gallup poll. Nor does it reflect any permanent increase in active-force troop strength, which Congress may insist on even over administration resistance. With ongoing peacekeeping missions around the world, not even help from worn-out reserve and National Guard units can prevent the armed forces from being stretched dangerously thin should a new threat emerge. In December 2003, only two of the Army's ten divisions were both uncommitted and in a high state of readiness. That same month, 54 of the 61 members of the House Armed Services Committee, joined by the top Republican and Democrat on the House Intelligence Committee, signed a letter to President Bush urging him to enlist more troops.

Whatever they may feel about Iraq, most Americans seem to agree with the president's premise that in the war on terrorism, the best defenses are a good offense and forward deployment. Along with augmenting the capabilities of its armed forces, the United States is sharing intelligence with friendly governments around the world and training and equipping their antiterrorist forces as needed. Sea- and land-based ballistic missile defenses, long under development, are now being deployed at a growing cost ($10.3 billion in the fiscal year 2005 budget).

But sometimes the best defense is a good defense. No matter how effective the United States is at global preemption and deterrence, it must also take effective measures to prevent terrorism within U.S. borders. Here, too, there is an especially large gap between the resources needed and those allocated in official projections.

Most CIA analysts predict that there is a high probability of a serious terrorist attack with WMD on U.S. soil over the next several years. Granted, there is no conceivable price at which the United States could make itself totally secure against such an attack. Yet it is possible, at reasonable cost, to take extra steps that would make the country significantly less vulnerable to future attacks, which could cause catastrophic human or economic losses. Thus far, the government has not taken many of these steps, nor does it plan to. It is only a matter of time before American voters will, or at least should, insist that more be done. Indeed, this insistence may crystallize overnight come the next serious terrorist scare.

Yet doing more to bolster homeland defense will, of course, cost more money. What follows are just a few of the areas that need action.

More dollars need to be spent on equipping first responders: the fire, police, and other emergency personnel who are first to act after a terrorist strike. Only one-tenth of all fire departments currently have the capacity to respond to a building collapse, only a third of firefighters on any particular shift are equipped with breathing apparatuses, and only half possess radios (a deficiency that directly contributed to the high fatality rate among New York City firefighters on September 11). Moreover, biochemical and radiation sensors are lacking; urban search and rescue is spotty; the 911 emergency phone system is still not available nationwide; and emergency communications are not interoperable. The estimated cost to rectify these deficiencies and prepare first responders for a non-nuclear attack is $62 billion over five years.

America's health-care system is also under-resourced. During last winter's flu season, health clinics had to turn away patients when vaccines ran out—not a good sign that the United States is ready to handle a major biological terrorist attack. Acute-care hospitals have few quarantine or decontamination facilities and very little "surge capacity" in beds. Vaccines for major biological threats (most notably, smallpox) remain understocked. National Guard and reserve personnel and even many professionals in the public-health network have little or no training in responding to a nuclear or biological emergency. The minimum estimated cost to improve health-care capabilities over the next five years is $36 billion.

Reducing the threat posed by cargo containers will require another large injection of government funds. Only two percent of the roughly 20,000 cargo containers arriving each working day at 300 U.S. commercial ports are ever inspected by federal authorities. One recent study concludes that the current odds of detecting a shielded nuclear weapon inside a container are only about 10 percent. Closing all U.S. ports for more than a month in response to the mere threat of smuggled WMD would throw the U.S. economy into recession. The minimum estimated cost to remedy these security flaws including the introduction of measures such as globally monitored packing, tamper-proof seals, and satellite tracking—would be $20 billion upfront, with an unknown yearly investment needed after that.

The fact that six of the September 11 terrorists possessed expired or fraudulent visas points to the manifest failure of federal agencies to prevent illegal immigration, to locate illegal immigrants within the United States, or to monitor noncitizens who enter legally. There are currently 8 million to 12 million illegal aliens in the country, including nearly 300,000 who are fleeing official orders of deportation. The FBI cannot possibly handle the caseload, and local authorities have historically been excluded from any data on illegal immigrants. Few terrorism experts believe that an adequate level of safety can be attained without a total overhaul of the U.S. immigration system, a reform that may ultimately introduce biometric national identity cards. The costs of such measures are unknown but likely to be very large.

Finally, the U.S. government must spend more on safeguarding critical infrastructure, which, if disabled, could trigger widespread public terror and serious economic loss. For example, few water reservoirs or grain silos are any better guarded now than before September 11; a large share of consumable energy flows through a relatively small number of pipelines and refineries in remote, unguarded locations; and a well-placed attack aimed at electronic communications could bring financial trading to a stop. Transportation lines have bottlenecks: for example, five bridges and one tunnel entering New York State account for 70 percent of all trade with Canada, the United States' main trading partner. Again, the minimum cost to rectify these deficiencies is unknown, but it is likely to be very large.

Any effort to assess the cost of needed homeland security improvements must, of course, be hedged with the language of probability. Most of the wild-card surprises (say, another major terrorist strike) clearly lie on the side of higher costs. Yet even absent dreadful news, it seems very probable that the United States will be spending progressively more on homeland security over the next decade or two. No one can foretell exactly which areas of spending will rise fastest; much will depend on what threats emerge as the war on terrorism wears on. Much will also depend on whether homeland security becomes ravaged by pork-barrel politics. Regrettably, Congress is allocating much of the early spending on a politics-as-usual formula (each state receives according to its population) rather than on an objective assessment of need.

For the first time in the post-World War II era, the United States faces a future in which every major category of federal spending is projected to grow at least as fast as, or faster than, the economy for many years to come. That means not just pension and health-care benefits for retiring "baby boomers," or increasing interest payments as deficits and interest rates rise, but also appropriated or "discretionary" spending for national defense, for foreign aid, and for domestic homeland security programs.

The Bush administration has adjusted long-term discretionary spending projections upward from where they were in the Clinton era—but it has not done so sufficiently. In the post-September 11 world, Americans should not be banking on significant reductions in the level of discretionary spending, at least not without assurance that the danger has passed. They certainly should not imagine that any such reductions would pay for further tax cuts or allow the U.S. government to postpone reform of unsustainable retirement benefit programs.

## SECOND GLOBAL CHALLENGE: A HARD LANDING

The United States is now borrowing about $540 billion per year from the rest of the world to pay for the overall deficit funding Americans' consumption of goods and services and U.S. foreign aid transfers. This unprecedented current account deficit is paid for through direct lending and the net sales of U.S. assets to foreign businesses or persons: everything from stocks and bonds to corporations and real estate. The United States imports roughly $4 billion of foreign capital each day, half of that to cover the current-account deficit and the other half to finance investments abroad. At 5.4 percent of GDP in the first quarter of 2004, this deficit is substantially higher than its previous record (3.5 percent of GDP) in 1987, when the dollar fell by a third and the stock market took its "Black Monday" plunge. And experts at the New York Federal Reserve Bank and the Institute for International Economics predict that this deficit will grow even larger.

The rise in the current account deficit over the past 30 years is linked to a long-term decline in U.S. national savings, which is in part driven by widening U.S. federal budget deficits. Over time, chronic borrowing has accumulated into large debts owed to other countries. U.S. citizens must pay for these increasing liabilities with a growing annual debt-service charge, consisting mainly of interest and dividend payments. This charge is very sensitive to interest rates—going up when interest rates go up and its growth over time will itself widen the current account deficit.

If nothing else were to change, borrowing would continue until foreigners accumulated all the U.S. assets they cared to own, at which point a rise in interest rates (choking off investment) and a decline in the dollar (choking off imports and stimulating exports) would gradually close the current-account deficit. It would not entirely disappear, but it would close sufficiently to stabilize foreign holdings as a share of the U.S. economy. Afterward, Americans would cease to borrow as much from the rest of the world. In the absence of an increase in the national savings rate, people would just have to get by with less investment in their own economy and debt-service payments would no longer rise. Instead, Americans would simply make do with less capital, slower growth in GDP, and, of course, a slower rate of increase in their living standards.

Dreary as this scenario is, this sort of "soft landing" is the very best outcome we could expect so long as the United States' future fiscal path and national savings rate remain unchanged. But according to many economists, it is quite possible that the dynamic of gradual adjustment will at some point be trumped by a sudden loss of confidence, leading to a run on the dollar. If the dollar were to overshoot in a large and sudden plunge, inflation and interest rates could well jump substantially and financial markets could ratchet downward. The United States has already experienced some sort of dollar run four times over the last 30 years—in 1971–73, 1978–79, 1985–87, and 1994–95—with far less daunting projections than those of today. They typically began after the dollar had already been declining gently for some time. None was as serious as the hard landing the United States may yet face.

The next dollar run, should it happen, would likely lead to serious reverberations in the "real" economy, including a loss of consumer and investor confidence, a severe contraction, and ultimately a global recession. Soaring interest rates would cause the federal deficit to jump, as U.S. Treasury bond buyers demanded much higher returns. If short-term Treasury rates were to jump back to the four to five percent range, federal interest outlays would climb by $30 billion in the first year and by as much as $50 billion in the second year. Rather than improve the prospect of fiscal reform, gloomy economic conditions could delay it further.

Virtually none of the policy leaders, financial traders, and economists interviewed by this author believes the U.S. current account deficit is sustainable at current levels for much longer than five more years. Many see a real risk of a crisis. Former Federal Reserve Chairman Paul Volcker says the odds of this happening are around 75 percent within the next five years; former Treasury Secretary Robert Rubin talks of "a day of serious reckoning." What might trigger such a crisis? Almost anything: an act of terrorism, a bad day on Wall Street, a disappointing employment report, or even a testy remark by a central banker.

Skeptics say not to worry because governments around the world would never allow a crisis to happen. They would intervene massively to support the American currency by buying dollars. Indeed, they might try. But foreign governments might lose their nerve sooner than place vast sums of their own taxpayers' money into declining dollar-denominated assets. And once the mood of private investors worldwide changed decisively, there would be little that governments could do, even if they had nerves of steel. The magnitude of tradable assets around the world (global stock markets alone are now capitalized at over $30 trillion) would overwhelm the efforts of even the most dedicated band of central bankers or treasurers.

The skeptics are right about one thing: most governments have no great desire to correct the current imbalance of global trade and finance. Foreign leaders are as eager to stimulate their economies with a bustling export sector as U.S. political leaders are to keep running budget deficits at low interest rates. Fred Bergsten, director of the Institute for International Economics, observes, "We finally understand the true meaning of supply-side economics. Foreigners supply most of the goods and all of the money." It is an ugly but politically convenient arrangement. But it cannot be sustained indefinitely.

Most economists assume some sort of readjustment is inevitable. For the United States to export more and import less, however, it follows by arithmetic that the rest of the world must do the reverse. What if the rest of the world refuses? In a deflationary era of slack demand, some world leaders may feel compelled to maintain their trade surpluses by whatever means available: buying dollars, cutting interest rates, subsidizing exports, or resorting to outright protectionism and capital controls. Such policies may succeed for a time in delaying the readjustment, but only at the cost of throwing the global economy further out of kilter and worsening Rubin's "day of serious reckoning" when it arrives.

The question is not just hypothetical. With the substantial fall in the exchange value of the dollar since the beginning of 2002, global investors may be telling markets that a partial readjustment of the U.S. current account deficit is overdue. Although this fall has largely been accepted by some countries—members of the eurozone and Canada, for example—it has been largely rejected by others, most notably Japan, Taiwan, South Korea, and China (the currency of which is pegged to the dollar). The resulting regional asymmetry means that those who follow the "euro path" get hammered, whereas those who follow the "Asian path" get off easier by resisting the readjustment. In time, without better global cooperation, those following the euro path may give up and resort to a variety of surplus-preservation measures, such as subtle import restrictions and other de facto protectionist moves.

Although no one can predict how the current imbalance in the global economy will play out, trade economists marvel at just how many ways this lopsided flywheel can spin off the axle. One thing that economists agree on is that for the world to readjust to a path of balanced growth, the United States must export more and save more while the rest of the world must import more and consume more. This will require major shifts of labor and capital, not to mention profound cultural changes within all these economies.

Yet if moving to equilibrium too fast (the plunging dollar scenario) is full of peril, so is moving there too slowly by keeping adjustments on hold. And so too, for that matter, would be the situation in which different regions work at cross-purposes. All of these risks will have to be borne, moreover, during an era in which a major act of terrorism or war could send shock waves through global financial markets at any moment. Of course, the United States will try to exercise its global leadership and get every region to cooperate. But what happens to the dollar and the global economy depends as much on what foreign political leaders and investors do as on any unilateral U.S. policy.

That is so because America's economic leverage is diminished. A quarter of a century ago, the United States was still the largest net lender on earth; 20 years ago, its global assets still exceeded its liabilities. Today, however, its net investment position is sinking below negative $3 trillion. Americans may hope that the rest of the world will go on lending unlimited funds forever. That wish, however, is unrealistic.

## THIRD GLOBAL CHALLENGE: A GRAYING FIRST WORLD

For generations, the United States has relied on the material assistance of other developed countries in pursuing global projects of common interest—from defending democracy to managing the economy to helping the poor and oppressed. Washington continues to rely on this assistance today, not least for helping the United States meet the global challenges discussed above: the war on terrorism and the financing of fiscal deficits.

In the future, however, this reliance will decline—not out of pique or unwillingness, but from sheer incapacity, caused by the explosive fiscal costs of aging and (ultimately) the accelerating population decline projected to occur in nearly all developed societies over the next several decades. This is the third global challenge facing the United States' long-term fiscal strategy. It will burden Americans by increasing the cost of the first two challenges and by forcing the country to assume global leadership on problems once relegated to others.

The primary cause of the coming demographic revolution is falling fertility. Since the 1960s, birth rates have declined steadily throughout the developed world (and in most of the developing world as well). But whereas in the United States fertility has stabilized at just under 2.1 births per woman, which roughly assures a stationary population, it has fallen much further in other countries: to 1.2 in western Europe overall, 1.4 in

Japan, and 1.2 in certain southern European nations such as Spain and Italy. In most of these countries, people live at least as long as in the United States and immigration is much lower. Together, these trends produce very rapid aging.

Superimposing these dramatic demographics on extravagant pay-as-you-go retirement systems creates the fiscal equivalent of a perfect storm. Monthly public pension benefits and tax levels in most of the countries in question are considerably higher (relative to worker wages) than in the United States, and their retirement ages have been dropping even faster. It is common for European workers to retire in their late fifties, often on special disability or unemployment arrangements. In France, only 39 percent of men aged 55 to 64 remain employed, versus 65 percent as recently as 1980. These superaging societies will also consume more health care. According to the Center for Strategic and International Studies, total public benefit spending on the elderly in Japan, France, Germany, and Italy is projected, on average, to climb from 15 to 28 percent of GDP over the next 40 years. That figure is greater than the total revenues collected at all levels of government in the United States today.

To pay for such costs, these countries may try raising taxes. But many of them already have tax burdens of over 45 percent of GDP and payroll tax rates of over 35 percent of wages. At these lofty rates, many mainstream economists warn that further tax hikes may slow the economy more than they will raise new revenue.

Of course, political leaders can propose trimming benefits, but here they will encounter stiff resistance, because the elderly in these countries are so dependent on public benefits, which in turn are vigorously defended by powerful trade unions and their political allies. In continental Europe, employers do little pension saving on behalf of workers. According to a Merrill Lynch study, only seven percent of Europe's workers are covered by corporate pensions and only one percent by 401(k)-type savings plans. Household savings rates are higher in Europe than in the United States, but the savings are heavily skewed by income. Most median-earning households have little to count on except the promise of a government check. Thus, whether in Paris, Berlin, or Rome, the political leader who suggests even minor benefit reductions is typically greeted by general strikes and mass demonstrations. Washington's foreign friends, in other words, will face the wrenching dilemma of whether to fund weapons or walkers even more than the United States will.

In the end, governments in the developed world will patch together some fiscal expedient to tide them over. But one thing seems certain: they will be subjected to intense pressure to slash other spending and run larger budget deficits. The cuts will probably include defense, security, and international aid. And leaders will grow even more reluctant than they are already to commit public resources to U.S.-led military actions or nation-building operations. Meanwhile, private sector savings rates are almost certain to fall as the number of retired households rises and the number of working-age households declines. Larger budget deficits combined with declining private savings will end, and perhaps even reverse, the large current account surpluses that these countries have historically generated over the postwar era.

Haruhiko Kuroda, special adviser to Japanese Prime Minister Junichiro Koizumi and former vice finance minister for international affairs, is a world-class financial expert. My recent conversation with him on the issue of aging in the developed world was illuminating. He confirmed that the combination of an aging society and low birth rates in Japan remains a big problem and that, with a 25 percent drop in the number of workers under the age of 30 forecast in the next decade, Japan will face unprecedented deficits in the future. How, I asked, will Japan fund these deficits? "As you know, we have a big savings rate and a big capital account surplus. For some period, we can use those resources," he responded. "But Mr. Kuroda, you are now financing about a quarter of America's current account deficit. Can you really spend the same money twice?" I asked. "Yes. It is a very difficult problem."

If nothing else forces a rebalancing of the global economy, demography will be the clincher, its impact slow but inexorable. In the longer term, low fertility will mean not just a vicious fiscal squeeze but also an accelerating population decline. This too will have profound consequences in developed countries. The rate of GDP growth can decelerate and even shift into reverse in those countries in which the rate of workforce decline exceeds productivity growth. Population decline will also surely reshape the politics of migration and protectionism, reorient geopolitical strategy, and recast the cultural mood. Outside the United States, the population of the developed world is peaking now. By the early 2010s, assuming no change in fertility, it will decline by about one million people per year; by the late 2020s, by about three million per year; and in the 2040s, by over five million per year.

The United Nations periodically publishes a list of the 12 most populous nations. Back in 1950, this list included six nations from the "first world" (the United States, Japan, Germany, the United Kingdom, Italy, and France) and one from the "second world" (the Soviet Union). By 2000, only four of these nations remained on the list. In the UN projection for 2050, only one "first world" country remains—the United States, still in third place. According to political scientist Samuel Huntington, "the juxtaposition of a rapidly growing people of one culture and a slowly growing or stagnant people of another culture generates pressure for economic and/or political adjustments in both societies." Over the next few decades, Americans will be asking just how these adjustments may reshape the geopolitical contours of tomorrow's global order.

## MORE WILL THAN WALLET?

One demographic reality is already clear: no one can substitute for the United States' global role. Yet the United States cannot fulfill this role without facing up realistically to its full cost. Leading nations cannot indefinitely borrow massively from those they intend to lead. As the economist Benjamin Friedman puts it, "World power and influence have historically accrued to creditor countries." Equally, leading nations cannot subscribe to a foreign policy that has been aptly characterized by historian Niall Ferguson as based on "the Wal-Mart motto: Always low prices." Global security has never been guaranteed on the cheap and that is unlikely to change in an age of fanatical passions and hand-held WMD.

A leader must be willing to assume burdens. A global leader must be ready to undertake continent-wide projects requiring great patience, larger resource commitments, a public sector unburdened by excessive political promises, and an economy whose long-term prospects are unquestioned either at home or abroad. To date, unfortunately, America's elected officials leave the impression that vaunted superpower status comes with few long-term costs or responsibilities. They imply that wars can be waged without a war budget and that great debtors can set great examples.

President George H. W. Bush once opined that "America has more will than wallet, but what we need is will." His point was that good intentions count for more in international affairs than mere material resources. This may be true some of the time, and for a short while, perhaps. But ultimately good intentions need resources to be effective; "will" must prove itself by persuading citizens to open their wallets and, if necessary, to forgo other outlays.

The United States would greatly benefit from a serious and realistic discussion of the total cost of its long-term security agenda. It is a discussion that would lend welcome urgency to efforts to control the federal deficit, and, in particular, to reform ballooning entitlement programs. It is a discussion that would reconnect the domestic and foreign policy communities by requiring every policymaker to make a tradeoff: "How much am I willing to pay in tax hikes or benefit cuts in order to fund my security priorities?" Most of all, it is a discussion that ordinary Americans would welcome. People know in their personal and family lives that they cannot call for new sacrifices or promise new benefits without carefully considering the consequences. Why, they wonder, should things be any different in national life?

# 46

# A New Direction for U.S. Climate Policy: Credible Alternatives to Kyoto

## LEE LANE AND SAMUEL THERNSTROM

The problem of environmental degradation has become a topic of great importance in international relations. Since the 1970s, a number of international treaties have been implemented, dealing with problems such as toxic pollutants, endangered species, and ozone depletion. In the 1980s and 90s, scientific and political concerns began to mount regarding the problem of global climate change. This involves the extent to which the earth is warming due to the accumulation in the atmosphere of carbon dioxide and other "greenhouse gases," and the potential impacts this may have. An effort to address the problem resulted in the Kyoto Protocol, an international treaty to limit greenhouse gas emissions worldwide. The Clinton administration supported the effort and signed the treaty in 1997, but never brought it before the Senate for ratification due to intense political opposition. The treaty was seen as being unfairly applied around the world and too costly to the U.S. economy. Since emissions are caused primarily by using energy, curtailing energy use would adversely impact economic growth. Subsequently, upon entering office, President Bush withdrew the United States from the treaty, which went into effect among signatories in 2005.

In this article, Lee Lane and Samuel Thernstrom consider the current state of American efforts to deal with global warming. The authors find that the goal of combating global warming is necessary, and that there is a need for strong political action. They argue, however, that the approach of the Kyoto Protocol—to cap emissions at a certain level within a prescribed time frame—is politically satisfying but unlikely to achieve the desired results of curbing global warming. Instead, they offer that the best solution is to invest in the development of technologies that will achieve significant breakthroughs in cutting energy use and greenhouse gas emissions. In addition, the authors call for a carbon tax as a way of providing incentives to cut energy demand among businesses and consumers.

This analysis is notable in how it reflects a growing consensus on climate change and the ways to address it. Disputes in the

Samuel Thernstrom and Lee Lane, from "A New Direction for Bush Administration Climate Policy," *Environmental Policy Outlook, AEI Online*, No. 1, January 2007, www.aei.org. By permission of the American Enterprise Institute for Public Policy Research.

United States have revolved around the certainty of the science, the wisdom of the Kyoto approach, and the need for taxation. The American Enterprise Institute (AEI), which published this article, is an organization whose policy proposals reflect the conservative side of American political thought. This view has been opposed to increased taxation, and has often questioned both the goals and the means of efforts to combat global warming. The fact that AEI is now calling for a carbon tax and a more robust federal effort on climate change is a strong indicator that greater political agreement on this issue is forming.

---

President Bush's rejection of the Kyoto Protocol in 2001 was well-publicized, but most Americans are only vaguely familiar with the reasons for that decision or the administration's alternative policies. Meanwhile, the Protocol remains a favorite of environmental advocates and their political allies, as well as a growing number of rent-seeking businesses that stand to profit under such a system, and America remains an international pariah for its refusal to participate in it. President Bush has been able to prevent ratification of the Protocol, but he has not made the effort needed to convince people that there is a better way to approach the issue.

Kyoto's advocates claim that the only possible solution to climate change is an international agreement that requires rapid reductions in greenhouse gas emissions. This intuitively appealing perspective has dominated the public debate in both the United States and Europe. But a successful climate policy requires a much broader and longer-range perspective. The scale of emissions reductions necessary to retard warming significantly is vast, and our ability to achieve such reductions is severely limited by existing technologies and economic realities.

## THE KYOTO PROBLEM

Given Kyoto's serious and insurmountable flaws, the unshakable international commitment to the Kyoto approach is one of the greatest obstacles to crafting a successful strategy to combat global warming. Paradoxically, it is President Bush, nearly alone among world leaders, who seems to understand this most clearly—although he has been nearly universally condemned for this insight. Unfortunately, the Bush administration has never capitalized upon this opportunity by making a sufficient effort to change domestic or international opinions on this subject. If the president really wants to overcome the Kyoto problem, he must accomplish two things in his remaining time in office: convince Americans of the futility of the Kyoto approach, and persuade them that an alternative is viable.

The first of those tasks should be easier, of course. Kyoto's numerous flaws are beyond repair. Three critical flaws are well-understood and largely undeniable: it would have been unreasonably expensive for the United States (and several other countries) to meet its targets; it did not (and will not, in any future agreement) require China, India, or other developing nations to reduce their emissions; and even if it was implemented faithfully, its emissions-reduction targets are too low to matter. Kyoto's reach is too short, its grasp too weak, and its costs too high.

Even if the United States had ratified Kyoto in its original, more stringent form, it would have had almost no impact on overall global emissions or temperature trends. Kyoto's basic structure was so unfavorable to the United States that we would have paid a disproportionately large share of the costs. It is unreasonable to expect America to bear such costs when emissions in developing countries remain uncapped—and can be expected to rise even more rapidly if America's energy-intensive industries are driven overseas.

Without emissions limits for China and India, no Kyoto-style international agreement can be effective—yet adopting such limits is not in those countries' national interests, so it is foolish to expect them to do so. (Indeed, Kyoto's Clean Development Mechanism perversely reinforces their incentives to avoid accepting emissions limits in the next commitment period.) Having agreed in Kyoto that the developing world has no obligation to reduce its emissions, it will be nearly impossible for the developed world to reopen that question in the future.

Meanwhile, among the countries that have accepted emissions caps under Kyoto, progress toward meaningful emissions reductions has been hesitant at best. Many European countries (and possibly Japan) will not meet their Kyoto targets; some will miss them by wide margins. Others may only meet them by buying large numbers of "hot air" credits from Russia—an act of pointless symbolism, since Russian credits are the result of natural changes in the post-Soviet economy rather than efforts to cut emissions. The net environmental benefit of Kyoto, therefore, will be nearly zero.

Perhaps the most fundamental of Kyoto's problems is its surrender to the politically irresistible desire for a quick fix (or, at the very least, tangible signs of short-term progress). Climate change is a challenge that must be met over the course of the next century, not the next few years; the scale of technological transformation that would be required to stabilize atmospheric concentrations of greenhouse gases can only be accomplished over the course of decades. The critical issue for policymakers, therefore, is not how *quickly* emissions can be cut, but how *much* they can be reduced in the long run. (Or, failing that, what else can be done to adapt to warming or prevent it through other means, such as geoengineering.)

# EMISSIONS REDUCTIONS: QUICK AND DIRTY OR SLOW AND CLEAN?

What changes in energy production and consumption would come from short-term emissions caps of the sort that the Kyoto Protocol or the McCain-Lieberman bill would require? In general, they would be fairly modest. Carbon-intensive fuels such as coal and gasoline would cost more, so we would see a shift toward greater use of slightly cleaner fuels such as natural gas, and somewhat greater use of hybrid or other fuel-efficient vehicles. Renewable (and nuclear) energy sources might get a small boost, and some consumers and businesses might focus modestly greater efforts on energy conservation. (In fact, these trends are already apparent, and federal policies are promoting them. For instance, the president's latest budget proposal shifts solar-energy funding from research and development [R&D] to tax credits for consumers, thus subsidizing the use of existing solar panels rather than the long-term development of new, more cost-effective technologies.)

Environmental advocates will find these changes pleasing. But will they really help us meet the long-term challenge of climate change? We fear not. These efforts may be worthwhile, but the real question is whether they will help develop the breakthrough clean-energy technologies that will be needed to make dramatic emissions reductions possible (and cost-effective) in the coming decades—and the answer to that is no. Emissions caps are likely to prompt businesses to switch from using one existing technology to another, rather than to develop radically new technologies—and the entire challenge of climate change, at this stage, is in technology development, not deployment.

The development of new clean energy technologies is also the only possible answer to the Kyoto problems. Only new technologies that dramatically lower the cost of emissions abatement will make real reductions possible for most major emitters. When these technologies become available, the challenges of developing and implementing an effective international agreement to reduce global emissions will be vastly reduced. Until these technologies are developed, efforts to compel rapid emissions reductions are essentially futile.

Environmental advocates will object that a strategy focused on long-term technological development will not sufficiently reduce near-term emissions. That is true—but no politically feasible plan does. Even the most aggressive version of the McCain-Lieberman bill would have reduced global greenhouse gas emissions by a mere 2.5 percent by 2025, not even enough to noticeably lower the global emissions growth rate. And that bill was abandoned, deemed too expensive to be politically viable.

President Bush has been roundly condemned for emphasizing the importance of technological development. These critics are wrong—and wrong to overlook the flaws in his current efforts. What is needed now is a more robust effort to develop climate technologies, not a greater focus on short-term emissions trends. There are real questions about how to best do that, but the options are clear enough.

Conservatives may be inclined to believe that such research is best carried out by the private sector. And indeed, that is generally preferable—but perhaps not in this case. The kind of fundamental breakthroughs in basic science that are needed for climate technologies are not likely to come from the private sector. Most companies invest their resources in developing technologies that can be brought to market quite quickly—within, say, five years. These are typically incremental improvements over existing technologies, not radically new ways of generating clean energy. Much longer-term projects are significantly riskier, making them poor candidates for substantial private-sector investments.

## REFORMING THE FEDERAL CLIMATE R&D PROGRAM

If the private sector is ill-equipped to conduct this basic science research, the obvious alternative is federal research. The president has embraced that strategy, but he has not done so aggressively enough to make it credible. Ironically, the president's critics concentrate so heavily on attacking him for his refusal to embrace short-term emission cuts they have usually missed or misdiagnosed the serious shortcomings in the administration's Climate Change Technology Program (CCTP). The president devoted some attention to crafting this policy in the beginning of his first term but has largely ignored it since then, leaving it to drift in a sea of bureaucratic malaise.

Although the president has supported development of some specific technologies, such as hydrogen fuel cell vehicles, the federal climate-related R&D effort is seriously flawed. Three problems plague the CCTP: its research agenda is insufficiently ambitious and too risk averse, given the need for such large scale improvements in technology; its strategic planning process is starved for resources; and its influence on program priorities is questionable. (Its funding is probably also too limited in light of the size of the challenge.)

The scope of the CCTP's research deliberately excludes several of the most promising technologies. Ironically, it concentrates excessively on making incremental progress rather than on making the fundamental breakthroughs needed to cope with climate change—thus reproducing the flaws of Kyoto's short-term vision in the very area in which they should be corrected. And the strategic planning process is underfunded and ineffectual.

One option would be to create a new R&D organization modeled on the Defense Advanced Research Projects Agency (better known as DARPA).

This would not be a panacea, but if properly implemented, it might significantly ameliorate some of the known institutional problems with the existing federal program, especially its unambitious style. An independent agency could study solar-radiation management strategies and other geo-engineering technologies, as well as strategies to help people here and abroad adapt to, and minimize the damage from, changes in the climate that are already underway.

With additional resources, there could also be opportunities for innovative engagement with the private sector. Environmental advocates think of President John F. Kennedy's challenge to put a man on the moon as a model for the sort of federal climate program they would like to see—a well-funded government-led enterprise—but history offers another model worth considering: in 1714, the British government offered a £20,000 prize (a vast fortune at the time) as an inducement for inventors to create a device that would allow ships to accurately determine their longitude, and consequently, to reliably navigate across vast ocean distances. It took John Harrison, a carpenter and amateur clockmaker, almost fifty years to win the prize, having invented the first marine chronometer. This is precisely the sort of long-term research effort that federal climate scientists need to undertake now. While much of that research will be done in federal energy labs, there is no reason why comparable prizes could not be offered to private companies as an inducement for the development of specific clean-energy or climate-related technologies.

## A CARBON TAX

The Bush administration faces two challenges: designing an effective long-term climate policy and stopping the growing momentum toward inefficient, Kyoto-inspired policies. These are complementary efforts; a long-term alternative to Kyoto may help lessen its appeal. But the desire for short-term action is irresistible; politics demand action. An R&D-focused "do nothing until the technology ripens" policy is simply not credible, either domestically or internationally. If for no other reason than to halt momentum toward economically inefficient Kyoto-style emissions-trading policies, the Bush administration needs to reconsider its long-standing opposition to mandatory greenhouse gas–emissions controls. Federal emissions limits are now inevitable; the only question is which president will craft them.

Given the importance of precedent in American politics, the answer to that question is critical: once the federal government embarks on a given approach to curtailing greenhouse gases, future policies are likely to follow that path. For the last decade, most Americans have assumed that emissions trading is the best approach to reducing greenhouse gas emissions.

Cap-and-trade programs have been effective at controlling conventional air pollution in the United States, but greenhouse gases are very different. Establishing economically efficient emissions caps is an exercise in arbitrary and inevitably politicized policymaking. Creating a well-run multibillion-dollar market in carbon emissions is a vastly greater logistical challenge than trading sulfur dioxide credits among a relatively small number of utilities. The evidence we see so far from Europe's experience with Kyoto is hardly encouraging.

Most economists agree that a carbon tax would be the most efficient way to limit greenhouse gas emissions. A carbon tax would apply moderate, even pressure across the economy to reduce emissions rather than selectively raising the cost of politically unpopular forms of energy production and consumption, such as automobiles and power plants.[1] A carbon tax may seem anathema to the Bush administration, but as several economists (including AEI's Kevin A. Hassett) have noted, carbon-tax revenues could be used to finance reductions in the marginal rates of other taxes.[2] The net result would be a revenue-neutral tax reform, not increased taxation.

In his remaining time in office, President Bush must think strategically about how to make his well-intentioned but anemic climate program robust enough to garner bipartisan support, and prevent his successor from reengaging, in some form or another, with the Kyoto system. A more robust R&D program must be the centerpiece of America's long-term climate policy, but establishing the principle that taxation rather than emissions trading is the best way to limit emissions in the short run may be the most important element of crafting an efficient near-term policy. Such a tax will be hard for President Bush to swallow, but it may be the price he needs to pay to make his alternative to Kyoto credible and buy time for the next generation of clean-energy technologies to develop. If that cannot be done, there may be no way to control global warming—but we will waste a great deal of money trying.

## Notes

1. A moderate carbon tax might be something in the range of $15 per ton of carbon, for example, which translates into a five-cents-per-gallon increase in the price of gasoline. A tax in the $10 to $30 per ton range would generate between $15 billion and $45 billion annually in federal revenues.

2. Kevin A. Hassett and Gilbert E. Metcalf, "What Would a Rational Energy Tax Policy Look Like?" *Tax Analysts*, November 27, 2006, available at www.aei.org/publication25199/.

# 47 China's Search for Stability with America
## WANG JISI

The rise of China as a major world power is a development that will
have a great impact on the course of global politics in the coming
decades, and this change may present a challenge to the United
States. China has experienced rapid economic growth in the last generation, and it now boasts the world's second-largest economy. This
has been fueled by a combination of manufacturing, foreign investment, and making itself an important trading partner to countries
around the world, above all the United States. The government of
China has spoken of its "peaceful rise," indicating a commitment to
strengthen the country through trade and economic integration, as
opposed to military conquest and strategic confrontation. However,
throughout history when the world's leading power is challenged by
a rising one, the two have had a difficult relationship.

In this article, the U.S. relationship with China is examined from
the point of view of someone who is not American, but from China.
Americans often consider their global hegemony to be beneficial to
others, or at least benign, but the same view of America does not
always prevail overseas. Wang Jisi looks at American actions toward
China and argues that the two countries have a number of similar interests: economic growth and cooperation, stable oil supplies and prices,
safe and open shipping lanes, prevention of a North Korean nuclear
arsenal, and avoidance of crisis over Taiwan. Because, he states, the
United States is the global leader in military power, economics, education, culture, technology, and science, China "must maintain a close
relationship with the United States if its modernization efforts are to
succeed." At the same time, however, Jisi sees significant potential for
conflict with the United States in Asia, especially with regard to issues
such as Taiwan's future, North Korea's nuclear aspirations, and Japan's
relationship to the United States and China. He points out that with
regard to certain issues, American policy exacerbates tensions.

The implications of America's relationship with China are significant. Jisi believes that the framework for cooperation exists. After all,
"like all relations between states, the Chinese U.S. relationship is fundamentally based on interests." Therefore, the United States is not
likely to regard China as its main security threat, and China will generally avoid antagonizing Washington. This view, however, embodies

Wang Jisi, "China's Search for Stability with America." Reprinted with permission from
*Foreign Affairs*, 84.5, Sept/Oct 2005. Copyright 2005 by the Council on Foreign Relations, Inc.

not only a degree of realism, but also a paradox: the strength, prosperity, and success of each country are not only mutually beneficial, but also potentially threatening. While China is not likely to challenge the United States in the same way the Soviets did—striving to keep pace in military terms, which is not realistic considering America's military advantages—it is likely to be able to use both its expanding economic strength and its increasingly effective political skills to achieve its objectives, sometimes at the expense of the United States. This will have a profound impact on global politics.

## AFTER 9/11

The United States is currently the only country with the capacity and the ambition to exercise global primacy, and it will remain so for a long time to come. This means that the United States is the country that can exert the greatest strategic pressure on China. Although in recent years Beijing has refrained from identifying Washington as an adversary or criticizing its "hegemonism"—a pejorative Chinese code word for U.S. dominance—many Chinese still view the United States as a major threat to their nation's security and domestic stability.

Yet the United States is a global leader in economics, education, culture, technology, and science. China, therefore, must maintain a close relationship with the United States if its modernization efforts are to succeed. Indeed, a cooperative partnership with Washington is of primary importance to Beijing, where economic prosperity and social stability are now top concerns.

Fortunately, greater cooperation with China is also in the United States' interests—especially since the attacks of September 11, 2001. The United States now needs China's help on issues such as counterterrorism, nonproliferation, the reconstruction of Iraq, and the maintenance of stability in the Middle East. More and more, Washington has also started to seek China's cooperation in fields such as trade and finance, despite increased friction over currency exchange rates, intellectual property rights, and the textile trade.

Although there is room for further improvement in the relationship, the framework of basic stability established since September 11 should be sustainable. At least for the next several years, Washington will not regard Beijing as its main security threat, and China will avoid antagonizing the United States.

## THE LONELY SUPERPOWER

To understand the forces that govern U.S.-Chinese relations, it helps first to understand U.S. power and Washington's current global strategy. Here is a Chinese view: in the long term, the decline of U.S. primacy and the subsequent transition to a multipolar world are inevitable; but in the short term, Washington's power is unlikely to decline, and its position in world affairs is unlikely to change.

Consider that the United States continues to lead other developed countries in economic growth, technological innovation, productivity, research and development, and the ability to cultivate human talent.

Despite serious problems such as swelling trade and fiscal deficits, illegal immigration, inadequate health care, violent crime, major income disparities, a declining educational system, and a deeply divided electorate, the U.S. economy is healthy: last year, U.S. GDP grew an estimated 4.4 percent, and this year the growth rate is expected to be 3.5 percent, much greater than the corresponding figures for the eurozone (2.0 percent and 1.6 percent). Barring an unexpected sharp economic downturn, the size of the U.S. economy as a proportion of the global economy is likely to increase in the years to come.

Many other indexes of U.S. "hard power" are also on the rise. The U.S. defense budget, for example, has increased considerably in recent years. In 2004, it hit $437 billion, or roughly half of all military spending around the world. Yet as a percentage of U.S. GDP, the figure was lower than it was during the Cold War.

Further bolstering U.S. primacy is the fact that many of the country's potential competitors, such as the European Union, Russia, and Japan, face internal problems that will make it difficult for them to overtake the United States anytime soon. For a long time to come, the United States is likely to remain dominant, with sufficient hard power to back up aggressive diplomatic and military policies.

From a Chinese perspective, the United States' geopolitical superiority was strengthened in 2001 by Washington's victory in the Afghan war. The United States has now established political, military, and economic footholds in Central Asia and strengthened its military presence in Southeast Asia, in the Persian Gulf, and on the Arabian Peninsula. These moves have been part of a global security strategy that can be understood as having one center, two emphases. Fighting terrorism is the center. And the two emphases are securing the Middle East and preventing the proliferation of weapons of mass destruction.

The greater Middle East, a region stretching from Kashmir to Morocco and from the Red Sea to the Caucasus, is vital to U.S. interests. Rich in oil and natural gas, the region is also beset by ethnic and religious conflicts and is a base for rampant international terrorism. None of the countries in the area is politically stable, and chaos there can affect the United States directly, as the country learned on September 11.

On the nonproliferation front, the United States' main concerns are Iran and North Korea, two states that are striving to develop nuclear technology and have long been antagonistic toward Washington. In 2004, the United States carried out the largest redeployment of its overseas forces since World War II in order to meet these challenges.

## NOT INVULNERABLE

Despite its many advantages, the United States is not invincible. The war in Iraq, for example, resulted in international isolation of a sort that Washington had not faced since the beginning of the Cold War. The invasion was strongly condemned by people all over the world and explicitly opposed by the great majority of nations. Washington split with many of its traditional allies, such as Paris and Berlin, which refused to take part in the operation. And tensions with Islamic countries, especially in the Arab world, increased dramatically.

Since then, the extent of armed resistance to the U.S. occupation of Iraq has exceeded the Bush administration's expectations. Meanwhile, revelations of prisoner abuse by U.S. personnel in Iraq and elsewhere have undermined the credibility of U.S. rhetoric on human rights and further damaged the United States' image in the world. U.S. "soft power"—the country's ability to influence indirectly the actions of other states—has been weakened. The United States also faces serious competition and disagreement from Europe, Japan, and Russia on many economic and development-related issues, and there have been disputes on arms control, regional policies, and the role of the United Nations and other international organizations.

Nonetheless, the points in common between these powers and the United States in terms of ideology and strategic interests outweigh the differences. A pattern of coordination and cooperation among the world's major powers, institutionalized through the G-8 (the group, of leading industrialized countries), has taken shape, and no great change in this pattern is likely in the next five to ten years. To be sure, some of the differences between the United States and the EU, Japan, Russia, and others will deepen, and Washington will at times face coordinated French, German, and Russian opposition, as it did during the war in Iraq. But no lasting united front aimed at confronting Washington is likely to emerge.

Meanwhile, many developing countries now boast higher growth rates than those found in the industrialized world, and they have enhanced their role in global affairs by strengthening themselves and coordinating their stances on major international issues. Rich countries, however—especially the United States—still occupy dominant positions in the UN, the World Trade Organization, the World Bank, the International Monetary Fund, and other global institutions. Moreover, they continue to maintain the contemporary international order and rules that serve their economic and security interests.

All of the changes described above have provided China with new, albeit limited, opportunities for maneuver. So long as the United States' image remains tainted, China will have greater leverage in multilateral settings. It would be foolhardy, however, for Beijing to challenge directly the international order and the institutions favored by the Western world—and, indeed, such a challenge is unlikely.

## EYE ON ASIA

There is one region where the United States is most likely to come into close contact with China, leading to either major conflicts of interest or real cooperation (or both): in Asia and the Pacific. Divining the direction of relations between the two countries therefore requires a comprehensive analysis of the forces in the region. Of all the recent developments in Asia, China's rise is attracting the most attention at the moment. But several other important developments are occurring simultaneously.

Thanks to a period of internal reform, Japan has recovered from the doldrums of the 1990s and is reinforcing its status as Northeast Asia's most powerful economy. Meanwhile, India's economy is growing very rapidly, and New Delhi has sought rapprochement with Islamabad and improved relations with Washington and Beijing. The Russian economy is growing fast as well, due in large part to the surge in world energy prices. As a result of these and other forces, most Asia-Pacific countries are growing closer diplomatically, and economic cooperation in eastern Asia is speeding up. Two worrisome security problems remain, however: the North Korean nuclear program and the question of Taiwan.

Among all the nations in the region, Japan has the biggest effect on the Chinese-U.S. relationship. Since the end of the Cold War, the U.S.-Japanese security alliance has strengthened, not weakened (as China once hoped it would). Unlike some other traditional U.S. allies, Tokyo has sent troops to support the occupation of Iraq and given substantive reconstruction assistance to Iraq and Afghanistan. In return, Washington has praised Tokyo's international role and endorsed (at least diplomatically) Japan's bid for a permanent seat on the UN Security Council. The prospect of conflict between the two allies, which many in the media once predicted, seems to have disappeared from the scene.

In sharp contrast, Tokyo's ties to Beijing have cooled significantly. A series of recent irritants have exacerbated a relationship already strained by Japanese Prime Minister Junichiro Koizumi's repeated visits to the Yasukuni Shrine (where Japan's war dead, including a number of war criminals, are commemorated). These incidents have included the accidental intrusion of a Chinese submarine into Japanese territorial waters in November 2004; a visit by former Taiwanese leader and independence activist Lee Teng-hui to Japan in December 2004; Japan's ongoing publication of textbooks that downplay its World War II atrocities; and, this spring, anti-Japan demonstrations in a number of major Chinese cities. As such cases show, the historical conflicts between China and Japan and the mutual antagonism of their peoples can easily become political problems. Unless the issues are handled with care, they can evolve into serious crises.

Rather than play a helpful role, the United States has pushed China and Japan further apart. Beijing fears that the consolidation of the U.S.-Japanese alliance is coming at its expense and that the growing closeness is motivated by the allies' common concern about the increase of China's power. As the "China threat" theory gains followers in Japan, right-wing forces there are becoming more assertive by the day and turning increasingly toward the United States as their protector. Japan has also used the United States to exchange military intelligence with Taiwan; indeed, Japanese right-wing forces no longer shrink from offending Beijing by making overtures to pro-separation forces in Taipei.

Japan has also failed to respond warmly to China's sponsorship of more institutionalized economic cooperation in eastern Asia. As its reluctance suggests, Tokyo is wary of Beijing's growing role in the region and does not want to cooperate with any attempts to create regional structures that would exclude the United States. Hard-liners in Washington may think that the United States benefits from a souring of the Chinese-Japanese relationship. In the long run, however, conflict between Beijing and Tokyo helps no one, since it could destabilize Asia's existing economic and security arrangements, many of which benefit the United States.

In the field of international security, the primary focal point in Chinese-U.S. relations is the North Korean nuclear issue. On this question, the Bush administration has little choice but to act cautiously, relying on the six-party talks to exert pressure on Pyongyang and using various mechanisms (such as the U.S.-sponsored Proliferation Security Initiative) to stop North Korea from exporting nuclear materials or technology. China, in its own way, has tried to dissuade North Korea from developing nuclear weapons but so far has declined to support multilateral blockades or sanctions on Pyongyang. If North Korea ever publicly, explicitly, and unmistakably demonstrates that it does possess nuclear weapons, the policies of the United States, China, South Korea, Japan, and Russia—all of which favor a nuclear-free Korean Peninsula—will have failed. The United States might then call for much tougher actions against North Korea, which would increase tension and narrow China's options. The result could be new friction between China and the United States and a serious test of their relationship.

If, on the other hand, the six-party talks are resumed, tensions between the United States and North Korea may ease, and China's role will then be more favorably recognized. Should that occur, the countries involved in the process might even consider expanding the six-party mechanism into a permanent Northeast Asian security arrangement, a development that would serve the interests of all the countries concerned and one that China should favor. Under the current circumstances, however, such a possibility is slim. The more likely outcome is that tensions between Washington and Pyongyang will persist, although without an actual war breaking out.

Meanwhile, at a time when political relations between China and the United States are basically stable and economic and trade links are expanding, Taiwan remains a major source of unease. War between China and the United States over Taiwan would be a nightmare, and both sides will try hard to avoid it. Despite their differences, there is no reason the two sides should have to resort to force to resolve the matter. Yet some people in Taiwan, looking out for their own interests and supported by outsiders— notably parts of the U.S. defense establishment and certain members of the U.S. Congress continue stubbornly to push for independence, ignoring the will of most Taiwanese. It is a mistake for Americans to support such separatists. If a clash occurs, these parties will be responsible.

China views the status of Taiwan as an internal matter. But only by coordinating its U.S. policy with its policy toward Taiwan can Beijing curb the separatist forces on the island. Despite U.S. displeasure at China's passage of an antisecession law in March 2005, policymakers in Washington have reiterated their opposition to Taiwan's independence and viewed favorably the spring 2005 visits by Taiwanese opposition leaders to the mainland, which eased cross-strait relations. Nonetheless, Washington has now asked Beijing to talk directly to Taipei's ruling party and its leader, Chen Shui-bian. To improve matters, Chinese and U.S. government agencies and their foreign policy think tanks should launch a sustained and thorough dialogue on the issue and explore ways to prevent separatist forces from making a rash move, dragging both countries toward a confrontation neither wants.

## LONG-TERM INTERESTS

The Chinese-U.S. relationship remains beset by more profound differences than any other bilateral relationship between major powers in the world today. It is an extremely complex and highly paradoxical unity of opposites. It is not a relationship of confrontation and rivalry for primacy, as the U.S.-Soviet relationship was during the Cold War, but it does contain some of the same characteristics. In its pattern of interactions, it is a relationship between equals. But the tremendous gap between the two countries in national power and international status and the fundamental differences between their political systems and ideology have prevented the United States from viewing China as a peer. China's political, economic, social, and diplomatic influences on the United States are far smaller than the United States' influences on

China. It is thus only natural that in their exchanges, the United States should take the offensive role and China the defensive one.

In terms of state-to-state affairs, China and the United States cannot hope to establish truly friendly relations. Yet the countries should be able to build friendly ties on nongovernmental and individual levels. Like all relations between states, the Chinese-U.S. relationship is fundamentally based on interests. But it also involves more intense, love-hate feelings than do the majority of state-to-state ties. The positive and negative factors in the links between China and the United States are closely interwoven and often run into one another.

As this complex dynamic suggests, trying to view the Chinese-U.S. relationship in traditional zero-sum terms is a mistake and will not guide policy well; indeed, such a simplistic view may threaten both countries' national interests. Black-and-white analyses inevitably fail to capture the nuances of the situation. If, for instance, the United States really aimed to hamper China's economic modernization—as the University of Chicago's John Mearsheimer has argued should be done—China would not be the only one to suffer. Many U.S. enterprises in China would lose the returns on their investments, and the American people would no longer be able to buy inexpensive high-quality Chinese products. On the other hand, although Americans' motives for developing economic and trade ties with China may be to help themselves, these ties have also helped China, spurring its economic prosperity and technological advancement.

This prosperity and advancement will naturally strengthen China's military power—something that worries the United States. Indeed, this issue represents a paradox at the heart of Washington's long-term strategy toward Beijing. Unless China's economy collapses, its defense spending will continue to rise. Washington should recognize, however, that the important question is not how much China spends on its national defense but where it aims its military machine, which is still only a fraction of the size of the United States' own forces. The best way to reduce tensions is through candid and comprehensive strategic conversations; for this reason, military-to-military exchanges should be resumed.

China faces a similar paradox: only a U.S. economic decline would reduce Washington's strength (including its military muscle) and ease the strategic pressure on Beijing. Such a slide, however, would also harm China's economy. In addition, the increased U.S. sense of insecurity that might result could have other consequences that would not necessarily benefit China. If, for example, Washington's influence in the Middle East diminished, this could lead to instability there that might threaten China's oil supplies. Similarly, increased religious fundamentalism and terrorism in Central and South Asia could threaten China's own security, especially along its western borders, where ethnic relations have become tense and separatist tendencies remain a danger.

The potential Chinese-U.S. conflict over energy supplies can be seen in a similar light. Each country should be sensitive to the other's energy needs and security interests worldwide. China is currently purchasing oil from countries such as Venezuela and Sudan, whose relations with the United States are far from amicable. Washington, meanwhile, is now thought to be eying Central Asian oil fields near China's border. Both Beijing and Washington should try to make sure that the other side understands its intentions and should explore ways to cooperate on energy issues through joint projects, such as building nuclear power plants in China.

History has already proved that the United States is not China's permanent enemy. Nor does China want the United States to see it as a foe. Deng Xiaoping's prediction that "things will be all right when Sino-U.S. relations eventually improve" was a cool judgment based on China's long-term interests. To be sure, aspirations cannot replace reality. The improvement of Chinese-U.S. relations will be slow, tortuous, limited, and conditional, and could even be reversed in the case of certain provocations (such as a Taiwanese declaration of independence). It is precisely for this reason that the thorny problems in the bilateral relationship must be handled delicately, and a stable new framework established to prevent troubles from disrupting an international environment favorable for building prosperous societies. China's leadership is set on achieving such prosperity by the middle of the twenty-first century; with Washington's cooperation, there is little to stand in its way.

# 48 Russia's Wrong Direction: What the United States Can and Should Do

## COUNCIL ON FOREIGN RELATIONS

The relationship between the United States and the Soviet Union was the most important relationship in the world during the Cold War, and American interaction with Russia, the successor state to the Soviet Union, continues to be of immense importance today, even after the Cold War. Russia is one of the world's great powers, its role

Council on Foreign Relations, from "Russia's Wrong Direction: What the United States Can and Should Do," Independent Task Force Report No. 57, March 2006. Reprinted by permission.

in regional and global affairs is considerable, and after several years of weakness and decline relative to its previous stature, the country has achieved strong economic growth and is asserting its interests to a greater degree in world politics.

When the Cold War ended, the United States and Russia enjoyed a period of close cooperation on a number of issues, including nuclear nonproliferation, trade and economic development, and inclusion in Western international organizations. After September 11, cooperation reached a peak, as both countries saw a similar threat in Islamist terrorism. In the last few years, however, there have been a number of areas in which the United States and Russia have diverged. Disagreements involving Russia's intervention in bordering states, energy, U.S. bases in Central Asia, and the growing authoritarianism of President Putin's government have been increasing. This report by the Council on Foreign Relations takes stock of U.S.-Russian relations. Cognizant of the fact that relations between these two countries are critical for global peace, stability, and prosperity, the report examines the sources of friction between the two countries and offers recommendations on how the United States should engage Russia.

---

Fifteen years after the end of the Cold War, it is time to take stock of what has, and has not, been accomplished in the effort to create a "strategic partnership" between Russia and the United States. Russia is not the same country it was a decade and a half ago. It is not even the same country it was when President Vladimir Putin took office in May 2000. U.S.-Russian relations have changed as well.

Since the dissolution of the Soviet Union, American presidents and policymakers have believed that the interests of the United States are served by engagement with Russia. This Task Force, too, began its review of U.S. policy—and concludes it—convinced of the extraordinary importance of getting U.S. relations with Russia right.

U.S.-Russian cooperation can help the United States to handle some of the most difficult challenges it faces: terrorism, the proliferation of weapons of mass destruction, tight energy markets, climate change, the drug trade, infectious diseases, and human trafficking. These problems are more manageable when the United States has Russia on its side rather than aligned against it.

Good relations between Moscow and Washington also bolster one of the most promising international realities of our time—the near absence of security rivalries among the major powers. That the world's leading states deal with each other in a spirit of accommodation is a great asset for

American policy, and the United States will be in a better position to protect that arrangement if relations with Russia are on a positive track.

Today's U.S.-Russian relationship can be credited with real achievements:

- Cooperative programs to increase the physical security of nuclear materials and sensitive technologies help to keep them out of dangerous hands.
- Growing trade and investment benefit Americans and contribute to Russia's social and economic modernization.
- Russian and American policymakers are—at least for now—working together to reduce the risk that Iran will acquire nuclear weapons. Containing Tehran's nuclear aspirations depends in large part on how closely and effectively Moscow and Washington collaborate.

Yet U.S.-Russian relations are now also marked by a growing number of disagreements. Cooperation is becoming the exception, not the norm, and what leaders of both countries have called a "partnership" is not living up to its potential.

- At a time when the president of the United States has made democracy a goal of American foreign policy, Russia's political system is becoming steadily more authoritarian. Russia is a less open and less democratic society than it was just a few years ago, and the rollback of political pluralism and centralization of power there may not have run their course.
- Russia has used energy exports as a policy weapon—intervening in Ukraine's politics, putting pressure on its foreign policy choices, and curtailing supplies to the rest of Europe. The reassertion of government control over the Russian energy sector increases the risk that this weapon will be used again.
- Russia and the United States may also be starting to diverge in their responses to the threat of terrorism. Russia has tried to curtail U.S. access to bases in Central Asia that support military operations in Afghanistan. President Putin raised further questions when, after agreeing with the United States and the European Union (EU) not to have high-level contact with Hamas, he invited its leaders to Moscow.
- Russia's policies toward the states on its periphery have become a recurrent source of friction between Moscow and Washington and are increasingly entwined with other issues, including energy, counterterrorism, and support for democratic reform.

With disagreements of this kind on the rise, U.S.-Russian relations are clearly headed in the wrong direction. Contention is crowding out consensus. The very idea of "strategic partnership" no longer seems realistic.

How should America deal with this downward trajectory? Some have suggested a narrower focus: choose one or two interests—nonproliferation, for example—and keep disagreement over Russia's growing authoritarianism from undermining cooperation on these priorities. Others favor a process of disengagement: exclude Russia from forums, especially those of the Group of Eight (G8), that are supposed to reflect common values.

We do not believe that either of these approaches is correct. In America's relations with Russia, the choice between interests and values is a false one. It misreads the connection between internal developments in Russia and the broader foreign policy interests of the United States.

- On an issue such as the proliferation of nuclear weapons, both sides are guided by calculations of national security. They will not cease to cooperate merely because they disagree on other matters.
- Moreover, disagreements between Moscow and Washington are not confined to the realm of "values." Russian and American approaches to major issues such as energy security and counterterrorism are also diverging. The gap between them will not be closed merely because the United States is less critical of Russian authoritarianism.

Above all, concern about Russia's domestic evolution should not be seen as a matter of values alone.

- It reflects growing doubt about whether Russia is building a modern and effective state that can cooperate successfully with other modern nations to deal with common problems.
- Despite rapid economic growth and social transformation, Russian political institutions are becoming neither more modern nor more effective, but corrupt and brittle. As a result, Russia's capacity to address security concerns of fundamental importance to the United States and its allies is reduced. And many kinds of cooperation—from securing nuclear materials to intelligence sharing—are undermined.
- Today, Russia seems stable, but its stability has a weak institutional base. The future of its political system is less

predictable—and the country's problems are less manageable—than they should be.

The list of issues that matter in U.S.-Russian relations is too long and too important to be shortened to one or two overriding security concerns. We believe that current American policy is right to have a broad agenda, but that the United States needs a more effective strategy to achieve its goals.

- To create a stronger foundation for working together on securing nuclear materials in Russia and to promote a common strategy on Iran, the United States should deepen its cooperation with Russia on a range of other nuclear issues as well. Moscow and Washington should negotiate an agreement that will for the first time create the legal basis for working together on civilian nuclear energy projects, including international spent-fuel storage.
- To limit Russia's use of oil and gas exports as an instrument of coercion—and as a prop for authoritarianism—the United States needs to agree with other governments, especially those of its European allies, on measures to assure that state-controlled Russian energy companies act like true commercial entities. Such an effort cannot succeed in a vacuum; it underscores the vital importance of developing a comprehensive energy policy.
- To ease Russian pressure on neighboring states, the United States should work to accelerate those states' integration into the West. Post-Soviet states that share America's approach to major international problems and can contribute to resolving them should be able to count on greater support.
- To go beyond mere expressions of concern about the rollback of Russian democracy, the United States should increase, not cut, funding under the Freedom Support Act, focusing in particular on organizations committed to free and fair parliamentary and presidential elections in 2007–2008. Russia's course will not—and must not—be set by foreigners, but the United States and its allies cannot be indifferent to the legitimacy of this process and to the leaders it produces. Working with Congress, American policymakers need to elaborate—publicly and privately—the criteria that they will employ in judging the conduct of these elections.
- To protect the credibility of the G8 at a time when many are questioning Russia's chairmanship of that group, the United

States should make clear that this role does not exempt Russian policies and actions from critical scrutiny. Keeping the G8 a viable international forum will require a de facto revival of the Group of Seven (G7). Without creating a completely new forum, the United States and its democratic allies have to assume a stronger coordinating role within the existing one.

Current U.S. policy toward Russia tries to capitalize on areas of agreement, while muting issues of discord. Our approach is different: We favor doing more to build on existing agreement, but more as well to advance American interests in areas where Russian and U.S. policies are at odds. This approach will help to get the most out of the relationship in the short run, while encouraging its transformation in the long run.

Urging Russia to take a more democratic direction must be done with great care. America will not succeed if it is seen to be hypercritical, hypocritical, or excessively meddlesome. It will be easy to alienate a Russian public, already prone to xenophobia, that knows of Washington's close relations with many states whose societies are not nearly as open as Russia's. The United States and its allies should not belittle Russia by subjecting it to double standards but should show respect by holding Russia to high ones. By speaking in unison, the United States and its allies can make clear that their goal is not to prevail in a post-Cold War test of strength, but to draw Russia back into the Western mainstream.

Over time, accumulating disagreements between Russia and the United States can have consequences that go well beyond a downturn in bilateral relations. They raise the prospect of a broader weakening of unity among the leading states of the international system. If growing consensus among the major powers gives way to a new line of division between democrats and authoritarians, if their energy strategies diverge, or if they respond in different ways to terrorism, America's chances of success in meeting global challenges will be reduced. At present, the risk that such divisions will emerge may seem remote, but policymakers should not fail to anticipate the tipping point. And Americans should understand how much Russia's future course—above all, whether its policies look West or East—can affect the outcome.

Since the end of the Cold War, successive American administrations have sought to create a relationship with Russia that they called "partnership." This is the right long-term goal, but it is unfortunately not a realistic prospect for U.S.-Russian relations over the next several years. The real question that the United States faces in this period is not how to make partnership with Russia work, it is how to make selective cooperation—and in some cases selective opposition—serve important international goals.

# 49 Is Washington Losing Latin America?
## PETER HAKIM

The United States' relationship to the countries of Latin America is one that, because of proximity, has long been different from U.S. relations with other parts of the world. Going as far back as Thomas Jefferson and James Monroe, American interest in Latin American affairs has been substantial. The association, however, has always involved a double-edged sword. While the region has often warranted special attention from the United States, such attention has brought both advantages and drawbacks. Latin American countries welcome American interest, support, and aid, but also bristle at American heavy-handedness. Moreover, Latin America seems to warrant active American engagement only when the region is in crisis, or when other parts of the world are not.

Peter Hakim addresses this ebb and flow in U.S.-Latin American relations, pointing out how since September 11, "Washington effectively lost interest in Latin America." The United States not only had other, more pressing interests, it was also unimpressed with the region's lackluster economic growth, and the sometimes erratic commitment to democratization. This estrangement has been compounded by Latin American wariness of U.S. immigration policies, a failure of American global leadership, what is seen as a narrow U.S. focus on terrorism, and an equally narrow focus on free trade and privatization as the only road to economic development. This is at a time when an increasing number of Latin American countries have elected leftist parties to power, itself a result of the economic inequalities that were exacerbated by adopting U.S. economic prescriptions in the 1980s and 90s. The result is that few countries in the region consider the United States to be a reliable partner. Many of them have welcomed Chinese investment and trade, and a smaller number support the openly anti-American policies of Venezuela's Hugo Chávez.

The U.S. relationship with Latin America is of great importance. Whether through trade agreements, such as NAFTA or the proposed Free Trade Area of the Americas, or by other means, the United States has a great stake in Latin American political and economic success. If the United States is not willing to devote time, resources, and energy to Latin America, if it cannot help create a better future there, in a region that is considered to be so important to American interests, then there may be little prospect that the United States can convince other countries to sign on to its policies regarding economic development, combating terrorism and illegal drugs, or other issues.

## DRIFTING DANGEROUSLY

Relations between the United States and Latin America today are at their lowest point since the end of the Cold War. Many observers in the 1980s had hoped that Latin America's turn toward democracy and market economics, coupled with Washington's waning emphasis on security matters, would lead to closer and more cooperative ties. Indeed, for a time, the Americas seemed to be heading in the right direction: between 1989 and 1995, Central America's brutal wars were largely settled; the Brady debt-relief proposal (named for then U.S. Treasury Secretary Nicholas Brady) helped end Latin America's decade-long, debt-induced recession; the United States, Canada, and Mexico signed the North American Free Trade Agreement (NAFTA); the United States hosted the hemisphere's first summit meeting in more than a generation; and in 1995 a bold Washington-led rescue package helped prevent the collapse of Mexico's economy. But much of this progress has since stalled, with U.S. policy on Latin America drifting without much steam or direction.

After 9/11, Washington effectively lost interest in Latin America. Since then, the attention the United States has paid to the region has been sporadic and narrowly targeted at particularly troubling or urgent situations. Throughout the region, support for Washington's policies has diminished. Few Latin Americans, in or out of government, consider the United States to be a dependable partner. U.S.-Latin American relations have seriously deteriorated—the result of failures of Washington's leadership, the United States' uncompromising stance on many critical issues, and the unwillingness of the administrations of both Bill Clinton and George W. Bush to stand up to powerful domestic constituencies.

The United States is not the only culprit, however. Latin American leaders have also performed badly. Most Latin American governments have only partially completed the political and economic reforms needed to sustain robust growth and healthy democratic institutions. They have mostly neglected the region's deep economic inequities and social tensions. Too often, Latin American governments have only grudgingly cooperated with the United States and one another. Some of the region's leaders have turned to populist and anti-American rhetoric to win supporters and votes.

So far, Washington's tattered relations with Latin America have mainly translated into a series of lost opportunities for both sides. At a time when the Bush administration needs partners and allies across the globe, the United States and its international agenda are discredited in Latin America. Democratic progress is faltering in the region, in large part because of the dismal economic and social performance in country after country. The United States still has a big market in Latin America, with U.S. exports to the region valued at more than $150 billion a year, almost as much as the value of its exports to the European Union. But two-thirds of that goes to Mexico, while Brazil and other South American markets remain relatively untapped in the absence of more productive hemispheric trade arrangements. The burgeoning Hispanic population in the United States is already providing important new links to countries throughout Latin America, but its potential contribution is constrained by Washington's muddled and unworkable immigration rules.

U.S. interests in the region are endangered in other ways, too. Oil and natural gas supplies from politically troubled Venezuela and other energy-rich Andean nations are less secure than ever. Several small and weak states in the Caribbean and Latin America are at risk of becoming permanent centers of drug activity, money laundering, and other criminal operations. Stability is threatened by the upsurge of crime and violence almost everywhere in Latin America. The United States could end up paying a stiff price for the region's economic reversals and unsettled politics. Unfortunately, there are a few prospects for a turnaround in U.S.-Latin American relations anytime soon.

## SOUTHERN EXPOSURE

At the beginning of his administration, President Bush declared that Latin America would be a priority for U.S. foreign policy. The White House hailed the region's progress toward democracy and market economics and set out to complete the ongoing negotiations for a hemisphere-wide free-trade pact, build broader economic partnerships, and resolve such chronic problems as immigration and drug trafficking. The administration was confident that it could reinvigorate relations with the region's two largest and most influential countries, Brazil and Mexico. In particular, it saw the newly installed government of President Vicente Fox, whose election ended 70 years of one-party rule in Mexico, as a special opportunity to reshape and deepen the relationship.

Five years later, the Bush administration's attitude has changed markedly. U.S. officials have been regularly disappointed by developments in Latin America across an array of issues. Economically, the region has been limping along for years. True, the past two years have brought mostly good news: foreign investment has started flowing in, trade has expanded at a strong pace, family remittances are surging, and inflation remains low. But few analysts are confident that the gains can be sustained. The region's economic improvement is mostly the result of a particularly benign global economy that has boosted Latin America's commodity exports and kept interest rates down, easing the burden of the region's high debt.

Even more troubling to U.S. officials has been the evolving political situation. Washington likes to tout Latin America as a showcase for democracy. Democratic politics are still the norm in the region; only Cuba remains under authoritarian rule. But in the past decade, nearly a dozen elected presidents have been forced from office, many by street protests or mob violence. Despite holding elections and plebiscites, Venezuela today barely qualifies as a democracy. The same is true of Haiti, which more and more is coming to resemble a failed state. In Bolivia and Ecuador, fractious politics are reinforced by deep social, ethnic, and regional divisions. In Nicaragua, an alliance of corrupt legislators from the left and the right has so paralyzed the government that next year's presidential election may restore to power Washington's nemesis Sandinista leader Daniel Ortega. [Ortega won the election and currently serves as President of Nicaragua.] And these are not the only countries in the region where democracy is under stress and could deteriorate quickly.

The Bush administration's disillusionment with Latin America goes well beyond the region's economic and political failings, however. Washington has bristled at Latin America's opposition to much of the United States' post-9/11 security agenda. The White House was outraged when Chile and Mexico, Latin America's representatives on the UN Security Council in 2003 and two of Washington's closest allies in the region, opposed a resolution endorsing the invasion of Iraq. In fact, of the 34 Latin American and Caribbean countries, only seven supported the war. Six of them (Costa Rica, the Dominican Republic, El Salvador, Honduras, Nicaragua, and Panama) were engaged in trade negotiations with the United States at the time. And the seventh, Colombia, receives more than $600 million a year in U.S. military aid.

## YOU SAY YOU WANT A REVOLUTION

More serious than Latin America's distaste for U.S. policies, however, is the emergence of Venezuelan President Hugo Chávez as a vexing and potentially dangerous adversary. Under Chávez, Venezuela has developed close ties to Cuba and is now generously subsidizing the island's economy. Some in Washington think this support could complicate Cuba's post-Castro transition by helping a repressive regime hold on to power. And there are more immediate concerns. Although the nature of Chávez's involvement remains murky, administration officials are convinced that he is provoking instability in some of the most volatile states in the hemisphere, including Bolivia, Ecuador, and Nicaragua. His alleged links to Colombia's leftist guerrillas and the sanctuary they enjoy in Venezuela also worry U.S. officials.

Furthermore, Chávez's ambitions are not limited to stirring up trouble in a few neighboring countries. He has made clear his intent to forge a wide anti-U.S coalition in order to replace Washington's agenda for the hemisphere with his own—one that rejects representative democracy and market economics. So far he is a long way from succeeding: no other government has followed his economic or political lead. Indeed, nearly every Latin American country still sees its future as being linked to the United States and wants to strengthen its relations with Washington. Nonetheless, the United States is alarmed by the prospects that Ortega could take power in Nicaragua and that a radical government could come to power in Bolivia if the left-wing indigenous leader Evo Morales wins the presidential elections in December 2005. [Morales won the election and currently serves as President of Bolivia.] Chávez has close ties to both leaders and is assisting them financially.

Despite his failure to export his "Bolivarian Revolution" thus far, Chávez, buoyed by enormous oil revenues and virtually unchecked power at home, is working to increase his influence in the region. On his watch, Venezuela has launched Petrocaribe, an energy alliance designed to deliver subsidized oil from Venezuela to the small states of the Caribbean, and begun financing Telesur, a regional news network intended to compete with the BBC's and CNN's Spanish-language programs. Venezuela is nearing full partnership in Mercosur, South America's most important free-trade zone, which also includes Argentina, Brazil, Paraguay, and Uruguay (Bolivia, Chile, and Peru are associate members). And Chávez has proposed the creation of Petrosur, which would be a confederation of the region's state-owned petroleum companies; he has also suggested forming a nuclear energy consortium with Brazil and Argentina and establishing a South American development bank.

## THE CHINA CARD

Washington also worries about China's growing presence in Latin America, a concern that has already been the subject of congressional hearings. In fact, some members of Congress view China as the most serious challenge to U.S. interests in the region since the collapse of the Soviet Union. They cite the huge financial resources China is promising to bring to Latin America, its growing military-to-military relations in the region, and its clear political ambitions there all as potential threats to the long-standing pillar of U.S. policy in the hemisphere, the Monroe Doctrine.

China's interest in Latin America is significant and expanding. The region has become a vital source of raw materials and foodstuffs for China. In the past six years, Chinese imports from Latin America have grown more than sixfold, or by nearly 60 percent a year. Beijing also faces a major political challenge in the region: of the 26 countries that recognize Taiwan, 12 are in Latin America or the Caribbean. China is intent on reducing that number through aggressive diplomacy and increased trade, aid, and investment.

Bush administration officials have watched China's growing commercial and political engagement in the region closely. Chinese President Hu Jintao traveled to Latin America twice in the past two years, spending a total of 16 days there. The White House could not have missed the warm welcome he received in the five Latin American countries he visited, the concessions the host governments offered him (such as the quick granting of "market-economy status" to China), and the enormous expectations his presence created of major Chinese investments in roads, ports, and other infrastructure. Hu's trips have been reciprocated by a long series of visits to China by Latin American heads of state, economic officials, and corporate leaders.

Many people in Latin America look to China as an economic and political alternative to U.S. hegemony. Although officials in some of these countries are concerned that China, with its lower manufacturing costs, will cut into their sales, profits, and investment, others (mainly South America's food- and mineral-producing nations) largely see China as a major potential partner for new trade and investment. Brazilian leaders, including President Lula, have said they want to establish a strategic relationship with Beijing that might involve trade in high-tech products, mutual support in international organizations, and scientific and cultural collaboration.

China is still a long way from threatening or even really competing with the influence of the United States in Latin America. But as in other parts of the world, China is pragmatically and aggressively seeking economic and political advantages there. A few commentators have suggested that with its strong ties to Cuba, growing interest in Venezuela, and presence in Panama, China represents an emerging security risk to U.S. interests in the hemisphere. Most analysts, however, doubt that any of China's initiatives in Latin America will provoke a confrontation with the United States. They point to Beijing's general caution in its relations with Washington, China's recognition of the preeminence of the United States in Latin America, and the far greater importance China assigns to other items on its agenda with the United States.

## AT ARM'S LENGTH

Disappointment with the U.S.-Latin American relationship is a two-way street. Anti-Americanism has surged in every country in Latin America. People in the region, rich and poor, resent the Bush administration's aggressive unilateralism and condemn Washington's disregard for international institutions and norms. A recent Zogby poll of Latin America's elites found that 86 percent of them disapprove of Washington's management of conflicts around the world. Only Cuba and Venezuela are openly hostile toward the United States, and most Latin American governments continue to seek close ties with the United States, including free-trade arrangements, immigration accords, and security assistance—even though many of them no longer consider the United States to be a fully reliable partner or want to be Washington's ally. The region's leaders are well aware of the overwhelming political and economic strength of the United States and are pragmatic enough to work hard to maintain good relations with the world's only superpower. But they view the United States as a country that rarely consults with others, reluctantly compromises, and reacts badly when others criticize or oppose its actions.

For many in the region, Washington's championing of human rights and democracy now rings especially hollow. Most Latin Americans were dumbfounded by U.S. actions at Abu Ghraib and Guantanamo Bay. The U.S. government has long scolded Latin American countries for their violations of human rights and their shabby judicial procedures, but it suddenly seemed to be playing by a different set of rules when its own security was at stake. Latin Americans, mindful of what have often been devastating U.S. military actions in the region, have never been comfortable with unilateral U.S. interventions and have steadfastly resisted the use of force to promote democracy. Washington's initial enthusiasm for the short-lived April 2002 coup against the freely elected Chávez government raised questions in virtually every country in Latin America about the sincerity of the Bush administration's commitment to democracy. So did Washington's pressuring President Jean-Bertrand Aristide to leave Haiti in 2004.

What the majority of Latin American countries most want and need from the United States are productive economic ties, such as the free trade agreements Washington concluded with Chile in 2003 and the countries of Central America and the Dominican Republic in 2005. These will bring sizable benefits to the countries involved, and they have kept the U.S. trade agenda active even as the negotiations for a free-trade area in the Western Hemisphere remain stalled. But Washington can do better. In the recent past, Latin Americans have particularly welcomed four U.S. initiatives: the Brady debt-relief plan, introduced in 1989; President George H. W. Bush's 1990 proposal for a hemisphere-wide free-trade area; the 1993 adoption of NAFTA, which prompted negotiations over the proposed Free Trade Area of the Americas (FTAA); and the rescue of the Mexican peso in 1995. There has been no U.S. economic initiative in Latin America of similar magnitude for the past decade.

Another sore point, particularly for Mexico, Central America, and the Caribbean, but also for an increasing number of South American countries, has been U.S. immigration policy, which has remained basically unchanged for two decades. Latin Americans see immigration as a solution both to their own high unemployment and low wages and to the huge demand for workers in the United States. They argue that the United States should accept larger numbers of immigrants. Instead, Washington has stiffened enforcement measures at its borders, an action that has not reduced illegal immigration but has raised the costs and risks of entering the United States and kept many immigrants in the underground economy, where exploitation is common. Worse, state and local governments in the United States are increasingly implementing harsh anti-immigrant initiatives, and armed civilian volunteers occasionally take it upon themselves to patrol the U.S.-Mexican frontier to keep immigrants out. A related issue concerns the U.S. practice of deporting convicted felons, including naturalized U.S. citizens, to their countries of origin, where many join extraordinarily vicious street gangs. All of this generates extensive press coverage in Mexico and other countries that send immigrants to the United States, making it appear that the United States is becoming increasingly anti-Latin American.

Perhaps what most troubles Latin Americans is the sense that Washington just does not take the region seriously and still considers it to be its own backyard. Less than a week before 9/11, President Bush made the stunning declaration that the United States' most important relationship worldwide was that with Mexico. No one was surprised by the dramatic shift in U.S. priorities in the aftermath of the attacks toward a reemphasis on security and the Middle East. But the virtual exclusion of Mexico and the rest of Latin America from the U.S. foreign policy agenda was brusque and unexpected. Today, Washington seems to notice only those developments in Latin America that look like direct challenges to its own interests, such as the growing influence of Chávez, the expanding presence of China, or the reemergence of Ortega. On issue after issue, Latin American officials feel they are not consulted, and when they are, they sense that their views carry little weight with U.S. decision-makers.

## A VERY LONG ESTRANGEMENT

There is little reason to expect that U.S. relations with Latin America will improve soon. More likely, they will get worse. The region will remain peripheral to the central concerns of U.S. foreign policy, which are the war against terrorism, securing and rebuilding Iraq, the Arab-Israeli conflict, and nuclear proliferation. With new presidents scheduled to come to power in nearly a dozen Latin American countries over the coming year, some important political shifts will certainly occur. But many conditions in

Latin America are unlikely to change much. At best, the region will sustain its recent modest economic growth, but it will not offer the trade and investment opportunities that U.S. businesses find in Asia and Central Europe. Latin America's social and political tensions will persist, and much of the region will remain alienated from the United States. Chávez is likely to continue his adversarial stance toward the United States for some time, and it may get even stronger if he further consolidates power at home and continues to earn and spend Venezuela's enormous oil profits. The elections in Nicaragua and Bolivia may even provide him with new allies.

Although U.S. relations with Latin America are at a low point and the prospects for improvement in the short term are not good, not all the news is bad. The United States and Latin America share many values and are still cooperating on many issues. Some bilateral relationships are remarkably strong. Washington has maintained an unusually productive relationship with Colombia over the past half-dozen years. U.S. aid programs, initially propelled by domestic concerns about increased drug trafficking, have helped make Colombia more secure and have strengthened the authority of its government. Similarly, Chile continues its exceptional economic and social progress, and its democracy has become more robust. Since 2004, when Chile's free-trade pact with the United States went into force, U.S.-Chilean trade has soared, further reinforcing the two countries' genuinely respectful and valued relationship (all despite Chile's opposition to the war in Iraq). At the United States' request, over the past year Brazil has led some 7,500 peacekeepers (mainly from Latin America) in Haiti, helping reestablish security and order there as the country prepared for elections in December.

Despite their disagreements and dissatisfaction with U.S. policy in the region, most governments in Latin America want to strengthen their relations with Washington. But the Bush administration has demonstrated neither the determination nor the capability to pursue policies in the Americas that would mobilize the support of the other nations of the hemisphere. Latin American countries, divided among themselves, are by no means clamoring for a renewal of hemispheric cooperation. Chávez's antics at the Summit of the Americas in November 2005 obscured the real tragedies of the gathering—that is, how little the leaders accomplished, how badly the hemispheric agenda has unraveled, and how deeply divided the countries of the Americas are. Despite enthusiasm in the region for economic partnership, Latin Americans' fundamental ambivalence toward the United States' foreign policies has forcefully reemerged.

The costs of this impasse may be high for both the United States and Latin America. Another financial crisis in Argentina or Brazil could have global ramifications. So would a political confrontation in oil-rich Venezuela and or an intensification of the armed conflict in Colombia.

Greater regional integration and political cooperation could benefit all the countries of the Western Hemisphere, as they have in Europe. But the United States and Latin America have demonstrated neither the will nor the ability to travel that road together.

# 50   New Rule Sets

## Thomas P. M. Barnett

The final reading in this book revisits the idea of grand strategy and prospects for the future. The war on global terror, a deteriorating war in Iraq, the specter of nuclear proliferation, and a sense that the United States has diminished its effectiveness in global politics have all prompted numerous analyses of American grand strategy and direction in global affairs. Concepts such as containment and democratic enlargement have defined U.S. grand strategy in the past, and in light of the limited effectiveness of "pre-emption," the United States is in a position of asking what comes next.

Thomas P. M. Barnett looks at the problem of American grand strategy and global security, considering them in the context of globalization and its expansion since World War II, but especially since the 1980s, when the Cold War was coming to an end. Barnett makes the argument that the problem of global security and the problem of global economic integration are one and the same. Looking at the world in terms of two types of states, those that are part of a connected "functioning core," and those that remain outside of this group in a "not-integrated gap," Barnett says, "show me areas where globalization is thick with network connectivity, financial transactions . . . media flows and collective security, and I'll show you regions featuring stable governments [and] rising standards of living . . . but show me where globalization is thinning or just plain absent and I will show you regions plagued by politically repressive regimes, widespread poverty and disease, routine mass murder and, most important, the chronic conflicts that incubate the next generation of global terrorists." To be successful, says Barnett, American foreign policy needs to realize that the expansion of globalization into the "gap" is imperative in order to diminish the dangers to both American and global security. A military strategy alone is simply insufficient to keep the world's troubles at bay.

This analysis speaks to the close correspondence between the international economic order and America's political and security goals and needs, similar to those provided by Walter Russell Mead, Stephen Cohen, President Clinton, and others in this volume. It also recognizes an important truth: The United States will have to create a compelling vision that will allow it to win the cooperation of other "core" states. This will entail not only the use of America's military and economic resources, but its soft power—its historic ability to set the international agenda and persuade other states to want what it wants. The paradox of American primacy and power is that the United States is the most powerful country the world has ever known, yet in spite of this, it still cannot achieve some of its most important objectives on its own.

---

Rather than dwell on the unpredictability of future threats or attacks, our strategic vision for national security needs to focus on growing the community of states that recognize a stable set of rules regarding war and peace, as in "These are the conditions under which it is reasonable to wage war against identifiable enemies to our collective order." Growing that community of like-minded states is simply a matter of identifying the difference between "good" and "bad" regimes, and rallying the former to work collectively to encourage the latter to change their ways, applying military power when diplomacy alone does not do the trick. But changing "bad" states to "good" ones requires that we generate some broadly accepted definition of what a "good state" is, meaning a government that plays by the security rules we hold dear—like "Don't harbor transnational terrorists within your territory" and "Don't seek weapons of mass destruction." Enunciating that rule set is the most immediate task in this global war on terrorism, and promoting the global spread of that security rule set through our use of military force overseas (e.g., preemptive war against regimes that openly transgress the rule set) is our most important long-term goal in this struggle.

But the growth of any global security rule set reflects the underlying economic reality of the world at large. In the Cold War, that security rule set reflected the bifurcation of the global economy into capitalist and socialist camps. So where do we draw a similar line today? In the era of globalization, we draw that line between those parts of the world that are actively integrating their national economies into a global economy, or what I call globalization's Functioning Core, and those that are failing to integrate themselves into that larger economic community and all the rule sets it generates, or those states I identify as constituting the Non-Integrating Gap. Simply put, when we see countries moving toward the acceptance of globalization's economic rule sets, we should expect to see commensurate acceptance of an emerging global security rule set—in effect, agreement on why, and under what conditions, war makes sense.

Where this global security rule set spreads and finds mass acceptance, the threat—by definition—will diminish. Because if the economic rule sets are fair and equitably applied, "losers" or "unhappy" players will find sufficient political opportunities, within the rules, to press their cases for adjustment, restitution, and the like (like Canada going to the World Trade Organization to protest U.S. tariffs on lumber—no soldiers, just lawyers). Moreover, as political and military cooperation grows among the states within the Functioning Core, their collective ability to absorb the disruptive blows unleashed by terrorists and other bad events will inevitably grow. In effect, that which does not kill globalization makes it stronger: the world gets blindsided by AIDS, wakes up a bit, and then handles SARS better, which in turn only makes us smarter and more prepared for the SARS-after-next. The preparations for Y2K had the same positive effect on our recovery from 9/11.

If we apply that sort of approach to the global security system, then we break out of the Pentagon's tendency to view U.S. national security as somehow divorced from—or worse, exacerbated by—the spread of economic globalization. Instead, we begin to understand the threat less in terms of anyone, anywhere getting his hands on dangerous technology and more in terms of which players, governments, and even entire regions count themselves either in or out of the expanding global rule set we call globalization. Up to now, the U.S. Government has tended to identify globalization primarily as an economic rule set, but thanks to 9/11, we now understand that it likewise demands the clear enunciation and enforcement of a security rule set as well.

When we view the global security environment as divided between those states that adhere to globalization's emerging security rule set (the Core) and those that do not (the Gap), we begin to understand that the real sources of instability in our world are not only concentrated in those "off-grid" areas but are likewise found anywhere that rule sets are out of whack—even at home.

What I mean by rule sets "out of whack" is when one aspect of life (say, security) seems to have fallen behind some other aspect of life (say, technology) in terms of providing sufficient rules to account for an unexpected turn of events. Identity theft is a good example: The technology of communications and finance simply leapfrogged ahead of the legal system to the point where criminals were committing crimes that we didn't even have names for not too long ago. Eventually enough people got burned by this new form of crime that the political system responded, passing new security rule sets that allow the police to prosecute the offenders. But until that happened, the rule sets were out of whack—too many rules in one sector but not enough in another.

Think about 9/11 for a minute. It told us that we didn't have enough rule sets in certain areas of our lives (e.g., airport security, visa policies), and that those rule-set gaps could easily be exploited by those who not only don't adhere to our general rule sets but actually prefer to see them overthrown or at least kept out of their neck of the woods (e.g., Muslim extremists who dream of a Middle East greatly isolated from the "infidel" West). This kind of diagnostic approach isn't about assigning blame or pointing fingers; that's what Congress is for. What this sort of rule-set focus is really good for is understanding where we are in history, what the main security tasks of the era truly are, and how we can forge a comprehensive strategy for not only protecting America but likewise making the world a better place for everyone over the long haul.

I believe that history will judge the 1990s much like the Roaring Twenties—just a little too good to be true. Both decades threw the major rule sets out of whack: new forms of behavior, activity, and connectivity arose among individuals, companies, and countries, but the rule sets that normally guide such interactions were overwhelmed. These traditional rule sets simply could not keep up with all that change happening so quickly. People were doing new things, both good and bad, for which we had to invent not just new names but entirely new rule sets to make clear to everyone what was acceptable and unacceptable behavior in this new era. That tumultuous situation of rule sets being disjointed existed within families, communities, nations—even the international security order itself.

Eventually the situation spins out of control and nobody really knows what to do. Economic crashes effectively marked the end of both tumultuous decades, followed by the rise of seemingly new sorts of security threats to the international order. In the 1930s, it was fascism and Nazi Germany, while today most security experts will tell you it is radical Islam and transnational terrorism. In both instances, the community of states committed to maintaining global order was deeply torn over what to do about these new security threats—try to accommodate them or fight them head-on in war? Most of the time we cannot even agree on what to call these threats—for example, what makes a government a "rogue regime," and when are terrorists legitimately viewed as "enemy combatants"? If there are no easy answers, then there are no common definitions, and that means rule sets are out of whack.

Meanwhile, the global economic order will inevitably grow brittle if there is widespread confusion over what constitutes legitimate threats to international stability and order (e.g., al Qaeda? America the out-of-control hyperpower?). Everyone becomes more worried about the future, and so trust decreases across the system, making compromises all the harder to achieve. If it gets really bad, states stop cooperating on economic rule sets altogether, and start turning on one another in security matters. In the 1930s, the global economy basically collapsed in on itself, as the major players put up walls around their economies in the form of tariffs and other restrictions on trade. Today, we face similar temptations as the Core and Gap fight over the former's high agricultural subsidies and the latter's high tariffs against industrial imports. In the 1930s, the world drifted toward global war, while today many around the world speak ominously of America's growing "empire" and the prospect of "perpetual war."

My shorthand for rule-set divergence in the 1990s is roughly the same as the one I would offer for the 1920s: economics got ahead of politics, and technology got ahead of security. In effect, we let the world get too connected too fast. Not that connectivity itself is bad, for I'm a huge believer in the free flow of mass media, ideas, capital, goods, technology, and people. Rather, we didn't construct sufficient political and security rule sets to keep pace with all this growing connectivity. In some ways, we got lazy, counted a little too much on the market to sort it all out, and then woke up shocked and amazed on 9/11 to find ourselves apparently invited to a global war.

The question that now stands before us is whether or not this decade ends up being a repeat of the 1930s, when, by God, we really did end up in a global, *total* war. World Wars I and II, in combination with the self-destructive economic nationalism of the 1930s, completely wiped out all the gains in global economic integration achieved by that first great globalization era of 1870 to 1914.

Taking to heart the lesson of the demise of Globalization I, the United States decided to institute a new global rule set following World War II, or one that restored some sense of balance to the economic, political, and security rule sets that defined what later became known as the West. I'm talking about the resource flows (Marshall Plan), the massive reorganization of the U.S. Government (Defense Act of 1947, which created the Defense Department, the CIA, and other entities), the creation of a slew of international organizations (United Nations, International Monetary Fund, World Bank), new economic rule sets (General Agreement on Trade and Tariffs, Bretton Woods agreement on a currency stabilization regime), and the forging of new military alliances (the most important being the North Atlantic Treaty Organization). This period of rule-set "reset" took the better part of a decade, consuming U.S. diplomatic and military efforts deep into the 1950s. This Rome wasn't built in a day.

Nor was it promulgated without a significant amount of long-range planning, or the sort we seem to have forgotten in the Pentagon, perhaps because the bulk of that historic planning occurred in the State Department. Here we had the so-called wise men, most notably George Kennan, who looked around the world and decided it wasn't hard to identify the main sources of mass violence in the system over the previous quarter-century: basically a militarist Germany, an expansionist Soviet Union, and an imperialist Japan. So they did the logical thing: they created a long-term strategy to buy off the two losers from World War II while waiting out the third.

Their dream was simple enough, but amazingly bold: perhaps by the end of the century both Germany and Japan would be so pacified and eco-nomically integrated into a resurgent West that they would never again pose a threat to global peace, and maybe—just maybe—the Soviet Union would collapse of its own accord and join the dominant Western rule set in perpetual peace. Now, of course, this is basically history. But step back to 1946, and that simple plan looks less like a strategic vision and more like a daydream. To many security experts of that era, the notion that we could rehabilitate Nazi Germany and imperial Japan while simultaneously stand-ing up to the Reds was simply ludicrous. We had neither the will nor the wallet after fighting World War II, and our experience in the Korean War made it seem like this new world would feature lots of U.S. casualties for very uncertain and unsatisfactory outcomes.

Sound familiar? This is why I prefer comparing George W. Bush to Harry Truman rather than Ronald Reagan. Reagan didn't win the Cold War but had it handed to him on a silver platter. Truman really got the ball rolling, just like Bush, who—if he plays his cards right—may yet set in motion a new strategic security paradigm that will far outlive his presi-dency. But that will happen only if the Bush Administration generates reproducible strategic concepts, or a compelling containment-like vision that other, successor administrations can also champion. Reproducible here means both Republicans and Democrats can understand them in the same basic way. Not identical, mind you, but we can't be forever arguing about definitions. Trust me, the military wants this sort of bipartisan consensus in the worst way.

This outcome, obviously, is far from certain. If I compare Bush favorably with Truman in terms of action, I'd be forced to give him a failing grade to date in terms of strategic vision, which is just a fancy way of saying how he explains his foreign policy to the public and the world. No doubt Bush has a far tougher task than Truman, because Truman's enemy was more clearly defined by its military threat, whereas Bush's enemy is characterized less by a direct threat to our way of life than a sheer rejection of it. The Soviets were really out to get us, whereas the antiglobalization forces—represented in their most violent form by an al Qaeda—don't seek our historical destruction so much as a sort of permanent civilizational apartheid.

Because we called the post–World War II period the Cold War, history remembers those decades mostly as a scary, strategic standoff between the United States and the Soviet Union. In reality, that was the sideshow of the containment strategy. The real goal of that visionary strategy was to resurrect globalization on three key pillars: the United States, Western Europe, and Japan. Between 1950 and 1980, we succeeded beyond our wildest dreams, as roughly 10 percent of the global population controlled the vast wealth of the resurgent global economy. But around 1980 it got even better, if you listen to the World Bank, which notes the emergence across the 1980s of roughly two dozen globalizing economies, to include such current globalization welterweights as South Korea, Brazil, and India, not to mention the emerging heavyweight of that class China.

That wondrous story of Globalization II (1945–1980) is the buried lead of all Cold War histories yet written. Truth be told, Globalization II was the Cold War's *raison d'être*, whereas Globalization III (1980 and counting) is its "peace dividend," the pot of gold we spent the 1990s fruitlessly searching for in the U.S. federal budget. But you know what? It was completely worth it, because globalization, with an assist from the spectre of nuclear weapons, has effectively killed the idea of great-power war—all-out conventional (nonnuclear) war among the world's most powerful states that concludes only when one side is completely defeated. But even better than that, Globalization II and III have lifted hundreds of millions out of poverty over the second half of the twentieth century. While the world's population has doubled since 1960, the percentage living in poverty has been cut in half.

For those of you who thought that globalization was invented in the 1990s, let me tell you why all this talk about rule sets is important. We let economic nationalism outpace political reason in the 1930s and we got a Great Depression for our failings. We let the technology of killing get ahead of our ability to manage security relationships among great powers in the 1930s and we got the Second World War and the Holocaust for our failings. We stand at a similar point in history now, having just gone through the "roaring" nineties only to wake up with a four-aspirin hangover called the Asian flu, the tech crash, 9/11, and the global war on terrorism. How we move ahead depends greatly on how we view our world and the rule sets that define it.

Despite being the world's sole military superpower, America needs to understand that it stands on the cusp of a new multipolar era defined by globalization's progressive advance. It also needs to realize that the emerging global conflict lies between those who want to see the world grow ever more connected and rule-bound and those who want to isolate large chunks of humanity from the globalization process so as to pursue very particular paths to "happiness." If we as a nation, through our diplomatic and security strategies, succeed in closing the rule-set gaps that currently exist, we will do far more than make our nation more secure or wealthier, we'll finally succeed in making globalization truly global.

The task that lies before us is no less historic or heroic than that surmounted by the so-called greatest generation over the course of the twentieth century. And, yes, this task will consume a similar length of time.

The only global future truly worth creating involves nothing less than eliminating the Gap altogether. . . .

America can only increase its security when it extends connectivity or expands globalization's reach, and by doing so, progressively reduces those trouble spots or off-grid locations where security problems and instability tend to concentrate. In sum, the best-case scenario for Globalization III must be its continued expansion. It is not enough for the Core to survive. It must grow. Conversely, the best-case scenario involves not just growing the Core but shrinking the Gap as well. Keeping with the theme of this opening chapter, the only way to accomplish Core expansion and Gap shrinkage is to extend the reach of rule sets. That means not only must Old and New School globalizers reach agreement on the rule-set reset for trade (i.e., better alignment of economic and political rule sets in the ongoing Doha Round negotiations of the WTO), but they must also come to a clear understanding on what the reset between technological and security rule sets must be.

Right now, the biggest proposal out on the table is the U.S. strategy of preemption, which, in effect, argues that whenever known rule breakers get close to obtaining weapons of mass destruction, it is only normal and right for great powers to strike preemptively for the avowed purposes of regime change. But again, focusing solely on that strategy does a great disservice to the task at hand. In many ways, the breadth of the rule-set reset on security is far wider than just the question of how we deal with bad actors in the system. In reality, it encompasses the far larger question of how we deal with all this rising connectivity in ways that do not hamper globalization's continued expansion.

Remembering that the rule-set reset following the Second World War took a decade or longer, we can see that some patience is clearly in order. Moreover, to get to that best-case outcome, America needs to understand that getting the rest of the Core to accept its new security rule set will require significant compromises along the way. This is crucial, because if the United States is viewed by the rest of the great powers as going off the deep end in its idiosyncratic quest for what other cultures consider to be unacceptable new rule sets, then America may well find itself belonging to a Core of one. That means the quickest route from the best- to worst-case scenarios runs right through the White House. No matter how logical or necessary our new rule sets may appear to us, if we cannot sell them to a large chunk of the planet, we lose our credibility as a competent superpower, and our rules will invariably be dismissed by other cultures as reflecting an American bias, not universal truths.

In many ways, nudging globalization in the direction of that best-case scenario is the ultimate example of global risk management: the quickest way to secure America absolutely is to run hog-wild with preemptive strikes against the most dangerously disconnected states like Iran, North Korea, Syria—or basically, the "who's next?" strategy. But a mindless pursuit of America's short-term security is likely to damage globalization's capacity for expansion, and therein lies our best hope for increasing our security over the long haul. Scaring the rest of the world to death with some half-cocked "World War IV" to-do list will divide up the planet pronto, not to mention send our own society into anguished upheaval.

America faced a similar situation during the Second World War, when President Franklin Delano Roosevelt and Supreme Allied Commander General Dwight D. Eisenhower were both pressured by public opinion, allies, and world events to end the war as quickly as possible. But instead of winning that war quickly only to lose the peace, they made a series of calculated compromises that not only kept the alliance intact but kept the American public firmly supportive of an activist postwar strategy as well. The global war on terrorism cannot be a multileg sprint from one "Berlin" to the next, because the United States simply cannot shrink the Gap by itself.

Ultimately, to shrink the Gap over the coming decades, the United States will need the combined assets of the entire Core. To bring that much of the world along as we seek to test out and propagate new rule sets in international security, America must carefully but forcefully enunciate a comprehensive vision of a future worth creating. That vision will have to sell on both Main Street and Wall Street, in both Berlin and Beijing, and in both the Core and the Gap. Anything less is a waste of our servicemen and -women.